For Chris and Margaret
with best wishes
Charles Whitney.

# At Close Quarters

LOGASTON PRESS
Little Logaston, Woonton, Almeley
Herefordshire HR3 6QH
logastonpress.co.uk

First published by Logaston Press 2009


ISBN 978 1906663 19 3 (hardback)
978 1906663 20 9 (paperback)

Set in Times New Roman, Garamond and Gill Sans by Logaston Press
and printed and bound in Poland
*www.polskabook.pl*

*TO THE MEMORY*
*of*
*T.M.A. Cooper,*
*The Revd R.F. McNeile OD,*
*E.S. Hoare OD & H.W. Osmond*

*and also for*
*Professor R.J.W. Evans OD,*
*M.A. Girling & R.C. Padfield OD*
*all of whom contributed significantly to the preservation of this School's history*
*and without whose efforts this volume would have been impossible*

*Also by C.E. Whitney*

*Discovering the Cinque Ports* (Shire Publications)
*Dover College Junior School, Westbrook House* (Dover College)
*A Pictorial History of Folkestone* (Phillimore)
*Bygone Hythe* (Phillimore)

# Contents


| | | *Page* |
|---|---|---|
| | Foreword | *ix* |
| | Acknowledgements | *xi* |
| | Preface | *xv* |
| Chapter 1 | The Foundation and Opening of Dean Close Memorial School | 1 |
| Chapter 2 | The Flecker Years | 13 |
| Chapter 3 | The First Two Decades of the Twentieth Century | 29 |
| Chapter 4 | Between the Wars, 1920 to 1938 | 49 |
| Chapter 5 | Desperate Times | 65 |
| Chapter 6 | Recovery, 1946 to 1968 | 81 |
| Chapter 7 | Genesis and Growth of Dean Close Junior School, 1886 to 1968 | 99 |
| Chapter 8 | Co-education Begins, 1968 to 1978 | 117 |
| Chapter 9 | Towards the New Millennium | 131 |
| Chapter 10 | Sport at Dean Close School, 1918 to 1968 | 151 |
| Chapter 11 | Sport at Dean Close School since 1968 | 169 |
| Chapter 12 | The CCF and Outdoor Pursuits from 1919 | 199 |
| Chapter 13 | The Performing Arts | 219 |
| Chapter 14 | School, Citizenship and Community | 253 |
| Chapter 15 | Junior School to Preparatory School and Beyond, 1968 to 2009 | 269 |
| Chapter 16 | The Advent of Tewkesbury Abbey Schola Cantorum | 303 |
| Chapter 17 | The Pre-Preparatory School | 313 |
| Chapter 18 | Old Decanians and The Old Decanian Society | 323 |
| Chapter 19 | Towards the Future | 345 |
| Appendix | The layout of the School buildings | 361 |
| | Select Bibliography | 363 |
| | Cheltenham and School Index | 365 |
| | Names Index | 371 |

# Foreword

## by Baroness Cox of Queensbury, President of Dean Close School

It was in November 1884 that the Cornerstone on which Dean Close School was to be built was laid. Now, 125 years later, there is an opportunity to reflect on what has been achieved and whether the original vision of the Founders has been maintained.

I have had the privilege of being President of the School for eight years, and I have come to appreciate that the education and opportunities offered are truly excellent and distinctive. This is not only because of the superb facilities and the positive, caring attitude of the staff and the Decanians themselves, but also because of the continuing commitment to the faith and values originally enshrined in the Christian Cornerstone, which have been preserved and nurtured in the ethos of the School.

Whenever I visit the School, I feel it is imbued with enthusiasm in two senses of that word: firstly, in the literal definition of 'God in us', and secondly in its everyday meaning: the vitality, commitment, joy and, where appropriate, fun which are evident throughout the School community. I can think of no more important attribute for a School. Neither can I think of a greater compliment to those who founded it and to those who have maintained the vision and enthusiasm of the Founders from the beginning through profound changes to the challenges of the present day.

This book faithfully records the sometimes difficult educational journey from a boys' Victorian boarding school to a leading co-educational community, with enviable resources, which enthusiastically reaches out to local and international communities in order to bring help to others. How the School has done so makes fascinating reading.

Dean Close School is making an outstanding contribution to the life of the country and this heart-warming story of faith has been admirably set out here. I warmly commend it, not only to all who have any association with the School, but also to anyone with an interest in education and our Christian heritage.

Caroline Cox

# Acknowledgements

*Ladies' maiden names are in brackets.*

My thanks goes to many people for making this book possible, not least to the Revd Tim Hastie-Smith for asking me to do it, and for his abiding interest in the project, observations and helpful suggestions. I am also grateful to the Revd Leonard Browne, Headmaster of Dean Close Preparatory School, and Sue Bennett, Headmistress of Dean Close Pre-Preparatory School, for their interest and support.

Grateful thanks to the Revd Canon Paul Williams, Vicar of Tewkesbury Abbey, for his understanding in supporting me in an almost three-month-long sabbatical together with the kindness of my clergy team colleagues at Tewkesbury Abbey – the Revds Carolyn Methven, Sarah Miller, Steve Short and Catherine Williams – in making it possible to have the time to complete this project. I am also grateful to the Revd Canon Dr David Hoyle for wise advice.

Thanks go, too, to Bridget Lyne, the Headmaster's Secretary, Watford Grammar School for Boys, for information on Percy Bolton.

Thanks to Fergus Read, head of the Department of Exhibits and Firearms, Imperial War Museum, for information on the institution of the George Medal and finding the citation for Dr Oscar M. Holden GM, OD. I also wish to thank the staff at Cheltenham Library's Local History Collection and the Gloucestershire Archives Office for their never-failing courtesy and help.

I would like to thank M.A.B. Radway OD, Dr Andrew Crowther and my brother-in-law Peter Stevens, for their help concerning the old railway line that used to run by the School.

Chris, Linda and Brendan O'Donovan from Leicester found additional information on the Green Bicycle Murder, for which grateful thanks.

Neil Arthur Williams, author and musicologist, very kindly gave me a significant amount of information on Emil von Holst OD (Ernest Cossart), Hollywood and Broadway actor, on whom Neil is involved in a long-term project.

My thanks to Olive Burkitt, widow of the late Dr Denis Burkitt, CMG, OD, and their daughter, the Revd Judy Howard, for details of Dr Burkitt's distinguished career.

Thanks to the Revd Douglas Graham's three sons, James, John and Tim, for their help on the history of Dean Close House, and also to the Martin family through three generations who have assisted on a number of topics.

Thanks to Heather Grundy and Alastair George for making the survey on loyalty possible and to the Housemasters and Housemistresses for their help. Rosie Fleming and Alex Bennion, both former DCS Sixth Form Archives researchers, helped on the survey and also on aspects of the text.

To Niall Monkton, Phil Sidey, Ben Earnshaw, John Didcote and Pauline Widdows of the IT team my grateful thanks for doing their very best to keep my computer working whenever I was able to be in School.

A very big thank you to the following ODs, past and present, and to any others inadvertently omitted who have provided helpful information either through interviews, letters, emails, articles, discussion or autobiographical material: R.A. Baylis; B.J. Barker; J.M.B. Bastow; C.H.R. Bell; J.S. Bell; John Boswell; Maddy (Norman) Bradshaw; Roy Brennan; C.J. Buckett; H.G.W. Clarke; John Cobb; F.I. Cooke; John Dravers; John Evans; C.N. Faulkes; M.E. Firth; Charlie N.E. Forbes; D. Garner; W. Clarke Graham; David Hanks; D.P.K. Havard; John Heskell; Georgina Hildick-Smith; Richard Hildick-Smith; the Revd Dr Jonathan Holmes; John Horsley; J.P. Howse; Richard Huck; A.L. Jayne; D.H. Jones; D.W. Jones; Nikki (Troughton) Kay; Sarita (Cawston) Khan; Dr L.M.J. Kramer; The Revd A. McFarlane; Philippa Martin; H.G. Mullens; A.S.R. Parker; A.A. Pilson; Sarah Pocock; Lucy Pomfret; Joshua Powell; Peter F.B. Preston; D.A. Pringle; Jenny A. (Gibbs) Pritchard; Derek Reynolds; Geoffrey Saunders; H.F. Shapland; D.R. Sharp; A.J. Simms; A.N. Smith; Lisa Marie Smith; Dr Rebecca (Millard) Smith; Malcolm H. Struthers; Dr Heather Whitney; Louise Whitney; Victor Whittaker; The Revd Arthur Wilcox; Emily Williams; M.P.L. Wright; the Revd Paul Youde and lastly to David Marsh for presenting a copy of *A Goodly Heritage: A History of Monkton Combe School* to the Archives Department. Chapter 5 was especially useful.

Thank you to a number of former staff who helped with various details: Richard Akenhead; Stephen Baird; Peter Cairns; Denys Carnill; Ian Ferguson; Margaret (Buchanan) Ferguson; Tony Forbes; Jane Harrington; Mike Hart; Ken Hollington; Tony Jones; Iris Long; Tony Marchand; Jean (Golder) Reeve; Joanne Reeves; Hilary Swan; Richard Taylor.

Mervyn and Mary Vaughan undertook a valuable study of the history of the School's medical department in 2004 for which I have been most grateful.

Various members of the present School staff have helped at numerous points and I would like to thank Jon Allen; Lloyd Allington; Laura Burton; Steve Cahill; Rebecca Chaplin; Karen Coward; Anthony Davies; Paul Davies; Martin Davies; Jackie Dunlop; Michael Ede; David Evans; Dominic Evans; Roz Fraser; Rhys Gwilliam; Jon Harris; Julie Kent; Chris Leigh; Paul Montgomery; Aron Needs; Benjamin Nicholas; Rod Pellereau; John Phillips; Helen Porter; Sue Raybould; Pam Shaughnessy; Pat Speller; Mike Titley; Dave Thompson; Gary Tredgett; Rebecca Vines; Kate Walton; Paula Watson.

I am grateful to the following for checking particular chapters or parts of them: Lloyd Allington, Dr Keith Aris, Vanessa Aris, Jill Bacon, Sue Bennett; Pat Bryan, Jim Burrows, the Revd Hugh Cocksedge, Professor R.J.W. Evans, Ian Ferguson, Margaret Ferguson, Mike Girling, F.J. Horsley, Mrs V-A Hutton, Chris Kenyon, Iris Long, Sue Padfield, Helen Porter, Hilary Swan, Viv Troughton, The Revd Christopher Turner, Lucia Turner, The Rt Revd P. St G. Vaughan, Sue Vaus, Brian Wilson and Val Wilson.

I am also particularly grateful to Sue Hardy OBE, Cecil Buckett OD, Patricia Napier and Peter Lynam OD, for patiently undertaking to read the entire first draft and thereby being able to give an overview of the whole project.

Warm thanks are due, too, to Tracey Colbert-Smith (from Dean Close School) and Rebecca Chaplin (from Dean Close Preparatory and Pre-Preparatory Schools) for their advice and for their professional help and skill in helping to put this project together and for assistance in the selection and use of the many photographs that have been used. They were essential members of the book's working party.

There are several people who have done much to support me and to whom mere thanks seem inadequate: Lucy Smith, Assistant Archivist, in addition to her normal tasks, dealt with much of the correspondence and permissions involved, spent hours searching out dozens of photographs and also did some most useful research into Old Decanians. Jonathan Lancashire, both as Bursar and Headmaster, was understanding on the financial side, interested, encouraging and practical on the writing side, read chapters, made detailed, helpful suggestions and came up with little gems of information that my research would not have found otherwise. It was he who found the apparent wartime shrapnel markings on the side of the Old Careers' Building. Richard Padfield OD, member of the Dean Close staff 1965-95, Old Decanian Registrar 1987-2009 and Old Decanian President 2005-2009, was equally supportive. Not only did he read and comment in detail on the entire first draft and then read and comment on various subsequent draft chapters but his patient corrections, suggestions and encyclopaedic memory for details of seemingly thousands of Old Decanians and former members of staff was more than helpful. He also contributed an interesting piece on hockey Blues. Sylvia Klemz gave me much help, excellent suggestions and a great deal of useful information from the Old Decanian Society. She also spent many long hours patiently and carefully checking what I had written, so that errors of spelling, grammar and punctuation should be cut to a minimum. Her ability to root out unnecessary words was invaluable. It is fair to say that without the committed help of those four this book would probably not have seen the light of day.

R.F. McNeile, in his original *A History of Dean Close School,* published in 1966, had C.A.P. Tuckwell as editor, former Second Master, Housemaster and Senior English Master, assisted by E.S. Hoare. A pleasure of this project has been working with an old friend who acted as an inspirational, supportive, conscientious yet gently demanding editor. Andrew Judge, former Senior Master, Housemaster and Head of English at DCPS, oversaw the text. However, I must also thank him for his work on DCS drama productions, the indexes and the master-minding of the selection and editing of the photographs. His care, patience, perseverance and good humour were always evident and I am deeply grateful to him.

Andy Johnson, of Logaston Press, was calm, professional, forebearing and always helpful. Very many thanks to him, and to Karen, too.

Anne, my wife, understood as days became more frenetic and much had to be done in a short period of time. I am more than grateful for her patient support and I hope she feels that the result was worth it!

While every attempt has been made to eliminate errors and omissions, please forgive any that may have slipped through, for which I apologise.

C.E.W.
March 2009

# Photographic Acknowledgements

The author gratefully acknowledges the contribution of many photographers to this volume, including Antony Thompson Photography; Stuart Robbie; Steve Cahill; Jeremy Winter; Paul Coleman; and Andrew Judge.

Grateful thanks also to: The Gloucestershire Echo; Cotswold Life; Cheltenham Borough Council; Gloucestershire Archives; David Gaine (Uppingham School); Bettridge School; Alison Primrose; the Revd Judy Howard; Sir Bernard Ribeiro CBE; Neil Jenkins; The Elsa Conservation Trust; Brian Jones Fan Club; Hugh Quarshie; Robert B. Stephenson (Glyngarth School); Happy Home Orphanage, Kenya; Pom Mbwanga; Professor R.J.W. Evans.

In Chapter 16 photographs are by kind permission of Miles Amherst and with thanks to Christopher Regan. In addition, the photograph of the Abbey is reproduced by kind permission of the Vicar and Churchwardens of Tewkesbury Abbey.

In Chapter 18 the photograph of Francis Bacon is from *The Times Review* for Saturday 3rd September, 1989.

# Preface

The Revd Tim Hastie-Smith, then Headmaster, invited me to take on the task of writing this book in the spring of 2006 so that it would be available for November 2009, the 125th anniversary of the laying of the School's Cornerstone. It had several tasks.

Firstly, it was to tell the evolving story of the School. To say that it was to be a history is stretching a point, as that suggests careful analysis, the weighing up of this course of action in contrast to the possibility of that. Although there are occasions when such reflections are made, it is more correct to see this volume as a chronicle.

Secondly, up to a limited point it was to be something of a reference book, so that child or adult, staff member, parent or Old Decanian (OD) could turn to it in order to try to verify some fact or resolve some point. This is one of the reasons that boxed text has been used containing lists of who did what and when, and also why there is a select bibliography and reasonably comprehensive index. It is clearly impossible to write about all the facts that some might feel warrant inclusion in such a volume, and so the reader's indulgence is requested where something has been omitted. Although considerable care has been taken over accuracy, inevitably there will be areas where this is called into question. Where this volume is found to be incorrect, I can only apologise.

Thirdly, this book was to be broader than merely a rehearsal of events in the three schools – four, if you include the International Summer School. It was to try to put the perspective of the children and young people involved from time to time as well as those of the adults concerned. It was also to say something about the locality in which the School is found, and something of other schools with which Dean Close School has had – or continues to have – any number of dealings.

Fourthly, it was to be a book into which people could dip without feeling that they had to read the whole volume. This was to be made easier by the use of a large number of photos, the index and the use of boxed text.

Fifthly, it was to say something about the three wars that have particularly affected the School thus far but about which little has been written from the School's point of view: the Boer War and the First and Second World Wars.

However, writing about an institution that has evolved over 120 years and more has inevitably produced problems. Sometimes they have been easily solved; the Junior School remains the Junior School in the text until 1999 when it became the Preparatory School; the Pre-Preparatory Department remains as such until 2003, when it became a School in its own right. Rather harder to determine was what the terms were to be called: Autumn, Spring, Summer appeared on some calendars in some years: Michaelmas, Lent and Trinity on others. There was sometimes a mix. As all three Schools now conform to the latter three, it was decided to stick with that throughout the book. A further problem was how to refer to members of the Senior School as, from the start of the School until about 1980, pupils were known as Decanians. In about 1980 it was decided by the Headmaster, Christopher Bacon, to refer to them all as Scholars. The idea behind that had been to attempt to improve the self-image and feeling of worth academically among those who were not necessarily too academically gifted. Feedback from a number of people who read early drafts of chapters where the word Scholar was used in this new sense, was that some were confused, especially if they had not come across the name in that context before; it was particularly difficult where those holding conventional scholarships, of whatever type, were involved. Therefore, it was decided to revert to the original Decanian, not least because it is a term that may be used perfectly correctly today.

This book has a number of brief biographies, and other material, set aside in boxes. Who to include and who to exclude became something of a vexed question. It would clearly be invidious to include this person but not that unless there was a clear rule. Ultimately, it was felt that it was appropriate that only Headmasters or Headmistresses were always to be included, whether dead or alive, together with those of the governing body, such as the President. No other living, present or former members of staff or pupils were to be included in their own individual box, although those who made a particular contribution but had since died might be included, e.g. C.A.P. Tuckwell.

Another question was which staff should be *listed* in boxes. In the end it was decided that Headmasters and Housemasters/mistresses, Bursars and Chaplains should be. However, it was felt that members of Senior Management Teams should not be as the number of lists involved would have been extensive, and changes of status of some positions over time would possibly be confusing. Moreover, many senior staff appeared in the text in their individual capacities anyway.

The value of money changes constantly and is most marked over a period of years. In order to help readers, the Bank of England values of money in December 2008 (shown in brackets) have been used to enable comparisons to be made.

One other matter needs to be mentioned. Roughly until the end of the 1960s, the amount of activity in the two schools, Senior and Junior, was very gently expanding. Admittedly, there were a total of nearly 540 children in 1968; over 900 by 2008, including the Pre-Preparatory School. However, from the end of the sixties to the present day there has been a veritable explosion in the amount of activity on campus and a major expansion in School initiatives off-site. This was caused in part by the advent of girls; in part by the enthusiasm of staff; in part by more money becoming available because of increased numbers; in part by widening academic, sporting and extra-curricula opportunities; in part by ever-improving facilities; and in part by the expectations of the Headmaster of the day, of parents and of the Decanians themselves. Hand in hand with the increase in activity has been a rise in the standards attained, be they academic, sporting or cultural, and a consequent feeling that more and more achievements should be referred to in any chronicle of the School. Moreover, the information concerning these activities might be found in an increasing number of School news and information outlets. The result for anyone writing about the School has been the necessity to look at an increasingly daunting quantity of material. Inevitably, this has meant that, at times, more recent achievements, incidents or occasions recorded in the text have become perilously close to looking like a mere list, although there have been determined attempts to avoid that if at all possible.

The observant reader will quickly note that in this book there are no footnotes and that the bibliography is 'select'. Given the 2,000 and more footnotes and the range of sources used in the first draft, it was realized that if they were included in the book itself the final price might be prohibitive. For the student who wishes to delve deeper, it is hoped to produce a more detailed version, though without illustrations, within a comparatively short time of this edition being published. Indeed, one of the hopes of this project is that readers will feel encouraged to undertake their own research. As it is, some may regret the omission of this person, that detail or that incident but the text and boxes together have considerably overrun the original anticipated length, so economy of words has had to be paramount.

Unlike R.F. McNeile's *History of Dean Close School*, the reader will find no specific chapter on Religious Life. It was felt such a chapter might suggest that the secular and the religious should be separated, when both should be seen as indivisibly part of the whole.

It is hoped that if this book does little else, it will at least show what faith can achieve. At times, disaster has been perilously close. Nevertheless, even in today's society, this book maintains that there is a valued place for a School that is rooted in the Christian faith and the ethos and positive values that flow from that starting point.

C.E. Whitney
Bushley Green, Tewkesbury
March 2009

# Chapter 1

## The Foundation and Opening of Dean Close Memorial School

At 11am on 11th November, 1884, – a time of year that would herald the Armistice 34 years later – a service began at St Mark's Church, Cheltenham before the laying of the Cornerstone of a new Evangelical Anglican independent school for boys. The School was to be named Dean Close Memorial School after Francis Close, one of Cheltenham's best known clergymen from 1826 to 1856, when he was appointed Dean of Carlisle. The stone laying itself was undertaken by the Mayor, George Parsonage, once a member of one of Francis Close's Bible classes, as the President of the future school (the 83-year-old Earl of Shaftesbury, famous Evangelical and social reformer) was unable to attend the ceremony.

Cheltenham Promenade *circa* 1900

## The Laying of the Cornerstone, 11th November, 1884

The Revd Canon G.P. Griffiths

To the Glory of God,
and in Memory of the late
**Francis Close, D.D.**
Incumbent of Cheltenham, 1826--1856,
and Dean of Carlisle, 1856--1881,
**The Building of a Middle Class School**
Was undertaken for the Purpose of
Training Youths for spheres of Future Usefulness
upon Scriptural, Evangelical, and Protestant Principles
in accordance with the Articles and Liturgy
of the Church of England.
**The Corner Stone**
after a Service of Prayer and Praise, was Laid by the
Mayor of Cheltenham,
on the 11th day of November, 1884.
Charles Dent Bell, D.D. Rector of Cheltenham.
George Parsonage, Mayor of Cheltenham.
"The Memory of the Just is Blessed."

The laying of the Cornerstone, with its Biblical allusions (I Peter, chapter 2, verses 6, 7) was thought more appropriate than referring to it as a Foundation Stone. It is located to the right of the black door leading to the main reception area at Dean Close School.

The service in St Mark's Church began at 11am. The prayers were led by the Vicar, the Revd G.P. Griffiths. The sermon was preached by the Very Revd W.H. Fremantle, Dean of Ripon and a noted Evangelical. The lessons were taken from Deuteronomy, chapter 6 and I Peter chapter 2. The first of two hymns was *Spirit Divine, Attend Our Prayers* while the second appears to have been written for the occasion, although its authorship is a mystery. The first verse began:

> 'Lord, at Thy mercy-seat we bow,
> Oh, hear the prayer we offer now!
> Stoop from Thy dwelling-place on high,
> Accept our fervent pleading cry…'

The verse finished:

> 'Be with us, gracious God, we pray,
> As now this Corner-stone we lay.'

Each of the three subsequent verses finished with '…As now this Corner-stone we lay…'. The Blessing was given by the Revd Canon Bell, Rector of Cheltenham.

A collection was taken that amounted to £93 15s 3d, a huge amount that approximates to about £8,700 in 2008.

After the service, everyone transferred across to Shelburne Road where, at 12.30pm, the second, shorter ceremony took place. It was taken by Canon Bell, the Revd G.P. Griffiths and the Revd T.H. Clark, a Governor who had been instrumental in the setting up of the School and was Honorary Secretary of the Governors for some time. After the singing of *All People That on Earth do Dwell* and some prayers, the Mayor of Cheltenham, George Parsonage, laid the stone with a special trowel. The hymn *O God our Help in Ages Past* was sung, followed by a prayer from the Dean of Ripon and the Blessing by the Rector of Cheltenham.

A further collection was made which realized £8 15s 0d (£814). The Mayor presented the School with £25 (£2,328), and a prominent local citizen, James Agg-Gardner, whose family had held the lordship of the manor of Cheltenham earlier in the century, promised a similar amount.

Francis Close's widow Mary and one of his sons, Admiral Francis Arden Close, attended the ceremonies, the Admiral acknowledging '…the generous manner in which his Father's memory had been honoured and the pleasure that it gave his family that such a memorial be raised to him…'.

There was a luncheon for 80 distinguished visitors and guests at the Queen's Hotel and the workmen had a celebratory meal too, though probably not in quite such genteel surroundings.

Landsdown and Queen's Roads *circa* 1900

The background to the decision to build a new day and boarding independent school for boys in Cheltenham was quite complex. In the 19th century, education for middle class boys and, to a lesser extent, girls, became increasingly important. The empire required educated administrators; industry and commerce entrepreneurs; the armed services, the professions and the Home Civil Service were all requiring increasing numbers of educated people. The existing public and grammar schools were too few to cope. During Queen Victoria's reign, the Roman Catholic Church in England, which had been legally re-established in 1829, and one Church of England faction, High Church in character, under the leadership of the Revd Canon Nathaniel Woodard, began to build schools that reflected the faith tradition from which they came.

Evangelical members of the Church, inspired by men such as Charles Simeon and later by Francis Close felt they must respond to what many of them saw as these developing signs of 'Popery'. Schools were founded such as Weymouth College in 1863. The cumbersome sounding South-Eastern Clerical and Lay Alliance, an Evangelical body, opened a South Eastern College in Ramsgate, Kent, in 1879 that was soon to be known as St Lawrence College, Ramsgate.

In 1882, Evangelicals in western England formed the Clerical and Lay Association (Western District) Middle-Class Schools Committee that decided to found a similar school to St Lawrence with a view initially to building it in Clifton, a suburb of Bristol. Such a school should be in or very close to an Evangelical Trustee-run parish church. It should be both day and boarding and should ideally have a similar school for girls nearby. The death of Dean Close, a leading Evangelical of his day, that same year, led to the decision to build the school in his memory in Cheltenham.

A suitable site for the School was found on the private and almost rural Shelburne Road. A 9½ acre field that formerly grew '…rich barley…' was sold by John and James Winterbotham, from a prominent Cheltenham family, at a price of £1,880 (£175,000). The sale was completed in April 1884 and a local firm of architects, Knight and Chatters, was engaged. The School was paid for by individual donations to an appeal for £20,000 launched by local Evangelical clergy, headed by Francis Close's widow, Mary, who gave £1,000 (£93,000).

**Evangelicalism**

An Evangelical is one in whose Christian faith the greatest importance is attached to the teachings of the Bible as the basis for belief and to personal conversion to following Jesus Christ as a necessity for true Christianity. There is a strong commitment to missionary outreach combining compassion with urgency, spreading the Faith to others. Many Evangelicals are in independent congregations as well as in the main denominations including the Church of England.

**The Winterbotham Family**

The Revd William Winterbotham was a famous non-conformist minister in the late 18th century connected with Plymouth. He certainly knew Cheltenham and suffered two years' imprisonment for his religious and political opinions. John Brend Winterbotham, his son, a solicitor, owned quite a lot of property in and around Cheltenham and was deeply involved in the incorporation of the borough of Cheltenham which occurred in 1877. James Winterbotham was also involved, being against one man one vote when it threatened to overturn the influence that property owners had been able to exert in the past. Miss Clara Winterbotham, great-granddaughter of the Revd William, was the first woman to be elected Mayor of Cheltenham (1921).

Early in the summer of 1886, work was completed on the Headmaster's House (where the School's reception is now, together with the Headmaster's Study, the staff Common Room and part of Gate House). Also completed was approximately half of the present classroom and boarding block attached to the old Headmaster's House. The question was how long the newly appointed Headmaster, the Revd William Flecker, would take to fill the initial 50 places. He had been the successful candidate from 18 replies to the following advertisement that had appeared in the newspapers after a first attempt had not attracted the right person: '…A Headmaster of decidedly Evangelical and Protestant principles, is required for the Dean Close Memorial School, Cheltenham. Applicants should be Graduates in

**The Revd Dr William Herman Flecker and Family**

He was born on 18th December, 1859 in Northamptonshire. His father, Issacher, was a Jew from Galicia in Austria, who emigrated to England, converted to Christianity, married and eventually became a teacher and non-stipendiary Baptist Minister. William's parents subsequently moved to London, where he attended a number of schools, the last being the Cowper Street School which he left at the age of 16. Always keen to teach, aged 17 he was working in a private school in Stoke Newington. Two years later he was awarded a scholarship by Durham University. He chose to read Mathematics.

At Durham he was deeply involved in music, Christianity, reading and his studies. These numerous activities told on his health. He graduated with a Second Class degree.

Aged 21, Flecker was appointed to an Assistant Mastership at Eastbourne College where he stayed for three years, during which time he married the highly musical Sarah Ducat, daughter of a Polish Jew who, like Flecker's parents, had emigrated to England and similarly converted to Christianity, and with whom he had fallen in love when he was only 16. On 19th May, 1883 he was ordained, serving as an assistant curate at St John's Meads. He became Headmaster of the new City of London Collegiate School in 1884 but left that in order to be the first Headmaster of Dean Close Memorial School in 1886, aged 26. L.M.J. Kramer writes that Flecker was '…dark, with a dark moustache and thick glasses and …that…he was tall, formidable, well built and imposing and usually seen in cap and gown…'. R.J.W. Evans described him as '…pious, energetic and determined, with a thirst for learning and a good business sense...'. Pupils said of him that he was '…kindly, just, strict but impartial…he had a sense of humour…yet he could be furious if the situation demanded it…'. He was also assistant curate of St Mark's Church for some years and remained Headmaster until 1924.

Thomas Cooper was a lifelong friend of Flecker's who joined him at DCS in around 1890. The two of them, when boys, walked miles '…to see Thomas Carlyle come out of his house in Chelsea and mount his horse for his morning ride…'. When their paths diverged for a time, Cooper suggested to Flecker that they should read some Plato every week and then write to each other, comparing notes.

Honours, and in Holy Orders. A stipend of £300 a year guaranteed, with house and the boarding of pupils…'.

The School was formally incorporated under the Companies Act and was finally enrolled in the High Court (Chancery Division) on the 4th March, 1886, the object being stated as '…chiefly to educate boys of parents of limited means for the spheres they are to occupy upon Scriptural, Evangelical and Protestant principles in conformity with the Articles of the Church of England as now by law established…'. Those principles were to be found again in the advertisements for the School in the press: '…the object of the School is to give a thoroughly useful education, based upon the Scriptural, Evangelical and Protestant Principles of the Church of England…'.

Mrs Flecker had oversight of all the domestic and health arrangements in the School. She was assisted by a team of young girl servants and a trained nurse.

The Headmaster and his wife had four children. The eldest was Herman, better known as the poet, James Elroy Flecker OD, who died of natural causes at the early age of 30 in 1915 (see chapter 18). Claire, the second child, married E.C. Sherwood, Headmaster of St Lawrence, Ramsgate while Joyce, the younger daughter, read Science at London. She taught Chemistry at Dean Close during the First World War, producing a text book used by the School in her day. Her fiancé, the musically talented Lionel Halse OD (briefly a Master at Dean Close), was killed in the First World War. She eventually married Arthur Bolton and worked in the schools of which he was Headmaster. Oswald, the youngest Flecker child, was also an OD. Invalided out of the Army in 1918, he taught at Marlborough College and eventually became Headmaster first of Berkhamsted School and then Christ's Hospital. He was awarded a CBE in 1949 and later became Principal of Lawrence College, Pakistan.

At Dean Close Memorial School, Dr Flecker taught most subjects except the Natural Sciences. He particularly tended to teach Scripture, History, German and Mathematics. After some years at Dean Close, he was awarded the degree of Doctor of Civil Law by Durham University for a thesis on 'The History of Roman Civil Procedure to the time of Justinian'. In 1916 he was also appointed a local Justice of the Peace.

He was Headmaster of Dean Close for 38 years. On his retirement he initially took a house in Croydon but subsequently took charge of a new church in Staines, Middlesex. Here he remained for the rest of his life. In the early summer of 1941 he celebrated his diamond wedding with Sarah, receiving 400 congratulatory letters and telegrams. He died on 26th August, 1941, aged 81.

The Headmaster, Mrs Flecker and their eldest child Herman (James Elroy)

The original school frontage, viewed from Shelburne Road, with Dr Flecker standing in front of the main door

The School opened on 5th May, 1886. The previous few days had clearly been busy, as the Headmaster wrote later: '…The east wind howled through the unfurnished building; workmen swarmed everywhere, putting finishing touches to their work – no blinds, no gas, no beds! Outside on the playing fields a few blades of grass were struggling up amongst a mass of weeds…'.

The School site was far more restricted than it is today; it only occupied the western side of Shelburne Road. One boy who came in 1887 recalled how it was '…unmade and very rough and dusty. There was a barrier across it just past the Headmaster's House [i.e. roughly where the bursary drive is now]. (It) must have been very annoying to people who turned into it from Lansdown Road unwittingly and found they had to turn back again…'. The road's upkeep appears to have been a School responsibility. As late as December 1888, Governors were ordering in 50 loads of stone, including 20 loads of Leckhampton stone, in order to repair the road as necessary. Soon afterwards, the road was taken over, presumably by the Borough Council, the surface improved and the barrier removed.

The School was bounded to the northwest by a fenced railway line to Andoversford and beyond to London; on the School side there was a low, straggly hedge. To the south, the grounds were bounded by the Hatherley Brook, a part of which has subsequently been covered over to create space for the hockey astro pitches. A.N. Smith, who entered the School in 1887, recalled that '…down the hill to the brook was out of bounds. A tall, straggly hedge with two crab apple trees in it crossed at right angles to

**The Branch Railway Line**

The present School shooting range was built on the old railway bed. The drive leading from Hatherley Road is roughly parallel to, and 20-30m the Cheltenham side of, the old track which was apparently originally the Banbury and Cheltenham Line. When it opened in June 1881, the single track stretched from Cheltenham to Bourton-on-the-Water via Leckhampton, Charlton Kings and Andoversford; eventually, it was routed through to London. It was bought by the Great Western Railway in 1897. In 1944 double tracks were laid. It was closed on 15th October, 1962.

the line of Shelburne Road from the School buildings to the railway line…'. Somewhere down there, towards the Hatherley Road but not as far as the field called Humpty Dumpty was a small field reserved as a grazing ground for Dr Flecker's pony. In those very early days, it was possible to go blackberrying without ever leaving the School premises.

J.H. Harvey, the only teaching member of staff apart from the Headmaster, was a friend of Dr Flecker, and was himself ordained while at the School. Initially staying only until the end of Trinity 1887, he brought eight boys down on the train from London – boys who had possibly been with Flecker at his previous school or, as R.F. McNeile suggests, the children of personal friends of the Fleckers, or both. These, together with some local day boys were the first members of the School. It has been suggested (and circumstantial evidence also supports) that the School opened with 12 boys although the Register

| Date of Entry. | Scholar's Name. | Name and Address of Parent or Guardian. | Date of Birth. | Music | German | Drawing | Workshop | Remarks. | Date of Removal |
|---|---|---|---|---|---|---|---|---|---|
| April 1886 | Young. W. M. G. | W.C. Young, 22 Windsor Road, Forest Gate, Essex | | | ✓ | ✓ | ✓ | | July 1887 |
| " " | Hopkins A. J. | Mrs Hopkins, 135 Green Lanes, London N. | 7th Sept 1873 | | | | ✓ | | July 1887 |
| " " | Wardroper J. M. | Rev. A. Wardroper, 21 Cloudesley Sq. Islington N. | 5th April /75 | | | ✓ | | | July 1892 |
| " " | Lewin A. H. | G. Lewin, 25 Woodberry Grove, London N. | 6th July /70 | | | | | | Dec 1886 |
| " " | Murray C. S. | Mrs Murray, 9 Eastfield Park, Weston S. Mare. [G] | 24th Feb. /74 | | | | | | Dec 1890 |
| " " | Philp F. R. E. | W. R. Philp, Eagle House, Highbury Hill, London N. | 21st Nov. /70 | | | | | | July 1887 |
| " " | Vickers E. W. | J. K. Vickers, 32 Aldersgate St London E.C. | 12th Apr. /72 | | | | | | Dec. 1887 |
| " " | Vickers E. S. | " " " | 12th Nov. /73 | | | | | | Dec. 1889 |
| May 1886 | Westley F. | C. Westley, Horton Villa, St Mark's, Chelt^m | 27th Nov. /73 | | | ✓ | | | July 1889 |
| " " | Westley E. | " " " " | 23rd Jan^y /78. | | | | | | July 1895 |
| " " | Searle G. M. | G. Searle, Marlboro' House, Woodberry Down N. | 16th June /73 | | | | | | July 1888 |
| " " | Summers A. | Mrs Summers, Cheltenham | 5th June /74 | | | | | | April 1889 |
| " " | Scamell A. W | W. Scamell, 4 St George's Parade, Chelt^m | 10th April /77 | | | | | | April 1889 |
| " " | Scamell H. M. | " " " | | | | | | | April 1891 |
| (Half Term) 1886 | Epps J. R. | Mrs Epps, | 1st April /76 | | | | | | July 1887 |
| " | Berry H. J. S. | J. A. Berry, Southcot House, Bath | 17th Oct. /73 | | | ✓ | | | Dec. 1892 |
| September 1886. Xmas Term | Ballance H. C. | G. Ballance Esq^r Blackheath Pk. London S.E. | | | | | | | July 1887 |
| | Campbell C. H. | Rev. C. Campbell, Highcroft, Weston-Super-Mare. | 1st April 1875 | | | | | | Dec. 1889 |
| | Nicholl G. T. B. | Mrs Nicholl, Hampton Villa, Weston-Super-Mare | 29th March 1873 | | | ✓ | | | July 1890 |
| | Smith C. C. | S.W. Smith M.D. South View, Pershore | 9th July 1872 | | | ✓ | ✓ | | |
| | Abbey W. B. T. | Mrs H. E. R. Abbey, Combe Down, Bath | 8th August 1872 | | | | | | July 1890 |
| | Pearson J. P. N. | W. J. Pearson, Essendine, Stamford | 19th May 1872 | ✓ | | ✓ | ✓ | | Dec. 1889 |
| | Read B. Moubray | Major M. Read, Beaumont, Cheltenham | 19th Sept 1874 | | | ✓ | ✓ | | July 1890 |
| | Read H. A. Moubray | " " " | 15th March 1876 | | | | | | Dec 1890 |
| | Jose S. W. | Rev. S. P. Jose, Churchill, Bristol | 16 Oct. 1873 | | | | | | Dec 1891 |

The first school register

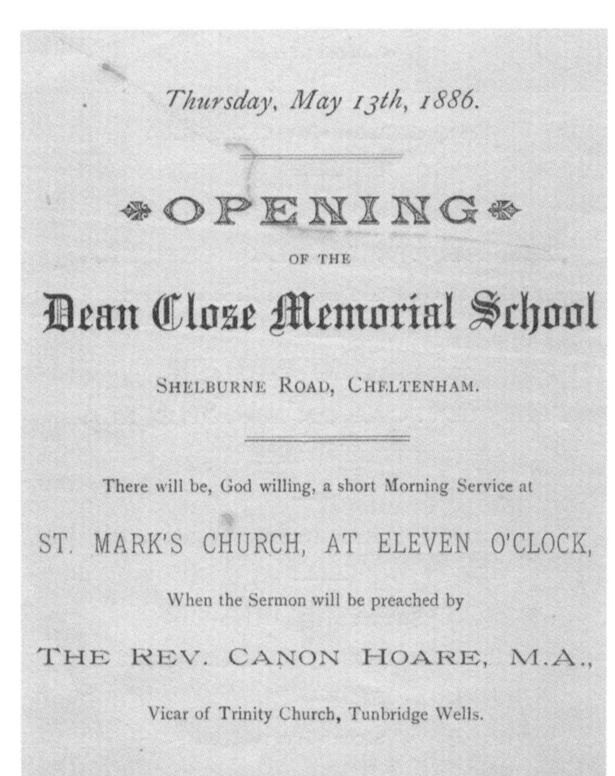
Thursday, May 13th, 1886.

OPENING

OF THE

Dean Close Memorial School

SHELBURNE ROAD, CHELTENHAM.

There will be, God willing, a short Morning Service at

ST. MARK'S CHURCH, AT ELEVEN O'CLOCK,

When the Sermon will be preached by

THE REV. CANON HOARE, M.A.,

Vicar of Trinity Church, Tunbridge Wells.

states that there were 14. All agree that numbers had risen by the end of that first Trinity Term: some suggest to 15; the Register shows 16 names while the Headmaster thought it was 17! After the first term, half a dozen boys also came from the parish where Dr Flecker had been assistant curate and where he had made a favourable impression.

The Register shows that one boy was eight, another nine and a third ten at the time of the School's opening. Of the rest there were two 11-year-olds, seven 12-year-olds, one aged 13, another 14 and a couple who were 15. There was, thus, a seven year spread of children. Initially, at least, there were more boys of preparatory school age than of normal public school. There may have been an arrangement whereby Mrs Flecker looked after the very youngest boys to begin with, though she probably wasn't paid.

The School was opened officially on 13th May, 1886 with a special service at which the Revd Canon

1895 cricket XI

Hoare of Tunbridge Wells preached. One of the last to be personally influenced by Charles Simeon at Cambridge, he was a staunch supporter of St Lawrence, Ramsgate, the school that was seen as something of a template for Dean Close Memorial School. There was a first special lunch in the new school buildings and then the School was operating in earnest.

The Headmaster recruited from Evangelical aspiring middle-class parents, word of mouth being his key recruiting sergeant initially. Entrants came from London, the west generally, Wales, Ireland, the ex-patriot community abroad and around Cheltenham. Subsequent careers are looked at in chapter 18.

Many years later, J.H. Harvey recalled what it was like playing cricket that first term. 'When the School was opened', he wrote, 'our field [now known as Chapel Close, as Big Field did not then belong to the School] had been sown with what was supposed to be grass seed, but the result was nothing but weeds and wild flowers. Some of our friends helped us by providing for the turfing of the triangular piece between the oak tree and the [then branch] railway, and meanwhile we had to play in a meadow below Brown's cottage. [Probably roughly the area where the current Swimming Pool and Bacon Theatre are.] Here we had thick spongy turf for our pitch and grass varying from six to 18 inches [½m] to field in. Under these circumstances a score of 20 or 30 was thought to be a good one for the whole side, and an individual innings reaching to double figures quite a rarity…There was considerable anxiety in the School when the time for the first match arrived, as one member threatened to get ill, and our only reserve man – we were but 12 in number all told – measured his height by inches rather than by feet…'. The Headmaster takes up the story: '…we formed our first cricket eleven, with [F.R.E.] Philp (aged 15) and [A.H.] Lewin (also aged 15) at the head, and a following of very small boys, the two junior members being eight and nine respectively. Some not discreditable matches were played, notably a most exciting game with the second eleven of the Grammar School, ending in victory for Dean Close…'. Unfortunately, it has not been recorded who the other matches were against, nor which of the two senior boys was captain. A.H. Lewin was also the first boy to leave the School, the only one to leave in December 1886, at the age of 16.

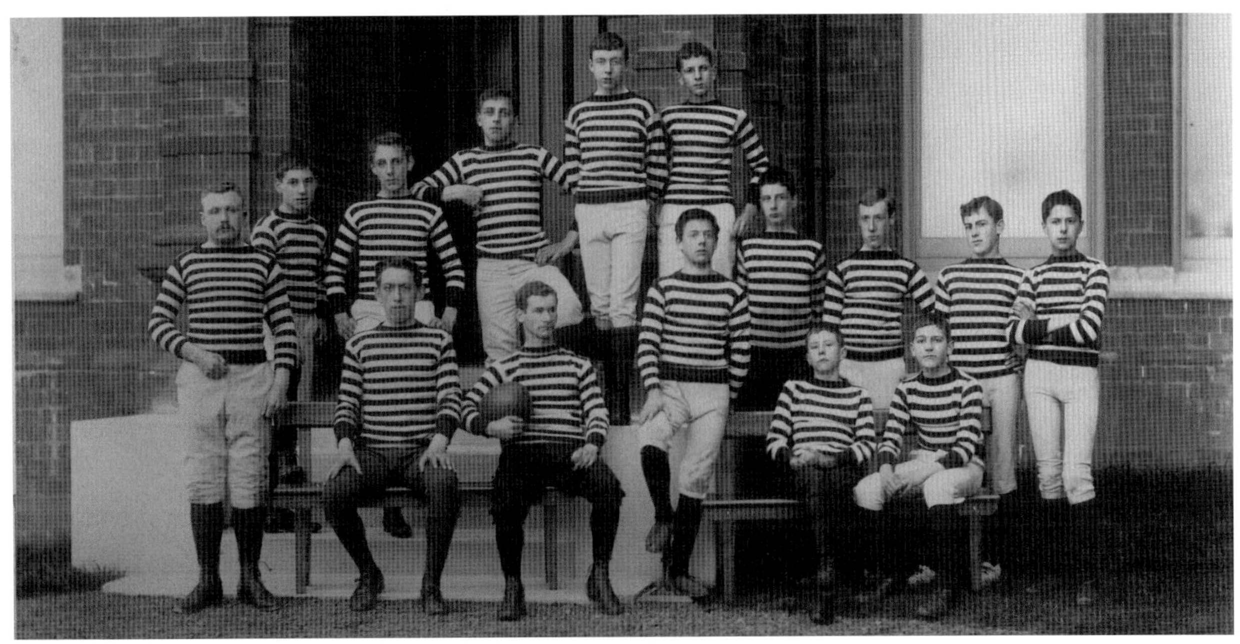

The rugby XV from the late 1880s

## Dean Francis Close

Born 11th July, 1797 at Corston near Bath, Somerset, Francis was the youngest son of the Revd Henry Jackson Close and his wife Mary who had five sons and four daughters. Francis attended Midhurst Grammar School, Sussex and Merchant Taylor's School, then in London. Subsequently, he went to Hull, at that time a well-known Evangelical centre, as the private pupil of John Scott who strongly influenced his Evangelical conversion in 1813.

Francis Close went up to St John's College, Cambridge in 1816, graduating in 1820 and gaining his MA in 1824. During his time in Cambridge he was strongly influenced by the Revd Charles Simeon, Vicar of Holy Trinity, Cambridge, a famous Evangelical who became, in Close's eyes, virtually a surrogate father, his own having died in 1806.

Francis married Anne Arden (1791-1877) in 1820. Subsequently, they had nine children together, five boys and four girls. One boy died aged only five months. Ordained in October, 1820, Francis served his title (that is, his first appointment as an assistant curate) at Lawford, near Rugby, moving to be assistant curate in Willesden and Kingsbury, Middlesex, in 1822. In 1824 he became assistant curate of Holy Trinity, Cheltenham, until 1826 when he became Perpetual Curate of St Mary's, parish church of Cheltenham. Effectively, he had the authority of a vicar or rector but not the freehold. He turned Cheltenham into something of an Evangelical stronghold and was noted for his work as a preacher, church-builder and educationist. He heartily disliked ritualism and anything that he felt was 'Papist'.

Close initiated the building of three chapels in Cheltenham: Holy Trinity, Portland Street; St John's, Berkeley Street (pulled down in 1967), and St James's, Suffolk Square (closed in 1976). He was also responsible for St Paul's, Christ Church, St Peter's (Tewkesbury Road) and St Luke's churches.

He played a key part in the development of infant education in the Cheltenham area from 1824, supported National Schools and contributed to the establishment of a school for what were then called the deaf and dumb. Close was deeply involved in setting up Cheltenham College which opened in 1841 and also Cheltenham Grammar School. He was influential in the foundation of The Cheltenham Ladies' College in 1854. He vigorously supported the setting up of a teacher's training college for men (St Paul's) and women (St Mary's); both opened in 1847 and are now part of the University of Gloucestershire.

In 1856, Francis Close was appointed Dean of Carlisle. Here he built two more churches. Anne died at the deanery in 1877. In December 1880, at the age of 83, Close remarried. Mary Hodgson (1806-1899) was the widow of a local wealthy landowner. In August 1881, aged 84, Close resigned the deanery and retired with his wife to Penzance, Cornwall where he died on 18th December, 1882. Mary died in Bournemouth on 8th April, 1899, aged 93. She left the School a legacy of £800 (£77,000).

Present day main school entrance with a detail, inset, of the replica of the school badge erected over the front door in 1986

For the first few years, what is now Chapel Close was a cricket pitch, a playground, and was where the annual sports events took place. Presumably it was also where all the other sport took place.

The first term as a whole was described by the Headmaster as being '...a very pleasant term...full of bright sunshine, long walks, kindly feeling and some good work...'. Dr Flecker finished the term with a community of under 40. Little could he have foreseen that same community today, now numbering over 1,000 pupils and staff, with more than 4,000 members of the Old Decanian Society.

# Chapter 2

# The Flecker Years

During the 1886 summer holidays, large parts of the dining room ceiling fell in, probably due to indifferent workmanship. Over the following weeks and months, more falls occurred elsewhere. In the end, all the boarders were moved out to 'The Ferns' in St Mark's Road in the summer of 1887 and every ceiling was taken down and renewed. The Headmaster reckoned that '…upwards of 10,000 feet of plaster had to be treated, and the dirt and inconvenience involved was simply indescribable…'. Despite the ceiling problem, recruitment continued promisingly. That September, the School began the academic year with 31 boarders and 12 day boys, 43 children altogether. 26 were under 13, including seven under ten years, while 16 were 13 or older, and could be said to be of public school age. Numbers do not always tally, as sometimes the age of the child was omitted. A second member of staff was appointed, J. Pritchard, who did not stay long, not least because he had problems keeping control. Numbers continued to rise during the year and so in the first half of 1887 a further teacher, L.G. Tugwell, was appointed, bringing the total full-time teaching staff to four, including the Headmaster.

Dr Flecker and his teaching staff in 1887.
Standing: J. Pritchard, L.G. Tugwell and J.H. Harvey

In March, the first Athletic Sports Day occurred that, given the few boys and the spread of ages at that time, cannot have been as competitive as later ones were to become! For the first few years it took place on what is now Chapel Close. By 1892 it was quite an event, with the Cheltenham town band playing, ODs returning, and the mile being won easily in a time of 5 minutes 13.6 seconds!

About the same time, the Revd G.P. Griffiths, who was not only the Vicar of nearby St Mark's but also a School Governor, began annual Confirmation Classes which he was to continue for some years.

The First School Photograph, 1887

The Flecker Library today

An anonymous writer (probably Edward Ellam) in the 1932 *Decanian*, having mentioned that in the early days all cricket matches had to be played on what is now Chapel Close, records that there were originally no boundaries: you hit the ball and ran. The record was a 'nine' where the ball was hit, and the batsman ultimately run out, through what is now the space occupied by the Beaufort building, through where the WAM Edwards Dining Hall building now is and trickled down to the bottom of the valley presently covered by the astro hockey pitches. Apparently the ambition of many boys was to smash the glass in the schoolroom (now the Flecker Library) where other boys might be sitting in detention. So real was this possibility that those in detention were sometimes required to vacate the window side of the room. A.L. Bodley is credited with hitting the ball sufficiently hard that it cleared the roof of the schoolroom and surprised a musician practising in a music room that in those days was immediately beyond the Library.

The new academic year that began in September 1886 brought with it a change in sport. The 43 boys played rugby! How this was achieved given the wide disparity in age and size is not recorded. According to one OD of the time, the School at one point '...had the temerity...to send a challenge for a match to Cheltenham College...'. This was something of a nerve as the College had been established for nearly 40 years and had a large number of pupils. No reply was received for some days but when it did arrive, it said simply: 'Eton we know and Harrow we know, but who are ye?' A terse put-down if ever there was one! It became clear that, notwithstanding the School's rising numbers, opposing teams to play at rugby were few and far between. Records do not say exactly when the change to football occurred but it was almost certainly in 1889. Almost immediately the School did well, the Headmaster noting at one point that '...the Football Team during the last term of 1891 had singular success, winning every match save one...'. One of their opponents was Cheltenham Town Football Club. They met in 1892 and the School won the first match 4-3, on the town ground. In the return match at the School, the Town won 3-2.

W. Page, carpentry instructor, in his shop

Other than sport, a key activity was carpentry. '... One of the useful things I learnt at School and it has stood me in good stead...' remembered one OD. There was a separate building used as a workshop, although it abutted the gymnasium. A working carpenter called Mr Bamber came out from Cheltenham several times a week to teach the boys, though he did not stay long. He was replaced by W. Page who became something of an institution; ODs returning to the School would make a point of trying to see him. By the end of 1891 between 50 and 60 boys were spending a minimum two hours a week in the cramped workshop. It consisted of two rooms: one for carpenters' benches and the second for the two lathes, while a loft was used for storage. Nevertheless, in the summer of 1891 an exhibition was staged during Speech Day including rabbit and ferret hutches and garden seats made by the boys. The enthusiasm was such and the conditions so cramped that an article, supported by correspondence, was written for *The Decanian* suggesting quite seriously that the workshops should take over the Gym as it was '...scarcely used at all for gymnastic purposes...'.

In 1888, Flecker allocated allotments to those boys who wanted them, encouraging them to garden. They were sited on the beginning of the sloping ground near what is now the old signal box.

Drill was part of the curriculum in the early years, taken in hour sessions two or three times a week by a former Sergeant from a Highland Regiment and subsequently by Sergeant Major Brown, Royal Engineers.

Punishments in those days have been described as 'innumerable'. Basically, beating, known as 'tanning' seems to have been the norm, administered almost every day. At the first Decanian Society (now Old Decanian Society) Dinner on 6th December, 1891, one OD referred to '...the rod which Dr Flecker kept for the purposes of physical chastisement...'. Detention seems to have been another favoured option, often for poor academic performance or effort. In time spent they ranged from 15 minutes to six hours for very bad work. Detentions were held every day after morning school and also in the afternoon on half-holidays. There was said to be a daily attendance of at least 20 boys. There were also 50 or 100 'lines' that could be imposed. Finally, one OD of the period has described being put on a diet of bread and water for some trifling offence and being served it in the Dining Room, where one of the Brown sisters (maids to the School and to the Flecker family for many years) would also dispense '...ever kind sympathy...with the meagre fare...'.

Detention in the Schoolroom

Edward Easterfield joined the staff in September 1887 from Corpus Christi College, Cambridge. He held an additional degree from France and was an ardent teetotaller, and ran a club in the School to persuade boys to abstain from alcohol. At the same time, a Debating Society was founded that has been refounded on several occasions since but is flourishing today. In the early part of 1888, 'Lantern' lectures were begun, the object of which was to '...impart pleasantly useful knowledge not actually included in the ordinary course of the School...' as the Headmaster put it.

Trinity 1888 opened with 130 boys, just two years after the School began. Its success was due in the first instance to the fact that it was comparatively cheap. Even as late as 1912, Dean Close Memorial School was charging £48 to £50 for boarders per year. St Lawrence, Ramsgate, in some ways its sister foundation, was charging £68 to £80 per year. Monkton Combe, the school near Bath with a very similar Evangelical approach, was charging £57 to £68. Of approximately one dozen Evangelical boys' schools quoted by the Church Association Register of Evangelical Schools at the time, Dean Close Memorial School was the cheapest. In the School Register, several families from Bath and one or two from Ramsgate chose to send their sons to Dean Close even though there were renowned Evangelical schools on their doorsteps. Dr Flecker managed to keep his prices comparatively low by undertaking all the administrative and bursarial tasks himself, having in his wife an apparently born administrator who watched over expenditure on the domestic front carefully, and by paying his teaching staff as little as he reasonably could – between £40 and £100 per annum compared to Cheltenham College's assistant teaching staff, for example, who were paid at least double and often more. He paid himself £300 (£25,700) a year plus some additional fees when the College's headmaster was said to be earning £800.

| Bursars | |
|---|---|
| 1886-1924 | The Rev. Dr W.M. Flecker, MA, DCL |
| 1924-1926 | T.M.A. Cooper, MA |
| 1926-1932 | Major A. Poe |
| 1932-1940 | E.H. Warr |
| 1940-1941 | E. Ellam, MA |
| 1941 | W. Crafnant Mould |
| 1941-1942 | R. George-Wallich, OD |
| 1942-1948 | Major B. Gaussen |
| 1948-1963 | C.E. Rowe |
| 1963-1964 | Brig. R.D.B. Taylor, OBE |
| 1964-1971 | Major D.A. Imlay |
| 1971-1983 | Brig. J.H. Montagu, CBE |
| 1983-1988 | Lt Col W.E. Spreadbury, MBE |
| 1988-1994 | Wing Cmdr S.G. Fowler |
| 1994-1998 | R.D. Hopkins, FCA (Acting) |
| 1998-2000 | Mrs N. Mosley, BA, ACA (Acting) |
| 2000-2008 | J.M. Lancashire, MA, FCA |
| 2008-2009 | Mrs K. Walton, BA, ACA (Acting) |

*Note: Two Headmasters acted as Bursar, The Revd Dr W.H. Flecker (1886-1924), i.e. throughout his headship. Christopher Bacon assumed the office of Bursar (1994-99), although delegated much of the routine financial work involved to R.D. Hopkins and Mrs Nicola Mosley, who effectively often acted as Bursars on a day-to-day basis.*

*One Bursar, Jonathan Lancashire, became Headmaster in 2008.*

*Two former assistant masters were Bursars: T.M.A. Cooper (1924-26) and E. Ellam (1940-41).*

Dr Flecker was also pragmatic when it came to recruiting boys. He was prepared to take boys as young as seven years old if necessary and as old as 16. He was also prepared to take day boys, though numbers of them had fallen to below 30 by 1890 and fell lower still thereafter. There were one or two unfortunate side effects: although many boys stayed some years, there were quite a few who stayed a year at most, making building a strong community more difficult. Moreover, Flecker's willingness to take in very young boys meant that for some parents, Dean Close Memorial School was treated as a preparatory school, their sons transferring to another, possibly more prestigious, public school when they reached 13. Yet Flecker took understandable pleasure in being able to say at the close of 1891 that '...Without advertisement or any aid, other than the good word of parents and friends, the numbers have gone on increasing...and we are still face to face with the problem of more applicants for admission than we can receive...'. The task of establishing the School as a *bona fide* recognized public school in its own right was helped considerably by Flecker's admission to that influential association of leading public schools, the Headmasters' Conference, in 1896 and Dean Close Memorial School's first appearance in the *Public Schools' Year Book* in 1898. About the same time the Headmaster decided to underline the School's acceptance as a *de facto* public school on the national stage by acquiring a coat of arms. He took advice from experts and in October 1897 the Executive Committee accepted what was proposed '...subject to such alteration in colouring as might commend itself to a sub-Committee...'.

According to Dr Flecker in an article in the first issue of *The Decanian* in 1892, in July 1888 the first formal 'Speech Day' (called a Public Day) was held, with the President of the School, John Deacon, presiding. The President gave the School a donation of £100 (£9,740). However, we do know that prizes had been awarded during midsummer of the previous year as one of them, awarded to P.T. Thornburgh for his Latin, is in the School Archives. This slim volume is of particular interest because it is probably the only item currently held by the School that contains the original motto – *Ad Majorem Dei Gloriam* – 'To God give the Glory'. It must have been shortly afterwards that it was discovered that this motto was the same as the Roman Catholic Society of Jesus (the Jesuits) that some Evangelicals would have looked at askance, and so the motto was changed '...after long and exhaustive consideration...' at a meeting of Governors on 31st January, 1888 to a very Scriptural Psalm 119 verse 105: *Verbum dei Lucerna*, which a modern translation has as 'God's Word (is) a Guiding Light', the transla-

**Dean Close (Memorial) School Coat of Arms**

Above: The Dean Close Memorial School Coat of Arms
Below: Cheltenham's Coat of Arms

The School uses the following arms, using the technical language of heraldry:

'Or, a chevron engrailed gules between two pigeons proper and a garb azure; on a chief gules an open Bible proper rayonne or. Motto: Verbum Dei Lucerna' ('God's Word: a Guiding Light' or 'The Word of God is a Lantern' from Psalm 119 verse 105: 'Thy word is a lantern unto my feet, and a light unto my path.'

For the lay reader, it can be described that upon a golden shield there is an inverted 'V' or chevron with scalloped edges, i.e. edges that are a succession of curves coming to points. Above the inverted V are two pigeons in their natural colours. Below the V there is a wheatsheaf in blue. On the red upper third of the shield (the Chief) there is an open Bible in black lettering on white pages, gold edges to the leaves and a red binding. The rayonne means that the Bible is encircled with, or formed of, rays or beams of light.

The top third or 'Chief' together with the inverted V or cardinal red 'Chevron' together with the pigeons are taken from the arms of Cheltenham Borough Council although the 'Chief' is blue, not cardinal red. Cheltenham were granted them in 1887, a year after the start of Dean Close Memorial School and, therefore, fairly fresh in Dr Flecker's mind. The pigeons represent the story of the discovery of the mineral waters that led to Cheltenham becoming such a noted spa town. The Bible is a reference to the School motto and the wheatsheaf comes from the arms of the Close family although the colour was, for technical heraldic reasons, changed to blue.

The School adopted the coat of arms in 1897 although they have not as yet been officially granted.

At the School's centenary in 1986, Houses devised their own badges based on heraldic concepts.

Original school motto

tion to be found in the present Dining Hall. This also seems to have been a motto connected to the six Morrison sisters of Cheltenham, the first of whom had just entered Cheltenham Ladies' College. No connection has as yet been established but the coincidence is curious.

Dean Close Memorial School expanded its facilities, including building the large schoolroom, now the Library, that opened in 1887, the extension to the boarding accommodation and classroom space that completed the familiar full frontage of the School a year later, together with the building of workshops and a dining hall.

In October 1890, Dr Flecker reported to Governors that the School had reached 200 pupils, of whom 170 were boarders.

**John Deacon, First President of Dean Close Memorial School**

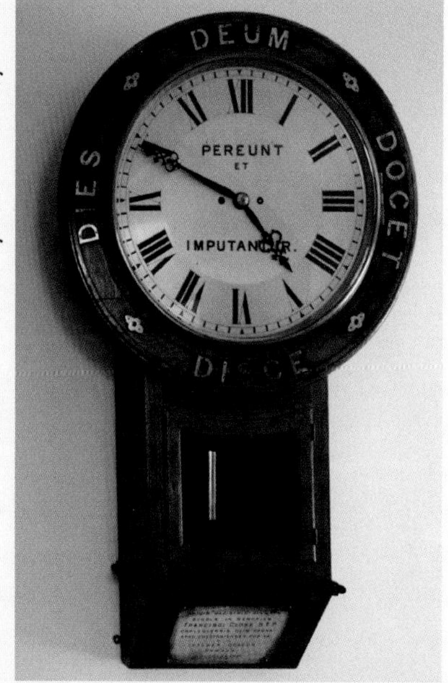


He took over as President in 1885 on the death of the inaugural President, the Earl of Shaftesbury.

Born in 1825, John was the son of John Deacon the elder of Battersea, London, a great friend of William Wilberforce, the social reformer. John Deacon the younger was educated at Oriel College, Oxford, before becoming a very successful banker. He was a leading supporter of Evangelicalism in the Church of England. He was one of the founders of Ridley and Wycliffe Halls of Cambridge and Oxford respectively.

Described at his death in 1901 as having '...untiring zeal in the cause of Religious Education...', John was one of the founders and a great benefactor of St Lawrence College, Ramsgate. Founded in 1879, it was seen as something of a model that Dean Close Memorial School should follow. John became the College's second President in 1895.

He is remembered in Dean Close School by the gift of a clock that is still in the hallway in reception, which he gave on the occasion of his attendance as President on the first formal Public Day (prize day) in July 1888. He is remembered in the Preparatory School by a day house, opened in 2001, that bears his name.

This was not achieved without difficulty. Already the School was using 'The Ferns', where Mrs Flecker's mother (Mrs Ducat) lived, as a Sanatorium.

The School simply could not house 150 or so boarders at that point. For a while a large house called 'The Myrtles' was rented where two masters and six boys were housed with space for perhaps another four. Then a boarding hostel was created out of two large semi-detached houses in St Mark's Road, almost a hundred yards townwards from the church, officially known together as Shelburne Villas.

New dining hall (ground floor centre) with boarding accommodation above and new swimming pool/gym building (right foreground) in 1899

Domestic servants in the 1890s

A sleeping cubicle in 1899

They were called 'Cora Lynn' and 'Atherstone' but quickly came to be called simply 'Cora Lynn'. They are still there. It was thought, somewhat optimistically, that the buildings could take 40 boys. L.G. Tugwell was put in charge but only 30 or so boys joined him. The house servants, the kitchens and Mr Tugwell, initially a bachelor but after two or three years joined by his bride Alicia, occupied most of the 'Cora Lynn' side, leaving the 'Atherstone' half to be occupied by the boys.

In the main School, the boys slept in cubicles, each closed off by a red curtain and each individual area usually adorned by family photographs. Later, these were to be joined by pictures of racing cars or sporting heroes. However, in Cora Lynn boys were in ordinary bedrooms, three or four to a room, according to its size. Breakfast and tea were taken in the house, in two basement rooms that had been knocked into one, but lunch was in School. Breakfasts were meagre unless a child's parents paid an extra guinea or two for 'special diet' that apparently consisted of an egg, a herring or a piece of bacon. Otherwise it was basically just porridge and bread and butter. After tea, prep was done in the house dining room. L.G. Tugwell remained at Dean Close School, and at Cora Lynn, until 1894. When he left, Dr Flecker had created enough space to be able to accommodate all the boarders back in the main part of the School. He may have been quite keen to do so, as a certain *esprit de corps* was beginning to develop, *The Decanian* remarking in 1892 that at the prize distribution that summer '...the applause...was especially loud when any past or present member of the Cora Lynn household came up for a prize...'. Tugwell himself took Holy Orders and eventually became Archdeacon of the Isle of Wight.

Back in the main School, boys washed in cold water using their own basins and ewers in their cubicles, which were used only for sleeping and games changing; there was no proper place to wash mud off legs after sport. Housemaids made the beds and cleaned the cubicles: boots were cleaned by an odd-job man and returned to boys' lockers in a gloomy boot room. 'At bed time, silence was the rule until the duty master turned out the gas lights', wrote one Old Decanian. Presumably silence was enforced after lights out, too!

Meals tended to be rather monotonous, with unvarying weekly menus. The pupils sat at tables in the dining room which was at right angles to where the school notice boards now are in the cloister area and covered some of the room space presently used by Fawley House and the IT Dept. One OD remembers that there were white table-cloths with aspidistras in pots down the middle of each table. Even when given chemicals spirited out of the laboratory by determined schoolboys, the tough plants refused to die. The slang word for bread was 'toke', said to be the word for it then used in prisons.

On Wednesdays but particularly on Saturdays, clutching their pocket money, boys made their way to Lansdown Castle Post Office and general stores, complete with its Victorian, crenellated walls that gave it its name, that did a roaring trade as the School did not have its own tuck shop. A 3lb (just over 1.3kg) pot of marmalade by Crosse & Blackwell cost 1/6 (£7.30). However, Dr Flecker was not the man to allow a potential area of profit to be denied him for long. He had a School Shop functioning by either 1888 or 1889 on Wednesdays and Saturdays, run at least in part by the Brown sisters, that

View from site of present Chapel showing Ellam's Oak

**Chaplains of Dean Close School**

| | |
|---|---|
| 1886-1911 | The Revd Dr W.H. Flecker |
| 1911-1915 | The Revd J.A. Luce |
| 1915-1918 | The Revd Dr W.H. Flecker |
| 1918-1919 | The Revd W. J. Allan Price |
| 1919-1935 | The Revd D.F. Horsefield |
| 1935-1937 | The Revd E.L. Phillips |
| 1937-1940 | The Revd G.W.H. Moule |
| 1940-1951 | The Revd E.V. Tanner, MC |
| 1951-1958 | The Revd P.R.W. Tidmarsh |
| 1958 | The Revd R. Walters |
| 1958-1960 | The Revd R.D. Page |
| 1960-1962 | The Revd K.N. Senior |
| 1962-1964 | The Revd R.D. Page |
| 1964-1965 | The Revd R.W. Hallett |
| 1965-1968 | The Revd J. Panting |
| 1968-1976 | The Revd D.I. Gibson |
| 1976-1983 | The Ven. C.C.H.M. Morgan |
| 1983-1999 | The Revd D.G.H. Young |
| 2000-2003 | The Revd L.J. Browne |
| 2003-2004 | The Revd S.J.N. Gray |
| 2004-2005 | The Revd T.M. Hastie-Smith |
| 2005-present | The Revd L. Talbot |

(In the early years there were as many as five ordained men on the staff. From 1925 to 1940 the Revd D.H. Bodley seems to have acted as Assistant Chaplain.)

was so successful that the profits were chiefly the means whereby the Fives Courts were opened roughly where the Upper Quad pond is now. In 1891, the School Shop total sales reached just over £200, realizing a net profit of £50 (£4,761).

The Brown sisters were not the only two ladies other than Mrs Flecker who were to remain vividly in the memories of Old Decanians. Miss Matilda Cogbill, the Matron, came to the School during the 1890s and did not retire until 1939. She was in charge of the servant girls who were mostly Welsh, all from the same district, and who were put on a list to join her when she had a vacancy. Later they tended to come from the Forest of Dean. She demanded the very best that the girls could give in terms of household skills and they were noted for their clothes-mending abilities. She also read prayers for her girls and made sure that they went to St Mark's on Sundays.

Prayers for the School were held daily, at around 9am and again in the evening at about 8pm, in the big schoolroom. Dr Flecker also took lessons in the Schoolroom on Sunday mornings to teach about services: Matins, the Litany, Holy Communion and Ante-Communion as well as to say something about the Reformation or Luther or some other aspect of Church history or faith. At other times of the week boys were encouraged to learn passages of the Authorized Version of the Bible. Some boys organized their own prayer meetings at which the Headmaster sometimes spoke and his confirmation classes gave '...sound evangelical grounding...'. He encouraged junior masters to hold their own Bible study groups in cubicles before lights out and occasionally invited outside speakers to visit, although their quality appears to have been mixed. As there was no Chapel at that time, the School went to St Mark's Church in a crocodile twice each Sunday, where the Revd G.P. Griffiths was incumbent. He was a venerable man with a long white beard, known as 'White Bear' to the boys. His nephew, who was also

Confirmation class of 1889

The big Schoolroom, now the Library

an assistant curate there, was known as 'Brown Bear'. A.N. Smith OD remembers the services being '…very long, very uninteresting and the sermons usually intolerable…'. However, it was felt that the influx and spiritual nurturing of Dean Close boys was sufficiently important that in order to accommodate them properly, rather than consigning them to the west gallery, which rapidly became inadequate owing to the growth of the School, a north transept should be built onto the Church especially for them, which it was in 1888. This move effectively put off the building of a School Chapel for 20 years. On Sundays the younger boys dressed in Eton suits, complete with Eton collars; wing collars, black jackets and striped trousers were worn by older boys, often with waistcoats. On Sunday walks, school mortar boards called 'Dabbers' had to be worn, adorned with the tassel in school colours. In the summer, straw boaters were worn, resplendent with the school colours on a band.

Church of St Mark

**School Colours**

It does not seem to be recorded when the School Colours were first used, who chose them or why the specific colours were picked. They were referred to by A.N. Smith OD in his memories of Dean Close School, published in *The Decanian* in 1962, about when he was a pupil (1887-1894). Recalling his contribution to the building of the first cricket pavilion, he writes: '...The boys themselves built the first cricket pavilion against the north-west corner of the workshop building...To this day whenever I read the verse in the psalms, 'In the time of trouble He shall hide me in His pavilion' I picture myself being shut up in a cupboard with a lot of smelly cricket pads in a building painted with cardinal [red] and cream stripes. Later, when the Big Field east of Shelburne Road was acquired and the cricket pitch transferred to it, a new pavilion of brick was built there...'.

Smith was a prefect, and so would have been extremely unlikely to have found himself 'shut up in a cupboard' that year. Moreover, the colours had already been painted. Thus it is very likely that he had his 'cupboard' experience either in 1892 or possibly 1893. It strongly suggests that the School colours of cardinal red (close to but not quite maroon) and cream must have been selected by the end of 1892 if not before.

Other evidence is given in a message from the Cambridge Old Boys (as they were then) to the annual Old Boys' Dinner in London, January 1893, when it was read out that '...a tie had been chosen for the society, and that the colours were a maroon ground with two narrow white stripes...'. The decision would have been made in 1892 by Old Boys, the majority of whom would have left the year before to go up to Cambridge. This indicates that the School Colours had been decided by 1891 at the latest.

There were occasionally expeditions out of School; for example, to mark Queen Victoria's Golden Jubilee in June 1887, the School was taken for a picnic in Cranham Woods. Coaches took the boys on a '...gloriously warm and fine day...'. The boys roamed the woods while School servants, who had preceded the boys' coaches, prepared lunch. There was also the 'Monthly Holiday' twice a term when boys were allowed to '...go off anywhere and do anything...'. However, this was curtailed when it became evident that some local hostelries were deriving undue benefit on such occasions!

In 1889 the first Chemical Laboratory was completed. It was a slightly grandiose title for what was apparently a small room in which only the legendary T.M.A. Cooper, who taught Science as well as Mathematics, and five or six pupils could squeeze. It was situated to the west of the workshops and behind the cricket pavilion. In short, it was well away from the main buildings and other pupils! It was, however, close to the first gym that had been built in 1886. It is said that when the teacher was not there, the laboratory was used by the boys to boil eggs in beakers.

This group of buildings (the first gym, the laboratory, and the 1892 pavilion) all occupied a position now largely covered by the fountains and rockery outside Tower House.

In 1889 the School was given the opportunity to buy Big Field, on the other side of Shelburne Road. Already it was very clear that the School was far too short of playing space for the children. The area on offer was a space of some 13 acres that stretched as far as the driveway that currently leads from the Tuckwell Open Air Theatre across to the Preparatory School. The asking price was steep at £400 per acre or a bargain £4,250 for the whole area. Initially, the Governors baulked at so high a price, preferring to rent it at £60 per annum. However, after lengthy negotiations with the Winterbotham family, a deal was done in December 1892, it being evident that if the School did not buy it then the space would probably be sold for building houses. R.J.W. Evans has described the newly acquired field as having

‘...the terrain better suited at that time to snipe-shooters than other kinds of sportsmen...’. One person who is certainly supposed to have shot snipe there was Canon Griffiths. Another described it somewhat ambiguously as ‘...rough pasture land...’. Draining it proved a major problem. After one holiday, the School returned to find Big Field a mass of mud and clay. However, corrective measures began to work. Lakes, that used to be inevitable after heavy rain, gradually became smaller.

Big Field was to be transformed over the years to a sports field thought worthy to host national trials in hockey and county standard cricket matches. That was in large part due to the enthusiasm and drive of one of the most enduring personalities to come to Dean Close School, the Classicist, Housemaster and Second Master, Edward Ellam. He had replaced the rather ineffectual C.H. Ayer, who had departed to be ordained, as senior Classicist in Michaelmas 1891.

The corner of the field nearest Lansdown Road, between Shelburne Road and what is now Caldecote House, possibly called ‘Absalom’ and including the area on which Shelburne is now built, was not part of the original purchase, and was only added to the main field after the end of the First World War. In earlier years, apparently, this parcel of land ‘...was a dismal swamp, inhabited by a goat [Archibald]

**Edward Ellam, staff member 1891-1941**

He was born in 1869 in Yorkshire, the second of three sons of his clergyman father’s first marriage. The other two entered Holy Orders.

Edward became Head Boy at King’s, Canterbury. Subsequently he won an Exhibition for Classics at St Catharine’s College, Cambridge. Although he was a reasonable runner, he was pressured into rowing for his College, though with indifferent results. He was not a team games player, although realised their importance.

After gaining a Second he came to Dean Close in September 1891. He remained at the School until his death in the School Sanatorium in May 1941. As well as being senior Classicist, Ellam at one time or another was the first Housemaster of Brook, the first to be appointed Second Master (in 1917), Acting Headmaster, briefly Honorary Bursar and the first teacher at Dean Close School to become a Life Governor. He acted possibly as a self-appointed superintendent of the grounds, librarian and extra-curricular activities co-ordinator. The idea of planting flower borders in the front of the School, in the area in front of Chapel and, originally, on the way to the Tuckwell Theatre were all his.

Possibly his greatest service to the School was in 1940 when at the 11th hour he managed to avert its closure through an emotional appeal and a cheque for £1,000 (£42,000), possibly the gift of an OD and himself, at the Governors’ meeting in Swindon, called to decide the School’s fate.

He was famed and feared for his vitality, no-nonsense approach, strict discipline and concern for high standards in academic matters and every other sphere of life. He has been described as being essentially a lonely man. He warmed to pupils as they grew older and many became deeply attached to him. Deeply, but unostentatiously, religious he was influenced by Dr Westcott at Cambridge and considered entering the Church.

Swimming Bath

of surpassing virulence, whose death took place under suspicious circumstances…'.

Late in 1889, a swimming bath was opened, roughly on the site now occupied by a part of the Dining Hall in the Edwards Building. It was 55ft (16.75m) long by 24ft (7.3m) wide with the depths ranging from 3ft 4ins (1m) to 6ft 6ins (almost 2m). This meant that boys wanting to swim no longer had to go into Cheltenham. The building was 25ft (7.6m) high. The pool was boarded over in the winter months so that the area could be used as a gymnasium. It continued in service until the present Swimming Pool and the adjacent Gymnasium were opened in 1964.

In 1891, the second (or possibly third) season that the School had played football, they entered the County Cup. The team usually consisted of eight boys and three members of staff. There seems to have been a certain amount of gamesmanship, for eventually they drew St George's, Bristol, the Cup holders, at School on a very wet day with a strong wind. The referee used ground conditions, a disallowed goal and the apparent onset of darkness to stop the game when the School were winning 4-1. They decided to try again a week later. On the Friday the referee declared the School ground to be unfit. There wasn't time to find another ground close to Cheltenham, so the School had to scratch and withdraw from the competition!

The School may have been less than popular locally because there were very few day boys, and the ones who were allowed in were usually hand-picked, 'trade' being rather frowned upon. Staff were largely recruited from elsewhere, and that included the domestics, so there was little employment generated for the local economy; even the vegetables were largely grown on site and the Fleckers, with the Governors at their backs, were always looking to drive hard bargains for goods or services. Thus the local economy was not boosted as much locally as some might have felt it should have been. There was also the perceived rather puritanical approach engendered by the Evangelical nature of the foundation. Moreover, the Fleckers were seen by some as being 'foreigners'. Nevertheless, in spite of all this, the School was thriving.

In the School of 200 there were just ten teaching staff, including the Headmaster. Yet many of those first boys made worthwhile careers in the professions, notably the Church, such as R.F. McNeile; medicine, for example F.P. Mackie OBE, as well as in business and commerce generally. Occasionally boys stepped out of line. Leonard Llewelyn came to the School with his younger brother Ivor in May 1888 from Aberdare, aged rising 14 and 12 respectively. While the younger boy stayed until April 1890, his elder brother was 'removed for bad conduct' in the summer of 1889. It is said that he was expelled because he had been more than physically aggressive and threatening towards the Headmaster, a situ-

R.F. McNeile

ation which, if true, could not be tolerated. No other child in the Register has that against their name until 1924, a remarkable reflection on the general level of behaviour, even though in 1894 the Headmaster expelled a pupil for having a revolver and cartridges in School after he had previously been warned. However, there were fights '...of the good old style...' as one OD put it, usually held in the Gym, now long gone, where spectators crowded up ladders on to beams to watch.

By 1896, the School had existed for ten years. Much had been achieved: the School numbers seemed to have settled at around 200; further buildings and grounds had been purchased; and it was beginning to accumulate respectable academic results. A highlight had been a prestigious scholarship to Balliol College, Oxford in 1895 by R.F. McNeile. Dr Flecker allowed a three day holiday to celebrate that but there were others, for example S.W. Jose's Scholarship to Christ's College, Cambridge in 1892. From the outset, Dr Flecker did not have classes as such: arrangements were far closer to the present day concept of 'setting'. Indeed, within Mathematics it was possible to be in different sets for Arithmetic, Algebra and Geometry. It meant that the whole School would do the same subject at the same time. This in turn required that, with few exceptions, every master was expected to teach every subject. R.F. McNeile noted that because of the lack of classrooms, the main Schoolroom might have to accommodate two or possibly three classes for each period. Music may not yet have been a strength, but certainly concerts of a type that encouraged staff as well as pupils to do a turn were well in place by 1892. Possibly Mrs Flecker's musical talent was also used. R.N. Green, the forerunner to W. Heller Nicholls, played and taught the piano, too. A Decanian Society for those who had left the School had begun to evolve in 1891 and *The Decanian,* the School magazine, was published for the first time in 1892, the first 99 editions overseen by the capable, modest, erudite T.M.A. Cooper, Flecker's lifelong friend, who did not retire from the editorial chair until 1925.

It is true that Flecker allowed little to devolve to others. The only exception was possibly 'Cora Lynn' and that was shut down as soon as L.G. Tugwell left the School. There was no Second Master at this point; the use of prefects took time to evolve; 'fagging' was never started. It has been suggested that in his organization of the School, Dr Flecker may have been ahead of his time and that in his use of 'setting', espousal of more liberal elements within the curriculum and lack of contrived tradition he predated the likes of J.N. Roxburgh of Stowe. However, his vice-like grip on all the key points of the School is reminiscent of traditional preparatory school headmasters or the patriarchal notion of how such institutions should be run, possibly harking back to his Jewish background.

On Tuesday, 21st July, 1896, there was a special Commemoration Service to mark the first ten years of the School. Dr Flecker himself presided at the Speech Day ceremony that afternoon: the prizes were given away by that morning's preacher, the Revd Prebendary Webb-Peploe from London. In his speech Dr Flecker referred to the evangelical character of the School and how supportive Evangelicals had been, but also noted the limited appeal such an approach had to a comparatively narrow base of the population.

Dr Flecker's friend, Thomas Cooper, and men like Edward Ellam (who was to stay until his death in 1941), Heller Nicholls (who arrived in 1894 to be Director of Music until 1936) and, later, William Judson (who began teaching at Dean Close in 1898 and stayed until his retirement in 1934) and others shared something of the Headmaster's vision for the School. They worked long hours for many years for indifferent pay and conditions. With his membership of the Headmasters' Conference and the possibility of a coat of arms, Flecker could begin to feel that the School that he had worked so hard to make a reality was being recognized by others in the educational world. Dean Close Memorial School was becoming truly established.

# Chapter 3

## The First Two Decadcs of thc Twentieth Century

Dr Flecker published a new prospectus in 1899. The first one, published on the establishment of the School, was probably fairly minimal. The support of the evangelical Christian community and word of mouth had proved sufficient for the first few years to build up the School, together with occasional advertisements in the press. The new prospectus was revealing in a number of ways. The School's adherence to evangelical principles was made clear on the title page; other than the Headmaster, there were 11 resident assistant masters who included not only Thomas Cooper, Edward Ellam and W. Heller Nicholls but also Edward Easterfield and F.W. Biennemann, who was ordained while at the School.

The new prospectus contained a photograph showing a much-improved Big Field named as the 'senior' playing-fields, while what is now Chapel Close was called the 'junior' playing-field. Another

The school frontage in 1892, viewed from Shelburne Road

Cutting the outfield on Chapel Close in 1901.
Note the Fives Courts behind the horse

picture shows the large schoolroom, now the Flecker Library, with desks formally arranged for over 100 scholars and a raised dais at the Shelburne Road end. It looks austere to modern eyes, with only a few bookshelves and a clock to relieve the monotony. However, it was well lit naturally by large windows augmented by gaslight during winter months. Initially there was no balcony.

The text mentioned that '... the Dormitories are divided into Five "Houses", all communicating with the Headmaster's House. All the boys in a "House" are of approximately the same age, the Junior House containing boys from 9-12, the Senior, boys over 17...'. A house contained about 30 cubicles, one for each boy. A master and a prefect slept in each house, the masters sleeping in cubicles that were larger but not very different from the boys', other than having doors. There was no attempt at house identity or the extended family ethos; the absence of 'vertical' houses in terms of ages would have made this difficult. The term 'Housemaster' was not used. The houses were effectively just dormitories and the Headmaster allowed little responsibility to devolve. All dormitories were in direct communication with the Headmaster's House, which meant he kept a tight grip on the School, even at night, and the new prospectus continued, '...There is unrestricted access to the Headmaster for boys of all ages, but a special afternoon is also set apart each week when a boy may consult Dr Flecker in private on any matter affecting his work or his well-being...'. There was no question of consulting another member of staff in quite the same way. At the same time, Dr Flecker's enormous energy and commitment have to be admired. As Headmaster of a school of 200 he taught every morning, with all the marking involved therein, his conscientiousness about which ODs attested. He sometimes taught a junior teacher's class for a whole week, to check the man's efficiency. He put aside an afternoon a week for pastoral work and also attended all the meetings to which he would inevitably have been committed. As Bursar he would have had a heavy administrative burden. All this suggests that he must have worked long into most evenings. Indeed, all his letters were written in his own hand. Afterwards, he walked to the pillar box at the end of Shelburne Road to catch the midnight post.

Inside the Tuck Shop

Apart from English, French, Greek, Latin, Mathematics, Book-keeping, Physical Science, Natural Science, Shorthand, Singing and Drill, in the normal curriculum much was made in the prospectus of a newly opened Engineering class. German, Drawing, Instrumental Music and Handicrafts were all seen as 'extras' and were charged accordingly. However, more space in the prospectus was given to Religious Instruction than to any other subject. Prospective parents were told that it included '...the Holy Scriptures, the Thirty Nine Articles [of the Book of Common Prayer], the Catechism, the Liturgy and the History of the Church of England – especially the period of the Reformation...'. This was taught daily by the Headmaster. The first mission came to the School for a week in the autumn of 1896, led by the Revd Norman Bennett; the Headmaster reported that he was '...very hopeful that real good was being done...'.

The prospectus was able to point to significant academic successes. In 1895 alone Decanians won scholarships to Cambridge, Oxford and Durham Universities. The School was a centre for the Cambridge Local Examinations, forerunners to GCEs, A and O levels and similar exams, and the School did well in them from the outset. '...In the Cambridge Local Examination the School has more than once done better in certain subjects than any other school in England...' the prospectus claimed modestly. '...The School has taken the first, second and third places in England in Religious Knowledge, the first and second in England in Arithmetic, the first in Mathematics, the second and fourth in Latin, the third and fourth in Greek, the first in Shorthand and the first in Drawing...'.

A large paragraph was given over to discussing the 'Junior School' curriculum which was effectively the same as the seniors. Unusually, they were taught '...once or twice a week...' by the senior masters in each subject and the Headmaster was said to teach them '...frequently...' himself. Thus both the Headmaster and his senior colleagues knew junior Decanians well from early on in their careers in the School. Moreover, the classes were said to be kept purposely small, though how small is not made clear.

A passage dealt with Victorian concern for health and sanitation and the work of Miss Cogbill was alluded to, though not by

**Early Staff who were Ordained either at Dean Close Memorial School or soon afterwards**

The Revd Dr W.H. Flecker was already ordained when he opened the School but was assistant curate at St Mark's Church for some years whilst also being Headmaster.

The Revd J. Pritchard was ordained soon after leaving Dean Close School *c.*1887.

The Revd J.H. Harvey was ordained while at DCS *c.*1890. He resigned in the summer of 1896. He was assistant curate at St Mark's after Dr Flecker.

The Revd C.H. Ayer was ordained soon after leaving Dean Close School in 1891.

The Ven. L.G. Tugwell was ordained after leaving DCS *c.*1894 and subsequently became Archdeacon of the Isle of Wight.

The Revd T.H. Senior, Assistant Housemaster of Cora Lynn, came in 1890 and was ordained soon after leaving Dean Close School *c.*1899.

The Revd F.W. Biennemann was ordained while at the School in 1899. He, also, was an assistant curate in St Mark's Parish. He died while Housemaster of the Hostel in 1901. He had served the School for nine years.

The Revd S.W. Payne was a lay member of staff 1905-06 but left to attend Theological College.

The Revd J.A. Luce was a lay member of staff from the beginning of 1907 but went away for two months in 1909 to prepare for Ordination.

The Revd J.F. Hepple sometime *Decanian* editor, was a lay member of staff 1901-11, then attended theological college, later becoming Rector of Nacton, near Ipswich.

The Revd C.C. Mountfort, who brought hockey to the School in 1907, was ordained while at Dean Close *c.*1910. In 1917 he returned to his old school, Uppingham, where he became a housemaster.

name. Health was a key issue, for numbers went down marginally during 1896 because the School closed early at the end of the Lent Term owing to an outbreak of measles affecting 21 Decanians. It may have become associated in the minds of parents with a '...severe outbreak...' of smallpox in Gloucester at about the same time. The net result was that a dozen or so boys did not return for the Trinity Term.

Mrs Flecker took the issue of health seriously. Junior boys were required to file past her each day and say to her, 'Yes, Mrs Flecker, and I had five (or three or whatever) for tea'. This coded sentence meant that the bowels of the child in question had been in action that day and how many slices of bread and butter had been eaten. If the child said 'No', then an aperient pill was prescribed. If fewer than three slices had been eaten, more had to be consumed there and then. She was said to have been momentarily put out by one stout boy who remarked, 'Yes, Mrs Flecker, and I had thirteen for tea...'.

Sport merited only a line more in the prospectus than was given to the Library! Nevertheless, money was being spent in this area. For example, *The Decanian* reports that E.N. Baker, who had been School cricket coach and groundsman 1895-98 was leaving to be replaced by R. Bell, the coach at St George's Club, Newcastle. The School must have been acquitting itself well at athletics, for in an 1898 article in the *Public School Magazine* the School was rated 17th in the list of all the public schools of England.

Perhaps one of the most interesting observations was at the end of the Prospectus. Having commented that the School attended St Mark's Church every Sunday '...where a Transept is set apart for their use...' which was slightly inaccurate as it was a specially built north nave aisle, the Prospectus announces that '...the Terminal Charge for Seat in Church is Five Shillings [25p]...'. It would have yielded approximately £150 per year (£14,450), a significant sum.

The Governors on the Executive Committee always looked after money carefully, especially as the purchase of Big Field had put them into considerable debt, but when appealed to by the Headmaster

The turning of the first sod prior to the construction of what is now Tower House.
Roland Brooke, Head of School, receives a memento

that unless he was given a Bursary, a boy called Claude Hart would be educated by Roman Catholics, there was immediate agreement that the boy should be helped!

In 1899 it was decided that a prefect's badge should be adopted, to wear on 'college caps', i.e. 'Dabbers' or the School mortar-boards.

More facilities were desperately needed. Initially this need was met by a dining hall block with a medical room close by and with boarding spaces on the upper floors and ground floor, rooms now used by the IT Department. It was completed in 1899.

There had to be still more accommodation for the boarders. The Governors may have had misgivings about the financial commitment but there was felt to be no other way to move forward. On 11th June, 1898 the School community gathered first to worship, using what had by then become the official School Hymn, *Now Thank We All Our God*. Then they witnessed the turning of the first sod first by Mr Roxby, Rector of Cheltenham, and then by R.G. Brooke, the Senior Prefect, who was given a gold pencil by Mr Chatteris, the architect, as a memento of the occasion. The building was to become the senior boarding house. Today it is Tower House.

The younger Flecker daughter, Joyce, wrote an article in the 1958 *Decanian* in which she described the end of the Michaelmas Term as Christmas approached at the turn of the century. In early December, her mother took her to Lance's shop in the High Street to watch her buy the dress lengths that were

Tower House today

given to the maids for Christmas, '…solid blacks for the upper servants, durable prints for the younger ones…' she remembered. A few days later, plum puddings were made in a huge earthenware crock. The wooden box arrived from Cambridge with the materials for the Cambridge Local Examinations. Mr Page and his helpers emptied the Gym of its apparatus and set out the long trestle tables with numbered labels marking each boy's place. There was also the important desk for the genial but unfortunately named Mr Pigg, the invigilator. He came to be well-known to generations of boys.

Excitement grew as the last day of term approached. On the last night there was a concert in the Big Schoolroom. The 'Band', composed of strings, was grouped at the end near the big window (where the Librarian's desk is situated in the Flecker Library); the boys were crowded into the desks and a row of masters sat on chairs from the library (now the seminar room) down one side. The music included lots of choruses to be sung by everyone. '…When there was a good musician in the School, his solo was listened to with respect and heartily applauded…'. Boys looked forward eagerly to the concert, and it was seen as a dreadful punishment if someone was naughty and had to be in detention in Rooms 1 or 2 instead.

Joyce Flecker continued: '…Towards the end of the concert came the exodus of the Irish boys going off to catch the night boat and being given their journey-money and exhorted not to forget their sandwiches. There always seemed to be a great many boys from Ireland in those days. Next day the rest of the journey-money was given out. My father did this himself; it was only towards the end of his time at Dean Close that he had any clerical help; with Mr Cooper in charge of the accounts they did everything between them…All letters were written by my father in longhand, and he never had either a trained secretary or a Bursar...'. Probably after the end of term, in the Library, '…there was always a very tall Christmas tree, rather over decorated in the German style by the Fraulein of the moment…'.

As the 19th century was closing, the School heard of the deaths of Mrs Close, the Dean's widow, and also of Canon Bell, a major supporter of the School, both in 1899.

Again, a sombre mood was struck by Dr Flecker at the OD Dinner on the 12th January, 1900. It was reported that '…he referred to the military situation in South Africa, which though painful to our beloved Queen [Victoria] and her subjects was bound to end in the overthrow of the Boer Republic. As a result of the lessons taught by the War, he anticipated that the use of the rifle would in the near future be introduced into the curriculum of our schools…'. This was to prove an accurate prophecy. Volunteers were already being sought to go to South Africa to fight. Some of the poetry written at the School at this time was almost jingoistic:

'England's call was not unheeded,
By Decania's loyal sons;
And if more should still be needed
There are more to man the guns…'
*(from 'An Encomium', anon. 1900)*

Moreover, the Boer War marked the first occasion the School was to suffer casualties. Roland Brooke, who proposed the health of the School staff that evening, was sadly to be one of them within six months. The first to be killed was T.W. Jenkins, then Brooke, while H.M. Wood was the only OD officer to die on active service in that conflict.

## Dean Close School and the Boer War

The Boer War usually refers to the second of two conflicts in South Africa, the first being in 1880-81 before Dean Close School existed. The second was 1899-1902, over 12 years after the School opened by which time over 700 boys had left, of whom 84 were members of the fledgling OD Society in January 1900.

The Boers were descendants of Dutch settlers. They and the English settlers fell out over self-government, voting rights and the discovery of gold in Witwatersrand near Johannesburg. The Treaty of Vereeniging was finally signed in May 1902, ending a war that had cost 75,000 lives.

Although the School did not suffer many casualties, the psychological impact of them was far greater in that initially it was seen as something of an adventure – other people might be killed but people one knew were in some way thought to be immune. Casualties were as follows:

**T.W. Jenkins**. Killed at Labuschagn, possibly in a skirmish; his body might have been taken to Dordrecht on 4th March, 1900. He was the eldest of three brothers who all joined Dean Close School in September 1887. He left the following year aged 16, and later bought land in South Africa, becoming a farmer. Dr Flecker, speaking of him, said, '…At the outbreak of the war he left wife and children that he might defend the country of his adoption. He was a magnificent shot…'.

**Roland George Brooke** (DCS 1891-99) Killed '…in a rearguard action...' Rietfontein Ridge, Heilbron, Orange River Colony, 7th June 1900. He was not quite 20 years old. This was a huge shock to the School (reflected in his 'In Memoriam' in *The Decanian* which covers six pages) as he had been Senior Prefect (Head of School) for three years less than a year before and was highly thought of – a good cricketer and also twice Victor Ludorum. He had volunteered to go out as a private while still a Scholar at Wadham College, Oxford, believing it was for 'Queen and country'. He was a member of the Oxfordshire Division of the Imperial Yeomanry. There is a memorial tablet to him in Wadham College Chapel.

**Hugh Maurice Wood** (DCS 1889-91) died of disease at Springfontein on 3rd May, 1902 aged 22. He was the only known commissioned officer from the School to die on active service during the conflict, being a 2nd Lieutenant of 1st Battalion, Royal Sussex Regiment. Earlier in the war he was a rifleman with the Cape Mounted Rifles and was recommended for a commission by Lord Kitchener.

Other ODs known to have participated include H.W. Hillier (Cape Mounted Police) wounded in the knee but recovered, near Kimberley, and experienced its siege; G. Moore (Rimington's Horse), a lengthy report of some of whose adventures appears in *The Decanian,* February 1900; W.H. Richards (Thorneycroft's Horse); J.G. Villar (North Somerset Imperial Yeomanry); Lt Col F.T.D. Wilson (2nd Suffolks); G. Stratton (Glamorganshire Imperial Yeomanry); K.H. Jones (Surgeon, RN – the only OD known to have been involved in the Boxer Rising, China, in 1900); and possibly E.T.R. Tyers in Natal; A.G. Hillier in Grahamstown; and A.F. Deacon, a vet, at the Cape. It seems, too, that P.S. Hill also fought in that war. A further list in *The Decanian* for February 1901 includes W.C.R. Savage, a Lieutenant in the Imperial Yeomanry of the New South Wales Contingent, who was with the advance of Lord Roberts to Pretoria; R.H. Greaves (Imperial Yeomanry); C.S. Frost served on the staff of the Imperial Yeomanry Base Hospital at Pretoria; E. Wait (1st Royal Scots (Volunteer Company); J.H. Williams of Baden-Powell's Police Force.

In February 1900, the Governors, at an Executive Committee Meeting, resolved that '…a free education should be given to some son of an officer who might lose his life in the South African War…'.

At that time the School had no Chapel, so that it was decided by ODs, with the firm backing of the Headmaster, that a memorial to Jenkins and Brooke would be installed in the Library, (the present Seminar Room), over a year before Wood's death. It is not known whether this idea came to fruition. There is no memorial plaque in the seminar room today; it is possible that any plaque was transferred into the original 'temporary chapel' in 1909.

Roland Brooke's death in particular jolted the School. When the new Bell Prize was offered for a prize poem later that year, the title was *The Dying Century*, a theme later also take up by Thomas Hardy in his poem *The Darkling Thrush*. A.S. Bell, the winner, included a verse about the fighting in South Africa that seemed to hint at the critical poems to come of the First World War, very different in tone to the poems of *The Decanian* an issue or so before:

> 'Blindly they go to their death; from the hill-side suddenly sally
> Flashes of flame and a roar; then the sound in a stillness dies,
> Birds on the slopes scarce pause in their songs, but down in the valley
> Horses and riders lie stretched on the sand whence they never shall rise.'

Training for warfare was a topic that the Headmaster broached again in his report at Prize Distribution the following July. The War Office had issued a circular giving directions regarding the formation of Cadet Corps in Public Schools. Dr Flecker suggested that if the War Office wanted such corps then they '…must provide the means…'.

Edward Easterfield left at Christmas 1900 to become Headmaster of Monkton Combe Junior School, having been head-hunted. He had been a positive, effective presence in the School. Arriving in 1887 from Cambridge University with an additional degree from France, he was an ardent teetotaller who ran a Temperance Society that reached 70 members in the School. He had run the Junior House, Hostel (the present Wilton) for six years. At that time, the house may have been known as 'Dormer', though how official that was is not clear. J.W. Kearns, Headmaster of Monkton Combe, said of Easterfield that '…his appointment…was the most important I ever made. (Easterfield) was a schoolmaster of outstanding ability, a fine scholar and a good forceful teacher with original methods…'. Easterfield stayed at Monkton Combe for the rest of his career. He died in 1941. The Revd F. Biennemann took over at the Hostel until he developed pneumonia and died only a few months later in 1901.

However, Easterfield's appointment had made Dr Flecker reflect on the School situation. In October 1900, soon after Easterfield's decision to leave was announced, the Headmaster mentioned the possibility of having a separate Junior School at an Executive Committee meeting of the Governors, an idea about which he said he was ambivalent. A sub-committee was selected to look into the whole question but before it could really get to grips with the issues, it was agreed to hold the idea '…in abeyance…' as '…all (the Headmaster's) energies were engaged at present in accommodating the increased number of pupils…'. It was not raised again for decades. Probably he could see the advantages of such a school but possibly there was the issue of personal control. He would have to rely on others, which he was disinclined to do.

Hardly had the School recovered from Roland Brooke's death than John Deacon died in the spring 1901; he had been a supportive, if largely absent, President for 15 years. He was succeeded by Lord Wimborne, a School Vice-President, who owned 83,600 acres of Dorset. His local connections were minimal but both he and his wife were evangelically minded. This was borne out in 1903 when the Governors had '…a long discussion…' about amalgamating many evangelical schools under one board, presumably in the same way the Woodard Corporation was doing for more anglo-catholic schools. Trent College was interested, as was a school company run by Lady Wimborne. The Dean Close Executive Committee decided to send four Governors to Lord Wimborne's home for a meeting on the subject.

The Schoolroom, now the Flecker Library, *circa* 1905

Meanwhile, in 1901, a balcony was constructed opposite the large window in the Big Schoolroom. Thus, more boys could be accommodated in one place. Electric light was finally introduced.

Queen Victoria died in 1901, succeeded by her son, Edward VII. 20 boys went to London in the summer of 1902 to see the Coronation while the other 150 plus were taken out for the day to Chepstow or Tintern. The new king asked headmasters to give a week's holiday: Dr Flecker compromised with four days.

The meeting between the evangelical schools agreed that the five unnamed schools involved would explore a federal approach. However, constitutional, theological and other difficulties made any sort of amalgamation impractical. Dean Close, for its part, was thriving with 218 boys of whom just ten were day boys in Trinity 1903. The amalgamation idea was unsuccessfully resurrected in 1912.

One of the longest-lasting prizes (the Charles and Elizabeth Prize) was donated in 1905, an anonymous gift from an admirer of the School, in memory of his parents. It was not until 1909 that the generous benefactor's name leaked out as a consequence of him visiting the School as a lecturer. He was A.W. Large, a lay worker at the China Inland Mission in the remote westerly province of Sechuan. The prize is still awarded today.

Maybe it was a perceived challenge to his own authority but in June 1909, Dr Flecker reported to his Committee that one of the assistant masters had married '…unsuitably…' during the Lent vacation and '…did not report to the Headmaster the fact of his marriage…'. When he had acknowledged it, but only under compulsion, the Headmaster had dismissed the teacher, paying him only up to the time of his dismissal. Exactly which member of staff and what was unsuitable about his bride were not revealed. Notwithstanding the difficulty he had admitted in recruiting teaching staff in sympathy with the School's religious stance, Flecker was prepared to be robust if he disapproved sufficiently of a colleague's actions.

The number of extra-curricular activities, other than the major sports of football and cricket and (from 1907) hockey, grew gradually. There were occasional debates; there was a Field Club for the scientifically minded; there was the surprisingly popular Temperance Society. For the more athletic, swimming (and the annual Swimming Sports) was already firmly in place; shooting, tennis and fives were available; fives had been popular since 1896. Boxing began in the Lent Term, 1905 and was to continue intermittently until finally banned in the late 1950s by the Headmaster, the Revd Douglas Graham, himself no mean boxer.

One activity that went from strength to strength was gymnastics. The key competition was the Public Schools' Gymnastic Competition held at Aldershot. On 6th April, 1906, F.J. and W.G. Lidderdale represented the School, beating the 40 other public schools competing, including such illustrious names

The 1913 Hockey XI of whom five were killed in the Great War.
Standing: B. Reed, B. Wreford, S. Wreford, R. Johnson
Seated: J. Warren, N. Herapath, F. Hoare (capt), B. Astley-Weston, V. Willington
On ground: E. Gonner, M. Willington

as Harrow, Cheltenham College and St Paul's, to win the coveted Silver Shield. The two boys also won medals for coming joint second overall in their individual performances. *The Decanian* records that: '... A crowd of congratulatory enthusiasts met the winning pair at the Great Western Station [Cheltenham] on their return home, and with the aid of a stout rope drew them in triumph to the School. Peace was restored at a late hour...'. A present of £2 (£180) was given by the Governors to the Sergeant who trained the gymnasts. This triumph was worth more to Dr Flecker than merely winning a prestigious competition. It signalled to other public schools and anyone else interested, including potential pupils' parents, that Dean Close Memorial School might be comparatively recent, and of only minority appeal, but it had already shown that it could win academic scholarships to universities and now here it was making an impact in sport. To any who may have had doubts, Dr Flecker's election to the Headmasters' Conference was now amply justified.

The Lidderdale brothers (seated) with their instructors and the Silver Shield

1906 was also the year in which the School celebrated 20 years' existence. Dr Flecker wanted to mark the year by beginning a fund that would lead to the building of a School Chapel. The Old Decanian Society was almost unanimously for it, the Executive Committee of the Governors was probably basically in favour but Canon Griffiths, Vicar of St Mark's where the School worshipped and who by then, apart from T.H. Clark, was almost the only member of the original Committee of the School still alive, was vehemently opposed, to the extent that the whole idea was shelved.

Mrs Flecker had decided to commission a portrait of her husband to mark not just 20 years

C.C. Mountfort

of the School but also their Silver Wedding Anniversary. The Fleckers were also presented with a service of silver plate, duly inscribed, presented by the Committee at that year's Prize Distribution.

That winter, C.C. Mountfort arrived as a member of the teaching staff. He is remembered for being the driving force behind two key initiatives that are still very much part of the Dean Close community's life today: hockey and the OTC. Until his arrival, there had been two terms given to football. Now former captain of the Cambridge University hockey team, he was seen as being not only a real enthusiast but also a stylish player with '…strong wrists and a powerful flick…'. Such was his drive that within four years the School had its own first Blue in H.O. Cooper of Cambridge.

The Officers' Training Corps (OTC) was the public school response to pressure from the government at a time of growing international tension. The formal offer to the War Office from the School in the Lent Term, 1909 was duly accepted, the War Office bearing much of the cost. It began at the start of the Trinity Term with 50 cadets and within a short time drills and miniature range shooting had started.

Mountfort also found time to study for ordination, taking Holy Orders in 1909 and continuing to be a major influence in the School until he left in 1917. He subsequently went back to his old school, Uppingham, where he later became a housemaster.

The death of the Revd T.H. Clark in 1907 (a founding Governor of the School and for many

**A Summary of the OTC Contract**

I. This section relates to uniform and to the financial assistance offered by the War Office to the funds of the School Corps.

II. Recruits are to drill two days a week; each drill is to last 45 minutes. There is to be a parade of one hour once a week.

III. Each cadet is to fire at least 14 rounds a week in miniature-range shooting. Range shooting is to occur at least three times a year.

IV. There is to be one whole Field Day every year.

V. All cadets who so desire can attend one of the Public Schools' Divisional Camps.

OTC camp 1910

years Honorary Secretary to the Executive Committee) led to his generous bequest to the School of £1,000 (£90,160), which allowed the building of the first 'proper' Science block, called the T.H. Clark Laboratories, to go forward as it represented nearly half the total expense. It is the building that, complete with its arch, stands next to the present Flecker Library, facing Chapel Close. The two laboratories, one above the other, were for Physics and Chemistry; they were opened without ceremony at the beginning of 1908.

The Governors were also incurring further expense as they bought almost four acres of land facing Hatherley Road so that houses could not be built on it.

The subject of the School Chapel would not go away. In 1908, Edward Ellam discreetly made it known that he was prepared to give £250 towards such a project. The magnitude of this offer cannot be appreciated until it is realized that his own salary as a senior member of the teaching staff was only £200 a year! Clearly, he must have had an independent income. The offer sparked another prolonged discussion in the Executive Committee. Canon Griffiths, although much against the idea, generously agreed not to split the Executive over the issue and so the decision was made to go ahead with a temporary Chapel so that in the future a fitting permanent Chapel could be built when funds permitted. Things then moved rapidly. The temporary Chapel, built next to the T.H. Clark Laboratories on the site now occupied by the Beaufort Science Block, was dedicated by the Bishop of Gloucester on the 23rd January, 1909, attended by the Archdeacons of Cheltenham and Gloucester and a number of Cheltenham clergy. The final hymn sung at that service was *Now Thank We All Our God.*

The Clark laboratories

## The Temporary Chapel

The temporary Chapel, seen at the far end of the Clark laboratories and, below, the interior

This was a large room, 69ft (23m) by 30ft (10m) wide with a vestry at the west end. The east end was raised for choir seats, lectern and pulpit, the communion table being raised further. The congregation sat on chairs. There was an open-boarded roof.

The building cost was over £600. Fixtures and furnishings brought the total up to £800 (£71,370).

The lectern Bible, with Dean Close's name on the cover, was a bequest to the School from the Revd T.H. Clark, for many years Honorary Secretary of the School, who in turn had received it from Admiral Close, Dean Close's son.

On 23rd January, 1909, after the Dedication by Bishop Edgar Gibson of Gloucester, Evensong followed which included the School Hymn.

## The School Hymn, *Now Thank We All Our God*

This was written by Martin Rinkart (1586-1649), minister at Martin Luther's birthplace, Eisleben, Saxony. Later, as Archdeacon of Eisleburg during the Thirty Years' War (1618-48), he suffered with local people at the hands of invading armies. Widespread plague followed, including Rinkart's wife among its victims, then devastating famine. Rinkart, encouraging and courageous, saved people from utter despair. Yet the School Hymn was written in 1647 at the height of his problems and difficulties. He died in 1649.

The hymn became popular in Germany. It was translated into English in 1858 by Catherine Winkworth (1829-78), who lived much of her life in Clifton, Bristol. It was not used as the School Hymn before 1888 but was in use as such by 1891 when there is a reference to it being sung at the Prize Distribution, now called Commemoration. The decision was probably Flecker's.

Johann Cruger (1598-1662) who composed the tune, originally came from Brandenburg, and was '…one of Germany's finest composers of the 17th century…'.

Through the hymn's writer there is a link with Martin Luther and the Lutheran Church, whilst as he was born on 23rd April, St George's Day, there is a tenuous patriotic element. Its protestant credentials are immaculate, yet its appeal is to all traditions within the Church. Its theme of peaceful yet joyful thankfulness in the works and Person of God is entirely appropriate in the School's worship.

It is unfortunate but understandable that the use of the School Hymn was curtailed as a probable result of the two world wars.

Under Dr Flecker, each child had his place and gradually moved up through the dormitory houses until the senior one was reached – the present Tower House. There was never any 'fagging', so revered in older schools. However, it was thought that a little healthy competition within the School would be a good thing, so around the end of 1908 a sports house system was set up. The four 'Clubs' as they were called were North, South, West, and South West, probably because the School was situated on the western side of England. Points were awarded for a club team in football, cricket, hockey, athletics and gymnastics, competing against the other three clubs. Other sports such as fives and shooting might be added. Each club would be split into two divisions, under and over 15 years. Points would be accrued over the year and the champion club would be announced at the end of the Trinity Term.

Fees had been stable for years but it was decided that from January 1911, a new tariff would be introduced. Boys under 12 years old would be charged five guineas a term for tuition: the older Decanians, six guineas: boarding for everyone, regardless of age, would be 11 guineas with an additional guinea for laundry.

Something else had to be decided, too. Lord Wimborne had resigned as President in 1908 because of poor health. It took some time to find a suitable successor but eventually Sir John Kennaway, a distinguished evangelical, was appointed. His first official duty was as Guest of Honour at the Prize Giving in 1909, when he spent much of his speech saying what a disaster a war with Germany would be.

As in the country, the School seemed to feel that war in the near future was a distinct possibility, a view buttressed by such people as the Dean of Canterbury, who, as Guest of Honour at the 1911 Prize Giving, publicly expressed his pleasure at seeing so many of the boys in Officer Training Corps uniform. He declared that '...the training of the corps had a moral value as well as a physical one, for in that training the first and last word was 'obedience'...'. Also in 1911, the School was approved by the Army Council as one of those entitled to nominate candidates for Sandhurst.

The mix of implied militarism, nationalism, preparedness and duty that had been hinted at by the Dean became more explicit in a letter that was published in *The Decanian* in August 1912 at the request of Field Marshal Lord Roberts, who was concerned that Britain was drifting towards war but was not prepared for it. The School received it without comment, save for one brief observation, buried in *The Decanian* 'Occasional Notes' section, which noted that '...the letter...is probably appearing in most (public) school magazines this summer...'.

The same year, the School embraced new educational thinking by undergoing its first ever inspection. It occurred from 3rd to 8th March, 1912, at the end of which their spokesman, a Mr Fletcher, reported to the Life Governors that the School reflected '...great credit...' on Dr and Mrs Flecker and the staff. The management was '...excellent...'. He commented on the fact that there was '...a large proportion of backward and difficult boys which indirectly testified to the excellence of the School and its teaching...'. Buildings were on the whole '...excellent...' being '...cheerful, bright and convenient...' though he thought a couple of additional classrooms were needed and also an Art room. Domestically, things were not so good; the area and rooms surrounding the kitchens needed improvement; one bath per 30 boys was not sufficient and he considered changing rooms to be '...necessary...'! He went on to praise the loyalty and devotion of the staff but commented that the languages side of the School seemed to be better than Mathematics and Science provision.

When they convened a fortnight later, the only inspection issue that the Executive Committee seemed to want to talk about was whether or not to take up the suggestion to grade things differently

**Letter to the Leaving Boys of Dean Close School from Field Marshal Lord Roberts, 1912**

NATIONAL SERVICE
TO THE EDITOR
Englemere,
Ascot,
Berks.
5th July, 1912.

Sir,
Will you kindly allow me to send through your columns the following message to the boys who are leaving school at the end of this summer term?

You boys are about to take your places in a larger life than that which you have hitherto led and your minds must be greatly exercised as to what the future may have in store for you. I would like to remind you that, while you are working for your own advancement, you must never forget that you owe a duty to the Country and the Empire of which you are members.

You have had great advantages as British Public Schoolboys, and as British citizens you will have even greater privileges. What do you mean to give to your country in return? It is in the power of every one of you to give personal service, that is, deliberately to work for your nation as well as for yourself; but personal service means some sacrifice of self, the giving up of some leisure and of some amusement.

At the present time your personal service is needed to persuade your fellow countrymen of the great necessity there is for every able bodied man being trained to defend his country in time of need. It is difficult to convince people ignorant of war of this necessity, or to make them realize that it is unpreparedness that leads to war, but the lessons of history will have taught you that disaster assuredly awaits the nation whose sons are unable to defend her, and I would earnestly beg of you to do all in your power to bring home to people the fact that if we continue to shirk this, the first duty of citizenship, we cannot hope to retain our great heritage.

As you know, some of our fellow-countrymen across the seas have already adopted the principle that it is the duty of every man to be trained in the use of arms; believe me, boys, you can give no greater service to your country than by doing your utmost to procure the adoption of the same noble principle in the Motherland.

Yours etc.;

ROBERTS, F.M.

academically. When the Headmaster observed that to do so would involve recruiting another full-time member of staff, the Committee took the matter no further! However, teachers were to be better looked after. By July 1913, after consultation with the staff, the first pension scheme was introduced. This was at the same time as many schools, but ahead of others by up to 50 years. The rooms by the kitchen were improved and a shooting range for the OTC was built in 1913 alongside the branch railway line. The changing rooms had to wait a little longer.

1914 began with a huge blow for the Flecker family and, to a lesser extent, the School. On Sunday, 3rd January, James Elroy Flecker OD, the eldest Flecker child, died in a sanatorium in Switzerland, aged 30, from tuberculosis. He was a noted poet. After his death, Mrs Flecker wore black for the rest of her life.

The First World War began. For the next four years the War would always be centre stage in *The Decanian* as the numbers of those involved from the School increased dramatically and casualties rose tragically. Each edition devoted the first few pages to news of casualties, extracts from letters from the front and information about who had joined up and where they were, as far as it was possible to say.

On 27th May, 1915, the School was addressed by Miss Hawley on behalf of the central committee of the National Patriotic Organization. Apparently her usual task was to try to recruit for the armed services but on this occasion she was more concerned to help in forming and maintaining '...a sound body of public opinion...'. In modern terms, her talk was an exercise in propaganda. On Friday, 11th February, 1916, the Revd William Temple, then Rector of St James, Piccadilly, a former Headmaster of Repton and future Archbishop of Canterbury, came to the School and stood by the lectern in the temporary Chapel, where '...he spoke for an hour, holding the attention of even the youngest among us. To hear him was a privilege which will long be held in grateful memory...'. His subject was the War, and the Church's responsibilities concerning it. He felt clearly that it was a Christian duty to take part and that the principle for which Britain and the allies were fighting was compatible with Christianity.

James Elroy Flecker

Compulsory rationing was only introduced late in the War but it was decided to accept bread rationing in the School while it was still voluntary. This had a poor impact on the health of the boys. S.C. Neill, later a Bishop, recalled that over a long period they simply did not have enough to eat, given that they were playing football through the long hard winter. '...By the time the school authorities realized that four small half-slices of grey bread and a large ration of stodgy boiled rice was not enough, the damage was done. For months I, for one, could not run or play any kind of game. I was lamed by a kind of sciatica, which has never reoccurred, and which I have little doubt was due to debility caused by malnutrition...'.

The pressures on Dr Flecker grew. The death of his son, the almost constant news of casualties of Old Decanians at the front and the sudden death of the Revd J.A. Luce who had been an excellent assistant master for ten years and Chaplain since 1909 all affected him. The supply of assistant teaching staff (never easy to find) virtually dried up. He was forced to try to keep the few younger staff he had by appealing to the relevant tribunal, not always with success. At least one teacher was 'poached' by a leading public school much further north. Reluctantly, he brought in female teachers: Miss Morris to teach Art and his own daughter, Joyce, to teach Mathematics and Chemistry. Prices were rising and that was having a detrimental effect on the School finances. His younger son, Oswald, was wounded in Mesopotamia in 1916 and that was quickly followed by the death of a 17-year-old boy in the School from pneumonia. In his account of these years, Professor R.J.W. Evans suggests that on top of their personal sensitivities about their Jewish background, the Headmaster and his wife were also subjected to mindless xenophobia concerning their Teutonic origins. Members of congregations were not above walking out, according to one observer, if Dr Flecker preached. Unsurprisingly, these cares, plus the sheer weight of his workload, proved too much for the Headmaster.

**Old Decanians and Staff Involved in the First World War**

The painstaking researches of the late Humphrey Osmond and related work by Richard Padfield OD have established that at least 124 Old Decanians died as a direct result of the First World War, of whom 122 are on the Roll of Honour and in the Memorial Book in the School Chapel. Four of those ODs were only 18 years old when they died and a further 13 were just 19 years old. A total of six sets of brothers, who were all ODs, died.

*The Decanian* records that at least 110 ODs were wounded, six of them three or more times. Major C.B. Bartlett MC, Royal Sussex Regiment, was wounded an incredible seven times before eventually dying of his wounds in Flanders in 1917. 18 ODs were taken prisoner, of whom 14 survived. 13 ODs were doctors in the Royal Army Medical Corps, of whom four won the Military Cross. A further 13 were Chaplains to the Forces, all save one in the Army; one of them, the Revd E.V. Tanner, who later became Chaplain to Dean Close School (1940-51), won the Military Cross and Bar, and another OD Chaplain, the Revd J.E.L. Warren, won the Military Cross. Two Chaplains were wounded and one was taken prisoner.

Nearly 700 ODs are recorded as having participated in the War, of whom a third were casualties, huge numbers for a school whose annual number of leavers was between 60 and 70.

Major Unwin RFC, who was killed in 1916

Old Decanians served on many fronts: the Western Front, Gallipoli, Italy, Palestine, Egypt and elsewhere. Most of the casualties sustained were in Flanders and France. The vast majority served in the Army. About 30 served in the Royal Navy with another half dozen in the Royal Fleet Auxiliary. Only a handful were part of the Royal Flying Corps that became the infant Royal Air Force.

Those decorated for gallantry included nine ODs with the DSO (Distinguished Service Order), 65 awarded the MC (Military Cross) with three awarded Bars, the equivalent of being awarded that medal a second time, while one was awarded a DFC (Distinguished Flying Cross) and 28 were Mentioned in Dispatches.

Other distinctions awarded included two ODs becoming Commanders of the Order of St Michael and St George (CMG), two Officers of the Order of the British Empire (OBE) and four foreign decorations being given.

Teaching staff also left to go to war. Among them were Messrs Elias, Claughton, Smith and Hitchcock, followed by Mr Talbot and Mr Strand. Mr Leslie Halse OD came back to teach Music and became engaged to one of the Headmaster's daughters but sadly died of his wounds in 1917 (see chapter 4).

Harry Seates, who was a gardener at the School, volunteered in 1914 and joined the RAMC. He was wounded in France, became a corporal but died on active service in East Africa in 1918.

ODs who served in the First World War and were killed are still occasionally coming to light. In November 2007 it was reported that Harold Wilton OD, a solicitor and a Captain in the Territorial Force in 4th Wessex Brigade, Royal Field Artillery, died in India in 1914. His memorial is on the Madras 1914-18 War Memorial, Chennai.

In the autumn of 1916, he was stopped outside the Army and Navy Stores in London and found to have on him several items for which he had not paid; he gave a false name and attempted to bribe the arresting police officer. Fortunately, the jury at his trial accepted the defence submission of 'mental prostration' and dismissed the charges. Dr Flecker for his part insisted on making a public confession to the boys at School, at the end of which, according to one astonished boy who was there, he said, 'Boys, it says in the Book of Proverbs "He that marrieth a wife getteth a good thing." The best advice I can give you is to marry a good wife as soon as you can. What I have owed my wife and daughter during these days I have no words to express.'

Flecker must have been very deeply moved to make such an uncharacteristic revelation of his innermost feelings, thought that boy. Dr Flecker also sent in a letter of resignation. When the matter came up before the Executive Committee of the Governors, there were letters in support of Dr Flecker, including one from the prefects. The Governors persuaded him to stay but insisted on a term's leave of absence, during which Edward Ellam was Acting Headmaster. Local support included Canon Waterfield, then Headmaster of Cheltenham College, who volunteered to come and preach in Chapel. Dr Flecker returned for the Trinity Term 1917. Although he insisted that he was much better but would delegate some tasks, the Governors decided that he must have a formally designated Second Master and, with the Headmaster's agreement, appointed Edward Ellam who took up his new responsibilities in September 1917, for which he was paid an additional £50 (£2,600) per year.

As the war progressed, so did the School's commitment to military training. When C.C. Mountfort, who was the officer commanding the OTC, returned to his old school, Uppingham, in 1917, Dr Flecker appointed his wounded second son, Oswald, in Mountfort's stead. One observer at the time felt that '...This meant that for the rest of the war he [Oswald] had guilty feelings which he tried to suppress by imposing the maximum military effort on himself and on us…'. The hours spent on drill grew until, as another master, also invalided out of the army, remarked, 'This place isn't a school, it's a depot'.

However, the Headmaster's trials were not quite over. In 1919, after the end of the war, the Fleckers decided to join in the Victory celebrations by the revolutionary step of taking the whole School to a variety show at the theatre. A troupe of personable young ladies called 'The Macpherson Sisters' came on, dressed in attractive kilts, and entertained the audience with a high kicking routine that exposed their equally attractive drawers. The School roared its appreciation, while Dr and Mrs Flecker bowed their heads in horror in the front seats of the stalls. It probably put back other theatre trips by the boys for some time.

A further unfortunate incident occurred because the supply of schoolmasters was so short. The Headmaster employed one Ronald Light as an assistant master. Unfortunately, his testimonials were forged and he was arrested and tried for the murder of a girl early in 1920, although he was later acquitted. This was the famous 'Green Bicycle' case.

During the war years the School kept going surprisingly well, notwithstanding the problems that it had experienced. Indeed, at the beginning of Michaelmas 1918, the Headmaster could report the School having 229 boys, of whom 19 were day boys. However, as 1920 approached, the School was

**The Green Bicycle Murder**

On Thursday, 3rd March, 1920 Det. Supt Herbert Taylor from Leicestershire Constabulary, accompanied by Sgt Iles from Gloucestershire Constabulary visited the School to see Dr Flecker about a teacher, Ronald Light, who was suspected of the murder of Annie Bella Wright, a 21-year-old Leicester millworker, found shot dead in a country lane near Leicester on Saturday, 5th July, 1919 at about 9.20pm. Her bicycle was by her. She had just left her uncle's house with a stranger who had struck up an acquaintance with her when he caught up with her on his green bicycle, hence the name of the case.

The stranger and bicycle disappeared despite much media coverage and handbills being widely distributed. On 23rd February, 1920 part of the green bicycle was found in the canalized section of the old River Soar in Leicester. It had been taken apart and dumped in the canal at different points. Although one identification number had been obliterated, another had not, and as it had been a special order it was eventually traced to Ronald Light.

Dr Flecker told the police that the War meant that male teaching staff were difficult to find. In December 1919 he had received an application from, subsequently interviewed and appointed Ronald Light. On 20th January, 1920, Light began as an assistant Mathematics master. He seemed to have zeal and intelligence, had interested himself in the extra-curricular activities of the boys and supervised the armoury.

Ronald Light was smartly dressed, tidy, well-groomed and well-spoken. Rather different from the unshaven, slightly unkempt person who had been with Bella Wright. However, he had the highly pitched voice on which everyone had remarked. He answered Supt Taylor unsatisfactorily and was eventually taken to Leicester, where he stood trial. He was acquitted because of a lack of perceived motive and less than conclusive forensic and other evidence. He himself falsified his testimonials to Dr Flecker.

In 2007, a supposed confession by Ronald Light was discovered in Leicestershire Archives among old police records. He confessed two or three days after his acquittal to a police superintendant, claiming that the death was accidental, and arose out of showing his service revolver to the victim. Experts are divided over the authenticity of the confession. Some still contend that the killing was deliberate while others feel that Bella Wright met her death at the hands of someone else entirely.

beginning to look somewhat old-fashioned. No building work had occurred for ten years. No proper house system, other than clubs for sport, nor a proper Junior School existed. Yet there was a handful of deeply committed schoolmasters. Bishop S.C. Neill, a Decanian at that time later wrote, '... Dean Close (was) extraordinarily fortunate. It...won and retained the loyalty and devotion of a remarkable series of assistant masters. Abominably treated, underpaid, overworked, ill-lodged and ill-fed, they... stuck it out year after year, in some cases perhaps because once (at Dean Close) they found it hard to move, more often, I think, from real concern for the place, for the boys, and for the ideals that it had striven imperfectly to translate into action...'.

However, there was the other side, too, for during the War, according to one source, 40 young members of staff came and went. One of them, the Revd Harold Taylor, must have been typical. Having been to Cambridge, entered the Church, been a Chaplain to the Forces in the latter days of the Great War and earned an OBE, he came to the School in 1919 aged about 28 to look after the boys in the Hostel, now Wilton. He lasted just a year before becoming Headmaster of Cheam where he was later responsible for the future Prince Philip's preparatory school education.

The Fleckers themselves had been deeply affected by the War and time was no longer on their side. Changes were needed, but it was questioned whether Dr Flecker could move forward into the post-war period, too.

# Chapter 4

# Between the Wars, 1920 to 1938

### *Carmen*, the School Song

It was first sung by the School on Friday 15th December, 1922 at the end of term concert. It was called *Carmen*, Latin for a song or poem. The School song, which is both, was originally in Latin, written by Edward Ellam, Second Master, with music by W. Heller Nicholls, Director of Music and a prolific composer. The melody is striking both harmonically and rhythmically, the chorus being in three/four time and the verses in four/four time. Although the original music appears no longer to exist, it has been recreated by Barry Barker OD. The words were translated into English by Hugh Elder when Headmaster. The original chorus ran:

Jam Deum nos adorantes,
Bona usque recordantes,
Meliora augurantes,
Discessuri canimus

Hugh Elder's English version is:

Now to God our praises bringing
In remembrance of his blessing,
Greater good in hope possessing,
We the parting song are singing.

There are three verses. The first talks about those Decanians who are leaving, the second about the duties and attitudes of those returning, while the third says:

Last, may those whose toil unceasing
Gave to us the School enduring,
Our inheritance assuring,
Rest with honour still increasing.

Each chorus after the first changes the 'Now' to 'Thus' in the first line.

Dr Flecker was approaching the end of his headship at Dean Close Memorial School. Even though the old 'Hostel' had been pressed into service and Walton Court (now Caldecote) was purchased for £3,100 (£120,000) in November 1919, it was still evident that fresh energy, drive and ideas were needed at the top. It is said that Dr Flecker could not afford to leave. Apparently, capital he had saved for a pension had been in Austrian bonds rendered worthless in the War: he owned almost nothing. Eventually, the Governors borrowed money to give him an honorarium.

However, new School traditions were being created. A School song, *Carmen,* was sung for the first time in 1922. Together with *Auld Lang Syne* and *God Save the King* it was used subsequently at the end of School concerts and on other end of term occasions until the 1950s.

## The Dean Close School Chapel

The permanent Chapel, aligned north and south rather than the more usual east and west because of the railway, was significantly larger than the temporary Chapel dedicated in 1909. The latter was 69ft long and 30ft wide, whereas the new building was 100ft long, 34ft broad and 54ft high to the roof ridge. It had been hoped to build it in Cotswold stone; however, the cost proved prohibitive, so it was built in brick although stone edging is to be found around the tall window openings. Cheltenham architect L.W. Barnard designed it. The decision to seat the congregation 'collegiate style', i.e. facing one another, is said to have been made at the last moment by Mrs Flecker.

The pulpit that was put in the Chapel in 1924, and is now to be found in the cloister immediately outside, was paid for by the memorial fund for the Revd J.A. Luce, a former lay member of staff (as opposed to the Revd C.E. Luce, who had been Junior House Housemaster in Hostel). It was designed by A. Linton Iredale OD. A Holy Table made by W.R. Page, the School carpentry instructor, was installed in 1926, as was the Chaplain's desk to the east of the main entrance. This was also designed by A. Linton Iredale and was given in memory of R.M. Weston OD who was at the School 1890-93.

Humphrey Osmond's researches have shown that the Headmaster's Reading Desk, now in the cloister, was presented as a gift in memory of Miss Bailey, joint Headmistress of Bryansford Place School, in 1961,

In 1923, the Headmasters' Conference honoured Dr Flecker by holding their first conference at a member school after the war at Dean Close School. The President, Mr Gilson, Headmaster of King Edward's School, Birmingham, heaped praise upon him, referring to the '...wonderful school...' that he had created almost single-handed.

In 1923 (5th-8th July) four Board of Education inspectors came to the School; two of them, Messrs Fletcher and Cookson, had inspected the School in 1912. However, as the Senior Inspector apparently communicated the team's thoughts to the Executive Committee on 6th July, one wonders what they did with the remaining two days! Their conclusion was that '...Dr and Mrs Flecker have done a great work for the School...'. The number of entries in 1911 was about the same in 1922 but the average age on admission had fallen from 14-15 to 13-14 which they saw as an improvement; there was a '...steady flow...' of boys to the universities; there had been '...considerable improvements...' to the buildings and grounds, although there were still buildings without fire escapes; the problems of recruiting young staff were acknowledged but the work was '... better organized...' than it had been in 1912. It was a pretty good report.

Dr Flecker's last major project for the School was close to his heart – a School Chapel built as a memorial to Old Decanians who had fallen in the Great War. Much fund-raising went on and in July

when the Luce Memorial pulpit which had been there was transferred to a point near the north east angle of the nave, virtually on the sanctuary step, so that Decanians in the congregation and later in the new balcony could see the preacher better. The carved figures of St Philip and St James at the back of the original pulpit were left in place so that they became a rather splendid seat back for the Headmaster.

The Vestry and Chaplain's Room date from 1954. The additional room beyond was for Natural History in memory of the Revd E.V. Tanner. The balcony, with its spiral staircase in an external turret, was completed in 1964 and was paid for by the Friends of Dean Close Chapel.

The original instrument to accompany worship in the temporary Chapel was an American harmonium. It was replaced in 1917 with a pipe organ of one manual and six stops, bought for £100 and powered by water, following the efforts of Lionel Halse OD. The organ itself was transferred to the new School Chapel in 1923, minus the water blower, and was hand blown until 1938 when it was sold to St Mary's, Dursley for £20 to be replaced by a Hammond organ. After the Second World War, Nicholson's supplied a two manual second-hand pipe organ. It was dedicated, together with the panelling in the sanctuary that included the memorial panels to those who had fallen in the two World Wars, on Sunday 17th June, 1951 by the Bishop of Gloucester. It was extended during a minor rebuild by J.W. Walker in 1960. The console for the organ was originally just east of the vestry doors but was relocated to the balcony in 1969. Since then there have been a number of adjustments to the instrument.

The pulpit in its original place in the Chapel

1922 the first sod was turned by the President of the School, the Bristol lawyer T.W.H. Inskip, KC, MP, who eventually became Lord Chief Justice and the first Lord Caldecote. The Foundation Stone was laid by Sir James Agg-Gardner, MP, in November 1922 over a copy, on vellum, of a list of the Names of the Fallen at a service where the OTC paraded with fixed bayonets and the Roll of Honour was read. The Chapel was dedicated by the Bishop of Gloucester at All Saints-tide, 1st November, 1923. It was austere; indeed, some referred to it initially as 'Flecker's Folly', but succeeding generations have made it more welcoming.

Dr Flecker's rule ended. It had been autocratic, economically Spartan, to the extent that possible charges of under-financing are not wholly fanciful, and lacked any real long-term vision or planning. Yet the School had thrived partly because of the devotion, pastoral care, example and stability provided by Dr Flecker himself (Cheltenham College had four headmasters over the same period) and the handful of generally like-minded masters who spent their careers at the School such as Ellam, Cooper, Heller Nicholls and Judson. The School's popularity was partly due to a feeling that there was a real attempt to inculcate Christian principles and partly because it was comparatively cheap. S.C. Neill, later to be a Bishop, was a boy under Dr Flecker from 1912 to 1919. His judgement was that Dr Flecker never really understood boys '…and his nervous rages made him terrifying to the more timid among them. He had high ideals and did his utmost to set them before us…'. As Dr Flecker was leaving, a second group of masters began to be recruited who were also to stay some time, possibly because changes were evidently afoot: Sgt Major A.W. Golder (who ended his 1914-18 war service as a PTI at Aldershot Gymnasium and School of Physical Training) came to the School in 1919, the Revd Douglas Horsefield became Chaplain also in 1919, F. Horsley, arrived in 1921, Hedley Warr started in September 1922, F.R.H. Brian came in January 1923, while B.O. Bradnack MC and C.A.P. Tuckwell arrived the following September. E.S. Hoare joined the staff in Trinity 1926. Their quality is evident, as three of them (Horsefield, Bradnack and Warr) eventually became headmasters, while F. Horsley, C.A.P. Tuckwell and E.S. Hoare became successive Second Master at Dean Close. F.R.H. Brian was senior Mathematics master for 39 years and Housemaster of Walton Court for ten. Sgt Major Golder, famous for his forthrightness, his immaculate copperplate handwriting on the blackboard and his glass eye, through his contribution locally in the Second World War, emerged as a Major and was awarded an MBE. These eight men averaged over 30 years' service to the School.

Letters from Mrs Gare to her sons (1920-22), which were unearthed recently from beneath floorboards

**The Revd Douglas F. Horsefield, Chaplain 1919-35**

The son of a clergyman, 'Tully' Horsefield came to the School in 1919 as Chaplain. He was tall, painfully thin, with a walrus moustache. His voice was '...shrill and strident...'. Yet he had '...an excellent brain and a heart on fire with religion...' He inspired generations of boys to take Holy Orders. His Jubilee as a priest was held at Lambeth Palace at the invitation of Archbishop Geoffrey Fisher, where large numbers of priests and bishops who had been his pupils met to do him honour. He held well-attended Crusader meetings at School. Scores of boys would go to him with their problems. He operated what one former member of staff called '...a sort of evangelical confessional ministry...'. Housemaster of Walton Court (1926 to 1935), he left in 1935 to become warden (headmaster) of Kingham Hill, then a grim charity and trade school for orphans and children in difficulties. He transformed it. Later he went back to parish ministry and was elected to the old Church Assembly. He was an honorary Canon of Chichester Cathedral, a Rural Dean and a Life Governor of Dean Close School. A former colleague from Dean Close days said of him, '...I began by almost mocking him as a 'ranter'; before he died I revered him almost as a saint...'. An OD said of him '...A dear man. He was always interested in you, kindly and comforting...'.

**Francis 'Fully' Horsley, staff member 1921-59**

He came to Dean Close School in 1921 with two degrees, a BSc from London and an MA from Selwyn College, Cambridge, to teach mathematics, becoming senior Mathematician in 1924. His early education was at the Grammar School, Wirksworth, Derbyshire. During the Great War he served in the Communications Branch of the Royal Navy, 1915-18.

He has been described as '...a rather jolly, fat man who had been capped for England at Soccer in his younger days...'. He coached the 1st XI football for 17 years and had been a noted sprinter. He was Head of the Junior School (1930-32), then a bachelor appointment, leaving to marry Mary who supported him faithfully in his subsequent career. They returned to head the Junior School during the War years and beyond, 1939-49, that included a brief spell being evacuated to Glyngarth Preparatory School, Cheltenham. He was given a rather struggling, small school of barely 40 pupils but handed over a healthy Junior School of 142 boys to Eadward Langhorne in 1949.

During Hugh Elder's illness he was, briefly, Acting Headmaster, having been appointed Second Master of Dean Close School in 1938, retiring from that role in 1955. However, he remained on the staff until 1959, a total of 38 years.

He died in 1985 aged 90, Mary having died in 1978. They had three children: Robert, who sadly died aged six, John and Margaret.

**Hedley Warr, staff member 1922-41**

He was born in 1899. He was a boy-chorister in the Choir of Westminster Abbey. In the First World War he was a Lieutenant in the Gloster Regiment and was wounded in the thigh by a shell splinter. He later served with the Northumberland Fusiliers. He came to Dean Close School in 1922, having emerged as a History graduate from Cambridge. He was much admired by the boys, one of whom described him as '…charming…'. Within a year he had become Senior Historian at the School. When Percy Bolton organised the house structure in 1924, Hedley Warr was one of the first Housemasters. His house became Gate. Hugh Elder (Headmaster) asked him, as Senior Resident Master, to be master-in-charge on a day-to-day basis during the evacuation to Monkton Combe, thereby allowing the Headmaster to remain at the heart of matters in Cheltenham. He left in 1941, soon after the School's return to Cheltenham, to become headmaster of Louth Grammar School. He died in 1978.

During Dr Flecker's final Speech Day, Thomas Inskip said of him '…If you want a monument, look around you…' using the comment applied to Sir Christopher Wren and St Paul's Cathedral. In looking, one would have seen the buildings, the sports fields, the staff and above all over 200 boys and a large gathering of Old Decanians who had come to do their Headmaster honour. When they left, he and his wife took the ever-loyal Brown sisters to his new parish in Staines, Middlesex.

The new Headmaster was Percy Bolton, aged 38, who had taught briefly at Cheltenham College in 1912, Berkhamsted and then Oundle. To younger boys he seemed '…a reserved dry stick of a man whom one did not get to know unless one entered the Science Sixth and was taught…Physics and Mathematics by him…'. '…He had a cold, even chilling, personality…' wrote another, who was to add a little later, '…Mr Bolton could give his boys individually good advice; but the dry, rasping tone in which it was delivered often robbed it of acceptability…'. However, he had his supporters, too. One OD spoke of him being '…an excellent Physics teacher. He provided us with handwritten notes duplicated by using a special ink and impressing the copy on a plate of gelatine – the precursor of the photocopier! Each foolscap page lucidly set out the essentials of a topic…'.

Percy Bolton later described much that he saw around the School as being 'drab', 'dismal' or 'dull' while he saw the new Chapel '…of distressing gauntness without and grim austerity within…'. There was a prevailing pattern of '…institutional severity…'. However, he found the dormitories far more comfortable and homely. He realized that much needed doing. As R.F. McNeile has remarked, '…the task confronting him was formidable: it was to bring the School quickly into the 20th century, and to do it on a shoe-string…'.

**The Brown Sisters**

Agnes and Mary Brown, together with another sister, gave long and devoted service to the School. Agnes, who was two years older, spent 55 years working for Dr Flecker. She was matron of the Senior and Junior Houses, besides helping in the Tuckshop. Mary was known to generations of boys simply as 'Brown'. She was for a long time Head Dining Hall Maid, and later Assistant Cook. Agnes and Mary went with the Fleckers in 1924 and stayed with them to the end. Mary and Agnes died in 1957 and 1958 respectively, the third sister having died some time earlier.

**Percy Bolton, Headmaster 1924-38**

Born in 1890, he was a Scholar of Queen Elizabeth's Grammar School, Blackburn. In 1911, he was Junior Wrangler in the Mathematical Tripos at Cambridge, as a member of King's College. In 1912 he also took the Natural Science Tripos. He spent a year teaching at Cheltenham College and possibly a brief spell at Berkhamsted before becoming, at the age of 24, head of Physics and Engineering at Oundle School, a pioneering post said by *The Times* to be '...ideally suited to his genius for invention and construction...'.

He married Miss Madeleine Scott, daughter of the Revd D.L. Scott, and had two children, James and Elaine.

During his time at Dean Close School he was president of the Cheltenham Scientific Society.

In 1938, Percy Bolton was appointed headmaster of Watford Grammar School, where he remained until his retirement in 1951. The Boltons then moved to Kimpton near Hitchin and divided their time between their home there and their cottage in Freshwater East in Pembrokeshire.

He died on 6th January, 1981 aged 91.

H.W. Osmond, Housemaster of Court 1965-73, later the first School Archivist. He finally retired in 2000

The first reform needed was social. Most junior boys came into Hostel (now Wilton) under the Revd C.E. Luce – not to be confused with the Revd J.A. Luce, a lay member of staff who left to be ordained. The boys were between eight and ten years old. Next door, Walton Court (now Caldecote) housed boys who were a year or two older. The Revd Douglas Horsefield was Housemaster, known initially as 'Tusko' because of a huge walrus moustache that hid a receding chin, but as 'Tully' subsequently, a jolly personality who was School Chaplain. From Walton Court, the Decanians moved to the Junior House in the main School, then to Middle House after a year or two, and finally Senior House under the Second Master, Edward Ellam.

Masters had little responsibility, as that was all vested in the Headmaster. Having spent some time consulting Edward Ellam, the new Headmaster changed the situation virtually overnight. One morning late in 1924, according to the late Lance Kramer OD, '...we assembled in the School Room [now the Flecker Library]. Instead of lessons that morning, Bolton said we would be re-arranged in three senior Houses, the boys in each varying in age from 13 to 18. He gave us our Housemaster's names, new cubicle numbers and which House we would be in: Warr's [called Gate from 1926], Neill's [Tower from 1926]

**Housemasters of Court (originally Walton Court)**

| | |
|---|---|
| 1926-1935 | The Revd D.F. Horsefield |
| 1935-1940 | E.R.B. Gray |
| 1940-1950 | F.R.H. Brian |
| 1950-1965 | J.S. Moore |
| 1965-1973 | H.W. Osmond |
| 1973-1975 | P.A. Oakley |
| 1975-1984 | The Revd D.I. Gibson |
| 1984-1988 | R.F. Taylor |
| 1988-1991 | S.W. Holliday |
| 1991-1994 | N.M. Blake |
| 1994-1998 | S.G.G. Aiano |
| 1998-1999 | J.P. Watson |

Walton Court House photographed c.1930. The building is now called Caldecote House

and Ellam's [Brook]... We then carried our own belongings from our old to our new cubicles, moved our books, and assembled in our new House's rooms...'. Initially, Hedley Warr had B.O. Bradnack as his Assistant Housemaster; Edward Ellam had F.R.H. Brian at first but E.S. Hoare arrived and became Assistant Housemaster within a couple of years; while H.C. Neill had C.A.P. Tuckwell. Hedley Warr noted, 'The coming of the Houses brought an upsurge of new life, enthusiasm and loyalty that had to be experienced to be believed.'

The Headmaster had to make arbitrary decisions as to where each House had dormitories and common rooms. Until then, the only boys who really had their own space other than in the Library (today's Seminar Room) were the six school prefects who had their own studies in what had been the Senior House. Ellam's House, (later Brook), did best out of the initial arrangements, as they were given the old Chapel. Here there were opportunities to create common rooms, aided by their Housemaster's

**House Magazines**

One of the immediate consequences of the development of the houses was the appearance of House magazines, laboriously typed and often including hand-drawn pictures or photographs, which tended to begin in 1927 and went through until the late 1960s. Apart from the descriptions of travel, they give valuable information about members of the house in question at that time and often useful descriptions of house matches or events. Walton Court had *The Courtier*, Tower had *The Turret*, Brook had *L.M.* and Gate House had *The Martian*. The last two require explanation. *L.M.* is a play on the surname of their first Housemaster, Edward Ellam. It was the first house magazine to cease production in 1951 or 1952, complaining of lack of material. The first Housemaster of Gate was Mr Hedley Warr; in honour of him, members of Gate referred to themselves as 'Warriors'; the mythical Roman god of War was Mars; the magazine took its name from that.

generosity. Warr's (Gate), used classrooms adjacent to the Schoolroom (the present Flecker Library), while Neill's (Tower) arguably had the poorest deal with the senior common room being one of the present Geography classrooms opposite the stone corridor and next to the old staff Common Room. The Junior Common Room was in what is now the Girling Room, then known as Room 5, where the light came in through skylights that leaked during heavy rain. It was also in close proximity to the Headmaster's study and was above a boiler room. One Old Decanian has left a vivid word picture of life in this Common Room: '...I still recall the atmosphere of Room 5, the noise of coal being shovelled into the stokehole and the high pitched voices of the women washing up in the kitchen nearby [now Gate Common Room] and the smell, particularly the smell, a mixture of fumes from the stoke hole and the curious cloying stink of decaying vermin beneath the floor, the whole leavened by an overall awareness, as it were, of boy...'.

**Housemasters of Gate**

| | |
|---|---|
| 1924-1941 | A.H. Warr |
| 1941-1951 | The Revd E.V. Tanner |
| 1951-1966 | A.S.R. Parker |
| 1966-1970 | H.F. Cocksedge |
| 1971-1983 | C.M. Kenyon |
| 1983-1990 | M.S. Symonds |
| 1990-1995 | R.F. Akenhead |
| 1995-2002 | D.J.R. Pellereau |
| 2002-2006 | R.I. Kirby |
| 2006-2008 | D.B.W. Marsh |
| 2008-present | M.D. Tottman |

1924-26 the House was known as *Warr's*

**Housemasters of Brook**

| | |
|---|---|
| 1924-1936 | E. Ellam |
| 1936-1959 | E.S. Hoare |
| 1959-1962 | G.V. Harries |
| 1962-1964 | E.S. Hay |
| 1964-1978 | P.E. Smith |
| 1978-1988 | T.G. Odell |
| 1988-1998 | R.P. Ryall |
| 1998-1999 | N.P. Moor |

1924-26 the House was known as *Ellam's*

**Housemasters of Tower**

| | |
|---|---|
| 1924-1926 | H.C. Neill |
| 1926-1929 | B.O. Bradnack |
| 1929-1952 | C.A.P. Tuckwell |
| 1952-1967 | M.A. Girling |
| 1967-1980 | B.K. Wilson |
| 1980-1988 | R.C. Padfield |
| 1988-2000 | R.F. Taylor |
| 2000-2004 | G.T. Williams |
| 2004-2008 | N.P. Stokes |
| 2008-present | B.W. Williams-Jones |

1924-26 the House was known as *Neill's*

Library, now Seminar Room c.1930

Interior of Brook House Common Room, situated in Old Chapel c.1930

The dormitories for Tower were on the first floor over the classrooms, the 'horseboxes' or almost double-sized cubicles for the Housemaster and Assistant Housemaster approximately in the centre. The floor above had a similar arrangement for what was to become Gate. Brook House took over the sleeping accommodation that had been the block for the old Senior House; today it houses Tower.

Walton Court across Big Field was different, not very large and housing only comparatively junior boys. The Housemaster, the Revd D.F. Horsefield, whose Assistant Housemaster, chemist R.F. Bomford OD, just down from Oxford, was given the option of having a few older boys to allow it to be a complete house from the ages point of view from the first. He elected not to do so but to allow the house to grow from the bottom up. It meant that they were not able to field senior sides for a year or two but the initial disadvantage was probably more than made up for in enhanced house spirit. Fortfield House, purchased in 1925, became the most junior boys' house.

Percy Bolton's second reform concerned changing rooms, which were considered essential. By 1930, these had been built parallel to but a little distance from what had become a part of Brook, thus creating a new, lower Quad. Brook's changing rooms were at one end, Tower's in the middle and Gate's at the other end. Today that extended building houses the Domestic Science classroom and the Sixth Form Centre. Their advent improved cleanliness and hygiene for boys to a significant extent.

The third reform was food. Several ODs have written about their diet which, to modern eyes (and their own), was poor. The most bizarre meal was Sunday Tea at 5pm. Let an OD describe what happened: '... a group, say, of half a dozen would sit together at table and each would produce a tin of something large enough for all members of the group to get a reasonable share...the mixture of foods owed little to any culinary theory as to what could go with what. Thus, tinned peaches and pineapple would rub shoulders, so to speak, with corned beef, baked beans, spaghetti, pilchards and beetroot, to rehearse but a modest menu...'. Another OD wrote '...We gorged ourselves. The result was catastrophic. It was quite a regular thing for five or six boys to go out of evening chapel (which was directly after Sunday Tea) looking green. Eventually one boy did not go quickly enough...'.

It was not easy financially but around 1934-35 'PB', as the Headmaster was called, found an excellent reason for improving diet. At Christ's Hospital (the public school), Medical Officer Dr Friend had divided boys into two groups: one received a dietary supplement that included additional milk, fruit and so on; the others did not. Dr Friend demonstrated a significantly greater growth rate in the group receiving the supplement. It had a big effect on the quality and variety of food at most boarding schools. Certainly, whereas in the mid-1920s Dean

**Weekly Diet in 1926**

Breakfast (served on alternate mornings):
a) Porridge; 'Jingles' (home made meat paste on half slices of bread and margarine); tea
or
b) One beef sausage (or one rasher of bacon); bread, margarine and golden syrup; tea

Lunch:
First Course: Cold meat (or possibly meat that had begun hot but was cold by the time it reached the child) and possibly stewed vegetables
Second Course: steamed pudding OR stewed fruit

Afternoon Tea:
Two half slices of bread and margarine for each child; cocoa (winter) or lemonade (made from a powder in the summer)

Tea (7pm):
Bread, margarine and golden syrup; tea

(...Boys lived out of their tuck boxes or went hungry...' A.H. Warr, Dean Close School staff, *c.*1926)

Aerial view *circa* 1930 looking west

Close School boys and sometimes masters '...were frequently plagued by boils...' both ODs and staff commented on the improvement in the boys' diet in the mid-1930s. There were fewer boils.

A different part of the food question concerned the Tuck Shop. Percy Bolton brought in two reforms. Using willing helpers among the boys, he transformed the old Walton Court stables into a permanent Tuck Shop, the reconstruction beginning in 1925. Second, its control was put in the hands of a small committee of masters and boys, the latter serving in the shop under the direction of a matron. It gave some boys the opportunity to manage, in part, something of their own affairs.

Percy Bolton's fourth reform involved developing the arts, particularly drama. Under Dr Flecker, ODs, military men or else missionaries or clergy came to give improving talks or to preach. While still supporting their visits, the Headmaster instigated a drama production on the Headmaster's lawn at his first Speech Day in 1925, the play being *Hamlet,* directed by C.A.P. Tuckwell, who also took the lead. An OD sets the scene: 'The play itself was done on the level at the bottom of the lawn and the seating was rather like an amphitheatre in front, with one's back to the Headmaster's House. The trees behind the stage allowed suitable entrance and exit points...'. Notwithstanding its success, there was still Dr Flecker's unhappy experience in 1919 at the variety theatre. This meant that when in Michaelmas 1925 Percy Bolton requested the Governors' permission to allow boys to attend theatrical performances, they insisted that parents' permission had always to be sought. All visits had to be reported to the Executive Committee. The Headmaster was careful to report that within a year boys had been to see a film called *New India* and to a production of *Macbeth*.

Before the advent of the house system, a group of fairly senior boys had traditionally been given Room 5, without any responsibilities, as an independent Senior Common Room. Their absorption into houses meant this practice ceased. As a final gesture, with the help of C.A.P. Tuckwell, they produced

***The Speckled Band***
by Sir Arthur Conan Doyle
17th December, 1924

| | |
|---|---|
| Sherlock Holmes | C.W. Thomas |
| Dr Watson | D.G. Ferriman |
| Dr Grimesby-Rylott | G.H. Shaw |
| Mr Armitage | H.J. Wood |
| Mr J.B. Montague | T.W. Tait |
| Mr Milverton | J.H.D. Crumplin |
| Billy | F.R. Lamb |
| Ali | G. Fowler |
| Rodgers | T.F. Cannon |
| Enid Stonor | W.H. Leach |
| Mrs Staunton | R. Hill |
| Prompter | R.C. Thomas |
| Producer | C.A.P. Tuckwell |
| Additional help by | Mr & Mrs P. Bolton |

Interval Jazz Band *The Warriors*
directed by C.S. Cates and L.J. Kramer

the play *The Speckled Band* by Sir Arthur Conan Doyle, on 17th December, 1924, thought to be the first occasion that only boys took part in a production in front of the School. It included interval music by a school jazz band called 'The Warriors'. Meantime, houses were encouraged to organize their own productions, Gate House and Tower House proving particularly keen to take up the challenge.

Marie Hall, a distinguished violinist, visited the School to give concerts (see chapter 13). With the development of houses, the House Music Competition began. Percy Bolton also strengthened the English Department by the additional appointment of G. Wilson Knight, who later became an international authority on Shakespeare, and the Music Department by appointing F.G.K. Westcott.

Fine Art, though represented, was not so fortunate. Percy Bolton brought in Adrian Daintrey, who had studied at the Slade. Although later well known as an artist, he almost certainly didn't teach Francis Bacon, then at the School and who later achieved international fame as an artist (see chapter 18). Daintrey did not stay long, his decision possibly influenced by the resources he was offered that were at best meagre, although there was by now an Art Room in one of the out-buildings. It was a later Art teacher, Miss K. Leavey, who was with the School for several years until 1938, who appears to have first organized some exhibitions of Decanians' work on Speech Day. The years 1937 and 1938 were particularly noted, not least because Seaton White, head of the Cheltenham School of Art, came to both exhibitions and offered opinions on the wide variety of work that was displayed. N. Sinclair-Hill was considered '…outstanding…' and he subsequently went to study Art in London, but this promising talent was tragically cut short as he was killed in action in the Second World War. In 1938 Seaton White was sufficiently impressed that he invited the entire Exhibition to his Art School where it became a part of a bigger show of work from local and London schools. However, Fine Art was still perceived as something of a Cinderella subject and its status did not begin to move forward even with the arrival of Cedric Kennedy later the same year.

In addition to reforms, Percy Bolton was keen to try and develop the School in a predetermined way: by December 1924 he had persuaded the Executive Committee to allow him to draw up a scheme of new buildings although, because of the financial problems he was to face, the changing rooms completed in 1927 became almost the only block of any substance built during his headship.

In 1924, School numbers were 240. The brief post-war boom stayed at the School longer than elsewhere, numbers reaching 270, its biggest to date, in Trinity 1927. It had hardly been touched by the General Strike of a year earlier, except that the Headmaster had to assure his Governors that the School's coal was being used with '…the strictest economy…' and that in order '…to economise lighting during the strike, the School clocks have been advanced one hour…', thus everyone was off to bed while it was still light! The University situation looked good, too, with 21 ODs at Cambridge, particularly Queen's College, and 16 at Oxford in December 1927, with eight of them representing their university at hockey, cross country running, football or swimming.

In 1932 William Judson retired; he died in 1951. He had completed 30 years at the School and had taught most subjects: Latin, Greek, French, English, Geography and Mathematics. He just taught the Fifth Form but laid the foundations for many university scholarships. He was a hard taskmaster who insisted on accuracy. A comparatively minor mistake would provoke the exclamation, as his pince-nez flew from his nose, 'Good heavens, man! A gross error!'

Aerial view 1934 looking east

**1** Branch Line. Opened 1881 to Leckhampton and beyond. Double tracks laid 1944. Closed 1962. **2** Old Chapel. Built 1908, dedicated Jan 1909. Chapel until 1923. Became Brook House Common Rooms, demolished *c.*1959 to make way for Beaufort Block (1960). **3** Old Pool. Built 1889. Demolished to make way for the Edwards building (1987) **4** Kitchen gardens. In use until the 1980s, now covered by Carnill and Ellam astroturf pitches, car-park for DCS & Bacon Theatre. **5** Shooting range. Almost certainly the indoor range opened in 1913. **6** Site of Tuckwell Theatre. Site part used as a shooting range from 1909, work began on the Tuckwell, Trinity 1934, opening Trinity 1937. **7** Benhall Farm fields. Part of the farm called Ryland's Land. First parcel of land bought in 1956., the second in 1961. **8** Chapel Dedicated 1923 in part as a memorial for the DCS fallen, 1914-18. **9** Clark Laboratories. Built in 1907, opened 1908. Half of it paid for by the will of T.H.Clark, first Hon. Sec to the Governors. **10** Brook. Built 1898, opened 1899. Senior boarding 1899-1924, Brook 1924-1964. Since 1964, Tower. **11** Dining Room Block. Built 1898, opened 1899. Ground floor Dining Hall & medical room until 1987, then day rooms for out houses. Now IT Department. Boarding accommodation above. Later upper storeys part of Brook, 1924-1964, then Tower. **12** Changing rooms. Built 1930. 1985, recital room created out of part of them; Home Economics also took a part. 1997, sixth form centre created. **13** Cottage. Date of construction unknown but certainly before the First World War. Used by resident estates/domestic/catering staff. 1975 converted to use as part of the Music Dept and from 1997 as the medical centre.

Sport at the School revolved around football in the Michaelmas Term, hockey in the Lent Term and cricket during Trinity. Football coaching was under Francis Horsley, himself a good player in his early years. The XI would be selected following some practice games at the beginning of term.

Hockey was in the capable care of C.A.P. Tuckwell, with E.S. Hoare assisting him. There was coaching in techniques, and in practice games the action would be stopped and players corrected. Playing Cheltenham College, Dean Close School always made a point of selecting an 'A' XI and not the full XI as they were more than capable of beating them and the glory seemed just that bit greater if the School won with less than a full strength XI!

Of the three major School sports, cricket was the most coached. There was a cricket professional who was also a groundsman. In the early 1930s, he tended to concentrate on the batting. The master-in-charge was the Revd D.H. Bodley OD, who coached the bowlers. Net practices were frequent for members of the XI and for others, too, if a little less often. In matches against Cheltenham College, the Dean Close XI always played the College 2nd XI.

During Percy Bolton's headship XXII Colours were introduced. These were awarded to those who had played for the first team in any major sport, even if only once. Full Colours were awarded by the master-in-charge of a sport based on an individual's performance over the season. They were never awarded automatically.

Apart from the major sports there were also athletics, fives, swimming and gymnastics all of which had their own Full Colours and, like the major sports, House Colours too. For various reasons Colours were not awarded for cross country or shooting.

Numbers began to drift downwards, beginning with the Junior House in Fortfield, at 36 no longer full. Its classrooms were in the newly-converted Fortfield stable block and on the ground floor of the Hostel. The Headmaster gave the perceived drop in the birth-rate during the First World War as the initial reason for disappointing recruitment. The general recession heralded by the Wall Street crash of 1929 finally caught up with the School in the mid-1930s. By 1935 there were 207 Decanians. The teaching staff gave 5% of their salaries to an emergency fund in the spring of 1932. Later the same year they increased it to 10% in order to assist boys already in the School to ensure that their education was not jeopardized by parental financial difficulties. Things were beginning to look grim.

Start of the 600 yards race in 1934

In Michaelmas 1935 the School roll dropped just below 200 for the first time in many years. A few months later the Executive Committee met and decided to cut accommodation to admit only 225 boys maximum; the number of teachers had to be reduced by three; Fortfield was to close at the end of 1936, a decision that was later rescinded. Moreover, bursaries were to be reduced and fees increased. Junior School fees became £120 p.a., while the main School fees rose to £136 p.a. (£7,250). The maintenance situation, too, was beginning to grow critical with a long list of outstanding tasks. These were tough decisions but are of interest, as there were only two sets of fee increases, indicating that Dean Close School had become a boarder-only school. This is confirmed by a Junior School prospectus (another almost unheralded development) that states starkly, '...as in the Senior School, no day boys are admitted...'.

At what point it was decided to exclude day boys is not clear, other than that it must have been after 1924; without them the School suffered more financially than it need have done. They were not to return during Percy Bolton's headship.

In the meantime there were things to be done on the campus, often by boys. The Headmaster reported to his Executive Committee that '...the electric lighting of several classrooms has been carried out by the boys, and that considerable savings had been thereby effected...'. Safety does not appear to have been an issue. Under the leadership of B.O. Bradnack, who discussed projects with them, boys who had no love for compulsory games were perfectly prepared to tackle such tasks. This

The OTC Band in front of the changing rooms in 1930

was at little or no cost to the School, now facing financial hardship. A labour corps was formed – The Pioneers. B.O. Bradnack explained the thinking behind it in a letter in the February 1937 edition of *The Decanian*. He also used the occasion to invite financial contributions from ODs and parents. By June the same year they had started to build a shed for 50 bicycles and remodel the Schoolroom stage in addition to assisting in the building of the Open Air Theatre. The latter project had begun some time earlier often using boy labour, '...under the direction of Mr Tuckwell with Mr Brian as Master Builder...'. What was to become the Tuckwell Theatre finally opened in 1937 (see chapter 13). The Pioneers, with a membership of 56, continued with a number of tasks until the School was evacuated at the beginning of the Second World War.

The careful husbanding of resources continued. Even the excitement of the Coronation of George VI and Queen Elizabeth on 12th May, 1937, when three Dean Close School cadets were sent to represent the School, failed to lift the general mood for long. The cadets were positioned just outside the main entrance to Buckingham Palace near the Victoria Memorial and had a good view of all that went on, even though they had to stand for 15 hours.

Thomas Cooper

One of the most important aspects of Percy Bolton's headship was to allow some measure of authority to devolve, both to staff, for example as Housemasters, and to boys themselves, whether as School or House Prefects, captains of sport, being on the Tuck Shop committee or helping to organize the Pioneers. With the retirement of Thomas Cooper who, apart from teaching and his other duties, was Editor of *The Decanian* 1892-1925 before becoming Bursar, boys were to run the editorial Committee of *The Decanian*, and also the house magazines that had now come into being. Percy Bolton felt that it was '...the guiding principle...' of his headship.

However, things were not going his way. By Trinity 1938 numbers had sunk to 139 boarders in the main school with 29 in the Junior House – 168 altogether. Despite his determined efforts, it has been suggested that the Governors not only called for economies but also brought pressure on Percy Bolton to go. His appointment to Watford Grammar School must have been something of a relief to him.

Percy Bolton made significant contributions to the School for which he may not always have been given full credit. His development of the house system and his encouragement of boys to take a real part in running areas of school-life were important internally. Externally, joining in national camps and seeing people in less privileged communities gave several boys experiences that would make some of them think seriously about working out their Christianity in society beyond the school gates. This encouragement, taken up by boys, Old Decanians and staff, was later to become the seedbed of the School's present day commitment to community service and participation in international aid, educational and pastoral activities (see chapter 14).

# Chapter 5

# Desperate Times

Hugh Elder began his headship in the Trinity Term 1938. He was a realist and understood that with the low numbers of boys, things were difficult financially and likely to get worse. However, as Hedley Warr, one of the Housemasters, later commented, '...He openly said to us that Dean Close was simply too good a school to go under...(He) brought new hope...'.

By 1938, all the senior boys were housed in the main buildings on the Shelburne Road site, as Walton Court was now a residence for masters. The Hostel was closed, the junior boys having transferred to Fortfield, the 'Junior House'.

At the beginning of his first term, Hugh Elder suggested to the Governors that the Junior House become the Junior School, with its own timetable and classrooms developed within the shell of Fortfield's stables; that as Fortfield could only accommodate 36 boarders, junior day boys should be admitted to make the numbers up to a viable preparatory school size. He would still act as Headmaster but a Senior Master would be put in immediate charge in Fortfield. This proved a most successful suggestion. The Junior School effectively came into being for Michaelmas 1938, quickly attracting a number of day boys. Another proposal agreed was that Dean Close School should play rugby and give up football. A

**Hugh Elder, Headmaster 1938-46**

Educated at the Edinburgh Academy, he gained a First Class Degree in Classics before entering Corpus Christi College, Oxford, gaining his second degree in 1929. He taught at Sherborne School and was then a House Tutor at Fettes College before coming to Dean Close School. He was 33 when he arrived, single and for the first 18 months his sister, Patricia, acted as his hostess before he married Mary Stagg who, at the age of 21 when she married, was said to be the youngest wife of a public school headmaster in the kingdom at that time. Their son, Hugh John Mainwaring Elder, was born on 15th August, 1948.

Hugh Elder resigned the headship of Dean Close School on his appointment as headmaster of Merchant Taylors' School in February 1946. In 1976 he retired, though he continued to teach a little at Millfield School, Somerset. A keen rugby player, he played for Edinburgh Academy and Corpus Christi College. He was elected a Senior Member of St John's College, Oxford, and a Freeman and Member of the Livery of Merchant Taylors' Company of the City of London.

further proposal, that there should be a Fabric Committee of the Governors, was not acted upon for some time.

The international scene was deteriorating. When School began again in September 1938, the Headmaster recalled that '...the nation was in a state of tension, for suddenly the hideous threat of war had come very near. The immediate danger was averted by the controversial Pact of Munich, which at least gave us a year's respite; but a grim prospect remained that was impossible to ignore...'.

At this point, Hugh Elder was struck down with appendicitis that developed complications and only the skill of the surgeons saved his life. The running of the School during Michaelmas was taken over by the Second Master, Francis Horsley, assisted by the Senior Resident Master, Hedley Warr. Edward Ellam had retired from being Second Master in 1937 and from his housemastership the year before.

The Headmaster was strong enough to return to work after Christmas. At the end of January a letter marked 'Secret' from the Permanent Secretary of the Ministry of Works informed him that in the event of war the buildings of Dean Close School would be requisitioned for national purposes. He would have to find other buildings for his School – and do it secretly. In the end, the Headmaster managed to arrange with K.M. Monie, the owner and headmaster of Glyngarth School, a Preparatory School whose old playing field is still to be found opposite Christ Church, to take in the boys from Dean Close Junior School. The Senior School was to go to Monkton Combe near Bath, a school with a very similar Christian outlook, founded in 1868 to train future missionaries. It, too, had a number of spare places and could probably arrange for some other properties to be let to them. Its headmaster, the Revd Edward Hayward, proved helpful and utterly discreet. Nothing could be announced to staff, pupils or parents.

At the same time, the School's financial position had become sufficiently serious that the budget for the academic year 1939-40 would have to balance even though the School was nowhere near full. The School could not even afford to pay for new hand basins in Brook House cubicles. They were supplied by an anonymous donor who was publicly thanked in *The Decanian.* Hugh Elder knew that the biggest item in the budget was teachers' salaries. He went to his colleagues, told them frankly what the situation was, and requested that they consider a temporary 10% cut. As he put it himself, their response was '...prompt and unanimous acceptance of my proposal...'. Other economies were made, too, by the Bursar, E.H. Warr.

**Other Schools in Cheltenham**

Cheltenham College evacuated to Shrewsbury School. Their premises were not used and after two terms they were allowed back. The Cheltenham Ladies' College under their Principal, Miss Margaret Popham, was required to vacate boarding houses and all other buildings so that government ministries could move in. The youngest girls went to Lilleshall Manor, Shropshire, and everyone else to large private houses around the town. Miss Popham demanded – and received – 20 army huts within 24 hours so that she had 40 classrooms available, erected on their playing fields. Showers and changing cubicles became study areas. Within three months the ministry agreed to vacate The Ladies' College in exchange for having the army huts back. Cheltenham College and Dean Close School waited a further four months or so before being allowed back into their buildings.

At the same time there were children moving into Cheltenham. The girls of King Edward's High School, Birmingham, shared Pates Grammar School for Girls while Moseley Grammar School boys shared Cheltenham Grammar School. Local children went to school in the mornings and evacuees in the afternoons. Over 1,500 children were evacuated to Cheltenham and the surrounding area.

Then the crisis happened. Hugh Elder later wrote, '...On the last day of the month (August) an official of the Ministry of Works arrived to inform me that he expected to serve the Requisition Order within a few days. On 1st September German forces invaded Poland; on the 3rd Britain and France declared war on Germany; on the 7th I signed a receipt for the Requisition Order, and the period of our exile began...'. Unbeknown to Hugh Elder, Cheltenham College and Cheltenham Ladies' College had both received similar secret letters and had dealt with them in their own ways.

Much happened at Dean Close School very quickly. It was still holiday time – just – and so the work had to be done by staff assisted by men from the local labour exchange. The Requisition Order required everything to be removed, but not everything was needed at Monkton Combe. The Chapel (which the ministry had said they would not need) was turned into a huge warehouse for unwanted school items. It was filled. Desks, chairs, bedsteads, chests, books and the entire contents of the Headmaster's House were stored there – it took five days.

Everything that was being taken to Monkton Combe School was put in the big schoolroom (now the Flecker Library). Hedley Warr has given us a flavour of what it was like:'...From the form rooms came stands of lockers and desks; from the dormitories cascaded – not infrequently with a shrieking maid mounted on them – piles of mattresses, blankets, pillows, hardware. A gaggle of maids would rush into the schoolroom with parcels of inadequately tied up books and dump them on the stage where they rarely failed to burst like bombs, until the stage looked like a picture of the mind of an erudite lunatic. Another carrying party was meanwhile heaping the other end of the school room with a kitchen assortment of food, cutlery, saucepans, magnums of jam and mountains of soap; while from the bursar's office came an arid harvest of stationery...'. Everything that it was thought the exiles would need at Monkton Combe was packed by men sent by the local labour exchange into large Great Western Railway furniture containers which they crammed full without much regard as to how the contents would travel. There is a suggestion that the member of staff supervising the move was R.M. Thomas, the Science master. It was certainly he who managed to create a workable timetable with the host school when Dean Close School arrived at Monkton Combe.

Meantime, civil servants kept arriving and departing. One spent days wandering around the buildings putting chalked numbers on doors. It was noted that the official in question '...showed a marked tendency to get lost in the corridors; when rescued, he began the round again, altering the chalk marks. It seemed a strange game...'.

It was very hard to dismiss a number of the domestic staff, some of whom had served the School for a long time (notably Miss Matilda Cogbill, the Senior Matron, who had served the School for 40 years) all with just a month's wages. The School would not be needing them at Monkton Combe. Miss Pruen, the Housekeeper, went to Bryanston. There was also a difficulty over the running of Fortfield at Glyngarth Preparatory School. The Housemaster, G.T. Clark OD and his wife, declared that the scheme was unworkable and wished to resign. Hugh Elder didn't argue. Francis Horsley, the Second Master, and his wife were asked to take over Fortfield, which they did while Hedley Warr, Senior Resident Master, became Hugh Elder's official deputy at Monkton Combe.

The furniture containers arrived at Monkton Combe School in their Farm Yard and were unpacked. 7lb jars full of freshly made plum jam, whose tops were not secure, had been packed on their sides in the drawers of the chests. Furnishings and jam were now one glutinous mixture that oozed onto the ground. As R.D. Hole, a member of the Monkton Combe staff recalled: '...the Yard remained sweet and sticky for a long time...'. But that wasn't the only problem. The beds brought were of a special pattern designed to

Monkton Combe School

fit over hot water pipes in dormitories: they did not dismantle as normal iron bedsteads do. The wire 'V's that made up the mattresses had become unhooked from one another: thousands of these 'V's cascaded onto the floor. Thus the first task for the Dean Close masters and other staff was laboriously to try to interhook the wire 'V's into usable mattresses again. It was a disheartening situation. However, things took a positive turn, as one anonymous member of the Dean Close staff observed, '...The Quad (Yard) was just a shambles. It looked as though nothing could be made out of the debris. And it was then that we began to appreciate the quality of the Monkton Combe Staff and their Serjeant Major (Mr Hanney)...they set to, wives and all, and began to learn the private and peculiar natures of the Dean Close beds, of which much might be written and more might be thought. As a result there were beds for all who came...'.

Ninety-five senior school boarding boys went to Monkton Combe and 36 to Glyngarth. The School was at a very low ebb. At Monkton Combe they were made most welcome by the Headmaster, staff and boys even though they had their own problems coping with the invasion. Dean Close boys slept at a number of different locations. Gate House was lodged in a furnished villa near the school but the main dormitory was in the roof where it was hardly possible to stand upright; Walton Court was assigned to a large house, possibly 'Crossways'; Tower House seniors slept in the attics of Combe Down Vicarage over a mile away while their junior boys slept in the billiard room of a large house with the owners in residence; the dormitories above Old Hall on the school site were assigned to Brook House boys.

The two schools had meals together, worshipped and were taught together. Otherwise they operated separately as far as was possible. Even CCF and games were separate in order to help Dean Close School maintain its

**DCS Staff at Monkton Combe**

Eight teaching staff from Dean Close School went to Monkton Combe:
A.H. Warr (Acting Deputy Head and Housemaster of Gate)
C.A.P. Tuckwell (Housemaster of Tower)
E.S. Hoare (Housemaster of Brook)
E.R.B. Gray (Housemaster of Walton Court)
F.R.H. Brian
F.G.K. Westcott (Director of Music)
R.M. Thomas
J.S. Moore

Also among those in exile:
Miss Patricia Elder, Hugh Elder's sister, who ran the Dean Close School office at Monkton Coombe and then stayed there as school secretary. She eventually married a member of their staff, A.W. Hurst, on 10th August, 1940. This was the first marriage service ever conducted in the Dean Close School Chapel and it was taken by the Revd E. Hayward, headmaster of Monkton Combe.
E. Ellam although technically retired since 1937, was described as '...not failing to take with him the continuity of (DCS) traditions...'.
Nurse, probably Miss Levett
Matron Lingley
Mr & Mrs Carter, domestic assistants

identity. Although the two schools were similar, in two respects they were different: Monkton Combe had fagging which Dean Close never introduced, and Monktonians were required to have cold showers every morning which Decanians were not. In the hard winter of 1939-40, Decanians were particularly grateful that they were not made to follow their hosts' customs.

The Juniors were allowed back to Fortfield for the opening of the Lent Term 1940, but it was a little longer before the Seniors were given permission to return, and it is thought that Viscount Caldecote, the School President, did his best in the corridors of power. However, the major problem arose as to whether, in coming back, the Senior School would be financially viable, with its reduced numbers.

A number of Governors' meetings were held. The future looked doubtful. A special committee deliberated over the figures for five hours. Hedley Warr maintained that while the School was in exile, numbers would slowly seep away. The School had to return. On the other hand as things were, the School simply could not pay its way. The masters had already accepted a 10% drop in their meagre salaries which at that time were a maximum of £480 (£20,000). They were now prepared to accept just two-thirds of their full salaries with the unpaid portion to be considered a debt of honour, to be repaid when times improved. The Headmaster undertook to do the same. Even so, the special committee was about to take the decision to close the School when Edward Ellam, by now a Life Governor, who was present and who had served the School for nearly 50 years, spoke out. It is said to have been '...a pathetic and passionate appeal. It ended with his breaking down and weeping...'. All are agreed about that. Exactly what he offered is not known but it was certainly at least a guarantee of £1,000 (£42,000) for the next year from his own resources – a significantly large sum. Another version suggests that an Old Decanian was behind Ellam's offer. It is not clear what swayed the committee – the sight of the weeping old man who had done so much for the School or the unexpected offer of an additional £1,000 if it were needed or a combination of the two – but contrary to what they had very nearly decided, and possibly against their better judgement, the committee voted to accept Hugh Elder's motion to advise the Governing Body to reopen the School in Cheltenham for the Trinity Term. The Governors agreed at their meeting on 14th March, 1940. Delighted, Hugh Elder told the Dean Close exiles the following day when he visited Monkton Combe to attend a unique joint Confirmation Service of the two schools.

The Lent Term must have been a somewhat anxious time for the authorities in both Schools as there appears to have been a prevalence of childhood diseases including mumps, chicken pox and severe attacks of German Measles that left the Monkton Combe sick bay overflowing with patients. However, the term ended with a farewell ceremony and an exchange of gifts between the staff Common Rooms. There was an electric clock in a walnut case from the Monkton Combe Common Room to their colleagues at Dean Close. The Dean Close Common Room gave a silver rose bowl made by George Hart of Chipping Campden, on which was inscribed: '*Hanc pateram exules in sodalitatem accepti hospites hospitibus D.D.D. MDCCCCXL*', that is 'We, the exiles who have been received into your community, ask you to receive this bowl as a gift from guests to hosts. 1940.' It was written by Edward Ellam. It was agreed that the experience for both schools had worked because both had gone out of their way to be courteous, thoughtful and tactful to the other. Dean Close School returned to Cheltenham on the understanding that there was a chance that they might have to evacuate again at 48 hours' notice if national circumstances warranted it.

The buildings were handed back to the School on 8th April with just under a month to sort out as much as possible before the Seniors returned for the start of Trinity 1940, and although the senior numbers were marginally better, Junior School entrants boosted the total to 150 – a hopeful sign. Indeed,

**Mr and Mrs Carter**

Mr and Mrs Carter served the School faithfully for 21 years. In the 1920s, Mr Carter was on the garden staff; Mrs Carter was a general domestic and catering assistant. They accompanied the School to Monkton Combe. In 1940 they returned to DCS and took over the garden cottage which is now the medical centre. Mr Carter became school porter while Mrs Carter was '...the mainstay of the domestic staff...'. It has been observed that '...It is no exaggeration to say that without them there might have been no resident domestic staff at all during the war. They began the day early and finished late, often working long hours in the holidays, too. Mrs Carter found time to be on daily duty at dining hall tea, and also to look after the Headmaster and Mrs Elder during four maidless years...'. Although they reached retirement age some time before, they were determined to see the School through the war. They retired to Winchcombe in 1945.

were it not for the success of the Junior School at this time, and the willingness of all the teaching staff to forgo a third of their salaries for a while, the School would probably not have survived.

It was at this point that E.R.B. Gray decided to take up a position at the Cathedral School in Hereford. Lt-Col Gray, TD, had been on the staff since 1922, Head of Modern Languages, Officer Commanding the Corps and Housemaster of Walton Court House. He had done much for the School.

That first summer back, Senior School Decanians had to adjust to the Ministry of Works furniture being everywhere, telephones seemingly in every corner and filing cabinets in every corridor. The Swimming Bath was occupied by '...an awe-inspiring mound of furniture of every description...' and each of the music rooms was half-full of books from the School and house libraries. It took a while to clear. That December, the editors of *The Decanian* remarked that '...All the Office of Works furniture has disappeared, and there is only a line of telegraph poles across Chapel Close to remind us of our exile...'.

There were now very few domestic servants around. Peter Preston, a Decanian at this time, remembers those staff, '...At the top was the Housekeeper who was in general charge. She was a tall, distinguished-looking woman [probably Miss Graham who took over as Housekeeper in the summer of 1940]. Mr and Mrs Carter, a diminutive couple, were school porter and cook and always seemed to be on duty (as did) Mr Finch, the boilerman...This last trio were the backbone of the School staff – hard working, friendly and very respectable. They were assisted by two maids, Lois and Edna, both attractive and doubtless admired by several generations of boys...'. Miss Cogbill also returned for a while to lend a hand. Miss Pearse, who had been at Walton Court, succeeded Miss Levett as school nurse in charge of the sanitorium.

One other school servant has been recorded at this time. He was T. Jeffries, who had been recruited by Edward Ellam, probably in 1932, to be a member of the grounds-staff, especially during the improvements that were being made at the time to Flecker's Piece and Humpty Dumpty. During the war, Mr Jeffries was the grounds-staff – there was no one else, other than the boys themselves. He died suddenly in 1946, and it is evident that he had a wide brief, '...Besides his splendid work on the grounds he showed himself at different times the artist in decorating rooms, in stone masonry, in painting, in caring for sheep...whatever job had to be done...', as his obituary recalls.

The boys now had to do much of the work themselves. *The Decanian* in June 1940 describes the changes that took place, '...we lay two meals each day, make our beds, and clean our shoes, and these

Kitchen pickets

duties seem very light when undertaken by so many hands. Owing to the reduction of the outdoor staff, each house is doing a certain amount of work in the school grounds, in addition to that which the Pioneers are doing. In order to economise in cleaning and lighting, only the Brook and Tower dormitories are now in use. Gate is in the upper Brook dormitory [now Tower] and Walton Court is at one end of the Tower dormitory [now Gate]…'. It wasn't long before things had to be taken further. Kitchen Pickets came into action. This consisted of three or four boys taken in turn from each of the four houses working under a house prefect instead of going into normal morning school. An OD has recalled that once, under supervision, he made all the pastry for a school meal. A large part of the duty was to peel potatoes and similar tasks, not to mention washing up. One story concerned a Decanian who said peeling potatoes gave him nightmares; rumour had it that once, at dead of night, he was found peeling his sponge with his tooth brush. Another OD recalls cleaning floors, dressed in rugby shorts and jerseys. '…Plenty of tea was on tap and slices of bread and dripping…'. Meals were served by orderlies. Hugh Elder later wrote, '…This was not altogether unpopular but the work was strenuous and messy, demanding ancient clothes and aprons of sacking…'. Some boys went down to stoke the boilers for hot water. One of them, Roy Brennan, found himself stoking three boilers every day in 1943, as he was not a games player and so could do it regularly. His father later gently observed that he thought it a bit rich that he should be paying fees so that his son could be a stoker. There was one boiler for the old dining hall; a second was virtually underneath the present Girling Room, a third served the Clark Science Building, a fourth the old swimming pool – and there were others.

There were daily chores that junior boarding members of the main School dealt with daily, including taking down the dormitory blackouts and dusting their common rooms, as well as the more familiar ringing of bells at prescribed times. If a boy was new, he would be asked if he wished to volunteer for the Pioneers. If he expressed no interest, the boy would be conscripted into doing '…very hard, back-breaking work sometimes, such as picking apples'!

Helping farmers

A third change was farming activity. Every half-holiday, working parties cycled (or were taken) to neighbouring farms, and in the summer holidays there was an annual 'camp' in the School itself, that served the needs of half a

Helping farmers

dozen farmers. Boys would harvest potatoes, do hedging and ditching, stack sheaves of corn into stooks, thin out plants, hoe weeds and so on. The great bonus was usually tea. Those who went to Barn Farm on the edge of the hills would sit down to a cooked tea, perhaps even egg and chips, then a real treat, followed by bread and treacle. At Fred Leech's farm, helpers would be taken to the local café where they sat in the garden munching plates of sandwiches. Two boys, who found themselves working hard in the large garden of a substantial country house owned by an elderly lady, were afterwards ushered into her old large kitchen where they consumed an entire, freshly-baked loaf, a block of margarine and a whole pound of home-made jam: at that time, sheer luxury. There were always boys eager to go to a Mr Lewis's farm as he sometimes handed-out bottles of home-made cider to quench the boys' thirst on hot afternoons. Decanians claimed to have contributed 1,200 hours' labour in one term on local farms.

**Fire Watching**

Air raids during the Second World War affected London and big cities but were also experienced in places like Cheltenham. This was because of its key position in the railway network and also because it had important technical firms such as Dowty and Smiths close by. GCHQ (or its earlier equivalent) was not located in Cheltenham at that time. Bombs used tended to cause extensive fires, therefore there had to be people on watch ready to fight them during attacks. These duties began early in 1941. The full picket consisted of a master and six boys. Boys on duty slept in the big schoolroom '…fully dressed with steel helmet, rake and shovel beside them…' ready to rise at the call of the master on duty. He used the Headmaster's study as his headquarters during the night, where he would 'rest' fully dressed on a camp bed by the telephone. Warnings were relayed to the School from a local Warden's Post, where people would be on watch all night, searching the sky. When an alarm was given the picket was roused from sleep and patrolled the buildings and grounds until the all-clear was sounded. It was their duty to give the signal that would bring the rest of the School down from the dormitories to shelter, and they were also prepared to deal with incendiary bombs.

There were eight teams of pickets at the School, each house supplying two. Each team was on duty for 24 hours. In addition, two other Senior boys slept at the Junior School every night for a week each, one on a camp bed by the telephone.

Supplies of fire fighting implements were placed at various points inside buildings. Stirrup pumps, buckets and sandbags were placed in the upper storeys and attics, with sand dumps outside the buildings.

In Trinity 1940, matters became sufficiently threatening for a Cheltenham local militia to be formed (later the Home Guard) in which the School was to play its part. The first alert at Dean Close School for a possible bombing raid was in June 1940, soon after the fall of France. The School descended from the dormitories to the passages which had been adapted as shelters. Thereafter, alerts during the night were fairly frequent. For senior boys, and for teachers, an additional responsibility asked of them from the early days of 1941 in addition to their other tasks was fire-watching pickets.

**Dean Close School and the Home Guard**

Dean Close platoon of the Home Guard 1940

Originally known as the Local Defence Volunteers, the Cheltenham Battalion paraded on Cheltenham College field for the first time in June 1940 and included a Dean Close Platoon made up of staff and senior boys. By the autumn, battle dress had been issued and the name changed to the Home Guard. Training progressed thanks to sessions on both Wednesdays and Saturdays and the Dean Close Platoon was fully equipped. An OD who experienced the formation of the DCS platoon noted that '...Home Guard parades were very similar to those of the Training Corps, with the main difference that the boys (in it) were probably better trained and considerably fitter than the masters...'! A grim note was sounded at the end of one report: '...another important part of our training is with the bayonet. Under Mr Golder's expert eye we have attained considerable proficiency in the handling of this weapon...'. In 1941, the Headmaster was appointed a Captain in the Battalion. And another member of staff, R.M. Thomas, did so well in the Home Guard that he eventually became a Major. During Michaelmas 1941 the platoon's strength was 31. A year later it had risen to 36 and had successfully taken part in an invasion exercise called '...the second Battle of Cheltenham...'. A few months later it was 40 strong. The Home Guard was not the same as the School OTC (Officer Training Corps) that had now, for some reason, been re-named the JTC (Junior Training Corps) that was the forerunner of the present CCF (Combined Cadet Force). The JTC was for boys aged 13 to 18. The Home Guard was really for adults who, for whatever reason, had not been drafted into the armed forces. The Dean Close School Drums and Home Guard Platoon paraded in Cheltenham on 3rd December, 1944 when the Home Guard was officially stood down.

Maj.or A.W. Golder

High explosive bombs only fell on the School once, on the night of 11th December, 1940, the boys having left for the Christmas holidays that day. Fortunately, only about a dozen boys were in School that night – they had stayed to take examinations the next morning. Everyone else had gone home. One bomb '...neatly removed the top of the swimming bath chimney in its downward path...' the swimming bath in those days still being partly on the site now occupied by the Edwards Building. The bomb went off, shattering every pane of glass on the south and west sides of the Senior School, damage that cost £400 (£16,800) to repair. The pit marks on the wall of the administrative building with a veranda next to the Bursary are most likely the result of shrapnel and indicate very accurately where the bomb exploded. Another bomb went off on the western edge of Big Field, and a third bomb also fell on Big Field but on the edge of the Hockey XI pitch (opposite the Pre-Preparatory building) which was subsequently known as 'The Crater Ground'. The bomb that did the most damage came down roughly where the Ferguson Block of classrooms is in the Preparatory School now, badly damaging the former Fortfield stables that were classrooms. They had only been opened in Michaelmas 1938. In the rest of Cheltenham that night, one street was almost obliterated and it is said that more than 20 people were killed. It took some time to repair the Fortfield classrooms, at a cost of £713 (£27,000) and it was not until Trinity 1944 that they were used again.

Bomb damage on Big Field

Map showing locations of bomb damage in and around the School

Bomb damage in the Junior School, where the Ferguson Building now stands

## Old Decanians and Staff in the Second World War

Records are not complete but it is known that at least 525 ODs served in the British, Commonwealth and Allied Armed Services during the Second World War. At least 90 served in the Royal Navy, of whom seven were in the Royal Marines, five were medical officers and a further eight were in the Fleet Air Arm. Over 300 were in the Army of whom nine were medics or dentists. Some 130 served in the Royal Air Force with just two being medics. There were no OD Chaplains in the Royal Navy as far as is known but there were ten in the Army and a further three in the RAF, virtually keeping pace with their contribution in the First World War. In addition at least seven ODs served in the Merchant Navy or Royal Fleet Auxiliary. Approximately 70 died as a direct result of the conflict, on whom the late Humphrey Osmond and also Richard Padfield have done much research. The first OD casualty of the war was Midshipman Stephen R. Mercer-Wilson, RN, killed on board *HMS Royal Oak* on 14th October, 1939 in Scapa Flow at the age of 19. 14 ODs were Prisoners of War, five of them being captured in the Far East, of whom one died. The figure for those wounded is not known.

Midshipman Stephen Mercer-Wilson

On the home front, ODs served in police forces, three as special constables. Four served as firemen, others in Bomb Disposal, AA batteries, as ARP Wardens, in Civil Defence, the Royal Observer Corps and the Foreign Office Naval Intelligence Section as well as in reserved occupations. Conspicuous among them was E.T. Paris, Principal Director of Physical Research and Signals Development, who was eventually knighted in 1954. The only known OD 'Bevan Boy' was D.J.M. Scowcroft.

Among those decorated for gallantry, four ODs won the DSO (Distinguished Service Order), five the DSC (Distinguished Service Cross), six the MC (Military Cross), two the DFC (Distinguished Flying Cross) and Bar, ten the DFC, one the CGM (Conspicuous Gallantry Medal) and one the DFM (Distinguished Flying Medal). In addition, 27 ODs were Mentioned in Dispatches, one of whom later also earned a Bar.

Among the civilian ODs, Dr Oscar M. Holden, then Medical Officer for Health in Croydon, was one of the first to win the newly instituted GM (George Medal), second only to the GC (George Cross) for '... great bravery...' that was not in the face of the enemy. The Royal Warrant instituting the decoration was signed on 24th September, 1940 and was published on 31st January, 1941. Dr Holden's citation appeared in the *London Gazette* on 7th March, 1941 less than two months later. A heavy calibre bomb had hit a Report Centre, demolishing it. Three of the five telephonists were killed outright. One survivor, severely injured, was trapped under tons of debris. '...Dr Holden, at great personal risk, crawled under the wreckage and proceeded in the most difficult conditions imaginable, to administer morphia to her. Owing to the abnormally confined space in which he had to work, Dr Holden was only able to come out by crawling backwards. During the time he was working, debris was continually shifting and he was in great danger of being buried under the ruins...'. Another OD, H. Jellings, won the BEM (British Empire Medal) for his work during the air raids in Swansea.

ODs received foreign awards including three Chevalier de L'Ordre de Leopold II, three Croix de Guerre, one Haakon VII Freedom Cross of Norway and one American Bronze Star.

ODs were also awarded British Honours including a CB (Commander of the Order of the Bath), four CBEs (Commander of the Order of the British Empire), five OBEs (Officers of the same order), three MBEs (Members of the same order), and six TDs (Territorial Decoration), of whom one OD had two Bars and another one Bar.

Among the staff, E.R.B. Gray, TD, already a Major in the Home Guard, and commandant of the OTC at Dean Close School was the first to join up, in May 1940. He had served the School for 20 years, six of them as Housemaster of Walton Court. He was followed by J.S. Moore who had taken over the OTC, now the JTC. He later returned and was Walton Court Housemaster for 15 years. C.J. Kennedy, the Art master, rejoined the RAF in order to be able to contribute his expertise on camouflage work. At the end of 1942, the Revd K.M.C. Melrose, the first Housemaster of Caldecote, also left on active service as a Chaplain to the Forces.

In the Cheltenham Home Guard, R.M. Thomas eventually became a Major. S.H. Findlay, also on the teaching staff, became a Sergeant.

A.W. Golder, the School RSM, who had done much for the Cheltenham Home Guard and for the local ACF, at last obtained a commission. He was promoted to Captain after 25 years with the School in 1944 and was awarded a special parade and presentation on Chapel Close. He eventually became a Major and was awarded an MBE.

A large number of incendiary bombs dropped uncomfortably close to the School a little while later – most of them coming down on Flecker's Piece, then one of the games fields, now given over to housing on the south side of Hatherley Road. One who saw it commented: '…There were enough there to have set the School ablaze from end to end, but not one touched any of the buildings…'.

Good relations that were developing between the School and the surrounding community were underlined in *The Decanian* December 1941 and again in December 1942. It reported that the Hatherley Platoon of the Home Guard provided fire pickets for a fortnight in the middle of the summer holidays. A party of boys remained at school after Trinity ended to help neighbouring farmers and act as fire watchers, while a second party that included some who had also been in the first party returned early for the same purposes.

However, not all the excitement was generated by enemy forces. In July 1943, R.T. Bell OD 'beat up' the School in his Tiger Moth training aeroplane, an exploit that is said to have resulted in a question being asked in Parliament.

The blackout regulations caused problems, not least with Chapel services. During the wartime winters, evening prayers on weekdays had to be held in the Schoolroom where the upper half of the windows were permanently blacked out, creating a depressing atmosphere. On Sundays, Evensong had to be earlier, as the Chapel could not be blacked out.

Everyone was rationed. There was no tuck shop, and although doing without sweets was tough, nevertheless the School ate tolerably well, supplemented by vegetables that the boys themselves helped to grow. One item the School found virtually inedible, though: cold meat pies of uncertain origin. An OD remembers very clearly that one lunch-time towards the end of the war, without any particular pre-planning, no-one among the 150 boys ate his pie. When the School rose and left at the end of the meal, the pies spelt out the word MUCK on each table, positioned so that those on the raised staff table could read the message. The 'rebellion' worked. The pies were never served again. However, they could not complain about the milk, delivered fresh every day from Mr Organ's Farm in Alma Road; his daughter, Joyce, brought it to the kitchens in churns on a horse and cart.

Clothes rationing presented difficulties, especially sports kit. Great ingenuity had to be shown in extending the life of such items as cricket trousers and hockey shirts, and resourcefulness in adapting whatever was to hand. An OD has recalled that, returning to school at the end of a holiday, the boys found bright red sheets on their beds. There was both difficulty and unwelcome expense in obtaining replacement bed linen and so sheets had been made from parachute material that had failed inspection.

Meantime, Old Decanians were heavily involved in defending the country at home and abroad, yet many made a point of visiting the School when they had some leave. As the war dragged on, each Dean Close School boy for his part imagined that he would follow in the footsteps of leavers the year before him and follow a rapidly developing School tradition that when the age of 18½ was reached, later 18

**The Tiger Moth Incident**

R.T. ('Dick') Bell (Brook House) came in 1937, leaving at Easter 1940. He was quiet, possibly overshadowed by elder siblings. His only noteworthy achievement at School was in the house diving competition which he helped to win.

A Tiger Moth

Dick trained in Canada as a pilot for the Fleet Air Arm, returning to England to complete his training at Eldom Airfield, known today as Birmingham International Airport. He learnt to fly solo in a Tiger Moth and on 25th June, 1943 he took his first solo flight.

He had to complete a number of hours solo flying, so on 23rd July, 1943 he took off, flying south, with what he noted was '...a strong tail-wind...'. He noticed presently that he was close to Cheltenham and decided to fly over his old school.

He decided to give a demonstration of his flying ability. He approached the School from the Hatherley Road side, just skimming the one storey high (25ft) (7.6m) swimming pool that was sited where the WAM Edwards Building is. He came even lower, just a dozen feet from the ground, then pulled back sharply on the joystick to clear the Chapel, with barely a foot to spare. The engine noise brought a number of curious boys out. He repeated the entire feat. By now, the crowd of boys was growing ever larger. Masters were beginning to appear, notably E.S. 'Monkey' Hoare, who was alarmed as he thought the pilot was bound to kill himself, and tried to persuade the boys back inside. R.T. Bell came round a third time, just missed the Chapel, then roared off as masters finally succeeded in ushering the boys from the scene.

The same day the Chairman of Governors, Sir Thomas Inskip MP, a former defence Minister in the wartime administration, happened to be visiting and was outraged to learn what had happened, not least because he had been involved in delicate discussions earlier in the War resolving what the role of the Fleet Air Arm was to be. He tried hard to find out who the pilot had been but without success. Some suggest that a question was asked in the House of Commons concerning the incident, but that cannot be confirmed.

R.T. Bell gained his wings and served on board *HMS Indomitable* and *HMS Formidable* in the Pacific. After the war he became a missionary. In Tibet he was involved in a motorcycle accident which he was lucky to survive. His missionary work subsequently took him to the West Indies. He died on 23rd April, 1972, aged 49.

and finally 17½, every boy would claim a half-day holiday to go and volunteer. It came to be expected. Several staff, too, either volunteered or were called up. Boys were reminded of the war daily, by media reports, intermittent bombing raids and the lengthening roll of Old Decanian casualties. Occasionally the Red Cross trains slipped slowly past the School on the branch line at their regulation three miles per hour, carrying large numbers of the badly wounded to appropriate hospitals or convalescent homes as far away from the front line as was practically possible.

At the beginning of 1941 the Art master, Cedric Kennedy, left the staff in order to rejoin the RAF where his considerable talents were used on camouflage work. H. Browning replaced him, though he only stayed until the end of the year and in January 1942 the new Art master was Professor Albert Reuss who stayed for the next three years. Cedric Kennedy returned in January 1945, his war work over. Within a few months, a number of his pictures were hung at the Cheltenham Art Group Exhibition.

**A Boy at the School in the Cheltenham Blitz**

Donald Duruty was in his penultimate year at Dean Close School, having joined in Michaelmas 1937. He was evacuated to Monkton Combe and returned, being one of the dozen or so boys due to take examinations on 12th December, 1940. He recorded his memories of the night of the 11th/12th December that were published in *The Decanian* in June 1945. Here are the highlights.

'...December 11th, 1940, was a lovely moonlit night...,' he began. They heard a bomb drop some way off and '...soon afterwards a red glow in the sky in the direction of Charlton Kings was noticed and flames could be made out. Feelings of mild anticipation were now aroused by a droning in the sky, feelings justified a short while afterwards by the whistle of bombs falling uncomfortably close. I happened to be in the Library at the time and narrowly escaped annihilation from the metal shield bearing the arms of Oxford University which was sent whizzing past my head...we flocked down to the cellars, where we heard the belated voice of the siren warning us to shut the stable door after the horse had escaped...We decided to settle down for the night where we were...we had not long to wait before the blitz began in earnest and the boomps of bombs interspersed with anti-aircraft fire could be heard at frequent intervals...It was by now 9pm and we (spent) the entire night seated in rows round the stove in the boiler room...The Headmaster read us P.G. Wodehouse, Mr Warr told us eerie stories of the supernatural and conducted a scripture resumé for the benefit of those taking the exam the next day...'.

'...The Chaplain [The Revd E.V. Tanner] brought down his radio set, and the announcer's urbane tones blended with the strains of song coming from the Cambrian elements of the domestic staff who were holding a miniature eisteddfod in the next cellar. Altogether we were a most cheerful crew. At midnight the company partook of refreshments; tea and hot Bovril prepared on a primus; lemonade, biscuits and buns. Mrs Elder's Dalmatian dog woke up at this point and took nourishment...'.

The Revd E.V.Tanner and Gate House in gas masks

'...So the night wore on. As the barrage seemed to have stopped by two o'clock in the morning, we dispersed to the corridors, where we slept, or tried to, on mattresses, till we were awoken by the all clear almost exactly twelve hours after the siren had gone...'.

In the summer 1942, advance detachments of the United States Army began arriving in Cheltenham, now the headquarters of the supply services. Although hotels were requisitioned for their use, schools were not. The Mayor of Cheltenham arranged a ceremony of welcome for them on 4th July (Independence Day) and the Dean Close School JTC Bugle Band took part. The 1943 Open Air Theatre production was *Abraham Lincoln* by John Drinkwater, a compliment to American Allies that was much appreciated by them. One of their senior commanders, General John Lee, returned the compliment by attending the School's Remembrance Day Service in Chapel on 7th November that year and afterwards inspected the School JTC. The presence of the Americans heralded the vast amount of planning that led eventually to D-Day and Victory in Europe. At one point, the building that had been called the Hostel (later a part of Walton Court, later still Rickerby and is today called Wilton) was a club for American Officers. When Trinity 1945 began, the end of war in Europe was approaching. As Hugh Elder later wrote, '...VE Day itself did not come unheralded, and it was possible to arrange for the first of two whole holidays. In the morning we assembled in Chapel and there gave thanks to God for a great deliverance. Afterwards the School vanished in all directions until the late evening...'. The Chapel Service included the hymn *Now Thank We All Our God*, though whether it was recognized as the School Hymn is not known. The School was in as exuberant a mood as the rest of the country. Hugh Elder had brought the School through the toughest of periods and he was bound to be affected by the strain of the experience. A new boy who joined the Senior School in 1943 later remarked that the Headmaster 'never had much of a smile' which was understandable seeing the demanding, difficult decisions and actions that he had had to initiate and see through.

C.A.P. Tuckwell as Abraham Lincoln

Commemoration had usually been held on 1st November, All Saints' Day. On 11th November, a two-minute silence was always observed across the land at 11am. In 1945, 11th November fell on a Sunday. Thereafter, the dead of two world wars and of later conflicts have been commemorated on the Sunday nearest 11th November, the Armistice Day of 1918. Commemoration Day from the School's point of view, therefore, ceased to exist as such, the Sunday being universally referred to as Remembrance Sunday. Commemoration as the School now thinks of it was begun (or revived) in a very different context as Commemoration of Benefactors in the Trinity Term during the headship of the Revd Douglas Graham.

The victory flag flying above the school

**Exuberance in the Schoolroom**

The end of the war seems to have heralded a practice that was apparently occurring in the big schoolroom. What was required was significant expertise, a 12" wooden ruler, an (old) penny coin and a postage stamp. The stamp, duly licked, was placed face-down on the penny which in turn was placed on one end of the ruler which was then flicked upwards. With skill and luck, the penny took the stamp up to the ceiling where it stuck. The penny fell back to be duly recovered, leaving the stamp permanently in position. One Old Decanian maintains that in 1946 he can recall roughly 25% of the ceiling being covered in stamps. History does not record how and when this practice was stopped or who had to retrieve all the stamps! Another OD remembers it happening in the old Dining-Hall.

The School had survived – just. Cautiously optimistic, it joined the Governing Bodies' Association from 1942, but it had changed significantly during the war as had the society from which it sprang. The servant age, in its pre-war sense, had gone forever. The Junior School was now a far more influential force within the Dean Close community. Day boys were an ever growing factor to be considered, especially in the Junior School. Thanks to the drive of the Headmaster, rugby, introduced by J.S. Moore, was very much part of the School scene where football had been before.

Several key figures had died – Dr Flecker and Edward Ellam in 1941 and Heller Nicholls in 1944. E.H. Warr, the Bursar since 1932, retired in 1940. Hedley Warr, who was a superb deputy for the Headmaster at Monkton Combe and had been on the staff for 19 years, departed in 1941 to become headmaster of Louth Grammar School. He, together with four other men who were DCS housemasters during this period – C.A.P. Tuckwell, E.S. Hoare, F.R.H. Brian and the Revd E.V. Tanner, and not forgetting the contribution of F. Horsley in the Junior – were the stalwarts of the School during the war years. One OD who was at the School during that time has described their collective contribution as being 'critical'. Dr Frederick Westcott, the Director of Music, also left at the same time to take up a similar post at the Royal School for the Blind, Worcester. R.M. Thomas, a Chemistry master at DCS for 15 years went to Whitgift School as head of Chemistry. Even a School landmark, the 'Flecker Elms', that had stood on the west side of the Headmaster's Garden had had to be felled because of Elm Disease early in 1945. However, the most important and hopeful factor in this time of considerable change was that parents had growing confidence in the School: the numbers were rising. In February 1945, senior boarders numbered 127, day boys 24, a total of 151. The Junior School accommodated 64 boarders and 59 day boys, a total of 123, a combined total of 274, an improvement of 27 on the same time the previous year. By the end of 1943, the improving finances were such that the masters' full salaries were restored. Future years looked at least equally positive, in contrast to the sombre situation in 1938.

It was at this point that Hugh Elder accepted the headship of Merchant Taylors' School and left in the Trinity Term 1946 on a hugely positive note. In his final year there were 156 Seniors and 142 Juniors in the two parts of the School – just under 300 in total – nearly double the number that had come back from exile. In June, the School had its photograph taken for the first time since 1942. Speech Day was revived for the first time in six years, in the Open Air Theatre, just in time to mark the School's Diamond Jubilee. Notwithstanding war, evacuation, financial desperation and a swiftly changing society, Hugh Elder, supported by his colleagues, had endeavoured to hang on to his concept of what the School was trying to produce, namely '...Christian gentlemen...', a view originally expressed in 1939. The way ahead looked exciting if a little uncertain. Yet there was much hard work to be done if desperate times were not to return.

# Chapter 6

## Recovery, 1946 to 1968

The new Headmaster was Antony (Tony) Gilkes. He was highly intelligent, suave, charming, administratively efficient, pastorally concerned, an able manager of people, and a preacher and speaker of note. He was also a disciplinarian. To some Decanians he could appear aloof and to youngsters somewhat cold and unapproachable. He would '…stride around the grounds with his walking stick rather like a country squire inspecting his estate…' in his trade-mark double-breasted suit. Yet he took the two lowest games of rugby, often including absolute beginners. In the summer, he tended to see how lower games of cricket were doing, appearing with a walking stick and sometimes umpiring. He was concerned about formality, politeness and particularly '…beastly bits of paper…' that might have somehow been dropped in the grounds. He was four years older on his arrival (45) than Hugh Elder was on his departure (41), and had a number of priorities to tackle.

Firstly, although numbers were improving, especially at the Junior School, the Senior School was only 170 strong. Finances were still precarious while the Sixth Form was too small to be able to offer a sufficiently wide selection of options at an economic rate.

Secondly, as M.A. Girling has written, Dean Close School, like many other schools, '…was at a low ebb…the standard of work had been lowered and extra-curricular activities were not thriving. For example, there was no orchestra at the time and (there were) few pupils learning music, though the Chapel Choir was an efficient body…'. This is not to decry the prodigious efforts of the previous Headmaster, Hugh Elder, governors and staff. They had achieved a huge amount by the School simply surviving the war and showing signs of recovery after it.

Thirdly, the School had a number of loyal members of staff led by the Second Master, Francis Horsley, currently running the Junior School. The four bachelor housemasters (C.A.P. Tuckwell, the Revd E.V. Tanner OD, F.R.H. Brian and E.S. Hoare) had each given themselves to the School community for a number of years, often at significant personal, physical and financial sacrifice. True, one or two fairly young former DCS teaching staff were returning to the School now the war was over, such as J.S. Moore, who had served in Burma but came back to continue to run Biology and take the rugby XV. As has been noted, Cedric Kennedy was back from his wartime camouflage work to continue as Art master. He tried to build up interest in Fine Art by encouraging outside speakers to visit. J.E. Barton spoke on 'Art and Enjoyment', illustrated by slides, in February 1947 although interest seemed rather superficial. However, there was a need to inject further new, younger life onto the staff which the Headmaster successfully did whenever possible.

## Antony Newcombe Gilkes, Headmaster 1946-53

Tony Gilkes, born in 1901, was 45 when appointed Headmaster of Dean Close School. He was educated at Dulwich, of which his father and later his brother were both Master (headmaster), and then Christ Church, Oxford. He was a Classical scholar reading Honour Moderations and Literae Humaniores.

He was an assistant master at St Paul's School, London, (1923-28), then Uppingham School (1928-46) where he was a housemaster. While there, he served as OC Rutland Army Cadet Force (1943-1945). He coached games, especially cricket. '…He was a fine athlete [a fact he was extremely reticent about], a fine orator and a very good administrator…'.

He also enjoyed cerebral challenges. On at least two occasions he won the *Church Times* Latin Verse Prize. On the second occasion, recorded in *The Decanian* in March 1950, the task was to turn the opening of the Epistle to the Hebrews into Virgilian hexameters. His first five lines ran thus:

> 'Ipse Deus, diversa utcunque prioribus olim
> Jussa dabat nostris, adflabat numine vates:
> Praescia vox veri partim non defuit ulli.
> Sed nostro iam dicta, haec edidit omnia saeclo
> Cara Dei suboles, Divi Patris incrementum…'

He was appointed High Master of St Paul's School, London (1953-62), later becoming Director of the Public Schools' Appointments Bureau.

He married Ruby Shaw, daughter of Bishop Shaw of Buckingham. They had four sons, David, Patrick, Robin and Roger. Ruby Gilkes shared her husband's '…passion for hospitality…' but was self-effacing yet able to give the Headmaster informed, sensible and quiet counsel. She also had '…a most charming, homely and serene character…' and was '…a wonderful foil to the energy and restlessness of Tony…'. She died in January, 1981.

A deeply religious man, A.N. Gilkes was '…an excellent speaker with a fine presence and a strong voice…' much in demand as a preacher and prize day speaker. He defended public schools and the Christian heritage, the latter with his *Faith for Modern Man* (1960) and *The Impact of the Dead Sea Scrolls* (1963). He died in 1977.

## Teaching Members of Staff who entered Dean Close School 1945-48

A.N. Gilkes recruited comparatively young men, many of whom had seen active service during the Second World War. Arnold Parker OD returned to take on the English Department and run the CCF; Vaughan Harries, having seen active service with RAF Intelligence, was senior Historian. Derek Gaye, who had been in the Royal Artillery, came as Director of Music after a spell at Clare College, Cambridge. Peter Chesshire, wounded on active service, including losing an eye, taught Classics and hockey. Dennis Foxall, a Cambridge 'Blue' for soccer, taught History, general subjects and ran cricket. By the end of 1948, E.H. Taylor, Mike Girling, C.B. Kiddell and A. Furnish had also been recruited.

**The Revd E. Victor Tanner OD, staff member 1940-51**

Born in 1886, a few days after the School officially opened, he became a Decanian in Trinity 1900. He left in Trinity 1905, going up to Emmanuel College, Cambridge. He subsequently entered Ridley Hall, Cambridge and was ordained deacon in 1909 and priest a year later. He served his title at St Luke, Maidstone (1909-11). He became chaplain to Weymouth College in 1911, staying until its closure in 1939, except for service as a Chaplain to the Forces (1916-19) where he won an MC and Bar. He returned to Dean Close School as Chaplain and Librarian (both posts requiring considerable fortitude) in 1940, and was Housemaster of Gate (1941-51). He spent a huge amount of his time in the house and all 'his' boys were 'good boys' according to him.

Both as a Decanian and later as a master, E.V. Tanner was a keen photographer, compiling valuable albums of his time at the School, while his passion for church architecture and his tendency for slightly unpredictable car driving became apparent. He also did much for the Field Club. He was a constant and generous host to anyone who visited him.

He retired to Preston in Dorset. He died in 1977.

Given his priorities, it is not surprising the Headmaster hardly initiated any building during his headship. Any available money was spent on staff – an anonymous gift of £1,000 (£31,388) allowed all back pay owed to teachers as a 'debt of honour' from the desperate financial situation in 1940 to be cleared. It was also felt right to improve slightly upon the newly created basic, statutory teaching pay scale (the Burnham Scale) – that was introduced in April 1951. Numbers of support staff improved, too.

A School inspection occurred in the Lent Term 1950. The inspectors found much to applaud: the Christian principles that undergirded the place; the management; the staff; the improving finan-

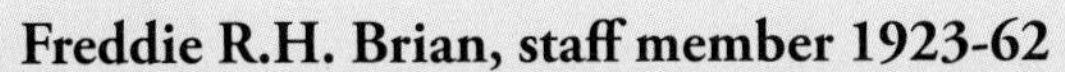

**Freddie R.H. Brian, staff member 1923-62**

Educated at Aldenham, he went to Cambridge to read Mathematics, and was a fine and enthusiastic teacher of all things mathematical. He was a useful athlete, a keen naturalist and an expert ornithologist. During the First World War he was an artillery officer. He arrived at Dean Close School in 1923. It was said of him that he was a modest, retiring man, an astute observer of human behaviour and capable of both dry and amusing remarks. His room was often in disorder, where garden forks, odd sticks, a hat or two and possibly some exercise books vied for space with a considerable number of ash trays, for he was a heavy smoker. Having been an Assistant Housemaster in Tower for some years, he became Housemaster of Court 1940-50.

He was often to be found tending, maintaining and beautifying the Tuckwell Theatre. At one time he led the Pioneers, where he was credited with producing their motto: 'Give us the work and we'll finish the tools!' He was also Chairman of the Young Farmers' Club.

He finally retired in 1962, having completed virtually 40 years' service. He went to live with his sister at Wadhurst to help look after her. He died in 1974.

**Geoffrey Lawrence, The Rt Hon Lord Oaksey, President 1948-60**

Born 2nd December, 1880 in London, Geoffrey was educated at Haileybury and New College Oxford. A lawyer, he was called to the Bar at the Inner Temple in 1906. He was a gunnery officer in the Royal Artillery in the First World War, being awarded a DSO. In 1925 he took silk and was appointed a judge of the King's Bench Division in April 1932. He was appointed a Lord Justice of Appeal in 1944, the same year he became a member of the Privy Council.

From 1945-46 he was the British President at the Nuremberg trials as Mr Justice Lawrence. There he '...discharged his difficult task with a calmness, courtesy and fairness which won universal approval, even from the defendants...'. In 1947 he was appointed a Lord of Appeal in Ordinary, having already been granted a hereditary peerage in recognition of his work at Nuremberg. That year, Oxford University awarded him a DCL (Doctor of Civil Law).

He became President of Dean Close School in 1948 after the first Lord Caldecote's death and took a considerable interest in the School.

He married Marjorie Robinson in 1921; they had a son and three daughters.

Lord Oaksey lived in Oaksey, Malmesbury. He died on 28th August, 1971.

cial situation; the social life. However, the academic standard was not as good as previously and on the whole children were not staying as long as they had in the years before the war. The comparatively new School President, Lord Oaksey, set up a small committee to consider the inspectors' findings and to make recommendations.

Already the Junior School was being allowed some independence. In 1949 Eadward Langhorne was appointed its first Headmaster when Francis Horsley declined the post, preferring to return to the Senior School full-time as senior mathematician and Second Master. Junior School boys had to sit the Common Entrance examination for the Senior School like any others – and Tony Gilkes was actively courting other preparatory schools so that the demand for places at the Senior School would be enhanced.

The last major link with the start of the School was broken in February 1949 with the death of Mrs Flecker, widow of the first Headmaster.

Tony Gilkes' efforts to recruit able teachers began to bear fruit. H.C. Neill OD, who had been Headmaster of Achimota College, Ghana, returned to the School where he had earlier made an impression as a young member of staff and before that

The Revd Philip Tidmarsh

as a Decanian. There was Denys Carnill, a versatile schoolmaster who was also a respected international hockey player; Derek Barker and Einar Hay who together were to transform the Science teaching; David Lepine, a most talented Director of Music and the Revd Philip Tidmarsh who updated and brightened the Chapel services after he arrived as Chaplain and started Lenten addresses. The latter's arrival virtually coincided with the installation of a pipe organ in Chapel, the console facing the Chaplain's pew but the other side of the aisle, with the pipes, swell-box and so on being in a specially constructed organ loft above and behind the organist.

The School was beginning to develop beyond the curriculum imposed by examination boards. For example, it was discovered in 1950 that the Higher Certificate examinations would be finished earlier than usual. A special programme was produced for the Sixth Form that included a change in the usual History taught (they explored Russian history); physics lessons gave way to a visit to Smiths factory at Bishop's Cleeve; papers belonging to officials in Gloucestershire at the time of Charles I were examined; and a lengthy visit was paid to the Princess Royal Colliery near Coleford in the Forest of Dean that involved crawling on hands and knees through shafts no more than three feet high, abandoned because of the '...incessant menace of water...'.

Meantime, Cedric Kennedy re-introduced the Speech Day Exhibition of Work in the Art room. Framed reproductions of famous paintings adorned the main corridor, including such different painters as Goya and Dame Laura Knight from early in 1949, that were replaced each term. Art Appreciation continued with senior boys, after public exams had been taken, using part of their Sixth Form Week to study a display of Modern Art at Cheltenham Art Gallery in 1952. A pottery, complete with kiln, came into being probably the same year, supervised by Ken Hollington from the Junior School for two evenings every week.

Outside School hours, societies began to flourish and during Gilkes' headship their number rose significantly embracing subjects as wide as science, light music, chess and the Young Farmers' Club, the latter rearing pigs on kitchen swill in sties situated where the maintenance department vehicle park meets the driveway to the Music School now.

One development that raised the morale of the School was the opening of a revamped Tuck Shop, closed during the war years. It reopened at 1.10pm on 22nd March, 1950 to the huge delight of the School, both Senior and Junior, in the former Walton Court, now Caldecote, stables. It was subsequently pulled down to make way for the Pre-Preparatory School in 2002-03. The front section of the 'Dean Close Shop' was termed the 'Buttery' where various kinds of foodstuffs could be bought, not least sweets and ice cream, while in the back area the Shop sold school uniforms and sports items as well as personal equipment for the schoolboy. It was initially managed by Selfridge's. *The Decanian* reported that the opening day was celebrated by the

The Tuck Shop

masters being invited to a party '... where they were regaled with free buns, much to the indignation of countless Juniors...'. A subsequent report by a young member of the Fourth Year gives a flavour(!) of the occasion.

'...amidst cheers the manager, rather unceremoniously, let us in. Manners were somewhat forsaken in the scramble. I managed to purchase an ice, and, at the expense of leaving a portion behind on everyone else's coat, I managed to reach the comparative comfort of the torrential rain outside...'. By the summer of 1954, Selfridge's had 'done a deal,' with Gorringes Ltd, who took over the shop but Mr Plumridge remained the capable manager. Older boys, though, sometimes sought refreshment elsewhere. One who left in 1953 remembered bicycling out to the Adam and Eve Pub that was then at Painswick; '...a bunch of us found (that) we could down a quick pint and just make it back to DCS in time for the evening meal...' he wrote. Consequences might have been serious had they been caught!

Inside the Tuck Shop

The School was short of property, especially for staff, so when Fawley Lodge in Lansdown Road came on the market in the summer of 1951 the School bought it. Initially, it was used to house staff and some 'overflow' boarders from the Junior School. No one could have foreseen that that name would eventually adorn a girls' boarding house!

On Sunday, 17th June, 1951, the Bishop of Gloucester dedicated the completed war memorials for both world wars at the East end of the Chapel. He also dedicated a second-hand two-manual organ supplied by Nicholson's which had originally been built for a private house in Stratford-upon-Avon in the late 1930s. A proper blowing chamber had to be constructed for it and the console was sited just to the east of the vestry door, in front of the organ pipes above. Here it remained for nearly 20 years, including a minor rebuild and extension by J.W. Walker in 1960. The console was transferred to the previously non-existent gallery in the major refurbishment of 1969.

A year later, on Speech Day 1952, a fund-raising body, the Friends of Dean Close Chapel, was formed. Its task was to solicit funds to provide stalls and wooden panelling in the Chapel.

Discussions concerning partnerships with local industry began as early as 1951 with Rotol Ltd and subsequently Dowty Equipment Ltd and Gloucester Aircraft Ltd. These discussions resulted in a room being found in the School, known as the 'Grease Pit' in 1953, for 48 boys to receive instruction in Mechanical Drawing and Metalwork; the equipment and instruction were provided by the firms who in turn hoped eventually to recruit from the pool of potential labour.

Nationally, the event of 1953 was the Coronation of Queen Elizabeth II. The School was granted a Coronation Holiday that ran from 1pm on Saturday, 30th May until 9pm Wednesday, 3rd June, so that many Decanians could spend the occasion with their families. The Rt Revd Basil Dale OD,

Bishop Basil Dale as a schoolboy

Bishop of Jamaica, represented the West Indies at the Coronation, having come to prominence as the organizer of the Jamaican hurricane appeal in 1951.

It was at this juncture that the Headmaster gave notice that he would be leaving in December 1953 to become High Master of St Paul's. As Mike Girling later observed, '...the School expanded and improved in every way except perhaps physically...' during the Gilkes years. Nearly half the Sixth Form were now Oxbridge entrants, and several scholarships had been gained with more in the pipeline.

The Dedication of the second Book of Remembrance of those who fell in the Second World War and of the oak caskets used to house both books, designed and made by C.G. Smith OD, was on Remembrance Day, 1953. The first Book of Remembrance for those killed in the 1914-18 war had been completed some years before and kept in a locked cupboard in the library (now the seminar room). Now both were displayed in Chapel.

Tony Gilkes achieved much in his seven years at the School, thus far the shortest headship of Dean Close School. He had raised numbers to 195 boarders and 48 day boys in the Senior School, and 108 and 98 respectively in the Junior School, a total of 449 – a substantial advance. He had brought in some excellent staff and gradually improved both their pay and the School's academic standards. He had enhanced the local and national standing of the School through his own charm and innumerable speaking engagements. The School had become less austere through such ventures as the School Shop but had preserved its ethos and discipline; he had encouraged growth in extra-curricular activities from extending the number of clubs and societies, to encouraging senior scholars to test themselves against bigger challenges – it was in his time that the first Decanian joined the British Schools' Exploring Society. He had fulfilled all expectations and more – but was now moving on, to be replaced on 1st January, 1954 by the Revd Douglas Graham.

Douglas Leslie Graham was the only Headmaster of Dean Close School, other than Dr Flecker, who had previously been a headmaster elsewhere. He was somewhat larger than life, a brilliant conversationalist possessed of great energy, outstanding abilities of organization and sound economic planning; abilities that have been described as '...bordering on sheer genius...'. He was generously compassionate, humane, hard-working and, at times, unpredictable. 'People either loved him or hated him but all respected him,' felt one member of staff. On education he always worried about over-specialization. Rather like Percy Bolton nearly 30 years before him, Douglas Graham found looking round the School somewhat depressing. There was a drabness about the buildings, mostly due to the twin problems of shortage of cash until comparatively recently and the restrictions imposed by rationing, that were only then ending. What he found inviting was the friendliness of the Chairman of Governors, Sir Ian Yeaman, and subsequently the 'feel' of the School, that of an extended family, a feeling of warmth, of pupils being loved but within a strong disciplinary framework, inherited from Dr Flecker via the likes of the housemaster body aided in no small measure by the work of a succession of Chaplains.

**Douglas Leslie Graham, Headmaster 1954-68**

He was born on 4th October, 1909 and educated at Portora Royal, Enniskillen and Trinity College, Dublin, obtaining a Double First in Classics and Philosophy. He was a Madden Prizeman of Dublin University and also studied at Munich. A lecturer at Dublin University (1932-34), he entered the Church, being ordained deacon in 1937 and priest the year after. He became an assistant master at Eton.

He played rugby for his university and was awarded an Irish trial cap in 1931. He was also heavy-weight boxing champion of Trinity College and is said to have represented the British Universities. He later became light heavyweight champion of the Royal Navy.

During the Second World War he was a naval chaplain (RNVR) for four years. He served on *HMS Trinidad*, *HMS King Alfred*, *HMS Daedulus* and *HMS Ferret*.

He was headmaster of his old school, Portora Royal, 1945-53 before coming to Dean Close School with his wife Ann, whom he had married in 1935, and their three sons James, John and Tim.

He left Dean Close School in 1968 to become assistant master and Chaplain at Williston Academy, Easthampton, Massachusetts, USA until his retirement in 1972.

He was a keen countryman, ornithologist, Cheltenham Races follower and a 'ferocious' bridge player. It was said that '...his motoring habits were more appropriate to Irish country roads *circa* 1929 where they had been learned...'. His brilliant conversation made creative use of incidents in his life.

His wife, Ann, was thought a '...superb hostess...'. She was seen as being '...a great strength in the pastoral life of the community...'.

He and Ann retired to Wiltshire, where he carried on a vigorous and extensive correspondence that had earlier included A.E. Houseman and Samuel Becket. He died in July 1991 aged 81. Ann died early in 1994.

**Miss Alice Schneider, staff member 1922-54**

Although when asked she couldn't quite remember, Alice Schneider almost certainly started teaching in the School in 1922. She eventually retired in 1954. She taught German and is one of the longest serving women teachers at Dean Close School as well as one of the first. She survived the prejudices concerning her name, during the Second World War, with aplomb. She referred to those to whom she had taught German as being '...one of mine...' and she followed their careers with much interest. Her hospitality was legendary and her support for School events, from Chapel to plays and from sport to concerts, unending.

Such was the new Headmaster's personality that few wished to leave: the only veteran teacher to retire at the end of his second term was Miss Schneider. The houses were still in very close proximity to one another; indeed, there was little room for a married man to run a house. Further, Douglas Graham felt an urgent need for '...more and better classrooms, laboratories, changing rooms, music rooms, art rooms and engineering workshops, and this process [just started by Tony Gilkes] took up the Fifties, together with the move in 1957 of the Headmaster...into Dean Close House...This last also allowed the start of a geographical loosening and relocation of the School's living quarters...'. Thus began a sustained campaign by Douglas Graham to achieve all that. Almost inevitably, given the fast pace at which the Headmaster wished to move, finances were often stretched. Governors' meetings with the Headmaster could be heated. One new OD Governor later wrote: '...When I first joined discussions

**Property Developments 1954-68**

| DATE | BUILT | BOUGHT | LAND BOUGHT |
|---|---|---|---|
| 1954 | | Lisnamoe (Hardy House) | |
| 1955 | Music Practice Rooms | Shelburne Hall (Turner Hall | |
| 1956 | Chapel Vestry & Classroom | | Smith's Land<br>Ryland's Land |
| 1957 | Rickerby Kitchen | Caynham (Dean Close House) | |
| 1958 | Industrial Fund Labs.<br>New Changing Rooms<br>School Shop extension<br>New CCF HQ | | |
| 1959 | Music School DCJS | | |
| 1960 | Beaufort Block | 9 Glencairn Park Road | |
| 1961 | Hard Hockey Pitch (Carnill's) | Ombersley (Yearlings/ Fawley)<br>Wilton House DCJS (sold to police) | More Ryland's Land |
| 1963 | | St Mary's Convent (Brook House; later sold for development) | |
| 1964 | Gym & Swimming Pool<br>Chapel Gallery | | |
| 1965 | Central Block (later Mead) | | Railway Land<br>Alma Road Land |
| 1966 | New Classrooms DCJS (built on Hardy House garden) | | |
| 1967 | Langhorne Hall DCJS | | |
| 1968 | Labs DCJS | | |

were often turbulent. Douglas Graham did not take kindly to governance while there was a group of governors with business experience who saw that the School could only survive if its financial affairs were conducted on sound business principles…'. Moreover, the Headmaster also believed in loosening rigid timetables if it suited his purpose. For example, a lovely spring morning might result in him announcing, '…There will be a roll-call at the top of Leckhampton Hill at 11am…'. Lessons would be abandoned in favour of a stimulating walk.

Although a Protestant Irishman, Douglas Graham was open to a broad approach to Christianity. While he insisted that during his time the churchmanship of the School was '…sound Church of England…' he felt it allowed him, on one occasion, to have an Anglo-Catholic, Fr Hallett, for a term, but by and large he stuck to the open evangelical approach of the Revd Philip Tidmarsh and the Revd Dick Page among others. However, he later observed that '…under my successors (the School) has acquired again a more evangelical tone, more in accord with the intentions of the founders and also a tone which has become more common in the Church of England…'. Douglas Graham initiated a discussion about celebrating Holy Communion, ensuring that an article advocating the Westward facing position for the President or Celebrant, as opposed to the North end or the more common Eastward facing position, was aired. Advised by The Very Revd Seriol Evans, Dean of Gloucester and School Governor, the Headmaster used gold leaf to help pick out some of the East end detail and make it more colourful. Today, of course, this has been added to further by the use of colourful banners. The School Chapel began to attract interest. In the summer of 1962, Sir John Betjeman, later Poet Laureate and something of a connoisseur of church architecture, pronounced the interior 'a little drab' but 'went into ecstasies' over the chancel arch which he felt '…must be the largest in brick in all England…'.

The Cheltenham Festival of Contemporary Art began in 1954. It was visited by Decanians who were studying Art the following year, principally to hear Sir Gerald Kelly, a former President of the Royal Academy, speak not just about contemporary art but also about the artists whom he had known in his youth: Manet, Degas, Moret, Lautrec and others. The boys were somewhat overawed!

The GCE examinations had just been introduced, and the School trumpeted the performance of the candidates, although they probably were not too good seen against today's pass rates (see box of examination results.)

The Headmaster's move into the newly acquired but unfortunately

**GCE Examination Results, 1955**

**A Level**

| Subject | No. | Subject | No. | Subject | No. |
|---|---|---|---|---|---|
| Greek | 1 | English | 3 | Mathematics | 1 |
| Latin (Classical) | 1 | History | 3 | Mathematics for Science | 4 |
| Latin | 4 | Geography | 6 | Physics | 1 |
| French | 12 | Music | 2 | Chemistry | 11 |
| German | 1 | General Paper | 10 | Biology | 8 |

**O Level**

| Subject | No. | Subject | No. | Subject | No. |
|---|---|---|---|---|---|
| Scripture | 10 | History | 9 | Elementary Mathematics | 58 |
| Greek | 1 | Geography | 12 | Additional Mathematics | 15 |
| Latin | 20 | Economics | 1 | Physics | 28 |
| French | 33 | Music | 2 | Chemistry | 22 |
| German | 7 | Art | 3 | Chemistry with Physics | 5 |
| English Lang. | 45 | Geometrical & Mechanical D'ing | 5 | Biology | 1 |

*At Advanced Level, A.C. Dann obtained Distinction in Latin.*
*Altogether 118 boys took 1 to 9 subjects, passing 0 to 9 subjects. 23 took A levels – Average 2.87 passes per candidate.*
*95 took O Level – Average 2.9 passes per candidate.*
*For a comparison, see 2007 results in the final Chapter.*
*(Source: Decanian, Summer 1955, Page 56)*

named 'Caynham House' on Lansdown Road, speedily renamed Dean Close House, allowed the re-designation of his former drawing room as a much improved Common Room for the teaching staff. Although the Headmaster continued to use the same study as before – now the Front Office of the Senior School – the rest of the former Headmaster's residence was quickly taken over by the bursary, housemasters and Gate House.

Dean Close House had an unused former servants' wing which was swiftly pressed into service as a newly-formed Yearlings House, designed initially for 16 boys entering the School who had yet to be formally allocated a house. The 'Yearlings' idea, that new boys should have a year in the School before entering their main houses, came from Marlborough but that school had no preparatory school, unlike Dean Close, and the concept never really worked well. A bachelor house tutor and Head of Science, Derek Barker, supervised them. Within four years land was purchased behind and between what is now Fawley House (then called Ombersley) and the much later buildings (Millennium and Rickerby blocks) of the Preparatory School, an area formerly known as Ryland's Land.

Ombersley House, too, was bought by the School but before it housed girls, it was used as an expanded Yearlings House from 1961-73 under the direction of Derek Barker. After Douglas Graham's departure the School came to feel that it was better to revert to former policy and the Yearlings House was disbanded in 1973.

During 1956 a small store room with a sink and running water, a Chaplain's Room and two classrooms, one of which was to double as the choir vestry, were added to the side of the Chapel, a much-needed facility. The same year, the Friends of Dean Close School Chapel gave the oak choir stalls.

Denys Carnill

September 1957 heralded the opening of the first day house. Until then, day boys had been attached to all four boarding houses, between eight and 12 of them in each at any one time. The overall size of each House had been just over 60 boys. Douglas Graham felt that day boys would be better served if they had their own House and Denys Carnill was the first Housemaster. He proved sympathetic and an effective champion of day boys when in many Schools the idea of a day house was frowned upon. He took trouble to liaise and get to know parents. He was also a gifted hockey-coach, a fine economics teacher and contributed to the School on many other fronts. When it opened, Field House had 54 boys scattered throughout the School in terms of age. House Colours were violet and white. The first Head of House was J.R. Hensman, a School Prefect, Company Sergeant-Major in the CCF and member of the rugby XV and cricket XI, winning his Colours in both. He was clearly respected throughout the School – an admirable person to have heading a fledgling house. He subsequently had a distinguished career in the Royal Marines. Traditionally, a house's name was ideally one syllable, for ease of use, and a new house name should begin with

**Housemasters of Field House**

| | |
|---|---|
| 1957-1972 | D.J. Carnill |
| 1972-1975 | T.N. Snow |
| 1975-1980 | R.C. Padfield |
| 1980-1984 | J.S. Richardson |
| 1984-1992 | C.M. Kenyon |
| 1993-2000 | L.S. Allington |
| 2000-2003 | C.J. Townsend |
| 2003-2005 | R.C. Boyle |
| 2005-present | P.S. Montgomery |

a letter not already in house use, hence B, G and T were already ruled out. It should have a connection of sorts with the School though not a person's name. Field was the answer. At the same time, Walton Court was shortened to just Court so that it was no longer WC.

At the end of 1957, Douglas Graham wrote to parents announcing that he had given each boy an IQ test and explaining its use as a general guide. It appears to have been the first occasion that the whole School had been tested and from then on they became a part of School procedure.

1959 was notable for the number of boys who contracted influenza. On 18th March, Douglas Graham wrote to parents saying that, as he had 88 cases in the School and the Medical Officer had told him a further 100 cases would probably occur within a very short time, and taking into account the need for proper convalescence, the School could not really cope and he was closing it early, a week before the Easter break. He noted that several other schools had shut, reopened but had been forced to close a second time. This all brought into sharp focus the work of the medical department, especially as influenza and poliomyelitis epidemics had created problems in the Cheltenham area in 1954. Influenza was again to be a problem towards the end of Michaelmas 1967. This was before efficient 'influvac' vaccines had begun to be in widespread use.

Before the Second World War, medical matters had almost certainly been under the overall umbrella of the matron of the day, notably Matron Cogbill. There was a treatment room just outside the old dining hall; after about 1968 it was relocated, but it was not long before a small pavilion to the rear of the entrance to Tower House flat was used until it moved to its present location in the old cottage in

**Nursing Sisters, Dean Close School, 1945 – 2008**

|  |  |  |  |
|---|---|---|---|
| Sister Alcock | 1945-1947 | Sister Shona Edmondson | 1986-1987 |
| Sister Sedgewick | 1947-1953 | Sister Catherine Gay | 1986-1987 |
| Sister Nancy Hudson | 1953-1955 | Sister Donna Palfreyman | 1987–1988 |
| Sister Frances Westmacott | 1955-1970 | Sister Wendy Guy | 1988 |
| Sister Mary Vaughan | 1970-1997 | Sister Naomi Woodcock | 1988-1990 |
| Sister Gillian Liverton | 1970 | Sister Anita Shepherd | 1989-1990 |
| Sister Vera Green | 1970-1971 | Sister Sally Fowler | 1990-present |
| Sister Mina Fordham | 1971 | Sister Claire Henle | 1990-1993 |
| Sister Penelope Langhorne | 1971-1974 | Sister Philippa Aiano | 1992 |
| Sister Jenny (LeSeelleur) Bowden | 1974-1976 | Sister Sarah Gallagher | 1993-2005 |
| Sister Jane Kvesic | 1976-1983 | Sister Gerry Dainty | 1997-2005 |
| Sister Mary Straker | 1983 | Sister Fiona Nelson | 2005-present |
| Sister Sue Webster | 1983-1985 | Sister Gill Thomas | 2005-2007 |
| Sister Ceri Davies | 1984-1985 | Sister Deborah Sharples | 2008-present |
| Sister Bridget Jacks | 1985-1986 | | |

**Sanatorium**

'The Ferns' in St Mark's Road was probably used as a sanatorium up until 1924. Later transferred across to the main School campus, it was for some time on the floor above what is now the IT workshop but which was the dining hall until 1987. In the mid 1960s, the ground-floor flat of Shelburne Hall (now Turner Hall) became the sanatorium, a sanatorium assistant occupying the flat above on the first floor. In 1975, it moved to 9 Glencairn Park Road. Patients were accommodated on the ground and first floors and there was accommodation for the assistant. Briefly, in 1983-84, it was decided to try the Churchill Nursing Home in Park Place but this proved too expensive. The sanatorium returned to Glencairn Park Road until 1998, when it was relocated with the treatment room and both are now at the former music cottage.

1998. From the Second World War until 1990, a specialist nurse/sister was resident, since when nurses have been on 24-hour call. The longest serving sister was Mary Vaughan (1970-97) who was not only concerned with medical matters but from 1977-82 also acted as Housemother to the fledgling Fawley House, aided by her husband Mervyn, although Fawley was still an extension of Mead House and thus still under Sue Vaus.

Cedric Kennedy, Art master since 1938, retired in 1960. His watercolours were becoming quite well-known, especially locally, as they were of the surrounding countryside. Not only had he sketched many boys for their parents; he had also painted the portraits of three Headmasters – Hugh Elder, Anthony Gilkes and Douglas Graham. They may be seen in the Dining Hall. Cedric Kennedy presided for most of those years, when he wasn't in the RAF war effort, in a so-called 'temporary' building, erected in 1926, that seems to have been somewhere near the present Art department and BonBernard Gallery, and also contained other classrooms.

Cedric Kennedy was succeeded by R.D.M. Spicer, who had studied Art in Tours, France and Norwich, knew something about pottery, fabric printing and photography and had made a study of Van Gogh. He attempted to open up Art by forming the Dean Close Society of Contemporary Art, through which he wanted to encourage more boys to 'dabble' in oils, rather than just drawing and sketching, and also encourage a far greater appreciation of Art. The initial take up was very encouraging but numbers soon fell away. Within three years R.D.M. Spicer had left, to the regret of *The Decanian*, to be replaced by G.M. Jones.

Among a large number of projects in the late 1950s through to the late 1960s must be included the building and opening of the Beaufort Block on the site of the Old Chapel in 1960, initially housing laboratories, a demonstration room, classrooms, the library and a scholars' gallery, common rooms and studies together with a cloister linking it with the Chapel.

Cedric Kennedy at work

Old St Mary's Convent (Brook House)

**Extract from Annual Report to the Governors 1964 by Sir Ian Yeaman, Chairman**

'...The removal of Brook House to St Mary's Convent led to the biggest internal upheaval in the history of the Senior School:-

i Tower House moved into Brook and occupied the Study Corridor
ii Court House went into the Main School to share it in vertically divided halves with Gate House
iii Gate took over the former Court Annexe dormitories (above the old School House), these being converted into studies.
iv The Dayboys (Field House) inherited Common Rooms from Court
v Four good classrooms were made out of the former Court dormitories.

Important results of these moves are that no classroom is any longer also a Common Room, and that new composite House areas have encouraged better control and discipline.

Final moves are due when the Central Block provides more studies and cubicles for Court and Gate, thus releasing to Dayboys all the Studies in the Beaufort Block...'.

The old St Mary's Convent, almost on the corner where Hatherley Road and Alma Road converge, was purchased thanks to the Headmaster's opportunism. The School had unsuccessfully bid for it at auction, but he went ahead and bought it at a considerably lower price, without authority, when an opening unexpectedly presented itself, but without the land originally around it. This was to become Brook House in Easter 1964 which led in turn to a massive internal change around. Not everyone was happy about it. E.S. Hay, Housemaster of Brook, felt very strongly that his house was losing so much in the move that he resigned his housemastership, to be replaced by P.E. Smith. The Headmaster subsequently reported to the Governors that '...Brook House is very happy in and proud of its new home but Mr Hay was unsettled and is off back to Australia...'

Another former Housemaster retired. F.R.H. Brian joined the School in 1923 as a mathematician. He did not finally retire until the end of 1962. He was Housemaster of Walton Court 1940-50.

Decisions about what were then new aspects of life were never far away. In 1962, it was the potentially intrusive use of small transistor radios. Douglas Graham decided to steer a middle, enforceable course and wrote to parents that although radios were banned '...the small transistor set which only one person can hear and that with an ear piece may be brought back for use in their cubicles only, though I think it would be wiser to advise boys not to bring them back...' This was later mirrored by the steps taken in the early 2000s to control the use of mobile telephones!

The development plan was momentarily dealt a blow by a fire in the main part of the old school during the early hours one day in August 1962. It is not quite certain where it began but was probably in the upper boot room. Flames were spotted on the first floor in the front building by a passing early-morning motorist who called out the fire brigade. Some say that the motorist in question was E.S. Hoare. Fortunately, all the necessary repairs were completed by the time term started on 20th September.

There were changes to the central block during 1964-65. The upper and lower Boot Rooms, what was called the Staircase Block and a number of '...other mean buildings...' between the Front Block and the Dining Hall Block, now the area where the Technical Services Department is based, were all demolished. A strong covered way, able to support three further storeys on top of it, was built from the

The Gym in 1964

The Swimming Pool in 1964

Front Block to where the present Design Technology Department frontage is. Presently those upper storeys would include Mead House. Once the old Rooms 6 and 7 were also swept away, the Upper (later Hooper) Quad came to bound the area it has today.

The building of a large, up-to-date swimming pool and gym was completed and opened in 1964. The pool, 25ft by 36ft, was far bigger than its predecessor and the gym measured a huge 110ft by 56ft in order to accommodate a full size basketball court. It was opened by the second Viscount Caldecote who had followed his father, the first Viscount, formerly Sir Thomas Inskip, as President of Dean Close School in 1960 when Lord Oaksey retired. The pool was quickly put to good use by both staff and Decanians.

The School had grown so much that the Chapel was no longer big enough. Its capacity was enlarged by building a West end gallery, with access gained by a turret staircase. This, too, was completed in 1964, the architect being the same Col Eric Cole who had designed the Chapel originally some 40 years earlier.

A feature of the Douglas Graham years was a succession of newsletters that were published, edited and produced by the boys. Usually, they were strongly supportive of the School, even though the first of them, the *Decanian Weekly*, was originally founded by M.A. White and A.B.W. Davies in 1955 as a platform to complain about the quality of the food. By the end of 1957 the newsletter had become fortnightly and had changed its name to the *Recorder*. It managed to keep going until 1960 when there was a fallow period for three years before *Impact* began as a monthly newsletter in January 1963 and carried on for some months. Although some material was of uncertain quality, a few insights these publications offered into the life of the School are interesting. For example, in February 1958, they organized their version of a Gallup Poll to try to discover the School's church-going habits the previous Christmas holidays. They took a sample of 100 boys – a very large group – and asked how many had been to church 'at least three times' the previous holidays. 54% claimed that they had. Of those who had gone to church, a narrow majority had gone with both parents, while nearly a quarter went on their own. 70% claimed to have gone to church on Christmas Day itself. The youthful editors were 'encouraged' by the result and suggested that it was still right to call Dean Close a Christian school.

The editors weren't above having a quiet 'dig' at their Headmaster. Rather like his predecessor Tony Gilkes, Douglas Graham was often tempted to join in rugby training, in the latter case sometimes without necessarily taking the precaution of changing into sports kit. His sessions on tackling were immortalized by one gently amusing poem, *Pateronage*.

Beyond the newsletters, however, Douglas Graham was encouraging useful extra-curricular activities and societies; there were 30 or so by the early 1960s, even including a falconry club briefly in 1962. There were trips out, such as by the Art and Pottery Society, that not only looked at local galleries but in 1964 '...a few aspiring artists...' went to London for the day to visit the Tate Gallery. Moreover, he kept

View of Chapel from Lower Quad c.1950

an eye on academic matters. In 1962, he announced in a letter to parents of Fourth Form boys that those who had studied Latin and French for some years but were not making much progress would be taken off both subjects and be subjected to a 'fairly intensive' course in basic German. The Headmaster wasn't beyond becoming involved in public issues either, his defence of Bishop John Robinson's position in the 'Lady Chatterley' obscenity trial in 1960 in a letter to Dr Robinson which the latter mentioned obliquely in court being a case in point.

Numbers registering for the School were always important. Advance calculation included the Headmaster extracting from *The Times* every year the number of male births and then working out from that the likely intake to the School. During Douglas Graham's headship numbers reached a record 341 in the Senior School in 1961-62, of whom 67 were day boys (the last gasp of the post-war bulge) but like other independent schools declined until by Douglas Graham's last year they had settled back to 324, of whom 69 were day boys. Apparently potential parents were almost always very impressed by the Headmaster. Junior School numbers were 218, including 103 day boys.

***Paternonage***

A keen headmaster said to me
A human bullet you must be;
Run past here and I will show
How to tackle hard and low.
I launch myself like this you see
Encompassing below the knee,
Hard and truly falls he so,
Squashed beneath from head to toe.

Such exercise just serves to show
To what extent headmasters go
That they may teach the young to see
How to tackle splendidly.

T.V.P.B.

The poet, Timothy Bliss, was then in his final year and was a House Prefect in Gate. Subsequently, he became a brain surgeon.

If there were changes concerning numbers of pupils coming to the School, buildings, activities and innovations, there were changes on the land front, too. In 1961, the Governors sold some land fronting the Hatherley Road – probably Flecker's Piece; in 1965 the land available on the eastern side of Barnfield (roughly opposite the pitch known as 'Humpty Dumpty' today) became available, so it was bought, as was railway land that became available as a result of the wielding of Dr Beeching's axe and the closure of the branch line that had passed the School since it had opened. The embankments finally disappeared in 1966. Ryland's land, near the present Fawley House, was now levelled and brought 'on stream' as a playing field in the summer of 1968.

**Clubs, Societies and Groups at DCS in 1963**

| | |
|---|---|
| Acton Club (History) | Junior Motor Club |
| Art & Pottery | Literary Society |
| Astronomical Society | Madrigal Club |
| Chapel Choir | Mathematical Society |
| Chess Club | Meteorological Society |
| Choral Society | Mission to Lepers Group |
| Christian Union | Model Railway Club |
| Cine Club | Modern Languages Society |
| Corinium Society (Archaeology & Classics) | Motor Club |
| Debating Society | Photographic Club |
| Euripdean Society (Greek & Modern Studies) | Rutherford Society (Science & Lit. VIs meet) |
| Gramophone Society | Shooting Club |
| Hobbies Group | Theatre Group |
| Jazz Society | Tovey Society (Music) |
| Junior Chemistry | Young Farmers Club |

There were lighter moments. Social occasions for the boys had to be supervised; Christopher Kenyon, then a young member of staff, was supervising one with colleague Brian Wilson in the latter half of the 1960s and remembers that '...School dances required inviting girls in from outside...(On one occasion), growing tired of a sweaty dance floor, BKW and I decided to go for a swim. It was dark; since we had no swimming trunks with us, we stripped off and dived in. At that moment, there was some movement in the gallery.

A "couple", having apparently also found the dance floor too hot (!), rose and made a hasty exit. We crawled out of the pool feeling somewhat exposed…'.

In March 1961, Douglas Graham wrote to parents to say that for the first time, on Saturday, 10th June, 1961, the Commemoration of Benefactors service would be on the same day as Prize-Giving with '…possibly a Matinee in the Open Air theatre…'. It is from that beginning that Commemoration Weekend may be traced, that came to include a display of '…paintings, photographs, sculpture and pottery…' in 1966 and beyond, together with the OD cricket match and other events, such as a concert.

Traditions were in something of a flux. Probably since the Second World War, the Last Post had been sounded by the CCF senior bugler from the flat roof of the Beaufort Building every Saturday night at 10pm. John Cobb OD recalls doing so as late as 1965, remarking that: '…If I forgot the School got complaints from local residents…'. When this tradition ended is not clear.

The end of an era was signalled in Trinity 1966. The 'Dabber', the School's uniform headgear that was a mortar board whose tassel used the School colours of cardinal red and cream was finally phased out, together with those of Cheltenham College and Pate's Grammar. No boy liked wearing one into Cheltenham, as they were targets for local youth. Day boys coming into School waited until the last possible moment to put them on. Within 18 months another small but significant change took place. The School Bell was replaced by the old ship's bell from *HMS Ariel* and placed on top of the centre tower, from where it was rung electronically.

In June 1967, the Executive Committee learnt with '…dramatic suddenness…' of Douglas Graham's wish to resign the following April in order to take up a teaching post at Williston Academy, Massachusetts, USA. He felt that he had accomplished what he had set out to do and that a younger man was needed to deal with impending changes, especially those that would arise from the imminent Newsom Report. W.A.M. Edwards, Chairman of the Executive, said of Douglas Graham in his 1967 Report to the Governors, '…The outstanding characteristics of the Headmaster's reign have been his imagination and boundless energy. Since the School's earliest years no period in its history has witnessed expansion and improvements on anything approaching the scale achieved during his 14 years' service…'.

Douglas Graham had been the inspiration and driving force for much innovation and change but arguably the biggest change of all was imminent – co-education.

# Chapter 7

## Genesis and Growth of Dean Close Junior School, 1886 to 1968

There have always been preparatory school aged children at Dean Close School (see chapter 1). When the School opened in May 1886, the youngest boy was E. Westley, aged eight, while A.W. Scamell, at nine, was only five months older. J.R. Epps was ten. Two boys were 11, seven were 12 and only four were teenagers, the eldest being 15. The initial age-range of seven years among so few children and staff posed a variety of challenges – academic, sporting and pastoral. No wonder Mrs Flecker was used to teach the youngest boys, as well as her considerable domestic and catering duties, never mind being Headmaster's wife and mother to her family.

The 1899 prospectus has the first reference to 'the Junior School', later called the Junior Department. The School roll stood at about 200, and 'Lower Classes' in each subject were apparently taught once or twice a week by senior masters. Greek and French were in the junior curriculum together with English, Mathematics, History, Geography, Physical and Natural Science, and Religious Instruction, the last taught daily by the Headmaster. Although there were one or two day boys, the vast majority were boarders. The prospectus revealed that '...all the boys in a House are of approximately the same age, the Junior House containing boys from 9-12 years...a House contains about 30 cubicles, one of which is assigned to each boy, becoming his own strictly private room. A master and a prefect sleep in each house...'. Thus boys of preparatory school age formed a significant part of the community.

The able Edward Easterfield's decision to leave at Christmas 1900, to become headmaster at Monkton Combe Junior School, having effectively been head-hunted, gave Dr Flecker pause for thought. The Revd F. Bienemann took over at the Hostel (now Wilton) until he contracted pneumonia and died in 1901.

In October 1900, soon after Easterfield's departure was announced, at a Governors' meeting, the Headmaster suggested looking at having a separate Junior School, about which he said he was ambivalent. A sub-committee was selected to explore the matter but before it could tackle the issues, it was agreed to hold the idea '...in abeyance...' as '...all (the Headmaster's) energies were engaged at present in accommodating the increased number of pupils...'. It was not raised again during his headship. Possibly the Headmaster realised the advantages of such a school but he would have to rely on others which he was not inclined to do. Consideration of a separate Junior School was put off for a generation.

As well as a Junior House, there were also junior teams and events. Among the most poignant must be R.G. Brooke's name as the winner of the U13 100 yards sprint in 13.2 seconds in the spring 1893. Within eight years, having been senior prefect, he was killed in the Boer War (see chapter 3). There were occasional events in the Swimming Sports that were for boys of preparatory school age; by the Lent Term 1894, a Junior XI for football had been selected, which beat local preparatory school Glyngarth 8-2. Glyngarth, which had a playing field virtually in front of Christ Church, Cheltenham, was to become a regular opponent in football and cricket until the First World War. In those days it was expected that each side would have two innings. There were also occasional cricket matches against a school called Cherbourg, from Malvern.

By the inter-war years, Cherbourg and Glyngarth had been replaced by Cheltenham College's Junior House, and honours appear to have been fairly even. At the distribution of prizes in the summer 1921, the School devoted some of the proceedings to 'Prizes in Junior School'.

The Hostel, where children aged roughly from eight to ten years were housed in 1921, is today known as Wilton. It operated as an extended part of Walton Court House (now Caldecote). Boys progressed from Hostel to Walton Court, leaving the latter aged about 14 to join the 'Junior House' in the Senior School. Housemaster of the Walton Court and Hostel area of the School was the Revd D.F. 'Tully' Horsefield who was also the School Chaplain, a jolly, caring person. Resident in Hostel was the Revd C.E. Luce, who has been described as '...a large man with pale watery pop-eyes (who) gave off a sour smell...' who was both Assistant Housemaster and Assistant Chaplain. Apparently, he did not know much about what happened in his own house. His wife was described as '...a large, dull woman who attended to the cascara and cod liver oil side of life...'.

Life for a small boy in the Hostel was tough. Dormitories were on the top floor, and had six or more boys in each. Douglas Pringle was a member of Dormitory 4 at this time, and vividly recalled being woken at 7am by Davis, the general factotum, a former Royal Artilleryman, bringing up warm water for the basins. That was followed by 'Morning Blub' when '...the biggest lout in the room would bait the youngest ones until he achieved the desired result. He must have been all of eleven years old...'.

During the day, Hostel boys wore shorts (which became grey flannels by the mid-1930s) their ties were red and white stripes, their shirts grey. Sundays necessitated the wearing of a 'bum freezer' Eton jacket and a wide, white stiff collar that were '...the very devil...' to fasten, as one OD put it, as they were so heavily starched. Black striped trousers were also worn together with the 'Dabber' or mortar board complete with its maroon and white tassel. Most of the uniform in those days was purchased at Thos. Plant, of the Colonade, Cheltenham. Main School timings were followed and the Hostel juniors had to attend all assemblies and lengthy Chapel services, including two on Sundays. Douglas Pringle remarked that '...We played games as a house, two terms soccer, one term cricket without any coaching in either, with a run on wet days...'.

Major Daniels

The arrival of Percy Bolton as Headmaster in 1924 heralded changes. Apart from creating a new house system where each house was a community in its own right, Bolton sought to create a Junior House. The Revd C.E. Luce left to be replaced briefly (1923-25) by D.B. Tugwell, a music master and son of one of the earliest members of staff. The purchase of Fortfield House in 1925 allowed Percy Bolton to create a Junior House more like a small preparatory school, Walton Court and Hostel becoming one main School house, as well as providing space for a Tuck Shop. On the departure of Mr Tugwell, the Headmaster appointed Major G.P. Daniels

**Housemasters of Fortfield (Boys' House), 1925-2001**
**Masters of Juniors as well as Housemasters**

| | |
|---|---|
| 1925-1930 | Major G.P. Daniels |
| 1930-1932 | F. Horsley |
| 1932-1939 | G.T. Clarke |
| 1939-1949 | F. Horsley |
| | **Housemasters/Houseparents** |
| 1949-1959 | C.S. Harwood |
| 1959-1967 | O.P. Outhwaite |
| 1967-1973 | J.C. Titterington |
| 1973-1977 | J.D. Hooper |
| 1978-1981 | A.D. Carpenter |
| 1981-1988 | Mr & Mrs D.A.J. Crawshaw |
| 1988-2001 | Mr & Mrs A.J. Judge |

*In 2001, Fortfield became a girls' boarding house. See chapter 15.*

Housemaster of Fortfield and effectively Master of Juniors. He was said to be a big man, always smart and perhaps somewhat flamboyant. To young boys he must have seemed somewhat larger than life.

Major Daniels stayed until 1930. He was succeeded by Francis Horsley, who in his turn left Fortfield in 1932 to marry – at that time it was bachelor accommodation only and anyway he wished to return to teaching in the main School. However, G.T. Clark OD, the next Housemaster and Master of Juniors had to be given married accommodation, at the top of the house.

Fortfield boys by the side door, 1931

Fortfield was only for boarders, with accommodation for 40 boys, as the prospectus for the middle 1930s makes clear. Its title refers to Dean Close Junior School, although, like the 1899 prospectus, it later reverted to being '...the Preparatory Department of Dean Close School...'. The curriculum consisted of Scripture, Classics, Mathematics, French and English and an introduction '...at a fairly early age to the elements of Science...'. A simple form of setting appears to have been in operation. Games played included football, hockey and cricket. Interestingly, given the earlier comments about a lack of coaching, now the prospectus claimed that '...coaching is undertaken by experts in the respective games and is not restricted to or concentrated upon the boys of special promise. It is a principle

Fortfield Cricket XI 1933

of the school both in work and in games to give every boy his full share in all the facilities available…'. Moreover, it is known that from 1933 onwards, football and possibly other matches were played against rival preparatory schools.

Drama experiences then were restricted, although at the annual Christmas party in 1931 there were no party games, as Dormitory 2 had produced a short play about Boadicea. In the previous two years some kind of brief revue had occurred. *Boadicea* included three acts of two minutes each and was over '…all too soon…', as G. Wilson Knight, later a distinguished expert and academic on Shakespeare but then House Tutor in Fortfield, commented in his appreciation in *The Decanian*.

Small boys were allowed a certain freedom. John Heskell, among others, recalled that, in the mid-1930s, as a comparatively young member of Fortfield, he went for unsupervised walks, often with a companion, near the railway line which passed close to the School Chapel then across a bridge over the Up Hatherley main road. Apparently there was a pedestrian crossing on the line further along, and it was there that occasional conversations between engine drivers and the boys '…were one-sided, full of expletives on their side because we were trespassing…'. The boys wanted to put pennies and half-pence on the railway-line, just as a train was on its way, in order to make them bigger.

In 1936, W. Graham Clarke entered Fortfield as a 12-year-old. He remembered the long walled garden to the rear of Fortfield, which included a tennis court, and at the end '…embraced a brick-built stable block…' Today, the latter is the site of the Ferguson Building. The stables housed ground staff equipment, including mowers. The tarmac path that leads around the corner of the Preparatory School

Fortfield Hockey XI 1934

cricket XI pitch was originally of cinders that came from the Senior School boilers and were also used to lay the path to the Tuckwell Theatre.

Football was played in brown boots with heavy toe caps and leather studs, long navy shorts and navy woollen stockings with the school colours woven into their tops. Shirts were cardinal red with white, and white trim. All clothing was freshly laundered after every game. Hockey in the Lent Term required the same dress as for football, while cricket in the Summer was played in white flannel trousers and shirts. Proper white kid boots with steel studs were worn. The cricket caps were navy blue, hooped with two ribbons in the school colours.

Fortfield's good sized basement was partly used as a changing room. Also, clothes could be dried and shoe lockers found. The kitchen was there, too, with a 'dumb waiter' that carried food up to the dining room above. On the ground floor was a large common room with open wooden lockers for books, a dining room, now the TV room, the Housemaster's study and a private sitting room. The first floor had four or five rooms used as dormitories, sleeping about five or six boys in each, and a small sanatorium/medicine room. There were washstands in the dormitories, one for every two boys. The maids came up each morning, filled the washbasins with hot water and answered the question 'What's for breakfast?' New boys arose and washed first, emptied the slops into a bucket and filled the basin again. The floor above was for the Housemaster and family, by 1936 Mr and Mrs G.T. Clark, and possibly a Matron, too, although Mrs Clark certainly fulfilled a Matron's role. There was also a nurse who looked after the boys when they were ill. It was not until the 1980s that the Housemaster's flat was relocated to the first floor.

In 1934, pupils from the Junior House attended main School Chapel every morning and had PE and carpentry lessons over there as well as having their own classrooms on the ground floor of Hostel; Senior School staff came across to teach them. Morning break provided an opportunity to buy a penny bun that saw the boys through until lunch, which was eaten in Fortfield. After lunch there was one more period, then games. There were classes again later and, after tea, prep in the evening.

Hugh Elder's arrival as Headmaster in April 1938 was decisive for the Junior School. Fortfield was 30 strong in a school of 170, all of whom were boarders. The Headmaster quickly decided that '...day

**Howard Graham Trevelyan Clark, OD, Housemaster 1932-39**

He was born in 1900 and entered Dean Close School in September 1916. He left in July 1919, subsequently entering Bristol University where he obtained a BSc in Science. At some point he dispensed with his first name. He later taught at Mill Mead near Shrewsbury. In 1932 he was appointed Housemaster of Fortfield, staying until 1939.

Graham Clark was said to be '...quite a big man with thinning light red hair...' and was known among the boys, not unsurprisingly, as 'Nobby'. He and his wife, whom he married while in Fortfield, often invited several boys to spend a couple of weeks with them at their bungalow on the banks of the river at Potter Heigham in Norfolk. The Clarks owned a large cabin cruiser called *Crusader* as well as two sailing dinghies.

The outbreak of the Second World War meant Fortfield was evacuated to Glyngarth School, Cheltenham. Some arrangements upset G.T.C. and he decided to leave. He opened his own preparatory school at Purton Stoke. 'After a short while' his school moved to Barton Court near Kintbury, Berkshire. Apparently it was '...the first school for many Decanians...'. Little if anything is known of his later life. He died in 1965, leaving a widow and daughter.

**Junior School Cricket and Football Opponents 1938-39**

Beaudesert Park, Brightlands, Glyngarth, Oakley Hall, Ryeford Hall, Stouts Hill. As far as is known, only Beaudesert Park has survived to the present day.

boys of a junior age should be admitted to the School, and that the juniors should be reorganized as a separate unit, to be known as Dean Close Junior School, with its own timetable and classrooms…'. As far as possible, the Junior School would have its own staff, answerable to him. Day boys were essential as Fortfield could only take 36 boarders maximum, an uneconomic number for a self-contained, self-supporting preparatory school. The idea was that the Junior School would provide much-needed entrants to the main School in due course. The scheme would begin immediately: during the 1938 summer holiday, three classrooms were constructed in the old stables at the end of Fortfield driveway.

Michaelmas 1938 began with the new Junior School opening with 31 boarders and six day boys called, initially, 'day-boarders', who arrived in time for Morning Chapel and left in the evening after all work, games and prep were over. The Junior School used the main School laboratories, gym, swimming pool and carpentry shop and had their own additional teachers, Mr Moore and Miss Henslow, who both arrived that Michaelmas. Dr Flecker's original thought had taken nearly 40 years to materialise.

Sport was not forgotten, although few schools whose sides the infant Junior School took on in the early years have survived. There was a parents' match in the 1938, and it is recorded that '…contrary to general preparatory school custom, the parents were not in any way handicapped, and it was an excellent performance on the part of the boys to be only 4 runs behind on the first innings…A.J. Simms's performance in taking 5 wickets for 36 runs and A.W. Kirby's excellent 53 were the highlights of a very successful two-day match…'. Rugby was not introduced to DCJS until 1947.

The Junior School's first play was at Christmas 1938, performed on the stage in the Flecker Hall. It was *Arise Sir Walter* by Falkland Cary with a cast of 19 – virtually half the School – with only one pupil taking two parts. The director was Mrs Clark. This was followed by a Christmas supper '…when parents and boys did ample justice to a host of delicious, delightful and devastating dainties…'. This is of interest in that parents were invited to the supper and not just pupils and possibly staff.

Fortfield House July 1939. G.T. Clark, master-in-charge, seated centre

On 3rd September, 1939, Britain and France declared war on Germany and on 7th September Hugh Elder signed the receipt for the Requisition Order. The Senior School evacuated to Monkton Combe (see chapter 5). The Junior School stayed in Cheltenham, thereby helping Hugh Elder's recruitment of junior day boys. Within days, the Junior School was transferred to Glyngarth as their Headmaster, K.M. Monie, whose own numbers were falling, agreed to find accommodation for everyone from Dean Close Junior School. There was another crisis. Graham Clark and his wife, on inspecting Glyngarth, told Hugh Elder that their part of the evacuation plan was unworkable and they wished to resign. The Headmaster did not argue, asking Francis Horsley to take over the Junior School. The Clarks left to set up their own school. However, the evacuation and the departure of the Clarks meant pressure on the Junior School numbers as parents, a little uncertain as to the School's future, began to remove children. When term began at Glyngarth on 22nd September there were 16 Junior School boarders and 20 day boys. The staff included Francis Horsley, A.W. Golder, Hugh Elder himself from Monday to Friday afternoon and Miss Henslow. Glyngarth staff included

**Glyngarth School**

Glyngarth School, a privately owned preparatory school, was located opposite Christ Church in Douro Road, its former playing field virtually opposite the church's west end today, thus comparatively close to Dean Close School. It was founded by the Misses Hill in 1876; in 1882 they sold out to the Misses Sanderson. The school was in the building adjacent to the playing field which is now occupied by a Cheltenham Ladies' College house, Farnley Lodge. A newspaper report in 1898 notes a sports day at Glyngarth and it is clear that there had been many before that one. From that report it is possible to deduce that there were boys aged between 7 and 13 years being educated there. This is confirmed by a series of football and cricket reports from *The Decanian* dating from 1894.

It is not clear how many boys were at the school at any one time, although it is said that they wore pink and white striped caps.

The only other newspaper report comes from July 1898, when, to the great surprise of parents, pupils and other interested parties the two principals, the Misses Sanderson, announced their retirement within days, after 16 years running the school.

The new headmaster/principal was T.C. Weatherhead, MA, an 'experienced' preparatory schoolmaster, who had been living in New Barnet.

In the Second World War, Glyngarth took in the slightly depleted ranks of Dean Close Junior School – while Glyngarth's numbers were by then severely down. The headmaster was K.M. Monie who stayed until the school's closure in the mid-1950s when the field and school building were bought by Cheltenham Ladies' College.

their headmaster and two assistant teachers. In addition to the teaching staff, Mrs Cocks, formerly matron in Brook House, was matron. The boarders enjoyed the '...separate cubicles in our spacious dormitory...' not to mention the excitement (and necessity) of fire-drills under Mr Golder's direction. There were joint football teams and they worked off '...a little healthy rivalry with practice boxing...'. Popular, quieter amusements appear to have been chess, model ships and aeroplanes. At the end of Michaelmas the government allowed the Junior School back into Fortfield and their classrooms, though not to any part of the main school campus. Amazingly, the Junior School returned with more boys than when they left – now 19 boarders and 21 day boys. Once the Junior School was back in Lansdown Road, the trickle of new entrants became something of a flood.

On 11th December, 1940, John Horsley, then a boy, recalled that: '...When the siren sounded my parents, younger brother, sister and I went into Fortfield basement with the domestic staff. Suddenly, there was a loud knock on the basement back door and four to six Senior School boys rushed in. They had been to the cinema in Cheltenham that evening and sought shelter until the 'all clear' was sounded...'. One of a stick of bombs destroyed part of three classrooms created from the old Fortfield stables, rendering the whole building unsafe. For the next two years the Junior School had to walk to and from the main School. Indeed, for a while the Junior School had to inhabit a range of wooden buildings behind the changing room corridor on the Senior School side of Shelburne Road. M.P.L. Wright, about eight years old at the time, recalls that those rooms had been used previously as an art studio, a laboratory and a room for the Field Club. He was intrigued by a slightly older boy, W.S. Lamprey, a talented painter who apparently had a tame owl. Nevertheless, the Headmaster continued to encourage the boys, directing *Scenes from A Midsummer Night's Dream* in 1941 in the Tuckwell Theatre. A one-act play, *Check to the King of France*, was directed by a Miss Evans in March 1943 in the Senior School's Big Schoolroom. With their usual ability to react rather late in the day, the authorities built '...a new, reinforced ARP shelter...' in the Junior School during the Christmas holidays of 1941-42, although where is not clear. In 1944 the classrooms were restored (if a trifle ramshackle) and life at the Junior School returned to near normal.

In the meantime, numbers of boys entering the Junior School had grown. In 1942, the empty Walton Court building was returned to the School. It had been decided to continue to allow the expansion of Junior School numbers to give the main School an even stronger feeder Junior School than had originally been envisaged. Walton Court was renamed 'Caldecote' in honour of the President of the School, Sir Thomas Inskip, KC, MP, who in 1939 had been elevated to the peerage as Viscount Caldecote of Bristol on appointment as Lord Chancellor. Caldecote began its career in Trinity 1942 as the Junior School's overall numbers reached three figures and initially 12 boys slept there, under the care of the Revd K.M.C. Melrose who acted as Housemaster, assisted by a Miss Allcock as Matron. However, that clergyman left to be a Chaplain to the Forces by the end of the year, to be replaced by P.M. Wilson from Oundle School who stayed as Housemaster of Caldecote for three years before moving on to Rossall.

**Housemasters/Parents of Caldecote (Boys), 1942-2009**

| | |
|---|---|
| 1942 | The Revd K.M.C. Melrose |
| 1942-1945 | P.M. Wilson |
| 1945-1949 | C.S. Harwood |
| 1949-1970 | E.J.B. Langhorne |
| 1970-1974 | A.D. Wood |
| 1974-1987 | Mr & Mrs M.J. Piper |
| 1987-1993 | Mr & Mrs T.C. Lewis |
| 1993-2005 | Mr & Mrs S.A. Cahill |
| 2005-present | Mr & Mrs J.E.B. Harris |

Classrooms were a problem. The old tuckshop was pressed into service and Christopher Bell OD recalls that, as winters were cold, most boys had chilblains, especially if they were those pupils assigned to the old tuckshop. They were allowed to wear mittens from time to time '…and there was great competition to grab desks next to the very old cast-iron stove…'. During the mid-morning break '…the boys would be given a half-slice of bread and margarine which were stuck on pencils or compasses and toasted on the sides of the stove. French Toast, we called it for some reason…'. He recalls, too, that for a year or two after 1939, junior boys still wore Eton collars with white shirts and dark suits but presently that lapsed, to his great relief. In a letter dated August 1940, Hugh Elder was clearly anxious to save parents undue expense, so relaxed the Sunday dress code for both Senior and Junior School boys.

Most if not all the ground floor of Caldecote was classrooms or the music room. Another room was used as a classroom for younger boys on the first floor. Expansion continued until Michaelmas 1945, when the Hostel, now renamed Rickerby, was reopened. During the war it served as furniture store, lodging for members of the ATS (Auxiliary Territorial Service) and a club for American Officers. When Hugh Elder left a year later, there were 77 boarders and 65 day boys in the Junior School – a healthy 142 boys altogether.

Although it is debatable how comfortable the Horsleys were with the preparatory school age-group, nevertheless they created a very solid foundation from which a fully-fledged preparatory school could evolve. Between 1939 and 1949 they had presided over a remarkable expansion of numbers from 36 to 160, equally divided between boarding and day boys. Indeed, the Junior School was now sufficiently large that in his last year at the helm, Francis Horsley created four sports houses, subsequently called 'Divisions', later still 'sets', namely Nomads, Ramblers, Rangers and Rovers, that battled enthusiastically against each other on various occasions, certainly in football and athletics and later in work and games generally.

Mary Horsley was as successful on the domestic front as her husband was as master-in-charge, although occasionally her resourcefulness was seriously challenged. One morning she suddenly found herself in Fortfield without a cook. There had been no notice, yet the need to feed large numbers of hungry mouths within very few hours loomed large. The Horsleys had a house in Mead Road, Cheltenham, and knew their next door neighbours, the Thompsons, well. Mary Horsley telephoned and appealed to Mrs Madge Thompson to come in '…just for the day…' to help out. Mrs Thompson came – and stayed, remaining for about five years. She proved a resourceful, some say brilliant, cook and was great fun with an infectious laugh. She must have thought a great deal of the School, for her son subsequently came to the Junior and then to the Senior School and later became that much-loved Bishop of Bath and Wells, Bishop Jim Thompson, whose sister, Mrs Barbara Abbatt, became a Governor.

In May 1949, A.N. Gilkes, the Headmaster, revealed in a letter to Old Decanians that the Governors, having decided the Junior School should effectively become a separate entity, offered Francis Horsley the opportunity to be the first Headmaster of the Junior School, but he declined the invitation. Instead, he returned full-time to the Senior School as Second Master and senior Mathematics master.

The Junior School was now set to become a proper preparatory school in its own right. Eadward Langhorne, already on the Junior School staff for a year, became its first Headmaster from September 1949, serving for a total of 22 years in that capacity with three Senior School Headmasters – A.N. Gilkes, the Revd D.L. Graham and C.G. Turner. The change went much further than a mere job title. From 1949 on, the Junior School Headmaster would 'hire and fire' Junior School staff, select pupil applicants and be entirely responsible to the Governors through the Senior School Headmaster for running the Junior School, both day-to-day and in terms of policy and strategic thinking. Entry to the senior School would no longer be automatic: Common Entrance would have to be passed by Junior

**Eadward J.B. Langhorne, staff member 1948-49, Headmaster 1949-72**

Eadward and Rosemary Langhorne

He was educated at St Edward's School, Oxford and Keble College, Oxford where he was a Varsity trialist both for rugby and cricket; he taught at a preparatory school near Exeter before entering the RAF during the Second World War. He became an instructor at the Central Flying School for which he received an MBE. He taught at the Junior School from September 1948 and was appointed by the Governors on the nomination of A.N. Gilkes, DCS Headmaster, to be the first Headmaster of the Junior School from September 1949. E.J.B.L. had connections in high places: his referees were the Dean of St Paul's Cathedral, London, and the Chairman of the English Cricket Selectors!

Rosemary, his wife, took charge of catering and domestic matters which included acting as Housekeeper, as well as helping to run Caldecote House, keeping an eye on the junior boys in Rickerby and bringing up a family; she was later to be described as being '...a wonderful hostess to children, staff and parents...'.

E.J.B.L. was known not only for his love of sport but also for his enthusiasm for Classics, photography and ornithology.

In the last few years of his headship, Eadward and Rosemary Langhorne moved from the Junior School and lived at Whistling Down on Cleeve Hill. He retired from the Junior School in 1972, and taught Classics at Wycliffe College before moving to be closer to the rest of his family near Chichester.

He died in 1995 at the age of 88.

School leavers. This level of independence made the Junior School Headmaster eligible for membership of the Incorporated Association of Preparatory Schools, duly confirmed in January 1950.

Both Francis Horsley and Eadward Langhorne in turn were known to be strict disciplinarians and both were certainly prepared to 'tan' boys. E.J.B. Langhorne is said to have used beating to inculcate determination into some school sports teams. One OD states that boys were '...simply terrified...' of him, as were some staff. While people today might be aghast at such treatment to comparatively young boys, many parents in that era felt such an approach, although possibly regrettable, taught boys how to behave and conduct themselves. Some who experienced that treatment took time to recover; enrolment of the next generation to the Junior School proved problematic at times as a direct result, although the insistence on striving for excellence that was a hallmark of Langhorne's years was a strong recruiting sergeant. Parents of potential pupils in the locality and beyond had wanted to send their boys to Francis Horsley at what was becoming a popular school, and continued to do so in ever increasing numbers during the Langhorne years, a very tangible sign of approval for what was being offered. Indeed, within a year of taking over, the President of the Old Decanian Society suggested that there had been over 70 candidates for the 30 places available at the Junior School for that September.

Among Eadward Langhorne's first actions as Headmaster was reordering boarding houses. The youngest boarders moved to Rickerby (previously the old Hostel and today Wilton House), under their own Housemaster, G.H. Harper, the senior English master, while the middle age-group went to Fortfield under C.S. Harwood, Second Master and senior French master. The seniors were housed in Caldecote under the immediate eye of the Headmaster where a flat was constructed for him and his family. For a

**Dean Close Junior School, September 1949**

In September 1949, the Junior School became a separate preparatory school with its own Headmaster. In its first term, its organization looked like this:

Headmaster and Housemaster of Caldecote: E.J.B. Langhorne, MBE, MA
Second Master and Housemaster of Fortfield: C.S. Harwood

G.H. Harper, MA
Major A.W. Golder, MBE
G.E. Bright, BA
P.M.W. Williams, BA
The Revd C.H. Dawkins MA
D. Gaye, MA, ARCO Director of Music
C.J. Kennedy, Art
Miss E.R. Henslow, Preparatory Forms
Miss A. Jarrett, Preparatory Forms
Mrs J. Reeve, Preparatory Forms
Miss G.M. Stone, Preparatory Forms and Music

The classes were arranged so that the eldest were in Form I and the youngest in Form V. There was a streaming policy at this time but under Langhorne each child was reviewed every year to check that he was in the appropriate class.

| Form | Boarding Houses | | | Total | | 1949 | *1954* |
|---|---|---|---|---|---|---|---|
| | Caldecote | Fortfield | Rickerby | Boarding | Day | Form Total | *Form Total* |
| *Crow's Nest* | | | | | | | *8* |
| *1A* | | | | | | | *15* |
| *1B* | | | | | | | *16* |
| I | 10 | | | 10 | 5 | 15 | |
| IIA | 4 | 4 | 1 | 9 | 16 | 25 | *23* |
| IIB | 5 | 12 | | 17 | 11 | 28 | *24* |
| IIIA | 1 | 18 | 6 | 25 | 10 | 35 | *24* |
| IIIB | | 4 | 6 | 10 | 7 | 17 | *24* |
| IVA | | | 6 | 6 | 11 | 17 | *22* |
| IVB | | | 4 | 4 | 15 | 19 | *20* |
| V | | | 5 | 5 | 6 | 11 | *22* |
| 1949 Total: | 20 | 38 | 28 | 86 | 81 | **167** | |
| *1954 Total:* | *23+14=37* | *42* | *28* | *107* | *91* | | ***198*** |

(*Source: Dean Close Junior School Michaelmas Term 1949 School List; the figures for 1954 were taken from Report by HM Inspectors on Dean Close Junior School issued 5th November 1954, Copyright: Controller, H M Stationery Office and the Summer Term Calendar, 1954)*

In the 1954 figures, 14 of the boys who were boarders and technically part of Caldecote were in fact boarding in the newly-acquired Fawley Lodge which was then on the north side of Lansdown Road. The Inspectors felt that 23 were still too many boys in Caldecote itself and recommended that the number be brought down to 17.

Wilton House, previously Hostel

while the overflow of boarders assigned to Caldecote slept in the newly acquired Fawley Lodge which was on the opposite side of Lansdown Road. 14 boys were based there at the time of the Junior School inspection of July 1954. Ken Hollington, and later W.M. Newte, were the House Tutors who shared the basement flat of Fawley and oversaw Junior School boys during this period. The arrangement was far from ideal for the boys had to cross Lansdown Road in a crocodile at least twice a day. The reason for the youngest boarders being in Rickerby became clear when Eadward Langhorne centralized the dining rooms and kitchens there, closing the Fortfield dining room, as well as making Rickerby the location for the Junior School sickbay. As it was close to Caldecote where the Langhornes lived, and Rosemary Langhorne was responsible for all domestic and catering arrangements, the proximity of the kitchens and the junior house allowed her to keep a particular eye on how the youngest boys were faring.

The new Headmaster kept one area as it had been under Francis Horsley. It was the so-called 'Pre-Preparatory' part of the School for children under ten. Miss E.R. 'Hetty' Henslow (later Mrs R.D. Campbell) was there from 1938-72. Appointed by Hugh Elder, she had been to Glyngarth, had taught in temporary accommodation in the Senior School and had been with the Junior School ever since. She is said to have been an enormously gifted teacher, especially on the creative side. Major Golder, who did not finally retire from the Junior School until 1969, was pleased that Mrs Jean Reeve, one of his daughters, taught there from 1944-1957. She, with Mrs Campbell and a third colleague who changed at regular intervals, developed a strong department. They were also required to take boys out for football and cricket

**Housemasters of Rickerby House (Junior Boys' Boarding), 1949-1961**

| | |
|---|---|
| 1949-1952 | G.H. Harper |
| 1952-1959 | P.G. Foster |
| 1959-1961 | K.W. Hollington |

*In 1961, Junior boy boarders transferred to (old) Wilton House. See box later in this chapter.*

**Major Alfred William Golder, MBE, staff member 1919-69**

He came from Petersfield, Hampshire, and was brought up in Liss. He was an able cricketer, possibly of county standard; he trained as a teacher, probably in PE. He married Edith Mary Thresher of Wilton near Salisbury before the First World War broke out.

Alfred Golder finished the First World War at the Aldershot Gymnasium and School of Physical Training as a Sergeant-Major. He came to the School in 1919 as Warrant Officer/SSI for the Officers Training Corps, the forerunner of today's CCF, coach for the cricket XI and PE instructor. He and Edward Ellam would both appear very early on the day of any home cricket match so that they could prepare the pitch personally and meticulously. He wrote out the school timetable in his own clear hand; he assisted in school dramatic productions and also taught in the classroom when needed. He became an established Western Counties Association referee for hockey.

In the Second World War he assisted the CCF and the Cheltenham Home Guard where he became Battalion Training Officer, being seconded into the ACF, initially as a Lieutenant, but became a Major. He, with Miss Hensley, went with Francis Horsley and the Junior School to Glyngarth during Michaelmas 1939. In 1944, Dean Close School marked Major Golder's 25 years with the School Corps by holding a special parade and presentation.

After the war he taught in the Junior School, although he was past retirement age. One of his daughters, Mrs Jean Reeve, was also teaching in the Junior School. He finally gave up teaching at the end of Trinity 1969 after a 50 year association with the Dean Close community.

Although he had lost an eye as a result of a gardening accident, and towards the end of his life suffered acutely from arthritis, A.W. Golder had an irrepressible sense of humour, a fund of stories and an unswerving loyalty to the School. He died in 1971.

sessions on Big Field. At one point Eadward Langhorne suggested that they might begin junior rugby sessions but they declined!

On the domestic front, the work and example of Matrons such as Miss Frances Baker had kept things secure and stable for a number of years while the Junior School was built up.

By the end of Trinity 1954, Eadward Langhorne had been Headmaster for five years and there was a Junior School inspection. A team of inspectors moved in for three days. Numbers stood at 198,

**Miss Frances (Fan) Baker, staff member 1947-78**

In September 1947 Fan Baker first became Matron of Fortfield, where the youngest boys were. She was a Leader in the Campaigners, a Christian youth movement run from St Mark's Church, Cheltenham, which she still managed to support for some time after her appointment to DCJS.

The junior boarders were moved to Rickerby House (now Wilton) in 1949 and Fan Baker accompanied them, also doing duty in Caldecote, then the senior boys' house. The supervision of young, resident domestics was also her responsibility for a time.

She was the first Junior School matron for female boarders when six pioneers joined the School in 1968. In 1972 the ground floor of Shelburne became the sanatorium. Fan was put in charge, caring for patients from both Senior and Junior Schools.

In 1975 she took over the larger and better equipped Sanatorium in Glencairn Park Road, which she ran with great efficiency until 1978 when she retired after over 30 years with the Junior School.

Realizing she was terminally ill, she returned to her family in Ireland where she died, it is believed, in 1992 aged 85.

of whom 91 were day boys, nearly 40 having been added during those first Langhorne years. At this point classrooms were to be found in a number of locations. The three most junior classes had their own rooms in the old Fortfield stables, together with a Craft Room and an individual Music Room. There was a small building that housed the Art Room, though exactly where this was is not clear. There were classrooms on the ground floor of Fortfield and also Caldecote. There were almost enough classrooms for each class but the 'Crow's Nest', as the Scholarship class was called, had to use the day room in Fortfield, which was not felt to be a very satisfactory arrangement. Indeed, no classrooms at this stage were purpose-built.

Nevertheless, the inspectors were almost euphoric over the Junior School Headmaster. The Governors were congratulated for having had the wisdom to select him. He was described variously as being a gifted teacher, having sensitive understanding of boys, a well-balanced judgement, something of a visionary in terms of where a preparatory school should aim to be, heading a school that was considered enlightened in academic matters and where the curriculum was judged to be wisely and well planned. The inspectors were deeply impressed by the quality of the staff who they felt were, as a whole, notably above average. They singled out C.S. Harwood, the Second Master, who they felt was an outstanding teacher of French and professional schoolmaster. In short, the Junior School could be favourably compared to the best preparatory schools in the country. The inspectors were impressed perhaps above all by the morning service held daily in the School Chapel which they saw as a particularly significant religious and musical experience.

C.S. 'Mac' Harwood 1954

One extra-curricular feature that was reported on very favourably by the inspectors was the Argonauts. The Junior School had a brief flirtation with Cubs and Scouts in the early 1950s that appeared not to work well as the Headmaster apparently did not favour them, although there was clearly a demand for 'outward bound' type activities. Instead the Argonauts were born, largely a Junior School version of Scouts but without the uniforms.

Apart from the inspection, 1954 was important for two further reasons in that the house between Fortfield and Rickerby, 'Lisnamoe', which was privately owned, finally came onto the market. It was duly purchased by the School and later renamed Hardy House in honour of Major H.H. Hardy, CBE, a Chairman of Governors who had also been headmaster at both Cheltenham College and Shrewsbury School. The building became the administration centre of the School, including the Headmaster's study, an office for his secretarial support, a school library, whose absence had been noted as one of the few blemishes by the inspectors, and a Common Room for staff. Initially, the overflow of Caldecote boarders who had been in Fawley Lodge were now rehoused in two dormitories in Hardy.

The second key event was that day boys, by now well over a third of the Junior School, were finally recognized in the appointment of W.M. Newte as their first Housemaster, although it was to be some time before they were to have their own facilities.

The Revd Dr Jonathan Holmes OD recalls that one way fine lunch breaks were occupied in the late 1950s was by train-spotting from the Shelburne Road end of the Corner Pitch.

At this time, Sports Day coincided with Speech Day, held in Cheltenham's Town Hall.

(Old) Wilton House was acquired in 1961. It stood on the same side of Lansdown Road as the Junior School, next door to the County Police Headquarters. As it was a little apart from the rest of

**The Argonauts**

Ken Hollington was the initial driving force. The Scouts' last term was Lent 1952 and the Argonauts were set up by Ken for his first term at DCJS, Trinity 1952. The original principal aim was to 'develop character through adventure'. The Argonauts were grouped in 'watches' of 13 boys, initially three numbered watches. In the Lent Term 1955, the watches were expanded to four and given names, Cheviot, Cotswold, Pennines and Quantocks. Each Watch was divided into two divisions – North Country and South Country – for instruction purposes. It was soon after that reorganization that the Argonaut Badge was introduced for which a boy had to complete a term's satisfactory probationer membership. The nautical flavour of some of the terminology was because both Ken Hollington and Philip Foster, another master who assisted in the early days, had spent time in the Royal Navy during the recent war. The Argonauts were concerned with trekking, camping, canoeing, sailing, hill-walking and associated skills. In later years there would be regular trips to the Hope Memorial Camp at Braithwaite in the Lake District. The Argonauts met every week, initially on Mondays at 6pm but later on Fridays, sometimes went out on Sundays and often camped during the holidays. The very first expedition, recalled by R.I. Ireland, involved two groups scaling the steep walls of the Black Mountain ridges on the edge of the Vale of Ewyas. By 1957 it was reported that '…there are minor treks almost every week-end and major expeditions generally once a term…'.

Michael Rowlands, who joined the staff in January 1958, became an enthusiastic Argonauts leader and conceived the idea of having a school bus, thus making transport to places of interest more flexible and arguably cheaper. He would take the boys on training sprees to the Forest of Dean. Later, he organised camping trips to North Wales, as did John Titterington and the Chaplain, the Revd Anthony Creery-Hill occasionally, while Bob Benson, who appeared even later on the scene, took the boys camping on the Isle of Mull.

By 1957 there were several small craft, the biggest being *Old Nog*, an 11ft 4ins Heron gunter-rigged sloop, together with some canoes.

The number of expeditions declined as numbers of day children grew, other activities became more numerous, and changing legislation made organizing such expeditions more challenging. The spirit of Argonauts lives on in such activities as the Year 8 Leavers' Course today.

the Junior School, it was decided to allocate it to what had been called the Pre-Preparatory but which now came to be known as Lower School, moving them out of the old Fortfield stables, thereby freeing up much-needed teaching space in the rest of the School. Wilton, after skilful adaptation of the top storey, was able to take 31 boarders. Thus Rickerby was vacated and the 'Junior' boarding house went to Wilton, many of whose residents were members of Lower School anyway. There was room, too, not just for a housemaster's flat but also for a resident matron, a resident mistress and a common room for the boys. Ken Hollington was Housemaster from its opening until 1969. Given that he was also the Art master, it made sense that after a while the Art Room was also transferred to the Wilton House site – but in a cedar wood semi-temporary classroom that was built at the back of Wilton.

In order to save costs, two similar cedar classrooms were erected on the old Hardy House vegetable garden in 1966, to be followed within a year by what is now known as the Langhorne Hall. It had a green room and facilities for showing films. A quite large science laboratory in 1968 was added to the block a year later. However, these improvements had been made on a comparative shoe-string.

**Housemasters of Day Boy House, 1954-1966**

| | |
|---|---|
| 1954-1955 | W.M. Newte |
| 1956-1963 | G.H. Harper |
| 1963-1966 | J.B. Widdowson |
| 1966 | M.D. Rowlands |

*In 1967, Yeaman House was founded for day boys and later day girls.*

**Housemasters of (Old) Wilton House (Junior Boy Boarders), 1961-1977**

| | |
|---|---|
| 1961-1969 | K.W. Hollington |
| 1969-1974 | The Revd A.T. Creery-Hill |
| 1975-1976 | M.S. Booth |
| 1976-1977 | A.D. Carpenter |

*In 1978, (Old) Wilton House became a girls' house. See chapter 15.*

**Housemasters/mistresses of Yeaman House, 1967-2009**

| | |
|---|---|
| 1967-1973 | M.D. Rowlands |
| 1973-1980 | P.J. Bryan |
| 1980-1986 | C.V.J. Rooke |
| 1986-1991 | J.T. Lovell |
| 1991-1995 | M.D. Turner |
| 1995-2002 | Mrs J.M. Dunlop |
| 2002-present | M.F. Davies |

In 1967, day boys were finally given a house name and a base. It was 'Yeaman', named after the famous Old Decanian, and was to be found in the old stables classrooms where Ferguson is now. M.D. Rowlands was the first Housemaster.

Gradually Eadward Langhorne had also managed to build up his Common Room. The Junior School now had its own Art master, Director of Music and Chaplain together with its own specialist heads of department for each subject. Further, as Gordon Harper wrote, '...Functions that we had formerly shared with the Seniors, such as Speech Days and Chapel services, took place at different times...(although) the Choir still attended both Senior and Junior services...its treble voices (being) in demand...'

It was at this point that C.S. Harwood ('Billy' to some, 'Mac' to others) gave up the Second Mastership. Cecil Stanley Harwood had come to Dean Close School in 1944 and transferred almost immediately to the Junior School as Second Master and Head of French, a position that he held until 1968 when G.H. Harper took over. He had

Old Wilton House, next to the Police Station

also been Fortfield's Housemaster (1950-59) during which time he had met – and married – the House matron, Mrs Jean Harwood, who had been there since 1952.

The Annual Reports to the Governors at this time show that there was some anxiety about the general financial situation of the two schools. W.A.M. Edwards OD, an experienced businessman and Chairman of the Executive Committee, reporting to the Governors in 1968, stated that numbers and quality of entrant needed to be better.

**New Court School**

New Court School, founded by 1950 in Lansdown Road at the Montpellier end, began as a co-educational nursery/pre-preparatory school catering for 3½ to 7 years. Boys moved on either to Cheltenham College Junior School or Dean Close Junior School aged seven. The girls' side expanded, catering for girls aged 3½ to 13, taking Common Entrance at 11 or 13. There were 140 pupils, possibly more in the late 1960s, and 50 boarders. Girls went on to Cheltenham Ladies', Malvern Girls' or other girls' public schools. Barbara Bradby of New Court won the top scholarship to Benenden the year that Princess Anne entered it. New Court became the place to send a young daughter in Cheltenham.

Sole owner and principal was Miss Eleanor Peplow. She was short, bespeckled, with greying hair, '...pleasant but not particularly approachable...', very determined and a natural entrepreneur. She began by buying a dilapidated former American hospital after the Second World War that became the school building. She taught Religious Studies and had high expectations, especially of pupils' turnout and behaviour. The girls were immaculately dressed, wearing pink dresses in summer with grey pinafore dresses and pink blouses in winter. Grey coats, little grey hats, white knee socks, brown shoes and gloves completed the uniform.

The school had a nautical flavour, each class being named after a famous sea hero or ship such as Nelson, Vanguard, Courageous or Illustrious. Each class kept a diary of what occurred during the preceding week in a 'ship's log'. The School also had a ship's bell, compass, gong and life buoy on the balcony known as the bridge! Several admirals were guests on speech days.

Juniors had a thorough grounding in 'the three Rs'. French, Latin and some Science were taught towards the senior end. The school used Dean Close School Swimming Pool, instructed there by Major Chapman who was '...a very good instructor if a trifle brusque...'. Classes were from Monday to Friday. By the late 1960s the housemistress, Mrs Wills, and the young but capable matron, Miss Liz Wilson, were in charge at weekends.

Towards the end of the 1960s, Miss Peplow's sight deteriorated. Day to day running of the school was increasingly left to Deputy Head Mrs Iris Long, a class teacher since 1952 who became Deputy Head in 1965, and Headmistress in 1968. There were proposals and willing backers to keep the school going and provide for Miss Peplow in retirement. At the last moment in December 1968, she decided not to sell. Uncertainty over the school's future drove parents and daughters away. She was forced to close in 1969, selling the property to Westbury Homes – although Dean Close School were interested at one point in buying it. Senior boarders went for the most part to Cheltenham Ladies' College and day girls to Airthrie and Berkhampstead schools. The biggest group of day girls with junior boarding girls went to Dean Close Junior School, who appointed Mrs Long, Miss Sanders (French) and Miss Barraclough (Elocution & Drama) to the teaching staff while Miss Wilson (later Mrs Young) and Mrs Harris joined the matroning staff. Mrs Phyllis Rigby joined the Senior School music staff. Pam Rowles, the first girl educated at Dean Close Senior School, was given her early education at New Court.

**Housemistresses of Rickerby (Girls Boarding)**

| | |
|---|---|
| 1969-1974 | Mrs I.E. Long |
| 1974-1975 | Mrs E. Collins |
| 1975-1976 | Miss P. Edge |
| 1976-1978 | Mrs P.E. Harper |

In 1978, Girls boarding transferred to (Old) Wilton House

It was just at that moment, C.G. Turner having arrived to succeed Douglas Graham, the outgoing Senior School Headmaster, that the answer began to emerge, partly driven by the increasing problem and possible opportunity of the comparatively small New Court School for girls further down the Lansdown Road. The answer would change the Dean Close community forever. It was to take girls, and to become one of the early co-educational preparatory and public schools.

# Chapter 8

# Co-education Begins, 1968 to 1978

Christopher Turner became Headmaster in April 1968. To Governors and staff he seemed a popular appointment, as he sought to improve discipline and academic standards. That same term, Pam Rowles, the first female Decanian, entered the School. She had come to complete A level work and had been admitted by Douglas Graham as a '…one off…' after consulting with Christopher Turner. Her advent was surrounded by media interest, as the School was one of the first to go 'co-ed'. She was the sister of a Decanian who had been through both Junior and Senior Schools and was followed later by a younger

**Christopher G. Turner, Headmaster 1968-79**

Christopher Turner was 37 when he became Headmaster in 1968. A scholar at Winchester, he was a Winchester Exhibitioner to New College, Oxford, where he read Mods and Greats. He rowed in his College boat which was Head of the River and was in the Oxford boat in 1951, thereby gaining his Rowing Blue. He was also in the Oxford Bach Choir. He moved to Radley, where he was in charge of the Rowing VIII and then Charterhouse, being the senior Classics master at both schools and adjutant of the CCF at the latter. He was Schoolmaster Student at Christ Church Oxford in 1967. He left in 1979 to become headmaster of Stowe School.

There were three children: Rosalie, who sadly died in her twenties in an accident; Matthew; and Catherine, who returned to the School to study for her A levels.

Later, C.G.T. was ordained. He and his wife have latterly split their time between Birmingham, where he has helped children learning to read in primary schools, and Chipping Norton, where he has served as a non-stipendiary minister. He is a keen violinist.

Lucia and Christopher Turner

Lucia Turner, Christopher's wife, a Fellow of Lady Margaret Hall, Oxford, was a daughter of Professor Stephen Glanville, Provost of King's College, Cambridge.

sister, Alison. She wrote her first impressions in *The Decanian* in the summer 1968. '...I enjoyed the first few days...' she recalled, '...with everyone genuflecting as I swept through the doors like a Dowager Duchess. It took the exploits of the press and a sudden awful realization of what I had done to shatter my state of advanced euphoria...'. She felt that the School was happy, liked the freedom she felt Decanians had and what was to her the informal relationship they had with staff. However, she felt the prefect system 'feudal' and prefects benevolent despots. She chided boys over how they approached mealtimes where: '...the delicate art of conversation is sacrificed to the all-important task of filling one's stomach...'. And her observations made her '...hotly deny...' that girls gossip more than boys.

During 1968 the Governors formally agreed to girls in the Sixth Form from September 1969 '...as an experiment...' for five years and as day girls only. In the Junior School day and boarding girls could come in equally experimentally from April 1969 aged 7 to 11 because of the imminent closure of New Court School (see chapter 7). Expert legal opinion suggested that neither decision was against the letter nor spirit of the Deed of Constitution. Writing some years later, Sir Leonard Hooper revealed that Governors had been advised that '...in the 20th century, the entry of girls could rightly be consid-

**The Arguments for going Co-Educational**

The Governors were enthusiastic for the experimental introduction of girls because:

Firstly, the 1963 Newsom Report on Secondary Education, chaired by Sir John Newsom, *Half Our Futures*, had confirmed the recommendation of an earlier report that the school leaving age should be raised to 16, and had underlined the values of equality of opportunity for all that also implied the value of co-education and comprehensive schools. It suggested a broader curriculum especially bearing in mind the less intellectually able. It stressed the importance of Religious Education and guidance on Sex Education. It followed on the 1963 Robbins Report that had advocated far larger numbers and greater opportunities for people to take up college and university education.

Secondly, the widening scope of subjects at O and A level that flowed from these and other reports and the government action that followed, necessitated larger sixth forms offering an increasingly varied academic choice that the School would have found difficult to offer in terms of viable numbers on boys alone.

Thirdly, given the necessary improvement and expansion of facilities that the School had just completed under the previous Headmaster, the School was struggling somewhat financially, not helped in that the 1968 intake was the smallest for some years. An injection of fees from girls would be welcomed, notwithstanding the initial additional expenditure that their introduction would inevitably cause and also the contribution of growing numbers of day boys.

Fourthly, Dean Close School, by being one of the first to go co-educational, might forestall either Cheltenham College or Cheltenham Ladies' College from doing the same and therefore corner the market in something that appeared to be the 'coming thing'. This was two-edged as it could equally be suggested that going co-educational might put off the parents of boys who felt that going to a co-educational school could regrettably 'soften' a boy. There were parents on both sides of the discussion. However, the 'clincher' was that a further group of parents found that having both sons and daughters at the same school was very convenient.

Lastly, they had just brought in a new Headmaster who was clearly in favour of co-education. He felt that pupils performed better academically and that the School was ideally suited for it.

Thus the Governors' decision to admit girls, albeit for an experimental period initially, can be seen to have been pragmatic as well as educationally principled.

ered a part of boys' education...'! Not everyone agreed. The Revd Canon F.H. Robathan, OBE, an OD with a distinguished war record, was said to have been particularly unhappy and one or two staff were less than enthusiastic. Nevertheless, the decision was made.

The presence of eight girls in the Senior School in September 1969 necessitated some reorganisation. The Old Library (now the Seminar Room) became a mixed Senior Scholars' Common Room. The Bursar's Office became a Girls' Cloak Room and the VIP Room at the Swimming Pool became the Girls' Changing Room. The Bursar was relegated to a Portakabin, but not for long. It was not until the following year that Room 5 (now the Girling Room) became available and this large room was sectioned off into individual and shared study areas specifically for girls and became something of a sanctuary for them.

Boys seemed to be in favour of the move towards co-education. A boy-written editorial in *The Decanian* of the time said: 'Eight girls are currently co-existing with 302 boys: we hope they are enjoying it as much as we are...'. By Trinity 1971 there were 15 day girls in the School. In September 1971 numbers rose to 25, the point at which the first girl boarders became a reality.

Two members of staff who retired at the end of Trinity 1968 had had a huge influence on the development of the School. C.A.P. Tuckwell (see chapter 13) had been the last surviving teaching appointment made by the first Headmaster, Dr Flecker, in 1923 and had served the School for 45 years, while E.S. Hoare's association went back to 1914, when he first entered as a boy, a connection of 54 years, 42 of them on the staff (see chapter 10). With their retirement, the School lost a major link with its foundation. Pam Rowles notwithstanding, they were the last two masters to have spent their careers in a boys only Dean Close School. C.A.P. Tuckwell was replaced by Peter Cairns and E.S. Hoare by the Geographer S.M. Evans.

To mark his departure, Stanley Hoare gave the Chapel a dossal curtain for behind the altar. With a new Headmaster, and a new Chaplain in the Revd D.I. Gibson who arrived in Michaelmas 1968, experiments were tried about times of services. For the first time since before the building of the first temporary Chapel in 1909, Decanians were very occasionally allowed to worship at a Cheltenham church on a Sunday morning rather than at School. The Christian Union that had perhaps become a little lacklustre was re-formed with apparently encouraging results. The 'new' Chapel Organ was dedicated by the Bishop of Gloucester on 26th November, 1969 and on the 29th Colin Sherratt gave the post-dedication inaugural recital, the first-ever recital on it having been by a very talented Sixth Former, Christopher Boodle, on 23rd October.

**The First Girls**

Pam Rowles (Mrs Baillie) (1968-69)
Pam returned to teach at Dean Close School, married member of staff Neil Baillie and later became Senior Mistress of Pocklington School.

*The girls mentioned below were also the first members of Mead House and were at Dean Close School 1969 -71*:

Susan Billington (Mrs Barrington-Earp)
Susan Bowes (Mrs Burke)
Jennifer Gibbs (Mrs Brown, later Mrs Pritchard)
Janet Moore (Mrs Skidmore)
Sally Robinson (Mrs Nutbeam)
Nicola Stanway (Mrs Troughton)
Sonia Stern
Prudence Stringer (came Lent Term 1970)

Susan Billington was the first girl who became a House Prefect and as such became the first formal Head of House, but in her second year she became a School Prefect while Janet Moore, Sally Robinson and Nicola Stanway were House Prefects 1970-71. Jennifer Gibbs stayed an additional term (Michaelmas 1971) and was Head of House and a School Prefect during that time, the house having already grown to 25 in number.

The arrival of girls on campus was accompanied by three initially part-time graduate women teachers in September 1968, the first since Alice Schneider. All three were married to men already teaching at the School. They were Lucia Turner, the Headmaster's wife, a former Fellow of Lady Margaret Hall, teaching English; Valerie Wilson, whose husband Brian was Tower's Housemaster, teaching Geography; and Joyce Barker, whose husband Derek ran the Yearlings House, teaching Modern Languages. Mrs Wilson

**The 1969 Chapel Organ**

The previous Chapel organ was built by Nicholson of Worcester originally for a private house in Stratford-upon-Avon in 1937. It was built on the 'extension' principle in which one rank of pipes does duty for many. The organ was sold back to Nicholson's ten years later. It had originally come to Dean Close Chapel and was first used at the beginning of the Lent Term 1951, thereby replacing an electric Hammond organ. The Nicholson organ was cleaned and enlarged by Walkers in 1960.

The School's 1969 organ, from St Mary's, Charlton Kings, was built by William Hill in 1902. In 1968 Percy Daniels & Co. of Cleveden oversaw its transfer to Dean Close School. However, on its acquisition by the School some old pipes were still used but several new ranks were added. The organ console was now in the comparatively new gallery, built in 1964 to accommodate an expanding School. The additional work put both the organ and the Chapel out of commission for the best part of two terms. Old days were revisited as the School worshipped in St Mark's Parish Church as well as the Flecker Hall.

**Specification**

| Pedal Organ | | Positive Organ | | Great Organ | | Swell Organ | |
|---|---|---|---|---|---|---|---|
| Open Wood (A) | 16 | Lieblich Gedact | 8 | Quintaton* | 16 | Geigen Diapason | 8 |
| Bourdon (B) | 16 | Suabe Flute | 4 | Open Diapason 1 | 8 | Rohr Flute | 8 |
| Quintation (Gt) | 16 | Gemshorn | 4 | Open Diapason 2 | 8 | Salicional | 8 |
| Principal (A) | 8 | Block Flute* | 2 | Hohl Flute | 8 | Voix Celeste | 8 |
| Flute (B) | 8 | Larigot* | 1⅓ | Principal | 4 | Gemshorn | 4 |
| Quint (B) | 5⅓ | Twenty Second* | 1 | Harmonic Flute | 4 | Nazard | 2⅔ |
| Fifteenth (A) | 4 | Scharf 22.26.29* | III | Twelfth* | 2⅔ | Spitzflute* | 2 |
| Octave Flute (B) | 4 | Krummhorn* | 8 | Fifteenth | 2 | Tierce* | 1⅗ |
| Twenty Second (A) | 2 | | | Mixture 19.22.26 | III | Mixture19.22.26.29* | IV |
| Sifflote (B) | 2 | | | | | DoubleTrumpet (C) | +16 |
| Double Trumpet (C) (Sw) | 16 | | | | | Cornopean | 8 |
| Trumpet (C) (Sw) | 8 | | | | | Clarion(fr.16) (C)+ | 4 |
| Clarion (C) (Sw) | 4 | | | | | | |

Usual couplers and reversible pistons.
6 thumb pistons to each manual.
6 pedal pistons to swell and to pedal.
General cancel
All pistons are adjusted at a board beneath the music desk.
The wind pressure is 3 in. W.G.

* Percy Daniel 1969
\+ Part Walker 1960

Brian Wilson, Mike Girling, Richard Padfield, and Richard Taylor

was the first Housemistress of Mead, the girls' house, followed by Mrs Barker in 1971. There was a debate as to what the House name should be. Mead was chosen because it was a single syllable – in accordance with the prevailing practice – and its Old English meaning of it being a meadow complementing previous House names such as Brook and Field, perhaps tying in with *A Midsummer Nights' Dream*, Act II. With girls in the School, women Governors were appointed. Val Hall, sometime Principal of St Mary's Teacher Training College, Cheltenham, was first in 1970, joined a year later by local magistrate and School parent Sue Hardy and in 1975 by Miss M. Challis, sometime Head of St Mary's, Calne. Entry for girls was competitive for a while, and as Christopher Turner had hoped, boys' academic standards began to improve.

A new intake of staff at the end of the sixties, notably some heads of department, worked with colleagues already in post to raise expectations generally. Decanians were challenged to aim for excellence in what they attempted, not only in the classroom but in other areas including the Chapel Choir, drama, and on the sports field. During this time and through to the 1980s there was also a strong lead given by the boarding boy housemasters – still pastorally responsible for the vast majority of the School. It significantly influenced not only the boys' behaviour but also how they reacted to the enhanced challenges and rising expectations made of them.

Initially, girls had neither uniform nor dress regulations, with the possible exception of a Dean Close scarf. Sixth Form boys at this time were wearing navy-blue blazers, white shirts and grey trousers. While most girls wore sensible clothes, a few felt the comparatively new mini-skirt should be shown off, causing several stolid male hearts to flutter. Issues such as dress codes had to be monitored with some care by Val Wilson.

It was made clear to new girls that while the same demands were to be made of them as of boys, male teaching staff appreciated girls needed different pastoral care. Some masters were apprehensive

**A.S.R. Parker, staff member 1945-68**

Arnold Parker OD left Dean Close School at the end of Michaelmas 1968. He was the third Old Decanian, after E.S. Hoare and E.V. Tanner, to spend a sizeable part of his career back at his old School. He followed E.V. Tanner as Housemaster of Gate where he was Housemaster for 15 years. He was officer commanding the CCF 1947-60 and also encouraged gymnastics and music but was principally an English teacher. He decided to take up the offer of becoming head of Literature at the Collegiate School, Wanganui, New Zealand at the end of 1968. He died in 1998.

about teaching them, and dreaded the possibility of tears. This was tantamount to giving the girls an emotional weapon to use from the word 'go' that was used effectively because it was used sparingly. On one occasion a long-serving former housemaster set a mixed class some homework. He subsequently tested them on it – but also asked further questions beyond the material covered by the prep. The boys were philosophical, the girls furious as they felt unfairly caught out. Presently, one girl burst into tears. Surprised, the master produced a handkerchief. She dried her eyes and went on her way. Later, he recalled the handkerchief had his name sewn into the corner and worried about either being seen as a bullying teacher who made girls cry, or the handkerchief being used to suggest erroneously that he was attempting to gain the girl's affection; both disturbing thoughts. At breakfast the next morning the same girl, smiling broadly, presented him with his handkerchief, returned carefully washed and beautifully ironed. The master was left reflecting on the very different reactions that boys and girls sometimes had to the same lessons.

| Housemistresses of Mead | |
|---|---|
| 1969-1971 | Mrs V. Wilson |
| 1971-1973 | Mrs J. Barker |
| 1974-1987 | Mrs S.M. Vaus |
| 1987-1989 | Mrs G.S. Macgill |
| 1989-1997 | Mrs V.E. Burroughs |
| 1997-2001 | Mrs J.D. Kent |
| 2001-present | Mrs P.S. Watson |

The initial sports situation for girls was not good. Some swimming was possible, taken by Major Chapman and there was a little tennis. Two girls, Nikki Stanway (helm) and Jenny Gibbs (crew), joined the Sailing Club and occasionally took a boat out with the others at the Sailing Club's base on the River Avon near Twyning. By Michaelmas 1971 there were enough girls to begin team games such as hockey and netball.

It might be thought that the School was preoccupied by the girls' arrival. But as the Headmaster was later to point out, '…school life is so full and diverse that its significance for the majority of Decanians in the 1970s should not be pressed too hard.' Matches, plays, and O and A level examinations were most important. There were the outside influences of the era, such as the year of universal youth unrest in 1968: barricades in Paris, riots in Berlin, demonstrations in Grosvenor Square in London, difficulties in universities that gradually gave way in part to other diversions – Flower Power, pot, pop festivals, free love, long hair and a seemingly universal challenge to authority. They washed up against the walls of the School but comparatively little got through. Modern popular music was becoming a part of everyday culture. Long hair was tolerated up to a point, though the few who were caught trying drugs were expelled. A few senior boys now had their own cars or motorcycles, although they could not take other Decanians as passengers unless they had the written consent of the passengers' parents. Authority was accepted, mainly because it was perceived as being both necessary for the running of any large community and was seen as being largely benign under the Second Master, Mike Girling.

Mike Girling's career at Oxford was interrupted by the Second World War and he served for most of it in India and Burma. On his return he went back to Oxford and graduated with an Honours degree in Geography. An able sportsman, he played regularly for the Greyhounds and Authentics as well as Oxfordshire at both cricket and rugby, being also captain of the latter. Tony Gilkes appointed him in 1948 and he came to teach Latin, Geography and English. His sporting prowess was harnessed to good effect as a coach and he was master-in-charge of 1st XI cricket for many years. He also had other strings to his bow and played the double bass in the school orchestra. In due course he became a Housemaster and was in charge of Tower (1952-67), whereupon he succeeded Stanley Hoare as Second Master and served in that role (1968-81), during which time he was instrumental in ensuring the School's reasonably smooth change to co-education.

In October 1969, Christopher Turner, an enthusiast for links with local business and industry, wrote to parents of Decanians who were in their third Sixth Form year who had just secured a place at university. With Denys Carnill especially, and also Jake Jarrett-Kerr, he had discussed with local firms the possibility of boys spending time on various 'shop floors', some industrial, some commercial, and had had '...a most favourable response...'. The boys would spend up to four weeks at the firm in the mornings and at School in the afternoons. Their experiences, observations and thoughts would form part of a dissertation, and parents would have a significant reduction in fees during these weeks. Interestingly, one of the advantages seen for the scheme was that '...by having first-hand experience of industry or commerce at shop-floor level (your boy) will come to the University less green and immature than so many have been since the abolition of National Service...'. It was the beginning of a dialogue between local firms and the School that still continues.

In September 1970 the sudden death occurred of the much-loved, cheerful, hard-working resident Sister, Frances Westmacott, two days before term began. She was also one of the longest serving, having been with the School since 1955 apart from a break when she did a course in mental nursing. She had dealt with many School epidemics, including one that closed the School for some days in 1957. Such was the feeling of loss that the School held a Memorial Service in the Chapel after the funeral in Chilfrome, Dorset.

An Inspection at the end of 1971 drew attention to the need for better accommodation for Music and Art, more space for Science, some overcrowding on the boarding side and a shortage of general amenities. Some of these were dealt with comparatively quickly, an Art School and the development of Court House across Lansdown Road being achieved by the end of 1973 when the new Bursary, which is still in use today, finally came into operation. Fawley Lodge, run by Major and Mrs Chapman, was still technically a part of Mead House under Sue Vaus. She had succeeded Mrs Barker as Housemistress late in 1973, by which time the girls' version of Fawley Lodge had opened in its current location on the old Yearlings site.

It did not taken long for the teachers' Common Room to consider that girls should be accepted at all levels in the School and not just the Sixth Form. The final vote as to whether to '...go the whole way...' that is, admit girls of all ages, both day and boarding, was unanimously in favour. In his speech at 1973 Commemoration, the Headmaster pointed out that there were now 100 girls on the campus in the two schools. He was asked '...five or six times a week...' if co-education worked; his response was that '...there is only one answer to the question: we could not now think of the school being otherwise...'.

Before 1967, everyone had been on surname terms. With Pam Rowles' arrival and the subsequent addition of many more girls, that approach was challenged. *The Decanian* editors capitulated right away – or perhaps they saw themselves as trend setters. M.G. Mowat and D.G. Readings with C.V.G. Harries as the staff editor in the summer 1967 edition had become Chris Jones and Robin Rusher the following year. The rest of the School did not follow with the same breathless haste but within five years Christian names were being used as often as initials for reports in *The Decanian,* the arts tending to lead the way. For girls pioneering the way towards co-education, their time at the School had its crises but also compensations. One girl who came in 1969 later said that '...I had to come out of my shell. My main skill that I developed before I left was that I came to be able to talk to anyone about anything. If I had stayed at my previous, single-sex school that would never have happened...'.

A combination of the Headmaster's views, co-education, changing social attitudes, and the impact of the Plowden Report (1967) that looked at children and their primary education led to the end of corporal punishment, which did not finally die out at Dean Close School until the 1980s. Prefects, led by Head of School, John Cutts, voluntarily gave up 'tanning' in Trinity 1968, after a suggestion from the Headmaster, who finally stopped in 1977. Corporal punishment totally ceased under Christopher Bacon. There were, apparently, Old Decanians and one or two potential parents who were concerned about possible falling standards of discipline that would result. However, discipline at that time was not an issue. Smoking, when discovered, became a fineable offence. The Headmaster ended the School Prefects' practice of each having a walking cane as a 'badge of office'. No-one is quite sure when this tradition began but it was certainly in use immediately post-Second World War. A more relaxed attitude to life was also signalled by the decision to allow boys (and presumably girls, too) to wear '...informal dress...' after Chapel on Sunday for the first time. 'Mufti' had arrived. The decision was also made to use the cafeteria system in the dining hall for the first time.

In March 1970, Christopher Turner wrote to parents about the implications of the Family Law Reform Act 1969 that came into force on 1st January, 1970. 18-year-olds still at school had now reached their majority, rather than having to wait to the age of 21, giving them rights and responsibilities of being able to vote, enter into contracts, sue and be sued and make a Will. The School could no longer be *in loco parentis* but so long as they were members of the School, such pupils were *in statu pupillari* and as such still had to accept and conform to its rules, yet it was not unknown for sixth-formers to visit pubs. It was carefully observed beforehand which staff went where – the Upper Sixth told the Lower Sixth year by year. 16-year-olds could now consent to surgical, medical and dental treatment without referring to their parents although the School was anxious to reassure parents that they would still be '...fully informed...' except in emergencies.

Growth in girl numbers meant that the Chapel Choir was no longer dependant on a Junior School treble line. Chapel in itself became something of an issue, and there were several years of sometimes heated letters to *The Decanian,* pointing out the perceived iniquities of compulsory Chapel even under a respected Chaplain such as the Revd David Gibson. It was not until 1973 that the Headmaster could report to Governors that '...murmurings against compulsory Chapel have been fainter than for many years. On the other hand, numbers at the occasional (voluntary) Choral Communion declined sharply during the year...'.

Bill Farquhason, Head Gardener for 20 years, retired in 1971, while Commemoration 1973 celebrated four men who between them had served the School for 100 years. Mike Girling, the Second Master, reached his silver jubilee. Bill Mason, the Head Groundsman, had completed his 25 years a few months previously and had had a memorable year: on the one hand he had had Princess Anne's helicopter touching down on 'his' hallowed cricket square and, on the other, a sewer collapse under the tennis courts necessitating much digging by the local authority. Ted Maslin, the carpenter, had instructed generations of Decanians while Ray Witts, formerly the boilerman for 24 years, became the School Porter when Jim Power retired from the post after 19 years in office. They had all known the School when its future was far from assured at the end of the Second World War and had supported it loyally.

Bill Mason

**G. Vaughan Harries, staff member 1946-74**

He was senior History master 1946-74, briefly Housemaster of Brook (1959-62) and was Sixth Form Master, Librarian, staff editor of *The Decanian* and a cricket and rugby coach. A contemporary of Harold Wilson (later Prime Minister) at Jesus College, Oxford, he visited 10 Downing Street with a DCS sixth-former on at least one occasion. One of his daughters, now Angela Brain-Gabbott, later became Housemistress of the Junior School's Wilton House (1982-87) when it was a girls' only house. G.V. Harries died in 2006.

In the classrooms and laboratories, the girls' preferences in the Sciences, and the Inspectors' observations, meant that at last Biology became a full School subject and no longer just a Sixth Form option. In any case, in a now more liberal climate, potential parents were seeking, and increasingly expecting to find, ever wider choices at O and A level. The situation was made rather more challenging as both Douglas Graham and Christopher Turner made clear by the apparent lowering of some of the entry requirements in the mid-1960s in order to keep numbers up, especially among boarders. This in turn meant that some Decanians were not finding it easy to select suitable public examination subjects and this was also a factor in expanding what was on offer. In Michaelmas 1968, as Christopher Turner pointed out, '...30 men assisted the Headmaster in academic teaching, music, art, metalwork and PE; there were 315 boys and one girl...'. There were a total of 16 subjects being offered at O or A level or their equivalent. Ten years later, '...47 men and women assisted and the school roll was 417...' of whom 125, or just under a third, were girls; the number of subjects on offer had now risen to 23. In 1973, the Headmaster was able to report that an academic subject (Mathematics) now had its own micro-computer to help it 'number crunch' – a significant advance. The numbers of teachers had increased in proportion with the number of pupils and this had a significant effect on fees.

**Housemasters of Dale**

| | |
|---|---|
| 1973-1978 | D.A. Barker |
| 1978-1982 | D.S. Macpherson |
| 1982-1988 | M.K. Paul |
| 1988-2000 | T.G. Odell |
| 2000-2002 | R.I. Kirby |
| 2002-2004 | N.P. Stokes |
| 2004-present | J.P. Watson |

Day boy figures had been creeping up; Field was comfortably the largest house in the summer of 1973. As Yearlings House closed, thereby creating further space for the Mead boarding 'overflow', Derek Barker, freed from Yearlings, became the first Housemaster of Dale, a second day boy house, which opened with 28 boys in September 1973.

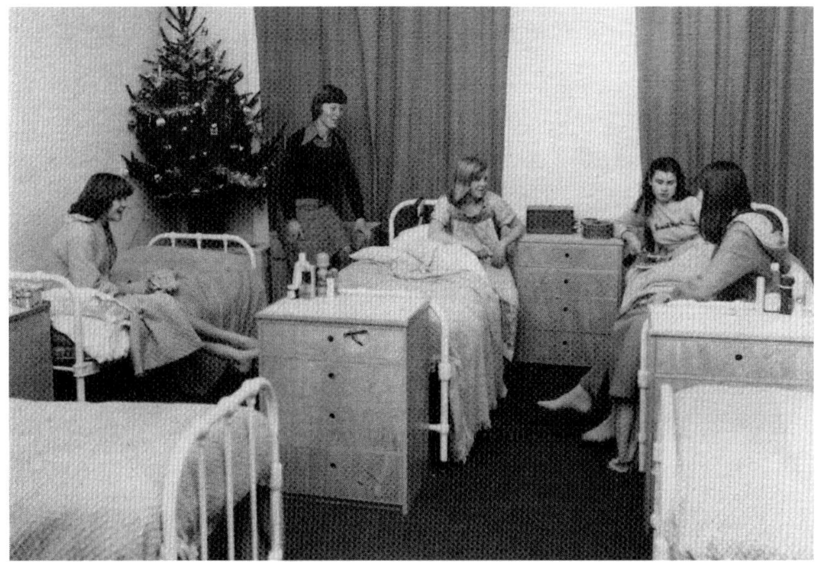

First Shelburne boarding girls, with their Housemistress Sue Padfield

Between Trinity and Michaelmas 1975 there were several changes, as Shelburne House (now Turner Hall) for boarding girls opened under Mrs Sue Padfield with 32 girls. This brought the closure of the girls' boarding wing in Dean Close

| Housemasters/Housemistresses of Shelburne | |
|---|---|
| 1975-1980 | Mrs S.E. Padfield |
| 1980-2001 | A.C. Forbes |
| 2001-present | Mrs J.D. Kent |

House, and the end of boarding out for girls, with staff and parents, for whom there had been insufficient room until then. Sue Padfield's husband, Richard, took over Field; Mead, under Sue Vaus, comprised 53 day girls together with 23 boarders in Fawley Lodge under Major and Mrs Chapman, who were later to be followed by Mervyn and Mary Vaughan. Sue Vaus had been running Mead on three sites – Mead itself, Fawley Lodge and Dean Close House. The Revd David Gibson, already School Chaplain, became Housemaster of Court.

The Manager of the School Shop, Mr Plumridge, celebrated 25 years with the School and threw a much-appreciated party for the Sixth Form. The School Sanitorium, which had been housed in Shelburne, had to move out to make way for the new girls' house and went to 9 Glencairn Park Road. There were 70 girls in Michaelmas 1974, when it was decided that there were enough of them to begin to play other schools at sport. With the opening of Shelburne, inter-house matches became possible, as did other competitions, such as music.

In the changing environment, several societies thrived. One was the Winemaking Society which by Trinity 1970 claimed to have produced orange, birch sap, apple, blackberry and elderberry wines, as well as visiting breweries and other places of interest. The Society's cellars were to be found in the floor below the official entrance to the School today. A new ceramics room and the arrival of additional art teacher Stuart Gane engendered a real enthusiasm for ceramics. There was a growing interest in Science and so in 1974 a Science Society was founded that did not meet regularly but came together for special events such as trips, talks or lectures on a variety of topics given by guest speakers.

Another was the Young Farmers' Club who, in an earlier era had kept pigs in sties roughly where the Estates Department car park is now. They fed their charges with kitchen slops and sent them off to the slaughterhouse to make a worthwhile profit. The Club funded more piglets with that profit while any surplus money went to buy Chapel furnishings. As an experiment in business studies, they decided to go in for rabbits. Guided by an advisor from the Commercial Rabbit Association, together with Mr Bone, the School Groundsman who looked after the rabbits during the holidays, the venture grew to the extent that at one point in 1970 they had 19 litters with an average five or six rabbits per litter.

Checking on the pigs!

There was the rather short-lived (Coarse) Angling Club with membership that briefly reached 30, which fished near Ludlow. There was a revised Chess Club and a Sixth Form Film Society that was run jointly with Cheltenham College and Cheltenham Ladies' College. A report in the Winter 1973 *Decanian,* when the School was clearly playing host, regretted that girls from the Ladies' College had not taken advantage of what the Dean Close reviewer called '...the entertaining showing...' of an evening of horror films.

Sixth Formers went to dig on an Archaeological site just outside Bourton-on-the-Water. The Sailing Club was in good heart. In short, the sheer diversity of activities beyond the CCF, the Social Service activity and the Duke of Edinburgh Award Scheme was becoming greater all the time. People were willing to try things, yet there were also complaints of widespread apathy. However, Christopher Turner spotted the growing trend, remarking in his report to the Governors in 1972 that weekend activity was growing and that '...climbers, CCF cadets, canoe club members, sailors and geographers...' were all cases in point.

Sailing Club

Another activity, and academic subject, gradually raising its profile was Art. Not only were its exhibitions at Commemoration appreciated but under Director of Art Keith Davis, who had arrived in 1967, drawings and sketches by Decanians were beginning to enliven the creative pages of *The Decanian*, often illustrating poems.

There was the Social Service Group concerned with the local area and its social problems and needs. Led by Denys Carnill, in 1974 it initiated a Midsummer Fair held on Big Field and elsewhere on site that made a net profit of some £850 (£6,640). Within a few years the Fair was making thousands of pounds and attracting a large following (see chapter 14).

Christopher Turner was attracting some pupils from abroad, too. One, Lucinda Costin from the USA, who came for a year, wrote of her reactions in the 1974 *Decanian*: '...I had pictured myself going into a cold, close-knit society where...masters emerged only for lessons in their mortar boards and black

Midsummer Fair in 1983

gowns and older boys 'flogged' younger boys who were not 'fagging' properly. I found instead a variety of people from Nigeria and Ethiopia to Hong-Kong and Singapore...Although very old, the archaic image I had always held in my mind (of the School) was shattered by the realization that it had a bigger library, better equipped laboratories, more tennis courts and a bigger swimming pool than my school in the USA. I found lessons far more challenging as they went into a much greater depth than I had ever attempted before...On the whole I have really enjoyed my year at Dean Close...Perhaps a year away from home...has enabled me to become a better person; to know myself better...It has given me a chance to realize that the friends I have made are my friends not because of my family or any status that I hold, but because of myself, and that they will be my friends for life...'.

The '... growing international element in the School...' as Christopher Turner reported to the Governors in 1976, included a number of pupils '...without any pretence of a Christian background...'. At the same time he noted that the leadership among the Christians in School in such areas as CU '...is growing stronger...'. Nevertheless, Christopher Turner was well aware of the School's tradition and *raison d'être* and was careful not to allow the numbers of those coming from abroad to change the character of the School substantially.

The Governors and Christopher Turner were also concerned with what they saw as another careful balance: the extent to which girls should be admitted. On the one hand there was the point cogently put by the Chairman of the Executive Committee, Sir Leonard Hooper, in 1975 in his Annual Report: '...Dean Close seems to flourish. It would not have continued to do so without the decision in 1968 to embark on co-education...The pressure for girls' places, including boarding places, continues and it is their numbers which are enabling the School to pay its way...'. It was the pragmatic approach acknowledging the help that girls' parents had given at a time of some political uncertainty, financial hyper-inflation and consequent soaring costs, of which the massive Houghton pay award for teachers was but one problem. Yet he seems to have wanted to have had his cake and eat it, for the following year he wrote: '...The Governors will no doubt wish to retain their objective of a co-educational establishment which nonetheless preserves the flavour of the traditional boys' school...'.

There were other concerns, too. In March 1972, Christopher Turner wrote to all parents about drugs (in this case cannabis) used by boys in School, so far as is known, for the first time. Two boys were expelled: several others were suspended. It was a most difficult time for all concerned. Many other schools were experiencing the same problem. Measures were put in place to inform Decanians and their parents about the effects of drugs. Even so, three more boys were expelled in October the same year when it was discovered that they had been using both cannabis and LSD. The Headmaster wrote to parents, '...Many young people honestly believe the underground propaganda that "there is no harm in it – it is just youth's version of adults' alcohol". Before they know what has happened they find themselves compromised and don't dare ask for help...'. His approach was measured but firm. There were to be no hysterical outbursts on the one hand and no sweeping under the carpet on the other. Everything would be exposed to the light of day and the culprits firmly dealt with in a spirit of sad yet supportive regret. That policy continues today.

A year later, John Moore retired after 38 years with the School, broken only by War Service. In fact, he was the only remaining member of the teaching staff with pre-war School connections. In 1975, in the interests of economy during a very inflationary period, and also less mess, school boilers that had served the School from the outset, though somewhat capriciously at times, were replaced by gas-fired plant, beginning with Tower and the Chapel.

**John S. Moore, staff member 1938-76**

During his 38 years with the School, John Moore was at one time or another Head of Biology, Housemaster of Court (1950-65), Officer Commanding the CCF, master-in-charge of rugby and athletics and also careers master. He made Hugh Elder's idea that Dean Close should become a rugby school a reality and was thought unfortunate not to have won a Blue. At his retirement he was the longest-serving teacher in Dean Close School by several years. He was much helped in his career by his wife, Binnie. He died in 2007.

Major Ben Chapman and his wife Evelyn retired in 1977. Major Chapman, who represented Great Britain in the 1936 Olympics as a gymnast, had been responsible for the School's PE for 17 years and had much to do with the design of the Gym and Swimming Pool that opened in 1964. He also supported his wife when she ran Fawley Lodge as a boarding extension of Mead House 1973-77.

Major and Mrs Chapman

The academic year 1976-77 saw the 400 pupil 'ceiling' well and truly cracked with numbers hovering around 420 Decanians, with girls numbering just on 120, now in three Houses – Mead, Fawley and Shelburne. The girls numbered some two-sevenths of the total, close to one girl for every three boys which the Governors thought would be the best ratio. The number of boarding boys stood at 207, roughly the same number as in Flecker's day. Numbers had risen in recent years because of the greater influx of day boys and now with the arrival of girls numbers had risen still further. The financial situation was also eased by the introduction of summer courses in the School. Christopher Turner was under no illusions, however, noting '...never have academic results been more important...', a cry heard with increasing frequency into the next century.

As the first ten years of co-education ended, the severing of some of the past with the present was underlined by the deaths of a former Chairman of Governors, Sir Ian Yeaman OD; a former Headmaster, Tony Gilkes; and a former Chaplain, the Revd E.V. Tanner. A visitor in 1977 who had seen the School in 1967 would have been amazed at the changes that Christopher Turner had quietly effected. Not only was there a sizeable number of girls; the previously all male teaching staff had increased from 28 in Michaelmas of 1967 to 47, of whom ten were women, ten years later. In 1977 the community 'feel' was more relaxed; the number of academic options at Sixth Form had been extended; Decanians were far less restricted; mufti could now be worn at times; corporal punishment was used far less often and badges of office like prefects' walking canes had vanished. There was a greater variety of activities; awareness of the problems of the wider community were developing; the intake was more international, up to a point, and the size of the School was greater than ever before. Problems Decanians faced that hadn't been grasped fully before, such as dyslexia, were acknowledged for the first time in a letter to parents in 1973. In 1975, the Fifth Form GCE O level results were even better than the record-breaking previous year, with a 74% pass rate (Grades A to E) and 122 Grade As from the 89 boys involved.

Yet it was still very much a Christian School with Chapel at its heart; it still saw hockey as its principal game; the Tuckwell Theatre was still used for Commemoration; CCF was still a key activity and, contrary to some dire predictions, the skies of good behaviour and a relatively high standard of discipline had not fallen in. Indeed, in 1975, Sir Leonard Hooper had written that: '…on the whole we seem fortunate in the vast majority of the pupils whom the school attracts. They are a welcoming and pleasant community…'. Christopher Turner, supported by Governors and staff, had skilfully yet almost unobtrusively worked a transformation of the School in just ten years.

**Sir Leonard Hooper, KCMG, CBE and the Hooper Sundial and Quadrangle**

A distinguished civil servant, sometime Director of GCHQ and formerly of the Cabinet Office, Sir Leonard became a Governor in the 1960s and was Chairman of the Executive 1974-84.

In 1990 the Hooper Sundial was unveiled in the Hooper Quadrangle, previously the Upper Quadrangle, designed by David Kindersley and his wife Lida Cardoza. The sundial was based on some found in historic houses and Oxbridge Colleges. Often such sundials had hidden meanings and statements and a similar approach was used in this instance. Christopher Bacon wrote in *The Decanian* in 1990, '…the overall design recalls the motif of Louis XIV of France – the Sun King. It is essentially a central orb with rayons surrounding…'. In the centre is the School Crest with its motto, *God's Word a Guiding Light* connecting the observer to the School on the one hand and the sundial and its use of light on the other through to God the Creator and Source in both. Above the sundial are the words *Dies Creatorem Spectat* (The Day Shows Forth the Creator), DCS also being a play on 'Dean Close School.' There are Hooper swans, too. The whole concept became a reality through the skill of stone carver and engraver John Williams of St David's, Dyfed. David Brown, Head of Physics at Kingswood School and a member of the British Sundial Society, assisted John Williams with the precise measurement of the compass setting on the wall and the calculations of the equation of time so that both the angle of the gnomon and the markings on the table of deviation could be calculated. The sundial is 'set' at BST and has been proven to be of '…the highest accuracy…'.

On one side of the arch, at eye level, there is a small tablet engraved with variations in time created by the elliptical nature of the earth's orbit.

# Chapter 9

# Towards the New Millennium

Christopher Turner had seen co-education established at Dean Close School over ten years. He had seen it through its teething troubles, seen the finances improve and had significantly helped it towards becoming a leader among smaller independent co-educational schools. '…He was…' remarked one who knew him well during this period, '…a typical Wykehamist: highly intelligent, utterly and always gentlemanly but perhaps sometimes a little lacking in humour…'. Others had also noted his contribution that may partly have led to his appointment as headmaster of Stowe. The Chairman of the Governors, in announcing the appointment, referred to ten years' '…accomplished and devoted service…' to the School. Peter Cairns, appointed Head of English by Christopher Turner, wrote that '…co-education has made the School a better place, and this is largely his achievement.' He also noted that '…Christopher Turner deprived Prefects of most of the trappings of power. They could not beat, carry canes or wear special uniform.'

When the Turners left, the outgoing Headmaster was interviewed by *Decus,* a School newsletter run by Sixth Formers. Drug-taking in 1972 had been '… worrying…' he revealed, as it had been to all headteachers. Asked what he thought his main contribution had been, he responded '…I think that a Headmaster influences a school by the principles he himself is guided by, by the staff he employs and by the activities that he encourages…'.

Mike Girling, who had been his Second Master, wrote, '…Today, 11 years after Christopher Turner was appointed, the Senior School numbers about 430 [it was 320 when he arrived], the Junior School 270 [it was 229 in Michaelmas 1968]…Co-education has been tried, fully accepted and approved of with success…As a School we are better off physically though there is still little or no spare room…our A and O level results have been increasingly good…and the School is much more widely known than it was 11 years ago…'. Mike Girling felt that Christopher Turner had three outstanding characteristics: he worked long hours; he was eminently approachable; and he took the School and what he considered it stood for well outside Cheltenham, '…whether as President of the Common Entrance Board, giving prizes away at Preparatory Schools or preaching somewhere…'. Writing of Mrs Turner, Mike Girling said, '…charming, undemonstrative, always ready to help anyone and quietly efficient, we owe Lucia also a great debt and shall miss her much…'.

The new Headmaster appointed for Michaelmas 1979 was Christopher J. Bacon, a Head of Science who ran a girls' house with his wife, Jill, at Oakham School. He came to a School of over 425 where co-education had progressed to a point where nearly a third of the Decanians were girls and where

**Building and other Projects During The Bacon Years, 1979-1998**
(Those projects that included new buildings are in **bold**)

| Year | Dean Close School | Dean Close Junior School |
|---|---|---|
| 1979 | Brook Dormitory extension opened | |
| 1980 | Two Squash Courts completed<br>Dean Close House reorganized to accommodate some of Shelburne | |
| 1981 | Computer Room equipped<br>Laboratories enlarged<br>Changing room block redesigned<br>Tower House modernized | |
| 1982 | Study annexe built for Brook House | |
| 1983 | Tower dormitory converted to study-bedrooms | **Bayley House built** |
| 1984 | Changing Room block converted to form Recital Room, Home Economics Room and VI Form Common Room | |
| 1985 | New Chapel Cloister incorporating stained glass | |
| 1986 | Seminar Room built<br>Seven hard tennis courts completed<br>New maintenance building constructed | |
| 1987 | Old dining room converted to day rooms<br>**New dining hall & kitchens plus complete**<br>**New Language Centre (Edwards Building)** | **Centenary Block completed (now Ferguson Building)** |
| 1988 | Old kitchens converted to CDT Centre<br>Hard surface laid on old railway land (Hoare's)<br>Gymnasium facility renewed<br>Astro-turf all weather pitch laid | |
| 1989 | Brook House remodelled throughoutCDT completed<br>Tower House modernized and refurbished | |
| 1990 | Hooper Sundial erected<br>Pavilion re-roofed and internally improved | **New Rickerby built** |
| 1991 | Laboratory modernization progressed<br>Computer networking initiated<br>**New Theatre/Concert Hall completed** | |
| 1992 | Chemistry Laboratories refurbished<br>New CCF accommodation built | |
| 1993 | Chapel super-structure restored & re-lit<br>Second astro-turf laid<br>DCS staff Common Room extension built | |
| 1994 | Two Physics Laboratories refurbishedPre-Prep extended & new library built<br>Cricket Pavilion extended<br>Hooper Quadrangle pond and fountain built | |
| 1995 | Gate House en-suite study bedrooms constructed<br>**New Art & Design School completed**<br>Astro pitch changing rooms completed | |
| 1997 | New Flecker Library completed<br>**New Music School completed** | (*Source: Dean Close Commemoration Newsletter No.9, May 1998)* |

**Christopher John Bacon, Headmaster 1979-98**

Jill and Christopher Bacon

Born in 1937, he was the eldest of six and was Head Boy of Cranbrook School, Kent. A big man at 6'3", he read Chemistry at Hertford College, Oxford, where he became an evangelical Christian, an 'abiding passion'. He taught at Canford School, becoming head of Chemistry, and was appointed head of Science at Oakham School in 1969, his task being to galvanize a decidedly flagging department. He began the Oakham Science Society, succeeded in turning Chemistry into Oakham's top A Level subject and, with his wife Jill ran the Round House, Oakham's first girls' boarding house of some 60 girls from 1975.

Christopher and Jill Bacon arrived in Dean Close House with their daughters Philippa, Stephanie and Tamsin for Michaelmas 1979. Jill combined the roles of mother and Headmaster's wife with numerous others, including leading two house Bible Study groups and a squad of young gardeners in and around the Tuckwell Theatre. She also organized the large children's party every Christmas in what is now the old gym, while her husband appeared as Father Christmas.

The Bacon family also owned 'Grosmont', a smallholding of some 17 acres in Monmouthshire where 'CJB' enjoyed cattle farming, building, the latest in technical invention and also classical and popular music, for Christopher played both the piano and flute. Christopher and Jill moved there on his retirement in 1998. As a licensed Reader (lay minister), he did much for the local church and community in rural Monmouthshire, including youth work.

Christopher Bacon died in April 2005, having battled against leukemia for 15 years.

virtually a third were day pupils, in three houses. When Christopher Turner had arrived there had been 320 Decanians, of whom only one was a girl, one day boy house, Field, and well under a quarter of the School were day boys. The School was obviously bigger, and that fact together with the growth of co-education, had meant greater diversification of resources and a more complex organization.

That first Michaelmas was marked by the deaths of two considerable servants of the School: John Bayley and Ray Witts. John Bayley was a local magistrate and Chartered Surveyor with the School firm of Rickerby's, a Governor for 17 years, many of them as Chairman of the Finance and General Purposes Committee, as well as being a School Trustee. Bayley House, where Headmasters of the Junior/Preparatory School lived, now the Chaplain's house, was named after him, for he had been particularly interested in the Junior School's development. Ray Witts had served the School for 32 years as boiler man, general factotum and latterly as the porter since coming out of the Royal Navy as a Chief Petty Officer, and was well known for cheering people up.

A term into his headship, Christopher Bacon gave an interview to *Decus*. In it, he was asked the direct question, '...Do you intend to make any dramatic changes?..' '...Yes...' he replied, '...in relation to the buildings...'. He was as good as his word, for over the 19 years of his headship changes to buildings or the appearance of new ones seemed to happen at almost breakneck speed. It was also about this time that he brought in the term 'Scholars' for members of the Senior School, as he felt it would improve their self-image.

Buildings, however, were not his only preoccupation, as he made clear at his first Commemoration Speech Day in 1980. He said staff should teach for change while holding on to the values and standards that had been the mark of the School. The Headmaster mentioned the arrival of computers and the necessity of having '…plans for other electronic equipment which would enable [Dean Close School] to enter the scientific era of the '80s with confidence…'. Finally, Christopher Bacon hoped that the 1980s would be a time '…of excellence and endeavour and expectancy…'. He put down the markers for his headship. He would pursue the goals of more, improved facilities together with up-to-date computer and electrical equipment. Traditional values and standards would be retained single-mindedly and enthusiastically, coupled with a pursuit and expectation of excellence in all its forms. This would include the quality of the state of the School grounds to the academic achievement of Decanians; from the standard of the preparation of a prospectus through to the quality of worship, content of the preaching and singing of the choir in Chapel; from the way visitors and staff were greeted to the food the School ate. Everything was to be open to scrutiny and often robust comment and searching review. As Brian Wilson later wrote, '…He set about galvanizing the School to improve on all fronts. He introduced a policy of assessment in the departments and openly linked advancement to performance, not an obvious popularity move!..' Christopher Bacon perceived the efforts of a number of staff to raise both standards and commitment among colleagues and Decanians in the preceding years and strove to build on it.

1980 was also the year in which a particularly severe outbreak of influenza resulted in two of the houses becoming temporary sanatoriums with house staff helping with the provision of meals from the kitchens. Such outbreaks have been less common in recent years, probably due to the 'influvac' vaccination policy.

Meanwhile, there were other important issues. The Governors decided not to participate in a Government Assisted Places Scheme; it could be withdrawn at any time, thereby possibly leaving both parents and the School stranded. There was national inflation; fees had to go up by 27%. '…A bad year for overall results…' was how the 1980 summer academic results were described and clearly the new Headmaster had to rectify that situation. A part of his solution was to adopt the approach outlined above. A second element was to cut down on those attending the Sixth Form for a year only. A third was to ensure that the teachers were paid a little more than before but performances were more carefully monitored. Some who found this more demanding approach difficult were encouraged to seek posts elsewhere. The increasing work-load caused by a widening choice of subjects and the growing demands of the National Curriculum resulted in the creation of the post of Director of Studies in 1985, its first occupant being Malcolm Davies. True to his word on keeping up with computing, within a year the School had five '3802' machines, and from September 1980, all Fourth Form Decanians, plus any in the Remove who wanted them, had lessons in computing, the administration for which was handled by the Mathematics department. Within a further year, the number of computers had risen to eight.

In Christopher Bacon's first term, Mead's Jennifer Morris became the first female Head of School, taking over from Tim Graveney, who had been Dale's first Head of School. In the Chapel, oak pews were bought from Salem Baptist Church in Cheltenham and some fine stained-glass windows came from Aston Magna Parish Church, near Blockley – a gift to Dean Close Chapel from Gloucester Diocese. That glass has been used to great effect in the Chapel Cloister, fulfilling a vision of John Lachlan, architect, parent and Governor. It was completed in 1985.

Christmas 1980 included one of the first solely DCS Balls. It was held in the gym and included parents, Old Decanians and staff and featured the School's Jazz Band that was under the gifted direction of Chris Carmel, Head of Modern Languages. A Scottish Dance band was also in evidence under the guidance of Tim Odell, Head of Strings, in the Music Department.

There were changes at house level when Tim and Dorothy Odell moved into Brook and D.S. Macpherson took over Dale in 1978. These were continued two years later when Tony and Lindy Forbes moved into Shelburne, Richard and Sue Padfield became Houseparents of Tower, having been running Field and Shelburne respectively, probably the first time that anyone had changed houses. John Richardson, later to become headmaster of Cheltenham College, became Housemaster of Field.

Mike Girling, who arrived in 1948, retired in Trinity 1981 after 33 years on the staff, having been Second Master since 1968. He had worked for four Headmasters – Tony Gilkes, Douglas Graham, Christopher Turner and Christopher Bacon. The Governors' Report for that year spoke of him as being '…a wise counsellor to Governors as to Headmasters, staff, parents and pupils; and as loyal a servant as a school could have…'. Christopher Bacon wrote, '…there can rarely be seen a devotion equivalent to his in any community…'. He was succeeded as Second Master by Brian Wilson who had been on the staff since 1958 and had wide academic, pastoral and sports experience at the School.

It was also in Trinity 1981 that Airthrie School, in Christchurch Road, came up for sale. Christopher Bacon and the Governors had a professional survey done, its 60 pupil capacity potentially a pre-preparatory for Dean Close Junior School. However, the asking price, repairs and alterations needed made the acquisition financially impractical. The disappointment was mitigated to a certain extent by the visit, and resulting excellent publicity, of Prince Charles and Lady Diana Spencer, who used Big Field for their helicopter when on a visit to the county Police Headquarters on 27th March that year. The publicity centred on one boy who seized his moment as *Time* magazine recorded: '…"May I kiss the hand of my future Queen?" asked Nicholas Hardy, 18, proffering one golden daffodil from the far side of a police barricade…Lady Diana took the flower, considered the proposition and smiled prettily…"Yes, you may," she said, extending her hand. Nicholas kissed, schoolboys laughed, and the Queen-to-be-giggled, "You will never live this down."…'. '…All the world knew within 24 hours of Nick Hardy's gallant gesture,' reported *The Decanian* later, '…although from subsequent correspondence there seems to be a certain amount of technique in hand-kissing that Nick has yet to learn…'.

Nick Hardy kissing Lady Diana Spencer's hand

At the end of that term Rebecca Millard, now Dr Rebecca Smith, left the Senior School Sixth Form. It is almost certain that she was the first girl to have been all the way through both Junior and Senior Schools, taking her 11 years.

John Butler arrived in 1981 as the first EFL (English as a Foreign Language) part-time teacher. On his retirement he was succeeded in 1993 by Kit Morgan. Since then, two other part-time teachers, Margaret Cormack and Elaine Banks, have joined what is now the EAL team – English as an Additional Language.

The front corridor of the School was reorganized, becoming a Humanities centre. The cause of having groupings of subject related classrooms was later greatly assisted by the English, Classics and Modern Languages suites being included as part of the Edwards Building, opened in 1987. Helpful receptions for local industrialists were developed and work schemes put in place. Brook House began to use video films for the first time while Shelburne House proudly announced the arrival of a colour television. There were 31 candidates for Confirmation that year, too. A Bridge Club team from the School reached the semi-finals of the *Daily Mail* Cup; 45 activities were now available, ranging from dri-ski to cookery, modern dance to picture framing and jazz appreciation to lacrosse, although the last-named did not last long. Visits outside School continued to expand. For example, in 1984, from their Art Room situated roughly where the Stanley Hoare Rose Garden is now, six A level Art and Ceramics students travelled to London to see exhibitions at the Tate and the Courtauld Institute. Within two years, they were back in the capital, this time visiting the National Gallery and the Hayward Gallery for a Renoir exhibition. Art History was developing under Martin Bowden: by the end of the decade, expeditions to Rome and Paris were undertaken to see some of the finest European art.

Martin Bowden

In the academic year 1981-82 the driveway from Hatherley Road to what is now the Bacon Theatre, Music Centre and the Estates Department was built. The valley through which the Hatherley Stream flowed was largely infilled, creating space for a second artificial hockey pitch. Grimshaw's, the builders, who had Decanian connections, moved hundreds of tons of spoil. Railway land, acquired as a result of the 'Beeching Axe' on the branch line some time earlier was also levelled, thereby collectively creating so much additional playing space – said to be six acres in total – that it was felt that Barnfield, directly opposite the School on Hatherley Road, could be sold for development, eventually realizing some £1.15 million in 1984 (£2.77 million).

It was in 1983 that the former Chaplain-in-Chief, Royal Navy, the Ven. C.C.H.M. Morgan retired from being School Chaplain which he had been since 1976. The Revd Daniel Young replaced him as Chaplain, bringing a more youthful approach, and stayed until 1999. This matched the longest previous Chaplaincy by the Revd D.F. Horsefield some 60 years before, both of whom served for 16 years.

Meanwhile, Decanian recruitment was proving difficult for two reasons. Following national trends, it was not easy filling boy boarding places; yet pressure on girl boarding places was intense. Apart from Shelburne, the only other place where boarding girls could go was Fawley Lodge, which at that time was on the other side of Lansdown Road and was technically a part of Mead; with 26 girls, it was already full. September 1983 loomed and there were 16 female boarders due to arrive without anywhere to sleep. The Sanitorium, then at 9 Glencairn Park Road, was pressed into service and saved the day but the Governors made it clear that it was a temporary arrangement only and could last no longer than one year.

As months progressed, no easy solution presented itself. Eventually the Headmaster, realizing that in the prevailing climate he could always fill a girls' boarding house but not every boys' house, proposed a swap of buildings. There was debate about whether the swap should be with Brook House or Court House. The decision was finally for the latter. Court House had taken over 17 Hatherley Road, formerly known as 'Ombersley', when the Yearlings House was closed in 1973 and had happily remained there ever since.

**Housemasters/Housemistresses of Fawley**

| | |
|---|---|
| 1982-1984 | Miss A.M. Stradling |
| 1984-1985 | M.R. Bowden |
| 1985-1997 | Dr & Mrs K.A. Aris |
| 1997-present | Mrs V.A. Burroughs |

That Fawley should transfer to 17 Hatherley Road and Court move in the opposite direction was greeted with some relief by the Governors, anticipation by Fawley girls and a mixture of reactions by the Court House community. Emotions ran high; feelings went deep. Boys' parents mounted a vigorous campaign to stop the decision going ahead. The upset Housemaster, the Revd David Gibson, made it clear that should the decision stand he would resign his housemastership. The decision did and he duly resigned, leaving the School itself a year later. His place as housemaster in the newly-located Court was taken by Richard Taylor with his wife Anne. He had arrived at Dean Close School in 1983 as Head of History, when Court House had been 43 strong. Now, in its new surroundings, it numbered just 30. Fawley, on the other hand, had expanded beyond the size that Court had been, and at Michaelmas 1984 numbered 58. Miss Annette Stradling, who had been a young, resident tutor in charge since 1982 – *de facto* Housemistress – stepped down and left the following year to take up a post in London. Martin Bowden took over the enlarged house in its new setting with the full status of housemaster, supported by his wife Jenny, who, not many years earlier, had been a DCS School Sister. Unfortunately, the Bowdens left the house after two terms, being replaced by Keith and Vanessa Aris in April 1985. Although the new Fawley House was some distance from the main School, a path from the house as far as the Junior School had been completed in Trinity 1978, thereby saving girls from having to walk to the main School via Hatherley Road.

Fawley House

The proportion of girls to boys in the School at large had continued to shift significantly from roughly 1:3 in 1976-77, noted in the last chapter, to 2:3 now, eight years later. This well exceded the Governors' original recorded intended ratio of one girl to three boys but there seemed little concern.

1978 was also the year when the Senior School had two Carol Services, the main one in Christ Church '...on the afternoon of the last Sunday in term ending nicely in time for tea...' and another, voluntary Carol Service in Chapel.

If the demand for different categories of places at the School was altering, ways of presenting the School to the outside world were also changing. The prospectus and newspaper or magazine advertisements and articles, used for nearly a century, were now joined by independent schools' 'trade fairs' called ISIS Exhibitions which Dean Close School first supported in 1983. Different schools took stands at an agreed venue and, armed with prospectuses, senior members of staff, possibly accompanied by a marketing manager or similar, would talk to potential school parents. Interested parents would then visit, perhaps on an Open Day, which first began at Dean Close in Michaelmas 1982. The School had a Registrar by 1988, promotional video by 1993, and by 1997 its own Marketing Manager, albeit part-time, in Tracey Colbert-Smith.

Sometimes publicity was highly individual. Possibly the best example was the World Speed Hair Cutting Record achieved by Allen Cresswell, the School Barber for 30 years (1973-2003), who on Sunday, 20th May, 1984 cut the hair of 100 boys in 2 hours 55 minutes, only having to go back to one boy. Central TV and the local press were on hand to record the event. Over £2,000 (£4,800) was raised to support research into Crohn's Disease, something from which his son suffered.

Academically, things were changing. In his letter to parents in March 1985, the Headmaster gave notice that GCEs would soon be giving way to GCSEs and that the first courses in these would begin in September 1986. In the event, the School took to GCSEs rather well, as the Headmaster wrote in October 1990, '...to be able to say that in both the GCSE and the A levels we had over 90% pass rate is truly gratifying...We record only A, B and C grades as a pass at GCSE. In addition, we are pleased that at 'A' level 49.5% of the grades were A or B...Our results place us far above national averages, and in the top third of HMC [Headmasters' Conference] schools...'. Christopher Bacon strongly resisted the charge that the School was an academic hot-house, pointing out that the intelligence range of the School's entry was wide. What the School did manage '...to a remarkable degree, was to motivate the young people to take hold of their own destiny, work for their own sakes and then achieve well up to their potential...(although) a few were disappointed...'.

Princess Alexandra on her visit to the school 1986

The cast of Oliver! on stage at the Everyman Theatre 1986

Other developments included the former changing room block being partially converted into an excellent Home Economics centre and a space being created next door that became a much-needed Music Recital room.

1986 was the centenary year of the School's opening, a year of celebration whose highlights included a visit by Princess Alexandra, a Centenary Concert in Tewkesbury Abbey with Dame Janet Baker as

Edwards Building

W.A.M. Edwards

**Derek and Joyce Barker, staff members**

Derek Barker was Head of Science (1953-86), responsible for the considerable development of the subject, including the original laboratories in the Beaufort Building. Assisted by his wife Joyce, he was the only Housemaster of the Yearlings (1961-73) and was Housemaster of Dale (1973-78). He also encouraged most sports, in particular tennis, and was stage manager of the Tuckwell Theatre for some years. He died in 1996.

When not assisting her husband in Yearlings, Joyce Barker joined the staff in 1968 as a Modern Linguist and was Housemistress of Mead 1971-73. The Joyce Barker Memorial Travel Award is in her memory. She died in 1986.

the guest soloist, and a week of performances of *Oliver!* involving both Dean Close School and the Junior School at the Everyman Theatre (see chapter 13). It was also the year that Derek Barker retired.

1987 and 1988 were the years of new starts, with the Dean Close School civic award-winning Edwards Building being opened by W.A.M. Edwards OD, School Governor and benefactor, where the old swimming pool/ gymnasium and some classrooms and huts formerly existed. It contained the new Dining Hall, kitchens and Classics, English and Modern Languages suites of classrooms. It was a great change to life in the School. Originally, Christopher Bacon's idea had been to have a dining hall for the entire campus located roughly where New Shelburne is now on the Junior School side of Shelburne Road. However, he later accepted that seven and 18 year olds would not go easily together; that supervisory, dietary and meal-time requirements might well be different and that separate dining halls were preferable, not least because moving over 400 young people across Shelburne Road without a proper crossing was potentially dangerous.

In addition to the opening of the Edwards building, six new hard tennis courts on Hoare's Ground (near the present CCF hut) and the opening of the CDT Caldecote Centre where the old kitchens had once been also took place. Stuart Gane, a former member of the Art Department, headed the new CDT Department that offered A level courses in Computer Science from

Michaelmas 1987. With 24 Amstrad PC 1640s and an Epson PC-AX that controlled a Novel Network, the School was moving from being merely an 'Educational User' of computers to being a 'Business User'. For the first time, computers were being seen not just as 'scientific' but as having cross-curricular uses and applications. The old Dining Rooms were converted into Common Rooms for the out-houses. Moreover, the upper Quad (the Hooper Quadrangle) had been made more beautiful with plants and a pond. Within a further year, an astroturf hockey pitch was in use as well as the artificial Redgra pitch.

Schools' Challenge Quiz team with Nancy Braithwaite

Also in 1987, a Dean Close team became the national champions in the Schools' Challenge Quiz, a general knowledge competition, beating six other schools in six rounds on their way to winning the Shield from Abingdon in the grand final. History teacher R.R. Osborne was the victorious team's manager while the team captain and only girl, Nancy Braithwaite, was the one Decanian to have been in every round. In 1987, Sue Vaus became the first official Senior Mistress, underlining the distaff side's ever-growing role. It was also the year in which Humphrey Osmond (a nephew of C.A.P. Tuckwell) formerly Housemaster of Court, a Modern Linguist, Lay Reader and Chapel Choir member retired from teaching at the School after 22 years but continued to play a valuable role as the first Archivist.

However, all was not entirely well, as there was a fire in Fawley during Trinity 1988. Fortunately, no-one was hurt.

**The Fawley House Fire**

The fire broke out in the trunk room of Fawley House at 9.40pm on Sunday, 15th May, 1988, caused by an electrical fault. The house of 58 girls was speedily and efficiently evacuated and there were no injuries, earning praise for their training from Graham Hinton, Divisional Fire Officer. The Fire Brigade arrived quickly and eventually employed eight appliances. The flames were under control fairly quickly but 'damping down' was not completed until 2.30am. Damage was confined to the top two floors. The girls spent the rest of the night as guests of Shelburne House but were back in Fawley the following night, sleeping in Common Rooms although two girls had to sleep in a study.

During the subsequent week the house was professionally cleaned. By the Friday night, three of the six rooms affected were able to be reoccupied. For the rest of the term two Common Rooms were converted into dormitories and by the following September the House was almost back to normal.

The Housemistress, Mrs Vanessa Aris, later wrote that one memory of that event was '...walking through the devastated top floor very early on Monday morning when all was still and realizing what might have happened and how we had really been looked after...(that) God must really have been watching over us – if it had happened even half an hour later...'. The sentence is not completed as the thought was too appalling to put into words.

In her end of year report, Head of House Joanne Jennings wrote that '...our thanks must go to Dr and Mrs Aris...not least in their careful washing of 59 charred teddy bears following the fire...'.

By 1989, the Christian Union was '…the largest single voluntary activity at Dean Close…' with about a quarter of the School attending – that is about a hundred at any one time from a total of 441 (201 girls, 240 boys.)

It was also at this time that Christopher Bacon was elected Chairman of the Headmasters' Conference (HMC) co-education group, and a year or two later Sue Padfield, the Senior Mistress, became Chairman of the Senior Mistresses' Group in HMC.

The 1989 Children Act came into force, requiring the vetting of all staff. Regulations concerned matters such as fire, health and safety issues and food standards. Central government administrative and regulative innovations flowed, culminating in local government social service departments being required to inspect boarding accommodation periodically and satisfy themselves that the boarders concerned were being properly looked after, in addition to the visits of the Independent Schools' Inspectorate. The amount of paperwork and the need for and range of records increased significantly. Computerisation had arrived just in time but numbers of administrative staff still increased.

Caroline Griffith opening the climbing wall

After additional training, it was Richard Padfield who in 1989 began to assist those who had been identified as having dyslexic problems, an issue that had first raised its head as early as 1973 in a letter of Christopher Turner's to parents (see previous chapter). After he retired in 1995, Richard Padfield's work was continued by Karen Butler and then John Watson before the appointment of a learning support specialist, Dr Stephanie Thomas, in 1999. Since then a department has developed able to offer appropriate help to those Decanians who may have a range of educational or learning problems.

Action on the Climbing Wall

The Girling Room (old Room Five) was opened in Trinity 1990. It was to house the Archives, an area in which Mike Girling, the former Second Master, had been one of the first to take an interest. It was also to be a meeting point for Old Decanians, who provided the leather furniture. It was named the Girling Room '…in recognition of Mike Girling's long association with the School and ODS…'.

Commemoration 1991 included the opening of the Talbot Griffith Climbing Wall on the back of the almost completed theatre. Talbot Griffith, a former headmaster of

Oakham, was a Governor of Dean Close School for many years and took up climbing in his fifties. His daughter, Caroline, herself a Dean Close Governor, performed the opening ceremony.

On Tuesday, 29th October, 1991, the long-awaited opening of the New Theatre, later renamed the Bacon Theatre, by the Lord Lieutenant of Gloucestershire, Colonel Sir Martin Gibbs, took place. The architect, Richard Slawson, had also designed the Edwards Building.

The Theatre, although it has been used extensively by the Senior School for productions, workshops, films, presentations, concerts, recitals and assemblies, was also used by the Preparatory School for productions, concerts, dancing displays and even Speech Days for a few years in the 1990s. It also came to be used not only by professional touring theatre and dance companies, groups and individuals but also by comparatively local amateur groups and organisations that included the annual 'Gang Show' of the Gloucestershire Scout and Guide Association.

The financing of the whole project, some £2 million, was partly funded out of land that had been sold off; partly out of very careful housekeeping and partly by an appeal. Even so, money became extremely tight and it was a considerable act of faith by the Governors, who realized that it would be a long while before such an opportunity would arise again. They decided to take the risk. Time has shown that they were right.

Peter Cairns, as Head of English and Drama, together with Richard Ryall, who had been the staff stage manager for many productions, had been invited to submit suggestions and requirements for a theatre over four years before the project reached fruition. Lloyd Allington, who was something of a newcomer to the School at that stage, also became involved. School theatres at Wycombe Abbey, Radley, and Brambletye in Surrey were visited. Peter Cairns, who put in a huge amount of time and effort on the project, wrote that '…The pressure by external expert advice was to construct a 'modern' theatre, '60s egalitarian in philosophy: no proscenium; in the round as far as possible; no windows…(However) everything we saw confirmed our desire for a building which was both a traditional, conventional theatre and a beautiful concert hall, with high clerestory windows and a proscenium arch. After much argument, this is what we were granted…'.

The Theatre also proved to be an excellent venue for an annual lecture that was inaugurated in 1992 – the Douglas Graham Memorial Lecture – that periodically reminded everyone of that remarkable former Headmaster who had died the previous July. Its first lecturer was Professor Robert Evans, PhD, FBA, OD, of Brasenose College, Oxford, who had been a pupil under Douglas Graham. After a few reminiscences concerning his old Headmaster, Professor Evans delved into his subject which was 'The Eastern European Revolution in Historical Perspective.'

1991 also saw the incorporation of Dean Close Services Ltd. This company, entirely owned by the School, was found to be the best way of providing services other than simply the education of Decanians. It became the agency through which accommodation in the School could be let during the holidays, from a classroom to the Tuckwell Theatre, from the swimming pool to a boarding house. It became the booking office for the New Theatre – for just a couple of seats for a particular performance, or for the entire Theatre – and for all non-school entertainment in the Theatre, Tuckwell Theatre and later the Music School, and also ran the School Shop. The early 1990s involved a reassessment of the catering that resulted in external caterers being used for the first time, a situation that has continued to the present day.

Other areas were upgraded, notably the Chemistry laboratories Sanger, Perkin and Dalton, which were completely redesigned, making them, in the words of the Head of Chemistry, Dr Keith Aris, who

**The New Theatre, later renamed The Bacon Theatre**

The Orangery is the Entrance Hall to the Theatre, so named because of several orange trees which initially provided pleasant greenery during intervals. It is a large marbled hall with a sloping roof – similar to that in the Dining Hall – complete with a Waterford chandelier. The marble floor, the chandelier and a concert grand piano were gifts from parents. It connects with the swimming-pool next door and a mezzanine walkway leads the audience into the auditorium galleries. The Orangery is large enough on its own, and has sufficiently good acoustics, to be a place for solo or chamber music. It is also used for displays and events.

Although it is possible to seat up to 650 people, the Bacon Theatre is only legally permitted to seat 566. The auditorium is on two levels, with balconies on both sides. The Lighting and Sound Box is computer controlled and connects with both stage and understage. There are high clerestory windows that give plenty of light but which can be completely blacked out.

The stage is large, 11m x 11m, which made it the widest though not the deepest in Gloucestershire when it was built – the Everyman Theatre in Cheltenham is deeper. At the back, extreme left and right, are steps leading under stage, and there is also the facility to access the covered bridge over to the Music School. The whole stage can be extended into the auditorium by an additional collapsible apron over the orchestra pit, which accommodates 30 players. The pit has a hydraulic hoist. There is a traditional proscenium arch, even though at one point there was speculation that the theatre would be 'in the round' as far as possible.

The under stage area includes two sets of dressing rooms and a large Green Room, where a plaque commemorating C.A.P. Tuckwell's contribution to the history of School drama has been relocated from its original site in what was the Flecker Hall but is now the Flecker Library. There are also rooms for storage, music practice and the making of props, together with toilet and washing facilities. An unobtrusive staircase to the side of the auditorium allows the swimming pool/old gym changing rooms to be used if there was a cast of hundreds!

The Architect was Richard Slawson, who also designed the Edwards Building.

spent long hours on the project '...the most technologically advanced and attractively designed (of) any school in the country...'. The practical areas were separated from the lecture areas using an L-shaped design. Dr Aris, Chemistry teacher since 1972, Head of Department from 1985, subsequently retired at the end of 1994. He ran Fawley House with his wife Vanessa 1985-97 as well as being the School's Examinations Officer.

Steuart BonBernard

Personalities among the Governors came and went. W.A.M. Edwards OD decided to step down from the Executive Committee after a record-breaking 45 years, eight of them as Chairman, and was promptly elected a Vice-President. Steuart BonBernard stood down as Chairman and also became a Vice-President, to be replaced by Colin Cocks. In 1994, Sir Leonard Hooper, himself a Vice-President of the School, died. He had been a Governor for 25 years and Chairman of the Executive for 11 of them.

1994 was also the year in which Rhod Pentycross retired after 33 years as a Chemistry master as well as being an effective rugby coach for many of them. He had also taken over the Duke of Edinburgh's Award Scheme from Hugh Cocksedge when the latter left in 1970.

The Marquess of Reading (left) with Colin and Gwyneth Cocks

Another departure was that of Wing Commander Stuart Fowler who had been Bursar since 1988. There was no replacement, Christopher Bacon convincing the Governors that he could do what was necessary in terms of strategic thinking and running the Bursary, so long as the Financial Controller (Robert Hopkins) did the accountancy work and oversaw the finance department on a day-to-day basis. The Estates Controller (Stuart Hay) would perform the same task in the maintenance and grounds department. Thus Christopher Bacon was the first Headmaster since Dr Flecker to be both Headmaster and Bursar at the same time, '...saving the Governors a lot of money...' as he put it. Not all Governors would necessarily have agreed.

A timely distraction was provided towards the end Michaelmas 1994 when the BBC programme 'Any Questions' was broadcast from the New Theatre. The team comprised Baroness Shirley Williams, the Rt Hon. Tony Benn, MP, the Rt Hon. Michael Howard, MP, and Anne Atkins, journalist, broadcaster and a Dean Close parent. The show was hosted, as was customary, by Jonathan Dimbleby before a packed audience.

Keith Davis, head of Art 1967-2003

The new Art School and BonBernard Gallery was opened by Lady Catherwood, wife of the President of the Evangelical Alliance, prominent public figure and businessman Sir Fred Catherwood, during Commemoration 1995. An area close to the Chapel, occupied for many years by CCF huts, had been turned into a small Quad whose focus was an attractive weeping willow in the middle of a lawn. The well-designed Art block around it included a pottery, senior studio, drawing research studio, a small seminar room and a junior studio. Apart from Keith Davis and Angela Ash, the Art

The BonBernard Gallery

**Commemoration Exhibitions at The BonBernard Gallery, 1995-2002**

Three Exhibitions by Joanna Haracz (Artist in Residence)
Chris Hoggett and Kay Wedgebury (landscape painting)
Chris Kenyon and Denys Carnill (watercolours)
A Still Life theme (with string quartet recital following)
ISADA (Independent Schools Art and Design Association) conference display (with jazz band accompaniment)
David Durstan (paintings and prints)
Emma Boyd and Ian Burch (paintings)
James Dunn and Keith Davis (paintings)
Wildlife Art Society (paintings and drawings)
Selma Parlour and Jane Baker (paintings and sculptures)
Prints and Printmaking Techniques
Richard Blomfield, Nigel Temple, Denys Delhanty (three artists)
Textile Art

Department now included Joanna Haracz, the first Artist in Residence, who used the old signal box which stood at the perimeter of the School grounds by the railway line. The BonBernard Gallery hosted an exhibition of work by artist Paul Hobbs in 1996 and subsequently many other exhibitions. A regular two page display of some Decanians' work was featured every year in *The Decanian.* However, neither the BonBernard Gallery nor the spread in *The Decanian* stopped A level artists from continuing to go up to London and elsewhere to view great artists in various galleries and draw inspiration from them. A great sadness in 2002 for the Art Department was when the Art Technician, John Harwood, died suddenly aged 52.

The CCF huts themselves were rebuilt, upgraded and moved closer to the tennis courts on Hoare's Ground.

At Trinity 1995, Brian Wilson retired. A graduate of Trinity College, Dublin, he came to the School in 1958 and served it for 37 years as Head of Classics, tutor, 1st XV rugby coach, Housemaster of Tower (1967-80) and an '... outstanding...' Second Master (1981-95). A noted golfer, he was seen as being tough but fair, was universally respected, and was '...renowned for his wit and perception...' as one colleague wrote. One small incident when he was housemaster demonstrates this. An OD recalled: '...over the years, BKW honed (his) method of creeping up a corridor, knocking on a study door and entering, all in one go...' This time the boy was quick and the radio was snapped off. 'Morning Sir'. 'Morning. Is everything all right?' 'Fine, thank you sir.' Huge sigh of relief as BKW left, only for the door to re-open. 'By the way – what's the score?' '227 for 8, Sir.' 'Thanks. I'll take the radio.' As the boy remarked rather ruefully, 'He was usually one step ahead of me.'

Richard Padfield also retired from teaching that Trinity Term. Entering the Junior School as a boy in 1955, by 1961 he was Senior Prefect, (Head of School) and Captain of Hockey and Cricket. After St Edmund's Hall, Oxford where he won a Hockey Blue and was an England trialist, he taught at Dauntsey's. He returned to the School to teach English in 1969 becoming Housemaster of Field (1975-80) and his old House, Tower, (1980-88). During his career, he has been Committee Member, Registrar, Honorary Secretary and President of the Old Decanian Society.

Christopher Bacon decided to look outside the School for his next Second Master and recruited Alastair Reid, head of History and a housemaster at Glenalmond and a keen sportsman. Sue Padfield, having been Senior Mistress since 1989 became the senior of the three deputy heads, the first woman appointed to that position as until that time, the Second Master had always been the senior deputy head. She was to retire in 2002 after nearly 30 years on the staff. The Director of Studies, Tony Marchand, continued to be the 'Third Deputy'. Eventually, he became Deputy Head (Academic), with David Evans as Director of Studies.

The 1997 General Election was replicated – to a certain extent – at Dean Close School under History teacher John Moule. Although the Conservatives won overall on a 91.6% turnout, both New

Labour and the Liberal Democrats scored significantly. Indeed, in the Upper Sixth, New Labour won.

At Commemoration in 1997 the preacher was the Revd Dr Alan Munden, Francis Close's biographer, whose book *A Cheltenham Gamaliel* had just been published. The Guest of Honour was the Archbishop of Canterbury, Dr George Carey, with whose appointment a former President and now Vice-President of the School, Lord Caldecote, had been significantly involved. Interestingly, the Archbishop's successor as Bishop of Bath and Wells was the Rt Revd Jim Thompson OD, previously Bishop of Stepney.

In addition to speaking at Prize Giving, Archbishop Carey opened the Flecker Library, unveiled the sculpture outside the Art School and also a plaque at the nearly completed Music School. In that year another plaque had appeared on the Climbing Wall, commemorating the life and service of Geoff Allen (Head Gardener 1983-96), who had sadly died while still in post.

The Flecker Library, housed in what had been the Big Schoolroom of 1888 and latterly a small and increasingly inadequate school hall, was totally internally rebuilt to give it a rather 'nautical' appearance. The books were transferred from the old library in the Beaufort Building to the new one by a human chain of Decanians of such length that a *Times* photographer came to record the event and it appeared on the back page of that newspaper the next day.

Mary Vaughan retired after almost 30 years with the School not only as a Sister but also, with her husband Mervyn, houseparents for a time of the infant Fawley Lodge in the 1970s which was then in Lansdown Road. Administratively, it had still been a part of Mead House under Sue Vaus.

The Music School

Michaelmas 1997 was the term the pavilion on Chapel Close was burnt down. It was rebuilt owing to the generous bequest of F.W. Morgan OD, himself a fine sportsman, who was one of several OD hockey players to be capped for Wales.

The academic year 1997-98 was Christopher Bacon's last as Headmaster before he retired. However, the pace did not slacken. There was a reorganisation of staff running the girls' houses. Keith and Vanessa Aris relinquished Fawley which they had run for 12 years. With the centenary in mind, Mrs Aris had designed the House crest that included elephants (symbolizing willingness), the quill (education), and the pigeons that were a part of the town and School crests; pink was associated with her husband. Viv Burroughs, who had been Housemistress of Mead since 1989, took over Fawley, and Julie Kent, a member of the Music staff since 1990, became Housemistress of Mead.

In addition to staff changes, Prince Michael of Kent came to open the Music School and name its concert hall 'The Prince Michael Hall'. The New Theatre was also re-named 'The Bacon Theatre' after the Headmaster whose particular project it had been. And Fourth Formers were all to have laptop computers.

Christopher Kenyon retired at the end of Trinity 1998. He was one of few in the modern era who devoted his entire career to one school. He joined the staff in 1962 from Jesus College, Cambridge, where he read Geography and Theology. He was Housemaster of Gate (1971-83) and Field (1984-93). He took over cricket from Mike Girling in 1964, having himself played for a Minor County (Norfolk) and continued in charge until 1997. The 1st XI pavilion on Big Field was renamed The Kenyon Pavilion in his honour at his retirement. He also played hockey and squash, both of which he supported in School, and also golf. He taught Geography and some Divinity when he arrived: by the time he left, he was Head of Divinity and had become a Licensed Reader (lay minister). His wife, Sarah, supported him wholeheartedly and generously throughout his career.

At the end of Trinity 1998, Christopher and Jill Bacon had completed 19 years at the helm of the School. After Flecker himself, 'CJB's' was the longest headship in the history of the Senior School. There were 453 Decanians, of whom 204 were girls, in the Senior School; of that total, 178 were day pupils. In an environment in which recruitment for boarding places at an independent school could be difficult, especially for boys, this was quite an achievement. It is too early to attempt to make a considered judgement of his headship but doubtless future generations will take into consideration factors such as Christopher Bacon's deep Evangelical Christian commitment, passion for education, single-minded drive, utter determination significantly to improve and extend the school facilities, academic and other standards of Decanians. He had the ability somehow to appear seemingly at all functions, matches and other occasions and to know everyone's name. He made huge demands upon himself – that sometimes included extra personal tuition – and upon others. His attitude was actively to encourage, if not require, excellence in all areas of the School's life, in the hope that a young person's potential could be realized. He was content with nothing less. His approach was most succinctly expressed in part of the conclusion of his annual report to the Governors in 1995: '...We can never rest...It is my task to keep the colleagues and the School as a whole up-to-the-mark and the higher that mark the greater the pressure must be applied. I praise God that He is always in the equation. Without His aid we could do nothing but with it 'all things' are possible...'.

The departure of the Bacons inevitably left a large gap to be filled. At least three Senior School generations of Old Decanians had known no other Headmaster. Virtually 80% of the full-time teaching staff had been appointed by 'CJB'. When he began as Headmaster, Margaret Thatcher was Prime Minister of

**The Revd Timothy Hastie-Smith, Headmaster 1998-2008**

He was educated at Cranleigh before reading History at Magdalene College Cambridge. He was lay chaplain at Felsted School, then studied Theology at Wycliffe College before entering the Church and served his title at St Ebbe's, Oxford. He was Senior Chaplain and Admissions Tutor at Stowe School and a member of the senior management team before his appointment to Dean Close School, aged 35.

At Dean Close School, Tim Hastie-Smith encouraged Decanians, not least by inculcating his own commitment to *Carpe Diem* ('seize the day'), initiated new management styles, saw through a number of building and refurbishment projects and was responsible for Tewkesbury Abbey Schola Cantorum coming to the campus (see chapters 16 and 19).

Outside the School, Tim Hastie-Smith was a member of the Gloucester Diocesan Board of Education, Chairman of TISCA (Teachers in Independent Schools' Christian Association), governor of eight independent schools at different times between 1995 and 2008 as well as Chairman of HMC in 2008.

Tim Hastie-Smith married Joanne in 1987, and they have three children, Emily, Edward and Alice. Joanne, like her predecessors, was an accomplished hostess and a strong support for her husband.

Since their departure in 2008, Tim has become Team Vicar at Kempsford near Fairford, Gloucestershire.

a Conservative government and the Falklands War had yet to occur. By the time he retired, Tony Blair was in 10 Downing Street and a Labour administration was running the country.

The Governors took some time to appoint Christopher Bacon's successor. The Revd Timothy Hastie-Smith was eventually selected. At 35, he was thought by some a little young for the post but Dr Flecker and Hugh Elder had been 26 and 33 respectively on their appointments as Headmaster, and both had been outstanding.

In an interview for *The Decanian* published a year after his arrival, the new Headmaster stated that he had arrived with '...no pre-conceived ideas about what needed to be done...(but) I arrived with the clear aim of examining all areas of the School with as open a mind as possible...'. He quoted Burke's dictum: 'a state without the means of reform is without the means of its own preservation'. He felt that there were few schools whose co-education was working as well as it was at Dean Close School; that for '...quite a small school...' it did incredibly well in a number of areas. Yet change was inevitable.

# Chapter 10

# Sport at Dean Close School, 1918 to 1968

***General***

At the end of the First World War sport had, not surprisingly, reached a low ebb at the School, notwithstanding inspirational moments like D.E. Green's 1915 cricket season when he averaged 51 runs including a top score of 163 at Worcester. Like many similar institutions, School teams were badly affected by senior boys and young male staff, who would normally coach, being called up or volunteering for the armed forces.

There was debate about the place of Games at School during hostilities. In the March 1918 *Decanian* the editor wrote, 'The question of the position that games ought to hold in a Public School during the war has been freely discussed during the last few months.' More time was being allocated to the Officer Training Corps (OTC – forerunner of the present CCF) at the expense of Games. However, it was noted that '…the Superintendent of Physical and Bayonet Training in the Southern Command inspected the PT [Physical Training] this term and asked about the games. He urged that the old 'sporting spirit' should be kept up, and that matches of all sorts should be encouraged…'. That spirit was helped by four sports 'clubs', started at the beginning of 1909, broadly representing home areas: North, South, West and South-West that competed in football, cricket, hockey, sports and gymnastics. Other sports/activities were added later. There were two divisions, senior and junior, the split being when boys reached 15.

Sports Day had moved from Chapel Close, where it had begun in the late 1880s, to Big Field which was smaller then, bounded by a rather rickety fence from the far end of the Tuckwell Theatre across to the present Bayley House, roughly following the line of the current path to the Preparatory School. Beyond the fence were two meadows, both belonging to Benhall Farm. These meadows were bought for use as additional pitches and athletics track in 1956 and 1961.

Organized PT

Thus football, hockey, cricket, athletics, fives, shooting, swimming and occasionally water polo were the only sports available in 1918, although boys also sometimes cycled or walked in the surrounding area.

Sports photo *circa* 1890

The decision by Percy Bolton (Headmaster from 1924) to create a house system embraced sport as well. The old 'League' of 'clubs' disappeared. Now boys found that their 'sports' house included the same pupils with whom they lived, their loyalty and enthusiasm for their own teams was greatly increased.

Percy Bolton encouraged senior boys to take on School responsibilities and a Games committee emerged run by the Senior Prefect (Head of School). It began during Michaelmas 1926 and dealt with vexed questions surrounding the awarding of Colours – how many and to whom, under what conditions, for what sports and by whom. The Committee comprised the Senior Prefect, the captain of the (main) game of the term in question and three other members, elected by secret ballot. A boy could only put himself up for election if he was a member of his house 1st team in the main sport under consideration. The electorate consisted of the 50 most senior boys in the School, together with anyone who was in a senior dormitory or holding School First Team Colours.

Percy Bolton also encouraged Physical Training, which occurred every morning for about 20 minutes before Chapel. Taken by Sergeant-Major Golder, each boy did two sessions per week. Hugh Elder changed this to include every boy for 40 minutes every weekday. It is not clear when this was abandoned.

Two incidents about Big Field are worth recording. Firstly, just after the end of term, on 11th December, 1940, a bomb explosion created a sizeable crater in the middle of Big Field (see chapter 5). The 1st XV rugby pitch that had one end by Shelburne Road and the other past the tuckshop subsequently turned ninety degrees to its current position. The pitch where the bomb dropped became known as 'Crater Pitch'.

Secondly, having received '... positive assurances from charming ladies...', the Headmaster permitted the West of England Ladies' Kennel Society to hold a one-day dog show on Big Field during the 1948 Easter holiday. On a gloriously warm day, 250 coaches and buses, nearly 4,000 dogs and 13,000 people arrived. But it took gangs of men took two days to clear up, whilst others filled in huge numbers of peg holes. Both School mowers had blades badly buckled by the sheer quantity of iron scraps left on the grass. It took a month before cricket was possible on Big Field. One commentator wrote, '...before you (next) meet your Delilahs with their honeyed words and positive assurances, (remember) our experience. Be firm. Remember Dean Close. You have been warned...'.

The fives courts, dating from 1890, were pulled down in 1957 to make way for the Beaufort Science Building.

Major B.D. Chapman DSO took charge of all PE in 1960. A gymnast from the 1936 Olympics, he was instrumental in raising sporting standards generally, and especially in athletics and swimming.

The opening of the state-of-the-art swimming pool and gymnasium in 1964 not only meant that traditional Dean Close sports such as swimming, water-polo and gymnastics were able to continue in enhanced surroundings but that other activities, such as badminton, basketball and weight training, became possible.

Before moving to Barn Field, athletics was on Flecker's Piece, the large field which became the Flecker's Drive housing development. This was also the main area for 'run of the mill' rugby and some hockey; it was often muddy. Under the devoted care of Edward Ellam and then Stanley Hoare, and also generations of groundsmen, the standard of Big Field was consistently high. R.F. McNeile wrote, '...From inter war days the names recur of Morse and Weaver and Brown and Jeffries, and the vision of a posse of them waiting on the touchline for the Saturday afternoon match to end, when they would step out and dig up the holes and lift the scrapes in readiness for the horse roller on Monday. And in post Second World War days there has been Bill Mason of the burnished head and flashing smile, friend and confidant of many generations...'. Also memorable was Ben Flint. After Neville Page, in our own generation, Neil Carter and his team have continued the tradition of care for the grounds.

***Athletics and Cross Country***

In athletics, Sports Day was a movable feast, being held in October in 1917, although previously it had been at the end of the Lent Term. The annual Hatherley Run, a little under three miles, was also held in October. Runners turned right onto Shelburne Road, right onto Hatherley Road and eventually came out near present-day Arle Court, worked their way back along Gloucester Road, turning right into Shelburne Road after crossing the railway bridge for the last desperate sprint to the School. R.M. Harvey, who was Captain of Football, won the Hatherley Run in 1917 in 16 minutes 12 seconds.

W.A.M. Edwards winning at cross country when at Oxford University

Cross country running was introduced in 1925 by B.O. Bradnack. It became popular, possibly because of the gifted W.A.M. Edwards, who won an Oxford Blue for it each year from 1925-27, with N.C. Moses not far behind, himself winning a Cross Country Oxford Blue in 1929. However, apart from R.P. Crabbe, who won a Cambridge Blue in 1905, those were the only Decanians who received such honours for that sport. Not only was there keen inter-house rivalry, W.A.M. Edwards brought a team over from Oxford to compete.

Cross country running matches against Cheltenham and County Harriers, Bristol University and St Paul's College began in 1938. Surprisingly, although they lost to Bristol University as might have been expected, they won their other two matches.

There was a reasonably good Cross Country season in 1939, especially as the School did not have many good senior runners; a highly encouraging athletic Sports Day in which C.E. Jensen came within 0.5 seconds of beating the School Record of 2 minutes 9 seconds for the 880 yards, J.A.D. Cox winning the Junior 440 yards in a new record of 56.6 seconds and R.S. Thompson jumping just over 5 feet to break the Junior record in that event. It was possibly the first School occasion ever filmed, with a sound track of sorts, featuring J.S. Moore as the staff commentator.

Athletic Sports were revived in 1948 but were split into two, the jumps being decided at the end of the Lent Term and the races at the beginning of Trinity, '...to ease the burden on the major games...'. The standard of jumping was described as being '...fearfully low...', while the quarter, half and one mile races were all won by runners under 16 years of age who had trained rather more than older boys. The following year, all the Athletic Sports were held just before Easter which *The Decanian* stated seemed '...the most suitable time to hold sports (that) has been found...'. Moreover, there was '...much more enthusiasm in evidence this year...'. In 1951 the Athletic Sports were abandoned because of the weather but they did hold the Hatherley Run, apparently for the first time since 1936. The winner, R.G. Hill, won in a time of 15 minutes, 54 seconds, slower than D.A. Pringle's 1930 record of 15 minutes 3 seconds but then, as *The Decanian* remarked, Pringle achieved that enviable time '...in less exacting traffic conditions...'.

First set up in 1925 and initially involving 33 runners, the Hatherley Run had ceased with the Second World War but determined souls, particularly Charles C.S. Neil, had rediscovered most of the course and lengthened it because of house building in the interim, though exactly where is not clear. In 1958 the Run was revived and modified yet again, the 1957 Captain of Athletics, R.L. Johns, suggesting that it was 'totally inadequate' at 2.75 miles, run over tarmac and through a dangerous built-up area, not to mention the problems of factories and petrol fumes from traffic. Mrs Graham, the Headmaster's wife, started the race, and the eventual winner from the 39 starters was A.T. Letchworth, who ran the revised 6.75 mile course in 38 minutes, 25 seconds.

Athletic Sports continued in Trinity, having been revived a few years previously. The highlight was probably J.R. Dickinson of Brook establishing a new School Record for the shot putt with a throw of 35ft 6ins. Other outstanding performances have included G.C.J. Ellis beating the 1906, 53 year record for the 100yds; E.G. Stephens' U17 100m in 11.6 seconds in 1960; and Henry Omenai's U20 200m and long jump performances in 1962. Sadly, further details of these achievements are not known.

### *Cricket*

Cricket was in better heart than other sports in 1918, largely owing to the efforts of an OD theological student and enthusiastic cricketer, Douglas Bodley, who had attended the School with his elder brother some seven years earlier. He visited the School when his studies allowed and, once ordained, joined the staff 1920-22 and 1925-40. In 1918, the XI won 4 matches, lost 2 and drew 1. The Second XI effectively played twice. Edward Ellam, who had become Second Master comparatively recently, was thanked for '...all the hours he spent looking after the grounds...' for he was continuing to act as a very effective but self-appointed superintendent groundsman, ensuring that the pitches were always in the best possible shape.

The School played Monkton Combe School for the first time in 1928 and won, but lost against King Edward's School, Birmingham and Cheltenham College 2nd XI. All other fixtures were against club sides or Oxford colleges. Understandably, the final tally was: played 12, won 4, lost 8; in addition, the School was beaten by the Old Decanians. Yet the School side contained an excellent captain and player in S.D. Rhodes, who later played for Nottinghamshire, and E.G. Righton, who later played for Worcestershire, like his OD father. E.S. Hoare, who played for the ODS that year, was also playing for Gloucestershire when time permitted.

In 1938, the XI played nine matches, although only three were against other schools. The Dean Close XI won 4, lost 4 and drew 1. A feature of the season was J.P. Crawford's 102 not out against Monkton Combe which he followed with a tally of 7 wickets for 45 runs after Dean Close had declared at 178 for 6. The 2nd XI were beginning to play more matches – they were now up to five, all against other schools – and a Colts XI played three matches, though they enjoyed no victories.

The School's return to Shelburne Road in time for cricket in Trinity 1940, when the Battle of Britain was at its height, allows glimpses of what conditions were like. *The Decanian* remarked that '...the weather was better for cricket than in any summer we remember but the use of water for the pitches was prohibited...Our field was rather rough after two terms' neglect and as a result our wickets

1939 cricket XI
Standing: D. Tugwell, E. Farmer, P. Turner, T. Backhouse
Seated: J. Hanson, R. Thomas, P. Dravers, N. Abraham, M. Struthers
On ground: R. Thompson, R. Baylis

Stanley Hoare, second from left,
coaching Colts cricket 1947

were 'sporting'...For our match wickets we relied on the [Hatherley] Brook, and by forming a chain of workers and using our fire buckets we lifted enough water on Wednesday and Thursday evenings to make the wicket roll out for Saturday's match. This was very hard work...The Eleven was young as the war had called away many of last season's team...'. And then again, later in the report '...Throughout the season, in spite of many difficulties, the field was always looking as good as ever it did. For this the devoted labours of two boys, W.St.C. Tisdall [Senior Prefect] and T.W. Backhouse [Prefect and XI member], were alone responsible...'. There was no other available ground staff. The season produced, understandably, mixed results, the XI winning 2 matches (one against Monkton Combe), losing 2 and drawing the match with the Old Decanians.

The 1948 XI depended too much on one batsman, P.J. Leech, who averaged 44. The best bowler, J.M. Oddy, averaged 7 per wicket. Yet they still managed to win 2, draw 4 and lose 5. They also had a new master-in-charge, M.A. Girling, who had played for Oxford, Berkshire, the Minor Counties and touring sides. The unfortunate 1949 XI lost nine matches and drew their last. Yet the 1950 cricket season included one of the most encouraging XIs for some years. It was not entirely due to the pitch, even though Denys Carnill thought it '...by far the finest playing surface in the county...'. Of the 12 matches played, Dean Close won 3, drew 7 and only lost 2, much of the credit for the improved form being given to Reg Santall, the former Warwickshire professional, recently arrived at the School as head groundsman and coach. When he died, the equally able Ben Flint from Trent Bridge took over. In one memorable match Moran, a left arm spin bowler, achieved 7 wickets for 11 runs against Monkton Combe School.

In the early 1950s, Tom and Selby Mudway were reckoned to be among the best wicket-keepers that the School had produced. M.G. Dash, captain in 1953, played cricket for Gloucestershire 2nd XI while still at School.

One of the best-ever School sides was said to be that of 1955 which included F.C. Welles as wicket-keeping captain, and notably W.J. Benton-Evans, J.H. Robinson, M.T. Robinson, R.I. Ireland, P.H. Knight, C.E.N. Blake and D.B. Grigg. They drew 6 matches, lost 3 and won 2, including defeating the Old Decanians by 10 wickets, the bald statistics not doing justice to the quality of the players, for example many of the draws would have looked different but for the intervention of the weather.

The 1957 season included such names as the legendary off-spinner P.H. Knight, the captain. A. Wilson, former Gloucestershire wicket-keeper who was at that point the professional coaching the School XI, rated Knight better than David Allen, the Gloucestershire and England bowler. Unfortunately, it was a very inexperienced XI that took the field in 1958 when it was not too wet to play. Of the matches they did play, they won 2, lost 5 and drew 2. The 2nd XI were also disappointing but the Colts were more hopeful, winning 2, drawing 2 and losing one.

1961's XI must be another contender for one of the best Dean Close XI sides ever. Captained by R.C. Padfield, it included R.D. Lane, M.K. Jones, R.J. Rose, T.L. Moore, J.C.B. Winter, D.B. Young and H.C.B. Shapland among others: they won 6 matches and drew 6. At the very end of the season, 'An' XI was beaten by the Barnacles. The top five School batsmen all averaged over 20 while the sixth, J.C.B. Winter, who averaged 17, was also top of the bowling averages.

Unusually two Decanians captained the 1st XI for two years each: R.C. Padfield in 1960 and 1961, and M. Bawden in 1964 and 1965.

In 1964, C.M. Kenyon, new to the staff and a former Minor Counties wicket-keeper, took over from M.A. Girling as master-in-charge, and continued for 33 years until 1997, a record.

One of the best XIs was that of 1966, unbeaten by any other school, playing 12, winning 3, losing 2 (to club sides) and drawing 4 while 3 were abandoned. Top batsman was M.J.O'H. Wigley who averaged 33 and the top bowler was S.A.H. Chapple with an average of 9.

The 1968 XI won 3 matches, with 6 drawn, 4 lost and 2 abandoned because of the poor weather almost all season. However, the 2nd XI faired rather better, winning 4 out of their 5 matches and drawing the fifth. Interestingly, their coach, T.N. Snow, observed that apart from the considerable contribution of their captain, S.V. Martin, one of the best aspects of the 2nd XI's game had been their 'smart' fielding – the best '…for some years…'. The School continued to use Willie Jones, formerly of Glamorgan, as the cricket professional.

Cricket in the 1960s, showing the old pavilion which was burned down in December 2006. Subsequent to this photograph it had a white picket fence at the front and the building was extended a little in the 1990s

***Football***

In Michaelmas 1917, the football team played a total of seven matches, winning two, losing four and drawing one.

In 1926, the XI, like all football teams, adjusted to the offside rule announced that year, bringing a rethink of tactics both in defence and attack. In 1927-28, the XI played 8 matches, winning 4 and losing 4, scoring 28 goals – and conceding 28! The 2nd XI only played 3 matches, winning 2 of them. J.S. Smith OD had just departed for Oxford, winning a Blue in both 1925 and 1927. Two earlier Blues were A.B. Wilson (Cambridge) in 1898 and H.S. Snell (also Cambridge) in 1900.

In 1938, Hugh Elder, who became Headmaster that April, was determined to replace football with rugby. Looking down the football XI match-card for 1937 would have strengthened his resolve, as the School was only playing club or collegiate sides. Nevertheless, the XI was said to have played 'splendidly' that term, probably due to the enthusiasm and determination of their captain, J.R.C. Sharp. He realized the importance of physical fitness and persuaded his team-mates to do 20 minutes or so physical training workout each morning after breakfast supervised by Sergeant-Major Golder. Thus Sharp's team were always able to play at full pressure throughout the 90 minutes. Their tally for the season was won 4, drew 1, lost 5, scoring 31 goals and conceding 26. The 2nd XI only had one set of opponents, Rendcomb College, whom they played twice.

The last football season was Michaelmas 1938. The XI played '…a very creditable…' final season, playing nine teams, none of them schools, winning 4, losing 4 and drawing 1 while the 2nd XI played a couple of matches with Rendcomb College, both of which they lost.

Thus football ceased to be a main sport. Since 1995 it has re-emerged as an activity.

***Gymnastics***

More than ten years after the School's first major sporting triumph in the national Public Schools Gymnastics Championship (see chapter 3), gymnastics was still very popular. The indoor swimming pool was covered by boards, turning it into a gym, on the site now occupied by the Residents' Common Room in the Edwards Building. One of the triumphant brothers, by now Dr W. Guy Lidderdale, judged the League Gymnastics competition in the Lent Term 1918 but the report in *The Decanian* noted: '…The calls of military duty seriously affected the numbers in the Gymnasium…'.

However, gymnastics was still keenly contested within the School. 1939 was the 25th consecutive gymnastics competition in which Instructor C. Smith had helped the gymnasts. He was presented with an engraved silver cup by the Headmaster.

Gymnastics post-war seems to have revived well by 1948 but sadly that year Dr W. Guy Lidderdale died, who with his brother, Dr Frank Lidderdale, had won the gymnastic shield for the School at the national public schools competition at Aldershot in 1906. The latter continued to come and judge the inter-house competition for over 50 years after that triumph. Instructor Smith finally retired in 1951, having begun as a PE Instructor at Dean Close in 1913 and, except for a short absence during the First World War, had stayed at the School ever since.

Brook tended to do rather well in the inter-house competition, not least because each boy in the house was rewarded with half-a-crown by the housemaster when an 'upstart', now called a 'chin-up', was achieved by a boy for the first time.

### *Hockey*

There is no record of external hockey matches in the Lent Term 1918. Much more interest was given to the 'club' 'League' matches, later called house matches.

In the early 1920s there was no coaching as such. Junior pupils learnt by watching seniors when possible and then copied them. Nevertheless, a Dean Close style did develop. It was centred round long, strategic, accurate passes from the backs, switching sides as required, moving the ball to the centre-half who would then distribute to the forwards as appropriate. The second main tactic was to deny ball to the opposition as much as possible. As the 1920s progressed, so coaching began to emerge. Two excellent coaches, C.A.P. Tuckwell and E.S. Hoare, made major contributions in other spheres of School life but in hockey their impact was very considerable. They coached the top game together for almost

**Ernest Stanley Hoare, OD, staff member 1926-68**

Stanley and Joan Hoare on their wedding day in 1958

Born in 1903, the youngest of four brothers, he entered the School in January 1914 with his two middle brothers. He was better known as 'Hoare Four' or 'Monkey'. He left the School in 1922 as Senior Prefect, captain of gymnastics (for four years), of cricket and hockey each for three years, and of football for two. He also swam for the School.

He read Mathematics and Geography at Queen's College, Cambridge. Playing at centre-half, he won Blues for hockey (1924-26) and played for England (1926-37), winning 35 caps. He captained Cambridge University and England and was the School's first international hockey player. In 1956 when Denys Carnill captained the Great Britain Olympic hockey team in Melbourne, Stanley was the coach and manager. He also occasionally played cricket for Gloucestershire under the great Wally Hammond's captaincy.

He returned to the School in 1926 as an assistant master. Together with Denys Carnill and C.A.P. Tuckwell among others, Stanley helped to raise the standard of games generally, and hockey especially, to new heights.

He was officer-in-charge of the CCF 1940-1946, Housemaster of Brook 1936-59 and Second Master 1959-68. He was modest, deeply devoted to the School, a man of integrity and faith. He is said to have attended over 60 consecutive Speech Days. His work for the Old Decanian Society was prodigious: Honorary Secretary 1927-57, Honorary Treasurer 1927-63, School Secretary 1957-68 and President 1965-66. He was the founding editor of (Old) Decanian News. He married Joan Edwards, sister of W.A.M. Edwards OD in 1958, retiring to grow roses in 1968.

Joan died in 1984 and Stanley died ten years later. The rose garden overlooking the artificial hockey pitches at the School is a memorial garden named after him. The sundial in the centre of it bears this inscription:

In sight of Hockey and roses,<br>
Remember Stanley Hoare,<br>
Brook was his love,<br>
Dean Close his life<br>
1903-94.

20 years. Tuckwell had been educated at Marlborough – a leading hockey school – and at St John's, Oxford, and may have been unlucky not to have won a hockey Blue. As it was, he played for the West of England and was a noted player and umpire. Stanley Hoare OD had been in the School 1st XI for four seasons and captained for three, won a Blue for three years at centre-half and captained both Cambridge University and later England (1928-1937) from that position although perfectly capable of playing elsewhere. Alan Milton OD, himself a hockey international for Wales, who had often played against Stanley Hoare, said of him that he was 'devastating' to play against because he was so 'absolutely solid'. In matches, he usually accurately anticipated what would happen next, if it was an opposition move, and moved to counter it before the opposition could react. His ability to stop and accurately pass a ball was legendary – not always easy on grass pitches however good and using the old English head, as opposed to the more modern Indian stick.

In the 1928 season, the XI won six of its eight matches, scoring 28 goals and conceding 20. The 2nd XI only played twice, winning one and losing the other. It was a vintage year for Old Decanians, for at the Varsity match, there were very nearly two Decanians on either side: F.W. Carpenter and T.N. Lamb represented Cambridge; A.J. Carpenter represented Oxford and should have been joined by G.H. Aldis. Unfortunately, the latter contracted measles and was unable to play.

The annual hockey tour started in 1925. Just after Michaelmas 1937 that year's tour took place with matches at Cheltenham, Marlborough and at Havant and Worthing. The team consisted of eight boys as well as staff members, Messrs Ellam, Tuckwell, Hoare and Phair. The quality of hockey had been rising, and in the early 1930s, B.R. Newman of Marlborough College, at that time by common consent one of the best hockey schools, wrote to Dean Close School asking for a fixture. It was played at Dean Close on 18th March 1933, Marlborough eventually winning 10-4. The next year Dean Close won, 2-1, at Marlborough.

In the Lent Term 1938, similar to the situation ten years before, the hockey XI played eight matches – and just as before a large number of the opponents were again club or college sides. Again, the tally looked less good: won 2, lost 2 and drew 4. It was a good season from the weather point of view, except for two days, on one of which '...we were cheered by the sight of a pilot drifting over Big Field on the end of a parachute, while his plane crashed in the High Street...'.

Unsurprisingly, because of the major disruption, the 1940 hockey season was described as being '...dismal...'. Uniquely, Dean Close School played – and beat – a Bath Hockey Club side on a pitch at Dean Close School which they were allowed to come back to use. However, because the School was at the time based at Monkton Combe, the match was recorded as being 'away'! Most of the other matches did not have quite such happy results and the XI ended the season with 3 won, 4 lost and 1 drawn.

Hockey in progress in late 1940s. Behind is the old stable building, repaired after wartime bomb damage

In 1941, the only victory was against what was '...a very scratch side...' from RAF Aston Down, and then only by three goals to two. The other eight matches were lost, although most of them were against club or university sides rather than school teams. These were possibly the worst results in a School hockey season ever. The XI scored a total of 13 goals while their opponents scored 42. Lack of reports on other sports at this time suggests that preoccupation with the war and survival meant that such activity was minimal.

By 1948, the hockey tour, that included ODs and one or two staff in the team, was flourishing again, war-time petrol rationing having recently been abolished. It began with a home match against a scratch Cheltenham Town side which the School won 3-0. Next day, the team played the occasional Wiltshire team, the Moonrakers, at Marlborough, who beat the visitors 4-1. A coach journey to Southsea for a traditional match against the United Services, Portsmouth, ended in a School defeat by seven goals. However, the other traditional match (against Havant Hockey Club) ended in victory for the tourists by 2-1. The whole thing was enlivened by some boys and ODs being at each match and cheering their side on. However, the hockey season itself showed only a mild improvement on the situation in 1941, although there were more matches scheduled, and a 2nd XI had four matches, as did a Colts XI but neither of these teams secured more than a single victory. 1950 was the 25th anniversary of the tour. Although the touring side sustained defeat consistently, Havant Hockey Club presented the XI with the hockey ball from their match with Dean Close beautifully mounted with a silver engraving marking the 25 year association.

In 1951, Denys Carnill joined the staff. After service in the RAF 1944-48, he read History at Worcester College, Oxford before coming to Dean Close School. He was captain of Oxford University, of England (45 caps) and of Great Britain (27 caps). He captained the Great Britain Olympic sides at Helsinki (1952, bronze medallists), Melbourne (1956 when E.S. Hoare was team manager) and Rome (1960). He had also played cricket for Hertfordshire.

Denys Carnill is seen off to the Melbourne Olympics in 1956 by Douglas Graham.
Looking on are Ralph Baldwin (exchange teacher from Melbourne),
the Revd Canon E.N. Spear (School Governor), C.A.P. Tuckwell, and Mike Girling

In 1957, hockey was '...never better...' with the outstanding captain, R.I. Ireland, later captain of Cambridge University, Wiltshire and England; W.J. Benton-Evans who played for Wales, while F.C. Welles played for the RAF and Scotland (and rugby for English Schoolboys) before being tragically killed in a flying accident.

By 1958 the number of boys at the School was increasing. Poor weather that Lent Term meant hockey had to be abandoned too often as pitches were in poor shape. Thus, when the different Dean Close sides did play matches, all too often they were outclassed by better practised teams. Nevertheless, efforts were made: Denys Carnill recalls that in the snow in the 1950s there were hockey training practices in which all 30 members of Game 1 would be involved, the goals at either end being some 200 yards apart, two balls in use and '...energy and injury expended and incurred...'. The weather was so poor in 1958 that among the five Dean Close sides there were only a total of 17 matches played, of which Dean Close were the victors on just five occasions.

At the end of the 1950s, C.A.P. Tuckwell and E.S. Hoare completed their 'stint' as inspirational hockey coaches. They had also initiated the construction of a small hockey 'quad' behind the changing rooms. A low wall and wire netting were put around, ice hockey goals stuck at each end, and throughout the week anyone could pick up a stick and practice or play a game. Denys Carnill commented '...in the opinion of many it was the practice gained on this quad, so near the changing rooms, so easy just to pick up a stick and knock a ball about for ten minutes, which did more than anything to maintain hockey excellence...'. It was in 1960 that the decision was taken that the old English hockey stick head should be abandoned quietly and the Indian style adopted. The Headmaster, the Revd Douglas Graham, underlined this in December 1960 when he requested that all new sticks should have the 'Indian' club.

The hockey world still thought a great deal of Edward Ellam's pitches because even in March 1961 they were continuing to be used for England trials. Yet things were moving on: also in 1961 a hard Redgra pitch was built, the first in any public school in the country, based on one that Denys Carnill had seen at the Central Council for Physical Research training centre at Lilleshall. It proved hugely helpful to the School. A Hockey Association XI that included six internationals played the School in the official opening match and were defeated 3-2. It was dug-up and resurfaced in 1984 after 23 years of hard wear and tear. Called Carnill's, it acknowledges Denys Carnill's huge contribution to the game at Dean Close School. However, there could still be problems, as in 1963 when there was more than a foot of snow on the ground and no games were thought possible. It was the Headmaster who decided that a different approach was necessary. He ordered that hardboard sledges, 5' x 3' with string handles, should be constructed, and that two dozen shovels be purchased. Boys, on a rota system, cleared the ground. As Denys Carnill later put it, '...Arctic hockey continued with the School timetable being turned on its head, hockey being played in the late morning while the pitch was bone hard and lessons taking place in the afternoon when the thaw came...'.

In the 1960s, Old Decanians were again being picked for high quality teams. In 1961 Richard Padfield (Captain) and others played for West Schoolboys Hockey XI. In 1965, *The Decanian* congratulated Ian Ireland on being selected to captain England; he played for Great Britain and England 1962-66. Also mentioned were: E.J. Sainsbury, goalkeeper for the West and an England trialist; D.N.A. Carpenter, Benton-Evans and Horton playing for Gloucestershire; Hodgetts and Reed for Kent; J.H. Lutley for Staffordshire; J.R.C. Watts for the Army; Richard Padfield for Oxford

University; Nelson and Benton-Evans in the Welsh trial; Bawden, Sharp, P.J. Harding and Horne playing in divisional schoolboy hockey – all in one season.

School hockey in 1968 included some key individuals such as Peter Mercer-Wilson (1st XI captain) who represented Wales at Schoolboy International level. There was also Peter Badger who reached the England Schoolboy Trials that year, while David Fitton, Peter King, William Bradstock and Simon Lansdown (who was captain of the 2nd XI) all played for their counties.

The hockey XIs in 1955, 1957 and 1961 were unbeaten by any school side, including beating Marlborough 3-0 in the 25th anniversary match in 1957. Denys Carnill handed over to Trevor Snow, an Oxford Blue and Welsh international, in 1966.

In 1960, the School and Cheltenham College sent a combined team to a hockey festival in the Hague. This was the beginning of regular tours abroad, especially to Holland.

One interesting fact that Denys Carnill has unearthed was that there was continuous Dean Close representation 1957-74 at the Cambridge v Oxford Universities match, except for one year. It is a measure of the number and quality of the players that the School produced between 1918 and 1968 that all four home countries have been represented by Old Decanians, and that in attempting to produce his 'ideal' paper XI, Denys Carnill effectively gave up the exercise when he found it a virtually impossible task.

***Rugby***

Hugh Elder, the incoming Headmaster in 1938, introduced rugby in Michaelmas 1938. *The Decanian* editorial that December remarked that '…an embryo 1st XV has forced all who cast aspersions on its abilities to eat their words, and a team of Colts has recently carried off its first victory…'. The principal coach in this new game to Dean Close was J.S. Moore, a biology teacher, fresh from teaching at King's School, Taunton, who was to spend nearly 40 years, when not involved in war service, at the School.

That first season, J.S. Moore noted an understandable tendency to kick and dribble the ball and '…a marked disinclination…' to handle it! However, he felt that the School had adapted '…extraordinarily well…' to the change of code and the 'friendly' matches played principally against Cheltenham College in order to gain match experience were valuable and enjoyable. Fixtures for the first 'real' season in Michaelmas 1939 had already been arranged with Cheltenham College, Bromsgrove, King's Worcester and Monkton Combe.

Michaelmas 1939 opened with the School, somewhat reduced in numbers, in exile in Monkton Combe, playing rugby which they were still learning. A number of trial matches (two against their hosts, three against King Edward's, Bath, together with a match against a Clifton College 3rd XV) gave valuable match experience and some hard lessons to the fledgling side. There were 6 'matches' in which the School won 2 and lost 4.

The first 'proper' rugby season with the XV at home was Michaelmas 1940. They beat their erstwhile hosts and, in part, mentors, the Monkton Combe XV, by 9 points to 6. Dean Close School won 5 matches and lost 3. The 2nd XV was still comparatively weak, small and inexperienced, as initially it had to draw on Colts age players to make up numbers. An anonymous commentator – almost certainly J.S. Moore – in *The Decanian* was clear what sides and individuals had to do to improve: passing had to be far more deliberate, accurate and better thought through; there were '…too many irresolutes…' when it came to tackling and that was '…as inexcusable as slack fielding by a cricket XI…'. There was also room for significant improvement in kicking, be it punting, dribbling, drop kicking or place kicking. All rugby took place on Flecker's Piece. In the opinion of the commentator,

'...the turf of Flecker's stands the wear and tear of rugby better than the Cricket Field [Big Field]...(so) during this season it was left under sheep...'. One wonders whose sheep they were – presumably from Benhall Farm.

In 1948, the XV won 3 matches, drew 2 and lost 6. The 2nd XV won 1 and lost 4 while the Junior Colts by contrast won 4 and lost 1. In J.S. Moore's report, one is aware of changes. The Junior Colts did well, and the captain of the XV, J.M.A. Parker, contributed considerably in changing attitudes to ones that were positive and determined. It was noted that success had been achieved in '...finally erasing the spirit of defeatism which had permeated into some previous teams...'. This was evident during Michaelmas 1950, when the XV won 7, drew 1 and lost only 1 game, a huge improvement – the best season to date. It was felt significant that every member of the pack scored during that season and J. Stanley-Smith's captaincy was marked by '...great dash and personal inspiration...'. Several players gained selected representative honours: J. Stanley-Smith played for Hereford and Worcestershire and was invited to play in the Western Division trial. M.P.L. Wright was selected to play for Dorset and Wiltshire. R.K. Flower played for Cornwall while I.F.C.S. Clayre was a reserve for Hampshire – and eventually claimed the School's only rowing Blue in 1957. In 1955, as in 1950, there was an excellent season under the captaincy of Jeremy Seavers when again only one match was lost, seven won and another drawn. It was arguably the 1970s before a XV improved upon those results.

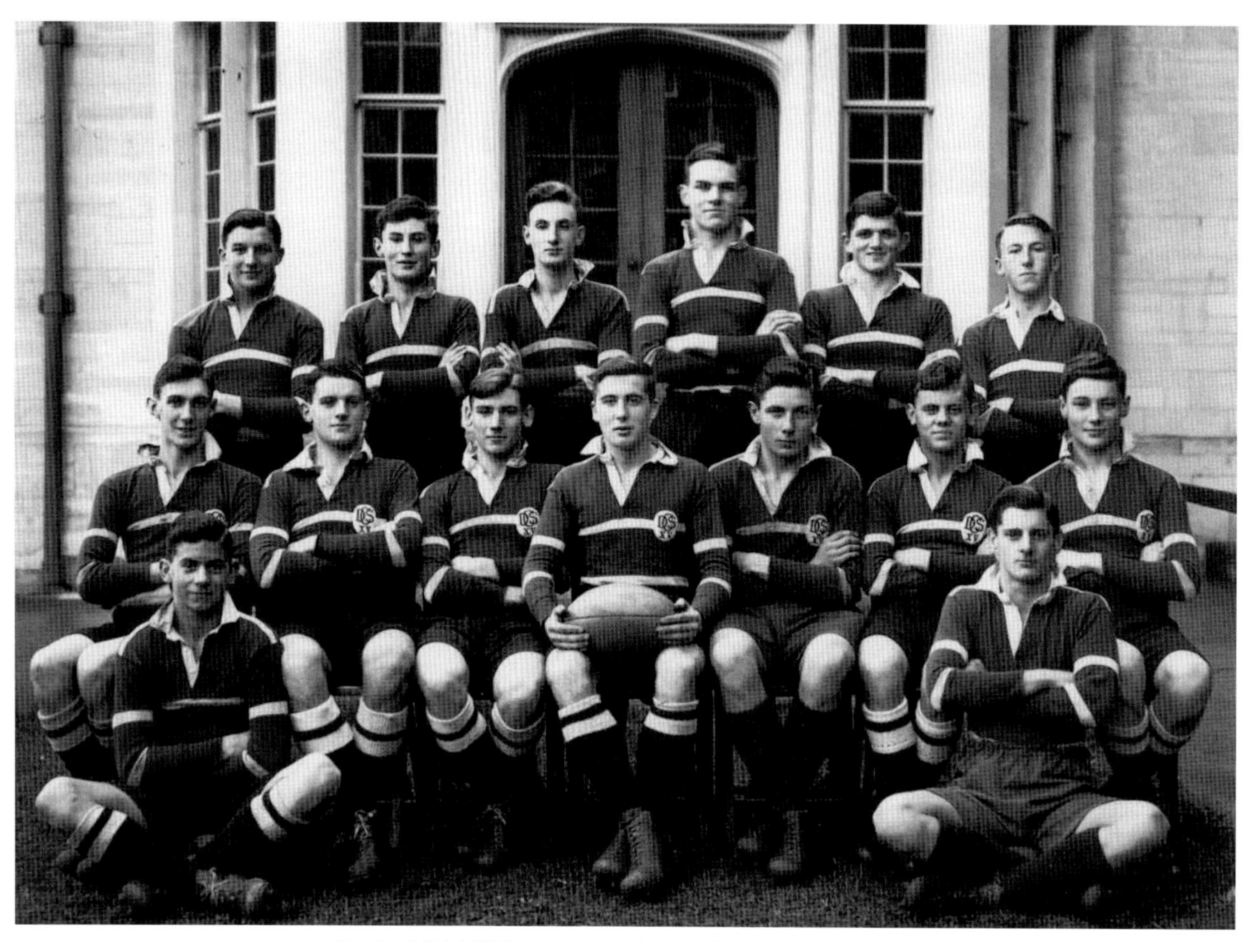

Rugby XV 1939, photographed at Monkton Combe

Rugby v Cheltenham Grammar School 1952

In the late 1950s, J.S. Moore, initially responsible for building rugby at the School, passed the 1st XV over to Brian Wilson, who had played for Trinity College, Dublin before joining the School staff. For J.S. Moore, Chris Welles (1955) was the finest player during his time and John M.A. Parker the best captain (1948). Unfortunately, both died in air accidents, in 1964 and 1983 respectively.

100 yards finish 1935

In the half-term break in Michaelmas 1961, Brian Wilson, assisted by Rhod Pentycross, took the XV on a brief tour of Dublin, Ireland, to play Belvedere College (which the School beat) and Terenure College (who beat the School). Even so, the XV was one of the best since the mid-fifties. Although the 1st XV looked good in 1967, injury and absence of four key players (D.J.M. Fitton, an excellent centre; R.H. Kinzett, a fine No 8; R. Major, described by Brian Wilson as '…the best schoolboy blind side wing forward I've seen…'; and Routledge, another good No 8) were big blows to sustain and even the considerable expertise of the rugby coaches was not able to resolve the situation satisfactorily. A total of 24 players appeared for the XV at one time or another during that season. By now there was not only a regular 2nd XV but also an U16 Colts side and U15 Junior Colts.

### *Swimming*

Water Polo continued to be popular in the (old) Swimming Bath in 1918, but '…owing to the large amount of time required by the Corps, it was found impossible to arrange as many games as in 1917…'. The League still dominated swimming and the Swimming Sports was keenly contested.

Swimming was popular but confined to competitions within the School, yet it would have been possible to mount teams of a respectable standard. L.W. McEwen, who left the School in 1920 went on to be Diving Champion of Wales five times.

In 1938 aquatic sports were quite popular, including diving, and a number of boys had begun to take Life Saving courses, including the Bronze Medal. 15 boys won various awards. However, there was no mention of water polo. In 1939, in addition to the usual Swimming Sports, School swimmers were invited to compete against the Worcester Royal College for the Blind where a former much admired Dean Close housemaster, B.O. Bradnack, was headmaster.

Partiality for aquatic sports gradually waned, although Life Saving classes and examinations continued as did Swimming Sports, held on the last Friday and Saturday of the Trinity Term. In the 1950s, enthusiasm returned.

The 1955 Captain of Swimming, J.M. Latham, resurrected inter-school swimming matches. In 1958, the swimming team beat Kingham Hill School and Bloxham but lost against Wycliffe College. In 1963, under captain I.D. Hutchinson, the School won all its matches.

The new swimming pool of 1964 was 25m by 36ft, with diving boards of up to 3m and a diving pit of 11ft 6ins; Denis Carnill wrote that '…there seem to have been no problems from this extraordinary mixture of metric and non-metric...'. In 1968 Philip Davies broke every School record except breast-stroke, helping the School to beat everyone including Millfield, and won a place in the Welsh team. He was thought to be the best swimmer the School had ever produced.

Swimming had grown in popularity by 1967. There were about 60 people competing for the 20 team places required for matches. Opposition now included Gloucester Swimming Club, Duffryn High School (Newport), Rugby and Stowe in addition to those already undertaken. With a total of 12 matches in a year, swimming had never had such a high profile, especially when the team only lost one match (and that only by one point) to Millfield School, which in 1967 was the fifth best swimming school in the country. The School had aspirations to be in the top ten swimming schools. Clearly, standards in the Dean Close team were rising. Inter-house swimming, too, was being up-graded, as an individual swimmer had emerged as Champion from all the events up until 1967, whereas the policy now was that each event was to be a championship in its own right.

In 1968, the swimming team captain, S.N. O'Neill, claimed the best-ever season in the School's history. The team beat all ten school teams that they competed against, including Millfield, and only lost to St Paul's Training College and the Gloucester Swimming Club.

### *Other Sports*

*Badminton*

Badminton came into its own with the new gym in 1964 and has been popular at times, although the beating of Rugby School in the first ever inter-school match in 1965 may not be repeated!

*Basketball*

Basketball also began in 1964 in the new gym. In 1965 there were house matches with inter-school matches beginning the following year.

By 1968 there were four matches (against St Paul's Training College, Kingham Hill, Marlborough and Cheltenham College) all of which the Dean Close team won, amassing 201 points and conceding only 75. Further opposition was becoming hard to find. The potential was promising as there was a strong U16 squad. The sport had already been recognized by the School for Colours purposes: P.G. Badger, K.E. Eames and K.P. Tarsnane were awarded colours in 1968, under the captaincy of W.F. Dwerryhouse.

*Boxing*

Boxing, in 1949, was sufficiently popular that one or two bouts at the end of the gymnastics competition had been justified. Instructor Smith was in charge with Mr Kiddell assisting from time to time.

There were a few matches against other schools, the last planned in 1955 but didn't occur. Boxing ceased during 1956-57 at the behest of the Headmaster, Douglas Graham, himself no mean pugilist.

*Fives (Dean Close code)*

The two fives courts that were roughly where the Beaumont Block is today were in demand. '…They could not be said to conform to the regulations of any known type of game, either Rugby or Eton…the Second World War prevented the making of any more fives balls…', according to R.F. McNeile. In 1918 a sequence of League games was re-introduced for the sport.

Walton Court often won the house matches in the 1930s but the only encounter that could be classed as a School match was against a staff VI in 1938, which the latter won.

*Golf*

After the Second World War it became possible for boys to play golf on local courses, and the game was gradually taken up. It was an 'occasional' sport but by the 1960s Brian Wilson was taking a few enthusiasts out. In 1967, the School raised a team that played Monmouth School on the St Pierre course at Chepstow, subsequently repeated.

*Sailing*

A Sailing Club opened in March 1960 as the result of a 'Cadet' boat being presented by the Midland Branch of ODs. Anchorages were found on the River Avon at Twyning near Tewkesbury as other boats had been promised. The Chaplain, the Revd Dick Page, lent his Heron and trailer before selling them to the Club subsequently. Numbers were at about 20 and rising, and trips over to Twyning Park occurred about three times a week. By 1962, inter-house and inter-school matches had begun.

That the Sailing Club prospered for over 20 years was in large part due to the enthusiasm of M.J.R. Cooper, Head of Chemistry at Dean Close School 1959-85. In early 1968, a 'graduate' class boat, donated by an Old Decanian, had been named *Tilly* and launched by Mrs Turner, the Headmaster's wife. By now, the Sailing Club was enjoying a full programme of up to 14 matches a year. Mike Cooper maintained that the first insurance claim for the Sailing Club was a boat cover, eaten by cows! A number of boys including Peter Pitt-Jones, Michael Robins and Denys Wells took advantage of by now six 'Graduate' boats and improved their sailing sufficiently that matches were won.

The 1968 summer sailing season went well, the team winning against every other school team and most clubs in their nine matches. They were only defeated by Tewkesbury Cruising and Sailing Club. The helmsmen at this time were G. Watt, P. Ellames, M. Hawkesworth and J. Cutts.

*Shooting*

Shooting was to be found on the miniature range built, some say, in 1910 but more probably in 1913. It was sited in an area beyond the then metal workshop that is now roughly underneath the bridge separating the Bacon Theatre from the Music School. By modern standards it was dimly lit, cold and sand-bagged but there were, and have continued to be, many .22 enthusiasts.

In 1948 the School VIII won all four matches. In 1958, L.H. Benians, the new master-in-charge, coached the boys. Standards improved and of eleven matches, the School VIII won six. In 1952 the School entered the Ashburton competition; in 1960 the team came ninth; in 1963 captained by Malcolm Baker, the School finished =2nd with Marlborough College behind All Hallows. The Spencer Mellish Trophy was won for the School for the first time by Michael Bowles in 1954 who beat 88 others and again in 1963 by David Langford, who the following year was selected by the British Cadets' Rifle Team.

*Tennis*

In the early 1950s '...highly selected...' boys were invited to play tennis and stay for tea on Sunday afternoons by Miss Kay Udell, Housemistress of Hatherley Court, Cheltenham Ladies' College. Courts at the School were few until 1950 when 'The Tip' (opposite the main entrance) was levelled and six grass courts, later hard courts, were created as part of a memorial to Edward Ellam. As early as 1954, boys were able to opt for tennis rather than cricket.

House matches began in 1955. Other hard courts were made available from 1961 on Hard Ground (later called Carnill's) so tennis became a recognized alternative to cricket. In 1958, tennis matches began with other schools. In this first year, the School won against Cheltenham Grammar School and Cheltenham College but lost to Wycliffe College. G.C.J. Ellis, Hamlett, Spurling, Walters, S.P.J. Ellis and D.M. Jenkins made up the pairs.

Derek Barker was the member of staff who particularly supported the game in its early years.

1968 was the last year in which boys' games were the only sports available at the School. In the next chapter sport in more recent years is looked at in the context of a school that had now embarked on co-education.

# Chapter 11

# Sport at Dean Close School since 1968

***Athletics***

In 1973, A.F. Sawyer's arrival brought renewed interest in athletics, then held on Barn Field.

Many track and field records were broken in 1977. Paul Calderbank competed at county level at 1500m, winning in a School record time of 4:26.1. M. Duffield (400m) and D. Bowen (800m) did the same in 1978. By 1978, only the 100m intermediate record set in 1960 by E.G. Stephens was intact.

In 1982, Alexander Kemp was one of the first Decanians to reach a national qualifying standard when, as a junior, he broke the U17 1500m record. Margaret Joyce was the first Dean Close School girl to compete at regional level at both 1500m and long jump, inspiring other girls to take up athletics in the early 1980s. Pittville's Prince of Wales Stadium's better facilities helped the sport considerably following the move there in the mid-1980s; nine School records were broken in 1984. Between 1980 and 1990 the results of inter-school matches were varied. 1984 was promising when the intermediate boys only lost to two schools out of nearly 20 against which they competed.

In 1991, outstanding Junior, Christopher Field, achieved two national qualifying standards in the javelin and 400m. The following year Daniel Honneyman came 4th, 10th and 4th respectively in the National Schools' javelin, hurdles and octathlon. The U16 boys' team put themselves in the top ten in the country in 1992 at the TSB Championships in Portsmouth. Matthew Butler finished 9th in the National Finals of the senior triple jump while David Wilkins finally broke Richard Padfield's 1960 senior high jump record of 1.62m with a leap of 1.9m at the South West Championships. Angela Blackwell, representing Gloucestershire, participated in the South West Championships both in 1992 and 1993, gaining a School record latterly with a national qualifying standard throw in the javelin of 37.34m. Vicky Youde ran for the county at 200m between 1992 and 1995.

In 1996, Anthony Pinches, representing Gloucestershire, achieved a School record with a national qualifying standard discus throw of 42m, while sprinter Rebecca Hewlett competed in finals of the English Schools Championships in the 4x100m relay team. She and Laura Bellwood both qualified for the English Schools Championships in 1998.

1997 was the first occasion Fourth Form boys won Cheltenham and District Championships. Intermediate Patrick Crowley reached the finals of the English Schools Championships 100m hurdles, competing at the same championships in the 110m hurdles in both 1998 and 1999. Intermediate Matthew Thomas's School record of 51.9 seconds for the 400m also sent him to the English Schools Championships in 1999.

In 2000, Laura Masterman (U19 long jump) and Laura Bellwood (U17 javelin) were county champions, while county runner Ben Dowty broke the School Intermediate 800m record.

The boys produced six county athletes in 2001: the girls seven. The girls' intermediate team was 3rd in the South of England Championships. Jo Safe (100m and 400m hurdler) represented the South West at the English Schools Championships and also qualified in the heptathlon. Laura Bellwood reached the English Schools Championships in the javelin.

In 2002, Ben Dowty, Dan Lane and Ben Tully were all county champions. Meanwhile, Jo Safe achieved county titles in the 400m and 100m hurdles.

The U17 team in 2003 enjoyed beating teams from Eton, Radley and Wellington at Radley. Nathan Thickett-Menghini became 400m county champion. Richard Hildick-Smith took three seconds off the 800m School record. Two years later, he broke the senior 800m and 1500m records set by Martyn Bowen in 1983. In 2005 Andrew Scrase became South West champion in the Junior 100m and long jump and qualified for the English Schools Championship Finals.

During 2007 Anna Glover succeeded in breaking the 100m record on two occasions, reducing the time to 12.8 seconds, while Dan Akenhead was the county senior long jump champion and Oliver Flannagan county senior high jump champion.

In 2008, the girls set up a new record time of 3:10.32 for the combination relay, which consists of 1 x 400m, 2 x 200m and 4 x 100m.

Richard Akenhead coached the boys and Sue Padfield the girls from the late 1970s until beyond the turn of the century, when present coaches (Ian Dunbar, John Alder and Rhona Donaldson) took over.

### *Cricket*

The constant in School cricket from 1964 to 1997 was the relaxed, enthusiastic master-in-charge, Chris Kenyon. With cricket professionals such as 'Willie' Jones, formerly of Glamorgan, Malcolm Heath, formerly with Hampshire, and Steve Hansford, Chris presided over cricket development including the introduction of overseas tours. Since his retirement, cricket has been in the successive care of Chris Townsend, Ben Barton and Ben Price. Internationally-respected New Zealand coach David Trist has enthused the cricket teams since 2002.

Some XIs achieved consistently good results, such as the 1976 side, captained by T.J. Lawrence, that won 8 matches, drew 6 and lost only 4. Highlights included P.M. Gilliam's 101 against Sir Thomas Rich's and A.J. Yearwood's 88 against Stowe while also taking 8 for 33 with his off-spin bowling against the XL Club. The 1978 XI benefitted from a remarkable all-rounder, Will Thomas, who scored 83 in 80 minutes on a wet wicket in poor light against Cheltenham Grammar School, returned 4 for 21 against the Free Foresters, and 4 for 26 against Dauntsey's as a seam bowler; he later played

for Worcestershire professionally. 1983 produced a good XI, although poor weather brought cancellations; it won 6 matches, drew 1 and lost 2, the most attractive victory being over Malvern, helped by bowling figures of 4 for 21 from Robert Lindsey and 5 for 25 from Paul Vincent as well as some good innings. The next year, Paul Vincent was captain. Now an impressive all-rounder, he scored 108 against Dauntsey's as well as another century against the XL Club on the one hand and achieved 4 for 15 against Free Foresters and 4 for 17 against the Old Decanians as a bowler, in a season that included victory against Stowe.

Anthony Thompson after setting the post war record score of 155 in 1996

The 2000 side won 6 matches, drew 3 and lost 3, captained by George Walker who took 3 for 19 against King's Gloucester while Alex Fateh hit 124. Chris Townsend, an outstanding cricketer who won the School's first Blue for cricket at Oxford before returning as master-in-charge of cricket, commented that the 2001 side was '...probably the most talented that Dean Close (had) seen for years...'. They played 17 matches, winning 10, losing 4 and drawing 3. The 2002 XI was often good, captained by Thomas Judge; Alex Fateh who scored over 800 runs during the season, including a record four centuries, 152 against Hereford Cathedral School being the highest. It was just short of the record 155 not out, set by Anthony Thompson in a match against King's Worcester in 1995. Alex Fateh's fourth century in 2002 and Alex Hume's first (103) combined in an opening stand of 250 against King's Gloucester – a record. Alex Fateh was selected for an England trial.

A highlight of 1984 was beating Stowe for the first time, bowling them out for 82, as the XI had been heavily defeated in 1981when Stowe's pair had scored 214, possibly a record. On another occa-

1st XI cricket with a thunderstorm looming

sion the School only managed 44 all out against Bloxham in 1992, the only season when the XI was beaten by ten wickets in a match – against Bromsgrove. However, that School side still managed to win 2 matches and draw 7. Perhaps the quickest unbeaten Decanian century was by Thomas Judge in 2000 against the Common Room, achieved in 78 balls that included 4 sixes and 12 fours. The 1989 XI included Simon Organ (Captain) and Jasper Bowditch who both took 5 for 16 in the same match against Bromsgrove.

Pommie Mbangwa

The first overseas tour, in 1991, was preceded by an inspirational visit to the School by West Indies 'great' Sir Gary Sobers. The XI went to Barbados, where pitches were often raised strips of mud, mown grass and sugar cane husks rolled into a hard compact mass: outfields were hard and often full of potholes. Of the six matches played under Chris Townsend's captaincy, the School won 3, drew 1 and lost 2. 1994 included a touring party to Zimbabwe. During their seven matches they lost to Peterhouse, one of Zimbabwe's best schools, whose headmaster was Mike Bawden OD. As a result of the tour, 'Pom' Mbangwa joined the School for two terms and played for the XI on a sports scholarship in 1995. He subsequently played Test cricket for Zimbabwe. The XI went to Kenya in 2000, where they won 3 and lost 5 matches, and to Uganda in 2005 where they won 3 matches and lost 3. The 2006 XI included Jonty Strachan, a talented bowler who went on to win a Blue at Oxford in 2008.

Other XIs of note have been the U15 XI of 1975, who were undefeated in 11 matches. The 1996 U15 XI did likewise under captain Paul Marchand, who that season scored 111 against Sir Thomas Rich's, probably the highest score yet at that level, complemented by left arm spin bowler Oliver Bretherton's 8 for 48 against the same side. In 2000, the 2nd XI only lost two of their matches. Nick

Chris Townsend, Chris Kenyon, and Mike Girling who between them ran 1st XI cricket for over 50 years

Cricket 1st XI 2004: Alex Carlisle and Les Gaylard, who both scored centuries in an unbroken stand of 240

Ball's 207 not out for the 2nd XI against King's Gloucester in 2003 is said to be the highest score ever by a School batsman in a match.

As yet, the only distaff contribution was in 1998 when a junior girls' XI beat Pate's Grammar School by 20 runs in '…a lovely game…' on Chapel Close.

***Cross Country Running***

The sport has had varied fortune since 1968. In 1969, all six boys in the team were either in the county team or reserves. Two, R.W. Holborow and Chris Jones, ran in the National Finals at Leicester. Teacher Trevor Park encouraged runners to 'pack' closely. This paid off in 1970-71 when Marlborough was beaten for the first time in seven years, as well as other schools.

The early 1980s were dominated by Margaret Joyce. In 1982 she competed at national level in Sheffield. In 1983 she won the county championship and other major races; came 2nd in the South West championship; 3rd in the Midland championship, and 15th out of 345 in the girls' English Schools championship in London – just missing selection for England. In 1984 she was 11th in the U19 girls' English Schools championship.

Meanwhile, in the inter-house cross country races in 1982, girls ran for the first time, Mead House winning, while the talented junior Court team with 1st, 2nd, 3rd, 4th and 7th positions achieved a record unlikely to be surpassed.

In 1985, a boys' VI under captain John Collins beat Bromsgrove and Kingham House.

In 1992, a staff and Decanians team finished second in the 'Crack Cancer' Relay Marathon in 2 hours 37 minutes.

In 1995, James Petrie and Alastair Judge ran in the National Finals. From then until the present there have been county runners but only two of national standard, Emma Lewis and Richard Hildick-Smith.

In more recent years there have been no regular School matches but regular entries in the Gloucestershire Schools' event leading to county representation. In 2007, Emma Lewis completed the London Marathon in 3 hours 59 minutes, coming 2nd in the 18-19 years age-group.

***Equestrian***

Riding began as a Monday Activity at Badgeworth Riding Centre in 1979. By 1982, jumping had begun, later fed in 1990 by Heather Newell becoming National Schools Eventing Champion. The first School riding team was captained by Kim Chester trying and tried a range of events in 1991. In 1992, Rachel Rank and David Eyres competed in the Independent Schools One-Day Event at Stonar, the former returning to come fourth in 1996. In 1994, Charlotte Moger, Rachel Rank and Amy Tucker-Brown completed the Cotswold Hunt Team Chase, while in 1996 a four-strong team came second in the VWH Hunt and Team Chase.

Paula Watson, who has overseen all Equestrian Activities since 1998, introduced polo in 2001, six riders taking part. An Intermediate team entered their first Polo Tournament in 2002 captained by Julian van Gils, who later played for English National Schools and the U19 England side. More riders began training in 2004, two teams entering the National Championships. Young talent emerging included John Whitehead, Ollie Duff, Elliot Lineham and Jenny Brown. Chloe Middleton captained the Cross Country team around Foxcote and also qualified for Great Britain Show Jumping. Pandora Bailey qualified in Show Jumping at the Horse of the Year Show.

Paul Whitehead riding to victory on Strathmore Heights in the national Under 18 Three Day Eventing championships at Chepstow in 2005

In 2005, training moved from Inglesham to closer facilities at Longdole Polo Centre, Birdlip where Arena Polo was played, giving invaluable playing experience before summer tournaments. John Whitehead was selected to play for the England U16 Polo-Crosse team that July, his brother, Paul, having won the U18 British Three Day Eventing Championship riding 'Strathmore High Spirits' that May. He subsequently represented Britain at the U18 European Three Day Event Championships in Saumur, France. That year, six riders participated in the Stonar Inter-School One Day Equestrian Event, possibly the biggest schools' competition in the country, in which Stephanie Boyd came 4th on 'Good Samaritan'.

The polo team, led by Robert McGuffie, won Division Three in both Open Arena and National Intermediate Tournaments in 2006. They were promoted to Division 2 but the floods of 2007 made competing impossible. In the 2006 National U16 Tournament, the School team, captained by a goal-scoring Ollie Duff, came third in Division Two. In September, Ben Peploe on 'Ashfield Alley Cat' took 3rd place in the FEI Intermediate class while Stephanie Boyd came 10th in the Senior Open at the Inter-Schools One-Day Event at Stonar against riders from 107 schools.

In 2007, Alex Edwards on 'Finis' and Ben Peploe riding 'Sportsfield Outline' continued Stonar successes with 5th and 8th places in the Intermediate and Senior Intermediate Classes respectively.

2008's Junior Polo team included Wesley Lineham, Jenny and Phib Brown and Jess Watson scoring 13 goals in their first Arena Tournament, earning promotion for the summer season, coming 3rd in the U16 Division 2 Tournament. The Senior team of Ollie Duff, Elliot Lineham, John Whitehead and Jenny Brown scored 8 goals in Division 2.

Equestrian Activities have come a long way over the last 30 years.

***Hockey (Boys)***

Since 1968, when the XI visited Spain and played in the 'Torneo Internacional de Reyes' as guests of the Real Club de Polo Barcelona, coming fifth out of eight schools, the standard of hockey has usually been high and sometimes exceptional. The drive and determination of talented coaches has helped, including John Nash, Richard Padfield, Trevor Snow, Alastair Reid, John Watson and Rod Pellereau, led by Tony Forbes, Director of Sport 1977-2006, and his successor, Rhys Gwilliam, a former Welsh international, together with the main specialist hockey coach and OD, Gary Tredgett.

In boys' hockey, county players have emerged almost continuously ever since Richard Padfield noticed seven Decanians in the 1981 U19 county side. In the late 1980s and 1990s, county caps often totalled over 10 each year from different age groups. In 1995, a remarkable year, there were 19; three in the county U21 side, nine in the U18, two in the U16 and five in the U14. Often, one or more players were in West of England sides, too. 1980 was exceptional, when two Decanians played for the U18, one for the U16 and four for the U14 teams. Possibly the best representative year was 2005, when William Pearce was in the England U18 XI, six boys were in West of England sides in various age groups while 23 boys were county players. In a school of under 270 boys, raising eight hockey teams meant roughly one in three played for the School – and that year one in 12 were county players. With standards rising generally, it has been more difficult winning representative honours but David Padfield (Cambridge) and Will Kinder (Oxford) attained hockey Blues in 1993 and 2001 respectively.

Tony Forbes wrote in 1989, '...the hockey season of 1988-89 (heralded) a transformation in hockey at Dean Close School. In 1961, D.J. Carnill, a former captain of Great Britain...was instrumental in obtaining the first Redgra pitch to be built in any school... [much later] the Governors were able to announce approval for a synthetic grass pitch to be built during the autumn of 1988. Situated next to the Redgra pitch it has created a perfect setting...All teams from all age groups and both sexes now have the chance of playing under ideal conditions...'.

The best season for matches thus far for the XI was possibly 1989 with 12 matches played, 11 won but the first – against Taunton – lost. Another might be the 1996 XI under Mark Pihlens' captaincy that was undefeated in school matches and came 5th out of 32 teams in the 53rd Hockey Interlyceale in the Hague with Hywel Lewis being voted 'Most Valuable Player of the Tournament'.

However, the best complete season for all the teams was possibly 2005. That year, the XI won all save one of their matches, the 2nd XI and U14 XI were both unbeaten. Yet 1998 must be seen as an impressive season when the XI, under its captain, Ben Marsden, won 10, drew 1 and lost 2 of its matches, scoring 72 goals but only conceding 19. For once Marlborough College was beaten (5-2), their coach, who went on to coach the England XI commenting that the Dean Close XI gave '...one of the best schoolboy displays...' he had seen for some years. Ben Marsden was an England U21 trialist, soon to be in the team; Ed Taylor, the goalkeeper, was in the U21 and U18 sides for Wales; Chris Price was in the U16 Wales side while James Davies was in the U15 Welsh Squad. It was also the season when the U16, U14 and the Junior School U13 sides all took their respective county cups while the U18 XI was runner-up in their cup but made up for it in the following season (1999) by being both county champions and West of England finalists under Paul Marchand's captaincy. Their match with Millfield for the West Championship was the only match they lost all season. Paul also captained the county U18 side while Christina Jones was captain of the U19 county girls' team, a 'double' that has been unique thus far. In a remarkable season, 24 boys represented the county at different levels.

Gary Tredgett

In 2007 the sports hall opened. Its much-improved indoor training facilities helped the boys' team qualify for the National Finals at indoor hockey for the first time – only one of four schools to do so – having in their coach, Gary Tredgett, a former England indoors international.

Ben Marsden and Tamara Fateh

Ben Marsden OD was selected for the Great Britain squad for the Beijing Olympics in 2008, an outstanding achievement. At School, the hockey XI was captained by U18 Welsh international goalkeeper Adam Williams. A new team had to be built up and 20 players represented the XI at one time or another. The statistics of played 10, won 3; drew 5; lost 2 were encouraging. Perhaps the 3rd XI (won 5, drew 1, lost 1) under Miles Beardsley's captaincy was the most successful of nine XIs the School fielded. The Indoor team of six (with six substitutes) also did well, reaching the National Finals for the second year running.

Under 18 National Hockey Champions 2009
Standing: Rhys Gwilliam (coach), Jack Ford, Tom Harris, Michael Strachan, Thomas Scrase, Richard Baker, Jeremy Gillman, Andrew Scrase, Simon Slabbert, William McAleer, Gary Tredgett (coach)
Kneeling: James Melville, Liam Brignull, Michael Penny, Benjamin Andrew (capt), Jonathan Cartwright, Alistair Parker, Thomas Pinnegar, Benjamin Miller

In March 2009, the U18 XI became West of England Champions for the first time. The team, led by Ben Andrew, became National Schools' Champions that April, beating Worksop College 3-2 in the final, Tom Scrase scoring a hat-trick. The School squad included nine current or former regional players and three county players. Gary Tredgett, the coach, said, 'This is the greatest achievement by any team we have produced during my 17 years here.'

**Hockey Blues**

Between 1924 and 1944 Dean Close won 15 hockey blues, 3 at Oxford and 12 at Cambridge. In the 60 plus years from 1945 to the present day the School has accrued a mere 8; 3 at Oxford and 5 at Cambridge. Yet in those years the standard of School hockey has improved enormously, so why the discrepancy?
Three reasons suggest themselves. Firstly, hockey is taken far more seriously by 'competitor' schools than it used to be and their numbers remain far larger than ours. Secondly, far fewer of our leavers win places at Oxbridge than before or between the Wars, and thirdly – probably most significant of all – many more post-graduates now fill University sides than heretofore; until National Service finished in the early 1960s those two years of growth and experience produced men able to compete with the top clubs in hockey, but these fixtures were threatened with the advent of leagues at Senior club level and with the arrival of undergraduates straight from school. So, although the School wins fewer nowadays, their value is arguably far higher!
The predominance in favour of Cambridge may have something to do with the combined influence of Edward Ellam and Stanley Hoare in directing Decanians towards Queens' College, Cambridge, that may have tilted the balance.

Richard Padfield

***Hockey (Girls)***

Hockey began gradually as girl numbers increased. In March 1973 a girls' XI first entered a tournament, captained by Jane Rowlands. The XI also lost to an all-male Common Room XI, 3-1.

1979 was the first year the 1st XI made any real impression, reaching the semi-final of the Gloucestershire schools' senior tournament, goalkeeper and captain Sara Joiner being selected for the Gloucestershire Schools' XI for two seasons.

1981 was the first year the 1st XI had a full fixture list. 17 matches were played, 12 won, 4 lost and 1 drawn, with 64 goals scored and 16 conceded. Claire Fletcher (captain Cheltenham and District U16 XI) and Stephanie Bacon were both in the Gloucestershire and West of England squads, boosting the team's confidence. A 2nd XI played four matches, losing only one.

1982 was a landmark season as the 1st XI was undefeated in any school match.

In 1984, Claire Fletcher was selected for the England U19 team and the U14 team made their mark, being undefeated all season except by one goal against Pate's.

Elisabeth Troughton led the 1985 XI to a first win of the U18 Gloucestershire championships, later being losing finalists at the West of England championships.

A skilful, fit touring team from Argentina beat the 1st XI 5-0 at School in the 1987 Lent Term. In 1988, an excellent U14 XI, led by Catherine McAdam, won all their 12 matches, scoring 60 goals and conceding only 3. Their success was replicated as the U16 XI, led by Lynn Burns, in 1990-91. They won the U16 national title, the first team of either sex from the School to achieve that accolade.

Numbers of girls grew: more participated in hockey. The 1991 season included, for the first time, three XIs and an U16 XI. Moreover, two girls were in the county U18 XI, three in the county U18 2nd

XI and two in the U16 XI, of which Joanna Kingston was captain, as well as playing for the West of England U16 XI.

The 1992 1st XI included seven newcomers, yet became Gloucestershire champions, captained by Lynn Burns. Suzanne Pike led the U16 team to be both county and West of England champions. Lisa-Marie Smith was in the U21 county and West of England sides. Camilla Robinson was both county and School U16 captain in 1993 when, for the second year running and for the third time in four years, the School were West of England champions. They came third nationally in 1994.

Pitch subsidence made practice more difficult than in 1994, yet both the 2nd and 3rd XIs were undefeated, the U16 XI was good and the U14 XI county champions. 10 girls were in county sides.

The 1st XI under captain and goalie Mary Black became county and regional champions, coming fifth nationally in 1995, a first for an U18 XI. The following March, the first girls' touring party to Western Canada won 5 of 6 matches.

Hilary Swan who, following Sue Padfield and later with Gary Tredgett, had really developed girls' hockey, retired from senior squad coaching in 1997, having coached the U16 national champions in 1991, though she was not away long.

Group photograph taken on Astroturf pitch
School Hockey players with county, regional, and national honours 1997-8
Back row (l to r): Gavin Curry, Joe Lane, Justin Forbes, Simon Stevens, Edward Taylor, Henrik Lehment, Alastair Judge, Ben Marsden
2nd row from back (l to r): Edward Hollows, John Keay, Rob Kinder, Nick Batten, Stuart Bond, Katy Hopkin, Lucy Johnson, Claire Godwin, Christina Jones, Tegan Faulkner, Paul Marchand, Tom Johnson, Douglas Crippen
Kneeling (l to r): Joe Jenkins, Tom Bacon, James Davies, Sam Barrett, Eddie Boyd, Andrew Martin, Alex Fateh, Garth Banks, Alex Hume, Tom Judge
Front row (l to r): Gareth Jenkins, Isy Shayle, Alix Reid, Naomi Reid, Tamara Fateh, Laura Macfarlane, Laura Bellwood, Sarah Downes, Jack Hunter

During the 1998 season, the 1st XI beat touring South African School Woodridge College and the following Easter joined the boys' XI in the UCL two day tournament in the Hague. The girls came 8th of 18 teams. That same season, for the first time, a School ladies' parents' team played, beating Richard Pate's parents' team 1-0.

The 1999 tour of South Africa took 18 days during which nine schools were visited, 10 matches played, 8 won, including that against Woodridge College, and 2 lost. The following season was exceptional. The seven teams played 64 matches losing only 5. The XI included, for the first time, the very talented Tamara Fateh, at 13 already an U16 English international, who had led the U14 county team to victory in the West Regional Tournament. The boys' and girls' XIs revisited the UCL tournament where the girls' XI reached the final. Tamara Fateh was awarded Best Player Prize – still aged 13.

The 2000 1st XI, led by Claire Godwin, came 3rd in the U18 national tournament. Tamara Fateh was awarded full Colours, the first U15 girl ever to win them. Playing without her, the U16 XI were still Gloucestershire champions. Altogether, 11 girls from the School were in county teams.

The 1st XI, captained by Sarah Downes, won all their matches save one in 2001 before touring Australia that summer with the 2nd XI. Tamara Fateh had represented England, while Dean Close also had girls in the county U19 and U15 teams and five in the county U17 team.

Hilary Swan returned to run girls' games in 2002, and the season was possibly the best ever. Blaire McColl and Tamara Fateh led the 1st XI, winning every school match played and being 'disappointed' at coming third in the U18 national tournament. The U14 XI, captained by Natasha Price, was also

Rebecca Smith in action for 1st XI

unbeaten and won the U14 national title. Out of eight teams, only the U15A XI lost more matches than it won.

In 2003, Tamara was in her fourth 1st XI season, her second as captain and in the U21 England team. Yet again the 1st XI were county and West champions. The first four XIs played 43 matches, won 32, drew 6 and lost just 5. 11 girls were playing for county sides. Gary Tredgett's sustained coaching skills were plain for all to see.

After a solid 2004 season, a touring party to Argentina, Chile and Brazil won all 10 matches. The U16 side, although undefeated, were runners-up on goal difference in the national championships at Nottingham. Natasha Price was in the England Performance Squad while Isobel Butland and Hannah Tredgett joined her in the U18 West of England XI.

In 2006 the School achieved the remarkable feat of the U18, U16 and U14 teams all being county champions.

2007 was sometimes frustrating. On the whole, match results were a little disappointing but in the National Schools' competition, Hilary Swan wrote, '...both U16s and U14s missed out on reaching the National Finals by the narrowest of margins – goal difference and 20 seconds!' Olivia Abbott and Abigail Porter, in addition to being in the U14 West squad, were also selected for England high performance hockey coaching. Hilary Swan retired, her coaching with that of Gary Tredgett having inspired girls to achieve beyond what they had thought possible.

Natasha Price and Isabella Fateh at U14 national hockey finals 2003

Girls' hockey tour to Argentina in 2005

**Centenary Hockey**

To celebrate 100 years of Dean Close Hockey in the Lent Term 2007, a Headmaster's International XI consisting of present and former England and Wales internationals, including four ODs, played a mixed School XI, captained by Matt Dring and Natasha Price. Although it was raining much of the time, the quality of play was high on both sides. The final score was 11-7 to the internationals. At the subsequent dinner, at which both Ben Marsden and Denys Carnill spoke, there were 18 captains together with past and present coaches.

***Headmaster's International XI***

Richard Alexander England & GB squad
Tom Edginton OD, Wales
James Fair, England & GB squad (goalkeeper)
Rhys Gwilliam, Wales (1996-2002)
Martin Jones England & GB squad
Simon Mantell England & GB squad
Ben Marsden OD, England & GB squad
Rob Moore England & GB squad
Chris Price OD, Wales U21
Matt Taylor England & GB squad
James Tindall England & GB squad
Chris Willis OD, Wales

***School XI***

Rachael Barraclough
Matt Dring (Captain)
Issy Fateh
James Gough
Jamie Legg
Helen Melville
Bryony Mintram
Will Pearce, England U18
Natasha Price (Captain), England U19
Tom Sword
Chris Tasker-Grindley
Tamara Fateh, England U19

**Manager**: Hilary Swan
**Coach:** Gary Tredgett OD, England Indoor Squad 1984-85.
**Pitch**: Ellam's

### *Netball*

The first netball VII was in 1974, captained by Caroline Whalley. The 1975 side appears unbeaten and by 1976 the county squad included Dean Close girls. The 1st VII was unbeaten in 1982 while the 2nd VII only lost one of six matches. A match against Old Decanians was organized for the first time in 1983.

By 1984, the School had four VIIs, the most successful being the U14 team captained by Tamsin Bacon. From 1986 to 1989 the School 1st VII won more matches than it lost, the 1989 and 1990 1st VIIs also being runners-up at the Wycliffe invitation tournament. The U14 VII won the Bromsgrove invitation tournament in 1992.

The 1996 U15 VII, led by Christina Jones, was first to win all their nine matches, including against Pate's Grammar, the county champions.

The 1st VII reached the final of the Marlborough Tournament in 2000 while the 2nd VII , inspirationally led by Lisa Fairclough, won all 15 of their matches, as did the 4th and U14A VIIs.

In the excellent 2002 season, the 1st VII, captained by Laura Bellwood, only lost to Pate's Grammar, while the 2nd, 3rd and 4th VIIs had undefeated seasons. The U19 VII reached the U19 West Midlands Finals. Helen Melville's selection for the South West Development Squad was in 2003.

The 1st VII achieved a milestone in 2005 when, led by Stephanie Parker, they won the U19 county championship. Helen Melville led them the following year when they were runners-up but in 2007 they had to be content with being quarter-finalists. In 2007 there was a netball tour – a first – to Malta during the Easter holidays. 23 Sixth Formers went and only one match was conceded of the half-dozen played.

Hannah Leger has developed the success of sides since starting netball coaching in 2006, building on the work of Hilary Swan, Beverley McKellar, Paula Watson, Pip Atkinson, Bridget Edkins and Laura Burton.

In 2008, the U16 team achieved 3rd place in the South-West Regional Finals, the best ever placement of a School side.

### *Rugby*

Senior talent was not plentiful, so the 1969 XV included four 15 year-olds. Consequently, the 1970 sides slimmed to four, not six, teams. The 1971 XV included S.W.E. Shaw, described by coach Brian Wilson as '...one of the finest centres we have produced...'. Another excellent player was 1974 captain and third season colour A.W. Milne, of whom Brian Wilson wrote '...what the team owed to (his) example, enthusiasm, strength and skill is incalculable...his training sessions should be a blue print for any future captain...'.

The 1975 XV was very successful, losing only 2 matches out of 13 played. It was Brian Wilson's last season after over 15 years with the XV. Richard Akenhead, formerly of Moseley, in his first season at Dean Close did much to sharpen up the three-quarters.

The XV of 1979-80 went to France in the 1980 Easter holidays but lost their three matches. The U15 XV were outstanding in the 1980

Richard Akenhead

season. Led by Peter Barnes, they played and won 14 matches, scoring 369 points and conceding just 36; in their short tour to Holland the 1982 XV won all three matches.

Thus emboldened, the XV went on tour to British Columbia at Easter 1985. Of seven matches played, the tourists won six, including winning the final in a knockout competition in Kelowna. ODs Lynn Burroughs, Howard Oliver and Stuart Taylor, all Canadian residents, entertained, supported and, in physiotherapist Miss Burroughs' case, patched up the tourists. The 1985 season began well but 'drifted' later, although David Morgans (centre) and Marcus Paget-Wilkes (full back) played for the county U18 XV.

The inexperienced 1986 XV were led by Tim Harmer, who in the match against Bloxham scored 24 points (4 tries, 2 conversions, 2 penalties and a drop goal) that may be a Decanian individual record.

The 1989 XV won 10 of 15 matches played and won both matches in a brief Holland tour. Experimentally, the OD match was usefully switched to the beginning of the season. The U15 XV was unbeaten in School matches and did well in the Daily Mail Cup, amassing 420 points and conceding 35. Captain Ben Hyde was described by coach Peter Cairns as '...the best U15 scrum half I have ever seen...'.

Ben Hyde

The successful 1991 XV – won 10, drew 0, lost 2 – profited from rule changes and also the emergence of Ben Hyde as captain and scrum half for two seasons, during which he also played in the England U18 XV tour to New Zealand.

In October 1992, the XV participated in the Third Benidorm International Tournament in Spain in sweltering conditions and won three matches, while in 1995 the XV toured South Africa, leading to a sound season culminating in a School win of the Gloucestershire Schools' Sevens Competition, 'sevens' having been played for some years.

The quality of the 1996 XV was reflected in the fact that captain James Mears was in the county U18 XV while Richard Lynall and Scott Curry were both in the county U16 side.

A fine 1997 XV won 9 of its 10 matches while the 3rd/U16 XV were undefeated, scoring 314 points and conceding only 36. Scott Curry and Christopher Hotchkiss were in the U19 and U16 county teams respectively.

In 1998, led by Richard Lynall, the School's sevens team reached the quarter-finals of the Rosslyn Park tournament on the second day.

The 1999 tour of Canada was possible largely through Rupert Lane OD, then headmaster of Ridley College, Canada. The XV and a junior XV went. The XV won matches and also reached the finals of the Ontario HSBC Sevens while the juniors reached the quarter finals. Paul Marchand amassed 100 points while Ross Pieters was Player of the Tour. In 1999, captain Tom Johnson represented the county's 'A' XV. The School U14A XV was virtually undefeated under Nick Ball's captaincy and Nick Akerman's coaching. Richard Lynall was in the county U18 XV while Paul Marchand also played for Gloucestershire against Dorset.

In 2000, the School VII were quarter-finalists at Rosslyn Park for the third year running. Joseph Purcaro was in the county U16 XV; Nicholas Marsh became the first OD to win an Oxford Blue for Rugby, later playing for the England VII in Hong Kong in 2001. Paul Marchand and David Marsh represented Cambridge and Oxford respectively in a rugby league match, the former scoring a try. The U14 A XV, led by Tom West, won all but one of the 10 matches they played.

In 2002-03, Nigel Melville, former rugby international, director of Gloucester Rugby Club and School parent presented a helpful session on defensive patterns of play. Alastair Smith and Benjamin Gibbons both represented the county XV. In Trinity 2003, the XV, together with an U16 XV, toured Australia. Both sides won in Singapore but the XV only won one match in Australia; the U16 XV lost only one. Matt Strong won the U16 XV Player of the Tour while XV Player of the Tour was Nick Ball, the new season's captain, whose young team subsequently had a good season, winning 8 of 11 matches, supported by a promising 2nd XV.

A fine 2004 XV was underlined in Robbie Newiss being county U16 XV hooker, Pete Browne (second row) in the county U17 side and Matthew Strong (No. 8) in the county U18 XV.

Pete Browne captained the 2005 XV that included a tour of Italy at Easter 2006 with an U16 XV. This was Richard Akenhead's last tour as XV coach, having been in charge for 30 years. He was presented with a watch by the XV. Pete was later selected to play for the premier league Newcastle Falcons.

Mark Tottman was the new coach in 2006 and implemented Nigel Melville's rugby plan that emphasized fitness. Sam Bailey was captain, Rob Newiss, now in his third season in the XV, vice-captain. The team drew with Bristol Grammar, a very encouraging result. Jeremy Gillman at No. 8 played for the county and South West U16 XV sides. The School VII won the Plate at the Bristol Grammar School Sevens. 2006 was also the first year that the School produced an U16 VII.

The 2007 XV, led by Declan Averiss, with 12 wins, 1 draw and 2 lost was very encouraging, especially with a 5-3 win over Bristol Grammar. An exciting tour of seven matches to New Zealand and the Cook Islands followed in the summer of 2008, the tourists winning 5, the hosts 2. Mark Tottman and Rhys Gwilliam have worked hard to improve commitment, fitness and techniques.

The advent of Pip Atkinson, former England international women's rugby player onto the staff in 1999 resulted in 12 girls training for the Rosslyn Park Sevens, March 2000, assisted by England women's team coach Peter Kennedy. Captained by Victoria Judge, the girls won several matches before losing to the eventual winners. Laura Bellwood, Georgina Fenton, Victoria Judge, Helen Thomas and Rebecca Hewlett were all nominated for the England Talent Identification Programmes. Unfortunately, Miss Atkinson left!

**Dean Close School, Cheltenham Rugby Club and The All Blacks**

On Tuesday, 6th December, 2005, Cheltenham Rugby Club held a centenary dinner to celebrate 'the greatest day in the history of the club'. On that day in 1905, the Club played New Zealand touring side 'the Originals', now called 'the All Blacks'. The Club lost 18-0, scarcely worse than the England side beaten 15-5 the week before. At the post-match High Tea, Grace was said by Dr Flecker, then Headmaster of Dean Close School. The Revd Tim Hastie-Smith was invited to say Grace in 2005 as Headmaster of the same School a hundred years later and chose a Latin Grace in line with the formal Grace almost certainly used by Dr Flecker.

1st XV Rugby 2007: Robert French dives over for a try

***Sailing***

The Sailing Club tried one or two sites on the River Avon but in 1969 they moved in with the Severn Sailing Club at Bredon. In 1970, the VI beat both Severn Sailing Club and Tewkesbury Sailing Club. In the County Schools' Regatta, Michaelmas 1971, John Gall and Richard Grace won the U15 event while Michael Malric-Smith and Michael W.G. Martin were second in the Seniors. During the same term, John Gall and older sister Diana won the Severn S.C. U18 trophy, the first occasion a girl was mentioned in any *Decanian* sports report. Christopher Collins and Philip Leopold won the Gloucestershire Schools' S.A. Regatta at South Cerney for the second consecutive year. In 1972, the School won five out of eight matches.

In 1973, only Malvern College beat the School in the April to October season. A new match against South Caernarvonshire Yacht Club gave the VI the opportunity to sail Schimitars at sea off Abersoch. At the South Midlands' Schools' Regatta at South Cerney, the U16s won two matches and lost one.

1974 was a particularly good year, Philip Poyner and Sue Hughes winning the Gloucestershire Schools' Regatta, with Bruce King and Rachel Garson runners-up. Simon Hawes won the U18 trophy at Severn S.C. Lt-Col C.E. Jarret-Kerr gave up the Sailing Club after 16 years in 1978 – and the battered old Ford bus was sold. Masters who also did much for sailing were Mike Cooper, Michael Hawkins and, later, Jon Brock.

The talented Fuller-Shapcott brothers did well as Juniors in 1981, although the girls lost possibly their first encounter with Cheltenham Ladies' College. Other than against Marlborough, the VI did not lose a match in 1982. At the beginning of Trinity, eight members of the club, with two members of staff, spent the weekend cruising in the Solent in a 38 foot Laurent Giles.

Two laser sailing dinghies appeared in the 1984 season for the club's use. Subsequent reports are sporadic. Rachel Garstang was possibly the first girl sailing captain in 1989 but by then most competitions were internal.

In more recent years, sailing has come under the wing of the naval section of the CCF and has ceased to be a School sport owing to health and safety regulations.

***Shooting***

Although it may once have been seen as a separate sport, shooting has increasingly been acknowledged as an extension of CCF activity over the last 40 years.

In 1969 the VIII, unbeaten in matches, came 4th out of 31 schools in the County Life .22 competition. .303 shooting was confined to the Pilning range near Bristol. In 1972, in the Country Life Competition Class 'A' event, the School came 8th nationally, winning a large shield as 'most improved' school. G.E.B. Whiting, master-in-charge, left, to be replaced by Major Harry Appleby.

Fortunes varied but in 1977 the School won the Elgood, a local competition between the School, Cheltenham College, Malvern and Bromsgrove, for the second year running.

In April 1982, Samantha Edwards and Susannah Rowles were the first girl cadet pair at Bisley. The new 7.62 rifle was introduced the next year but had teething problems that Major Appleby solved before retiring in 1984.

In 1990 the CCF RAF section won the national Assegai Trophy. Katy McAdam and Zoe Griffiths shot for the county in small bore shooting in 1992. In 1993 a county reserve team included Mary Black, Kirsty Herbertson and Thomas Pegg, who came joint first in the county championships.

Mary Black and Robert Newton shot for the county U21 small bore shooting team in 1995 with Ashley Foale, Kirsty Herbertson and Katy Hopkin shooting for the county reserve team. The VIII won their division in the county league, the Mere Cup and the 43 (Wessex) Brigade Falling Plate while a five strong School team came 2nd in the class 'B' competition of the Green Howards Country Life Competition, beating 170 teams. The small bore team also won the U21 county League and were ninth in the National Country Life competition.

In the 1996-97 season, Katy Hopkin led the small bore team to sixth place nationally in the Stamforth Competition. Katy also won an individual Gold Medal for a 'possible', that is, achieving a perfect score, in the Lambert Cup (snap shooting) in 1996-97 which the School team won.

Chris Mullen amazingly achieved 'best shot' in every small and full bore competition the School entered in the 1998-99 season. The School beat 220 teams to win the Country Life 'B' (small bore) competition and in full bore won the Lambert Cup for snap shooting they had first won the year before.

Two teams entered the 2004 Green Howards Country Life Competition, coming in the top dozen out of 200 teams participating. In 2005 the 'B' team of Jack Peploe, John Preston, Rowena Gibbins and

Richard Bolton won Bronze Medals in the same national competition and the Gordon Winter Silver salver, as the best 'B' team in the country. Rowena Gibbins claimed second best shot of the competition – a remarkable achievement.

After an indifferent year or two, in 2008 the team came first in the Green Howards Country Life 'class B' competition, with Richard Bolton 3rd. The School also won the Gordon Winter trophy.

Through the 1990s and the early years of this century, shooting coaches have been Mick Pegrum, Mike Hart and Ron Williams under the auspices of the CCF.

***Squash***

Five members began the Club in 1970-71. By Christmas 1972 there were over 30, plus a waiting list, overseen by housemaster Chris Kenyon and captain R.T. Davis. The local East Gloucestershire Club was used two afternoons a week. The girls played Cheltenham Ladies' College and the boys Cheltenham College, King's Gloucester and a 'select team' from the Common Room, all 'somewhat unsuccessfully'. Lack of facilities on site contributed to continued defeats. Supported by a sympathetic bursar, Brigadier Montagu, a Squash Ball was held in Cheltenham Town Hall in September 1978 that raised £467 (£2,000) and in March 1980 two courts opened, boys and girls using them in almost equal numbers, often before breakfast! Sarah Ball was captain 1981-82.

Even with coaching, progress was patchy – only 8 out of 20 matches were won by the School in the 1983-84 season, for example. However, within two years James Roth was in the county squad while Julian Ray was in a junior county team. Mrs Elgood, a former Scottish international, improved standards. In the 1986-87 season the team was promoted to division 2 in the Junior Sunday League. In 1988, Julian Ray led the team to the top division in the same league and the following year to the first division of the county U19 league, as well as successfully against other schools and clubs. There were now inter-house and individual competitions within the School, too.

In 1989, Helen Godwin, a Remove Decanian, was a semi-finalist in the U19 county squash championships and was in the U19 and U16 county girls' squash teams. She went on to represent the West Midlands.

The boys' team drifted back to division 2 in the county league in the early 1990s, though by 1995-96, led by Michael Jary, the team finished 3rd in that league while the girls' U19 team came top of their league. At U14 level, Christina Jones, winner of the U14 county closed tournament, and Catherine Spence both represented the county, as did Emily Barwell, Katherine Qualtrough and Joanna Batten at U19 level. It was 2004 before the girls did as well again.

Chris and Sam Tasker-Grindley

The early 2000s were dominated by the Tasker-Grindley brothers. Unfortunately, Sam had to give up owing to a knee injury; Christopher won the national title at Pontefract in 2003 and came 9th in the British Open, making him 9th in the world and the best squash player for his age in the northern hemisphere. He continued to represent Great Britain at U17 level, being ranked 1st in the UK in 2004, winning the U17 British Closed Championships that October, despite injuries to his right hand! He also won the Spanish Open Tournament in 2005 and in 2006 represented England at the U19 European Squash Championships in Switzerland, being ranked 7th in Europe.

Wesley Howell in 2008 was ranked in the top ten in England at U15. He helped to win the U15 County Team event for Gloucestershire the same year. In January 2009, he came 12th in the U15 British Open Tournament at Sheffield, in which there was large international representation, effectively putting him in the top six players for his age in England.

***Swimming***

The 1969 (boys') junior swimming team was undefeated, beating Millfield, unlike the seniors. During that season, 75% of School records were bettered. In 1970, swimming became a major sport. Vivian Davies beat five of his own records and won on 13 occasions for the School, eventually competing at the British Junior Trials. F.J. Wilson was outstanding at breaststroke; P.J. Weighill and D.H. Harper at diving from 1970-72. In 1971, Major Chapman introduced a structured training programme and performances improved. For the first time, 'A' and 'B' teams were entered for some matches. Apart from St Paul's Training College and Millfield, no team beat the School.

A girls' team, led by Jane Rowlands, ten strong, competed for the first time with mixed fortune in 1973. Anna Righton was the first girl to win the Diving Cup; Wendy Fredjohn the first to win the Victrix Ludorum. In 1974, Sue Walters wrote: '…It was not without considerable pressure that Mead (entered) the senior house swimming competition. The apparent mirth…turned to apparent humiliation when Mead came third, out of seven houses, the others all male, leaving not only surprise, but also a victory for the so-called 'weaker' sex…'. By the end of 1976 Elizabeth Robertson and Antonia Machin were permanent members of a swimming team that won all its seven matches.

In 1978, a School U17 relay team won the Cheltenham Schools Webb Shield for the fifth consecutive year. Linda Hewitt won the U15 county championships' 100 metre backstroke. School diver Linda Williams won a Bronze Medal in the Malaysian Games.

In 1982, the School won 13 of 14 matches. Senior girls events were beginning to be included. Cameron Smith broke freestyle and butterfly records while the U14 won, and the U19 team drew, the Cheltenham Secondary Schools Gala. The following season the U14, U16 and U19 teams were all runners-up in the same Gala.

Life saving competitions became popular. In 1984, the School received the Alderman Stanley Life Saving Award Trophy for senior schools, while Richard Jacob led the team to winning 12 out of 13 matches, drawing 1. Angela August led a victorious girls' team over four opposing schools' teams. The School regained the Webb Relay Shield for the 7th year out of ten, and also regained the Gloucestershire Trophy for Life Saving.

Again, in 1986 both boys' and girls' senior teams only lost one match. By the end of 1987, RLSS Bronze Medallion Award holders at the School totalled over 25.

Captain Chris Chandler led swimmers to an unbeaten season in 1988, breaking three School records himself. Jonathan Peskett and Patrick Ip also broke records. The senior relay team came second of all British Isles Schools in the Aldenham Cup. Cathy Alger, swimming captain, and Beth, her sister, came to hold nine records between them as well as both being county swimmers. This was in 1989, when the swimming teams won all 12 of their matches. For the first time, a girls' senior relay team qualified for the English Schools National Freestyle Team Finals. In the Cheltenham Secondary Swimming Gala, the School won the 14-16 and 16-19 boys' shields and the girls' 16-19 shield. Christopher Bacon, Headmaster, wrote that in school matches: '...both boys' and girls' teams are totally unbeaten this year and last...' and paid tribute to Marion Venn, the coach. Life saving, too, continued to be well supported.

1991 was memorable. The boys' teams were unbeaten for the fifth consecutive year, the girls for a fourth in school matches. Robert Holmes, Hugo Hunton and Chris Field all set new records. The girls' relay team came 5th nationally in the freestyle relay. The boys medley relay team had won the 1990 Otter 'B' Relay for Public School Teams in the British Isles, setting a new record – but were runners up in 1991. The freestyle team came 6th in the 4 x 100m of the Aldenham Cup.

Marion Venn's international swimming star nephew Duncan Goodhew visited the School on 28th April, 1991 for a sponsored swim. The £2,000 raised was divided between the Cheltenham Mayor's Fund for CLIC, Gloucestershire Dyslexia Association and the School's swimming tour fund. The Headmaster, Christopher Bacon, William Bullingham OD and Mayor of Cheltenham, and Duncan Goodhew had a two length race. Duncan Goodhew won but started much later than the others! 200 people from School and the local community, aged from four to nearly 80, then took part.

Marion Venn

1992 included swimming triumphs similar to 1991 with James Wilson and Sarah Kenny as captains. 1993 maintained the standard for the boys although the girls were not as strong as before. It was also the year that two former swimming captains, Richard Jacob and Tracey Dorrell, were married.

The 1994 team, led by Tim Brown and Katherine Wall, the latter for two years, were never defeated overall. Eleanor Rankin dazzled, setting records in the freestyle, butterfly and individual medley events.

In 1996, Chris Ong swam at U14 level for the county. At the end of Trinity, 23 swimmers aged from 12 to 18 left on the first School swimming tour – to Canada. The main feature was entering the Paul Hauch Open Meeting in London, Ontario against 500 swimmers from 28 clubs from Canada and the USA.

Victories continued to outnumber defeats significantly in school matches 1997-99.

Marion Venn retired in 2000, having been the swimming coach since 1977. She had improved swimming standards and introduced water polo and life saving programmes. Anthony Davies became swimming coach and has encouraged the development of water polo.

The 2001 season was very encouraging, as the U16 teams won 12 out of 14 matches. In the medley and freestyle relays at Crystal Palace, the girls came 9th out of 39 teams, the boys 14th out of 41 teams. However, in 2004, the girls came 9th, the boys 7th out of 69 teams.

Richard Jacob and Richard Hildick-Smith in 2005

Richard Jacob OD offered a financial incentive to anyone who could beat his 50m freestyle School record of 26.2 seconds. In 2005, Richard Hildick-Smith met the challenge with a time of 25.2 seconds.

In 2006, the girls' relay team achieved 4th place in the individual medleys at the National Schools' Swimming Competition.

The girls again succeeded in reaching the finals at Crystal Palace in 2008, coming 4th. Only one girls' match was lost – all other matches for girls or boys were either won or drawn.

2008 successes included reclaiming the Webb Relay Shield while the girls yet again reached the Crystal Palace Finals.

***Tennis (Boys)***

Roy Simpson and John Hill, the School 1st pair in 1969, won the Gloucestershire Schools' Doubles Championships but despite coach Mrs Bouquet's efforts, nothing more was won. Her successor, Bob Griffin, faired little better, the 1970s being bleak with few matches won even in competitions. Tennis was more popular in the 1980s among boys but still results were disappointing.

However, 1991 saw 1st pair Myron Askwith (captain) and Alexander Fitzgerald win four out of five matches, a major improvement, while the VI generally did better. The 1992 season was excellent, the 1st and 3rd (U16) VIs being undefeated in school matches. The U15 IV of Tom Gower, Jon Hammond, Christopher Newman and Frederik Foss-Pedersen reached the regional finals of the Midland Bank Tournament – a remarkable achievement.

1993 saw a generally good season under Richard Brice's captaincy. The School IV reached the semi-finals of their section of the Midland Bank Trophy being undefeated in school matches, as were the U15 VI. It was also Penny Allberry and Dudley Georgeson's last season after 15 years as the School's tennis professionals.

The excellent 1994 season included the first three VIs being undefeated in school matches. The VI, captained by Richard Harrison, reached the regional finals of the Midland Bank Tournament.

The U16 VI won all their matches in 1996 while the U15 team reached the final of the county Midland Bank competition. The talented Allan twins became the first pair in 1997 when Gordon Proctor was the tennis professional and Stephen Lunt the master-in-charge.

Veteran of five years in the VI, James Banks, was 1999 captain, winning the boys' singles tournament for the fourth year in succession, probably a School record.

At played 12, lost 12, 2000 was the worst year on record and even captain Garth Banks could not revive fortunes much in 2002. However, there was a contrast in 2003 when the U15 IV of Nick Sword (Captain), Chris and Sam Tasker-Grindley and Henry Staelens emerged as 3rd nationally for their age group in the HSBC competition. Neil Kynaston was now the coach, later replaced by Chris Neal.

By 2007, the School game was '...very healthy...' according to Aron Needs, the master-in-charge, as more boys than ever were playing. Under coach Mark Jacobsen, the IV reached the regional quarter finals in the Glanvil Cup while the U15 VI had an unbeaten season in matches.

The 2008 season included 6 matches. The two top VIs both won and lost three each of their matches and did not go far in the Glanvil Cup.

***Tennis (Girls)***

1973 saw Ann Nicholls captain the first ever girls' VI. It lost one match but won against Wycliffe College. The Old Decanians won the first match against the VI in 1978.

Sheila Milne and Cathy Edginton won the Gloucestershire Schoolgirls' Doubles Championships in 1984 while match results also improved. An U15 VI won all but one of seven matches in 1986. Improved facilities helped the 1988 season, when the 1st VI and 2nd VI won 14 out of 17 matches played.

The U15s were undefeated in 1989 and were area league winners in the Midland Bank Competition. Charlie Forbes and Martina Calvert won the county Schoolgirls' Doubles Championships. Again, in 1990, the 1st VI and 2nd VI won 14 out of 17 matches. Frances Allberry, captain in 1991 and 1992, led the 1st VI to victory in all but one of their nine 1991 matches. Indeed, out of five School VIs, 36 matches were played of which only six were conceded. The U15 VI reached the county finals of the Midland Bank competition.

Tennis team 2005.
Standing: Mrs Hilary Swan, Nadia Charania, Natasha Price, Emma Lewis, Isabella Fateh, Mr Neil Kynaston
Seated: Alexandra Cameron, Rebecca Saunders (capt), Francesca Downes

In 1993, the 3rd and U14A VIs were both undefeated in matches. Penny Allberry and Dudley Georgeson retired as tennis coaches after 15 years' improving standards at the School.

By 1994 there were eight girls' VIs as well as an U15 IV of Rachel Rank, Joanna Fulton, Linsey Bell and Selina Dowty who were county champions and finalists at regional level in the Midland Bank competition.

From 1995 to 1997, results tended to be similar to the early 1990s but in 1998 Hilary Swan retired as coach, returning part-time until 2008, together with Bridget Edkins, Chris Neal and later Mark Jacobsen.

In 1999 the 3rd VI was unbeaten in their matches. 1998-2003 were seasons where the talented Blampied sisters – Katrina, Eleanor and Amelia – were all strong players and all captained the sport in turn. Amelia, with Jo Crisp, won the county Schools' U18 Doubles' Championship in 2001 while members of the VI reached the 4th round of the U18 HSBC National Schools' Aberdare Cup. The U18 county Schoolgirls' Doubles' Trophy was won by Amelia Blampied and Helen Perry in 2003.

The U15 age group teams were undefeated in matches in 2004 while in 2005 the VI, 2nd and 3rd VIs won all but one match each. The 2006 season saw the 2nd VI undefeated in their matches, a feat also achieved by 3rds and U14A VIs the following season. An U15 team competed in a BSTA competition, winning the area final. 2008 was a solid if unspectacular season.

***Water Polo (Boys and Girls)***

Water polo first appeared as a 'boys versus girls' game, part of a swimming spectacular at Commemoration, 1974.

In 1981, junior and senior teams unsuccessfully entered the English Schools' Water Polo Championship. In the 1983-84 season, both teams successfully reached the quarter-finals, as well as playing other school matches. A first Old Decanian side was beaten 12-4 by the School in 1994. Steve Ong was picked for the county and the West for Junior Water Polo. In 1995-96 the U16 team reached the 2nd round of the English Schools Championships.

In 1997 and 1998 both junior and senior teams reached the quarter-finals of the English Schools' League. The team won all three of their school matches in 1999 while Chris Egan's team in 2000 beat all four opponents; a suitable send-off for retiring coach Marion Venn, who introduced the sport to the School.

The boys' team won the Plate trophy in the English Schools Water Polo in 2001. They toured Holland, playing four matches – and lost every one! Meantime, a girls' team beat Cheltenham College – twice! Jenna Mac, Sophie Davies and Rachael Corry represented the Western Counties at the U17 regional water polo tournament.

In 2003, the water polo team lost to SVH of Holland at Commemoration. However, in 2005 the girls, captained by Kate Batty, achieved the Bronze Medal in the U16 English Schools Swimming Association Water Polo Tournament, winning the Silver under the same captain the following year. In 2007, an ESSA water polo tournament was held at the School, possibly for the first time. Led by Rosie Pushman, the U16 team did well, reaching the quarter-finals.

The U16 girls reached the semi-finals and won the Bronze Medal in the English Schools water polo competition in 2008. The U18 boys' team came 4th in their competition.

## *Other Sports*

*Badminton*

In the 1971-72 *Decanian* report it is evident that a boys' VI had been playing '...for many years...' less than well. In 1977 a girls' team entered for the first time. The game was revived by A.N. Baillie in the early 1980s, Junior and Senior VIs being formed. Matches slowly accumulated until, in 1985, there were six matches against other schools, the VI winning three. The game was largely confined to fiercely fought inter-house matches.

In 2004, Rebecca Pantanay, Commonwealth Gold Medallist, began coaching at the School. Matches are now being played, those against Cheltenham College being particularly keenly fought.

*Basketball*

Well established before 1969, the team, captained by S.R.A. Weighill, won five of ten matches that year. Under D. Petrencik's dedicated coaching, the game became a minor sport. However, Mr Petrencik left in 1972, Mr Whitting being his successor. In the 1977-78 season, captain Drew Mitzner led an unbeaten team in school matches and reached the semi-finals of the Gloucestershire Schools Knockout Cup that also included some clubs, only losing to St Paul's College. In 1979 and again in 1980, the team, consisting at various times of Bahamians, Germans, Egyptians, Americans, Palestinians and Chinese as well as English won the Gloucestershire Schools' County Cup. Four players were selected for the U19 county team. 1980 also saw Colours awarded for the first time, Full Colours being awarded to Roland Hover.

In 1981-82 the team reached the semi-finals of the Gloucestershire Men's Division 1 Cup. Sam Abbas played for Gloucestershire and the West Midlands in the Junior National League. In 1988, the senior side won the Gloucestershire League and reached the final of the knockout cup, led by Tom Edginton and hugely aided by English Speaking Union scholar Jim Battle. Since then, the side has played half a dozen or so matches a year with varying fortune, although it appears that the side is not at present entering competitions.

Girls' basketball began with eight girls in September 2002 but quickly spread. Captain Lisa Kemp led a team to the finals of the South Midlands Independent Schools' Cup the same season.

In 2004, a girls' squad entered the South West tournament and competed in the Gloucestershire League where they won Division 3. Duncan O'Neill followed by Laura Burton have coached with some success.

*Chess*

The January 1983 *The Decanian* noted that there were 11 School chess matches per term, not two as before! M.E. Garbett, master-in-charge, entered the team in the local league. Robert Keiller and Christian Allen were selected to play for the Cheltenham U18 team. Chess became a School sport in 1987-88, challenging other schools and even winning the regional section of *The Times* Knockout Competition a year or two later. It has since had a very variable following, helped by Decanians such as Sam Gilbert, Farman Kaveh and Will Batten and staff such as John Moule and Sue Padfield. Recently, there has been a revival of interest under Peter Garner, who organized the biggest ever voluntary School knockout competition in 2008 in which over 200 Decanians took part, the senior winner being James Savage and the junior Wesley Howell, Gate winning the senior house cup and Field the junior.

*Clay Pigeon Shooting*

In 1990, a team of six came 22nd in the Independent Schools Clay Shooting Championships with Alastair Negus coming 12th individually out of over 500 competitors. In 1991, the team improved to 16th. In 1992, master-in-charge Chris Carmell produced two boys' and one girls' team. One boys' team was 11th overall and the girls were 4th overall at the Nationals. In 1993, the School came 3rd out of 15 schools in the 'Warwick Challenge' and was 'Best Invited School'. In the South West Schools competition, the School came 3rd out of over 20 schools.

In 1996 and 1997, the girls' team of Kirsty Herbertson, Katy Hopkin and Zoe Westwood won the Heart of England Trophy, with Katy winning the individual ladies' section in 1996, and the High Gun in 1997. In 1997 they also won the West Midlands competition, with Kirsty Herbertson gaining the High Gun.

In 1998, Anna Richardson, Katy Hopkin and Kirsty Herbertson won the National Schools Clay Pigeon Shooting Competition with a score of 95 out of 150, 12 points ahead of their rivals.

Eric Lai

*Fencing*

In the 1994-95 season, David Spanner qualified for the U14 National Fencing Competition. By 2000, Eric Lai, who began Fencing in the Junior School, was U16 Gloucestershire event winner and won the South West U18 Championships in 2001, qualifying him for the Nationals. In Budapest, he finished in the top 64. He was selected for the U17 Great Britain team that went to Belgium in 2002.

*Golf*

In 1972, a small but keen Golf Club won 5 out of 10 matches. David Williams played each opposing team's number one and won all but one match.

By 1988 golf was well established and an 18 hole putting-green was briefly created thanks to head groundsman, Neville Page. That year, the School was Gloucestershire Schools' Golf Champions. The courses at Ullenwood Manor and the Cotswold Hill Golf Club started to be used in 1989. Ten years later, Brickhampton Court GC tended to be the School's main golfing venue.

In 1991 in the County Schools' Championship, a weakened boys' team still managed to finish runners-up. Beth Alger was selected to represent the county – the first female Decanian to achieve representative honours in golf.

In 1992-93, golfers began to use the complex at Tredington; PGA professional David Finch coached them. Richard Brice represented Gloucestershire and was the School's only single handicap player. The next year the School team came 4th out of 16 schools in the British Heart Foundation Schools Competition.

1999 was Paul Marchand's year. He was selected for the British Independent Schools' Golf Tour of the USA, a team called the Swifts. 85 schools nominated players for this prestigious event. Paul performed well on the course and was a fine ambassador off it. In the USA with the team, he travelled 25,000 miles, played 19 courses and 13 competitive matches, winning 11 of them.

Golf team 2008.
Standing: Andy Swarbrick (coach), Thomas Dowler, Matthew Dowler, Adam Williams, Andrew Maxwell
Seated: Simon Marlow, David Barron (capt), Joshua Powell

In 2002, golfers reached the semi-finals of the HMC (Head Masters Conference) foursomes. Alex Carlisle won the inaugural Odell Cup (an internal stableford competition). Lilleybrook was now the regular venue. 2004 was Garth Williams' last year as master-in-charge, handing over to Ben Barton, then to Andy Swarbrick. House matches have developed and Gate triumphed for the three years up to 2008.

In 2008 there were several matches with mixed results but a Sixth Form v Common Room match was introduced, played at the Cotswold Golf Club, which the boys won 3-1.

*Gymnastics*

There was a revival of interest in gymnastics in 1970, and from then on there was a team that did a display every Commemoration, certainly up to the late 1980s. Initially, they were coached by Major Chapman and later by G.E.B. Whiting.

Pippa Mason and Anna Righton were the first two girls to take part in 1973, and the squad was 14 strong the following year, seven boys, seven girls. The display team increased to eight boys and eight girls and two reserves in 1976. The display was a part of Commemoration in 1985, although it is difficult to pin-point when it finished.

*Lacrosse*

In 1990, Charlotte Dyer won a place in the U18 Welsh Lacrosse team, '...for which we can take no credit...' as the Headmaster, Christopher Bacon, remarked.

*Martial Arts and Associated Sports*

Jo Hanks won the Silver Medal in her class at the National Ju-Jitsu Championships in 1998. In 2001 a range of martial arts and alternatives, from power yoga to Tai Bo, an ancient form of self defence similar to kick boxing, were tried, sessions attracting about 25 students.

*Modern Pentathlon*

Richard Hildick-Smith represented Great Britain at Modern Pentathlon in September 2002, when he was in the Fifth Form. Since then he has continued to do so in that and related events, being 6th in the Biathlon World Championships in 2004, 2nd in the National Triathlon Championships in 2005, champion in 2006 and ranked 3rd in the UK for the Pentathlon in 2007. By the end of 2008, Richard had been awarded two Blues for Swimming, two for Modern Pentathlon and 1½ for Athletics, with the probability of two more before leaving Oxford University. He has been awarded more Blues than any other Old Decanian.

*Orienteering*

In 2002, Tessa and brother Chris Hill came 8th and 33rd respectively in their age groups in the British Schools Orienteering Competition. Tessa built up her expertise while at the School (2001-05), coming 3rd in her age group in the World Schools Orienteering selection qualification race and 6th in the British Schools Orienteering Championships in 2003. She eventually received a Bronze Medal as a member of the English Senior Girls National Team at the World Schools Orienteering Championships in Belgium in 2004.

In 2005, Ian Collinson, Chris and Tessa Hill competed in the British Schools Orienteering Championships, held at Sandringham. Tessa Hill, a Great Britain team member, won the girls' individual title in 42.02 minutes on a 5½km course. Ian completed his course but Chris had to retire. Tessa Hill also came 3rd in the UK International Festival, thereby becoming the British Elite Champion at Middle Distance in the U20 competition. She also came 3rd in the U18 Long Distance Competition.

Tessa Hill

*Rounders*

1999 included the first *Decanian* report on rounders. An U15 XI, led by Alix Reid, and an U14 XI, led by Georgina Hildick-Smith, played four matches in all, winning three, scoring 82 rounders and conceding 71. Alix Reid and Katie Lea also attended England trials for possible selection into the 'C' team during the summer.

The following summer, both the U15 team, captained by Jacky Allen, and the U14 team led by Elizabeth Pratt, were unbeaten, although neither played more than three matches.

Through the 2000s, two or three matches have been played each season, 2008 ending with two victories and one defeat, led by captains Rosie Pushman and Miriam Mangue. Paula Watson has been the coach since 1999.

*Ski-ing*

In the British Senior Ski-ing Championships in 1991, Giles Barton was ranked number one in his age group when he won the Slalom and the Super Giant Slalom. In the British Junior Championships he came 12th, 17th and 28th overall in the Slalom, Giant Slalom and Super Giant Slalom respectively. The same year, Katherine Pallett, Rachel Darke and Joanne Marston all participated in the British Schoolgirls' Invitation Ski Races in Switzerland.

Ten years later, in the winter of 2000-01, Sixth Former Sergei Terent'ev became the Russian National Downhill Ski Champion for the second successive year, with a place in the Russian Ski team for the fourth time.

Chris Gregory

*Soccer*

In 1996, football reappeared at the School for the first time since 1938. In November 1997, Nick Anderson led a School U16 XI to victory over Cheltenham College. The game has continued to be played spasmodically ever since.

*Sporting Giants*

This was the name of a programme set up by Sir Steve Redgrave, the Olympic oarsman, to find potential Olympians for 2012. In 2008 he selected 6'9" Sixth Former Chris Gregory to be in the volleyball stream, one of only a handful to be selected out of over 4,000 applicants.

*Trampolining*

Trampolines were first acquired in September 1985. Within weeks, Julian Acheampong came 3rd in the South West Schools Championships while the U15 boys won the team event. In October 1985, Ruth and Lucy Robinson won the Sychronized Event while Hanna Steplewska and Nadia Stradling came 3rd in the Welsh Tariff Competition. In the Welsh Championships, Julian Acheampong came 2nd in the men's events while the Robinson girls came 5th and 7th in their event, Moira Davies finishing 5th in the U18 girls' age group. In the South West Closed Championships, Matthew Herbert won the U15 competition.

In 1986, Julian Acheampong partnered coach Tony Jones to win the men's synchronized event in Group 2 of the Welsh Tariff Competition, and also came 3rd in the individual competition. In Group 1, Lucy Robinson and Hanna Steplewska won the sychronized competition, Lucy also coming 2nd in the individual competition. In the teams, Matthew Herbert and David and Gareth Jones won the men's section.

1988 was another good year, the U15 girls 'A' team winning the Gloucestershire Schools' Championships, the 'B' team coming 3rd. Kate Tilley won the individual title; Christian Oliver won the boys' U15 event, Julian Acheampong the U19 event. In 1991, in the Gloucestershire Schools' Championships, Gareth Jones beat brother David, the previous year's winner, into 2nd place. Matthew Winstone won the U19 event, aged 14.

However, with the departure of Tony Jones the coach, the sport fell into something of a decline until Naomi McBane arrived to coach it in 2003, since when it has become a popular activity.

**Sports in which Decanians have reached International Status**

- Bowls
- Cricket
- Curling
- Equestrian
- Fencing
- Fishing
- Hockey (boys)
- Hockey (girls)
- Lacrosse
- Modern Pentathlon
- Orienteering
- Rugby
- Ski-ing
- Squash

*Cheltenham Sports Achievement Award*

In 1992, Decanian David Ferguson was selected by Whitbread Breweries to be the first recipient of the Cheltenham Sports Achievement Award, created to give recognition to individuals who have made a contribution to any aspect of sport despite particular problems. David completed a number of half-marathons after undergoing extensive neuro-surgery. He raised money through his running for the Neurological Research Fund of the Bristol Royal Infirmary's radiotherapy centre.

**ODs Selected for Olympics**

| | | | |
|---|---|---|---|
| D.A. Pringle | Pentathlon (reserve) | Berlin | 1936 |
| R.I. Ireland | Hockey | Tokyo | 1964 |
| Ben Marsden | Hockey | Beijing | 2008 |

# Chapter 12

# The CCF and Outdoor Pursuits from 1919

The formation of the Officer Training Corps (OTC) in 1909, forerunner of the CCF, was C.C. Mountfort's second major contribution to the School, who two years previously had initiated boys into playing hockey. He was the first Officer Commanding. A type of CCF had been foreseen by Dr Flecker when speaking at the Old Decanians' Dinner in January 1900 (see chapter 3). An outdoor miniature shooting range, 35 yards long, was constructed in 1909, roughly where the Tuckwell Theatre is, necessitating removal of part of the bank and creation of a causeway. A second, indoor, range followed possibly in 1910 but more likely 1913, sited roughly between today's Bacon Theatre and the Music School.

Initially, few joined the OTC but during the First World War every physically fit boy was expected to enrol. An Orderly Room was fitted up, bugling and semaphore signalling began and one boy constructed a heliograph. By 1919, no officer was left to command other than the wounded son

OTC camp 1911

OTC parade 1918. Top left, note Walton Court stables before conversion to the (old) School shop

of the Headmaster, H.L.O. Flecker, who held things together for a few months, possibly assisted by J.W. Talbot. Sergeant-Major Golder also arrived, remaining for many years as RSM/SSI. Major G.P. Daniels became Officer Commanding in 1920.

The School Corps supported the annual Public Schools' camp from Trinity 1910 when 30 went and virtually every year thereafter, entering competitions in Physical Training, Drums and Guard Mounting and apparently never fell below third place.

The contingent gradually evolved. In 1937, a riding class began '…at Mr Parry's School…' for beginners and advanced riders and, more adventurously, an Air Squad was formed. Participants had to have passed their Certificate 'A' training. Eight cadets enrolled at the Cotswold Aero Club with flying instructor Pilot Officer 'Red' Walwin. Three cadets were learning to fly, a fourth joining in 1938. Within months two of them, Anthony Mathias, aged 18, and Roy Lawson, 16, had 'gone solo' after only 5½ hours dual instruction, flying biplanes. Sadly, both were killed in the Second World War, Pilot Officer Mathias, RAF, in July 1940 over South Holland and Flight Sergeant Lawson, RAFVR, over Malta in December 1941. The School was possibly the first to include flying as part of OTC training. The Air Section was not refounded until January 1952.

The contingent's standards remained consistently high, even during the evacuation to Monkton Combe at the beginning of the Second World War (see chapter 5).

The School Home Guard platoon in 1940

Presentation to Major Golder in 1944

Captain E.S. Hoare was in charge during the war years, when the OTC provided a platoon of the Cheltenham Home Guard with the extra training involved. The School also co-operated in starting the Cheltenham Schools' Squadron of the Air Training Corps (ATC).

On Commemoration Day (allied to Remembrance Sunday in November 1943) the JTC paraded with drums on Chapel Close, to be inspected by General John Lee of the US Army, the only inspecting officer thus far not from UK forces. Many US troops were billeted in Cheltenham in preparation for D-Day.

The Cheltenham Home Guard was disbanded at a ceremony on 3rd December, 1944, Captain Golder having passed 25 years' service with the School contingent in the previous Trinity Term.

The 1946 Annual Inspection report by Colonel A.A.E. Chitty, Inspector of Training Corps and Army Cadet Force, was glowing: '…a very good unit, well commanded. There is a really fine spirit throughout this contingent and Dean Close is rightly proud of its JTC…'. Captain Hoare stepped aside

Admiral Lord Tovey leaving Chapel after the Remembrance Day service 1948 accompanied by the Headmaster, A.N. Gilkes

for Captain W.A. Davies, now commanding a contingent of 171 cadets. Unfortunately, Captain Davies left in 1947 and his place was taken by Captain A.S.R. Parker, who continued as Officer Commanding until 1960.

In January 1948, the JTC occupied new huts, where is not clear but equipment could now be brought together. That year the contingent became a 'Combined Cadet Force' (CCF). After basic training, cadets might opt for the Army or, if available, the Royal Navy or RAF.

The 1948 Remembrance Day visitor was Admiral of the Fleet Lord Tovey, responsible for the sinking of the German Battleship *Bismark* in the War. The 1949 Remembrance Day dignitary was the Duke of Beaufort, KG.

In 1949 a CCF shooting team entered for Bisley for the first time, under Lieut C.B. Kiddell. That summer, Major Golder retired from the CCF, though not entirely from the School.

**The British Schools' Exploring Society (BSES)**

The British Schools' Exploring Society is the oldest youth adventure society in the world. Surgeon Commander Murray Levick, who, with two other men, had been imprisoned in a snow-hole for months with two weeks' rations during Scott's last, ill-fated expedition to the South Pole, realized that their survival had depended on teamwork. He wanted young people to learn, like him, the value of living in remote, challenging conditions while pulling together as a team. He founded the British Schools' Exploring Society in 1932. Its objects are to advance the education of young people and promote the development of their confidence, teamwork and leadership skills through the provision of inspirational challenging scientific expeditions to remote, wild environments.

Since 1953, over 30 Decanians have been on these expeditions all over the world. Co-educational expeditions have existed since 1981.

Currently, Dean Close is a BSES Star School, that is it has produced four or more pupils who have gone on expeditions between 2004-07. Only 20 schools in the country have that accolade.

Those Decanians who have participated include:

| | | |
|---|---|---|
| M.R. Greening | British Columbia | 1953 |
| D.J. Foster | Northern Quebec | 1955 |
| I.G. Handy | Northern Quebec | 1955 |
| Sarah Ball | East Greenland | 1982 |
| Simon Derry | Arctic Norway | 1984 |
| John Collins | S E Iceland | 1985 |
| Dominic Faulkner | Yukon, Alaska | 1986 |
| Kathryn Watson | Himalayas | 1988 |
| Matthew Newall | Arctic Norway | 1989 |
| Emma Garrett | Arctic Norway | 1993 |
| Will Garrett | Arctic Norway | 1994 |
| Richard Ball | Alaska | 1995 |
| Nicholas Ball | West Himalayas | 1997 |
| George Walker | Lesotho | 1998 |
| Christopher Price | Alaska | 1999 |
| Robert Kinder | Greenland | 2000 |
| John Lee | Malawi | 2000 |
| Edward Forrester | Malawi | 2000 |
| Sam Barrett | Himalayas | 2001 |
| Garth Banks | Alaska | 2001 |
| Joe Moor | Upper Amazon | 2002 |
| James Davies | Upper Amazon | 2002 |
| Vicki Cooper | Amazon Forest | 2002 |
| Ben Hadfield | Arctic Norway | 2002 |
| Guy Huckvale | Arctic Norway | 2002 |
| Samantha Jackson | Arctic Norway | 2002 |
| Lana Kettle | Lesotho | 2003 |
| Samantha Jackson | Footsteps of Shackleton | 2003 |
| Guy Nield | Arctic Norway | 2004 |
| James Townsend | Arctic Norway | 2004 |
| Rebecca Craig | Greenland | 2006 |
| Megan Howell | Peruvian Andes | 2006 |
| Natasha Price | Peruvian Andes | 2006 |

*Miss J.A. Crane (Leader, Greenland 1988; Leader, Arctic Norway 1989) taught at the School 1986-89, returning as Mrs J.A. Davis, Senior Mistress, in 2007.*

On Friday, 16th March, 1951, Princess Elizabeth visited Cheltenham and inspected a School CCF guard of honour in Shelburne Road.

During 1951-52 at the Remembrance Day parade, Air Vice-Marshall L. Darvall, CB, MC was the first RAF officer to inspect the contingent, and the only visiting RAF officer to hold the Military Cross rather than the Distinguished Flying Cross (DFC). In the following Lent Term the Air Section of the Corps was refounded with 25 boys. It was led by E.S. Hay, assisted by the Revd P.R.W. Tidmarsh, both members of staff having had RAF war-time experience.

1953 was Coronation Year. Outdoor Pursuits began at the School, with M.R. Greening being selected for the British Schools Exploring Societies' (BSES) Expedition to British Columbia. A glider was purchased and, apart from six hours of static training, there were 62 launches recorded by the RAF Section. Corporals Foster and Seavers both won Flying Scholarships. Corporal Paget-Wilkes later also achieved a Flying Scholarship, the first three of many, yet only 90 were awarded per year in the whole country.

In 1955, Sgt R.A. Ellis returned from Bisley with the Silver Medal in the *Sunday Times* Rapid Competition. The contingent was the best in the district according to Inspecting Officer Brigadier Shacklock and his staff officer. That Trinity R.A. Ellis, Captain of Shooting, also won the *Sunday Times* Medals Competition.

During Michaelmas 1955, the full Remembrance Parade on Remembrance Sunday was discontinued, it being felt that the elaborate Inspection and March Past was becoming less appropriate, and so a simple Guard of Honour and Colour Party took its place.

In 1956, Air Vice-Marshal S.O. Bufton was the first OD to be Inspecting Officer. A CCF Corps Hut was built, roughly where the BonBernard Gallery is now.

Over the Easter holidays, an officer and nine cadets made the contingent's first visit to BAOR. They, together with some Westminster School cadets, were guests of the 5th Royal Inniskillin Dragoon Guards. The highlight was a night exercise in which cadets '...saw and experienced...' the massive centurion tanks in action.

Duke of Edinburgh Gold Award expedition 2007-8.
Matthew Dowler, James Savage, Adam Williams, Andrew Maxwell, Lucy Howell and Eleanor Stone

The unassuming, friendly, interested Lt-Col J.P. Carne VC, DSO, whose courage in the Korean War had captured the imagination of many, was Inspecting Officer that Trinity.

Hugh Cocksedge, an RAF officer, arrived in Michaelmas 1958 and revived the RAF section. Under him, the School became one of the experimental units of the Duke of Edinburgh's (DoE) Award Scheme and first year cadets took part in training for Bronze Awards, helping to develop the syllabus. The course involved '...much camping and endurance…'. The initial camp for 20 cadets was in the first week of January at Plasterdown on Dartmoor. Several cadets survived a night out on the moor without food, tent or lights. The camp was seen as an unqualified success, notwithstanding '…ferocious…' weather, escaped convicts, '…shaky…' map reading in some quarters and the '…general necessity to learn as one went…'.

The House Drill Competition was revived in Michaelmas 1959. The Band continued to play at the War Memorial in Sherborne Village at the British Legion's Remembrance Service as it had done for several years.

During the Lent Term, 1960, Wing Commander Rayner, Director of the BSES, presented DoE Award Scheme Bronze Medals to qualifiers. They were the first Decanians to receive these awards. After achieving the Bronze Award, cadets could move on to the Silver and, upon completion, attempt the Gold Award.

In Michaelmas 1960, the Inspecting Officer, Brigadier G. Laing, presented 12 Silver and 44 Bronze DoE Awards, the first time Silver Awards had been achieved by Decanians. That autumn a group of NCOs who had been training juniors for Bronze Awards completed their own Golds and were presented with them by Prince Philip at St James' Palace.

The following May, Colonel E.C. Pickard OD, who had been the CCF CSM 32 years before, inspected. The CCF sent its first ever team, that included Sgts Gorton and Taffinder, L/Cpl Seymour-Smith and Cadets Millward, Prior and Wright, on the Ten Tors exercise. Together with 152 other teams, they covered 50 miles starting from Haytor Rocks in 36 hours, of which 10 hours were compulsory rest over the Saturday night. Although making one error costing 45 minutes to rectify, they reached the Hexworthy finish with 2½ hours to spare, winning a medallion as the team was complete. Later, Sgt M.A. Taffinder, writing in *The Decanian*, hoped the School would send a team or two annually, feeling that '…a more worthwhile expedition would be difficult to find…'.

The Corps buildings were extended by Christmas 1961, with a Signals HQ, lecture room, office, Arduous Training equipment, RAF and drums stores. Asphalt paths were laid and grass sown around the weeping willow the following spring.

Arduous Training was on the Brecon Beacons for the first time in January 1962. That Trinity among Army Scholarships to Sandhurst, RAF Scholarships to Henlow and Flying Scholarships, ten more boys achieved DoE Gold Awards. The main camp was at Leek in North Staffordshire; the First Years' Camp was at South Brent on Dartmoor. At the end of this latter camp the equipment and staff remained to run a specialized camp, largely for boys from the County who were attempting Silver and Gold expeditions. For the next 40 years and more, Gold, Silver and especially Bronze Awards were to be made every year. Records are incomplete but suggest that since 1960 over 130 Gold Awards have been made under increasingly difficult and stringent regulations.

Old CCF buildings, where the BonBernard Gallery is today

Arduous Training in the 1963 Easter holiday was near Aberystwyth, centred on an old house by a lake in the centre of a group of 'bleak' hills. It consisted of some of the DoE's Silver and Gold Award Expeditions as the Army had cancelled the original Arduous Training the previous January. Elements of the DoE scheme were becoming part of the cadets' programme. The First Year Cadet Camp was the biggest ever, at Abernefal in Mid-Wales, and included Silver Award expeditions.

Ten Tors Trek

That June, the CCF Shooting VIII entered the Sussex County Rifle Association Public Schools Open Meeting at Bisley. Out of 41 schools, Dean Close came third in the Cusack-Smith Bowl, was runner-up in the Cox Cup and won the Royal Sussex Regiment Challenge Cup, while Cpl J.S.R. Hawkins won the Silver Medal in the individual Aylesbury Cup.

New CCF training patterns were implemented from Christmas 1963. New, Fourth Form, boys trained for DoE Awards but received help from the CCF both in staff and materials. Most cadets were in the CCF for nine terms, their second, third and fourth years at School. The Army Basic Test was abolished, allowing Cadets to enter the RAF Section directly as recruits. Cadets could aim either for Advanced Proficiency in the Army CCF, or for Specialist qualifications in Signals, Motor Transport, Civil Defence or First Aid. In the final two years, genuine university scholarship candidates could be excused any form of service. The remainder were required to choose: to remain in the CCF as a senior NCO, numbers for which would be limited; help train boys for their Bronze Awards as non-Corps instructors; or join a Pioneer squad working on projects around the School. Changes did not result from a decline in the appeal of military matters: on the contrary, just after Christmas 1963, five boys from the School entered Sandhurst, a high number.

In 1964, training changes now in place meant the annual junior Fourth Year or 'Yearlings' Camp during Trinity became compulsory, happening during the last ten days of term, thus being part of the School curriculum rather than an optional extra. Naturally, it was larger than before, 75 cadets plus officers and some senior NCOs going to Aish Ridge on the southern edge of Dartmoor. It concentrated on basic instruction in camping, map reading, compass work, giving opportunities for completing a DoE Award Silver expedition, and encouraging Bronze Award completion. Its success continued for more than ten years. As usual, it was in addition to the annual camp which was at Plasterdown, near Tavistock, Devon.

The 1964 CCF shooting team captain, D.E. Langford, shot for UK cadets in Canada and again when the Canadians came over to the UK for the Graham Bell Trophy. The UK team won with a new record score of 759, and D.E. Langford was the third highest scorer with 95 out of a hundred.

Arduous Training in January 1965 involved boys attempting Gold Award expeditions. Unfortunately, the weather around Okehampton was so appalling that attempts were abandoned for the first time, only half the 50 miles having been completed. Later, at Whitsun, a second Ten Tors

**The 50 Mile Walk by T.J. Linford, M.S. Reynolds and P.R.H. Webber**

The object was to walk 50 miles across-country in under 15 hours, thereby beating the time of two boys from another public school. It meant walking at a constant speed of just over 3.3 miles per hour. The three Decanians did no particular training, although they were fit. The walk was attempted on Tuesday, 7th December, 1965, supervised by RSM Benians, assisted by two senior boys, B.G. James and A.W. Horncastle, who covered the course in a car bringing the team hot food.

They started near Tewkesbury at 5.10am. The route was via Bredon Hill, Elmley Castle and Hinton which was reached on time at 8am. They walked on to Broadway, up Fish Hill, to Lynes Barn Farm and from there to Syreford. At dusk the team were on top of Cleeve Hill, then they dropped down to Winchcombe, by which time over 40 miles had been walked. The finish at Aston Cross was reached by way of Gretton and Teddington Hands at 7.40pm, exactly 14½ hours after the start.

expedition was mounted in which four participants (S.G. Barnes, J.F. Cobb, P.R.H. Webber and M.S. Reynolds) were joined at short notice by the inevitably slightly less fit B.G. James and T.J. Linford. Notwithstanding a number of blisters and a twisted ankle, the team completed the 50 mile challenge with 2½ hours to spare, finishing in roughly the same time as the first expedition from the School, four years earlier.

Arduous Training in January 1966 at Okehampton was in some appallingly wet weather so only three of the 11 who started completed the course for their Gold Award 50 mile expedition. However, the previous month, having read that at another school two boys had walked 50 miles in 15 hours, three Dean Close boys, T.J. Linford, M.S. Reynolds and P.R.H. Webber, decided to attempt to beat it. They succeeded.

The School entered two teams for the Ten Tors Expedition at Whitsun 1966. One was for the 60 mile course for 18-20 year olds, the second for the 35 mile course for the 14-16 year olds, both for the first time. Regulations had been significantly tightened. Only two of the senior team were over 17 but they completed the course with one hour left of the 26 allowed. The junior team, which comprised four Yearlings (13-14 year olds), also had two older boys, J.R.B. Cook, the leader, and M.W. Eaton. They finished with five hours to spare.

Companies A and B were scrapped in Trinity 1967, being replaced by House Platoons. The Inspection was by Field Marshal Sir Claude Auchinleck. He presented a new Cadet CSM's stick to the Corps, the first to use it being his relative, Mark. Captain Trevett, Adjutant for nearly ten years, moved on.

The end of Trinity 1969 marked the end of an era, for from the beginning of September 1969, CCF membership became voluntary, Decanians having a choice between that and other forms of training or service.

In shooting, the VIII did well – during the Lent Term 1969 it was unbeaten in school matches. Later, it came fourth out of 31 schools in the Country Life Competition, R.L. Lemon achieving the highest individual score.

By 1969 the Drum Corps had been disbanded. Those volunteering for the CCF did so knowing that they would be in for a minimum of two years. However, the DoE's Award Scheme was still required in the first year at the School. An Adventure Section was formed, with the hope that canoeing, mountaineering and similar activities might be possible. Interestingly, while the overall number in the CCF went down, the RAF section actually increased.

Decanians sometimes 'did their own thing' in outward bound terms. The Trinity 1970 *Decanian* included a graphic account by Stephen Oxlade (Fifth Former) of his climb with two others of Kilimanjaro, on the border between Kenya and Tanzania. Meanwhile, the CCF and 'Adventure Training Section' had their annual camp at Leek in Staffordshire, as well as the Yearlings' camp on Dartmoor. This was the last camp organized by Hugh Cocksedge, who left at Michaelmas 1970. Rhod Pentycross took over.

Hugh Cocksedge had been the architect of the Duke of Edinburgh Award Scheme within the School, and being one of the first in that field had been trained by Sir John Hunt of Everest fame. By the time he left, over three quarters of the School were involved. He was Housemaster of Gate 1966-70. He left to become warden of an educational centre near Wisbech for London schools and later entered the Church, serving in Turkey.

Thirteen cadets on Dartmoor during Easter 1971 all completed the 50 mile expedition for the Gold DoE Award.

The CCF adapted successfully in Michaelmas 1972 to new requirements, under their Officer Commanding since 1970, Major the Reverend D.I. Gibson, who had taken over from Major J.S. Moore.

That autumn, a DoE climbing weekend was spent in Snowdonia for the first time. Returning at Easter, they experienced '...glorious climbing in shirt sleeves...'. In the following holidays it was reported that '...a few climbers joined the DoE Gold expedition camp and, despite some good days climbing, spent most days and nights rescuing the DoE groups...'. In addition to a further climbing weekend in Snowdonia, in the Trinity Term there was climbing in Glencoe and the Avon Gorge. Two eventful weekends were spent white-water canoeing and a canoeing trip was also made on the Rivers Severn and Avon that involved camping out just north of Tewkesbury. By the end of that term, 36 boys had been on one or more rock climbing trips and 15 were able to handle a canoe competently.

The DoE Scheme at the School passed another landmark in Trinity 1974 when there was a girls' camp as well as the usual boys'. The climbers for their part made two major trips to the Lake District and a brief one to Chepstow.

In Trinity 1975, climbers Simon Reeve, Tony Long, Jo Trickey and Gordon Heaton-Jones climbed Ben Nevis. Four boys completed their Gold expedition on the Isle of Mull; another four completed theirs in the Lake District. In October 1974 and May 1975 there was rock climbing in Snowdonia; in August 1975 it was in Glencoe; much of the organization for this was undertaken by Rhod Pentycross. There had been whitewater canoeing at Glasbury that April, too. There was canoeing on the River Wye that November; rock climbing in Snowdonia in March and the Lake District in April and June 1976. Mountaineering on the Isle of Skye occurred in August/September, although an attempt to traverse the Cuillin Ridge was unsuccessful.

During 1976, Major Gibson relinquished command of the CCF, and Lt-Cdr M.J.R. Cooper became Officer Commanding. By 1980, the CCF had been reorganized. Of 125 cadets, the Army had 80, the RAF 29 and a relatively new (*c.*1974) Royal Naval section 16.

Scouts were part of the School during the early 1980s, led by Mike Hawkins, who had been a keen Scout. Rhod Pentycross, together with Richard and Sue Padfield, also assisted. It included both boys and girls, offering another option to boys disinclined to join the CCF whilst for girls it was a time when the School was ahead of the Armed Forces in having suitable facilities for them. Activities included field trips, badge acquisition, life-saving and lengthy walks of 16 miles along the Ridgeway. Three patrols of six to eight Scouts each were planned.

**Dean Close School Dartmoor Letterbox**

Chris Tonge OD placed a Dartmoor Letterbox on the southern slopes of Dartmoor in 1986 to commemorate the School's centenary. The site overlooks Yalland, where many summer camps had been held. The visitors' book in it briefly outlines the School's history and the aims of the camps which were from 1959-80. The box is sited under a granite boulder about 70 paces north of the hunting gate in the wall at map reference SX692634.

1980 was the last time the CCF and DoE Scheme were able to use Farmer Codd's Yalland Farm, South Brent on Dartmoor. 40 Fourth Formers went, accompanied by staff. As usual, there were training walks, orienteering exercises on the moor, cooking over open fires and an expedition. Richard Unwin captured something of the memories, recording that he would have: '…a hard day spent erecting HQ tents and digging large holes in stony ground; an evening swim in the River Avon and a walk over the moor through sheltered valleys where wild orchids grow, then the descent into Holne and the smell of hay and honeysuckle…'.

That Trinity was when Chris Tonge OD and John Nash decided that after helping on numerous camps it was time to go. John Nash had led three expeditions – two of them successful – to traverse the Cuillin on Skye, one of the major rock climbs in the British Isles and exceptional for a school group to tackle. There was a Scout camp to Beddgelert, North Wales, near the foot of Snowdon, led by Richard and Sue Padfield.

In Michaelmas 1980, the CCF took overall responsibility for the DoE scheme, as the army declined to fund it unless the participants wore uniform, did drill and so on. In the same term, the CCF entered a team for the Black Mountains Trek for the first time. Organized by *HMS Royal Arthur*, it involved a 30 hour orienteering competition. The School finished a very creditable third.

The RN Section sailed at South Cerney, possibly for the first time, in 1981.

Lt-Cdr Cooper relinquished command of both CCF and RN Section in 1982. Major Harry Appleby became OC.

In 1983, the Army Section camped on the Brecon Beacons and Dartmoor. The shooting team won the South West District Rifle Meeting at Bulford Ranges, beating 18 schools, the Number 4 Rifle appearing for the last time, having been used by Major Appleby in the Western Desert in the Coldstream Guards.

In 1984, Marcus Paul led five rock climbing Fifth Formers on a trip to Borrowdale for four days. 'Little Chamonix' and other climbs were attempted, usually successfully. Work on rock climbing continued in 1984. In 1985 he and two Decanians spent a weekend at the mountaineering centre at Plas y Brenin in North Wales learning fresh techniques and refining old ones. Cleeve Hill and Symonds Yat provided useful training on Field Days. Specific training for attempting the Cuillin Ridge in July was held on the Malverns and the Black Mountains. The party were all very fit but when the attempt was made the weather gradually deteriorated and so no-one progressed further than the Thulach-Dubh gap. However, as one participant wrote,'…none of us would have missed the experience for anything…'.

At Michaelmas 1984, Major Jim Burrows became OC the CCF with a new RSM/SSI, Mike Hart. In March 1985, a selected group were entered for the South West District's Jubilee Trophy where they were joint runners-up. The summer camp was held at Okehampton, a team successfully entered the Ten Tors expedition while others faired similarly in the Black Mountains Trek. Mark Hughes was selected to be the Lord Lieutenant's Cadet.

Jim Burrows

The School lecture in October 1985 on the Falklands campaign by the articulate, self-effacing Major David Nicholls RM, mountaineer, photographer and expert in Arctic warfare, was thought-provoking. He was responsible for 'yomping' the press corps from San Carlos Bay to Port Stanley and for briefing them. He considered the campaign from a purely professional angle and discussed the options facing the British Commanders at different stages.

1986 was the School's centenary year and the thirtieth anniversary of its DoE scheme beginning, celebrated by OD Dominic Faulkner's inclusion in a BSES expedition to the Yukon in Canada. It was also celebrated by the 'World Record Walk' from John O'Groats to Land's End (see chapter 14).

In the CCF, basic training had become a combination of useful skills and techniques for a cadet as well as taking the DoE Bronze, the whole course being four terms long. The Annual Camp changed from Okehampton to Penhale, Cornwall. The Army Section CSM hoped he might join the Glosters – where there were then 13 serving ODs. Teams were successfully entered for the Ten Tors and Black Mountains Trek Competitions. The Motor Transport Section managed to build a working hovercraft. The RAF Section highlights included flying Chipmunks and the senior Cadet winning his wings for gliding. The RN Section benefited from the arrival of School Porter Mick Pegrum, a former Fleet Chief Petty Officer.

The RAF Section expanded still further in 1987. The School entered the only mixed team in the Black Mountains Competitive Trek and success was achieved in both that and the Ten Tors Trek. Canoeing was becoming popular, 30 having completed the three week course that year.

The academic year 1987-88 was the first occasion the School was asked to undertake interviews on behalf of the 1988 BSES Expeditions.

In 1988, the contingent entered a successful junior team in a very hot 35 mile Ten Tors Competition for the first time for many years. The senior team was forced to withdraw. In October, the School entered their first girls' team in the Black Mountains Competitive Trek, and they came close to beating the boys' team. In shooting competitions, canoeing, climbing, MT, signals, lifesaving and band much was achieved.

**Dean Close School CCF**
**Lord Lieutenant's Cadets**

| | | |
|---|---|---|
| 1985 | CSM | Mark Hughes |
| 1986 | CSM | Eleanor Cocks |
| | WO | Richard Long |
| 1987 | CSM | Tamsin Bacon |
| 1990 | RSM | Nicola Chick |
| | CSM | Steven Odell |
| 1992 | CSM | David Wilkins |
| 2003 | Sgt | Richard Hildick-Smith |
| 2004 | CSM | James Townsend |
| 2008 | C/Sjt* | Samuel Leakey |

* correct spelling!

In the 1989 Lent Term, a boys' and a girls' team competed in the Jubilee Trophy Competition. Despite it being their first time, the girls' team won, hotly pursued by the boys' team as runners-up! In the Easter holidays, Iain McAdam, Stephen Brett and Nicola Chick enjoyed an Inter-Service camp on Gibraltar, where all three distinguished themselves, Iain becoming camp RSM, Stephen a Flight Sergeant and Nicola being interviewed on local radio on the CCF and life at Dean Close School. During Trinity a junior team completed the Ten Tors 35 mile course for the second year in succession, the senior team completing the more arduous 45 mile course. The Royal Navy Section was proud of Claire Cole, who was selected to join an all-female crew for the Cutty Sark

The Lord Lieutenant of Gloucestershire, Col Sir Martin Gibbs, flanked by senior cadets Nicola Chick and Steven Odell in 1990

Tall Ships' Race from London to Hamburg. She was one of a crew of seven sailing the *TS Martin*, a 43-foot Morgan Giles yacht. They came third in their class and fifteenth overall.

Service cutbacks ended the Royal Navy's organization of the CCF Black Mountains Trekking Competition. Major Burrows, assisted by Mike Hart, took over the administration and organization for 12 selected schools of Southwest District, later 43 (Wessex) Brigade until, after about ten years, increasing regulation made the competition impossible.

During the academic year 1989-90, RAF cadets won the Assegai Trophy for .22 shooting while RSM Nicola Chick and S/Sgt Steven Odell were the Lord Lieutenant's Cadets. For the first time there was an inter-house CCF competition for the RCT Trophy consisting of five sections: Inspection, Shooting, Drive, Assault House and Command Task. Field won for the boys and Fawley for the girls. In DoE there was a surge of interest while three previous Gold Award winners (Tamsin Bacon, Kathryn Watson and Elizabeth Thomas) received their awards at Buckingham Palace.

During 1990-91, the RN Section had four days at sea with *HMS Daene*, a two day trip to *HMS Kent* and a challenging day at Yeovilton to the Helicopter Dunker, a real 'heart-stopper' as the simulator crashed into the water in total darkness with the cadets trapped inside. However,

**The Talbot Griffith Climbing Wall**

(Grosvenor) Talbot Griffith, known as TG, headmaster of Oakham School for some years, became a Governor of Dean Close School in 1966 until his death in 1981. In 1978, he became a Vice-President. He began climbing aged 53, and was a noted artist.

The opening ceremony was performed on 25th May, 1991 by Miss Caroline Griffith, TG's daughter, who unveiled a plaque dedicating the wall to his memory. Miss Griffith referred to the support that her mother, Mary, gave TG through 47 years of marriage. Miss Griffith, herself a Trustee of the School, held a sale of TG's paintings to raise the initial sum for the wall.

12 metres wide and 15 metres high, the wall is one of the highest in the country. It was designed by Don Robinson of Leeds, designer of the famous Acker's Trust outdoor climbing wall in Birmingham and the indoor wall at Leeds University where the World Championships were held in 1990.

The Talbot Griffith Climbing Wall has five belay shelves – i.e. large, jutting slabs big enough for three or four people to stand on – three at the top, one two-thirds of the way up and one half-way up. The wall includes a mantle-shelf and various cracks that may be used for the lay-back technique and chock replacement.

One boy is said to have slung a hammock and slept there overnight – for charity.

perhaps one of the most significant occasions that year was the opening of the Talbot Griffith Climbing Wall on the south side of the New Theatre (now the Bacon Theatre). The Wall enabled a variety of climbing training to take place.

The contingent's 1991 Annual Camp at Okehampton created such a favourable impression that the Colonel of Logistic Support Command arranged a trip for a handful of cadets to see the British Army working in Norway. Led by Lt Tony Jones, five cadets left RAF Lyneham on 13th February, 1992, touching down at Bergen. They experienced using snow shoes, used a variety of weaponry on ranges, went cross-country skiing, were involved in air drops and the rescue of a BV (general purpose tracked vehicle used by the British in Norway) which had nose-dived into a frozen lake. Five exciting days.

In the 1990s, Major Burrows re-started reading parts of the Roll of Honour on Remembrance Sunday at the wreath-laying. Up to 20 names from the Second World War were selected, as they had belonged to houses. Their names were read out, their house, age at and date of death and where they died. Many found it intensely moving.

In 1993, Sub-Lieutenant Montgomery took over the RN Section which was now 30 strong. Eight Decanians were awarded DoE Gold, four of whom were invited to attend a Garden Party at Buckingham Palace. In shooting, four Decanians represented Gloucestershire in the U21 County League.

In 1994, the Senior Boys, Senior Girls and Junior Boys all won their respective competitions in the Black Mountains Competitive Trek. Teams also did well in the Ten Tors, the senior team being led by Richard Ball, the junior by Sam Gilbert. The boys' team were runners up in the Jubilee Trophy competition near Bath while the girls' team won for the third year in succession. Richard Ball and Ashley Foale participated in a survival course where '…they learnt the skill of fattening a chicken before killing and eating it…'.

Remembrance Sunday 2004

In a memorable shooting year, the School won the South West District SNAP competition with Ciaran Dyer and John Hopkin coming second in the cadet pairs. Louise Harriss '… won everything she…entered and is still the best military shot in the district…'.

1994 was the first year that a girls' house, Mead, won the inter-house Royal Logistics Corps (RLC) Trophy. Alice Sturdy was the first girl to win a Flying Scholarship. The Gloucestershire Regiment trooped its Colours for the last time at a service of Commemoration at Gloucester Cathedral, a sad but proud occasion at which cadets laid wreaths to commemorate the many campaigns in which the Glosters had been involved. The School was privileged to send a contingent of cadets who, with others, represented the CCFs and ACFs of Gloucestershire.

The 1995 Black Mountains Competitive Trek had 'the usual' four teams competing. The junior boys and girls both won their competitions. Deteriorating weather and a wrong turn put paid to the chances of the senior girls' team. The senior boys tried an ambitious approach that did not quite come off as, owing to a case of hypothermia in the team, they coped with a casualty evacuation in an isolated situation and in darkness.

In 1996 Captain Muriel Hocking RN was the first female Inspecting Officer to visit the School. The subsequent report was '…quite superlative…' as the Headmaster wrote, '…we have clearly been named as the best CCF contingent in the Wessex Brigade and they think they are the best brigade in the country…'. Two cadets, Claire Simmons and Clare Marchand, both gained the senior Cadet Instructor Cadre, while Zoe Westwood completed the Air Cadets Gliding Course by flying solo. The Annual Camp was at Penhale, Cornwall, where the contingent impressed so much that Colonel Harris, site commandant, wrote informally to Major Burrows congratulating him, a gesture rare if not unique. The Army sponsored a Prize for Leadership at the School, the Officer Commanding informing the Army of each year's winner.

In 1997 in the Jubilee Trophy, the DCS boys' A team came first, the B team third, while in the girls' event, the DCS girls also came first, only the second time in the history of the competition that DCS teams carried off both trophies.

The Royal Navy section began a sailing course at South Cerney, it being three years since competitive sailing restarted at the School.

The Royal Air Force section took 60 of its cadets to RAF Bruggen in Germany visiting the control tower, seeing Harrier jets in action, the RAF regiment and its Napier surface to air missiles and training on Napier simulators, RAF and police dog handlers at work and a moving visit to a Second World War cemetery.

In 1998, statistics produced gave an idea of the CCF situation. For example, 96% passed Army Proficiency, 91% DoE Bronze Awards and 100% Red Cross awards and RN and RAF exams. Over 20 cadets attended external and adventure courses; 47 cadets gained Air Experience, 4 won Flying Scholarships and 3 completed gliding courses. 122 cadets attended Army camp, 17 the RN and 12 the RAF camps. 16 of the RN section 'did' sailing including work on luggers, single-man toppers and two-man sailboats; of these over 90% passed the Royal Yacht Association (RYA) level 1 sailing certificate. The RAF section did well in the RAF inter-CCF competition, winning three of six competitions. The shooting team won the Cadets of Gloucestershire competition and was second in the Green Howards' Country Life competition.

In the Ten Tors Expedition that year, the School was one of the few teams to be still complete by the end of the expedition.

Further regulations and limitations on adventurous pursuits made it increasingly difficult for Decanians to complete Silver and Gold Awards, notwithstanding the work and effort of teachers such as Jon Brock – but it did still occur, two completing their Gold Awards just after leaving the School. They went to Buckingham Palace, together with their Commanding Officer, by now Lt-Col J.R.J. Burrows, to receive their Certificates and meet Prince Philip.

In 1999 two former School cadets distinguished themselves at Sandhurst. Anthony Bird (1993) was awarded the Sword of Honour and David Wilkins (1992) the Sovereign's Medal. The two girls' teams won their respective classes in the Jubilee trophy, the boys' teams coming second and third respectively in their classes. Two teams completed the Ten Tors Challenge, 43 cadets gained Air Experience, four being awarded Flying Scholarships, while three completed gliding courses. The RAF Section won the South West ground Competition.

Shooting was impressive in 1999. At .22 level, the School VIII came 12th out of 138 teams in the country. In the Green Howards Country Life Competition, the School entered two teams. The B team won Bronze Medals and the Gordon Winter Silver Salver and were the highest placed B team in the country. The A team came 17th out of 220 teams taking part. In the Assegai Trophy for the RAF Section, 60 CCFs entered and the School RAF team came third. In the Full Bore Shooting, Dean Close was victorious in the Mere Cup for the fourth year in succession, beating 12 teams to win Gold Medals. Patrick Nasralla and Henry Pratt won the Cadet Pair Gold Medal. The team came second in the Langport Snap Competition, as they did in the Elgood Schools meeting. Guy Routledge and Michael Harwood-Smith won the cadet pair. This was the last occasion that 5.56mm cadet rifles were used as the new 7.62mm rifles were issued later that year.

The DoE scheme had a new format in September 2000, requiring changes at the School. Although making the Awards no easier, it was hoped to make them more accessible to Decanians, particularly at Silver level.

In 2001, the Motor Transport section built a kit car, the focal point in the School's drama production of 'Grease' that year. The Signals section was active while Climbing thrived, both on the School's Griffith Wall and at Symonds Yat. A Scuba Diving section developed. The RN Section at South Cerney now offered windsurfing, kayaking, sailing and Canadian canoeing. During the summer holiday, Katie Lea and Robin Davies attended a week's leadership training at the Joint Services Mountain Training Centre at *HMS Indefatigable* at Anglesey.

Christopher Lomas, Jamie Hall and Tom Bacon, together with a boy from Oundle School, planned, practised and eventually completed a detailed cycling exploration of the water resources of the sand dunes of North West Holland from Haag to Texel and back to Petten through the canal system. The boys were used as subjects for training the first DoE expedition assessors in Holland, who were new to the Award scheme.

In the 2001-02 academic year, teams participated in the Ten Tors and in the Jubilee Trophy. In the inter-house RLC trophy, Shelburne triumphed, only the second time that a girls' house had won. Liz Weitz of the RAF section represented Dean Close School in Cyprus at the National Air Cadets Overseas Camp. She also completed the RAF gliding scholarship and achieved her Silver Wings allowing her to fly solo in a Vigilant glider.

In 2002-03, in the national Jubilee Trophy, the senior boy CCF cadets won a silver medal – they won the outdoor assault course section. The senior girls won a bronze – and the indoor assault course section. The RN section highlight was visiting the Submarine *HMS Courageous* in Plymouth. The RAF

CCF Band in Shelburne Road in 1955

section had been expanding; three went on an Easter camp for the first time, at RAF Cranwell, as well as the usual summer camp at RAF Halton. Ian Collinson was selected for the National Air Cadet Adventure Training camp at Llanbehr in Wales while Roisin Rowley-Brooke won a place on the Air Cadet Leadership course at RAF Stafford.

The Ten Tors team successfully completed the challenge, the full team arriving at the finish an impressive 3½ hours before the cut-off time.

Kilimanjaro expedition 2005

In October 2003, a new competition was begun, known as the Cheltenham Schools' CCF Challenge Cup. Both the boys' and girls' six-strong teams from the School came first in their respective competitions involving an obstacle course, watermanship, which involved ferrying all team members plus boxes across a lake, camp craft, a tank range, mountain biking, a range and a command task. They were delighted to be the first winners of the cup.

The RN section rose to 40 in the course of the academic year while the RAF section sent four of their number to the National

Cadet Adventure Training Centre at Windermere for the first time. Nick Sword was selected for the Air Cadet Leadership course while Ryan Hill and Jonty Strachan gained gliding scholarships.

A Ten Tors team completed the Challenge. The Silver Jubilee Trophy competition saw the School sweep the board in all three categories, and thereby come first overall, taking four cups back to the School in what was the last competition with Lt-Col Jim Burrows as OC before his retirement. At 20 years, he had been the longest serving OC and with Mike Hart had planned, worked and presided over the contingent's marked improvement over that time until it had become arguably the best CCF in 43 (Wessex) Brigade of 41 schools, seen by some as the best Brigade in the country. In addition, he had fostered Outdoor Pursuits and largely through him the School was seen as being one of the best in the BSES.

Jenny Brown, Vicky Brenninkmeijer, and Mike Penny about to board a Gazelle helicopter for a test flight at a CCF Summer Camp

In shooting, the Green Howards Country Life competition included two teams entered from the School. The B team came 7th out of 275 teams, the A team 11th. John Preston was the best shot from the School, coming 6th overall.

Capt Edward Taylor OD, flanked by his parents, Anne (School Registrar) and Richard (Second Master)

The Field Gun Competition

**The Origins of The Field Gun Competition**

'The origins lie in the Second Boer War in South Africa,' Major D.D. Evans has written. The legendary story tells of the British garrison in Ladysmith being besieged in 1899. To support the British Army, the Royal Navy landed guns from *HMS Terrible* and *HMS Powerful*. The sailors transported guns over difficult terrain and brought them into action against the Boers. It is possible that sailors carried a 12 pounder gun for two miles after a wheel collapsed. The siege of Ladysmith lasted for 120 days until February 1900. Once home, the sailors concerned paraded their guns through London and appeared at the Royal Naval and Military Tournament at the Agricultural Hall, Islington. Displays of Field Gun Drill continued in subsequent years, leading eventually to the competition.

In 2004 S/Ldr R.I. Kirby took over as contingent commander. Lt D.D. Evans became responsible for the Army Section. Flt Lt Boyle looked after the RAF Section for a year before A.R. Swarbrick replaced him.

The School won the Cheltenham Challenge Cup again by the narrowest of margins. The girls' team won their part in the Jubilee Trophy Competition while the boys' team came fourth in theirs. Senior and junior teams both successfully tackled the Ten Tors Challenge.

The RAF Section, now allowed to recruit the Remove year, was 50 strong.

In shooting, the CCF did well once more, the B team coming 7th in the country in the Green Howards Country Life competition, and as the best B team, won the Gordon Silver Plate.

In 2005-06 Major Dominic Evans took over the CCF as contingent commander. During 2006-07, the School contingent again succeeded in winning the Jubilee Trophy, a matter of considerable pride.

The event that caught the eye was the inaugural Inter-School Field Gun Competition, based on a similar competition held at the Royal Tournament from 1907 to 1999, between Cheltenham College and Dean Close School. On Wednesday, 14th March, 2007 a Decanian crew comprising five girls and ten boys went to the College to take part. The gun crews gave their all, racing head to head. Major Evans described it as '...a magnificent display of skill, teamwork and attention to detail...'. It was finally decided on penalties and Dean Close won by a good margin. The return match the following year ended in another win for Dean Close School.

General Lord Guthrie inspecting

General Lord Guthrie came to witness the Inter-House RLC Trophy and to attend a Dinner held in his honour. He was sufficiently impressed to indicate that he would be prepared to come again on another occasion.

RSM/SSI Mike Hart retired at the beginning of 2009 after 25 years with the contingent. He worked hard to help achieve the

CCF's current enviable position. Brian Lloyd is now RSM/SSI.

The CCF has grown from the original OTC of 1909 and is now among the finest of any school in the land. Survival, fieldwork and a variety of other skills from signalling to sailing, together with the opportunity to gain leadership, instructional, arduous training and other valuable experience make the organization a huge asset, equipping many to attempt the various levels of the DoE's Award Scheme. It has also produced a number of Decanians who have had distinguished records in the Armed Services. As the School marks the 125th Anniversary of the Laying of the School Cornerstone in 2009, so the Combined Cadet Force celebrates its Centenary at the School.

**Dean Close School Winners of The Sword of Honour**

| | | |
|---|---|---|
| 1952 | J. M.A. Parker | Cranwell |
| 1955 | T.R. Morgan | Cranwell |
| 1999 | A.R. Bird | Sandhurst* |

* The winner of the Sovereign's Medal was D.M. Wilkins

T.R. Morgan receiving
The Sword of Honour at Cranwell in 1955

# Chapter 13

# The Performing Arts

*Drama and Theatre*

Francis Close regarded drama and the theatre with deep suspicion. Dr Flecker's views may have been more accommodating but the Macpherson Sisters incident in 1919 (see chapter 3) and the moral concerns of Governors meant that progress towards a proper place for drama and theatrical production at the School would take time.

A small chink appeared in March 1921 when the Cheltenham Branch of the British Empire Shakespeare Society performed *Twelfth Night* in the Schoolroom with a cast of 15, including four women. Musical direction was by Heller Nicholls. The arrival of C.A.P. ('Ambi') Tuckwell in September 1923, and the appointment of Percy Bolton as Headmaster in 1924, brought changes. By the end of 1924, a group of boys were allowed to act in A. Conan Doyle's *The Speckled Band* directed by C.A.P. Tuckwell (see chapter 4).

**C.A.P. Tuckwell, staff member 1923-68**

Former Head Boy of Marlborough, he was commissioned into the Grenadier Guards, later going up to Oxford University where he read Greats. He came to the School in 1923 as Head of English and Drama, and apart from classroom teaching, he was notable as a hockey coach, having played for the West of England and was unfortunate not to have won a Blue. Pre-eminently he was a Shakespearian actor and director. However, as R.F. McNeile points out: '...C.A.P. Tuckwell was entirely without stage training, knowledge or experience, and his methods of production were largely intuitive...'. A.S.R. Parker, a former colleague wrote: '...In [Tuckwell's] view, Shakespeare as a dramatist knew his business better than his critics, and if one bothered to find out what the words meant, clothe them in clear and audible speech and interpret them in meticulously rehearsed action, the play...would take care of itself...'.

He directed over 30 productions during his time at Dean Close School.

He was a much respected Tower Housemaster for over 21 years (1929-52) and would hold holiday parties for boys and staff at his cottage on Exmoor. He was Second Master (1955-59). One colleague wrote to *The Times* commenting that C.A.P.T. epitomized the Arnoldian ideal of a Christian gentleman.

**The First Production of Hamlet at Dean Close School, 1925**

There were one or two unique features about this first major production. Firstly, it did not use the full text. *The Decanian* declared that '...the play, as Shakespeare wrote it, is too long even for an ordinary professional representation...Mr Tuckwell's version of the play contained 12 scenes, arranged in four acts...'. Secondly, it was first performed on 1st April, so that by the time they came to do it on Speech Day, it was for the second time – but performances were separated by several weeks! Thirdly, four members of staff were members of the cast: Claudius was played by B.O. Bradnack, Hamlet by C.A.P. Tuckwell, who had first acted the role as a boy at Marlborough, Polonius by A.H. Warr and Laertes by H.C. Neill. Lastly, *The Decanian* was so overwhelmed by the performance that they witnessed on 1st April they hoped to '...enrol on the staff of the Magazine a dramatic critic competent to give his opinion...From us as we are, anything beyond an expression of gratitude would be impertinent...'. Such humility on the part of an editor is most unusual.

At the instigation of the new Headmaster, his first Speech Day in 1925 included a performance of a shortened *Hamlet* with C.A.P. Tuckwell in the principal role, thereby setting a precedent whereby he both directed the play and took the lead, which he was to do virtually throughout his time at the School. *Hamlet* was performed on what was described as a '...miniscule...' stage in the Schoolroom.

The introduction of houses in 1924 suggested house plays: Percy Bolton was encouraging and Tower House under its Housemaster H.C. Neill, who was to be followed by B.O. Bradnack in 1926, and Gate House under its Housemaster Hedley Warr were both keen to take advantage of the new situation. Tower House offered *Grumpy* by Horace Hodges in December 1926 – both C.A.P. Tuckwell and B.O. Bradnack taking key parts. Gate responded with Shaw's *Arms and the Man*, Drinkwater's *Oliver Cromwell*, Barrie's *The Admirable Crichton* and Anstey's *Vice Versa.* The Juniors – possibly of preparatory school age – offered scenes from *Henry V* in the Lent Term 1927, the first time G. Wilson Knight's name appears associated with any sort of Shakespeare production by the School.

Performances were on the Headmaster's Lawn, now part of the garden the Common Room, Gate and Tower Housemasters share. It was not until after the 1933 production of *Macbeth* that C.A.P. Tuckwell's thoughts turned seriously towards creating another theatrical space that became the Open Air Theatre and eventually the Tuckwell Theatre.

**G. Wilson Knight, CBE, staff member 1925-31**

He came to Dean Close School in 1925 thereby strengthening the English Department. A First World War dispatch rider in the Middle East, he attended St Edmund Hall, Oxford, where he gained a Half Blue at Chess.

He was a Shakespeare enthusiast, and his first book, written at Dean Close School, was the classic on Shakespearian tragedies, *The Wheel of Fire*, published by O.U.P. in 1930 with an Introduction by T.S. Eliot. The book resulted in his appointment to the Chair of English Studies at Trinity College, University of Toronto. During his time at Dean Close School he directed *A Midsummer Night's Dream* and *Twelfth Night*. He supported and underlined C.A.P. Tuckwell's drive to establish a Shakespearean tradition at Dean Close. Returning to England in 1940, he taught at Stowe and at Leeds University, from where he retired as Professor Emeritus in 1962. He wrote over 20 books, roughly half of them on Shakespearian topics.

Professor Francis Berry OD, who eventually became Professor Emeritus of English Literature of Royal Holloway College, London University and a minor poet, was initially inspired as a boy by G. Wilson Knight when he taught at the School.

**The Building of The Open Air Theatre (later called The Tuckwell Theatre)**

Originally, it was suggested that the stage should be a raised platform, and that the audience should be on the flat with their backs to the stream. This proved impractical. For what is now the auditorium, there was a slight natural slope in existence, and the stage did not need much levelling. However, the raised back of the stage caused '…a formidable amount of excavation above the brook…'.

Work started in Trinity 1934, when the path was cut out at the side and back of the stage. In the winter, work stopped altogether. The honorary architect, Herbert Thompson OD, qualified architect and First World War Royal Engineer, was also an amateur actor who founded the Cheltenham Operatic Society in 1914, and therefore understood many of the issues and problems and was in an excellent position to offer technical advice and encouragement. Edward Ellam, retired as Second Master but still keeping watch over his beloved grounds, also offered help and practical instruction.

C.A.P. Tuckwell noted that '…all the time work was in progress there was a steady supply of boys and masters to do the rough jobs of digging out and wheeling. They were attracted partly by public spirit, partly by the idea of having a new kind of occupation, and partly by the chance of removing their upper garments and acquiring the sun tan which is *de rigeur* on bathing beaches. The task would never have been possible without the example and leadership of senior boys. Prefects and members of first elevens alike were to be found scraping and shovelling with the rest. And it was all voluntary labour. Boys came and went as they liked…'. F.R.H. Brian acted as an indispensible Master Builder and Clerk of Works.

During 1935 the two levels of the stage were laid out, the low stone walls built enclosing the banks of earth where bushes were to grow. The platform for the orchestra was levelled; bushes, poplars and the long hornbeam hedge that separates theatre from field put in by the gardener. A groundsman laid turf on the stage and another cemented the cross steps and the steps at the back.

A significant problem was working out a method of supporting tiers of seats. It was solved by the industrial architect and School Governor Sir Philip Stott, owner and preserver of Stanton village. He designed and paid for between four and five hundred concrete blocks, each shaped to dovetail with its neighbour, linked by an iron rod, which was held back at one end by the row behind, '…all making it difficult even for the amateur builder to go far wrong…' as C.A.P. Tuckwell put it. Other gifts included funds for an army hut to act as a dressing room from Mr and Mrs Henderson, parents of three Gate House boys; bushes and trees paid for by Governors and masters; paving stones, bricks and walling stones were gifts from parents past and present. Some money was available from Mr Ellam's School amenities fund but a point of honour was that the building of the theatre would not cost the School at a time when funds were tight. Thus the Theatre opened in 1937.

Since the war, four rows have been added to the back of the auditorium; permanent underground cables have been installed to light the stage and the hut, and floodlights have been bought, a vast improvement on the early days when car headlights were used. The upper stage has been raised one step and paved. The sides of the lower stage and its two entrances have been paved. The grass slope that ran down towards the audience was chopped off and a stone retaining wall installed. The stage right entrance was raised and three rounded steps added. Finally, two 12 foot walls have been erected, one on each side.

**Prologue to the opening of the new Open Air Theatre (since renamed The Tuckwell Theatre), Dean Close School, Saturday 12th June, 1937, written for the occasion by John Masefield, Poet Laureate**

Friends, take this scene to heart, for well you may:
The man who built this wished to see a play.
He had no theatre, but wished, until
The living wish became an act of will.
The act of will approached his friends, and said:
'Come, let us build, and let a play be played.'
'Right,' said his comrades, 'that's the way to do it.'
It is the way, and very soon they knew it.
You can imagine what a task they had;
Good builders all begin by being bad.
They persevered, and lo, the stage, a fact.
'Now, friends,' said he, 'fall to, and let us act.'
'Right', said his comrades; now they're here to play;
But, ere they start, a poet bids me say:
'Good luck, friends. That's the spirit; that's the way!'

The lines were read by Randle Ayrton, the distinguished Shakespearean actor, and were followed by a performance of Shakespeare's *King John*. At the close of the performance, after a short speech by C.A.P. Tuckwell, a presentation was made to Randle Ayrton by J.D. Wakeling on behalf of the cast. J.D. Wakeling himself later entered the Church, eventually becoming Bishop of Southwell.

In August 1933, groundsmen cleared the chosen site. In Trinity 1937 it was officially opened by Randle Ayrton, described as '...the leading actor from Stratford-upon-Avon, one of the most humble and charming of men and the best Lear of his time...'. He was shy of speaking his own words in public, so he asked his friend, John Masefield, the Poet Laureate, to write dedicatory lines that Ayrton duly delivered.

There was a Summer Play annually in the Open Air Theatre between 1937-97 except for 1962 and 1965. It was usually, but not always, Shakespeare. The Second World War and the School's forced evacuation to Monkton Combe did not occur until after the 1939 production of *The Tempest*. The School returned in time for the 1940 production, which was *The Merchant of Venice*. The 1944 production of *King John* was topical as it included an invasion of France. Apparently that was why it was featured in *Picture Post* that summer. According to one OD, the standard of wardrobe and makeup was so high that some of the boy actors as 'ladies' looked quite glamorous, attracting the attention of US servicemen attending the performances.

C.A.P. Tuckwell's last major production for the Open Air Theatre was *The Tempest* in 1964. For two years the annual production was taken on by Ian Mullins, Director of the Everyman Theatre in Cheltenham, who produced first *Murder in the Cathedral* in 1966, followed by David Monaco's *Of Cabbages and Kings* in 1967, which raised the hackles of some parents and Old Decanians on the grounds that it was '...considered profane, indecently suggestive, offensive to parents, relations and friends...' as Douglas Graham, the Headmaster, put it. However, he defended its anti-war and anti-power stance and that '...when it portrayed the worldly bishop and cynical rulers, the author was himself expressing genuine Christian insights and that the discussion on God by the three soldiers, so far from being profane, was indeed both edifying and touching. So much for profanity...'. Yet that said, he was not sure it was appropriate for Commemoration.

By the following year, Tim Murray had been appointed to the staff on exchange from Australia, and he directed the 1968 production of *A Man For All Seasons* with C.A.P. Tuckwell as Wolsey in his last performance in the Open Air Theatre, and also Pamela Rowles, the first female Decanian to be involved in a production, playing Margaret. The following year Tim Murray directed *Waiting For Godot* by Samuel Beckett, a play that it is said made '...the audience come out bemused, even irritated at having such a play at Commemoration...'. More complaints. No review of the performance ever appeared.

Peter Cairns

In 1970 Peter Cairns produced his first Commemoration play, Shakespeare's *Henry IV, part I.* Over the next 30 years, he carefully balanced Shakespeare productions with other playwrights for the Commemoration Play such as Anton Chekhov, Tom Stoppard, Bernard Shaw, Oscar Wilde, Alan Bennett and Georges Feydeau. He has commented that the '...hunger to act...' within the School was remarkable. A third of the School signed up to act in *Henry IV, part I* and a similar number signed up for his first Junior Drama Group production the same year, *The Importance of Being Earnest.*

Tim Murray founded a Junior Drama Group during Michaelmas 1968, mainly devoted to mime and play readings. In the same term the School won the Everyman Youth Drama Festival with Decanian Chris (Lloyd) Wood's production of *The Long and the Short and the Tall.* It was an 'all-boy' production, the first time a Sixth Former had directed a play. Tim Murray only stepped in when the young director fell sick a week before production. The star of the play, and winner of the award for the Best Actor in the Festival, was Chris Jones as Private Bamforth.

The following term Tim Murray presented a *Modern Drama Night*, with four modern sketches and 'a half play' in the Flecker Hall. In the Lent Term, he directed *See How They Run* that included actors from Court, Mead and Field Houses. The critic on this occasion, who wrote a balanced yet penetrating critique for *The Decanian*, was one Hugh Quarshie, then a Fifth Former, who had already played Pozzo in the 1969 production of *Waiting For Godot.*

The winter of 1971-72 included two house plays, *A Penny For a Song* by Court House and *My Three Angels* by Gate House, both supported by girls from Mead. The latter play was only the second to be directed by a boy, this time Colin Martin. Given that the School had mounted a mighty *Othello* as the Commemoration production the previous summer with Hugh Quarshie '...a triumph...' as the Moor, Peter Cairns' offered a contrast the following Commemoration with *Forty Years On* by Alan Bennett for the 1972 Commemoration, followed by a Junior Drama Group production the following Lent Term. A very rough and ready cycle began to emerge of the houses producing something every other year; Commemoration having a Shakespeare play every other year; the Junior Drama Group usually also performing in alternate years.

During the 1970s and up to the turn of the century, following *Of Cabbages and Kings*, directors were often verbally attacked for themes, deeds or language in productions from both within and without the School. *Othello*, *Forty Years On* and many subsequent plays were criticised, leaving Peter Cairns and, later, Lloyd Allington somewhat frustrated.

Occasionally, a house would go for a musical production, such as Court's *Pirates of Penzance* in 1975, directed by David Watson, a History teacher who was a fine musician, too. Unusually, Major General Stanley was played by a member of staff, Ricky Akenhead.

Peter Cairns' direction of *The Three Sisters* by Anton Chekhov at the Youth Drama Festival at the Everyman Theatre in Cheltenham in December 1976 was highly praised and also resulted in one of the three sisters, Masha, played by Jane Scott, being joint winner of the Forest Leach Cup for the most outstanding performance.

It was not until October 1981 that the first all-girl house production took place, Shelburne producing *Toad of Toad Hall*, following it up early in 1983 with another all-girl production, this time of the far more serious *The Lady's Not For Burning* by Christopher Fry. Mead went one better in 1984 by teaming up with Tower House for a combined production of Noel Coward's *Fallen Angels*, and the practice of a girls' house combining with a boys' house' for productions has continued ever since.

Meanwhile the annual Commemoration plays were continuing as well as fairly regular Junior Drama Group productions. The latter's *Twelfth Night* in 1983 caused a stir when, as reviewer, I.D. Davies, writing in *Decus* and *The Decanian* observed '...it was a stroke of inspiration which prompted Peter Cairns [the director] to make Aguecheek a Danny la Rue and so transform a jarringly tragic figure when played by a male into a really laughable one when played by the effervescent Nancy Braithwaite...'.

1986 was centenary year: there were three big productions. The first was the Junior Drama Group's *Much Ado About Nothing* in March, presented in the Flecker Hall, enhanced, or, as Richard Padfield in *The Decanian* put it '...transformed by a superb Gibson backdrop of typical Tuscan scenery...'. The Revd David Gibson, Chaplain, scenery designer and painter *par exellence* had again made a major contribution to the production. Then there was the Commemoration production in the Open Air Theatre of *Caesar and Cleopatra* by G.B. Shaw. Dai Davies described the production as '...a gripping drama, a hilarious show, a visually memorable piece...'. Will Turnau was '...great...' as Caesar, Sarah Warren, '...at the climax of a brilliant series of dramatic performances ... triumphed as Cleopatra...'.

The third major production was with the Junior School. It was Lionel Bart's *Oliver!* with Anthony Bird and Giles Watson both playing Oliver. It ran from 18th to 22nd November 1986 and included two matinées as well as five evening performances in the newly refurbished Everyman Theatre, directed by Peter Mills assisted by Andrew Judge, with Ian Little directing the Music. On this occasion Junior and Senior Schools, staff, Decanians and pupils were all on stage and '...the whole enterprise formed a triumphant conclusion to the School's centenary year...' as Humphrey Osmond put it.

In addition, the Lower Sixth put on Tom Stoppard's *The Real Inspector Hound* and Brook House performed an *Extravaganza*, or '...(an) evening of fun and frivolity...' the theme being 'A Day in the Life of DCS'. The Drama Department tried to steer houses onto more solid and challenging fare, although Stephen Aiano, Housemaster of Court 1994-98, went further than most with Ben Jonson's *The Alchemist* in 1995 and Gascoigne's *A Larum for London* in 1997.

*The Decanian* the following year indicated that plans were '...well under way...' for the building of a theatre. It was made clear that the site for this needed to have direct access from Hatherley Road so that outsiders would be able to attend performances.

Lloyd Allington joined the staff in Michaelmas 1987, initially being responsible for house plays. The first play he directed was a Tower/Shelburne production in December 1987 of Arthur Miller's *The Crucible.* Humphrey Osmond referred to its '...sustained tension...the compelling power of the play itself and certainly of this performance...' in his review in *The Decanian*, and came out at the end '... drained but thrilled...' at the quality of what the 26 actors achieved, together with the support crew.

From November 1989 to the end of the Commemoration play in 1990 there were five plays and two entertainments that included *Love's Labour's Lost*, put on by the Junior Drama Group, directed by Peter Cairns who cut '...whatever was obscure or obscene...', unveiled in March 1990. He also directed a '...stylish...' production of *Lady Windermere's Fan* as the 1990 Commemoration play in the Tuckwell Theatre. Half a dozen productions a year were becoming increasingly common.

On Tuesday, 29th October, 1991 the New Theatre was opened by Colonel Sir Martin Gibbs, Lord Lieutenant of Gloucestershire (see chapter 9). The Gala Evenings that followed included musical items together with scene three from Act Two of *Twelfth Night* and *A Close Thing* described as being '...a mini musical based on *Much Ado About Nothing*...'.

With the opening of what came to be the Bacon Theatre, named in honour of the Headmaster whose drive and enthusiasm had overcome every obstacle, Drama at Dean Close School continued to develop.

The first major production in the New Theatre was *Twelfth Night* in November 1991, a few weeks after the opening. Directed by Peter Cairns, there was an acknowledgement of an old School tradition in the inclusion of two members of staff in the cast – Richard Taylor as Sir Toby Belch and Lloyd Allington as Malvolio. With David Pihlens (Orsino), David Wilkins (Sir Andrew), William Odell (Feste), Kim Chester (Olivia), Frances Allberry (Viola) and Julie Cooper (Maria) in the key parts, there was '...a lasting impression of a coherent, professional and wholly entertaining production...' as *The Decanian* put it. The following May, the Commemoration play, *Hamlet*, was held, as usual, in the Tuckwell Theatre, with David Wilkins in the title role and Lloyd Allington as an evilly moustachioed King Claudius.

There were exceptional occasions, such as the remarkable end of Trinity 1997. *Welcome Home: A Trivial Comedy for Trivial People* involved a cast of seven, written by sixth-former Sam Gilbert, set to music by another sixth-former, Paul Hodges, and directed and produced by the two of them. It was the work of one hectic week after A levels – after the rest of the Upper Sixth had left. Peter Cairns later wrote: '...It was an amazing achievement: Peter (Cairns) and Lloyd (Allington) were as proud of this as of anything that has happened in the new Theatre...'. The following summer, Edward Scott, another sixth-former, directed *Oedipus Tyrannus* in the Tuckwell Theatre. Members of the School increasingly took up the challenge to direct.

*My Fair Lady*, May 1998, was possibly the most sumptuous production to date, put on to honour Christopher and Jill Bacon on their retirement. It was a Peter Cairns production with Lloyd Allington as co-producer and Richard Knight directing the music. Richard Ryall, who had created numerous imaginative sets not just in the New (Bacon) Theatre but also in the Flecker Hall and the Tuckwell Theatre since the 1980s, in what was to be his last DCS production, was once more Stage Manager. Jenny Bowden, with her team, master-minded and made a reported 168 costumes. Victoria Barritt as Eliza, Edward Scott as Pickering, Douglas Paine as Higgins and Rebecca Rimell as his mother were particular stars.

In 1999 it was Tower's *The Duchess of Malfi*, directed by Lloyd Allington with Phillip Birch making a remarkable acting debut in the demanding role of Bosola with a characterisation described as '... masterly...' that really caught the eye.

In 2000, for the first time since the 1920s, a Headmaster took a hand in directing a production. Tim Hastie-Smith and Lloyd Allington co-directed *Lord of the Flies* in the Tuckwell Theatre, that was both compelling and disturbing.

Later the same year, Tim Hastie-Smith went one step further and played Vince Fontaine, radio personality, in Lloyd Allington's production of *Grease*, a spectacular production with choreography by Janet Marshall and marvellous musical direction by Ciara Allen. A complete contrast was *The Agamemnon* produced by Jon Allen, Head of Classics, the following March also in the Bacon Theatre: a 'towering tragedy' as *The Decanian* described it.

In 2002, Peter Cairns retired to France after 34 years and nearly 60 productions at Dean Close School. He had built on the foundations established by C.A.P. Tuckwell and seen drama flourish and become an essential part of the School scene, though not without challenges that some saw as ill-informed attempts at constraint and censorship from plays selected to language used, but others felt were attempts to maintain perceived conventional standards. Peter Cairns was later to comment that Timberlake Wertenbaker's *Our Country's Good*, which was put on in 2001 and again in 2008, would have been '...inconceivable...' before 2000, as also would have been the case with several other plays. Theatre Studies has now been introduced for A level and at GCSE. Lloyd Allington became Director of Drama that incorporated Theatre Studies from 2000, while Sean Hamill became Head of English in succession to Peter Cairns in 2002.

John Preston as Macbeth 2004

Rebecca Vines

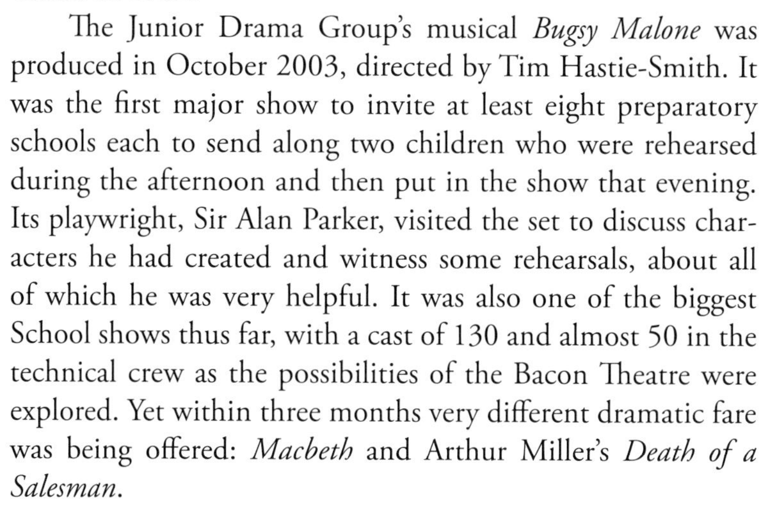

The Junior Drama Group's musical *Bugsy Malone* was produced in October 2003, directed by Tim Hastie-Smith. It was the first major show to invite at least eight preparatory schools each to send along two children who were rehearsed during the afternoon and then put in the show that evening. Its playwright, Sir Alan Parker, visited the set to discuss characters he had created and witness some rehearsals, about all of which he was very helpful. It was also one of the biggest School shows thus far, with a cast of 130 and almost 50 in the technical crew as the possibilities of the Bacon Theatre were explored. Yet within three months very different dramatic fare was being offered: *Macbeth* and Arthur Miller's *Death of a Salesman*.

The same academic year, Rebecca Vines joined the Drama Department. She was concerned with developing Speech and

William Martin and Heather Simons
in *Amadeus* in 2005

Drama, which had prospered under Tim Goodwright's guidance over several years, particularly at the Cheltenham Festival, before he returned to the stage himself. He had followed Rosemary Bourne and Sheilagh Pragnell. Rebecca suggested, and with Lloyd Allington, organized, the School's first foray to the Edinburgh Festival Fringe in 2004. The group, called Close Up Theatre, presented themselves as drama students working together rather than coming from a school. This was so that reviewers would take them more seriously. They took four plays. The Scotsman was unimpressed but other reviews were generally excellent. Apart from Rebecca Vines and Lloyd Allington, adults included Jane Davies, there to assist generally, while Phil Sidey and Dave Thompson provided the technical expertise to ensure that sound, light and effects all worked. In subsequent years, they have enjoyed packed houses and appreciative media criticism, which have resulted in 'elite sell-out' status each year from the Festival Authorities.

The academic year 2004-05 was remarkable for three major, superlative productions: the musical *West Side Story*, directed by Lloyd Allington with Andrew Cleary as musical director; Brecht's parable play *The Resistible Rise of Arturo Ui*, Rebecca Vines' first production in the Bacon Theatre, the first time that Brecht had been performed at Dean Close School; and sixth-former James Townsend's remarkable production of Peter Shaffer's *Amadeus*, described by Lloyd Allington as '…one of the best things he had seen on the Dean Close stage…'. More Dean Close thespians converged on the Edinburgh Fringe Festival than in the previous year – 70 in all, bringing five plays! Apart from *A Midsummer Night's Dream*, the other plays were all new to the School repertoire: *Look Back in Anger, A Day in the Death of Joe Egg, Abigail's Party* and *The Browning Version*.

Joe Hill as King Lear 2005

The following year, Lloyd Allington tackled *King Lear* for the first time. The only other Dean Close School producer to direct it was C.A.P. Tuckwell, and the three times he did so – 1942, 1951 and 1958 – he took the part of the King himself. Thus Joe Hill, barely 17, was the first Decanian to attempt it and gave an '…extraordinarily mature performance as the flawed monarch…' as Emma Taylor (Senior Mistress) commented in *The Decanian*. There was also a rash of house

*The Crucible* in performance 2006

Lloyd Allington performing in *Talking Heads* 2006

plays: Shelburne's *After Juliet* with a cast of 60 girls and ten Tower boys; Mead House with *The Prime of Miss Joan Brodie*, with Heather Simons' '...towering performance...' as Miss Brodie, both productions being master-minded by Rebecca Vines. The Fawley and Dale production was a marvellous *Oh! What A Lovely War* directed by Chris Haslam and Kate Miller. *The Crucible*, directed for the fourth time by Lloyd Allington was the sole entry for the Edinburgh Festival by the Close Up Theatre, whose distinguished President, Patricia Routledge, was in School on a couple of occasions to encourage.

Actor Nigel Havers opened the new Drama Studio during Michaelmas 2006. It was originally the old trampolining room converted to a Speech and Drama area, rehearsal space and a place where small-scale dramatic pieces could effectively be performed to audiences of up to a hundred or so. Within a couple of months, the Studio began its first production with an evening of four of Alan Bennett's *Talking Heads*. At the other end of the spectrum in the Bacon Theatre was a truly magnificent *Guys and Dolls* directed by Lloyd Allington, with musical direction by Ciara Allen; the Junior Drama group did *Pygmalion*, Field House came up with *Twelve Angry Men*, co-directed by Chris Haslam and Sean Hamill while Brook Court offered *The Winslow Boy* and Rebecca Vines directed *An Evening of Comedy*.

Isabella Richards and Ed Burgon in *Anything Goes* 2008

Such are the opportunities available to budding thespians that there is now a 'Ten Play Challenge' in which Decanians try to act in ten productions – or more – whilst at the Senior School.

Lucinda Lee (centre) leads the cast in *Anything Goes*

Alex Carden and Beatrice Lawrence in *Our Town* 2008

The main production at Michaelmas 2008 was a towering production of *Les Miserables*, directed by Lloyd Allington, with a cast of 100, a production crew of 50 and a 20-strong band.

Thus the Drama side of the School now has formidable resources in its directors and in its three production venues – the Tuckwell and Bacon Theatres and the Drama Studio, not to mention at the Edinburgh Fringe. Apart from the years 1966-67 when Ian Mullins of the Everyman and then the Australian Tim Murray, also for two years 1968-69, directed productions, the overall responsibility for Dean Close productions since 1924 has been in the hands of just three men – C.A.P. Tuckwell, Peter Cairns and Lloyd Allington. It has developed different strands through house plays, the Junior Drama group, workshops, Theatre Studies, Close Up and full School productions, yet can allow informal groups to put on productions, too, encouraging student directors.

Today, in Phil Sidey, David Thompson and Martin Stewart, there is considerable experience and expertise on the technical front. Gary and Sue Winrow are versatile set designers. Jenny Bowden, after years being a resourceful Wardrobe Mistress, has now made way for the equally talented Sheila Charania. If it is a musical, Janet Marshall and her sister, Carol McDowall, achieve wonders as choreographers. In recent years, Ciara Allen has been available to be Musical Director as she was so successfully for *Guys and Dolls*, *My Fair Lady*, *Grease* and *Les Miserables*, together with the considerable talents and resources of the Music Department. It is to that area of the School's history that attention now turns.

*(Readers wanting to know more about the Open Air/Tuckwell Theatre may obtain a copy of its history of productions from the Old Decanian office.)*

Two scenes from *Les Miserables* 2008

*Music*

Dr Flecker and his wife were both musicians. The first Director of Music was R.N. Green (1886-94), but with the second, Heller Nicholls, there were often small-scale concerts at the end of terms. Usually, parents were not admitted, the Schoolroom (now the Flecker Library) and on rare occasions the Library (now the Seminar Room) being too small. Sometimes, music staff from Cheltenham College or Cheltenham Ladies' College performed for the boys. The repertoire was 'light classical', punctuated by the whole School singing songs from 'The School Song Sheet'. Occasionally Joyce Flecker, one of the Headmaster's daughters, arranged small concerts where, with perhaps four or five members of staff, works by composers from Corelli to Sir Edward Elgar, who was still very much alive, would be performed.

There was also music in Chapel, the choir certainly singing Christmas carols and John Stainer's *Crucifixion* most years during Lent.

The School Song, *Carmen Decaniense*, written in Latin by Edward Ellam, music by Heller Nicholls, was first sung at a School concert on 15th December, 1923. Thereafter, with *Auld Lang Syne* and the National Anthem, it was regularly sung until the Second World War.

'The Warriors' Jazz Band had formed by 1924, and the following year they took part in a School concert, playing a total of six numbers among duets, songs and a harp solo from other participants.

Very occasionally, outside artistes would perform. On one occasion in 1916 Alice Gardner arrived with her all-female Russian orchestra. However, without doubt the best-known internationally was Marie Hall, a near neighbour, who gave three recitals at the School.

The House Music Competition, initially a House Singing Competition, began in Lent 1925, for which the overall winners' cup was presented by Joyce Flecker. The first winner was Neill's (today's Tower) House. Perhaps the most distinguished adjudicator of the House Music Competition was the

**Heller Nicholls, Director of Music 1894-36**

Over 40 years he proved to be a prodigious composer and arranger. He would totally rearrange a piece of orchestral music if he felt certain boys were having too many difficulties coping. He played a wide range of instruments himself though not necessarily to a very high standard. His best known compositions included *The Masque of the Magi* and the School Song *Carmen Decaniense*, together with his *Toy Symphony*. He was also Director of Music for the five live BBC broadcasts from the School in the 1930s.

One observer said of him that he was '...an indifferent executant, but the best raconteur in my experience, with a lovely, unmalicious sense of humour...'. He spoke fluent German and was the friend of Marie Hall, the distinguished international violinist and also of Frederick Delius. He was apparently sent for in a hurry on one occasion to interpret for Sibelius who was in the country to conduct but had no English.

He introduced the song *Waltzing Matilda* to the British public through one of the five broadcasts he did with the School at the beginning of the 1930s.

**Marie Hall, 1884-1956**

Born in Newcastle, violinist Marie Hall's debut in Vienna 1903 began an international career. She first came to Cheltenham in 1905, making the town her permanent home from 1911, when she married Edward Baring, living at 9 Eldorado Road, close to the School.

Marie Hall became friendly with Heller Nicholls but it was not until 11th February, 1928 that she gave a recital at the School, promised the previous autumn. *The Decanian* reported that '...her exquisite playing held the School spell-bound until the end...'. Her programme consisted of lesser known composers from the 18th, 19th and early 20th centuries, as well as the better known Austrian, Fritz Kreisler.

Marie Hall returned to Dean Close on 18th March, 1930, with the doyen of all accompanists, Gerald Moore. Her programme included Sonatas by Grieg and Schumann and, generously, one of Heller Nicholls' own pieces, *Slovak Legend.*

On her third and last recorded visit, Marie Hall brought her daughter, Pauline Baring, as accompanist. It was a concert honouring the centenary of Brahms, in which the School Choral Society, Junior Choir, Senior Choir and Chapel Choir all participated. *The Decanian* reported, '...both artistes had a great reception from the School, and the Senior Prefect presented a bouquet of flowers...'.

During Marie Hall's lifetime, Ralph Vaughan Williams composed especially for her, and dedicated to her, the breathtaking *The Lark Ascending* which she first performed in 1921. In 1984 a plaque was unveiled to commemorate her residence at 9 Eldorado Road by Ursula, widow of Ralph Vaughan Williams. Although Marie Hall never played it at the School, *The Lark Ascending* has been played at Dean Close School by Helen Hewitt whilst a scholar here and also by Robert Bishop, the current Head of Strings.

35-year-old Dr Thomas Armstrong of Christ Church Cathedral, Oxford, later a knighted Principal of the Royal Academy of Music (1955-68), who visited in 1933. Apparently his summing up was masterly, '...tempering instruction with humour...'.

Through contacts, possibly Hedley Warr, Heller Nicholls and the whole School were invited to do a live broadcast, principally of folk songs, by BBC Midland Radio in late October 1931. This was so successful that there were annual, live, broadcasts from 1932-35.

Heller Nichols retired in 1936. His assistant, Dr Freddie Westcott, took over, (1936-41) and programmes became slightly more serious. A tradition of Sunday afternoon concerts began – often recitals – usually given by adults visiting the School. In 1938, a Hammond organ was installed in the Chapel. Christmas Services of Lessons and Carols began, the one for Christmas 1938 finishing with *Now Thank We All Our God* – the old School hymn.

Dr Westcott seated at the Chapel organ in its original position

The coming of war, and the evacuation to Monkton Combe meant few reports of musical activity. Having returned, by mid-summer 1940, the School Choir, complete with cassocks presented to them by an anonymous donor, expressed the hope

**The Dean Close School Annual BBC Broadcasts, 1931-35**

BBC Midland Radio gave Heller Nicholls just over a month to prepare a broadcast on Tuesday 27th October, 1931 at 7.50pm – live – for 40 minutes. It included the whole School. The broadcast was light-hearted but varied. Heller Nicholls certainly ensured this as it included his specially composed *Toy Symphony* '...in three movements, founded on American airs and arranged for strings, piano and...cuckoos in C and F, toy trumpets in C and G, nightingale, side drum, triangle, glockenspiel, bells, cymbals, kazoos and cock-crow...'. In addition there were contributions from Freddie Westcott on the harpsichord, the Junior Choir, the Senior Choir, the Music Club (of singers) as well as the whole School and orchestra. The broadcast must have been thought successful because a second took place a year later on 24th October, 1932 and was five minutes longer. It included another Toy Symphony as well as the School's *Carmen Decaniense*, i.e. the School Song, among the negro spirituals and folk songs. This time they were picked up as far away as Lausanne, Switzerland. The BBC Midland Regional Director wrote: '...I must...tell you what a success the broadcast was from Dean Close School...We have already received several very appreciative letters...' The third broadcast was on 2nd November, 1933, and the letters received showed that a large area was being covered, from County Meath to Lowestoft, from Southport to Ramsgate and from Sunderland to Liskeard.

The fourth broadcast, on 17th November, 1934, was of interest for two reasons; it was the first occasion that the later well-known Australian Bush song *Waltzing Matilda* made its debut to the English public. The radio critic W.R. Anderson, writing in the *Musical Times* said: '...The concert is now an institution...Dr Thomas Wood's *Waltzing Matilda* from his 'Cobbers' experience, had a first performance: a jolly swinger...'. Dr Walker Robson, of *Musical Opinion* wrote '...the programme is always one which can be enjoyed by either low or high brow listeners...'.

The second item of interest was at the very end of the concert and escaped public comment. It was entitled *Vesper Decaniensis* apparently composed by Frederick Delius. Closer inspection shows that the Latin words were by Edward Ellam with the music adapted by Heller Nicholls in 1923 with the permission of the original composer whom Heller Nicholls knew. At present, this potentially most interesting piece has not been re-discovered.

The fifth and last broadcast was on 2nd December, 1935. This time there was a theme –Bonnie Prince Charlie – that changed the style of the broadcast a little. The reception was not as good as in previous broadcasts, although better than had been the case in the Post Office tests the preceding afternoon. All 12 items were arranged by Heller Nicholls from a collection of Scottish music published in Edinburgh in 1848. Apart from 'numerous' letters of congratulation from England and Wales, Heller Nicholls also received them from as far afield as Cairo, Gibraltar, the Isles of Scilly, Bordeaux, Strasbourg, Cologne, Aberdeen and Dublin.

of singing a few anthems the next academic year. Later that same year, Dr Westcott left to join his former colleague, B.O. Bradnack, now headmaster of the Royal College for the Blind, Worcester while Dr E.A. McLellan became Director of Music (1941-47). The choir was also part of the Public Schools' Choirs' Festival held in Gloucester Cathedral. Despite the war, boys still went to the Town Hall to see world class performers, such as Benno Moiseiwitsch playing Tschaikovsky's *First Piano Concerto* in 1942, or William Walton conducting his *Façade Suites* in June 1945.

On Sunday 28th March, 1943, the last day of term, the Choral Society sang much of Handel's *Messiah*, augmented by Cheltenham and Gloucester Choral Societies. The Headmaster, Hugh Elder, was the bass soloist. The performance was accompanied by H. Byard on the Hammond organ.

Dr McLellan, who had conducted the performance, was married next day in the same Chapel to a Junior School colleague, Joyce Sadler, Dr Westcott returning to the School to play the organ.

The House Music competition was revived on 29th March, 1947, the last recorded having been in March 1939. Brook House won. At the end of that Trinity Term, Dr McLellan left after six years at the School.

Derek Gaye

Derek Gaye was Director of Music 1947-53. The distinguished musician and composer R. Sterndale Bennett '...delivered a lecture to the school entitled *How a Symphony is Made*... illustrated by the speaker himself on the piano; and simultaneously, the playing on records of Schubert's *Unfinished Symphony*, and the showing of lantern slides of the score...'; possibly the first interactive audio-visual presentation! The School Choir learnt five anthems during Trinity 1949, together with Stanford's *Jubilate* and a further anthem on Commemoration Sunday. The School Orchestra, a war time casualty, was resurrected.

In November 1949, the Chapel Choir gave a concert in Dursley Church, invited by its organist, C.S. Adams OD, the first known occasion that the nearly 40-strong choir had sung outside the School, other than in the Cathedral for the Public Schools' Choirs' Festivals. There were two Carol Services for the first time, one for the main School and one for the Junior School, although the full Chapel Choir sang at both.

On the last Sunday of Michaelmas 1951, for the first time for many years – possibly ever – a boys-only School instrumental concert was held; just two sets of songs were the only vocal items in a ten item programme. Derek Gaye and also Alfred Furnish, a wind instrument teacher, had encouraged instrumental music making. A small orchestra played some Haydn, together with violin, clarinet, flute and piano solo items. Derek Gaye made sure that another appeal for instruments – particularly brass ones – went into the next *Decanian*.

Mozart's *Requiem* was performed in Christ Church, Cheltenham, in June 1953 by the Choral Society with the ladies of St Mary's Training College, Cheltenham. Derek Gaye left later that year, becoming Director of Music at Bradfield College. He had significantly improved choral singing and had galvanised the instrumental side of the School's musical activity.

David Lepine, was Director 1953-61. He conducted Haydn's *The Creation* with the School Choral Society augmented by Cheltenham Ladies' College. Held in Christ Church, Cheltenham in March 1954, it was the first occasion the two schools had co-operated in such a way.

The Chapel Choir, re-equipped with new surplices and cassocks in royal blue, sang Evensong in Tewkesbury Abbey for the first time on Whitsunday 29th May, 1955, while the Headmaster, the Revd Douglas Graham, preached. There were many parents and boys in the congregation. Since then, the Chapel Choir have sung in the Abbey every year.

In November 1955, David Lepine inveigled Dr Bernard Rose, then a Fellow of Queen's College, Oxford, to the School as adjudicator of the House Music competition.

In 1956, there were the requirements of worship in Chapel; the Choral Society's performance of Bach's *St John Passion*; an instrumental and choral informal concert; Evensong at Tewkesbury Abbey and the developing Madrigal Club, invited to perform music by Schutz and Purcell to the Cheltenham

Music Society. A concert at the end of the Trinity Term included the rapidly improving orchestra playing Beethoven, Purcell and Grieg.

In December 1957, the Madrigal Club sang Fauré's *Requiem*. A.S.R. Parker, then Housemaster of Gate, wrote in his critique that of those listening '...none of them had probably ever heard (it) before...' and that it '...deserves more hearing than it gets in England...'. That seems incredible, given its popularity 50 years later.

In 1958, the Chapel Choir recorded for the first time an LP record for private circulation. Tape recorded in Christ Church, the result went to a firm in Manchester for processing. It included two anthems for trebles: *O Turn Away Mine Eyes* (Boyce) and *My Joy, My Life, My Crown* (Montgomery); and the whole choir singing the *Nunc Dimittis in C* by Stanford together with Wood's *O Thou the Central Orb*.

In June 1959, when the Music Masters' Association conference came to the School, it was given a recital in Chapel that included solo instrumentalists, small chamber groups, the Choir and finally a specially commissioned Festival Jubilate for Congregation, Choir, Brass, Percussion and Organ by Tony Hewitt-Jones, a rising and respected composer, formerly Junior School Director of Music, later Assistant County Music Advisor for Gloucestershire.

The Michaelmas 1960 edition of *The Decanian* noted that '...The 'temporary' building which lies on the south side of the Hockey Quad has been converted into a most successful Music School, (originally) erected in 1926...The 'old' Music School which was built on the north side of the Hockey Quad has been renamed the Band Room and this provides a further seven practice rooms...'. The area involved in this Hockey Quad with the old and new Music Schools is roughly where the Gym and Swimming Pool are now. They were both wooden huts.

In March 1961, Dean Close Choral Society joined with Cheltenham Ladies' College under David Lepine's baton to sing Mozart's *Requiem* in the Princess Hall at The Ladies' College. The reviewer noted that the Dean Close tenors only numbered eight, basses few more, and both were occasionally understandably swamped. David Lepine left that year to become organist at the new Coventry Cathedral and Music Adviser to the city of Coventry. He had effectively developed choral singing, encouraged instrumentalists and had watched over the burgeoning singing talent of Neil Jenkins.

Graham Smallbone became Director (1961-66). His first major project was *Messiah* in December, 1961. He kept the chorus and orchestra as small as he believed Handel originally intended. The soloists were all drawn from the School and included sixth-formers Neil Jenkins, Martin Oram, Christopher Brown and Martin Campbell-White, together with M.S. Reynolds, from the Remove, and Mrs Harries. The occasion was seen as '...an unqualified success...'.

The Princess Hall at The Ladies' College was again the venue in March 1962 when the Dean Close Choral Society, with The Ladies' College, presented a programme of Haydn, Handel and the comparatively new *St Nicholas Cantata* by Benjamin Britten with Gerald English as the tenor soloist.

Bach's *St Matthew Passion* in 1963 which the Choral Society, Junior School choristers and girls from The Ladies' College performed in Christ Church was memorable and a personal triumph for Neil Jenkins. Still only a schoolboy, he sang the demanding part of the Evangelist and succeeded '...with considerable ease...' reported the *Gloucestershire Echo.*

Amongst other musical activity, the Chapel Choir sang Evensong in Tewkesbury Abbey on Whit Sunday then three days later sang Evensong in Coventry Cathedral for the first time. In November 1963, the Junior School, Dean Close School itself and Cheltenham Ladies' College combined to present, on two evenings, Britten's *Noye's Fludde* in Christ Church under Graham Smallbone. It was thought to be its first performance in Gloucestershire.

The *Gloucestershire Echo*'s reviewer described Graham Smallbone's next major musical venture in the Lent Term 1964 as '...one of the largest and most ambitious musical enterprises ever to be attempted by local school children...'. It was Verdi's *Requiem*, performed in Christ Church with a sizeable contingent from The Ladies' College – trained, as always, by Anne Foster – as well as the School's own Choral Society. A soloist was Neil Jenkins, now a choral scholar at King's, Cambridge.

In 1964 the School, with the Bishop of Wakefield, commissioned the distinguished composer John Joubert to compose a setting of the Holy Communion Service for choir and congregation which the Chapel Choir hoped to use when they revisited Coventry Cathedral in 1965. With the additions of singing Evensong on the Saturday and Sunday this they duly did, the setting being called *Joubert in D*. It was reported that '...Mr Joubert himself was among the congregation to hear his work performed...The choir did not dominate the Communion Service...its function being to lead the congregation rather than to sing alone...'.

Progress was being made regarding Decanians' instrumental competency. At the informal concert held in November 1965, some wind players tackled Beethoven's *Quintet in E flat*, Opus 16, while the String Orchestra tried three of Hindemith's *Eight Pieces*, Opus 44. Neither would have been possible by Decanians a few years earlier.

Graham Smallbone departed to become Director of Music at Marlborough College in 1966. His impact on the musical life of the School and Cheltenham had been considerable. He was succeeded by Joe Polglase, Director 1967-74, a former Choral Scholar of Magdalen College, Oxford who was Assistant Musical Director at The Leys, Cambridge.

In 1967 there was a jazz concert, 'Jazz '67', featuring the Tony Baines' Big Band and the Jimmy Horsfall Sound, which packed the Big Schoolroom. A.C. 'Tony' Baines, a clarinettist, had arrived as a member of staff in 1965, while pianist J.S.C. Horsfall was a member of the Sixth Form.

Joe Polglase

In 1969 an organ loft was built to take a new organ. Services were held in the School Hall and, on Sundays, at St Mark's Church. The Commemoration Service was held in St Matthew's Church. For possibly the first time, a Decanian took on a movement of a concerto, Christopher Boodle playing the first movement of Mozart's *A major Piano Concerto* at a concert given in the gym. Meanwhile, a major choral work performed in the Town Hall for the first time was Brahms' *Requiem*, assisted by choristers from both Cheltenham Ladies' College and Pates' Grammar School for Girls. Joseph Polglase conducted.

Between March 1971 and 1972 the School Choral Society, together with girls from The Ladies' College and Joseph Polglase as conductor, tackled three major concerts. The first was Verdi's *Requiem*, with Peter Cairns the bass soloist. Then Fauré's *Requiem*, sung in Chapel in January the following year, again with Peter Cairns. Thirdly, in St Matthew's Church in March 1972 a concert included the *Sixth Chandos Anthem* by Handel as well as Haydn's *Nelson Mass* with a '...highly effective and stylish...' orchestra, though this time Head of History, David Watson, was the bass soloist.

In 1974, Joe Polglase moved to Cranleigh, and was succeeded by George Howarth, 1974-83, then an Assistant Director of Music at Malvern College.

The first 'Rock 'n' Roll' group that played to a paying audience emerged in 1975, in time for the Midsummer Fair, playing their own material apart from one Bob Dylan track. The Chapel Choir went to Winchester Cathedral to sing services, giving Coventry a rest, while the final concert in the Trinity Term was a Serenade on Chapel Close. It featured Bach's *Double Violin Concerto* with the new Head of Strings, Tim Odell, and the Headmaster, Christopher Turner, being the two soloists. Few headmasters would have undertaken so demanding a task in the dying days of a School year. The Lent Term Concert in the Town Hall, was Haydn's *The Creation*. This time, the Choral Society sang with Pate's Grammar School for Girls. Felicity Lott was the soprano soloist, with Neil Mackie and the School's David Watson the other soloists, conducted by George Howarth.

Highlights in 1976 included the Chapel Choir singing the Evensong opening festivities at Malmesbury Abbey, marking the 1300th anniversary of the Abbey's foundation, and a performance of *Messiah* in Cheltenham Town Hall which, for the first time, did not call on any other school.

Michaelmas 1976 was the first occasion when the Chapel Choir sang Evensong at Tewkesbury Abbey on Remembrance Sunday. This tradition has remained unbroken for over 30 years since. In 1977 the School gave its first-ever concert in Tewkesbury Abbey, a performance of Monteverdi's *Vespers*.

In Trinity 1978, concerts at Commemoration and the end of term allowed instrumentalists to show their paces, Andrew Blair being possibly the first Decanian to play a complete concerto as the soloist in Mozart's *Second Flute Concerto*.

Chris Carmell and Martin Fothergill formed a Jazz band in January 1979. Within a year it grew to 13 personnel although fewer played at any one time. It gave concerts in the Flecker Hall, at the Deerhurst Wine, Cheese and Music party and the School's Christmas Ball, where Peter Cairns was vocalist.

The Chapel Choir sang at Chichester Cathedral and also assisted in St Paul's Church, Cheltenham's 150th Anniversary celebrations. School instrumental playing was now impressive, for in 1980 a School quintet won the Challenge Cup for Chamber Music in the Cheltenham Competitive Festival, two other Decanians – Nicola Johnson (woodwind) and Charlotte Holloway (brass) – won Gold medals.

Chris Carmell's Jazz Band

George Howarth left in the summer of 1983 and the School was without a Director of Music for a term. Peter Cairns, the Head of English and Drama and a former choral scholar of King's College, Cambridge, who had sung in the School Chapel Choir since 1968, was invited to be its Choirmaster. The standard of the Choir, already considered reasonable, rose significantly to '…a very high standard…' as Colin Sherratt, Chapel Organist and Head of Keyboard at the time, later wrote.

Ian Little was Director of Music 1984-89. He had been Director of Music at Coventry Cathedral. While preserving much of the traditional in Dean Close School Music, he wanted to be adventurous at times. Thus in the Lent Term 1984 Choral Society Concert in Cheltenham Town Hall, where the Choral Society was augmented by pupils from Charlton Park School and Dean Close Junior School, things were different. After Handel's *Zadok the Priest* and *The King Shall Rejoice* there was a first performance in Cheltenham of David Fanshawe's *African Sanctus*, with Timpani, Rock Drums and electric guitars, conducted by Trevor Owen, while Ian Little himself played the piano. The majority of the audience were apparently '…very impressed…'.

1985 was when Decanian parent Marion Montgomery, an internationally well-known singer of American popular music, together with pianist and composer Richard Rodney Bennett, gave an Endowment Concert for School Funds in the Town Hall. The Chapel Choir went to France, singing in Le Mans and Chartres Cathedrals and also the Chapelle Royale where some French royalty are buried – the first continental tour for the Choir.

1986 was centenary year. The Chapel Choir, directed by Peter Cairns, produced an LP recorded in Tewkesbury Abbey that included items from Jacob Handl and Orlando Gibbons to Ralph Vaughan Williams, Sir Lennox Berkeley and Benjamin Britten. There were centenary services in both Gloucester Cathedral and Christchurch, Cheltenham. The Centenary Concert, also in Tewkesbury Abbey, was a recital by Dame Janet Baker with her accompanist Geoffrey Parsons in October. Earlier, at the end of the Lent Term, a performance of Verdi's *Requiem*, described as being '…intensely moving…' had been given in the Town Hall by the Choral Society, augmented by Charlton Park School and by Dean Close Junior School, with the Gloucestershire Concert Orchestra, conducted by Ian Little. Neil Jenkins OD gave a song recital as part of the Cheltenham Festival of Music. Sir Richard Luce, Minister for the Arts, was in the audience of the School's centenary recital in the Pittville Pump Room. Items included the compositions of two ODs, John Metcalf and Christopher Brown. The year finished with a massive production of the musical *Oliver!* that had a cast of over a hundred (see Drama section).

The Chapel Choir sang Evensong at Carlisle Cathedral as well as Tewkesbury Abbey in 1987; the Small Choir – a select group from the Chapel Choir – came into being and gave a number of concerts both within and without School.

Dean Close Choral Society on its own sang Mozart's *Requiem* in the Town Hall in March 1988. A measure of how good the Chapel Choir were becoming was that they were part of the Morning Service broadcast from the School on 6th June by the BBC. That July the Chapel Choir, as part of the Cheltenham Music Festival, sang all the items in 'Byrd to Lennox Berkeley – A Recital of English Cathedral Music'.

Ian Little, having achieved much, notably chorally and with the brass group, moved on to Ampleforth, to be succeeded by Richard Knight (1989-2001). One of the latter's initiatives was to insist on regular orchestral and wind band rehearsals rather than *ad hoc* rehearsals for concerts. This helped to raise instrumental standards significantly and eventually led to the formation of a chamber orchestra. One of the first musical events of Michaelmas 1989 was the Preparatory Schools' Choral Course that

Colin Sherratt

began the year before. The demand spilled over to two days, choristers coming to learn about singing in the setting of the Chapel, finishing the afternoon with Choral Evensong. In December 1989 there was a performance of Mendelssohn's *Hymn of Praise* in the Town Hall. Held in December, it was conducted by Richard Knight.

At Trinity 1990 the Chapel Choir recorded a CD, *From Michaelmas to Whitsuntide*, in Tewkesbury Abbey under Peter Cairns' direction, with Colin Sheratt on the organ.

The academic year 1990-91 included masterclasses from Colin Sauer, the distinguished violinist, and April Cantelo, recitalist and opera singer, and a recital from the American virtuoso organist Carlo Curley on the Chapel organ. A Chamber Orchestra of 28 players was founded, playing its first concert in Chapel in February 1991. Subsequently, in the year of the bicentenary of Mozart's death, it went on a highly successful three concert tour to Salzburg during the Easter holiday, the first time that an instrumental group had toured. Another excitement was the gift of the Nightingale/McConnell Music Library to the Music Department.

The opening of the New Theatre in October 1991 had an impact on the Music Department almost as great as on the Drama Department, as it offered a venue for concerts other than Chapel or an outside church or concert hall. The New Theatre came with a magnificent Steinway Grand Piano, the generous gift of the Sorensen and Bulgarides families. This Steinway gave Colin Sherratt the opportunity to give two memorable recitals each year – usually in the Michaelmas and Lent Terms, begun in September

**The Nightingale/McConnell Music Library**

This unexpected gift to the Music Department was in 1990 by Mrs McConnell, a Prestbury resident. The collection was begun by her grandfather, Moses Nightingale of Crawley, Sussex, when he began to provide copies of the music needed for an amateur orchestra that met weekly at the Nightingale residence. The tradition was subsequently continued by Mrs McConnell's father and also by her late husband.

Over one hundred years, the collection developed considerably. Several hundred works are included; the most represented composers being Handel, Mozart and Haydn. 50 of the latter's symphonies are in the library. There are also works by Albinoni, Boyce, Schumann, Smetana, Tchaikovsky, Delius and many others. Despite the age of some of the sets, the music was well looked after and was in marvellous condition, with numerous copies of each part. The School's orchestras have already played some of the pieces and the library is of great use to the School.

The School continues to be most grateful for this generous donation.

*(Adapted from an article in the Decanian, 1990-91, by Richard O. Knight, Director of Music, 1989-2001.)*

1992 – that were also platforms for senior music students to show their abilities. There were numerous concerts in 1992 and 1993. The Chapel Organ was overhauled in 1992 and two stops – an 8ft Solo Trumpet and a 16ft pedal Trombone – were added by Messrs Percy Daniel & Co. There was another recording by the Chapel Choir, also directed by Peter Cairns, with Colin Sherratt on the organ, in Tewkesbury Abbey in June 1993. This one was called *Christmas to Easter*, recorded by Priory.

In 1993-94, musical Decanians went to Bushley, Kemerton, Deerhurst, Bideford and Slimbridge to give concerts in the parish church of each village. In 1994 the orchestra toured part of Poland. Nearly 50 musicians with several Music Department teachers led by the Director of Music played five concerts in and around Krakow. Decanian violinists Helen Hewitt and Susie Henley became Associates of the London College of Music before leaving School, while Melissa Bastin (viola) joined the National Youth Orchestra and Matthew Martin won an Organ Scholarship to Magdalen College, Oxford.

The Advent Concert had become so popular that not everyone could attend, so in 1995 it was held on two consecutive nights. Richard Knight, himself a published composer, usually penned a composition for the end of each concert. On this occasion his *The Night Before Christmas* used two soloists, chamber orchestra, choir and Jazz Band.

The academic year 1995-96 also meant more villages were visited by musical Decanians to give recitals or concerts. A feature of 1996 was the orchestral tour of the Czech Republic that included concerts in Jachymov, Prague and Tabor, singing a Mass in Tabor.

In 1996 Peter Cairns stood down as Chapel Choirmaster after 13 years. He had insisted on the very highest standards, taking the Choir to sing in numerous cathedrals and abbeys in this country and on the continent. They had broadcast for Radio 4 and the World Service, and recordings had been played on BBC Radio 4, the World Service, Classic FM and local radio. Records and CDs had been made and future professional singers such as Robert Johnston, Emma Brain-Gabbott, and Julie Cooper had developed under his direction. Colin Sherratt finally retired after 30 years as a hugely talented yet utterly self-deprecating Chapel Organist, Head of Keyboard, accompanist and virtuoso soloist whether on piano or organ. In June 1996 he gave as his 'finale', a wonderful interpretation of Grieg's *Piano Concerto* with the orchestra.

The 1996-97 highlights included the Choral Society's *Messiah* in the New Theatre with soloists Julie Cooper (soprano) and Robert Johnston (tenor) being ODs and the other soloists – Diana Walkley (contralto) and Philip Brooke (bass) – from Dean Close and Dean Close Junior staff. There were the Advent and other concerts; the Chapel Choir sang in Winchester Cathedral, and were the semi-chorus in Elgar's *Dream of Gerontius*; visits to Birlingham and Deerhurst parish churches to make music; the Jazz Band as well as other combinations at Commemoration.

The Music School was formally opened by Prince Michael of Kent on 8th November, 1997. There was a Gala Concert in the New Theatre that, apart from many Decanians, also included Old Decanians who were now professional musicians and one OD, Christopher Brown, and one former Junior School Director of Music, Tony Hewitt-Jones, who were both composers. There was a Festal Evensong in Chapel the next day. The Jazz Band, Chamber Orchestra, Choral Society, informal and other concerts, Chapel Services, competitions and musical activities generally, such as the entertaining, glamorous and celebratory *My Fair Lady* in honour of the retiring Headmaster, Christopher Bacon, and his wife Jill, brought the Trinity Term to a memorable conclusion.

Over the next year or two, a selection of concerts with a range of musical Decanians continued not just inside but outside the School walls. The Chapel Choir sang Choral Evensong in Wells Cathedral

**The Music School**

The Music School was officially opened on 8th November, 1997 by Prince Michael of Kent.

The Prince Michael Hall is licensed for an audience of 120. It is used for rehearsals, Lunchtime Concerts and some evening performances. The roof is higher than the rest of the Music School, and this allows for high clerestory windows on the south side. A versatile stage system allows for concerts to be 'in the round' if required, and there is also a narrow gallery accessible from the upper floor. The level of resonance is adjustable using artistically designed acoustic curtains. A high-tech Recording Studio is to one side of the Prince Michael Hall. In addition there are two class teaching rooms, one with networked PCs, a library and work room, four offices for full-time staff, as well as rooms for individual instrumental teaching/practice and store rooms, together with a staff common room.

and a small group of instrumentalists and singers went off to Bushley Parish Church; a first-ever May Day Concert at the School and the Jazz Band in Pittville Park and at Winchcombe Park, all added to their experience while giving pleasure to others.

Tim Odell, who was Head of Strings since 1974, retired in 2000. He and his wife Dorothy, a piano teacher, had also been successful Houseparents of Brook House for ten years and Tim was also the longest serving Housemaster in Dale with 12 years' service. Richard Knight, after 13 years at Dean Close, moved to be Director of Music at Millfield School.

Highlights of the year included the Chapel Choir visit to York Minster to sing Evensong and the Millennium service in Gloucester Cathedral in which all three parts of Dean Close School – Senior, Preparatory and Pre-Preparatory – combined. There was a wonderful performance of Haydn's *The Creation*, at Tim Odell's request, by the Choral Society; the Jazz Band appeared at the Upton-upon-Severn Jazz Festival; Julian Gale emerged as an up-and-coming counter tenor who gained a Gold Medal for achieving one of the highest marks in the country when he took his Grade 8; and Olivia Hornby and Beccy Searle's achievements at becoming Associates of Trinity College, London, both on the clarinet.

Andrew Cleary

It took the School time to find the right person to take over from Richard Knight. Ciara Allen acted as Director 2000-01 during which she conducted Rutter's *Requiem* with the Choral Society. Andrew Cleary became Director (2001-04), having previously been at Oundle School; at his first Advent Concert he included Rutter's *Gloria*.

His arrival coincided with the beginning of a period when there were some particularly musically gifted Decanians. There was Ashok Gupta, pianist and organist who was to play Gershwin's *Rhapsody in Blue* as a 13-year-old in 2002, later to become Gloucestershire Young Musician of the Year, a composer, an excellent jazz pianist and bow out of the School with a performance of Rachmaninov's *Concerto No. 2* before taking up an organ scholarship in Cambridge. Another was violinist Ben Powell, who showed astonishing virtuosity in tackling concerti from Vivaldi, via Mozart (*G major*) to Max Bruch (*No. 1 in G major*) as well as many other pieces including many jazz numbers; leader of the 2nd violins in the National Youth Orchestra, he won a scholarship to Berklee, USA, for jazz violin. There was, too, saxophonist Jonathan Faull, who combined a prodigious talent for jazz with thoughtful and mature playing of classical pieces which, among other things, brought him the coveted Sherratt Prize; he also played piano and double bass. Then there was Edward Jones who not only played the piano to a very high standard but also played the violin so well that his performance of Mendelssohn's *E minor Concerto* brought a standing ovation. And this is in no way to belittle the talents of such musicians as Lee Axford (piano), Julian Gale (counter tenor), Olivia Hornby and Beccy Searle (clarinet), Jessica Hayes (cello), Rachel Mackinnon (bassoon), India Webb and Philippa Martin (flute), James Gough (brass), Alistair Reid (organ), Joshua Powell and Helen Reid (violin), while Alice Clayton, Paul Sutton, Harriet Colley, Rosemary Coombs and Henry Neill all won choral awards at Oxbridge.

Philippa Martin

The Jazz Combo: Jack Losh, Ben Powell, Ashok Gupta, Josh Powell, & Jonathan Faull

In 2001, the Jazz Combo were given the chance of working with Randy Becker, a world class trumpet player, who came to the New, now Bacon, Theatre to run a master-class as part of the Cheltenham Jazz Festival.

The Commemoration Concert in 2002 was almost certainly the first occasion that three concerto performances by School pupils were offered in one concert.

The Chapel Choir sang Evensong at St Paul's Cathedral the following January, having sung there on a previous occasion. The choir toured France in Trinity 2003, including singing Mass at Église St Roch in Paris, a concert in Église La Madeline and later also in the Cathedral Notre-Dame. Then to Normandy and a concert at the Eglise de Port-en-Bessin, whose audience gave a standing ovation! There was a final concert in Rouen Cathedral.

The Chapel Choir were at Tewkesbury Abbey on Remembrance Sunday and also recorded a CD of Christmas carols, called *On Christmas Night* there in February 2003. The Abbey was also used for the Preparatory Schools' Choral Day that March when Ralph Allwood, Precentor at Eton College, was in charge for Choral Evensong. 350 children from 11 preparatory schools took part.

Part of the school orchestra in 2004

During 2003, the Spring Concert moved to the Pittville Pump Room. This was so successful that the format was continued in 2004. One, two or even three concerti might be performed as well as other pieces. Robert Bishop, former co-leader of the BBC Symphony Orchestra and the School's new Head of Strings, made his debut as conductor of the School Sinfonia and School Orchestra.

In 2004, the Jazz Combo played at the Town Hall's Pillar Room as part of Cheltenham's International Jazz Festival and also at 'The Daffodil'. In the same year, RocSoc began as a new Monday afternoon activity for budding guitarists, drummers and singers that culminated in a two-hour rock concert in the Bacon Theatre.

Andrew Cleary left in December 2004, appointed Director of Music at Portsmouth Grammar School. A replacement was not easy to find. He had raised standards where they weren't already high. In the meantime, Benjamin Nicholas, Director of Music at the Abbey School, Tewkesbury, became the School's first part-time Director of Choral Music, while Helen Porter, who had been on the music staff since 1987, became acting Director of Music. She was later confirmed in that post.

The academic year 2004-05 had as its highlights the first-ever 'Strings Day' when 100 junior and preparatory school violinists, violists, cellists and even double bassists from 20 schools gathered in the Prince Michael Hall under the inspired direction of cellist Philip Sheppard; the Chamber Choir and the Sinfonia giving a lunchtime concert to a packed audience at St Martin-in-the-Fields, London; a wonderful Spring Concert in the Pittville Pump Rooms; and Commemoration Concert in the Bacon Theatre. That summer, the Chapel Choir toured Venice and Tuscany, performing concerts and also singing Mass on two occasions. Apart from singing in Venice, the Choir also sang in the Duomo in Florence, and churches at Pistoia and Montecatini.

In 2005-06 and into 2007, there were superlative concerts such as the Advent and the Spring Concerts, the latter including a performance of Mozart's *Requiem*, conducted by Helen Porter.

10th anniversary concert, Prince Michael Hall in November 2007. Yshani Perinpanayagam, Sarah Ings, Robert Bishop, Helen Porter, Ashok Gupta, Henry Neill and Benjamin Powell

Apart from the Advent Concert and carol services, the end of Michaelmas 2006 included a visit by the English Mozart Ensemble, a distinguished group of musicians who visited the School for a day, taking ensembles and masterclasses involving the Senior, Preparatory and Pre-Preparatory Schools. There were items in the subsequent concert by the Preparatory School children, Decanians, the English Mozart Ensemble and, finally, Robert Bishop, who played Vaughan Williams' *The Lark Ascending*.

In 2007, the Chapel Choir visited New York, singing in the Cathedral of St John the Divine and also at St Mary the Virgin in Times Square. On the Sunday they sang at St Thomas' Church. The service was broadcast on the internet.

During Lent 2007 in Tewkesbury Abbey there had also been the *St Matthew Passion*, that included Dean Close Choral Society, Dean Close Preparatory School Chamber Choir, Tewkesbury Abbey Schola Cantorum (see chapter 16) and soloists that had Dean Close connections headed by Neil Jenkins OD as the Evangelist, who had originally sung the part in 1963. The orchestra was led by Robert Bishop, the performance conducted by Benjamin Nicholas.

2007 was also the year when rock bands grew – there were at least four – as did opportunities to perform, such as the RocSoc Concert in February, Jazz and Blues in the Quad in April, and Rock in the Marquee at Commemoration. Jazz also did well, being an integral part of Jazz and Blues in the Quad but also having a Jazz workshop with renowned trumpeter Neil Yates as part of Cheltenham Jazz Festival.

A Gala Concert marking the 10th Anniversary of the opening of the Music School was held on Thursday 8th November, 2007 in the Prince Michael Hall. It opened with Robert Bishop and Helen Porter playing Beethoven's *C minor Sonata for Violin and Piano*, while Ashok Gupta (left 2006) played three Chopin Waltzes, Jess Hayes (2004) and her accompanist played Brahms' *Sonata for Piano and Cello in F*, Henry Neill (2007) sang Finzi's *Let Us Garlands Bring* and Sarah Ings (1999) played some modern saxophone pieces. Benjamin Powell (violin) (2005) was joined by Ashok Gupta to finish the concert with some jazz numbers played in their own inimitable style.

Edward Jones

The 2008 Spring Concert at Pittville Pump Room was also notable, not least for Laura MacKenzie's fine performance of Weber's *Concerto for Bassoon and Orchestra* and Edward Jones' '... very special performance...' of Mendelssohn's *Violin Concerto in E minor* that earned him, and the '...absolutely magnificent...' School Orchestra, a standing ovation. It was a performance that Edward repeated at the Commemoration Concert in the Trinity Term. That concert also included Rosemary Wendon and Lucy Howell playing Stamitz' little known *Concerto for Two Clarinets*, Yi-Lun Lin playing the slow movement from Mozart's *Concerto No. 21*, the Sherratt prize-winning saxophonist Jonathan Faull playing Milhaud's *Scarramouche* and the evening finishing with Joshua Powell's performance of Lalo's *Symphonie Espagnole.* It was a vintage year.

The following Spring Concert had as its solo highlight a remarkable performance of Elgar's *'Cello Concerto*, played by Edward Marshall. It was balanced by the Choral Society, under Benjamin Nicholas, singing Mozart's reconstructed *Mass in C minor*.

Musical activity has expanded hugely over the last 25 years, and the standard has also risen very significantly to a high level. There is a catering for a wider taste in music, and everywhere new challenges are being offered.

## Productions: 1924 to 2009

General entertainments (including house), short one act plays, revues, vaudeville and words & music have not been included

| | |
|---|---|
| Producers | C.A.P. Tuckwell (CAPT); H. Warr (HW); E.M. Phair (EMP); G. Wilson Knight (GWK); T.C. Murray (TCM); P.M. Cairns (PMC); L.S. Allington (LSA); R. Vines (RV); C.R. Haslam (CRH); S.G.G. Aiano (SGGA); H.D. Watson (HDW); R.C. Martin (RCM); L. Forbes (LF); * denotes a pupil |
| Venues | **B**acon (previously New) Theatre; **T**uckwell Theatre; **A**trium; **E**dinburgh **F**ringe; **S**tudio; **F**lecker Hall (previously Schoolroom); **H**eadmaster's **G**arden |
| Groups | **S**chool; Houses by initial; **J**unior **D**rama **G**roup; **C**lose-**U**p **T**heatre; Year Group: **LVI**, **V** etc; **D**ean **C**lose **P**layers |

| Year | Play (Playwright) | Producer | Venue | Group |
|---|---|---|---|---|
| 1924-25 | Hamlet (Shakespeare) | CAPT | F | S |
| | Speckled Band (Conan Doyle) | CAPT | F | Room V |
| | The Death Trap (Munro) | CAPT | F | Staff |
| | The Boy Comes Home (Milne) | HW | F | Staff |
| 1925-26 | As You Like It (Shakespeare) | CAPT | HG | S |
| | Grumpy (Hodges) | CAPT | F | T |
| 1926-27 | The Tempest (Shakespeare) | CAPT | HG | S |
| 1927-28 | Julius Caesar (Shakespeare) | CAPT | HG | S |
| 1928-29 | The Merchant of Venice (Shakespeare) | CAPT | HG | S |
| | Oliver Cromwell (Drinkwater) | HW | F | G |
| | Tons of Money (Evans) | CAPT | F | T |
| | Twelfth Night (Shakespeare) | GWK | F | Remove |
| 1929-30 | A Midsummer Night's Dream (Shakespeare) | GWK | HG | S |
| | Ambrose Applejohn's Adventure (Hackett) | CAPT | F | T |
| | The Admirable Crichton (Barrie) | HW | F | G |
| | Oliver Cromwell (Drinkwater) | HW | F | Acton |
| 1930-31 | Twelfth Night (Shakespeare) | GWK | HG | S |
| | Yellow Sands | Thomas/Westcott | F | WC |
| | Arms and the Man (Shaw) | HW | F | G |
| 1931-32 | *No play* | | | |
| 1932-33 | Macbeth (Shakespeare) | CAPT | HG | S |
| | The Devil's Disciple (Shaw) | HW | F | G |
| 1933-34 | The Tempest (Shakespeare) | CAPT / EMP | HG | S |
| | The Old Adam (Hamilton) | HW | F | Acton |
| 1934-35 | Richard II (Shakespeare) | CAPT /EMP | HG | S |
| | Journey's End (Sheriff) | HW | F | S |
| 1935-36 | No play (King George V's death) | | | |
| | *Tuckwell Theatre opened* | | | |
| 1936-37 | King John (Shakespeare) | CAPT | T | S |
| | Vice Versa (Anstey) | HW | F | G |

| | | | | |
|---|---|---|---|---|
| 1937-38 | Henry IV, Part 1 (Shakespeare) | CAPT | T | S |
| 1938-39 | The Tempest (Shakespeare) | CAPT | T | S |
| 1939-40 | The Merchant of Venice (Shakespeare) | CAPT | T | S |
| 1040-41 | The Zeal of Thy House (Sayers) | HW | T | S |
| 1941-42 | King Lear (Shakespeare) | CAPT | T | S |
| | Trial by Jury (Gilbert & Sullivan) | CAPT | F | S |
| 1942-43 | Abraham Lincoln (Drinkwater) | CAPT | T | S |
| 1943-44 | King John (Shakespeare) | CAPT | T | S |
| 1944-45 | Much Ado About Nothing (Shakespeare) | CAPT | T | S |
| 1945-46 | Macbeth (Shakespeare) | CAPT | T | S |
| 1946-47 | Richard II (Shakespeare) | CAPT | T | S |
| | Trial by Jury (Gilbert & Sullivan) | CAPT | F | S |
| 1947-48 | Twelfth Night (Shakespeare) | CAPT | T | S |
| | Grumpy (Hodges) | CAPT | F | T |
| 1948-49 | The Zeal of Thy House (Sayers) | CAPT | T | S |
| 1949-50 | The Tempest (Shakespeare) | CAPT | T | S |
| 1950-51 | King Lear (Shakespeare) | CAPT | T | S |
| 1951-52 | Much Ado About Nothing (Shakespeare) | CAPT | T | S |
| | Ambrose Applejohn's Adventure (Hackett) | CAPT | F | T |
| 1952-53 | Othello (Shakespeare) | CAPT | T | S |
| | See How They Run (King) | M Stanley-Smith | F | DCP |
| 1953-54 | The Merchant of Venice (Shakespeare) | CAPT | T | S |
| 1954-55 | Macbeth (Shakespeare) | CAPT | T | S |
| 1955-56 | A Midsummer Night's Dream (Shakespeare) | CAPT | T | S |
| 1956-57 | The Zeal of Thy House (Sayers) | CAPT | T | S |
| 1957-58 | King Lear (Shakespeare) | CAPT | T | S |
| | Tons of Money (Evans) | P McGhie* | F | DCP |
| 1958-59 | King John (Shakespeare) | CAPT | T | S |
| | Journey's End (Sheriff) | V Walters*/J Hensman* | F | DCP |
| 1959-60 | Richard II (Shakespeare) | CAPT | T | S |
| 1960-61 | Twelfth Night (Shakespeare) | CAPT | T | S |
| 1961-62 | | | | |
| 1962-63 | King Lear (Shakespeare) *rain stopped play* | CAPT | | |
| 1963-64 | The Tempest (Shakespeare) | CAPT | T | S |
| 1964-65 | | | | |
| 1965-66 | Murder in the Cathedral (Eliot) | I Mullins | T | S |
| 1966-67 | Of Cabbages and Kings (Monico) | I Mullins | T | S |
| 1967-68 | A Man for all Seasons (Bolt) | TCM | T | S |
| 1968-69 | Waiting For Godot (Beckett) | TCM | T | S |
| | The Long, the Short and the Tall (Hall) | C L-Wood*/TCM | Everyman | S |
| | *Junior Drama Group established* | | | |
| 1969-70 | Henry IV, Part 1 (Shakespeare) | PMC | T | S |
| | The Importance of Being Earnest (Wilde) | PMC | F | JDG |
| 1970-71 | Othello (Shakespeare) | PMC | T | S |
| | Much Ado About Nothing (Shakespeare) | PMC | F | JDG |

| | | | | |
|---|---|---|---|---|
| 1971-72 | Forty Years On (Bennett) | PMC | T | S |
| | A Midsummer Night's Dream (Shakespeare) | PMC | F | JDG |
| | A Penny for a Song (Whiting) | HDW | F | C |
| | My Three Angels (Husson) | C Martin | F | G |
| 1972-73 | Hamlet (Shakespeare) | PMC | T | S |
| | Romeo and Juliet (Shakespeare) | PMC | F | JDG |
| | Rosencrantz and Guildenstern are Dead (Stoppard) | S Toms | F | Fi/M |
| | Hotel Paradiso (Feydeau) | HDW | F | C |
| | Charley's Aunt (Thomas) | C Martin | F | G |
| 1973-74 | The Recruiting Officer (Farquar) | PMC | T | S |
| | The Housemaster (Hay) | J Groslin | F | G/M |
| | Tons Of Money (Evans) | PMC | F | JDG |
| 1974-75 | Twelfth Night (Shakespeare) | PMC | T | S |
| | The Importance of Being Earnest (Wilde) | PMC | F | JDG |
| 1975-76 | The Cherry Orchard (Chekhov) | PMC | T | S |
| | The Admirable Crichton (Barrie) | PMC | F | JDG |
| | Lord Arthur Savile's Crime (Cox) | S Serpell | F | G |
| | The Pirates of Penzance (Gilbert & Sullivan) | HDW | F | C |
| 1976-77 | Three Sisters (Chekhov) | PMC | Everyman | S |
| | HMS Pinafore (Gilbert & Sullivan) | HDW | F | C |
| | The Magistrate (Pinero) | S Serpell/PMC | F | JDG |
| | The Ghost Train (Ridley) | R Entwistle/K Baggaley | F | G |
| 1977-78 | Pygmalion (Shaw) | PMC | T | S |
| | The Beggar's Opera (Gay) | HDW | F | C |
| | Love's Labours Lost (Shakespeare) | PMC | F | JDG |
| | Arsenic and Old Lace (Kesselring) | D MacPherson/H Carter | F | G |
| 1978-79 | Much Ado About Nothing (Shakespeare) | PMC | T | S |
| | Crowns and Hearts | PMC | F | JDG |
| | Joseph and the Amazing Technicolour Dreamcoat (Lloyd Webber / Rice) | D MacPherson | F | D |
| 1979-80 | The Importance of Being Earnest (Wilde) | PMC | T | S |
| | Le Bourgeois Gentilhomme (Moliere) | PMC | F | JDG |
| 1980-81 | A Midsummer Night's Dream (Shakespeare) | PMC | T | S |
| | Charley's Aunt (Thomas) | RF Akenhead | F | G |
| | Tons of Money (Evans) | PMC | F | JDG |
| 1981-82 | Romeo and Juliet (Shakespeare) | PMC | T | S |
| | Hay Fever (Coward) | RCM | F | T |
| | The Mikado (Gilbert & Sullivan) | HDW | F | Fi |
| | A Penny for a Song (Whiting) | RF Akenhead | F | G |
| | French Without Tears (Rattigan) | RCM | F | T |
| | Toad of Toad Hall (Milne) | LF | F | Sh |
| 1982 83 | Rosencrantz and Guildenstern are Dead (Stoppard) | PMC | T | S |
| | The Lady's Not For Burning (Fry) | LF | F | Sh |
| | Gigi (Colette) | PMC | F | JDG |

| | | | | |
|---|---|---|---|---|
| 1983-84 | Twelfth Night (Shakespeare) | PMC | F | JDG |
| | Fallen Angels (Coward) | RCM | F | T/M |
| | Mystery at Greenfingers (Priestley) | | F | Fa |
| | She Stoops to Conquer (Goldsmith) | LF | F | Sh |
| | The Sleeping Prince (Rattigan) | PMC | T | S |
| | The Way of the World (Congreve) | E Paul | F | Fa/D |
| | Journey's End (Sheriff) | | F | C |
| 1984-85 | The Cherry Orchard (Chekhov) | PMC | T | S |
| | Pygmalion (Shaw) | PMC | F | JDG |
| 1985-86 | Lady Windermere's Fan (Wilde) | | F | D/Fa |
| | Caesar and Cleopatra (Shaw) | E Paul | T | S |
| | Plunder (Travers) | PMC | F | G |
| | Antigone (Sophocles) | RF Akenhead | T | |
| | The Pirates of Penzance (Gilbert & Sullivan) | P Mills | F | M/Fi |
| | Much Ado About Nothing (Shakespeare) | PMC | F | JDG |
| 1986-87 | Oliver! (Bart) | P Mills | Everyman | S+DCJS |
| | The Winter's Tale (Shakespeare) | PMC | T | S |
| | The Lady from Maxim's (Feydeau) | PMC | F | JDG |
| | Dial M for Murder (Knott) | LF | F | B/Sh |
| | The Real Inspector Hound (Stoppard) | D Breese* | F | LVI |
| | Le Bourgeois Gentilhomme | E Paul | F | S |
| 1987-88 | Cyrano de Bergerac (Rostand) | PMC | T | S |
| | The Importance of Being Earnest (Wilde) | PMC | F | JDG |
| | The Crucible (Miller) | LSA | F | T/Sh |
| 1988-89 | Romeo and Juliet (Shakespeare) | PMC | T | S |
| | A Midsummer Night's Dream (Shakespeare) | PMC | F | JDG |
| | Pinocchio | O Cullen | F | G/Sh |
| | Black Comedy (Shaffer) | LSA | F | T/Fa |
| 1989-90 | Lady Windermere's Fan (Wilde) | PMC | T | S |
| | Love's Labours Lost (Shakespeare) | PMC | F | JDG |
| | Teahouse of the August Moon (Patrick) | M Symonds | F | G |
| | HMS Pinafore (Gilbert & Sullivan) | S Holliday | F | C/Sh |
| | A Man for all Seasons (Bolt) | LSA | F | T/Fa |
| 1990-91 | Daisy Pulls It Off (Deegan) | LSA/RED | F | Fa/T |
| | Dracula Spectacula (Gardiner) | R Hilton | F | B/M |
| | Tons of Money (Evans) | PMC | F | JDG |
| | Three Sisters (Chekhov) | PMC | T | S |
| 1991-92 | *New / Bacon Theatre opened* | | | |
| | Twelfth Night (Shakespeare) | PMC | B | S |
| | Hamlet (Shakespeare) | PMC | T | S |
| | Rhinoceros (Ioneco) | SGGA | B | JDG |
| 1992-93 | The House of Bernard Alba (Lorca) | SGGA | B | M |
| | Billy Budd (Coxe/Chapman) | LSA | B | B/T |
| | The Real Inspector Hound (Stoppard) | PMC | B | JDG |
| | Krapp's Last Tape (Beckett) | SGGA | F | B |
| | The Admirable Crichton (Barrie) | RE Dowdney | B | C/Fa |
| | The Lady from Maxim's (Feydeau) | PMC | T | S |

| | | | | |
|---|---|---|---|---|
| 1993-94 | A Midsummer Night's Dream (Shakespeare) | PMC | B | S |
| | Volpone (Jonson) | SGGA | B | B |
| | The Winslow Boy (Rattigan) | R Taylor | B | T/Sh |
| | Bugsy Malone (Parker) | LSA | B | JDG |
| 1994-95 | Much Ado About Nothing (Shakespeare) | PMC | T | S |
| | Pygmalion (Shaw) | C Masterman* | B | T/Sh |
| | The Comedy of Errors (Shakespeare) | LSA | B | Fi/D |
| | The Sleeping Prince (Rattigan) | PMC | B | JDG |
| 1995-96 | The Alchemist (Jonson) | SGGA/J Moule | B | C |
| | Guys and Dolls (Loesser/Swerling) | LSA | B | S |
| | Wild Mink (Delderfield) | R Cole | B | M/B |
| | Browning Version (Rattigan) | D Laszlo | B | M/B |
| | Le Bourgeois Gentilhomme (Molière) | PMC | B | JDG |
| | On the Razzle (Stoppard) | PMC | T | S |
| 1996-97 | Henry V (Shakespeare) | LSA | B | Fi/D |
| | The Waste Land (Eliot) | J Moule/SGGA | B | Lit Soc |
| | Frogs (Aristophanes) | J Allen | B | JDG |
| | Love's Labour's Lost (Shakespeare) | PMC | B | S |
| | Welcome Home (Gilbert & Hodges) | S Gilbert* & P Hodges* | B | UVI |
| 1997-98 | My Fair Lady (Lerner / Loewe) | PMC | B | S |
| | Accidental Death of an Anarchist (Fo) | S Blackwell* | B | D/Fi |
| | A View from the Bridge (Miller) | R Rimell* | B | Sh/T |
| | The Real Inspector Hound (Stoppard) | PMC | B | JDG |
| | A Larum for London (Gascoigne) | SGGA | B | C |
| | Oedipus Tyrannus (Sophocles) | E Scott* | T | LVI |
| | The Dumb Waiter (Pinter) | R Garner* | B | UVI |
| | The Importance of Being Earnest (Wilde) | L Richardson* / E Kingston* | B | Fa/G |
| 1998-99 | Arcadia (Stoppard) | PMC | B | S |
| | A Man for all Seasons (Bolt) | PMC | B | JDG |
| | Women Are Like That (du Garde) | T Goodwright | B | LVI |
| | The Duchess of Malfi (Webster) | LSA | B | T |
| 1999-2000 | An Inspector Calls (Priestley) | J Whitehead* / J Lee* | B | L VI |
| | Bouncers (Godber) | C Bagshaw | B | L VI |
| | Lord of the Flies (Williams) | LSA /TH-S | T | JDG |
| | Blithe Spirit (Coward) | A Lyne-Pirkis*/K Nipperess* | B | Sh/T |
| | Daisy Pulls It Off (Deegan) | LSA | B | M |
| | Tons of Money (Evans) | PMC | B | DG |
| 2000-01 | Black Comedy (Shaffer) | A Saunders* | B | Fa/G |
| | The Farndale Macbeth (McGillwray/Zerlin) | CF Bagshaw | B | Sh/BC |
| | Grease (Jacobs/Casey) | LSA | B | S |
| | The Agamemnon (MacNeice) | J Allen | B | Classics |
| 2001-02 | The Roses of Eyam (Taylor) | CRH | B | BC/M |
| | Our Country's Good (Wertenbaker) | LSA | B | S |
| | Journey's End (Sheriff) | A Saunders* / G Routledge* | B | D |
| | Educating Rita (Russell) | LSA | A | |
| | Steel Magnolias (Harling) | S Tognazzi* | B | Sh |
| | All My Sons (Miller) | S Roebuck* / J Michell* | T | LVI |

| | | | | |
|---|---|---|---|---|
| 2002-03 | Cabaret (Isherwood/Masteroff) | LSA | B | S |
| | The Crucible (Miller) | LSA | B | T/Fa |
| | The Government Inspector (Gogol) | CRH | B | Fi |
| | Twelfth Night (Shakespeare) | LSA | T | UVI |
| 2003-04 | Bugsy Malone (Parker) | TH-S | B | S |
| | Macbeth (Shakespeare) | LSA | B+EF | S |
| | Death of a Salesman (Miller) | LSA | B+EF | G/D/Sh |
| | A Tale of Two Cities (Dickens) | CRH | B | BC/M |
| | Bard Inn (Decanians) | LSA/RV | EF | CUT |
| | Mother Said I Never Should (Keatley) | LSA/RV | EF | CUT |
| 2004-05 | West Side Story (Bernstein/Sondheim) | LSA | B | S |
| | The Resistable Rise of Arturo Ui (Brecht) | RV | B | DG |
| | Amadeus (Shaffer) | J Townsend* | B | VI |
| | A Midsummer Night's Dream (Shakespeare) | LSA | EF | CUT |
| | Look Back in Anger (Osborne) | RV | EF | CUT |
| | The Browning Version (Rattigan) | RV | EF | CUT |
| | A Day in the Life of Joe Egg (Nichols) | RV | EF | CUT |
| | Abigail's Party (Leigh) | LSA | EF | CUT |
| 2005-06 | King Lear (Shakespeare) | LSA | B | S |
| | After Juliet (MacDonald) | RV | B | Sh |
| | The Prime of Miss Jean Brodie (Spark) | RV | B | M |
| | Oh! What a Lovely War (Littlewood) | CRH / KMiller | B | Fa/D |
| | The Browning Version (Rattigan) | C White | EF | CUT |
| | The Crucible (Miller) | LSA | EF | CUT |
| | *Drama Studio opened* | | | |
| 2006-07 | Talking Heads (Bennett) | LSA / RV | S | DG |
| | Guys and Dolls (Loesser/Swerling) | LSA | B | S |
| | Pygmalion (Shaw) | RV | B | JDG |
| | Twelve Angry Men (Rose) | CRH / SHamill | B | Fi |
| | The Winslow Boy (Rattigan) | J Slade/LSA | B | BC |
| | The Importance of Being Earnest (Wilde) | LSA / RV | EF | CUT |
| 2007-08 | Anything Goes (Porter/Wodehouse) | RV | B | D/S/T |
| | Blithe Spirit (Coward) | RV | B | Fa |
| | Entertaining Mr Sloane (Orton) | L Lee* | B | V |
| | Suddenly Last Summer (Williams) | LSA | B | S |
| | Our Town (Wilder) | L Lawrence | B | JDG |
| | Educating Rita (Russell) | J Litt* | S | |
| | Our Country's Good (Wertenbaker) | LSA / RV | EF | CUT |
| 2008-09 | To Kill a Mockingbird (Lee) | RV | B | M/BC/G |
| | Separate Tables (Rattigan) | RV | S | V |
| | Blue Remembered Hills (Potter) | I Richards* | S | LVI |
| | Les Miserables (Boublil/Schönberg) | LSA | B | S |

# Chapter 14

# School, Citizenship and Community

For Decanians, the word 'community' has had several meanings. Firstly, those who use the School buildings – Decanians, staff and their families alike. Secondly, the later concept of Houses that Percy Bolton began created smaller communities within the School itself that had their own marked feelings of enthusiasm and loyalty. All this has been described in earlier chapters. 'Community' was later to include the immediate locality beyond the gates and subsequently the national community.

Given the School's Evangelical Christian roots, Dr Flecker, the first Headmaster, was very conscious and supportive of the world Church community and especially the work of missionaries abroad. Several boys were missionaries' sons. He encouraged the School branch of the 'Gleaners Union', designed to 'glean interest, support and blessing of the Church Missionary Society' (CMS), itself rooted in the Evangelical wing of the Church. Out of a School of 200 boys 'over 100' were said to belong to the Union and on 'Missionary Sunday', held every month, each contributed 1d (69p). Boys' interest was fed by regular visits of missionaries back from foreign climes. Between 1892 and 1906 missionaries gave 22 talks to the School. It was implied and occasionally suggested that a Christian citizen of the world community under God could do nothing better or nobler than offer himself either for ordination or missionary work or, even better, for both.

In addition, between 1900 and 1906, church dignitaries were the only guests of honour at Prize Giving, where acceptance by CMS of three Old Decanians for missionary work on one occasion merited a special announcement. There were often Lent courses or accounts in *The Decanian* of a boy meeting some notable Christian, such as W.T. Money meeting Dr Barnado in 1898. There were confirmation courses, Temperance movement activities within the School, a regular round of services and, for quite a few, Bible reading. Therefore, it is hardly surprising that numbers of Dean Close boys entered the Church, of whom a good few became missionaries. By 1918 many Old Decanians were abroad doing missionary work; so many, in fact, that four ODs, the Revd G.B. Davis, the Revd C.L. Richards, the Revd A.I. Kay and Dr C.S. Clark, all ended up together in a Punjab Mission Station. Yet one of the only times that Decanians saw the outside of the School was when they went to worship at St Mark's Church – and that ended when the temporary Chapel was built in 1909. Thus to a number of Decanians, School and Community was expressed through the worldwide Anglican Communion, especially in the mission field.

That the School at this time was well-intentioned, but did not quite know what to do concerning wider community involvement other than encourage boys to go into missionary work, was underlined by an article that appeared in *The Decanian* in July 1923. It was about the comparatively new National Council of Social Service that had been set up in 1919, written by a member of its Executive Committee. It explained that its role was to co-ordinate the '...innumerable associations and a vast army of volunteers...' that wanted to help in a variety of social and community situations, and where to write for more information if anyone was interested. There was no reaction from School or editor. The article was left to stand or fall by itself. However, its mere inclusion suggested a School interest in social and community issues.

On Percy Bolton's arrival as Headmaster in 1924, he immediately instituted the house system. Boys and staff were now taking responsibility within each house, thereby creating smaller communities; they would take greater responsibility within the School, too. It was the mark of a mature citizen. Thus the prefects' role was enhanced; schoolboy representation encouraged, not only on the new Tuckshop Committee but also among the Pioneers (a group begun by B.O. Bradnack, a history teacher, that set out to do practical things around the School grounds); senior boys taught to take responsibility for their decisions and cut maintenance costs, yet also an expression of involvement in community.

Dean Close School never had a 'fagging' system; why was never clear. It may have been Dr Flecker's express wish. It may have been because when the School first began, most of the boys were 14 or under. There was simply no call. Rather, with the move towards greater responsibility for senior boys, the School was effectively asking some of the older to serve the younger in the interests of community.

Thus far, community activity had been very restricted – either listening to visitors or else within the confines of the School. There was no tradition of external community service. Percy Bolton, together with comparatively new staff such as Hedley Warr, B.O. Bradnack and the Chaplain, the Revd Douglas Horsefield, clearly felt that at least an awareness and understanding of the immediate world was a part of what School community should be about. Thus each year from 1927 to 1939, two senior boys attended the Duke of York's Camps, subsequently called the King's Camps, held at New Romney, later Southwold Common, and later still at Abergeldie Castle on the borders of Inverness-shire and Perthshire. The camps brought 200 public schoolboys to meet 200 'boys from the industries of the land' for a week-long camp so that each knew rather more than before about the other. Run by approximately 100 staff, boys were divided into five colour groups, then subdivided into sections of 20. There was an emphasis on team games, notably rugby, football, tug-o-war, bench hurdling and relay racing. There was sea bathing, a daily concert in a marquee in which community singing was a particular feature (one concert was apparently broadcast each year, initially), worship, informal trips out and meals together culminating on the final day in a 2½ mile cross-country race later followed by a concert, and finally a gathering round a huge camp fire on the beach at the very end of the evening sometime after midnight.

Soon a second, rather more homegrown initiative began. It first appeared in a letter to Old Decanians from the Revd Douglas Horsefield, in *The Decanian* of October 1930. Parishioners from St Peter's, Greenwich visited the School for a summer's day out from 1929. The scheme was referred to as 'The School Mission'. The School's connection with Greenwich was that the Vicar of St Peter's, the Revd William Money, was an OD. Douglas Horsefield's idea was that the visit should be reciprocal, and that '...a round dozen members of the School staff, and senior boys, have already expressed their intention of coming during the week-end...'. The idea was that they should be joined by ODs.

In January 1931, a return visit was made. It included a large number of ODs, Decanians and staff. There was a football match and a concert. Decanians and staff contributed to services and Sunday

**The Revd Canon W.T. Money OD, 1873-1964**

Son of a founder of the School, he entered Dean Close Memorial School in January 1888 and left in December 1891. From Emmanuel College Cambridge, he went to Ridley Hall, Cambridge. He was ordained in 1897. In the First World War he was a Chaplain to the Forces in France.

He subsequently became Vicar and later Rural Dean of Greenwich and an Honorary Canon of Southwark Cathedral. He was founder of the Greenwich Scouts and Guides Association and became Commissioner of Scouts for London. He was on the Greenwich Board of Guardians for 28 years and was its last Chairman.

He was President of the Old Decanian Society and was a Life Governor of the School.

Schools by speaking and playing the organ. Dr Flecker preached at the morning service. This pattern of visits to and from Greenwich continued up until Douglas Horsefield left in 1935.

1937 included King George VI's coronation and the Golden Jubilee of the School, held over from the previous year because of the death of King George V. Moreover, some senior boys were drawn into thought-provoking community service, for Britain was by now deep in the Depression that affected not just numbers in the School which was struggling to survive but whole communities. One such was Pengam, a mining village in the 'distressed area' of South Wales.

A party of nine from the School (three masters and six boys) led by B.O. Bradnack spent the first week of the Easter holidays at Pengam, living as paying guests in the homes of unemployed men, and during the day helped to dig the allotments of old and sick miners. They also spent some time down a coal mine. It was clearly an experience that affected those in the Dean Close party. One boy wrote: '...We gained far more than we gave. We learnt at first hand much that we had only read about in newspapers. We now know something of what it means to work in the pit, or to live on the 'dole'. And we made some delightful friends. In spite of the apparent hopelessness of the economic situation, there is plenty of humour and hospitality in the Welsh valleys, and a spirit for which the word 'heroic' is not ill-chosen...'.

Several returned the following year, B.O. Bradnack's last on the Dean Close staff, and in 1939 a party of nine (four boys, two ODs and three masters) spent Holy Week at an Unemployed Social Centre at Pontypridd.

A participant (possibly Hedley Warr) later wrote that, '...we gave very little, infinitely less than we gained...the Social Centre, with a membership of 450 unemployed men, almost all over 40, was a live community built over the ruins of a derelict one...'.

Thus concern for, and interest in, the wider community was growing, albeit slowly. However, the intervention of the Second World War meant that the old School life and community was brought to a peremptory end with the evacuation to Monkton Combe.

When the School reconvened in Trinity 1940, a new community emerged from the old. Boys played their part in the practical running of the School, from stoking boilers to cooking, from being groundsmen to firewatching. They helped the wider community, notably local farmers. Some gave up part of their holidays to attend School work-camps to help get the harvest in. Additionally, some staff and boys were part of the Home Guard; each house 'adopted' a British prisoner of war and sent five shillings monthly so that he could be sent a parcel. The whole School raised funds towards the local war effort. These activities certainly allowed Decanians to experience different forms of citizenship to which they would not otherwise have been exposed (see chapter 5).

Boys operating the mowers in the early 1940s

Visit to a Forest of Dean colliery in 1950

In the immediate post-war years, the School was primarily concerned with its own survival and, where possible, the improvement of its facilities. Little was happening in terms of community and the wider world. There were Sixth Form weeks in the early 1950s when groups met German Sixth Formers (potentially a sensitive encounter though it apparently worked well), toured the British Rail workshops at Swindon, or went down a Forest of Dean mine. In other years there were opportunities to visit a court in operation, dealing with debtors; visit an Ebbw Vale steel works or a pin manufacturer in Lydney. These trips, while opening up new aspects of society and communities, were little more than a brief introduction at best. Apart from Chapel, there were one or two groups trying to do what they could for particular communities. For example, in the School there were the Lamplighters, a junior branch of the Mission to Lepers that consisted of about 16 stalwarts who kept interest and support alive in this field for some years.

Tony Gilkes was concentrating on building up the School itself as a community and he was doing it effectively, for when he left in 1953 to become High Master of St Paul's, London, *The Decanian* said of him: '...under (his) guidance, the School has achieved the reputation of being a happy and friendly community...'.

Within a year of becoming Headmaster, the Revd Douglas Graham had sanctioned two boys to go to the Bishop of Stepney's Sixth Form Conference in the East End of London, to find out what the Church and society in general were doing about the appalling conditions that were found there. Essentially, the conference was asking the same but important question each year: 'What should the Church be doing in an Industrial Society?' From 1954 until at least 1963, boys fairly regularly attended this conference that in 1956 brought them face to face with Trades Unionists, then seen by many associated with public schools as dangerous socialist radicals. M.S. Howells remembered the meeting well: '...To traditional Tory diehards such as Public School boys are supposed to be, this meeting promised to be one long tirade of Socialist propaganda, instead of which we were treated to an extremely interesting discourse on how the Trades Unions originated and how they operate...Most of us do not remember, nor have we read about, the appalling conditions for workers up to 1939 (including) the dreaded Means Test...'.

It was clearly an eye-opening experience, seeing people living in houses that were already condemned, visiting the youth clubs and the docks, the main employer, but also finding out about the sense of community that the East End had.

However, apart from the work done in the depressed Welsh mining villages and also, in a more superficial way, at Greenwich, the School had really only had observers that were going, looking and reporting back.

But things were beginning to stir on wider levels. From the end of 1957, articles began to appear in *The Decanian* on two matters that increasingly concerned the international community: nuclear warfare and apartheid in South Africa. The latter subject was explored in June 1959 when Father (later Archbishop) Trevor Huddleston, CR, who had been working among the South African blacks, came to the School to be questioned by the Vth, VIth and staff. He was clear that a clash between black and white was inevitable unless apartheid was dismantled. He encouraged a sporting boycott and for his audience to find out all they could about the situation. The same *Decanian* reported on A.L. Cornwell's visit to St George's Crypt, Leeds and its work among the people whom '…the state has failed to accommodate…', a visit that he clearly found moving. In February 1960, James Goudie, a member of the School, spoke at a meeting on Cheltenham's Promenade concerning apartheid and South Africa. Meantime, in the March 1960 *Decanian*, M.J.H. Harry of Walton Court tried to interest Decanians in marching to Aldermaston.

During the 1960s the School had two general responses to the need to train caring, resourceful, responsible citizens for the future. The first, developing from an already highly effective CCF, was to encourage boys to be involved in the Duke of Edinburgh's scheme and also compete for a place in the Ten Tors adventure walk on Dartmoor (see chapter 12). Both the activities encouraged self-reliance, teamwork, concern for others and initiative.

Secondly, at the beginning of 1965 the Social Services activity began. The following remarks were in the initial report: '…One of the arguments levelled at public schools is that instead of integrating with the local community, they become insular establishments, existing solely for their own benefit, and consequently contributing very little or nothing to the town in which they are situated.

'This term the Chaplain [the Revd R.W. Hallett] and Hugh Cocksedge [the member of staff responsible for the Duke of Edinburgh scheme], feeling that the School could well make a more effective contribution to the Cheltenham community, appealed for volunteers to do social work in the town. The tasks included jobs for the elderly and the infirm that were unable to help themselves, and ranged from hunting mice in an old house and teaching a blind person to use a typewriter to carrying out repairs in an old folks' home and a children's nursery and taking dogs for walks. Response throughout the School was good, and all the tasks were arranged under the auspices of the Cheltenham Health Visitors…'.

In October 1965, Ullenwood Manor, a centre specially designed for physically handicapped and other disadvantaged young people, was opened. An appeal was launched for funds and the School responded by making a collection from 2,000 houses in the neighbouring estates of Benhall and Warden Hill using over 100 boys. In the end, the collection amounted to just over £118 (£1,700) for what was now called the Star Centre.

The group experienced troughs – especially just prior to the advent of girls in the late 1960s – and peaks but later expanded into the Community Action Group, of which more presently.

Denys Carnill took on overall responsibility for the Social Service activity and he extended its role to taking a party of handicapped people to Slimbridge and bringing them and others to various

School functions. Other group activities included personal social work, i.e. visiting an old person and doing small tasks for them as well as talking to them. Another activity was visiting a home or institution, meeting the people there and helping to organize events for them and for others. Eildon and Cheshire Homes had ties as did Nazareth House, Dr Barnado's and Ullenwood, not to mention Arle House, Dowty House and Bettridge School, where links were to be particularly strong with Dean Close Preparatory School, especially, in years to come.

In 1973, a wheelchair was needed by the Social Service activity but there were no funds. Denys Carnill organized a Chapel collection that Harvest Festival Sunday, raising £80 (£725), easily paying for the chair, with money left over for other charitable needs. Together with Dr Keith Aris and Miss Purchase, he organized a fête on the last Sunday of the School Year in 1974 on Big Field, through which over £900 (£7,000) net was raised for charity. The profits from that first Midsummer Fair were shared by the Association for All Speech Impaired Children, Help the Aged and a smaller donation to Youth Action, with the residue being kept by the School's Social Services Group for further work. The entire School community was involved. In the following year, the gross total was £2,400 (£15,000). The proceeds were split three ways between the Home Farm Trust, who provide whole life residential care for the adult mentally handicapped; Bettridge School for physically handicapped children and the School

The Bishop of Tewkesbury, the Rt Revd John Went, a School Trustee, conducts a baptism and confirmation in the School Chapel in 2008

Social Care with the elderly – 1980s

Social Service Group which by now was running weekly visits in the wheelchair bus for the immobile. It had grown to a point in 1976 that it needed a larger umbrella committee to manage the Fete, and so Denys Carnill handed over to a committee of ODs, staff and parents under the chairmanship of the Headmaster's wife, Mrs Lucia Turner. In 1977, nearly £3,000 was raised. Local charities benefited as well as Dean Close Social Service Group that, among other things, was planning an Over Sixties Yearbook as their contribution to Age Action Year.

By 1978, the Group was almost 100 strong visiting about 60 elderly people every week. A year after that, the Group became involved with the Home Farm Trust at the 'Old Quarries' near Avening. Unfortunately, the sheer distance involved meant sessions were impractically short and so had to be discontinued, but links with the Sue Ryder Home in Leckhampton developed well.

In the early 1980s, led by Dr Keith Aris assisted by four colleagues, the social service activity was dominated by the Sixth Form. While dozens of old people were still visited, occasional outings were organized as well as a tea party for old people at the School on the Michaelmas term Field Day that by now had become something of a tradition. Some Sixth Formers involved took their role very seriously. In 1984 two, Bridget Harper and Simon Kirby, attended a weekend Community Service conference and came back with new ideas.

The Midsummer Fair was still growing, its connections with the local community becoming ever stronger. 1982, for example, saw the Fair just successfully beating the 1981 record of £5,000 profit (£13,225). Donations worth hundreds of pounds were made to the Physiotherapy Unit at the Delancy Hospital; the Gloucestershire Dyslexia Association; Speech Therapy in Cheltenham; Thirlstone Court for specially adapted tricycles for the children and to the School's own Social Service Group. However, the largest cheque – for £1,500 (£4,000) – went to the Cheltenham Association for Transport for the Disabled.

1982 was the first year that Sixth Formers were involved in work experience, albeit for a maximum of three days. Decanians experienced working in Cavendish House during the summer sales, while some worked in the Hospital, others with local manufacturers, accountants, solicitors, insurance companies, estate agents, advertising and PR firms. One boy spent his time at Cheltenham Racecourse. In all this, while learning a lot about the world of work, it was also an opportunity for the wider local community to see something of the kind of young men and women the School was producing.

The Revd Richard Martin (on the staff 1981-85) took over the Social Service activity from the Arises, and also helped the School to think more internationally by being the founding President of the International Club. By now Decanians were being drawn from around the world, and such a Club helped understanding between cultures to be appreciated within the School.

There was no Midsummer Fair in 1986 because of the School Centenary organization and events. Nevertheless, the Fair continued for two more years. The 1988 Fair was the last; the organization had

Midsummer Fair on Big Field, *circa* 1987

**World Record Walk from John O'Groats to Land's End, July 1986**

Stuart Fuller-Shapcott, deputy Head of School and captain of Brook 1984-85 wanted to contribute in a major way to buying a new RNLI boat. He talked with the Remove year from his house and the idea became a project: to walk from John O'Groats to Land's End, some 876 miles, and attempt to break Dr Barbara Moore's record of 12 days, 21 hours, 15 minutes. It was apparently permitted to attempt this in a team of 12 walkers. The difference would be that Dr Moore only counted her 'road time' whereas in this attempt, relays would be walking around the clock and all 'stop' time – if there was any – would be included in the final time. In the walking team of 12, each individual would do 20-odd miles in each 24 hour period.

Four vehicles were involved: a Land Rover as escort to those actually walking; a 'nippy' car to link the up-front walkers with the two hired 'mobile home' vehicles that leap-frogged in support. The latter had bunks. In the larger of the two, mothers Jane Herbert and Maureen Robinson turned out constant meals for the 21-strong team.

The attempt began at 10am on 16th July, 1986, at John O'Groats, signalled by a local lifeboatman with a rocket. The team was encouraged both by the sound of bagpipes and by personal messages from Prince Philip, Prince Charles, Princess Anne and Prince Michael of Kent. Early on, they halted at Thornhill, north of Dumfries so that they could visit the home of the Earl and Countess of Buccleuch who were holding a Garden Party for the RNLI.

En route, problems varied from leg and foot ailments to total apathy from onlookers. Reaching Cheltenham, they were received by the Mayor at the Municipal Offices, though not entertained. The course was completed in 10 days, 14 hours, 17 minutes, beating the old record by nearly 2 days 7 hours. If all the sponsors paid up, the RNLI stood to gain some £40,000 (£87,850).

Those who took part included Stuart Fuller-Shapcott, Gordon Heaton-Jones, Chris Gibson, Allan Trapp, Ken Robinson, Scott Ainslie, Pat Key, Chris Walker, Nigel Registe, Sven Awege, Tom Edginton, Matthew Herbert, Rodney Hunt, Toby Jarvis, Sam McCloy, Paul Robinson, Paul Young, plus two more adults, Dai Davies and Steve Robinson.

grown large and unwieldy, security was a problem and it was becoming a victim of its own success. At least £13,000 (£26,000) was raised and a range of charities benefited. However, the fundraising efforts of the Social Service group did not diminish: that year, three sponsored Decanians and a member of staff ran the Tewkesbury half-marathon. A cheque for £700 was given to Cheltenham Samaritans.

In 1989, Andrew Marsh, then in the Fourth Form, proposed and, in part, organized the recycling of quality paper at the School, possibly the first effort on the campus to look seriously and practically at green issues. It was certainly a year or two ahead of the popular adoption of such ideas.

In 1990 the International Club was confined to 30 members of the Sixth Form that quickly went up to over 50, roughly half British and half international. It was to be run by the sixth-formers themselves with backup from Richard Taylor, Housemaster of Tower. As before, it met once or twice each term. The Club's role and use in the area of understanding within both the international community and within Dean Close School was shown early on when German reunification was in full swing. An evening was organized, hosted by a Decanian who was a Greek German; led by a German member of staff, it largely comprised a discussion between visiting Germans, one from East Germany who was clearly facing huge problems as well as considerable hope, and another who was a university graduate from Munich, who put the views of the West Germans. Sixth Form understanding of international issues was hugely assisted by such encounters. Again, the international dimension of 'community' was underlined by the work of the Amnesty International group within the School, led by Housemaster Steven Aiano. In 1995-96 this group focussed particularly on the plight of Fernando de Araujo, an imprisoned Timorese student leader, sending 350 postcards to him and writing to the authorities. Great was the joy when a reply arrived, in English, warmly thanking them and encouraging the group.

Dr Peter Anstis with the International Club

It was felt that a wider appreciation of community was needed. Therefore, during Field Days, a programme began to be drawn up bringing in professionals from other spheres within the School's orbit. Thus in the early 1990s, visits were made to the Department of Social Security offices, the County Social Services, Gloucestershire Constabulary, the Nature Conservancy Council, the County Planning Department, the National Waterways Museum, Gloucester and to 'Big Pit' – a coalmine in South Wales. At one stage there were exchanges with the Sidney Stringer Comprehensive School, Coventry. Shades of the 1963 Bishop of Stepney's conference were evoked in 1995 and the following year when members of the Social Services Group went to Tower Hamlets in London to see for themselves something of the Inner Cities Young People's Project. In 1996 a party from St Paul's Community School, Tower Hamlets spent 24 hours at Dean Close School. In 1997, Decanians returned to Tower Hamlets also for 24 hours, visiting the Inner Cities' Young Peoples' Project again and also an inner city school. Several staff were involved in co-ordinating Social Services during the 1990s, especially Dorothy Odell.

Several DCS school leavers – 'gappers' – were now spending time abroad, working with organisations such as Voluntary Service Overseas, by assisting at the Happy Homes project for orphans in Kenya. Other than rather more outward-bound schemes, this was the first School based attempt to help a community abroad through personnel being there rather than through just monetary contributions. The only remote parallel was the assistance given to the mining communities in the 1930s.

**Happy Homes Orphanage near Kisumu, Kenya**

This is a Christian orphanage for about 40 children. 'Pastor Johana', who founded and ran it came to the School to speak in Chapel on several occasions in the 1980s and 1990s before he died, when the Revd George Ochola took charge. Over a number of years, several School volunteers assisted in the project, such as Thomas Eagleton, Andrew Jessop, Esther Colwill, Charlotte Timson, Louise Whitney and Kathryn Young. Since 2000 there have been attempts to reopen channels of communication. The orphanage is believed to be expanding and upgrading its facilities on the new Kopere site.

**Hebron School, Ootacamund, Nilgiri Hills, South India**

The school has just over 360 pupils, 65% from missionary families. 31% of the children are Indian, 27% British and the rest from a variety of nationalities. Ages range from five to 18.

The original school was founded by a Miss Orlebar, who had run the Brooklands Missionary Home, Coonoor, South India. In the late 1890s, missionary children often had to 'go home' to England or elsewhere to board, perhaps not seeing their parents for several years. Miss Orlebar began by taking two girls in 1899. Named Hebron School in 1902, it was a girls' school that also took boys up to ten. 'Breeks', a secondary school for boys, was close by. They amalgamated between 1974 and 1976 on the Lushington Hall campus. Initially just over 200 strong, recent years have seen steady growth up to its present level. It remains predominantly a boarding school and has had '...two strands which have always been present. First, it is thoroughly and unashamedly Evangelical, low-church Christian, and second – it is English – not even really British...'.

Its links with Dean Close School were strengthened in August 2000 when Second Master Alastair Reid became Vice-Principal, subsequently taking over as Principal. Rosalyn, Alastair's wife, taught there for some years, too, and their children have represented Hebron School at sport. Alastair Reid has been the driving force that has encouraged ever closer links between Hebron School and Dean Close School.

Hebron School has been visited by Dean Close Headmaster, the Revd Tim Hastie-Smith and others from the Dean Close community including Andrew Bruckland (Trustee), his wife Diane and daughter, Sarah; Vanessa Aris (DCS academic staff); Michael Ede (DCPS academic staff) and Sue Brown (Health Centre Matron). Decanians such as Sally Smith and others have visited or worked there. Alastair and Rosalyn Reid and colleagues have also been to Dean Close School. Jeremy Niblett, who was Head of Physics at Hebron now has a similar position at Dean Close School.

A different angle on citizenship and community was seen in the General Election of 1997. For on this occasion, the School held its own election with candidates from the three main parties together with the Communists, the Green Party and the Radical Ranting Ravers (see chapter 9).

In 2000 there was the Millennium Walk on 2nd May for 400 Decanians and 40 members of staff that included Shurdington Hill and Crickley Hill. It raised £5,500 for the Lotus Primary School in South Africa and the Teenage Cancer Trust, emphasizing both the concerns of the world community and those communities closer to home.

Two people took up roles over the Millennium that affected how the School was to view the world community and themselves as citizens of it. The first was the appointment of Baroness Cox as President of the School (see chapter 19). She famously described herself as 'a nurse by profession and a peer by astonishment'. However, the House of Lords gave her a platform from which, as International President of Christian Solidarity Worldwide, she has been able to exert influence on powerful people about the ways minorities are persecuted, speaking out on behalf of the Karenni people of Burma, the persecuted Christians of the Juba mountains of Southern Sudan and the Armenians of Nagorno-Karabakh among others. She has also been outspoken on people trafficking and slavery. Her warm personality, deep Christian faith and real concern for the down-trodden and persecuted have influenced many Decanians.

The other was the appointment of the School's Second Master, Alastair Reid, to be Vice-Principal of Hebron School in the Nilgiri Hills, South India, with a view to becoming Principal within a couple of years. It was founded in 1899 and is an international Christian School, the only British boarding school in India.

The increasing awareness of the worldwide dimension to community, underpinned by other School activities such as sporting tours and the British Schools' Exploration Society expeditions to various places on the globe, meant that there was real interest in developing the link with Hebron. Staff and students from both schools have visited each other's campuses.

Headmaster Tim Hastie-Smith's speech at Commemoration in 2001 focussed on three issues: citizenship, the spiritual dimension in a person's life and the concept of living in communities, seeing all three together as '...the very essence of education...of infinitely more value to the individual scholar and to society as a whole than any number of A levels or GCSEs which...are only one facet of a good education...'.

Two years earlier, Saskia Cole joined the staff of the School as a member of the Chaplaincy team but also with a brief to overhaul the Community Action arrangements. Old connections were maintained but new ones begun, such as a Fairtrade group, a stronger link with Bettridge School, a group to make 'storysacks' for special needs children at Battledown School, the setting up of a wheelchair basketball squad, Decanians assisting in a homeless project as well as other schemes including 'the Noise'. This last was a nationwide initiative 'to build community'. Youngsters, including those from the Fourth Form and Remove, were involved in projects including arts and crafts, gardening, ground clearance and car washing. At the end of the day, the Decanians met up with other involved young people at a barbecue. Some DCS Sixth Formers were involved with English as an Additional Language work with Turkish refugees. Although she left after two years to set up youth community projects in East Ham, Saskia Cole had begun a process that culminated in the production of a small handbook – 'Dean Close School Community Action' – that set out how the disparate parts of the various elements that made up Community Action were to come together.

One of the results of Saskia Cole's work was the Remove week on Citizenship, reserved for the last week of Trinity. There were talks from those concerned with ethnic minorities and the disabled; there was an exercise with the Ministry of Defence schools' team in which teams, each headed by a 'Prime Minister' had to deal with a fictional disaster relief operation in a fictional country – and then answer for their actions before a critical 'press corps'. There was a day on the hard realities of the business world, a Community Action Day and another on social inclusion.

It was about this time that Julie Kent became the co-ordinator. In 2005 she published a booklet 'Community Action', that laid down what was on offer that would help the School community, the local community or specific communities in the world. The Sixth Form were involved the most as they had the choice of being in the CCF, doing Outward Bound or being involved with Community Action; of the three activities, Community Action is the one with most adherents. The Remove Week and other

**The Emily Kent Charitable Trust**

Emily Kent was born in March 1992 and died in 1995 of Medulloblastoma, just as she was about to enter the Pre-Prep. Her father Bernard and mother Julie, a saxophone teacher at Dean Close School, later Housemistress of Mead and subsequently Housemistress of Shelburne, determined to set up a charity in Emily's memory. Although there were people who supported this charity who were nothing to do with the School community, nevertheless, much fundraising for it went on within Dean Close School. To date, there is an Emily Kent Unit in Gloucester Royal Hospital for children who suffer from leukaemia or forms of cancer. There is also the Emily Kent Day Unit at the Bristol Children's Hospital. The Emily Kent Charitable Trust has scaled back its activities in recent years.

occasions such as organizing a charity event often encouraged younger Decanians to become involved. There have also been charities founded from within the life of the School – the Emily Kent Charitable Trust and Claudia's Closet. By 2005, the whole business of citizenship and community had become a very significant part of the Dean Close School education package.

**Claudia's Closet**

Fay Sullivan was a member of Shelburne House. In Trinity 2006, her close life-long friend Claudia Paul died aged 16 from a rare form of cancer, Ewing's Sarcoma. Although Claudia was not a Decanian, Fay and several other girls in her house who had suffered the loss of friends or family due to cancer, decided to refurbish a recreational room for teenagers with cancer in the Emily Kent Unit at Gloucester Royal Hospital where Claudia was treated. Claudia was a keen horsewoman and her racing colours of blue and yellow were included as part of the improved décor. The room has been planned to be welcoming with new sofas, a computer with internet connection and a plasma screen with an Xbox. There is to be a specially commissioned landscape painting involving horses. By the end of 2007, the girls had collected approximately £2,000, on the way being awarded the first ever Service Recognition Award by the Sunrise Rotary Club of Cheltenham.

The girls plan to extend their activities on behalf of Claudia's Closet to other hospitals if sufficient funds are forthcoming.

Claudia's boyfriend Jonathan, Lucinda Lee, Imogen Stebbings, Fay Sullivan (behind), Anna Legg, and Sarah Duffin

In the meantime a second link school had expanded its relationship with Dean Close School: St Andrew's, Turi, Kenya. This is a Christian school for children aged five to 16. Its major link was through the work of the Revd Dick Drown OD (1933-38) who was headmaster of St Andrew's 1965-73. Although connections have continued, it was not until the turn of the millennium that they were strengthened by the efforts of the Dean Close Headmaster, Tim Hastie-Smith, resulting in several students from that school entering the Dean Close Sixth Form, a process that has continued ever since. One or two teachers from the Kenyan school have come onto the staff, notably Alistair Groom and also Adrian Palmer who, having spent four years as deputy headmaster at St Andrew's, came to Dean Close School for a year (2006-07), before returning to St Andrew's as its headmaster. Eric Harris, now Senior Master at Dean Close Preparatory School, was also on the St Andrew's staff as deputy head and lay chaplain. Moving in the opposite direction have been new ODs who have spent their gap year teaching at the Kenyan school.

Another school that has become linked to Dean Close School has included Nyakatukura Memorial School, a Secondary School situated in the bush in Western Uganda. This came about through the good offices of OD David Bristow's father, Chris Bristow, whose local church knew and had supported the Ugandan school. Dean Close School Community Action Group set up a project and raised funds for over a year to pay for new facilities, including cemented floors, plastered and painted walls, solar electricity and their own water supply. A party from Dean Close School visited to install the facilities in the Ugandan school in 2005. They were accompanied by the Revd Canon Tim Watson, a former Rector of Cheltenham, former General Secretary of the Intercontinental Church Society and a Dean Close School Governor who had many connections in Uganda and who became a Canon of Kitgum Cathedral, Uganda in 2005. In 2006 and 2007 Dean Close School sixth-formers and staff, led by Laura Burton, Head of Religious Studies, revisited the school. In 2008, 14 teaching staff, two husbands and Trustee Canon Timothy Watson returned to Nyakatukura School. They taught, met the 15 primary and eight secondary school orphans whose education members of the Dean Close community are supporting, and took funds to help building and furnishing expenses for their new assembly hall.

Tim Hastie-Smith signing school agreement in China 2007

The link between Dean Close and Shanghai No 2 School, China, happened through Carter Zhou OD, who had been taught at both schools. He finished his Sixth Form course in 2007 at Dean Close School as a School Prefect. As a result of Carter Zhou's initiative, Tim Hastie-Smith visited the Chinese school in April 2007 and signed an agreement with the Principal, Professor He Xiaowen, whereby a dozen scholars, accompanied by two staff, would visit each other's school every year.

Bishop's School, Cape Town, South Africa, runs an exchange programme for Sixth Form boys, of which Dean

Close School is now a part, whereby members visit each others' school for over a month. Several visits have taken place in both directions.

There has also been a link with Christ Church Grammar school, Perth, Western Australia that began when their 'Midnite Youth Theatre Company' came to Dean Close School in January 2006 to perform Anne Ridler's *The Trial of Thomas Cranmer*. James Townsend OD spent some months with them in Australia in his gap year and several of their students have since come to Dean Close School.

The spirit of individual initiative is far from dead, especially when it comes to charities. For example, in July 2005 Jon Allen, Head of Classics, led a team of 12 Decanians and four members of staff on an expedition to conquer Mount Kilimanjaro in Tanzania. The temperature dropped to –10ºC at one point but the top was reached and £1,900 raised for Christian Aid in Africa.

Vanessa Aris with her MBE awarded for services to education

Among all the competing worthwhile causes, the School decided that abroad they would focus particularly on Nyakatukura School, while at home the focus would be on the Family Space Project in Hester's Way, Cheltenham. In the latter case, Dean Close School has organized fund-raising and has hosted the children from the five local primary schools in the scheme every Field Day so that they could use the School's facilities for drama, swimming, art, games and other activities. Further, Decanians have been involved in Community Action concerning Asylum Seekers, several helping new arrivals to gain some command of the English language. Ten members of the School were each awarded a 'Certificate of Citizenship' by Gloucestershire County Council '...in recognition of (their) enthusiasm, commitment and willingness to support bilingual students...'. In addition, the School has continued to support 'Genes for Jeans' days and in 2006 also raised considerable sums of money for Breakthrough Breast Cancer, Muscular Dystrophy, Comic Relief and Unicef. The Duke of Edinburgh's Award Scheme has a Community Service element at every level, and so further Decanians have been drawn in.

In May 2006, a booklet called *Reaching Out* was published. It was the result of an audit among all 'stake holders' within the School, namely all teaching and non-teaching staff, pupils aged 10 or over from the Preparatory School and Decanians from the Senior School, as to what they were doing for the community both within and without the School. It was compiled by Vanessa Aris. In so doing they are continuing to encourage by example current Decanians to play their part in local, national and international communities.

**The Common Room's Contribution**

In the year 2005-06, when the audit was done, members of the Common Room were contributing in many spheres outside the School as well as within.

Within education, there is at least one Foundation fellow of the University of Gloucestershire. Several are governors of state schools – mostly primary schools – but also some special schools and secondary schools, including a governor trainer. Some staff are governors or trustees of independent schools while others provided science help for state schools, and leadership for cubs and scout groups. There are members of Common Room who adjudicate poetry, public speaking and music competitions in both independent and state schools. Some are lecturers in specialist interests such as mathematics, art, nature conservation, invertebrates and learning techniques. Teachers are members of academic societies in all the major disciplines. Staff have also helped pupils from other schools with coaching for public examinations, and there has been special needs support, adult literacy and adult dyslexia support and information.

Outside education, staff have been members of parish councils, village hall committees, Young Farmers' groups, Scout, Guide and Cub Scout troops, a Mountain Rescue team, Neighbourhood Watch, railway preservation, local health trust members and helpers in old people's homes. One particularly noteworthy is the Philomusica of Gloucestershire and Worcestershire which is a choir of 80: Dean Close supplied the President, Artistic Adviser, Vocal Coach and Conductor and allows them to practice in the School Chapel.

Many can be found on the organizing committees of charity fundraising occasions or playing musical instruments while some raise money themselves by running in marathons or competing in events such as Tough Guy.

# Chapter 15

## Junior School to Preparatory School and Beyond, 1968 to 2009

The first girl at the Junior School was Shân Harper, daughter of Gordon Harper, Head of English, and his wife Liz, in Michaelmas 1968. The imminent closure of New Court School meant 19 girls transferred to the Junior School before New Court's final term, Trinity 1969. Like girls entering the Senior School, at first there was no uniform.

In Michaelmas 1969, 35 girls were in the Junior School, six boarding in Rickerby. New Court's former Deputy Head and briefly Acting Head, Mrs Iris Long was in charge of them. She had an up-hill battle enlightening an overwhelmingly male Common Room of the needs of her flock. Initially, there was no provision for games, let alone activities like dancing. Iris Long was allocated the upper storeys of Rickerby – the old Hostel – as the girls' base. The pressure on day boy, now day child, places had risen since the early 1950s and continued beyond the founding of Yeaman, the first proper day house, in 1967; Oaksey, the second day house, was founded in 1971. This house was in Rickerby's basement, for the Junior School had acquired their own separate dining hall and kitchens in 1972, built in the space between Rickerby and Caldecote, and so the former house dining rooms were no longer needed.

**Sir Ian Yeaman, 1889 – 1977**

Sir Ian Yeaman entered the School in 1903, leaving in 1905 as a prefect with Colours in football. He became a successful solicitor, eventually becoming President of the Law Society. Elected a Governor in 1923, he was Chairman of the Governors' Executive Committee 1939-49 and 1959-66. He retired from the chairmanship aged 77. As Chairman, he had been much involved in the desperate decisions concerning the survival of the School before, during and after the Second World War. He died a Vice-President of the School, having served on the governing body for over 53 years.

**Headmasters of Dean Close Junior School**

| | |
|---|---|
| 1949-1972 | E.J.B. Langhorne MBE |
| 1972-1975 | C.A.W. Sanders |
| 1976-1981 | T.M. Thornton |
| 1981-1997 | I.F.M. Ferguson |
| 1997-1999 | S.W. Baird |

**Headmasters of Dean Close Preparatory School**

| | |
|---|---|
| 1999-2003 | S.W. Baird |
| 2003-present | The Revd L.J. Browne |

Eadward and Rosemary Langhorne retired in 1972. Although his health had suffered in his final years, he had continued to run the Junior School very tightly. His achievement was to expand Junior School numbers significantly, including introducing girls. Originally, admitting just day girls up to the age of 11 was felt appropriate. However, in 1972 the Governors agreed to allow girls throughout the Junior School with a ratio of one girl to five boys, subsequently eroded to one in three and later reduced further. When Eadward Langhorne left, there were 255 children in the Junior School, of whom 46 were girls, compared with 167 boys in 1949. W.A.M. Edwards OD, Chairman of the Executive, wrote that '...during (Mr Langhorne's) 23 years in office, the Junior School...gained a leading place amongst the preparatory schools of this country...'.

The new Headmaster was Colin Sanders. As the Langhornes had their own house on Cleeve Hill, the Governors bought 65 Hatherley Road for the incoming Headmaster and his family. He was, essentially, a gentle man. Although he did not stay long, Colin Sanders devolved onto senior colleagues some of the duties and responsibilities that his predecessor had carried. He introduced prep being done in the dining hall; began the second-hand shop; improved the uniform for girls; started parents' evenings, and encouraged parents to become more involved than before. He encouraged charity swims and loved cricket. He reintroduced firework parties, that had previously been enjoyed in the 1950s, and possibly the early 1960s, for the first time in November 1974.

Ken Hollington retired in 1973. He had been Art master since 1952, was the first Science master, played a key role in founding Argonauts, and had been a housemaster, too.

**Colin A.W. Sanders, Headmaster 1972-75**

He was educated at Clifton and Wadham College, Oxford, where he was a classical scholar, reading Mods and Greats and was also a member of Oxford University Dolphins. He first taught at Sevenoaks School, followed by Loretto where he was a housemaster of two houses before moving to DCJS; Carol Sanders had taught at Haslemers, specializing in PE and RE. They had two children, Ian and Ruth. C.A.W.S. was a keen cricketer and a deeply committed Christian. In 1975 he resigned on his appointment as headmaster of a new international school at Toddington Manor, not far from Winchcombe. He was later ordained.

### *The Young Decanian*

Originally, intermittent articles appeared in *The Decanian*, usually about Junior School sport, in the 1940s. In 1957 a termly magazine was published, called *The Lantern*, a mere 16 pages long. It survived only for a second edition. There may have been other attempts but they have not survived.

Ian Ferguson's *Young Decanian*, founded in 1974, was 64 pages long in A5 format. Editors experimented with different sizes over time, settling for its current A4 size in 1990. Pat Bryan, Housemaster of Yeaman, edited it 1977-83. Becoming Second Master (1981) made it increasingly difficult for him to continue and David Winpenny, Head of English, edited the 1983-84 edition, but he left soon afterwards. Julian Lovell took over for one year. For over 20 years, from 1985 to 2006, the editor was Andrew Judge, Head of English, Housemaster and later first Senior Master (1999-2007). The 2006-07 issue of *The Young Decanian* was edited jointly by Andrew Judge and Mrs Rebecca Chaplin, since when Rebecca Chaplin, Marketing and Admissions Co-ordinator for the Preparatory School, has been editor.

In terms of the number of pages, *The Young Decanian* has grown, and the page size has doubled! Publication started in July to coincide with Speech Day. However, it switched in 1977 to the end of Michaelmas so that the entire previous academic year could be reported in one issue. From 1992 it carried ever-growing reports on the Pre-Preparatory Department, later School, until in 2007 *The Young Decanian* was backed by a 25 page publication entitled *The Youngest Decanian* that subsequently became a separate Pre-Preparatory magazine in 2008.

Ian Ferguson founded *The Young Decanian* in 1974. It has been an annual publication ever since, like its Senior School sister, *The Decanian*.

In 1975, Colin Sanders resigned and Gordon Harper (Second Master) became Acting Headmaster for two terms. Tim Thornton was the new Headmaster, arriving in June 1976. Over the next four years, he instigated some internal reorganization. The girls' house moved from Rickerby to Wilton – next door to the Police HQ. The vacated Rickerby became largely a teaching block while the comparatively newly-acquired Hardy House became a second girls' boarding house. Tim Thornton initiated the Covered Play

### The Covered Play Area (CPA)

The idea was first conceived in 1976. It took two years of fund-raising to collect enough money to make it possible. £4,500 of the total cost of £12,000 (£64,700) was raised by parents, friends, staff and pupils. The opening ceremony was performed by Graham Wilshire, at that time Gloucestershire County Cricket Coach, in September 1978. By Michaelmas 1979, the CPA had been expanded to five bays, covering virtually the whole of the Fortfield playground area. The low brick walls were added a few months later.

Area (CPA) that began to take shape. The changes were such that Ian Ferguson, in his editorial for the 1979 *Young Decanian* describing the start of Michaelmas 1978, wrote: '…Even old timers at the School took a little while to get accustomed to the new use of many of the buildings this term, which starting from the West [Senior School] end, is now as follows: Caldecote, senior boys' boarding; Rickerby, classrooms, library, staff Common Room and in the basement Oaksey, day children's house; Hardy, Headmaster's study and secretary's office, music school [and second girls' boarding house that opened in 1980]; then Langhorne Hall and, behind, a classroom block; Fortfield, junior boys' boarding and lower school classrooms; behind it the art room, covered play area with Yeaman, day children's house, classrooms and carpentry workshop [on the site now occupied by the Ferguson Block]. Beyond Dean Close House and Shelburne of the Senior School there is Wilton House, girls' boarding…'.

One sad event was in February 1977, when the cheerfully enthusiastic Jonathan Hibberd, in the Junior School since 1973, and taking Common Entrance, died from a brain tumour, even though he had had a couple of operations. The plaque to his memory in the current pottery is a result of his parents' suggestion.

Phillippa Thynne became the first 'Old Girl' of the Junior School to return as a member of staff, as matron in Fortfield for two terms from Lent 1979.

In March 1981, Tim Thornton resigned the headship of the Junior School over his handling of a grave disciplinary matter concerning Adrian Carpenter, Fortfield's Housemaster. Both men having left, Ian Ferguson (Second Master since 1978) became Acting Headmaster. The abrupt loss of the Headmaster and a housemaster meant that confidence in the Junior School was now fragile at best, and Ian Ferguson worked hard and successfully to improve matters. He was later confirmed as Headmaster, having been selected from a short list of five. Now, for the first time, the Headmaster DCJS reported directly to Governors in the Annual Report and at meetings and not, as before, through the Senior School Headmaster. However, the Headmaster DCS still retained authority and responsibility for 'whole campus' issues.

After their marriage in October 1983, Ian and Margaret Ferguson lived in Bayley House, on the site of the old Yeaman

| | **Hardy (Girls)** |
|---|---|
| 1980-1982 | Mrs W. Gregory |
| 1982-1983 | Miss M.E. Buchanan |
| 1983-1988 | Miss J. Smith |
| 1989 | Mrs J. Herbert |
| 1989-1996 | Miss D.V. Norman |
| 1996-1999 | DCS overflow |
| 1999-2001 | Mr & Mrs T.J. Goodwright |

**Tim M. Thornton, Headmaster 1976-81**

He arrived as Headmaster from The Hall, Hampstead, where he had been Second Master, in June 1976, moving into the Headmaster's residence, 65 Hatherley Road. Lyndall, his wife, taught part-time in the Junior School. They had three sons, Samuel, Barney and Magnus, usually called Jake.

His lasting legacy to the Junior School was the Covered Play Area.

Tim Thornton resigned in March 1981, moving with his family to Stratford-upon-Avon where he bought The Croft School. In 1986 they moved it to a Georgian building on a 30-acre site on the outskirts of the town. The school currently caters for over 400 pupils aged 2-11. Mrs Thornton is still Principal, while Samuel is Head of Upper School.

Tim Thornton died in June 2003.

**Ian F.M. Ferguson, staff member 1970-81, Headmaster 1981-97**

Margaret and Ian Ferguson

He was educated at Westwick Lodge and Barnard Castle School before going up to Keble College, Oxford to read Geography and take his Diploma in Education. He played cricket and squash for his college. He taught at the Royal Masonic School, Bushey, coming to the Junior School in 1970 as Head of Geography, and games coach with particular interest in hockey, cricket and golf. He was initially House Tutor in Fortfield. He became Housemaster of Oaksey in 1973, founding editor of *The Young Decanian* in 1974, Second Master in 1978 and Headmaster in 1981. During his headship he was Chairman of IAPS District no. 10 for some years. His faith was particularly expressed in his ministry as a Diocesan Reader (lay minister).

In January 1982, Margaret Buchanan, a graduate of Exeter University, became Senior Mistress at the Junior School, having come from Oakham School where she was a tutor. Apart from having overall control of the girls, by then numbering over 100, she also taught Science and Scripture. In Michaelmas 1982 she was appointed Housemistress of Hardy.

In October 1983 they married in the Chapel, setting up home in the newly-built Junior School Headmaster's residence, Bayley House.

From 1983 until I.F.M.F.'s retirement in 1997, they steered the Junior School towards the goals of endeavour and excellence in everything attempted, coupled with an unapologetic, direct Christian faith. During this time, too, facilities were improved out of all recognition and the Pre-Preparatory Department was born. They retired to Wensleydale in 1997 where he has developed his ministry as a Reader.

House 'padder-tennis' court and garages. The former Miss Margaret Buchanan came to the Junior School in 1982 as Senior Mistress. Their house was named after John Bayley, JP, Chairman of the Finance and General Purposes Committee of the Governors for seven years, who had been a Governor for 16 years at the time of his tragic death from a brain tumour in November 1978.

1986, Centenary Year, began with a burst water pipe in Caldecote during the Christmas holiday, causing flooding and other problems. It continued with a flu virus sufficiently virulent that half-term had to be extended by two days.

The Lent Term was brought to a suitable and glorious climax by the Centenary Service in Gloucester Cathedral at which the School Visitor, the Bishop of Gloucester, John Yates preached.

The Trinity Term included a joint celebration service for both Schools in May in Christ Church, the month that the School first opened in 1886. Princess Alexandra visited both Junior and Senior Schools on 9th June, accompanied by much security,

Princess Alexandra at the Junior School, 1986

Aerial view *c.*1985.
**1** Cricket pavilion. **2** Stable block and porter's lodge. **3** Langhorne complex. **4** Tuck Shop

many dignitaries and the Band of the Royal Marines, who beat the retreat before a spectacular, if rather damp, firework display. The Princess saw and inspected, albeit briefly, Junior School activities: shooting, judo, art, science, gymnastics, heraldry, Argonauts, dancing, music, trampolining and cricket. Although several staff left at the end of that term, the most enduring had been Gwen Constable, the resident cook, who retired after 27 years at the Junior School.

Yeaman House left the adapted old Fortfield stables that they had occupied for several years as new classrooms were about to be built on the site. Their new home was the top floors of Rickerby.

In 1987, Lisa Smith won the calligraphy section of the SATIPS handwriting competition; Michael James's poem and Catherine McAdam's illustration, were winning entries that featured in WH Smith's book of the 1987 Young Writers' Competition. In Michaelmas 1995, Mary Wenham was a winner in

WH Smith Young Writers award winners 1990:
Morag McCulloch, Sarah Brick, Vicky Youde, Mark Pihlens, Chris Hill, Anna Thompson, Lucy Bruen and Naomi West with Miss Tracy Brown of WH Smith and the Headmaster, Ian Ferguson

Pat Bryan

the SATIPS poetry competition, with Suzanne Pike a runner-up. Five pupils won certificates in the WH Smith Young Writers' Competition in 1995 and a certificate of commendation was presented to the School for the general standard of its entries; the fourth such award in five years. In 2006, 14 children from Year 6 had their work published in a poetry anthology. Since the 1990s there have also been Mathematics Challenges, organized in recent years by Michael Ede.

The 1987-88 academic year began with the new Centenary Block providing classrooms and two laboratories. There was the new library where the laboratory had been, close to the Langhorne Hall, appropriately opened by Gordon Harper. There were two new families in charge of houses; Trevor and Liz Lewis in Caldecote, (boys' boarding); and John and Rosie Phillips in the girls' boarding house, Wilton.

Derek Crawshaw retired, having been on the staff since 1971 as Head of Mathematics, Housemaster of Fortfield 1981-88, briefly Second Master, i/c both cricket and rugby and into numerous other school activities. Bridget, his wife, who had really given girls' games the skills and confidence they had badly needed in the 1970s and 80s, continued to teach junior forms at the school until 1991 having officially first joined the staff in 1974. Andrew Judge, having run Oaksey for a year, now took over Fortfield with his wife, Margaret.

In Michaelmas 1988, the £2,000 (£4,020) raised at the Christmas bazaar was put towards a DCJS adventure playground. It was said to be the longest term in the Junior School's history, stretching from Monday, 5th September to Saturday, 17th December. Julie Smith, who had a high reputation as Housemistress of Hardy and junior forms' teacher, left to marry at the end of term after five years.

Pat Bryan retired the following summer. He had been Second Master as well as Head of Classics since 1981, a former Housemaster of Yeaman and member of staff for 20 years. In his final term he masterminded (and was the first to try) an adventure playground for the children situated between the Covered Play Area and the field.

Fortfield Stabl;es, wqhere the Ferguson Building is today.
Standing outside are members ofYeaman House, summer 1986

That summer, the porter's lodge next door to the Centenary – later Ferguson – Block was demolished. An administrative block was built, linking to a new building that from 1990 was called Rickerby, accommodating the two day houses, junior forms, the staff Common Room and changing rooms for staff and pupils.

Ian Ferguson was aware of government educational policy,

The porter's lodge viewed from the field in 1987-8

introducing the National Curriculum for state schools and independent schools, too, if they wished to participate; most did. All children would be tested at seven, 11 and 14 years, requiring additional administration, assessment, in-house curriculum development, policy decisions and extra parental contact. Ian Ferguson decided to create the senior post of Director of Studies, responsible for academic matters, and appointed the able, ambitious Paul Brewster, Head of Mathematics, to the job. A successor to Pat Bryan as Second Master was also required. Here again, Ian Ferguson decided on innovation: he did not promote internally as usual but looked externally, for the first time for either School, for this particular post. Charles Whitney, from Dover College Junior School, was appointed, having had many years' experience as a boarding housemaster and head of department.

In May 1990, Oaksey and Yeaman Houses, two classrooms, the staff Common Room and the Second Master's and Senior Mistresses' studies all moved from 'old' Rickerby to the new, an operation involving much furniture removal that took just 90 minutes. 'New' Rickerby was formally opened by the Marquis of Reading, President of the School. The 'Wilton Crocodile' of female boarders who had walked daily from their house next door to the police station disappeared, as Wilton House transferred lock, stock, barrel and name to the now vacated old Rickerby, formerly Hostel, where it has stayed ever since.

### *Hermes*

*Hermes* was first published on Friday, 28th January, 1994. Its founder and first editor was Paul Brewster, Director of Studies, who stated that its aims were: '...not only to help communication between School and parents but also to bring to a wider audience some of the achievements of the children as they occur...'. It was partly based on *Newspaper*, produced by Mark Turner in the Junior School that had concentrated on articles by the children, several editions of which came out between 1990 and 1993.

Paul Brewster left in March 1995, after edition 41. The editorship passed to Charles Whitney, who continued until his retirement in Trinity 2003, at which point there had been 300 editions, the most memorable being the 100th issue, the first in colour. Andrew Judge became editor in September 2003 and continued until his retirement in Trinity 2007, by which time over 400 editions had been produced. Currently, it is edited by Alastair Brown and Rosie Green. In September 1997, *Hermes* was made available on the internet by Paul Coleman. Since then, all editions have been similarly available. It claims to have been the first Dean Close Schools regular publication to have taken that step.

*Hermes* is the only School weekly produced publication that has survived for longer than ten years. It has had more editions than any other School publication, including *The Decanian*.

Bridget Crawshaw retired in Trinity 1991, having served the Junior School for 17 years. Julian Lovell completed his period as Housemaster of Yeaman and was succeeded by Mark Turner.

The 1992 Speech Day used the New Theatre for the first time, having been held in the Gym previously. Clive Rooke, a former Housemaster of Yeaman and Head of Science, retired after 18 years at DCJS. Pam Carnill, at Dean Close School for over 30 years, as Headmaster's Secretary and housemaster's wife, and a Year 3 form teacher at the Junior School for 15 years, also retired. Peter Mills (Director of Music) and Faith Jameson (English and Christian Union) moved on. Julie Rooney, the Junior School Catering Manager who had raised standards of food to a peak of consistent quality seldom experienced in a preparatory school, also left.

September 1992 included the launch of the long-awaited Pre-Preparatory Department in the Junior School (see chapter 17).

Iris Long

The final farewell to Iris Long, after a quarter century of service, was in Trinity 1993. The war widow of a decorated bomber pilot, she had known both 'Dam Buster' Guy Gibson and Eadward Langhorne during the War. After the closure of New Court, she brought many girls and some staff with her to the Junior School. Initially Girls' Tutor, she championed girls' needs to not always sympathetic colleagues. She became the first Senior Mistress as well as Housemistress of Rickerby and English teacher, retiring in 1977, having been described as '…the driving force…' behind the quality of co-education offered at the Junior School. She subsequently returned, and before her final retirement, aged 76, developed the 'Special Needs' Department, now called 'Learning Support'. In the Millennium wing, the current department suite is named after her. A skilful flower arranger, she was a sought-after counsellor to children, staff, parents and headmasters – of both Schools – and governors.

Year numbering changed to reflect the National Curriculum in Michaelmas 1993. For example, seven-year olds, previously Year 1, were now Year 3. Those children attaining their 13th birthdays and who had been in Year 6 now found themselves in Year 8. That term, inspectors from the Independent Schools' Joint Council visited; they were very complimentary about what they saw.

Paul Brewster edited the first *Hermes* weekly newsletter during Lent 1994 and a promotional video of the Junior School was made.

In 1994, the Headmaster and his wife flew to the Far East for 16 days. They represented the whole Dean Close community, recruiting boarders from the expatriate and foreign national communities and making contact with past and present parents. Several children came to the Schools as a direct result.

Michaelmas 1994 was the first time Year 3 had two classes, a consequence of the opening of the Pre-Preparatory Department in 1992.

Lent Term 1995 was the last for Paul Brewster, the first Director of Studies. He had helped all departments make huge advances with the National Curriculum, improved pupil assessments and been a vital link between a child's home and academic performance in School. With his wife, Debbie, he moved to St Mary's, Lincoln, as headmaster. He subsequently became headmaster at Foremarke Hall before moving on to the English School in Prague. His place was temporarily taken by Carol Huckvale,

Head of Learning Support, until September 1995, when the new Director of Studies, Alison Primrose, took over.

During Lent 1996, smart new railings appeared on part of DCJS frontage. They were extended over the next few years, until they were not only a part of the Lansdown Road frontage but also both sides of Shelburne Road, replacing some rather tired, elderly railings.

On Speech Day, for the first time there was Latin Drama by Year 7, initiated by Matt Dobbs, in the Tuckwell Theatre. Julian Lovell, at DCJS 18 years, mostly as Head of Geography and Housemaster of Yeaman for five, left, as did Viv Troughton, who retired after 15 years that included a key role in the opening of Pre-Preparatory. As Miss Sutcliffe she had also been on the staff 1968-70. Jacky Skinner, Sally Crabb and Jane Herbert, long-serving matrons, all retired within a short time of each other.

Alison Primrose

Diana Norman, Housemistress of Hardy, left at the end of Michaelmas 1996 to become Head of Junior Boarding at the Royal Masonic School, Rickmansworth. Falling numbers of boarding girls in the Junior School and burgeoning numbers of female boarders in the Senior School meant that Hardy had to be temporarily closed as a Junior School boarding house.

Ian and Margaret Ferguson retired in 1997. In 16 years as Headmaster, Ian Ferguson speedily arrested any decline in confidence or numbers that may have threatened the Junior School's stability when Tim Thornton left in 1981. In the ensuing period he took his cue from the Headmaster of Dean Close School, Christopher Bacon, who was determined to improve standards. Ian Ferguson tightened discipline and later emphasized the closeness with which the two Headmasters worked together, the longest partnership to date between Senior School and Junior School Headmasters. Ian Ferguson was tireless in promoting excellence at DCJS, whatever the context. He weathered the storms of decreasing interest in preparatory school education in the early 1990s. His reward was to see facilities greatly improve and standards (academic, in the arts, sport and behaviour generally) rise significantly during his headship. His warm support for all Christian matters was key, not only to the life of the School but also to its reputation.

Ian's wife Margaret contributed much, often suggesting positive solutions to difficult situations; her part in her husband's achievements was crucial. At the same time she was Senior Mistress, with wide responsibilities both for girls and staff, while also ably fulfilling the social role of Headmaster's wife as well as being a Science teacher, Head of Religious Studies and key supporter of Christian Union.

To mark the retirement of Ian and Margaret Ferguson, the whole School went to Alton Towers for the day in the Trinity Term. Ian and Margaret Ferguson's departure also signalled that of Mary Emm, who had been Headmaster's Secretary for many years. Jean Pope succeeded her. Leaving too, was Philip Brooke, off to Dulwich College Preparatory School, to arguably the biggest preparatory school music job, after raising Junior School music to new heights.

Into this situation came Stephen and Liz Baird and their family. He was in his late thirties. His task was to guide and update the Junior School into the 21st century without losing the best of the pursuit of excellence upon which Ian Ferguson had insisted. Alison Primrose had become Senior Mistress in addition to her responsibilities as Director of Studies.

Later in Michaelmas 1997, Prince Michael of Kent visited the Junior School to rename the Centenary Block as the Ferguson Building, in honour of the previous Junior School Headmaster, who attended with Mrs Ferguson.

Early in 1998, Don Cormack, a teacher and former missionary who had remained in Phnom Penh even during the horrendous Cambodian genocide, found his book on the subject, *Killing Fields, Living Fields*, selected as 'Christian Book of the Year.' That summer, the School bade farewell to Christopher Bacon, the retiring Headmaster of Dean Close School and Mike Herring, who was also retiring after 10 years as Housemaster of Oaksey and Head of Modern Languages. 1998-99 was a milestone: the 25th year of *The Young Decanian* and the 50th year since the Junior School became a member of IAPS.

Michaelmas 1998 included the arrival of the Revd Tim Hastie-Smith and his family as the new Headmaster of Dean Close School and also of Michael Ede as Head of Mathematics at the Junior School. During the Lent Term 1999, Stephen and Liz Baird flew to Oman on a recruitment trip and met a number of current parents. Trinity 1999 ended with farewells to the Chaplain, the Revd Dan Young and his wife Sue. Dan Young had been Chaplain to the whole site since 1983 and, at 16 years, his was the longest chaplaincy to the Junior School in its history.

The School was renamed Dean Close Preparatory School in Michaelmas 1999, for some had thought the term 'junior' referred to a maintained sector primary school. Moreover, the Pre-Preparatory department was growing and it seemed better to progress from 'pre-preparatory' to 'preparatory'. This included job title changes; Charles Whitney and Alison Primrose became Deputy Head and Deputy Head (Academic) respectively. Hardy became a girls' boarding house again, run by Tim and Vicky Goodwright, although this was only to last until 2001. There was also the recently completed Millennium Building, attached to Rickerby. It included the Iris Long suite for Learning Support; a new Harper Library; a Design and Technology suite that Paul Coleman developed well beyond National Curriculum requirements; and an Art suite where Mary Padley, who had done much to stimulate and improve Art in the School, was in her element.

**Stephen W. Baird, Headmaster 1997-2003**

He read English at St David's University College, Lampeter, and obtained a Post Graduate Certificate of Education from Bristol. He taught at Cheltenham College Junior School, St Michael's Tawstock and Exeter Cathedral School. He was a houseparent, with his wife Liz, of a boys' house at Catteral Hall, Giggleswick, where he was also Head of English and Drama and part of the senior management team.

S.W.B. had wide-ranging interests including sport, the performing arts, nature, literature, church involvement and preaching. Particularly remembered were his discos where he would preside as 'Rock HM'.

Liz Baird also qualified as a teacher, with a BEd for those at the pre-preparatory stage. She was to be Registrar, Housemistress of Wilton (briefly), teacher of Geography and an endless supplier of match teas as well as mother of their children.

Dickon, George and Edmund are their three sons. Dickon and George joined the Junior School while Edmund joined Reception in the Pre-Preparatory Department.

Stephen Baird subsequently became an author and later returned to teaching.

Wilton Year 8 girls raised money for the Emily Kent Charity (see chapter 14) at the end of Michaelmas. For a week they lived and dressed as their Victorian counterparts of 1900 would have done, had there been any, eating mostly savoury, period meals in silence. They had to sit bolt upright – which they found demanding – brush their teeth with bicarbonate of soda, wash their hair with soap and attempt some of their homework by candlelight; there were no CD players, hair dryers or television. They found it tough but raised £340.

Jean Robinson

Lent Term 2000 included a wonderful Millennium Service in Gloucester Cathedral, in which all three Schools took part. John Went, Bishop of Tewkesbury and a School Governor, preached. The congregation numbered nearly 1,000.

Speech Day included the formal opening of the Millennium Building by Professor Gervase Phinn, school inspector, lecturer and author. This was the year that Speech Day itself moved from a week before the end of term to the last day itself. It was also the last term at the School for Frank Howse, electrician, and Jean Robinson of the kitchen staff, both of whom were retiring after over 25 years.

At the beginning of the new academic year, the Preparatory School, in partnership with the Senior School and other Cheltenham independent schools, began their own bus service for day children from many outlying towns and villages.

A visit to Bettridge School

The highlight of Michaelmas 2000 was the pilgrimage to Gloucester Cathedral. The distance by foot taking a country route was just under 12 miles. Stephen and Liz Baird also visited the Far East in November, recruiting for both Schools and meeting up with former and current parents.

That term, children from the Preparatory School began visiting nearby Bettridge School that caters for children with disabilities and learning difficulties. An ongoing, regular visiting pattern began, to the advantage of both sets of children, overseen at the Preparatory School end by Sarah Davies.

Among staff leavers in Trinity 2001 was Alison Primrose, Senior Mistress, whose sheer efficiency and pastoral gifts complemented her further improvement and development of academic matters. She left to become Head of Bristol Grammar Lower School. Mick Pegrum, porter for 20 years and whose house had stood where Rickerby now was, retired.

That term was also the 200th anniversary of the birth of Lord Shaftesbury, the School's inaugural President. John Phillips, Oaksey Housemaster, accompanied by Alexander Harrison and Emma Brown, represented the School at a London Reception organized by the Shaftesbury Society.

**The Millennium Pilgrimage**

48 children from Year 8 plus ten accompanying adults walked the whole route, leaving after prayers led by the Headmaster at 8am on 22nd September, 2000, first completing a circuit of the field, with banners made by Mary Padley held aloft.

The pilgrims met the second group, consisting primarily of Year 7, at Brickfield Lane near Chosen Hill School. Now 120 strong, they met the Year 6 party of 36 children and 7 adults where they had been dropped off at Frog Furlong Lane. Numbering over 160, the pilgrimage took over 15 minutes to negotiate one stile! After more countryside, the A38 at Twigworth was gained, taking 20 minutes to cross. Lunch was then eaten. The pilgrimage was joined by Years 3, 4 and 5 at Sandhurst Lane and the Globe Inn. Everyone walked along the narrow banks of the River Severn and towards Gloucester. The pilgrimage, some 250 strong, was about half a mile long. After a pause at Westgate Gardens, the pilgrimage met up with Years 1 and 2 from Pre-Prep at Tesco's supermarket. Banners were unfurled as the year groups walked through the city on their way to the Cathedral. The youngest members of Pre-Preparatory walked from St Mary's Gate on the perimeter of the Cathedral Close. Everyone arrived in good time and was entertained by a brief play about the Garden of Eden performed by five senior pupils directed by the Headmaster.

At 4pm, a special act of worship on pilgrimage was led by the Very Revd Nick Berry, Dean of Gloucester, in the Cathedral, attended by about 370 from the School. Then adults and children returned to School by coach.

Change was in the air at the beginning of Michaelmas 2001: more day places and fewer boarding places were needed. Steve and Jo Cahill continued to run Caldecote, the boys' boarding house. John Phillips, who, with his wife Rosie, had looked after Wilton as a girls' house for 11 years had, since 1998, run a day house, Oaksey, instead. In their place Colette Virgin, having married another member of staff, Matt Dobbs, briefly ran Wilton. Then for a year, Liz Baird somehow managed to combine being Headmaster's wife, Wilton Housemistress, Registrar and mother; the situation couldn't continue. Andrew and Margaret Judge completed 13 years in Fortfield boys' boarding house. As boys' boarding places far exceeded demand, Andrew Judge set up and ran a new day house, Deacon, named after the School's first President, John Deacon (see chapter 2). It was located on the ground and basement floors of Wilton. The top floor was used, for a time, by Caldecote for its 'overflow'. Fortfield became a girls' boarding house. John Bunce, who had just been appointed the first lay Chaplain to the Preparatory School, and his wife Liz, a qualified teacher, became Fortfield's new houseparents.

Artslink, where Year 6 children from local primary schools joined Year 6, was a day of art, music and drama at the Preparatory School and in the Bacon Theatre. There was also a very successful inspection from the Independent Schools' Inspectorate.

In Lent 2002, *Hermes* reached its 250th edition and a new Director of Studies arrived. Wendy Tyler was from Alleyn's Junior School, Dulwich; she was a Biology and Education graduate from Homerton College, Cambridge, completing an MA from the Institute of Education. The next term, Jackie Dunlop completed seven years as Housemistress of Yeaman and handed over to Martin Davies. Rebecca Chaplin joined the Preparatory School at Michaelmas 2002 with a marketing brief. She quickly took on many associated tasks, notably press liaison and later also became Registrar.

In Trinity 2003, Michael Ede (Head of Mathematics) and Howard Newton (who taught at Hebron School in South India) swapped jobs for a term. Both found it challenging but rewarding.

At the end of the academic year, Charles Whitney retired after 14 years as Deputy Head, in order to complete his studies for ordination. Carol Huckvale, who had been Head of Learning Support for 10 years, also left, to pursue a career in child psychology. Dorothy Odell, peripatetic music teacher since 1979 and junior choir conductor, also retired after over 20 years.

The Baird family departed for their home in Cornwall, Stephen Baird spending some time writing before accepting an appointment at the King's Junior School, Canterbury. The departure of the Headmaster and the retirement of the Deputy Head posed a potential management problem. However, the Senior School Chaplain, the Revd Leonard Browne, was appointed Acting Headmaster of the Preparatory School for the start of Michaelmas 2003.

The new academic year began not only with an Acting Headmaster but also with a new Deputy Head, Robin Davies, fresh from a Sussex preparatory school. Both quickly fitted in and fears that some sort of 'hiccup' might occur were dispelled. As in the case of Ian Ferguson over 20 years before, Leonard Browne was required to apply for the headship, as did others. By the end of term, both Governors and Tim Hastie-Smith unanimously elected him to the vacant post.

In 2004, Mary Padley retired after 15 years as Head of Art at the end of that academic year. Under her, the variety and quality of art-work had improved hugely. Mrs Jackie Dunlop became Senior Mistress. At Michaelmas 2005, Jon and Fiona Harris moved into Caldecote to take over from Steve and Jo Cahill, who moved to Wilton to open a mixed Junior Boarding House up to Year 5. Giles and Rachel Wadsworth became Fortfield houseparents, the Bunces having left. All three Schools welcomed a new

| Wilton House (Girls) | |
|---|---|
| 1978-1982 | Mrs S. Guest |
| 1982-1987 | Mrs A. Brain |
| 1987-1998 | Mr & Mrs J.L. Phillips |
| 1998-2000 | Miss C. Virgin |
| 2000-2001 | Mrs E.J. Baird |

| Wilton (Co-ed Juniors) | |
|---|---|
| 2005-present | Mr & Mrs S.A. Cahill |

| Oaksey House (Co-ed) | |
|---|---|
| 1971-1973 | J.D. Hooper |
| 1973-1981 | I.F.M. Ferguson |
| 1981-1987 | R.A. Benson |
| 1987-1988 | A.J. Judge |
| 1988-1998 | W.M. Herring |
| 1998-present | J.L. Phillips |

| Deacon House (Co-ed) | |
|---|---|
| 2001-2005 | A.J. Judge |
| 2005-present | Mrs S.A. Davies |

| Fortfield House (Girls) | |
|---|---|
| 2001-2005 | Mr & Mrs J.D. Bunce |
| 2005-present | Mr & Mrs G. Wadsworth |

**The Revd Leonard J. Browne, Headmaster 2003-present**

He was educated at St Catherine's College, Cambridge, where he read History, graduating in 1981. He represented the university at both rugby and athletics, winning a Blue for the latter as a shot putter. He represented his country in the two sports at appropriate age levels, captaining Ulster Schoolboys at rugby but achieved full international honours in athletics. He taught at Clifton College, subsequently training for the Church at Trinity College, Bristol. He was ordained deacon in 1989, being priested a year later. After a curacy in Reading he became Vicar of St Barnabas, Cambridge in 1992. Somehow he managed to spend a little time assisting in the coaching of The Leys, Cambridge, 1st XV. He came to Dean Close School as Chaplain and Head of Divinity in 2000.

Leonard is married to Alison, who is Head of Religious Studies at the Preparatory School. They have three children, Katherine, Peter and Rebecca, all of whom attended Dean Close School.

Chaplain, the Revd Libby Talbot (the first ordained female Chaplain at Dean Close) and her husband John. She and her family came to live in Bayley House as Leonard Browne was to remain in the former Chaplain's House across the School Field on Hatherley Road. An inspection painted an excellent picture of the Preparatory School.

A significant episode occurred near the beginning of Trinity 2006 when the Abbey School at Tewkesbury, the Choir School for the Abbey, announced its closure. How its internationally known choir was saved, most of the choristers entering the Preparatory School, is examined in chapter 16.

At the end of Trinity, Wendy Tyler, the indefatigable Deputy Head (Academic), moved to Oxford on her marriage, her place taken by Laura Sorrell from Godstowe.

At Michaelmas 2006, Deacon House moved from Wilton's basement and transferred to the Rickerby/Millennium building. The size of the library had to be halved but it was felt the advantages outweighed the disadvantages. Admissions, though not the Headmaster's Study, returned to Hardy after 15 years, where more space was made for the Music Department. Additional games changing space was added in Rickerby. Partly because of the larger size of the School but also the increasingly complex timetables for both staff and pupils, a cafeteria system was introduced in the Dining Hall. For the first time, too, there was a dedicated medical treatment room close to the main office.

Although formally opened by Sir Geoff Hurst in April 2007, the magnificent new Sports Hall was in use from Michaelmas 2006. Trinity 2007 was the term when Paul Coleman (Art, DT and ICT teacher, Chelonia expert, latterly whole campus ICT Systems Manager), who had come in 1979, left, as did Caroline Allbut, Laboratory Technician for 22 years.

At the end of Trinity 2008, Robin Davies, Deputy Head, left after five years, to become headmaster at Barfield School. Alastair Brown, his successor, already a deputy head from Coram House, Pontefract, had also been director of sport and head of Geography at St Andrew's, Turi, Kenya. His wife, Ruth, is the daughter of a previous Headmaster, Colin Sanders.

The Preparatory School has continued to expand its horizons not just academically but in all areas: artistic, sporting, outward-bound, cultural, and pastoral.

### *Performing Arts*

A highlight of the academic year 1978-79 was various choirs singing in a variety of venues including Pershore and Tewkesbury Abbeys, Gloucester Cathedral, Redmarley and Upleadon parish churches and also at Christ Church, often under the Junior School Director of Music, J.M. White. In 1979, encouragingly, 185 children were learning instruments.

From 1979 there have been numerous plays – the junior forms in the Langhorne Hall, while senior productions were in the Tuckwell Theatre or the Langhorne Hall. For a while there was even a staff pantomime!

In September 1982, Janet Marshall began teaching dancing at the Junior School: Ballet, Tap and Modern Dance. Over 25 years and more, she, her sister Carol McDowall, and their team, became an essential part of DCJS life. They contributed hugely to many productions, and put on annual dancing displays – notably in the Bacon Theatre since 1992 – of a uniformly very high standard. They assisted with Senior School productions, too, achieving enviable results from seemingly unlikely material.

Musically, things improved under Elizabeth Brazell's leadership. When she arrived in 1982, she introduced informal, lunchtime concerts. Even beginners on their instruments were encouraged to play a piece to an audience, a tradition that has continued in DCJS and spread to the Senior School. Meanwhile, the four-part Junior School Chapel Choir improved greatly under David Watson, the Senior School's Head of History, who was also a gifted musician. Elizabeth Brazell was followed as Director of Music by Peter Mills. With David Watson's departure, Peter Mills was aided by the gifted choral input of the Senior School's Director of Music, Ian Little, a former Master of Music at Coventry Cathedral.

In drama, since the School Hall's completion in 1967, later called the Langhorne Hall, productions could now happen throughout the year. However, Gordon Harper continued to put

**Main Productions at Dean Close Junior School 1974 to 2007**
(T) = Tuckwell Theatre

Gordon Harper:
1974 The Taming of the Shrew (T)
1975 The Servant of Two Masters (T)
1976 The Liar (T)
1977 The Buck Basket (T)
1978 A Midsummer Night's Dream (T)

Tony Boardman & George Long:
1979 Ernie's Incredible Illucinations
The Sword of General Frapp

Gil Paltridge & George Long:
1980 The Fire Raisers (T)

Gil Paltridge & Martin Piper:
1981 Star Warps

Susan Burgess:
1982 The Thwarting of Baron Bolligrew
1983 The Phantom Tollbooth (T)
All the King's Men (T)
1984 Toad of Toad Hall

Elizabeth Brazell:
1984 Joseph & the Amazing Technicolour Dreamcoat

Martin Piper:
1984 The Ghost Train
1985 A Special Fire

Peter Mills:
1985 Smuggle Me a Secret (T)
1986 Oliver! (Everyman)
Noye's Fludde (T)

Andrew Judge:
1987 The Italian Straw Hat
1988 The Streets of London
1989 The Hound of the Baskervilles
1990 Bottom's Dream
1991 HMS Pinafore
1993 The Tinder Box
1994 The Servant of Two Masters
1995 The Pirates of Penzance
1996 The Silver Sword
1997 Salad Days
1998 The Ghost Train
1999 Smike

Stephen Baird:
2000 Destiny!

Tim Goodwright:
2001 The Happiest Days of Your Life

Andrew Judge:
2002 The Streets of London
2003 Oklahoma!
2004 Bottom's Dream
2005 Pinafore Pirates
2006 Annie
2007 The Boy Friend

on Junior School plays in the Tuckwell Theatre. His final production was *A Midsummer Night's Dream* in Trinity 1978.

With Gordon Harper's retirement, things changed. In the academic year 1978-79 there was a junior, or lower school, play, *The Scatterbrained Scarecrow of Oz* during March. The seniors presented two one-act plays just before and on Speech Day in July 1979, *Ernie's Incredible Illucinations* by Alan Ayckbourn, produced by Tony Boardman, and *The Sword of General Frapp* by John Harris, produced by George Long, both in the School Hall. A further innovation was that there were two performances, rather than one.

However, the Tuckwell Theatre was still used for *All the King's Men* in 1983 and *Joseph and the Amazing Technicolour Dreamcoat*, a major production by Elizabeth Brazell in Trinity 1984. In 1986, *A Special Fire* was written and directed by housemaster Martin Piper.

The musical and dramatic offering in Trinity 1986 was *Noye's Fludde*. The first performance was in the Tuckwell Theatre while the second had to be in the Gym as the heavens opened!

The Michaelmas Term included the musical *Oliver!* This was the biggest dramatic enterprise that had been attempted by either School, involving a cast of 116 giving 7 performances – of which

**Gordon and Liz Harper, staff members 1946-78**

Gordon Harper, an Oxford graduate and intelligence officer during the Second World War, began teaching at DCJS in September 1946. In 1947, Liz Griffiths became a Junior School matron and they married in 1951. Gordon was senior English and Drama master and librarian. Annually, he presented a play or programme of poetry in the Tuckwell Theatre. He was Housemaster of Rickerby, then the junior boys' boarding house (1947-51), Housemaster of the Day House (1956-63) and became Second Master in 1969. He was Acting Headmaster in 1970, 1976 and 1977.

Gordon played for Cheltenham Town Wednesday hockey XI at wing-half for many years, and was a noted coach of the Colts side.

Liz gave up being a matron, although still significantly involved in the welfare of boys and girls, to bring up their family of Miles and Shân, the first girl admitted to the Junior School. Liz made many of the costumes used in her husband's productions. E.H. spent the last two years before her retirement as Housemistress of Hardy (1976-78).

They retired to their house in Tivoli, often attending Junior School services and events. Gordon opened the Library that bears his name, in Lent 1981.

Liz died in 2005 while Gordon died in April 2007.

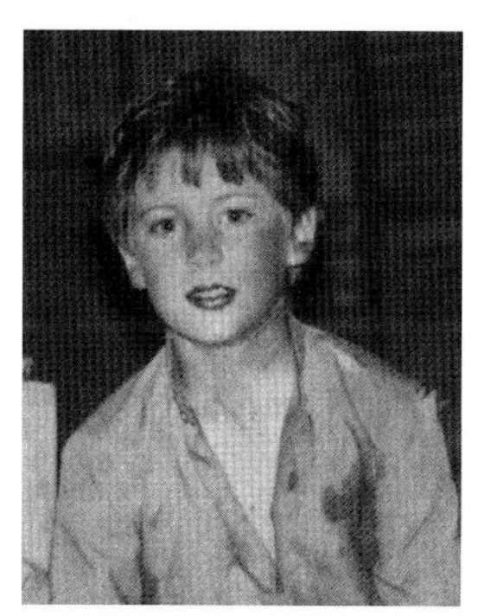
Anthony Bird as Oliver in 1986

two were matinées – at the newly-restored Everyman Theatre in Cheltenham (see chapter 13). The Chapel Choir brought out their first cassette – *I Was Glad* – in 1987-88. In the Cheltenham Festival, two cups were won for verse speaking; three and a gold medal in the music festival. The Chapel Choir ventured across the Channel, singing at mass and giving a concert at Caen in Normandy.

In 1988-89 the Cheltenham festival awarded four cups and gold and silver medals for musical performances to pupils; Melissa Bretherton reached the regional finals of Choirgirl of the Year.

An ambitious production of *HMS Pinafore* was staged in 1991. There were two productions during 1992-93: *The Tinder Box* and the junior forms' production of Steve Cahill's *Postman Wayne and the Big Bad Wolf* – the first time for some years that the playwright was also the producer.

*The Pirates of Penzance* was produced by Andrew Judge during Lent 1995. It had a cast of 43, including many members of staff, such as the Headmaster, Second Master, Director of Studies, a Housemistress, two Housemasters and the Chaplain, a number of whom had not been in any production before, nor since!

**DCJS/DCPS Junior Plays 1978 to 2008**

| | |
|---|---|
| 1979 | The Scatterbrained Scarecrow of Oz |
| 1981 | The Big Noise at Fort Issimo |
| 1984 | The Travellers |
| 1985 | The Other Children |
| 1986 | The Real Spirit of Christmas |
| 1987 | Ernie's Incredible Illucinations |
| 1988 | - |
| 1989 | Do It Yourself |
| 1990 | The Emperor and the Nightingale |
| 1991 | The Snow Queen |
| 1992 | - |
| 1993 | Postman Wayne and the Big Bad Wolf |
| 1994 | Percival the Performing Pig |
| | Captain Blackboot's Treasure |
| | 'Twas the Night Before Christmas |
| 1996 | Charlie and the Chocolate Factory |
| 1997 | - |
| 1998 | The Voyage of the Jumblies |
| | Postman Wayne and the Big Bad Wolf |
| 1999 | 'Twas the Night Before Xmas |
| 2000 | - |
| 2001 | Dandelion Time |
| | Christmas Around the World |
| 2002 | Santazia |
| 2003 | Babes in the Wood |
| 2004 | Charlie and the Chocolate Factory |
| 2005 | Peter Pan |
| 2006 | Wizard of Oz |
| 2007 | The Lion, The Witch and the Wardrobe |
| 2008 | A Christmas Carol |

During 1995-96, Chapel Choir recorded a cassette – *A Guiding Light* – in the Chapel. Clive Bailey and Isobel Shayle won places in the IAPS National Symphony Orchestra, Sarah Hayes, Olivia Hornby and Beccy Searle to the IAPS Concert Band while Claire Godwin won a place in the IAPS Training Concert Band.

A feature of the Trinity 1996 Speech Day was the first – if fairly brief – production in the Tuckwell Theatre of a Year 7 Latin Play. It was repeated immediately afterwards – but in English. It was the brain-child of Rosalyn Reid and was so successful that it became a tradition.

During Michaelmas 1996 half-term, the Chapel Choir toured Italy, singing in Lucca, Siena, Florence (the Duomo and also a concert in Santa Maria dei Ricci in the Via del Corso), and visited Pisa. The confidence gained was put to good use in a memorable production of *Salad Days*.

In Trinity 1997, Philippa Boyle won a Bronze Medal at the Cheltenham Festival. The next year, violinist Edgar Bailey won three cups at the Cheltenham Festival and Isabella Fateh won a Gold Medal at Gloucestershire dance festival in 1999.

*Destiny!* written and produced by Stephen Baird, was performed on the last three nights of the Lent Term 2000, a first in the Bacon Theatre. It was one of the biggest Preparatory School productions,

Cast of 'Bottom's Dream' 1990.
Chris Field (centre) surrounded by Benjamin Whetter, Ashley Foale, Savvas Koufou, Justin Upton, David Auckland, and Alexander Rose-Innes

The Chapel Choir singing in the piazza, Siena 1996

Oliver! in the Langhorne Hall 2008

with 120 parts. It had visual impact, foot-tapping music, excellent choreography, amazing costumes and effective scenery. All the children involved and the audiences loved it.

Early in 2006, wanting to do well in the Cheltenham Festival, the Preparatory School was particularly impressive with the children picking up awards '…left, right and centre, …' as the Headmaster, the Revd Leonard Browne, put it.

*The Boy Friend*, the main Preparatory School Lent 2007 production, was Andrew Judge's last before his impending retirement, having directed over 20 productions since arriving in 1986.

***Sport***

Since the mid-1990s, DCPS sport has been co-ordinated for boys by Jon Harris and later John Sutherland, and for girls by Claire Huxtable followed by Emma Krick. The co-ordinators and each team have been supported by committed coaches, latterly led by Martin Davies, Director of Sport. A key principle developed in the Preparatory School since Michaelmas 2001 has been that every child should have the opportunity to represent the School in a major sport. First tried by Jon Harris for boys in Years 7 and 8 and quickly also taken up by Emma Krick for girls, it spread through the Preparatory School. By 2004, every child in Year 4 and above had played for the School. It has meant a multiplicity of teams in any major sport. The use of the sports centre from September 2006 has created further opportunities for sport. In recent years, participation in the Severnside Tournaments in all major sports, for boys and girls, has resulted in frequent success.

Jasmin Head, Onyinye Chukwueke, and Victoria Harris in a Sports Day sprint final in 2007

*Athletics*

In athletics, both boys and girls began to participate in the five star award scheme from 1974 and athletics developed through the 1970s, encouraged particularly by teacher Julian Lovell. The first athletics meeting in which the Junior School participated was in 1975, though results were mixed. In 1982, Sven Awege won the U13 Javelin at the Oxford Area Preparatory School Meeting of 30 schools. In 1983 both boys' junior and senior teams won the Cheltenham Schools' Junior Championships. Long jumper Jeremy Hall qualified for the National Preparatory Schools' Athletic Sports Finals, representing the South West, while Matthew Herbert qualified similarly for Oxford having won the 400m.

The athletics team was outstanding in 1987. Richard Cooke (400m), Victoria Winch (100m) and Jason Piney (400m in a different age group) all won their events at the finals of the National Preparatory Schools' Athletics Championships. Richard also came second in the 800m and Victoria second in the 200m. In 1989-90 Christopher Field became Gloucestershire U15 400m champion while Victoria Youde became both 100m and 200m U13 Gloucestershire champion. A further ten new records were set in the Prince of Wales Stadium at the DCJS Sports Day that year, only surpassed in 1992 when 12 new records were established. During Trinity 2001, Enyinna Chukwueke won a shot put Gold Medal at the IAPS athletics championships. In 2003, Andrew Scrase came 5th in the IAPS national championships in the hurdles while Jeff Chiu came 8th in the shot put with a put of 9.44m.

*Cricket*

In 1974, the XI was coached one afternoon by Basil D'Oliveira, Norman Gifford and Glenn Turner, all Worcestershire and international players at the time. In 1977, DCJS hosted a new six-a-side cricket competition for the Tredgett Trophy, presented by the father of the XI captain. The competition continued annually for 20 years. In 1978, Huw Davies-Thomas scored 111 n.o. against Stouts Hill. The first Junior School cricket tour included Hazlegrove House (King's Bruton Junior School), Perrott Hill, and Kings' Junior School, Taunton.

The 1979 XI was undefeated in 13 matches and on tour, led by the '...outstanding...' Paul Vincent, who also led an IAPS XI, and in Huw Davies-Thomas, '...a wicket-keeper of the highest class...' wrote Ian Ferguson, then master-in-charge of cricket. Paul Vincent captained Gloucestershire U13 XI, with Huw Davies-Thomas and Robert Lowe in the same side. Paul Vincent scored a record 665 runs for the Junior School that year and was the first Junior School boy to score 1,000 runs in three years for his school. In 1987, Andrew Odell took 67 wickets during the season, thereby beating Peter Badger's record of 57 set in 1965, while Michael James took 49 wickets, both he and Andrew Odell being leg spinners. Most memorable in 1989, perhaps, was Hisham El-Marazki's 105, the first century since 1984. Andrew Judge, master-in-charge of cricket, wrote in *The Young Decanian* that the 1989 1st XI records were: '...183 for the 5th wicket between Richard Chubb and Hisham El-Marazki; 42 for the 8th between Tom Gower and Giles Barton; 38 for the 9th between Giles Barton and Neel Bhandari and finally 62 for the 10th between Anthony Bird and James Butler...'. In 1991, the XI scored 200 runs or more on four occasions, a feat not achieved since 1959. There were centuries from Nicholas Marsh and Duncan Gilroy.

In Trinity 1995, the School won the six-a-side cricket tournament for the first time in 15 years while Joe Lane and Gavin Curry each scored a century in the last week of term, Gavin being the only Year 7 boy thus far to achieve this. Alex Fateh and Thomas Judge became Gloucestershire Players of the Year at U11 and U12 respectively in 1996, the latter being the second boy to reach 1,000 runs in three years for his school in 1997. That year, he was also selected for the prestigious England U13 cricket development squad at the Lilleshall National Sports Centre. The cricket team won the six-a-side in 1997, it being the only XI other than that of 1979 to be unbeaten all season. During the season Thomas Judge (1st XI), James Fick (2nd XI) and Joe Jenkins (U12) scored centuries – possibly the only occasion when three Junior School cricketers have done so in the same season. In 1997 county cricket, both Joe Jenkins and Alex Carlisle won Player of the Year Awards in their respective age groups. In 1998 Douglas Crippen and Simon Ensor both played for the county.

1st XI cricket 2007

In 2001, the XI played a touring side from Soweto, South Africa. Although outplayed by superior cricketers, nevertheless the match ended in a draw and good friendships were made.

In Trinity 2002, under the positive encouragement of David Trist, a former New Zealand national cricket coach, team performances improved, including beating Cheltenham College Junior School for the first time since 1970.

In 2007, Lloyd Evans played county U11 cricket and scored only the second ever colts century – 117 n.o. following that of Liam Brignull in 2004. Tom Warren set a 1st XI record score of 167 n.o. against Wycliffe.

Among later success stories has been Alex Gidman, a former Colts cricketer who won the all-rounder cup. In 2009 he became Captain of Gloucestershire C.C.C.

*Cross-country*

Alastair Judge in 1993

The first major season for Junior School cross-country was in 1983-84 when the senior team was second in the North Gloucestershire Schools' League. Matthew Pickard and Martyn Smith ran for the county and in the same season the Junior School staged its first cross-country meeting, coming first out of six schools.

The boys won the senior and junior events in the 1988 DCJS invitation cross-country. In 1989-90 Christopher Field and Alastair Judge won the senior and junior cross-country races at an event at Malvern College and both won at two other events that year. In 1991, the cross-country teams either won individually or as a team everything for which they were entered, Simon Buckett winning two events. In 1992, the U13 girls' team won every event they entered, Melissa Furno usually being the individual winner. In 1992-93, Alastair Judge won the National Preparatory Schools cross-country race at Marlborough, with the boys' team winning the team event against 54 other schools. The girls came 4th out of 15 teams. The U11 runners won the Cheltenham Schools' competition. During Lent 1994 and in 1995, the senior girls came second in the National Preparatory Schools' Cross-Country Championship with Rebecca Orr achieving an individual third position in 1994. It was also the year that the inter-house competition was begun with Junior, Intermediate and Senior categories. During Michaelmas 1995, Edward Boyd was selected for the county cross-country team. From Michaelmas 1991 to 1996, the U11 boys and girls retained their trophies in the Cheltenham Schools' Cross Country League every year.

In 1995-96, Edward Boyd and Ben Dowty won county honours in cross-country. 1997-98 was when Peter Mullan won the U13 boys' county championship and Tamara Fateh the girls', both qualifying for the county's cross-country squad, the latter winning both district and county races for the second year in succession and subsequently qualifying for the national squad in her age-group.

In 2007, Jack Evans became county cross-country champion and with Will Woodcock, who had finished fourth, ran in the national championships. They were awarded full School Colours.

*Hockey (Boys)*
The groundwork for the strength of Dean Close hockey has been in the Preparatory School.

Since the astroturf pitch became available in 1989, 1st XI sides have won more matches than they have lost every season with one exception. Thanks to the coaching skills of Gary Tredgett and innumerable others, the seasons have usually ranged from good to exceptional.

The XI was unbeaten in 1991, 2002, 2004 and 2006. Over the last 20 years, the XI has either won or drawn 84% of the matches it has played. In addition, the mini-hockey team reached the regional finals on six occasions and the national finals twice, in 1999 and 2005. Since 1993, some 40 boys have played representative hockey at U13 county level. West of England hockey players have included Thomas Judge and Alex Fateh in 1996, Douglas Crippen in 1998, who went on to be included in the England national development squad in 1999, Simon Ensor who was in the England squad in 2001 and Liam Brignull, who in 2007 was selected for Great Britain in his age-group.

In 1974, in the first boys' hockey festival at the Junior School, the hosts won, scoring 17 goals but conceding none. In 1986, Richard Padfield presented the Padfield Trophy for boys' hockey for the winning team in a festival that has been contested annually ever since. In 1991, the boys' hockey XI, 3rd XI and Colts XI were all unbeaten in matches, the XI also winning the Padfield Trophy at the Six Schools' Festival.

The Colts A team won the prestigious Clifton College Preparatory Schools U11 Tournament in 2000 that subsequently became the U11 National IAPS Boys' Hockey Tournament. In 2004 the Colts A team triumphed again, now becoming official national IAPS champions. The team was captained by Liam Brignull, hailed by many as the player of the tournament. John Phillips had masterminded both successes as manager/coach. Meanwhile, at U13 level, the Padfield Trophy was won by the School for the sixth consecutive year in 2004 and the mini-hockey team was fourth in the National Finals.

In 2006, out of their 13 matches, the XI was again unbeaten, thus losing only one match in three seasons. The team won the Foremarke Tournament for the third year in succession, the county title for the eighth time in 11 years and also for the third year in a row. They were runners-up in the West of England tournament. The Colts won the county championship and were also runners-up in the IAPS National Tournament, having won it in 2004.

Liam Brignull (r) in action at the West of England finals 2005

The U13 team became Gloucestershire champions in Lent 1998, eventually coming third nationally. Chris and Sam Tasker-Grindley with Simon Ensor made a major contribution to the Senior School's U14 hockey team winning the national title in 2001. At Michaelmas 2001, five boys represented the county at U14 or U13 level. In the Lent Term 2002, the 1st,

2nd and Colts XIs were unbeaten in school fixtures. In the county championship, the 'B' mini-hockey side beat the 'A' side and went on to be county tournament runners-up!

In 2007, the Colts team became county champions without conceding a goal, and reached the semi-final of the IAPS championship. Liam Brignull, captain of both hockey and cricket, was selected for the Great Britain hockey team in his age group.

The XI were once more Gloucestershire mini-hockey champions in 2008. In 2009, the XI went further and were regional champions, finishing as national finalists, while the U11 team were county champions.

*Hockey (Girls)*

Girls' results were better as numbers increased and skills improved, coached by Carol Sanders, who arrived in 1972, Bridget Crawshaw, recruited in 1974 and later Lyndall Thornton.

In 1975, with only 55 girls over 11 years in the School, the U13 XI won two and drew one of 10 matches. The U13 XI felt fully established when they won all their matches in 1978, led by Claire Fletcher, an inspirational captain, later an international. In the following two years they remained unbeaten, and only lost one match – to The Ladies' College – in 1981. Christine Lee (née Parfitt) joined DCJS as a girls' PE teacher in 1980, the same year that an U11 team was launched that won both its first two matches.

Phoebe Bolton receiving her Player of the Tournament award at the national hockey finals, 2005

From 1986-90 the U13 XI were unbeaten in all their school matches, a remarkable five year record. The 1987 team also won the inaugural seven-a-side tournament at Blue Coats, Birmingham. In 1989, all the girls' teams were unbeaten; the three XIs amassed 154 goals but conceded just one! The opening of the new astroturf pitch helped training.

The U13 XIs were unbeaten in their school matches in 1993, 1998, 2001 and 2004 and, since 1989, have won or drawn 84% of their matches. In 1990, the VII became Gloucestershire mini-hockey champions. The U12 XI was unbeaten, too. Since Michaelmas 1995, over 20 girls have played for the county. The U13 mini-hockey team reached the national finals in 1998, 2001 and 2004-05.

In 1996, the girls' U11 had an unbeaten season. The U13 team were Gloucestershire champions in 1998. Tamara Fateh and Laura Macfarlane were selected for the national U13 hockey development squad while Naomi Reid and Frankie Downes were included in the West of England squad. During the summer 1999, Tamara Fateh and Naomi Reid were selected for the national hockey U14 development squad, Tamara Fateh being subsequently included in the U16 development squad. In Lent 2000, the girls' hockey U11 team were county champions.

In the Lent Term 2002, the U13 girls mini-hockey team came fifth nationally. Although still in the Preparatory School, Beth Moos contributed to the Senior School girls' U14 side, which became national champions in 2003.

In 2004, at U13 level, the School were county champions but progressed no further. During Michaelmas 2004, the U13 girls' team were county and West of England champions. At the National Finals, they came third. Phoebe Bolton, the girls' captain, was Player of the Tournament. In 2009, after a remarkable season, the U13 XI were again National Finalists, being both county and regional champions.

*Netball*

Junior School netball is first mentioned in 1975. By 1977, the VII improved, winning 9 matches, drawing 1 and losing 2. The VII won six out of seven matches in 1980 and 1982.

The VII (A) has won the Cheltenham and District U13 Netball Competition in 1983, 1986, 1988 and 1989. They were unbeaten in 1983, 1988, 2002 (both A and B teams) and 2006. In 1984 the U12 VII (A) won all its matches and reached the quarter finals in the IAPS National Tournament at Crystal Palace. They were also unbeaten in matches in 1990, 1993 and 2001. In 1988, the U13 VII won the prestigious IAPS National Netball Tournament in London, having benefitted from Christine Lee and Sue Warren's coaching. Led by Lynn Burns, they scored 302 goals, conceding 69, in the course of the season. They were finalists in 1991. Sue Warren finished as organizer of the IAPS Netball Tournament in 1989. The U11 team was unbeaten in Lent 1997. In 2004, Becky Bunce was selected to play for the county while the U13A, U12A and U11A sides only lost one match each all season. In 2007, the U12A team were regional champions and finished fourth nationally in the IAPS tournament. The U10A team won the Bromsgrove Tournament.

*Rounders*

The IX had their first successful season in 1977 when they won all their three matches. The Junior IX won their three matches, too, and also reached the semi-finals of the Cheltenham Schools' League.

In 1979 and 1980 the U11 IX were unbeaten in their nine matches in both seasons. In 1979, Claire Fletcher set up a record of hitting seven rounders in one innings. The IX won all their six matches in 1981, 1982 and again in 1988. The IX nearly repeated this in 1983 but lost one match.

Things were rather different in 1997 when the four teams could only manage three wins in the season between them but two years later

Rounders: Molly White in a close call

they had recovered and the IX, using the new rules concerning the award of half rounders, managed to win most of their matches.

In 2001, Emily Challenor was selected for the England U13 squad and the U12 side team won every match it played.

In 2006, the IX reached the third round in the JET competition for the first time. Both the U12A and B sides both won their respective Severnside competitions.

*Rugby*

The 1973 XV won six out of seven matches played, amassing 122 points while conceding 24. The 1983 XV is said to have been the best for 20 years – 15 matches were played: 10 won, 5 lost. The 1989 XV won all their matches, coached by Peter Mills, scoring 276 points while conceding 36, also winning an invitation tournament. This was particularly important, as whispers locally were that 'co-ed' boys were not as tough as those in single-sex preparatory schools. Here was positive proof that this was not the case. The Junior School has played seven-a-side rugby since at least the early 1970s, notably at the Dragon. In 1993 and 1994 the Junior School won the 'small schools' Dragon tournament. In 1995 they were 'promoted' to the 'bigger' schools' tournament but still managed to reach the semi-finals. In Michaelmas 2004, the XV, coached by Matt Dawson, was unbeaten in matches for the first time since 1989. Towards the end of 2005 and into 2006, Nigel Melville, a parent, former England rugby captain and coach of Wasps and Gloucester before he went to the United States,

Unbeaten 1st XV 1989, with coach Peter Mills

1st XV rugby 2005: Charlie Coaker goes for the line

put together a coherent plan to improve the standard of rugby across all Schools. That, and the first floodlit match the XV played, against the Cheltenham Tigers in 2007 seem to be pointing the way ahead. In 2009, winger Edward Bolton succeeded in joining the elite English Preparatory Schools Barbarians Team.

*Swimming*

In 1992-93, Christopher Morgan was the outstanding swimmer. In 1999 Ffion Evans came fifth in the IAPS National Championships for the U12 25m Butterfly, Francesca Hornby sixth in the U13 50m freestyle and two U12 relay teams qualified for the final for the first time. In 2000, Nick Sword achieved a new record in each of the four races he entered in the Swimming Sports, having also won a silver medal at the U13 50m freestyle at the IAPS National Championships. It is said that when he left, Nick had set 17 Junior School swimming records. With Marion Venn's earlier retirement, and Di Giles' departure, Anthony Davies became the swimming coach. During that year, four School relay teams competed at the finals of the IAPS National Championships and Stephanie Boyd won a bronze medal in the U13 breaststroke. Simon Hughes won the U13 50m breaststroke at the IAPS National Championships in 2002 while in 2004, a girls' relay team won a silver medal, another first for the School, all these results in addition to many successful matches against other schools over the years.

In 2005, for the first time, the Swimming Sports became a fully house-based event, increasing the number of competitors involved.

*Tennis*

1981 was the first year the School entered the Cheltenham and District U13 Tennis Tournament, through Sarah Martin and Louise Ruskell, who came second in their doubles section. In 1982, Junior School players were able to use the grass courts in the evening and the hard courts at week-ends for the first time. However, in general only girls played tennis, usually once a week, using four courts 'strategically situated at the furthest points of the School grounds', as Margaret Ferguson later remembered. One court was alongside old Wilton; one on Caldecote playground and two where the Estates Department in the Senior School now is, beyond the astroturf. The Shelburne courts were then grass and were often not in use because of the weather. Over the years, coaching for girls was introduced and later for boys. Facilities gradually improved so that today there are over 20 all-weather courts available in the Trinity Term.

By 1984, inter-school matches were being played. Boys began to be involved from 1985, the year Sarah Hague and Frances Allberry reached the semi-final of the area tournament. Charles Le Bargy was the first Junior School boy to play in the IAPS National Tournament and managed to reach the last 32 out of the 240 who started, in 1986. In 1988, the girls' VI won most of its matches while Martina Calvert, the captain, reached the semi-finals of the IAPS National Tournament, and so played at Wimbledon, the first Junior School player to do so. She and Charlie Forbes reached the quarter-finals of the doubles. The girls' VI in 1990, 1991, 1992 and 1993 and the U11 IV in 1992 won all their matches. Sian Harrison reached the IAPS U12 National Tournament semi-finals in 1990. Selena Dowty, captain in 1993, also reached the singles semi-final of the IAPS National Tournament. In 1998 in the Midland Bank competition, the U11 boys became county champions. In 2000 and in 2001, Chris and Sam Tasker-Grindley won the boys' IAPS Doubles National Tournament. In the latter year, the girls qualified for the HSBC Gloucestershire Finals for the first time.

*Other Sports*

Anna Wilkin, on her mount 'Artful Miss' was successful locally as a show-jumper in 1988. Rosanna Brown, Edward Boyd, Alex Fateh and Harry Dowty took part in the Stonar One Day equestrian event – a new venture – in 1996. In 1997, Rosanna Brown and Annabel Forbes, members of the Cotswold Pony Club, represented the UK in Germany.

Junior School fencing began in 1992. In 1994, a team won the Silver Medal in the Tor Trophy competition covering schools in South West England. Eric Lai came third in the U12 Gloucestershire Fencing Foil Championships in 1996. He also won Bronze in the Southwest Area Fencing Championships (epée) in 1997.

Golf was played for some years before 1975 but that was the first year that any Junior School boy played in the national preparatory schools' competition called the Stowe Putter. Nigel Newport-Black and David Wilson were the first two to compete and apparently did creditably well. In 1976, David Wilson established a new course record for Junior School pupils at Ullenwood of 34, which George Lane improved to 32 in 1992. In 1990, the Junior School came 13th out of 26 schools in the Stowe Putter. In 1991, Mike Harper presented the Ullenwood trophy; its first winner was Hywel Lewis. The same year, Nicholas Burns achieved a hole in one. Girls first joined in 1993, though their interest has proved sporadic over the years. 1993 was also the first year that the driving range at Tredington was used. In more recent years, notably from 2001, greater use has been made of the golf course at Brickhampton.

Connie Chan (Green Belt) and Tim Brown (Orange Belt) competed in the National Judo Championships during Trinity 1996. In 1997, Joanna Hanks won a Bronze Medal at the National Jujitsu Championships in her class.

In 1986, centenary year, the shooting team not only retained the St Patrick's Shield Preparatory School Championship, won the previous year; they won the U15 Championship, too, making the School VIII the strongest team for their age in the country. It was a worthy send-off for Charles Lee who had encouraged and led shooting in his time at DCJS. In 1992-93, the shooting squad won the Ardvreck Cup with Katy Hopkin gaining a maximum score of 100. The shooting team won promotion to the second division in the IAPS league in 1997. In 1999 the shooters won Division 3 of the Preparatory School League, gaining promotion to Division 2. In the PSRA League they gained promotion from Division 2 to Division 1.

Giles Barton

Outstanding individuals in 1988 included Giles Barton, downhill skier. Early in 1989, he represented Great Britain in the U16 skiing team. He came second in the British Dry Ski Slalom Competition in 1989-90.

Squash was first played at the Junior School in the early 1970s and for a while there were fixtures. Interest revived at the beginning of the 1980s and in 1982-83 season, matches were resumed, the School winning two out of three. In 1984-85, the outstanding boy was Julian Ray who was selected to play for the county. Michaelmas 1995 was marked by Lucy Johnson and Laura Hanks representing the county. By 1986, all 24 places on the squash ladder were occupied and a second V was started. During the 1990s probably the best player was Jonathan Sharpe. In Lent 2000, Chris and Sam Tasker-Grindley and Matthew Dring were county squash players, helping to win the South West League Championships. Chris and Sam Tasker-Grindley won the IAPS squash doubles for the second year in succession in Trinity 2001. In 2007, Wes Howell helped the county U15 squash team to reach the national finals. He came 10th out of the top 16 players in the country at the All England U13 Grand Prix Tournament in 2008.

In 1989, David and Gareth Jones, Justin Upton and Adam Pearson came third in the U13 British Schools' Trampolining Championships.

### *Activities*

Broadly speaking, activities divided into two: those that were concerned with the great outdoors and those that tended to be inside.

Of the activities that were outdoors, Argonauts, which had originally been in patrols (see chapter 7) still had camps, usually in North Wales, for some years into the mid-1970s, sometimes attracting nearly 50 children. Argonauts was popular among seniors and lengthy walks, including the 12½ mile trek over the peaks of the Black Mountains in 1984, were well supported. There was rock climbing

Walkers on the summit of Pen-y-fan, Brecon Beacons 1996

for 36 enthusiasts and over half the Junior School – 154 all told – participated in orienteering on one occasion.

Argonauts changed over the 1980s and into the 1990s. It eventually became the name for the senior part of the Junior School's walking activity that took place on a Sunday up to four times a year, and included all the senior boarders and any senior day children who wanted to come along, perhaps venturing to the Black Mountains. The Pathfinders, founded in 1972, was initially for boys from the middle part of the School and for senior girls, divided into four patrols. By the 1990s it, too, was the name for the middle school equivalent of the Sunday walking activity. The Ramblers were the most junior members of the School of either sex whose walks were naturally less demanding. Pathfinders and Ramblers often went to local beauty spots such as Broadway Tower, Painswick Beacon and the Forest of Dean Sculpture Trail. They, too, were primarily for boarders but some day children also participated.

In the 1970s there was also a junior/middle School expedition in the summer. It was called 'Beddgelert Week' and was in Snowdonia. The idea was to give younger children an opportunity to '...walk in the mountains and see the countryside without any need for camping...'. Accommodation was found in a guest house and a cottage. In 1975, for example, 17 boys and two girls went with five staff, including the Chaplain, the Revd Anthony Creery-Hill and also John Titterington, both having just completed some years as housemasters. By 1977, the week attracted 22 children and continued for several years. In July 1984, 18 junior children went for a part-holiday, part-camp, part-development of Argonaut skills based at the YMCA National Centre at the southern end of Lake Windermere.

Other outdoor skills were also on offer, notably cycling proficiency which became part of the Junior School scene in 1979 and were later known as the 'Silver Cycling Awards'. They were discontinued in 2003. In 1976, riding began with nearly 20 children involved at Badgeworth Riding Club. This activity continued into the 2000s. In 1977, to mark the Queen's Jubilee, Clive Rooke, Head of Science, set up a nature reserve project that included the planting of 25 trees, creating a habitat for small wild animals.

Skiing began in 1983 with a joint holiday with the Senior School. The first Junior School only trip was the following year when 40 children went for a week to Chatel in the French Alps; Charles Lee was

IAPS Cruise 1996

the member of staff behind the idea. Since the end of the 1980s, Andrew Judge was the organizer but trips ceased in 1996.

Travel was becoming more popular. Junior School children went on special IAPS preparatory school cruises over the years, often on the *S.S. Uganda*. Initially led by Pat Bryan and Iris Long, they were known to happen in the 1970s through to the 1990s. The itinerary usually included a selection from: Italy, including Venice, Pompeii or Rome; Turkey, including Istanbul or Ephesus; Greece, including Athens, Crete and the Greek Islands; Egypt, Palestine, Israel and sometimes Cyprus.

Travel slightly nearer to home was organized by the French Department under Martin Piper, whereby up to 40 children spent four days in Paris each year from the mid-1980s. In 2000 and thereafter, expeditions to France under Jackie Dunlop, Colette Dobbs and Sarah Davies came to involve the whole of Year 7 journeying to Château de la Baudonnière in Normandy, a centre for English schoolchildren, to learn about the culture and heritage of France as well as its language.

Travel even closer to home came in 1991 when teacher Paul Coleman and his wife Maggie began their annual canal boat holidays in the Easter break which continued for most of that decade.

The Leavers' Course, begun in 1991, included a large outdoors element. Initially developed by Trevor Lewis and later Selina Ramm, it sought to bridge the gap between the end of Common Entrance and the end of term by introducing new experiences, new skills and attempting to encourage initiative, all of which would be of use at the Senior School. It included a week-long camp at St George's House, North Devon, and many of the experiences that earlier generations would have found in Argonauts – canoeing, rock-climbing, orienteering – with one or two new ones, such as abseiling and water skiing. There were problem-solving days, such as the Cheltenham Trail, and a citizenship element, meeting thought-provoking people, such as those working in the field of drug-addiction or someone coping with disability, or meeting a magistrate and learning what they do. The course proved flexible and useful and in adapted form continues to be a part of the Preparatory School today, under Steve Cahill, the Head of Boarding, who also organises the Year 7 annual trip to Snowdonia.

Christian Union (CU) also did many outdoor activities as well as indoor ones. Bob Benson began it in the late 1970s, assisted by Viv Troughton. It received real impetus from the arrival of Susan Burgess in September 1981, and Margaret Buchanan in January 1982. It was initially for the top three years of the Junior School. In the Lent Term 1982 a small CU Drama Group was formed. By the end of 1983, the CU finished the year with a barbecue on Hardy lawn, a visit from ACORN, a Christian repertory company, as well a number of outside speakers during the year. A CU library and an after-meeting prayer group both began. The group felt encouraged by the new Chaplain, the Revd Daniel Young (1983-99). In between, it developed outdoors. By the end of the 1980s with Faith Jameson now the leader, CU was organizing summer holidays for 22 children. There were hikes and Easter holidays at St George's House, North Devon, with summer holidays at Hebron Hall near Cardiff. By 1991 there was Junior CU, led by Steve and Jo Cahill. It, too, took children out, but for long week-ends rather than full weeks. Briefly, CU split into three but soon returned to two groups. Into the new century, although there have been camps, there have tended to be activity days, such as kayaking on the River Wye or a ropes course in

Year 7 pupils on the French holiday in Normandy 2008

**Heads of School – DCJS**

*Records before 1981 are either non-existent or unreliable*

| | |
|---|---|
| 1981 | Abigail Churchill |
| 1982 | David Breese |
| 1983 | Stephen Ellard |
| 1984 | Michael Reicher |
| 1985 | Jonathon Tyce |
| 1986 | *not appointed* |
| 1987 | Catherine McAdam |
| 1988 | Anthony Bird |
| 1989 | Christopher Field |
| 1990 | Beth Williams |
| 1991 | Elizabeth Herber-Davies |
| 1992 | Charles Prentis |
| 1993 | Rebecca Orr |
| 1994 | Victoria Judge |
| 1995 | Tegan Faulkner |
| 1996 | Thomas Judge |
| 1997 | Laura Macfarlane |
| 1998 | Anna Bruckland |

**Heads of School – DCPS**

| | |
|---|---|
| 1999 | Jessica Burns |
| | James Dowler |
| 2000 | Megan Howell |
| 2001 | Natasha Price |
| 2002 | Tom Wood |
| | Eleanor Stone |
| 2003 | James Melville |
| | Rebecca Browne |
| 2004 | James Bunce |
| | Hannah Bailey |
| 2005 | Liam Brignull |
| | Rebecca Smith |
| 2006 | Timothy Brecht |
| | Claudia Stebbings |
| 2007 | Arbi Autarkanov |
| | Elizabeth George |
| 2008 | Benjamin West |
| | Catherine Hodgkins |

Train Club in the 1980s

the Forest of Dean. And in amongst all this activity, there has also been much teaching about the Bible, prayer and the Christian way of life.

Associated with CU, Alastair Reid, Senior School Second Master, visited Rempstone Adventure Camp in Dorset when it first opened in 1974. In 1998, he and his wife Rosalyn led nine Decanians and 29 Junior School pupils to sample it in its 25th anniversary year, the first of many subsequent visits for which Michael Ede has been largely responsible.

The Railway/Train club was begun by Michael Rowlands in 1958, in a basement of what is now Turner Hall. It had to move several times before taking over the old Argonauts' Hut in the 1980s which is presently better known as the Speech and Drama Room, close to Fortfield and next to the Langhorne Hall. There it reached a point under the supervision of Paul Coleman where timetabling for eight trains simultaneously was possible. In more recent times the club and its stock have transferred to the IDT Department under the care of David Jones.

The Junior School has been concerned with raising money for charity for some time, especially through the Autumn Fair and also Red Nose Day and similar occasions, but the £5,300 (£9,000) that staff and pupils raised for the St Paul's Maternity Hospital during 1990-91 was a particularly impressive achievement. The Preparatory School has continued to be active in this area in recent years, under the Senior Master, Eric Harris, such as in 2007-08 when the appeals supported included the Burma Tsunami fund, the cystic fibrosis appeal, Operation Christmas Child and the National Children's Orchestra. Red Nose Day, Winston's Wish and Jeans for Genes are also regularly supported.

There have been other activities, too; the slightly exotic such as origami, croquet and Chelonia and the more conventional, such as hobbies, art and craft, modelling, natural history and carpentry.

# Chapter 16

## The Advent of Tewkesbury Abbey Schola Cantorum of Dean Close Preparatory School

To understand how it was that Dean Close Preparatory School became a choir school for one of the leading abbey choirs of the land one has to look first at the history of the Abbey School, Tewkesbury.

A choral foundation at Tewkesbury Abbey was the inspirational idea of Miles Amherst. In 1952 he visited Tewkesbury Abbey and was captivated by its magnificence and special atmosphere. In 1973 he finally decided to found a school in Tewkesbury for the proposed choir. The Vicar, then Canon Cosmo Pouncey, and the Abbey organist, Michael Peterson, were both enthusiastic. One churchwarden was deeply concerned about the effect such an arrangement might have on the parish choir. Following discussions with him an unusual, possibly unique, agreement was reached – the new choir would sing on weekdays while the parish choir would sing on Sundays. This meant that the Abbey School Choir was the only choir school where the choristers were free to go home at weekends and at Christmas and Easter.

Michael Peterson, organist

**Miles Amherst, Founder and First Headmaster, The Abbey School**

Born in 1931, he was a science graduate of Cambridge University, and was also a gifted musician, having had experience as a Lay Clerk at Worcester Cathedral and later at Ely Cathedral. He was also a keen brass player. In 1973, after 15 years of teaching, mainly at the King's School, Ely that included a housemastership, he decided to open a choir school in Tewkesbury. It was the only privately owned choir school in the country until he retired as 'Sole Proprietor' in 1998 – the school's Silver Jubilee – and the school became a registered charity run by a board of governors, of which he was the first chairman.

The Amherst family had had dealings with Dean Close School generations earlier. Miles' father, William, an accountant in Minehead, Somerset, appointed Howard Shapland OD in 1938 to be an accountant with him in his practice. In 1946, when William retired, he left the practice to Howard.

Miles Amherst found premises for his school in buildings formerly used by the town's High School for Girls, close to the Abbey. The Abbey School opened its doors for pupils on 9th September, 1973, with five boys that within days became half a dozen. The first Evensong was sung on 8th May, 1974, '...with eight or nine boys...' and a tenor and a bass 'borrowed' from the parish choir. The music was

The Abbey School in 1978

simple: ferial responses, psalms for the eighth evening, the canticles sung to Arnold in A with Henry Ley's *The Strife is O'er* as the anthem. Initially, they only sang Evensong once a fortnight but by the end of the Summer Term 1975 it was four nights every week. The early staff included a former Chief Petty Officer Engineer who proved to be a versatile and resourceful maintenance man for some years; local people who put their teaching talents and expertise at the disposal of the school; a number of young men who came to be choral scholars and tutors and finally Mrs Joanna Chorley, Domestic Bursar, who '...did everything except teach...' that included being the secretary, housekeeper, cook, matron and PR person who also looked after the first boarders in her own home before the boarding house became available.

**Headmasters and Directors of Music, The Abbey School**

*Headmasters*

| | |
|---|---|
| 1973-1990 | Miles Amherst |
| 1990-2001 | Jonathan Milton |
| Ian Griffin/Jenni Wilson ran the School for some months in 2002 | |
| 2002-2004 | Gareth Jones |
| 2005-2006 | Neil W. Gardner |

*Directors of Music*

| | |
|---|---|
| 1973-1985 | Michael D. Peterson |
| 1985-1989 | Paul Brough |
| 1989-2000 | Andrew Sackett |
| 2000-2006 | Benjamin Nicholas |

In 1976 a Choral Scholarship fund was set up, while in 1980 the Choir made its first record and also appeared on the television programme *Pebble Mill at One*.

The school became co-educational in about 1983.

The Choir joined the Choir Schools' Association, which held its 1988 AGM in the Abbey School's newly-built hall and then attended Choral Evensong which was broadcast on BBC Radio 3. From then on it broadcast on several occasions.

The Choir undertook several tours to the United States and also went to France, Moscow, Sweden, Belgium, Germany and Venice, Italy. It released a number of recordings and CDs. It also gave first performances of Gabriel Jackson's *Tewkesbury Service*, commissioned to mark Miles Amherst's 75th birthday, Geraint Lewis's *Tewkesbury Service* and John Caldwell's *Latin Magnificat*.

In 2002, Tewkesbury Abbey celebrated 900 years as a Benedictine Foundation. Among other celebrations that year was a Choir Schools' Association Choral Evensong in March, in which choristers from Bristol, Exeter, Gloucester, Hereford, Llandaff, Salisbury, Truro, Wells, Winchester and Worcester came to sing with their colleagues from the Abbey School.

However, in 2005 the Abbey School governors realized that the school of 85 pupils, that had reached just over 100 in earlier years, was probably not financially viable. The bulk of the children left at the end of Year 6, when they were 11. All too often the top two years were in classes of fewer then six, populated almost exclusively by choristers.

After agonizing over the situation for some months and discussing possible alternatives, it was most reluctantly decided by the Board of Governors, led by their Chairman, Simon Chorley, that voluntary liquidation had to occur and the relevant administrator was put in place during the week commencing 24th April, 2006. It was agreed that the staff and children would be told that Friday. The evening before, Neil Gardner, headmaster of the school, rang round his fellow preparatory and public school headmaster colleagues explaining the situation. He included the Revd Tim Hastie-Smith in his round of calls, who asked whether it would mean the end of the Choir. When Neil Gardner said that, sadly, it would, Tim Hastie-Smith asked what would be the reaction if Dean Close School took on the Choir, to which idea Neil Gardner responded positively. It was agreed that the next day, after the news of the Abbey School's closure had been announced, Neil Gardner would ask Benjamin Nicholas, Director of the Abbey School Choir, to telephone the Dean Close School Headmaster. To rescue the Abbey School itself was regrettably impossible.

Tim Hastie-Smith's reflection had a certain edge to it as Benjamin Nicholas had joined the Dean Close Staff the previous September as part-time Director of Choral Music, when not at the Abbey School, at which he had been a notable success. The rescue of the Choir would mean that not only Benjamin Nicholas remained at Dean Close School – and be available to more Decanians than before – it would also mean an infusion of musical boys into the Preparatory School that would supply a never-ending, high quality stream of musical talent for the Senior School. It would raise the profile of the School in the musical world. It would mean also that Dean Close School would have a closer relationship with Tewkesbury Abbey and the area around it – an area where the School's name was not as well known as some other schools. However, Tim Hastie-Smith thought that others, closer to the Abbey School, might wish to mount a rescue for the whole Abbey School community. He felt that Dean Close School should be the school of last rather than first resort, not least because Dean Close Preparatory School was already virtually full for the following year. Any major alteration would mean an additional heavy administrative and logistical load for its senior management team. The initiative had to be with the parents. They might want nothing to do with the School, especially as it was in Cheltenham. He was also conscious that while the Abbey and Dean Close School had enjoyed excellent relations for many years, nevertheless they came from different traditions within the Christian faith, the Abbey being of a wide, broadly anglo-catholic approach whereas the School was decidedly more evangelical both in its foundation and ethos.

Benjamin Nicholas

As scheduled, Simon Chorley, chairman of the Abbey School governors, told shocked staff and pupils at the Abbey School of the sad decision to close. Benjamin Nicholas telephoned Dean Close School and spoke to the Headmaster. The following day the two men met. It was decided that there would be an attempt to put together a plan to save the Choir if it became evident that other proposals would not work. It would be Tim Hastie-Smith's task to persuade the Governors. Benjamin Nicholas would try to hold the chorister parents together as a group in the hope of saving the Choir. He achieved this by ringing the parents of every chorister almost daily for the next month. Meanwhile, the senior management teams of both Dean Close School and the Preparatory School, together with the Bursar, began to discuss initial thoughts on the idea.

The next day, Sunday, the Bishop of Gloucester, the Rt Revd Michael Perham, was at Dean Close School for a Confirmation

Bishop Michael Perham

The Revd Canon
Paul Williams

Service. As the School's Visitor, as a parent, and with his episcopal interest in and responsibility for Tewkesbury Abbey, he was deeply concerned about the Abbey School Choir situation. After the service, an informal meeting developed in the Orangery. The Bishop, both Headmasters, Benjamin Nicholas and others with an interest in both Dean Close School and the Abbey were present. Already, several other choirs were looking at some of the Abbey School Choir's top boys. Offers were beginning to be made: there was no time to be lost. It was essential to make sure that the Vicar of Tewkesbury Abbey, Canon Paul Williams, himself a governor of the Abbey School, was made aware of Dean Close School's willingness, in principle, to rescue the Choir and to seek his support for the idea. This was duly done and Canon Williams met Tim Hastie-Smith on the Monday.

During the ensuing week, the Preparatory School's senior management – the Revd Leonard Browne, Robin Davies (Deputy Head) and Laura Sorrell (Director of Studies) – worked enormously hard: '...the Headmaster and the two deputies have talked themselves to a standstill...' was one comment – and the Bursar for his part was close behind, not only investigating the financial implications of taking on the Choir but also looking at what the Ouseley Trust, the Friends of Cathedral Church Music and other bodies, such as the appropriate Trust for Choral Music at the Abbey, might be able to contribute.

The decisive meeting was probably on Friday evening, 12th May at 7.30pm in Dean Close House at a gathering of chorister parents. It was hosted by Tim Hastie-Smith, who gave an informal, low key presentation of the Dean Close School proposals. If a suitable scheme was launched in Tewkesbury to save the choir school, Dean Close School would immediately back away, although it stood ready to help. He did not mention it, but he had received a number of letters from distinguished musicians urging him to save the Choir, including John Rutter (composer), the Master of Music from St Paul's Cathedral, the Master of Music from Westminster Abbey, and the internationally known singers Sarah Connolly, James Bowman and Bryn Terfel.

The practicalities of the Dean Close Preparatory School package were spelt out by the Revd Leonard Browne, while the musical implications were discussed by Benjamin Nicholas. He indicated that, assuming that the Dean Close option went ahead, Evensong would initially be cut to three evenings a week – Monday, Tuesday and Thursday – at 5.30pm. It would only work – whatever the school in charge – if the majority of the choristers and their parents stuck together. Time was of the essence as children and their parents needed to know what was to happen next term; other choir schools required answers to offers that had already been made. Jonathan Lancashire, as Bursar, underlined the offer that included keeping fees at the Abbey School levels for a year and then adjusting them in the second year and being at Dean Close Preparatory School levels in the third year, all subject to the appropriate scholarships as choristers and acceptable performances in the entrance tests. After some discussion, the chorister parents slipped away, most feeling that the Dean Close option was probably best.

Meanwhile, Simon Dennis, a parent of a daughter in the Abbey School, supported by one choir parent and some other parents was working on an alternative plan. It became evident, however, that it was unlikely that the proposals would adequately support choristers. One or two other schemes were mooted but did not make headway.

The DCS Trustees, led by their Chairman, Patricia Napier, were kept informed of developments. On the morning of Friday, 12th May, she and the Finance and General Purposes Committee gave the go-ahead to the scheme in principle, subject to the final say of the whole Board of Trustees that was not due to hold a meeting for another fortnight.

Given that decision, a letter was sent out immediately to all chorister parents with the full details of the proposal, underlining the point yet again that the initiative as to whether the offer was taken up and the choir saved was with the parents.

The choristers and their parents attended an Open Morning at Dean Close School and Dean Close Preparatory School on Saturday, 13th May and were duly impressed. They went into the Dean Close Music School and heard Ashok Gupta, then a member of the Upper Sixth, practising his interpretation of Rachmaninov's *Second Piano Concerto* that he was due to play from memory at the Commemoration Concert a few days later, with his teacher playing the orchestral part.

The time for decision had arrived. In the event, ten choristers transferred to Dean Close Preparatory School: three elected to go elsewhere. Benjamin Nicholas was very pleased that ten boys had chosen the Dean Close option. His minimum number, if the scheme was to stand any hope of working, had been six: ten, a significant majority of the boys, made the continuation of the Choir that bit easier.

Tewkesbury Abbey

On 25th May, Rebecca Chaplin, Marketing and Admissions Co-ordinator at the Preparatory School, sent out a press release announcing that the Choir had been saved. The Tewkesbury Abbey community and many others heaved a huge collective sigh of relief and thankfulness, mingled with very real sadness that the Abbey School would be no more.

As the press release made clear, there were already a number of links between Tewkesbury Abbey and Dean Close School. Apart from Benjamin Nicholas' links with both, the Dean Close Chapel Choir had sung Evensong at the Abbey on at least one occasion every year since 1955. Since 1976, that Choir had sung Evensong every Remembrance Sunday at the Abbey without missing a single occasion. The School's Archivist, the Revd Charles Whitney, formerly on the Preparatory School staff, was on the staff at the Abbey; the Abbey's organist, Carleton Etherington, taught at Dean Close School while his wife, Katie, had recently been teaching full-time in the Preparatory School.

Thus a youthful wish of the first Headmaster of Dean Close School, the Revd Dr William Flecker, had come about in a totally unforeseen way. When a student at Durham University, he gave time in order to try to: '...reconcile the two great factions, Low and High Church, represented here...so that something unanimous may be done...'.

On Thursday 13th July, the Abbey School Choir sang its last Choral Evensong that included Balfour Gardiner's *Evening Hymn* as the Introit, Herbert Howells' *St Paul's Service* and his *Te Deum (Collegium Regale)* as the Anthem. The next day, the Abbey School held its Commemoration and Prize Giving in the packed nave of the Abbey. In his speech, Neil Gardner expressed the thoughts of many when he not only paid tribute to Miles Amherst's vision but also said: 'Although we all wish that we could have maintained the *status quo* we can't and so we must rejoice that out of it all at least Choral Evensong will continue to be sung in this Abbey just as Miles intended...I know that you and all of us here wish in our hearts that this wasn't happening but we must face what lies ahead of us and embrace the future with hope and with courage.'

During the service, the Choir sang Sir Edward Bairstow's *Blessed City, Heavenly Salem*, the School Crest was handed back to the Vicar for safe keeping and after *God be with you till we meet again*, the Choir completed its choral contribution by singing John Rutter's *The Lord Bless You and Keep You* before the Vicar gave the Blessing.

**Choristers from The Abbey School who transferred to Dean Close Preparatory School**

Benoit Andre
David Bath
Oliver Bullock
James Deans-Sidgreaves
Marcus Emmerson
Oliver Gay
Aaron King
Nathan King
Thomas Ooi
Hector Watson

*Those who joined from Dean Close Preparatory School for the First Evensong:*

Andrew Gamman
William Northcott
Robert Wilks

The term was over. Ten of the choristers made their way to Dean Close Preparatory School. If they expected to see a completely fresh teaching staff awaiting them in the September, they were wrong. Lisa Bailey (Year 4 teacher) and Lindsay Gooch (Modern Languages), both from the Abbey School, joined the DCPS staff, too. Thus, with Benjamin Nicholas there were three people who were familiar to them. The boys themselves rehearsed in the main first floor front room in Hardy House. A musical 'gap year' tutor was appointed to assist in the business of ensuring choristers were in the right place at the right time – sometimes quite a feat in a large, busy preparatory school.

At Evensong on Monday, 11th September, 2006 at the Abbey, the Choir sang under the new banner of Tewkesbury Abbey Schola Cantorum of Dean Close Preparatory School, Cheltenham for the first time. In addition to the ten boys who had transferred from

The first trebles of the new Schola Cantorum, 2006

Break time from rehearsal

the Abbey School, three new boys immediately joined from Dean Close Preparatory School itself, so that 13 boys sang the service. It was boys' voices only, the responses were Plainsong, the setting was Long in F and the Anthem was the *Pie Jesu* from Fauré's *Requiem*. The next day, the full four-part choir, including a number of Lay Clerks who had been a part of the Abbey School Choir, sang Evensong that included in the congregation members of the Prayer Book Society. A major test of the reconstituted choir occurred on Wednesday, 27th September, when they broadcast Evensong live on Radio 3 from St Michael's Church, Tenbury Wells to mark the 150th Anniversary of St Michael's College. Originally, it had been agreed before it was known that the Abbey School was to close but Benjamin Nicholas saw it as an opportunity to begin to establish the Schola Cantorum in the minds not only of the BBC but also of interested members of the public.

It was not long before the Choir joined the Cheltenham Bach Choir for a performance of Bach's *St Matthew Passion* conducted by Stephen Jackson in Gloucester Cathedral, at which several of the boys were presented to the Princess Royal. One of the choristers, Oliver Gay, reached the final four of the Chorister of the Year competition, and found himself broadcasting on BBC Radio 2. Although he did not win, he gave a very good account of himself.

A small yet significant step in the closer relationship between the Dean Close community and Tewkesbury Abbey was taken on 1st November – All Saints' Day – when, at Choral Evensong, the Revd Leonard Browne, Headmaster of Dean Close Preparatory School, was installed by the Vicar in the Abbey Quire in the same stall – opposite the officiant's stall, on the south side – that had previously been occupied by the Headmaster of the Abbey School. It was a poignant moment as Leonard Browne was presented to the Vicar for Installation by Miles Amherst, the symbolism of which was not lost on the congregation.

Having successfully negotiated the broadcast, the Choir joined forces with the Abbey Parish Choir to sing Fauré's uplifting setting of the requiem Mass on All Souls' Day. The Advent Carol Service in the Abbey was made special for the young choristers by boarders from Caldecote House coming to support them. There were a number of concerts as Christmas grew closer.

In the Lent Term, Pergolesi's *Stabat Mater* was a much admired major project, performed in the Pittville Pump Rooms. That same term, the Choir, together with the Preparatory School Chamber Choir, the Dean Close School Choral Society and soloists who were all former Decanians or associated with the Abbey School Choir, sang Bach's *St Matthew Passion* in the Abbey. The orchestra, too, had many Decanians in it and was led by Robert Bishop, Head of Strings. The performance, conducted by Benjamin Nicholas, was memorable.

The Choir embarked on their first CD – *The Three Kings* – a recording of Christmas music. It came out just in time for Christmas 2007 and was reviewed in *The Church Times* by Roderic Dunnett who wrote: 'I doubt whether there are many more admirable choirs outside Westminster, Oxford and Cambridge than the Tewkesbury Abbey Schola Cantorum…their future is now assured, thanks to the foresight of Dean Close School in Cheltenham…On Tewkesbury's new Christmas disc…Nicholas's choir give proof yet again of the qualities that place them firmly in the front rank: flair, acumen, versatility and poise…'.

In Trinity 2007 the Choir went on a nine concert tour of France, to considerable acclaim, having also been involved in two very popular concerts with Aled Jones at the Abbey.

It is a measure of the impact that the Choir has had on the musical life of the School that another school's Musical Director observed to Helen Porter, Director of Music at Dean Close School, at a conference that he'd '...never heard of Dean Close School before but recently it seems to have been in the (choral musical) news every month...'.

The fitting in of Abbey services on the one hand and Dean Close School commitments on the other meant that there were too many occasions when Carleton Etherington and Benjamin Nicholas were hard pressed to cover them. The solution was to appoint a well qualified musician as an organ and choral scholar assistant. Such a person arrived in September 2007 in the shape of Alexander Eadon, who initially came for a year but stayed a little longer! He played both the Chapel and Abbey organs as well as conducting various choirs, helping to train the choristers and assisting the teaching in the Preparatory School.

The boys currently rehearse every day during the week at School, and in addition rehearse with the lower parts at the Abbey for at least half an hour before each service. Since September 2007, the Evensong pattern has returned to four evenings a week: Mondays, Tuesdays, Thursdays and Fridays, as Wednesdays are match days.

Under present arrangements two groups are specifically concerned with the well-being of the choir and especially its boy choristers, apart from the School and Abbey authorities. The first are the Trustees of the Choir, chaired by Miles Amherst; among their main concerns are choral scholarships and associated financial topics, tasks that a sub group under Francis Rundall address. Funding choral scholarships is vital but never easy, yet a few concerned, kind individuals have supported this cause. To underline the fact that the Choir is an integral part of the School community, the Old Decanian Society is also generously currently funding a choral scholarship. The Clerk to the Trustees is the Bursar of the School.

The second group is a choir liaison group who meet every term in order '...to represent the Abbey to the School and the School to the Abbey...' as the Vicar has put it. Staff from the Abbey and the Preparatory School, as well as key musicians involved, meet in order to consider problems concerning logistics, liturgy, the well-being of the choristers, facilities and any perceived problems that may be emerging.

Miles Amherst's dream to maintain the tradition of a superlative abbey choir has not only continued but shows every sign of developing to still greater heights in the future. Another live Choral Evensong, this time from Tewkesbury Abbey itself, for Radio 3 on 1st June, 2008, was acknowledgement of the standard they have achieved, as was the worldwide appreciation of their efforts after the broadcast had gone out.

Jonathan Milton

They have been accepted by and integrated into the broad life of the Preparatory School while still being aware of their roots. This was underlined in Trinity 2008 when the Guest of Honour at the Preparatory School's Speech Day was Jonathan Milton, Chairman of the Choir School Association, Headmaster of Westminster Abbey Choir School and a former master and later headmaster of the Abbey School, Tewkesbury.

In December 2008, the choristers represented Great Britain at the closing event of the French Presidency of the European Union in Strasbourg. This was broadcast live in 39 countries, and Benjamin Nicholas described the choir's selection as 'a great honour'.

# Chapter 17

## The Pre-Preparatory School

What might be called a pre-preparatory school has meant different things to different people at different times. In the 1970s, the lower forms of the Junior School, i.e. those aged between seven and ten years old, were sometimes referred to as the pre-preparatory forms. For others, pre-preparatory forms covered five- to ten-year-olds. Dean Close Pre-Preparatory School is concerned with the education of those aged from rising-three up to seven.

It might have been thought that children so young would not have come to the School until the 1990s. However, this is not the case. The School was in a very grim financial situation after the main School came back from Monkton Combe in 1940 and closure was averted by the narrowest of margins (see chapter 5). Hugh Elder, the Headmaster, needed all the financial assistance that he could find. As well as re-introducing day-children as quickly as possible, another move was temporarily to lower the age at which the Junior School would accept children to below seven years, although this was probably unofficial. The Old Decanian Register shows that between Michaelmas 1940 and the end of 1941, the School accepted three boys aged six, five aged five and one aged just over four. Once 1942 had been reached, finances improved and there was no need to recruit that young, although several rising-seven-year-olds were still allowed in from time to time. Few stayed all the way through the main School, although Christopher Schneider – now a member of the OD Committee – was in his thirteenth year at the School when he left at Christmas 1952, having arrived in September 1940, and Richard Emms was at the School for nearly 12 years.

It was not until the 1980s that the question of taking children under seven arose once more. Ian Ferguson, Headmaster of the Junior School, noted that it was becoming harder to recruit children at seven because they had already settled into schools, formed their friendships, their parents were satisfied with their choice taken certainly by the time the children were five years old and sometimes as early as two or three; they felt no need to move their children until they were, perhaps, 11. Conveniently, Airthrie School, on Christchurch Road, a small privately owned school that catered for children up to the age of 11 came up for sale towards the end of the 1980s, and the School looked carefully into the possibility of purchasing it with an eye to turning it into a pre-preparatory school, but the scheme was not thought workable.

In 1992 Ian Ferguson persuaded the Governors that a pre-preparatory department was not so much a luxury as a necessity. Year 3 at the bottom of the Junior School was very small – sometimes beginning the year on fewer than double figures. Year 4 was better but often barely justified having two classes. The big inflow tended to be in Year 7, when children moved at the end of their primary schools. A far better supply of children lower down the age-range was needed. A pre-preparatory department, where friendships and peer groups could be forged early on, was the answer. Indeed, one of the additional problems was that other local independent schools already had flourishing pre-preparatory departments and Ian Ferguson felt they were drawing potential pupils away from Dean Close School. The Governors were very cautious. They were concerned that a child who had been through the pre-preparatory department, then the Junior School, might well not wish to come to the main School at 13 but go elsewhere. The investment that had been put into attracting pupils in the first place would thus have been shown to be counter productive. Moreover, there were other priorities in other parts of the School, not least a theatre and a music school.

Eventually, the Governors were persuaded to open a pre-preparatory department 'on a shoe-string', not least because interesting pupils and their parents was proving something of a challenge at the time, notwithstanding the quality of what was offered and Ian Ferguson's best efforts. The three classrooms immediately behind the Langhorne Hall were used as the first pre-preparatory base. One of them, the classroom that acted as the Green Room for the Langhorne Hall, could be used by the new department so long as it was clearly understood that it must continue to be available as a Green Room when needed. The grass between the classrooms was replaced by an all enveloping infant-friendly rubberized matting.

The first business meeting concerning a forthcoming pre-preparatory department was held in Bayley House on the 22nd April, 1992. It was attended by Ian Ferguson (Headmaster); his wife Margaret who, as Senior Mistress, was concerned with uniform, the children's health, welfare and related issues; Paul Brewster (Director of Studies), concerned with the curriculum; Viv Troughton, a widely experienced and very enthusiastic junior forms teacher, who had taught at the Junior School for some years both before and since her marriage and had extensive contacts with many parents locally and was to teach in the new department; Hilary Crofts, a young Year 3 teacher and boarding house tutor who was also to have her timetable adapted so that she could teach in pre-prep; and Charles Whitney (Second Master) who was concerned with some of the logistics, how the teaching cover would work and related topics, and who acted as secretary to the meeting.

That the meeting was convened as it was says something about the shoe-string nature of the venture. Although Viv Troughton's hours were to be extended there was to be no full-time teacher commitment at the beginning; equipment was barely adequate; classroom space effectively came from spare capacity at the time rather than anywhere particularly special. The only real building expense was for appropriate lavatory and cloakroom facilities.

The meeting suggested that the pre-preparatory department might be called Francis House – Francis having been the Christian name of Dean Close. The term 'House' was added to tie in with other areas of the Junior School. 'The Squirrels' was mooted but at that stage there was concern over other schools that had apparently already adopted that name and the possibility of confusion that might result. The uniform was to be blue and/or preferably bottle green, and apart from sweatshirts was to include boiler suits in bottle green with poppers or zips. Subsequent meetings on uniforms changed the colours completely to the cardinal red of the rest of the Dean Close community! The eventual design, of a cardinal red jersey with the School crest in the area where a breast pocket would have been was made more child-friendly by three embroidered squirrels scampering almost diagonally across the front. 'I used to love the pre-prep jersey with the three squirrels,' said one former member of the Pre-Prep.

Pre-Prep's first location, behind Langhorne Hall

The suggested hours were 9am to 3.30pm Monday to Friday, though there would be a crêche from 8.25am and also after school, possibly until as late as 5pm. Matrons might be used then to assist Hilary Crofts. A need for two qualified teachers each morning for the 'three Rs' was anticipated, although they might not be necessary in the afternoon. Specialist qualified teachers from the Junior School would teach art, music, swimming and games. Lunch would not be with the rest of the Junior School but at midday on specially raised benches. The only major problem might occur when the Junior School Year 8 sat their Common Entrance examinations or music candidates had their Associated Board examinations in the adjacent Langhorne Hall and silence was vital!

The meeting closed with groups agreed to finalise uniforms, curriculum (including leading up to the national curriculum Key Stage 1), liaison with the estates department, and the preparation of a prospectus pamphlet.

The first time that a specifically pre-preparatory function happened in the Junior School was on Thursday, 3rd September, 1992, when pre-preparatory parents were called to a meeting in the early evening to discuss the opening of the department the next week. That Thursday had also been the first day of the new term for the rest of the Junior School, the idea being that the Junior School should be up and running a few days before the pre-preparatory department officially began.

Rosie Phillips with her Year 1 class

On Monday, 7th September, the Term Calendar proudly announced: '...Pre-Preparatory School opens...'; 12 children were there to begin the new venture. Three academic years only were covered – Reception, Year 1 and Year 2. Children were at least four years old on entry.

That first term, and indeed for the year, much learning (and fun) was had by all. In addition to the work of Hilary Crofts and Viv Troughton, Mary Padley created Art with the children; Philip Brooke enjoyed making music with them; Sue Miliffe worked on their PE, games and swim-

**The First Pre-Preparatory Pupils, September 1992**

| | |
|---|---|
| Year 2 | Kate Pellereau |
| Year 1 | Alastair Cook |
| | William Martin |
| | Elizabeth Scarrott |
| | Nicholas Sword |
| Reception | Daniel Akenhead |
| | Lucas Bliss |
| | Charlotte McElhinney-Kent |
| | Michael Phillips |
| | Charlotte Scarrott |
| | Kyle Stovold |
| | Thomas Sword |

Alexander Allen joined Year 2 and Thomas Furnish the Reception class the following January, while Sian Darch-Hopkins joined Year 1 and Matthew Constaninou the Reception Class in April 1993.

ming; and Rosie Phillips taught some Science and Geography. There was a nativity play, a sports day and a concert. There were expeditions to the Troughtons' farm at Tredington and to the Cotswold Wildlife Park. Numbers gradually increased.

It became evident that September 1993 would see a department of 26 children and a head of department was needed. Hilary Crofts was leaving to be married; Viv Troughton was needed to spend more time with Year 5 in the main Junior School. Margaret Lehane was appointed as the first Head of Pre-Preparatory, having had valuable experience at Orley Farm Pre-Preparatory near Harrow, Middlesex. Jane Oke was appointed to the department and Rosie Phillips continued to teach some science, too – later, she was to teach full-time. Further occasions began to occur in the pre-preparatory year, such as Harvest Thanksgiving and Mothering Sunday and as well as a Sports Day there was also a Swimming Sports. However, numbers did not seem to be expanding as hoped or predicted, barely reaching 28 by Michaelmas 1994.

As the academic year progressed, it became evident that numbers would probably not alter a great deal. In the end, it was decided that, although the Head of Department was a good and sympathetic teacher, the department needed a rather more robust, although equally kind, leader and so Sue Bennett succeeded Margaret Lehane as Head of Department in September 1995.

Three things immediately struck Sue Bennett. Firstly, there was a real need to expand downwards to include a Kindergarten class; secondly, that the learning environment had to be brighter, more child-friendly and more stimulating; and thirdly, that there was virtually no paperwork about curriculum or much else, a situation that had to be rectified swiftly. However, there was Pre-Preparatory Sports Day, which was always popular: '…I always used to love Sports Day, with its dressing-up races, egg and spoon races and sack races…' remembered one former Squirrel from the period, Philippa Martin, '…it was such fun…'.

Assemblies were, and remain, important. Whilst Pre-Preparatory were in their old haunts around the Langhorne Hall, the top two Pre-Preparatory years joined in with the junior members of the main Junior School on Thursday mornings when they had their own special assembly.

Margaret Lehane with Daniel Akenhead

**Mrs Sue Bennett, Head of Pre-Preparatory 1995-2003, Headmistress 2003-present**

Sue Bennett was educated at Colston's Collegiate School, Bristol. Her teacher training was at Dudley College of Teacher Training at the University of Birmingham. Subsequently, she taught at Coaley Village School near Dursley, Gloucestershire having had experience working in a voluntary capacity in local schools and clubs and also for some charities. She took some years out to have her children (James, who is now a teacher himself, and Catherine, who is a probation officer), after which she taught in several schools with varied age ranges up to 11 year olds before joining Wycliffe College Pre-Preparatory Department in 1989. She came to Dean Close Junior School as Head of the Pre-Preparatory Department in 1995 and was appointed the first Headmistress in 2003.

Sue Bennett was a founding member of the IAPS Pre-Preparatory Heads' Advisory Group in 1997 and continues to sit on its committee. She was its Co-Chair 2006-07, organizing the annual conference of 250 Heads of Pre-Preps that year, spread over several days. She has been an Independent Schools' Inspector since 1998 and was elected to membership of IAPS (Incorporated Association of Preparatory Schools) in November 2006.

Michaelmas 1995 began with 27 pupils. It took considerable discussion and a visit to another pre-preparatory to convince other senior staff of the new Head of Department's proposal to introduce a Kindergarten year. The Kindergarten class appeared in 1996. By Trinity 1997, Ian and Margaret Ferguson's last term, the Pre-Preparatory was well over 40 pupils with 60 expected the following term. The decision to change the Head of Department, though painful, had been vindicated.

Stephen Baird, the new Junior School Headmaster, and his wife Liz, who was herself infant teacher trained, were both very supportive of the Pre-Preparatory, or the Squirrels, as it increasingly came to be called.

The Reception Year was becoming rather big and so, in order to split the year-group, terrapin classrooms appeared on Hardy Lawn. With greater numbers, classroom assistants were appointed, beginning with Claire Parker in Reception in Michaelmas 1998. Annette Reynolds, the first Old Decanian to work in the Squirrels, joined the Nursery Class leader, Jane Holyfield (who had set up the class the term before) in Lent 1999, while Lesley Minchin joined the staff to fulfil a similar role with Year 1 that summer.

A Nursery Ofsted inspection praised the excellent academic, social and pastoral care standards. Things started to become somewhat cramped, and the move by the Junior School, now re-named Preparatory School, into the new Millennium Building in September 1999 allowed the Pre-Preparatory Department to take over not only the old library, which became a Pre-Preparatory staff common room, but also the old art and CDT block next door, as the Department now numbered 80 children. The same year the Department welcomed Rachel Shouksmith as an additional Year 1 teacher, and the first music specialist in Pre-Preparatory, which was always particularly helpful when there was an assembly or a production. Oral French had become a part of the curriculum for Years 1 and 2, starting in the academic year 1994-95 with specialists from the Preparatory School, although by 2007 Pre-Preparatory had their own French teacher.

The Lent Term 2000 was special, not least in that the Pre-Preparatory were invited to be an integral part of the Millennium Service in Gloucester Cathedral in January. Not only did they behave impeccably for two hours but they delighted the rest of the almost 1,000-strong congregation with their spirited rendition of *Stand Up, Clap Hands, Shout Thank You, Lord.* They also enjoyed joining in the end of the Millennium Pilgrimage which the Preparatory School walked from the School to Gloucester Cathedral. Even the smallest Squirrels walked from the edge of the Cathedral Close.

In the Lent Term 2001, the Pre-Preparatory Department reached 100 pupils. By now, two other terrapins had been brought into service, positioned at the end of the Covered Play Area, for Year 2. Such was the feeling both of optimism and of realization that most of the Pre-Preparatory classrooms were rather old and had seen better days that the Pre-Preparatory was to have its own hall in the first of a two-stage plan, and that the second stage was to build classrooms, offices and so on around the hall so that the Department could have its own purpose-built quarters. The old Caldecote stable block that had done sterling work as tuck shop for the whole School had to be demolished to make way for it. Part of Caldecote playground

**Pre-Preparatory Productions**

|  |  |
|---|---|
| Michaelmas 1992 | Nativity Play (*with Junior Forms*) |
| Michaelmas 1993 | The Very Big Turnip |
| | First Harvest |
| | Nativity Play |
| Michaelmas 1994 | Nativity Play |
| Trinity 1995 | Major Green's Garden |
| Michaelmas 1995 | Stone Soup |
| | The Little Angel |
| Trinity 1996 | A Summer Holiday |
| Michaelmas 1996 | The Gigantic Star |
| Trinity 1997 | Entertainment |
| Michaelmas 1997 | Baboushka |
| Trinity 1998 | The Time Machine |
| Michaelmas 1998 | The Grumpy Sheep |
| Trinity 1999 | Alice in Wonderland |
| Michaelmas 1999 | The Bossy Fairy |
| Trinity 2000 | Moving On |
| Michaelmas 2000 | The Best Gift of All |
| Trinity 2001 | Pinocchio |
| Michaelmas 2001 | The Shepherd Boy |
| Trinity 2002 | Snow White and the Fourteen Dwarfs |
| Michaelmas 2002 | The Little Angel |
| Trinity 2003 | Thumbelina |
| Michaelmas 2003 | The Donkey's Tale |
| Trinity 2004 | The Time Machine* |
| Michaelmas 2004 | Baboushka |
| Trinity 2005 | Alice in Wonderland |
| Michaelmas 2005 | The Broken Manger |
| Trinity 2006 | Pinocchio |
| Michaelmas 2006 | The Little Christmas Robin |
| Trinity 2007 | All Aboard the Flying Squirrel |
| Michaelmas 2007 | The Bossy Fairy |
| Trinity 2008 | Snow White and the Seven Dwarfs |
| Michaelmas 2008 | The Best Gift of All |
| Trinity 2009 | Thumbelina |

* *First performance in the new Pre-Preparatory School Hall*

Music practice for Nina Raghuram

The Pre-Prep School, viewed from Big Field, that first opened for classes in 2003

had to go, too. To add to the curriculum offered, Jo Cahill joined the Pre-Preparatory Department in Lent 2002 as the first part-time Learning Support teacher.

Soon after the Hall was completed, work began on the classrooms. During the Easter holiday in 2003, everything was moved into the new Pre-Preparatory building. This meant that Pre-Preparatory assemblies were now further away from the Preparatory School. Nevertheless, members of the Preparatory School senior management team continued to take assembly from time to time as well as members of the department's staff and others, such as the School Chaplain, the Revd Libby Talbot, and visitors from outside the Dean Close community including both the Bishop of Gloucester and the Bishop of Tewkesbury.

However, the Squirrels had to wait another year before the official opening by Professor Lord (Robert) Winston in Trinity 2004. This happened because one of the Kindergarten Class, Helena Young, was one of the children selected for the BBC documentary 20 year nature/nurture programme project *Child of Our Time* that was presented by Lord Winston. The Squirrels waited until they knew he was to come to a conference in Cheltenham and then asked if he would open the Pre-Preparatory School and he agreed.

Professor Lord (Robert )Winston at the official opening of the new Pre-Preparatory School, 2004

Meanwhile, at the end of Trinity 2003, Stephen Baird, Headmaster of the Preparatory School, left and

Mark Collier with James Hunt

Vicky Stokes at the computer with Grace Stuart

Playtime for Cerys Williams-Jones, Rufus Davies, Anabelle Wells, and Matthew Hodgkins

it was felt that the Squirrels were now large enough to warrant their own Headmistress. Sue Bennett had proved a very capable manager on numerous occasions. With a roll of around 130 and a staff of 15, the Squirrels was rapidly approaching the size that the Preparatory School was when its first Headmaster was appointed in 1949. The Trustees felt it right that Tim Hastie-Smith appoint Sue Bennett as Headmistress of the Pre-Preparatory School, thereby allowing her greater managerial freedom.

During the academic year 2003-04, Amy Naylor joined the staff as Early Years' Co-ordinator while Marion Badham, who had joined in 2001, became Key Stage One Co-ordinator. That year, the Pre-Preparatory School was awarded the Gloucestershire Quality Assurance Award in recognition of the quality of education that the Pre-Preparatory provided, the only independent school in Gloucestershire to receive it. Following that, it was among the first to be accredited with being 'Investors in Children'. About the same time, the Squirrels entered into Early Years' Partnership with Gloucestershire County Council that meant that there was local authority funding for children to come to the School up to the age of five.

Amy Leeke, Deputy Head

As a result of the Early Years Partnership, there was an Ofsted inspection in January 2005. The report was highly complimentary: '...(the School) offers high quality nursery education...leadership, management, partnership with parents and teaching across all areas of learning (are) very good...Behaviour and teamwork are excellent...staff provide a wide range of stimulating activities to help children develop in all areas of learning...'. The range of opportunities for the children and the 'excellent' levels of pastoral care were also praised.

In 2005, Amy Naylor (who married Ben Leeke OD in 2008) was appointed Deputy Headmistress and, with Sue Bennett and Marion Badham, formed the senior management team of the Pre-Preparatory School. During that year, each member of the teaching staff became responsible for an area of the curriculum.

January 2007 included the introduction of Forest School for the Squirrels on a wooded site by the Hatherley Brook, close to the

**How The Squirrels Grew**

| September | Number of Pupils |
|---|---|
| 1992 | 12 |
| 1993 | 26 |
| 1994 | 28 |
| 1995 | 27 |
| 1996 | 35 |
| 1997 | 59 |
| 1998 | 66 |
| 1999 | 78 |
| 2000 | 93* |
| 2001 | 110 |
| 2002 | 108 |
| 2003 | 113 |
| 2004 | 121 |
| 2005 | 130 |
| 2006 | 129** |
| 2007 | 136 |
| 2008 | 138 |

* In the Lent Term 2001, the Pre-Preparatory Department reached 100 pupils
** In the Trinity Term 2007, the Pre-Preparatory School reached 151 pupils.

Tuckwell Theatre. This concept, imported from Sweden, focuses on outdoor learning where children build confidence through hands-on experiences in a woodland environment. The children build bridges and shelters, learn the names of trees and wild plants and imagine amazing events that might take place there. A member of staff (Jane Baylis) is Forest School leader. At the beginning of Michaelmas that same year, with careful reallocation of space, room was found for the Squirrels to have their own computer suite, comprising 16 small-scale workstations.

Forest School site in the brook area

The Pre-Preparatory School is now usually just over 130 each Michaelmas and reaches a maximum of about 150 in Trinity as children reach an age when they can come into School initially for short, and then ever lengthening, periods.

In the brook area

# Chapter 18

## Old Decanians and The Old Decanian Society

The first boy to leave Dean Close Memorial School and so, arguably, the first Old Decanian, was A.H. Lewin from London, possibly one of the group that followed W.H. Flecker to Cheltenham from his old school in London. A.H. Lewin was one of the oldest of the founding boys, being almost 16 when he arrived for the opening term in May 1886. He left at the end of the same year but sadly is said to have died shortly afterwards. 13-year-old E.S. Jones left at the end of Lent Term 1887 to go to Uppingham and the first leaving group, of three, left at the end of that Trinity.

**Honorary Secretaries of The Old Decanian Society**

| | |
|---|---|
| 1891-1894 | G.B. Webb |
| 1895-1896 | S.W. Jose |
| 1896-1898 | A.C. Gardiner |
| 1898-1899 | E.S. Vickers |
| 1899-1906 | A.N. Smith |
| 1906-1910 | H.I. Jones |
| 1910-1913 | E.W. Willett |
| 1913-1915 | J. Price |
| 1915-1917 | H.I. Jones |
| 1917-1920 | The Revd T.H. Senior |
| 1920-1923 | F.J. Phillips |
| 1923-1927 | E.W. Willett |
| 1927-1957 | E.S. Hoare |
| 1957-1973 | C.P. Lynam |
| 1973-1974 | C.J. Buckett |
| 1974-1981 | J.N. Fuller-Shapcott |
| 1981-1988 | Miss J. Gibbs (now Mrs Pritchard) |
| 1988-1989 | Miss V Robertson (now Mrs Crawley) |
| 1989-1992 | R.C. Padfield |

*Between 1896 and 1957, the Hon Secretary of the Society was also the Hon Treasurer.*

*From 1987 an OD office was established at the School. Sally Hill was the first of a number to provide part-time professional secretarial support to the Society. 2006-09 that support was provided by Sylvia Klemz, (formerly a PA to the Preparatory School's Headmaster) who was designated OD Secretary, as were predecessors. Some of the other former OD Honorary Secretary functions are presently undertaken by the OD Registrar.*

However, forming an association for former pupils began in 1891, five years after the School's opening. That summer there was the first cricket match of Past versus Present – the School (the Present) winning – followed by a dinner. What occurred is recounted by R.F. McNeile: '...the Old Boys then present decided to form an association; no rules seem to have been made, except that members should agree to pay an annual subscription of two shillings and sixpence [£6.25]. G.B. Webb, then a medical student at Guy's Hospital, was elected secretary...'.

The association's first annual dinner was held that winter at the Holborn Restaurant, London. The first issue of what was to become *The Decanian* suggests that it took place both on Tuesday 6th December, 1891 and Wednesday 6th January, 1892, depending whether you read page 17 or page 31. The balance of probabilities is that it was the latter rather than the former. Seventeen Old Boys were present, plus the Headmaster, Dr Flecker, who was in the chair, and five members of staff, the Revd J.H. Harvey together with Messrs Green, Pargiter, Cooper and Tugwell.

Although he said that he had come unprepared to make a speech, Dr Flecker nevertheless made suggestions as to what the objects of an Old Boys' association might be. First, it should support the School. If this was to include sending pupils, then he asked them to ensure that such boys were '...upright and clean-minded...'. Secondly, he asked them to support the School magazine, the first edition of which was about to be published. He suggested, too, that membership of the association should be tied in with subscription to the magazine and a combined subscription of three shillings and sixpence was introduced (£6). The Old Boys were to look upon the magazine as their '...means of intercourse with the School and with one another...'. Thirdly, he asked Old Boys to help one another, especially if one of them was in distress. Lastly, he asked that Old Boys '...muster in strong force at the School on Speech Day...' because present boys liked it, as did parents, governors and the Fleckers themselves. Interestingly, none of the original pupils was on the provisional committee, although

**Presidents of The Old Decanian Society**

| | | | |
|---|---|---|---|
| 1894-1913 | The Revd Dr W.H. Flecker | 1958-1960 | Major Gen W.A. Dimoline |
| 1913-1921 | T.M.A. Cooper | 1960-1962 | Rear Adml E.L. Tottenham, RN |
| 1921-1926 | Dr N.H.M. Burke | 1962-1963 | Capt R.H. Johnson, RN |
| 1926-1927 | E. Ellam | 1963-1964 | A.S. Dick |
| 1927-1928 | E.W. Willett | 1964-1965 | W.A.M. Edwards |
| 1928-1929 | F.G. Smallwood | 1965-1966 | E.S. Hoare |
| 1929-1930 | P. Bolton | 1966-1967 | D. Powell |
| 1930-1931 | I.D. Yeaman | 1967-1968 | Lt Col R.J.H. Gaunt |
| 1931-1932 | A.C. Iredale | 1968-1969 | H.C. Neill |
| 1932-1933 | The Revd W.T. Money | 1969-1972 | Grp Capt P.H. Gibbings |
| 1933-1934 | E. Dodd | 1972-1974 | Dr L.M.J. Kramer |
| 1934-1935 | W.H. Nicholls | 1974-1976 | G.M. Metcalf |
| 1935-1936 | Dr F.J. Lidderdale | 1976-1978 | C.P. Lynam |
| 1936-1937 | The Revd R.F. McNeile | 1978-1981 | Major D.J.G. Howarth |
| 1938-1939 | The Revd R.P. Dodd | 1981-1982 | J.H. Lawrence |
| 1939-1946 | C.G. Tottenham | 1982-1984 | A.D. Lewis |
| 1947-1949 | H.E. Newnham | 1984-1986 | Sir John Leonard |
| 1949-1950 | H. Elder | 1986-1990 | The Rt Revd J.D. Wakeling |
| 1950-1952 | The Revd A.J. Wilcox | 1990-1993 | Prof. D.K. Fieldhouse |
| 1952-1953 | The Revd D.F. Horsefield | 1993-1995 | Dr A.G. Blyth |
| 1953-1955 | A.N. Gilkes | 1995-1997 | M.P.L. Wright |
| 1955-1957 | W.A.M. Edwards | 1997-2005 | Prof. R.J.W. Evans |
| 1957-1958 | The Rt Revd S.F. Allison | 2005-2009 | R.C. Padfield |

*The Revd Dr W.H. Flecker formally became the first President in 1894 but had effectively fulfilled that role certainly since 1892, being 'in the chair' at dinners.*

*W.A.M. Edwards is the only OD to have been President twice, from 1955-57 and again from 1964-1965. E. Dodd and the Revd R.P. Dodd and C.G. and Rear Adml E.L. Tottenham are two sets of brothers who have been President. Four Headmasters have also been President as have three members of staff not originally Old Decanians, T.M.A. Cooper, E. Ellam, and W.H. Nicholls.*

*While female Old Decanians have been Honorary Secretary, Honorary Treasurer and Honorary Assistant School Secretary, the first female President has yet to be elected.*

**Honorary Treasurers of The Old Decanian Society**

| | |
|---|---|
| 1891-1895 | H.C. Ballance |
| 1895-1898 | A.C. Gardiner |
| 1898-1899 | E.S. Vickers |
| 1899-1906 | A.N. Smith |
| 1906-1910 | H.I. Jones |
| 1910-1913 | E.W. Willett |
| 1913-1915 | J. Price |
| 1915-1917 | H.I. Jones |
| 1917-1920 | The Revd T.H. Senior |
| 1920-1923 | F.J. Phillips |
| 1923-1927 | E.W. Willett |
| 1927-1963 | E.S. Hoare |
| 1963-1966 | J.N. Fuller-Shapcott |
| 1966-1973 | C.J. Buckett |
| 1973-1974 | J.K. Barker |
| 1974-1978 | A.R.M. Milne |
| 1978-1980 | C.J. Buckett |
| 1980-1981 | Miss J. Gibbs (now Mrs Pritchard) |
| 1981-1982 | M.A. Girling |
| 1982-1983 | C.J. Buckett |
| 1983-1991 | T.H. Lavis |
| 1991-present | I.M. Bassett-Smith |

*The Hon Treasurer is the only position in the OD Society that has existed throughout its history.*

**School Secretaries and Registrars of The Old Decanian Society**

| | |
|---|---|
| 1957-1968 | E.S. Hoare |
| 1968-1969 | A.S.R. Parker |
| 1969-1979 | M.A. Girling/R.C. Padfield |
| 1979-1981 | M.A. Girling/R.C. Padfield/Miss P. Rowles (now Mrs Baillie) |
| 1979-1981 | (R.H. Fraser acted as a separate Registrar) |
| 1981-1982 | M.A. Girling/R.H. Fraser |
| 1982-1987 | M.A. Girling |
| 1987-2009 | R.C. Padfield |

**Deputy Presidents/Chairmen of The Old Decanian Society**

| DEPUTY PRESIDENTS | | CHAIRMEN | |
|---|---|---|---|
| 1967-1968 | H.C. Neill | 1981-1988 | H.F. Wickham |
| 1968-1969 | J.M. Fitton | 1988-1989 | T.R. Morgan |
| 1969-1970 | T.F. Cannon | 1989-1991 | C.P. Lynam |
| 1970-1971 | Dr L.M.J. Kramer | 1991-1993 | Dr A.R. Bailey |
| 1972-1974 | G.M. Metcalf | 1993-2001 | P.D. Gaine |
| 1974-1976 | C.P. Lynam | 2001-present | N.R. Akerman |
| 1976-1978 | Major D.J.G. Howarth | | |
| 1978-1991 | J.H. Lawrence | | |
| 1981-1982 | A.D. Lewis | | |

three, A.J. Hopkins, C.S. Murray and E.S. Vickers were members of what was then the Dean Close Society by September 1892. However, four members of the provisional committee, including G.B. Webb, the first Honorary Secretary, and H.C. Ballance, the Honorary Treasurer, came the second term, Michaelmas 1886. Apart from committee members, it was not until 1957, when E.S. Hoare gave up part of his many-faceted role as both Honorary Secretary and Treasurer, that the position of School Secretary and Registrar was begun so that a direct link with the School could be maintained and a particular eye kept on what was happening to the membership, not only in terms of numbers but also the constant attempt to keep up with changes of address and generally keeping in touch. The position of Deputy President was introduced in 1967, evolving into the position of Chairman at the beginning of the 1980s.

The first membership list was issued in the September 1892 *Dean Close Memorial School Magazine* and contained 38 names. One pressing matter was what Old Boys should call themselves. There had been a range of suggestions, including Old Closians, Old Franciscans (after Francis Close), Old Dean Closians and Old Decanians. By April 1894, the Cambridge University branch of the Society were referring to themselves as 'Cambridge Decanians'. In the same issue of *The Dean Close Memorial School Magazine* – April 1894 – a correspondent calling himself 'Decanian', suggested that the school magazine should also be called *'The Decanian'*. This was adopted, with the first issue in January 1895. The first time the term 'Old Decanian' was used was in the first letter from Durham University (as opposed to the regular letters from Oxford and Cambridge) to the School Magazine in June 1895. It was not until 1896 that the 'Old Boys' Society' was dropped in favour of 'Old Decanian Society'. However, no formal announcement was made until June that year when

OD Dinner in Cambridge in 1906, Dr Flecker presiding

Jeremy Winter,
OD Cricket secretary

it appears very much at the tail end of the London meeting. The Old Decanians decided on their blazer in 1898. '...The colours chosen were cardinal in broad stripes, and cream in narrower stripes, separated by black lines...'.

Cricket having already started between the School and the Old Boys, football soon followed, the first match played in December 1892, when the School won 9-2. However, the School side contained four members of staff, who apparently did not tire as quickly as the Old Boys did! In 1899, Old Decanians began their General Knowledge Paper, open to the whole School as a competition, won that first year by the tragic, gifted R.G. Brooke who was so soon to die in the Boer War. Although he won easily, he only amassed half marks. He was given two '...handsome volumes...' of Ruskin and the ODs also gave a cup for the Mile event in the Athletic sports.

The Society itself had gone through a difficult phase, for example only attracting 13 to its Annual Dinner in 1899, having entertained 35 three years earlier. It was A. Niemann Smith, elected Honorary Secretary in 1899, who with two who followed him, H.I. Jones and E.W. Willett, gave life to the Society. A.N. Smith later vividly recounted the situation when he was elected Honorary Secretary: '...I had to take over what can only be described as a more or less moribund concern. From my predeces-

The gathering to celebrate 100 years of hockey

sors I received no Minute Book, no list of members, no constitution or rules or funds – nothing, in fact, except the name…'.

Membership barely seemed to exist. However, a businesslike committee began to have an effect; by 1902 the Society numbered 147 and by 1905 had reached 218. From there on it gradually grew. In 2009, the Old Decanian Society was in touch with approximately 3,500 worldwide, there being many more who had lost contact.

As the OD Registrar and Secretary of the Endowment Fund, Mike Girling did much work behind the scenes in preparation for the centenary celebrations in 1986. He edited a collection of essays on the history of the School – *The First Hundred Years* – with Sir Leonard 'Joe' Hooper, a former Chairman of Governors, and his preparation was such that he came across and stored away numbers of papers, letters, documents and other ephemera that were to become the beginning of the present archives collection. He was the first to attempt to make a systematic record of key appointments among the staff and senior boys.

The Old Decanian Society has done far more than be a point of contact for former members of the School. It has had regional branches – brainchild of H.E. Newnham – in South Wales, the North West, North East, Midlands, East Midlands, London, and Reading and District as well as having overseas contacts around the globe. It has played the School at a number of sports – rugby, cricket, shooting, hockey and tennis (both boys and girls), netball, sailing and water polo and has sometimes raised teams to play other opponents. Old Decanians play a significant role as Governors and Trustees of the School, currently notably C.J. Buckett and C.P. Lynam who have both, together with various offices in the OD Society, contributed over 40 years each. Cecil Buckett's contribution included 22 years as School Treasurer. Old Decanians also award a prize for service in the Preparatory School and travel bursaries in the Senior School. The Society supports Tewkesbury Abbey Schola Cantorum with an Old Decanian Choral Scholarship. It has always sought to support the School in building ventures from the end of the

First World War when the present School Chapel was built largely in memory of Old Decanians who had fallen, right through to the present day. In recent years, Old Decanians have contributed both information and artefacts to the School's archives, and some have been able to assist present-day Decanians over their choice of career. One or two Decanians have reached a ripe old age, the first Decanian known to reach his century was George J. Money on 27th March, 1976, having come to the School in Michaelmas 1988 aged 12; he died in December 1976.

Naturally, Old Decanians have followed a variety of careers, and what follows must be a comparatively arbitrary selection of what ODs have done. According to research undertaken by Lucy Smith, Assistant Archivist, among those whose career choices have been known, over the years careers in business particularly, teaching and academia and in the finance sector have become more popular, while the Armed Forces and the Church have lost ground.

Quite a few Old Decanians have made their careers within schools. H.G. Mullens was headmaster of Lord William School, Thame and also the Royal Masonic School, Bushey; The Revd Preb. E.E.F. Walters founded St Chad's Cathedral School, Lichfield; B.S. Raine was headmaster of the Red House Preparatory School, Norton-on-Teesdale for 35 years, while Rupert Lane was headmaster of Monmouth School before becoming headmaster of Ridley College, described by some as the 'Eton of Canada', and R.H. Perry was headmaster of Ashbury College, Ottawa. W.E. Morgan was headmaster of Mbeya School, in present-day Tanzania in the 1960s, for five years H.C. Neill was headmaster of Achimota College on the Gold Coast, and Mike Bawden became headmaster of Peterhouse School, Zimbabwe in 1993. Christopher Reeve ran a Language School in Granada in Spain. There have also been others, such as Christopher Schneider and Peter Court-Hampton, who became heads of primary schools in this country, or Duncan Harper who has been headteacher in a school for pupils with behavioural difficulty in South East London since 1994.

Moving to higher education, there have been a number who have carved out distinguished university careers, notably Professor Andrew Goudie, a Geographer, who became Master of St Cross College,

**Known Broad Career Choices made by Old Decanians**

| OCCUPATION | 1910-12 | 1935-37 | 1960-62 | 1985-87 | | |
|---|---|---|---|---|---|---|
| | % | % | % | | % | |
| | | | | M | F | T |
| Armed Forces | 74.9 | 25.5 | 6.4 | 4.9 | 1.6 | (6.5) |
| Doctors/Dentists/Vets | 4.8 | 19.5 | 10.6 | 3.2 | 4.9 | (8.1) |
| Clergy/Missionaries/Church | 3.9 | 9.8 | 3.3 | 1.6 | 0 | (1.6) |
| Lawyers/Govt Offices | 4.8 | 3.7 | 10.6 | 1.6 | 1.6 | (3.2) |
| Accounts/Finance/Banking | 2.9 | 7.3 | 10.6 | 11.3 | 0 | (11.3) |
| Agricultural | 1.9 | 4.9 | 13.8 | 4.9 | 1.6 | (6.5) |
| Architects/Designers/Scientists | 1.9 | 11.0 | 8.5 | 9.7 | 1.6 | (11.3) |
| Business | 3.9 | 14.6 | 26.6 | 24.0 | 11.3 | (35.3) |
| Teachers/Academic | 1.0 | 3.7 | 9.6 | 1.6 | 8.1 | (9.7) |
| PA/Secretarial | - | - | - | - | 6.5 | (6.5) |
| | 100.0 | 100.0 | 100.0 | | (100.0) | |

Note: The numbers of those who did not know – or we could not find out – their career choices rose as a percentage each time the calculations were made. Thus the earlier the figure, the more accurate it will be, as those who had not chosen (or chose not to say) in 1910-12 were about a quarter of the whole group, whereas by 1985-87, this had risen to about three-quarters. *Source: OD Directories and the Decanian*

Professor Robert Evans

Oxford in 2003, thus far the School's only head of an Oxbridge College. Professor G.H. Luce of Rangoon College, a poet, was a member of the Kanchenjunga Expedition of 1914. He came to be '...generally recognized...' as the world authority on Burma and its neighbouring areas of South East Asia, India and China. After his death in 1979, his important library became part of the Australian National Library, Canberra. Another distinguished academic is the historian, Professor Robert J.W. Evans, FBA, Regius Professor of Modern History at Oxford since 1997. Of his several books, *The Making of the Hapsburg Monarchy* (1979) won the Wolfson Literary Award for History in 1980 and the Anton Gindely Preis (Austria) in 1986. Professor Peter King has been Professor of History at the Open University since 2004. Professor Francis J. Berry was Professor of English Literature at Sheffield and from 1970-80, Professor of English Language and Literature at Royal Holloway College, London, retiring as emeritus professor. Apart from his academic achievements, he also published his poetry in a number of volumes beginning with *Gospel of Fire* (1933) through to *From the Red Fort* (1984); his *Collected Poems* appeared in 1994; he also wrote radio plays, a novel and several critical works. Anthony Faulkes is currently Professor Emeritus of Old Icelandic at the University of Birmingham while Piers Chapman is Professor and Head of the Department of Oceanography at the Texas A&M University. Professor Alan Milton, an educationist, served the University of Rhodesia and subsequently the University of Ulster until 1975. Professor Christopher Brown of the Royal Academy of Music is also a composer, particularly noted for his sacred music and in 1976 was the first British composer to win the Monaco Composition Prize against entries from 26 countries. Ian Eales-White became Professor in Performing Arts, Chicago and Professor Noel Witts is Professor of the same subject area at De Montfort University in this country. Professor Richard D. Russell was Professor of Furniture Design at the Royal College of Art.

At one stage in 1970 the School boasted three Professors of Pathology at the same time – Professor G.C. Cunningham (Medical College of Virginia), Professor J.N.P. Davis (Albany Medical College, New York) and Professor C.V. Harrison (Royal Postgraduate Medical School, London). Professor Harrison was described in *The Times* obituary as '...one of the most distinguished pathologists of his generation...' being a founder Fellow of the Royal College of Pathologists, a Fellow of the Royal College of Physicians and the man who set up a department of Pathology at the University of Nigeria as its first Professor after he had officially retired in 1972. Professor James Turnbull became a Clinical Professor of Psychiatry in Johnson City, Tennessee.

Dr Denis Burkitt

Such academic posts serve as a reminder of the contribution numerous Old Decanians have made to medicine. Among those of particular interest, Dr Denis Burkitt CMG, FRS, not only discovered what came to be known as Burkitt's Lymphoma but also a cure while working in Africa. Later, he realized the importance of fibre in the diet and became known as 'the fibre man'; among many other awards, he received the Gold Medal of the General Medical Council in 1978; he received degrees from six universities in four different countries, wrote six books and 300 articles. Dr Cyril Davies was as modest and humble as Denis Burkitt and he, too, went to the Third World but to the jungles of Paraguay where, with two other doctors, he founded and built the Primavera Hospital – 'the hospital in the wilderness'. Built by hand from local materials, it was entirely stocked with equipment supplied by American charities. Eventually he was asked to run the medical services in the southern city of Encarnacion, and later moved to a town in Eastern Paraguay where he retired at the age of 80; he has been called 'South America's Schweitzer'. Another OD doctor whose contribution was international was Dr Gerald Webb, described in one article as 'America's leading authority on tuberculosis,' who represented the USA at international congresses on the subject in Paris, Rome and London and was President of the American Association of Physicians in 1939. The Gerald B. Webb Memorial Building was added to the medical centre of the University of Colorado in 1954.

A. Dighton Stammers, Professor of Physiology at Witwatersrand University from 1927-49, eventually became Dean of the Faculty of Medicine, St John's College, Cambridge. Dr N.H.M. Burke OBE was a distinguished psychiatrist who ran Cell Barnes Hospital Colony near St Albans and was a member of the Standing Advisory Committee on Mental Health for over 20 years, while Sir Alexander Ewing, at Manchester University, did much for the deaf. G.W.M. Findlay was in the RAMC in the First World War and subsequently did much pathology work for Imperial Cancer Research and research for the Wellcome Research Institute; in the Second World War he was a Brigadier in the RAMC in West Africa; it appears that he was awarded a military CBE in the First World War – and then a civilian CBE in 1935! Col John Holman MC was both in the RAMC and later in the TA as a medical adviser to the Department of Health and Social security. He won his MC at Cassino, Italy.

Among surgeons, Sir Bernard Ribeiro CBE was elected President of the Royal College of Surgeons in 1998. J.M. Fitton MBE was a consultant orthopaedic surgeon in Wakefield who, after the Second World War, spent three years in Mauritius developing a hospital for polio sufferers. He spent 25 years at St James' Hospital, Leeds.

Sir Bernard Ribeiro

Anthony Davies was a Consultant Radiologist at Abergavenny. E. Fowler became consultant Anaesthetist at St Bartholomew's Hospital, London and later at the Kent and Sussex Hospital.

In dentistry, perhaps the most distinguished OD has been Sir Rodney Swiss OBE who became President of the General Dental Council in 1975. For four years while his brother was President, Kenneth G. Swiss, (also an Old Decanian), was Chairman of the General Dental Council, possibly a unique double.

In ophthalmology, F.A. Burnett-Hodd was awarded the First Research Medal of the British Optical Association in the 1950s. F.A.B. Hodd was a Consulting Optician and a Fellow of the Spectacle Makers Company who had a strong involvement in the advance of contact lens development. He was President of the British Optical Association twice, from 1968-69 and 1977-78. Dominic Tunnell is a Dispensing Optician specializing in partially sighted children and adults and has strong links with the RNIB College in Worcester where a former DCS housemaster, B.O. Bradnack, became headmaster in 1929.

Veterinary Science ODs have included H.H. Skinner, who was awarded the J.T. Edwards Memorial Medal for '...outstanding work in the field of Virology...' over 25 years at the Research Institute (Animal Virus Diseases) at Pirbright in Surrey. Peter Darke held a senior academic post at Edinburgh for 25 years before becoming a Home Office veterinary adviser.

Among health and hospital administrators, George Lister was Chairman of the Management Committee '...for the city and county of Gloucestershire...' in the 1960s.

In a related field, Dr V.P. Whittaker has been Director of Scientific Research in Gottingen at the Max Planch Institute, the first Englishman to be so honoured. In 1978 he was given the American Philosophical Society's Carl Spencer Lashley Award for his contribution to Neurobiology.

In the legal profession, the Honorary H.A.D. Oliver became a Supreme Court Judge in Vancouver, receiving *en route* the Cross of Merit (First Class) from the Federal Republic of Germany for his legal services to the German Consulate in Vancouver and later receiving from the French President the Ordre National du Merite in the rank of Chevalier for juridical services to France. Sir John Leonard was a High Court Judge of the Queen's Bench Division in the early 1980s. Stuart McKinnon is currently a High Court Judge, too. Richard McGregor-Johnson became a Circuit Judge around the turn of this century. Sir Ian Yeaman was President of the Law Society as well as a long term committed Governor of the School, being Chairman of the Executive 1939-49 and again from 1959-66. Sir Arthur Weston, CBE, was another distinguished solicitor who eventually became Legal Advisor to the Ministry of Agriculture and Fisheries after the Second World War. There have been a large number of ODs who have become solicitors and several have also contributed to local government, such as Lewis Rose OBE in Derby.

Few Old Decanians have ventured into politics. The exception has been Robert Moreland, who was Conservative MEP for Stafford East 1986-98. A management consultant, he was also a member of Westminster City Council 1990-98 and its Conservative Chief Whip 1993-94.

In the Armed Services, Rear Admiral C.L. Tottenham CB, OBE, RN was a Paymaster for 43 years in the Royal Navy and spent so long in the water after his ship, HMS Fiji, was sunk during the evacuation of Crete during the Second World War that his health was permanently affected. Later, he was both President of the Old Decanian Society and Deputy Lord Lieutenant of Hampshire. Commander H.N.A. Richardson DSO, DSC commanded a gunboat in the Yangste River during the Chinese Civil War; he won the Gold Award of the Royal Humane Society for successfully rescuing a sailor who had been washed overboard in stormy weather. Commander J.M. Lefeaux was a pilot and Engineer Officer specializing in aircraft; leaving the Royal Navy in 1966, he joined British Rail Hovercraft, eventually becoming Managing Director, and wrote a book on the history of the hovercraft. The distaff side is also represented in the Royal Navy, such as Claire (Bayley) Harding, who entered in 1976, and was later awarded a Reserve Decoration, not only for her work in the Royal Navy but also later in the Royal Naval Reserve.

Possibly the senior Royal Marine from Dean Close School has been Col Jake Hensman, OBE who is currently also a Deputy Lord Lieutenant in Scotland.

In the Army, ODs have included Lt-Col P.F. Bodvan-Griffiths, who supplied arms to Resistance Movements in occupied countries during the Second World War, becoming Chief Patriot Officer to the Allied Military Government of Venezia Giulia near Trieste, Italy, in 1945. Another in the same mould was Col E.C. 'Pick' Pickard who won the Norman Medal while at Sandhurst, served 18 years in the Indian Army with the Frontier Force Rifles, winning the DSO in Slim's offensive to retake Burma, largely at the Battle of Kanlan Ywathit, and subsequently served for 14 years in the Royal Artillery after Indian independence in 1947. There were also the exploits of Major R.C. Pringle, a Signals officer, in Wingate's special force, the Chindits. He was one of only ten survivors from one escapade 150 miles behind Japanese lines, and in another incident, had the extraordinary experience of discovering that a line which his party had just laid was connected to a Japanese exchange, and for ten days, important information was gathered.

Perhaps the most distinguished military man from Dean Close School was Major General W.A. Dimoline CB, CMG, CBE, DSO, MC. He served in France during the First World War where he won his MC, in India and notably in East Africa, culminating in the Madagascar campaign of 1942. In the latter stages of the Second World War, he commanded a brigade in Burma. He retired from the army in 1953, becoming Secretary of the Inter-Parliamentary Union for Commonwealth Governments in 1954. In 1962 he was also appointed Secretary of the Overseas Organization of the Duke of Edinburgh's Award Scheme. He was a Life Governor of Dean Close School.

In a letter to *The Decanian News* in 1993, Major Stephen Oxlade – later Colonel – in the Glosters, remarked upon Dean Close School connections with the Glosters, there being at least three other officers who were also ODs in the same regiment with him. He was followed as CO of the 2nd battalion, Royal Gloucester, Berkshire and Wiltshire Regiment, by another OD, Mike Motum. Lt-Col Sir Geoffrey Inkin OBE left the Army in order to pursue a second career in public service, notably as Head of the Cardiff Bay Development Agency. Jonathan Cook reached the rank of Brigadier before retiring in 2002, while Captain David Wilkins was awarded an MBE (Military) in 2004. Charles Letchworth retired from the Army in 1986 and then spent 11 years as a Queen's Messenger. B.K. Martin rose to be Officer Commanding the 4th Parachute Regiment before becoming a manager of the Humanitarian Division of Christian Aid, responding to emergencies and crises around the world which to date has included working in Darfur and in the aftermath of the Asia earthquake of 2005.

In the Royal Air Force, one of two utterly outstanding officers was Air Vice-Marshal S.O. Bufton CB, DFC a significant contributor to the forming of the Pathfinders in the Second World War. In *The Times* obituary, it noted that '...It was widely believed that Bufton, a quiet, unostentatious man, might have climbed higher, but for his refusal to compromise his beliefs...'. He had also been an international hockey player, a championship boxer and diver with a golfing handicap of five. He became High Sheriff of Radnorshire in 1966. The other outstanding officer was Wing Commander Geoffrey Page DSO, OBE, DFC and Bar, a Battle of Britain pilot who was horrifically injured but largely restored by the work of the celebrated plastic surgeon Sir Archibald MacIndoe. Geoffrey Page eventually went back to war, achieving a total of 15 kills, before breaking his back, necessitating more operations. He is said to have undergone at least 40 operations. He was the first chairman of the Guinea Pig Club, whose membership was only open to those who had been treated by Sir Archibald at the Queen Victoria Cottage Hospital, East Grinstead. He was the founder of the Battle of Britain Trust that raised £1m, with which the Battle of Britain memorial overlooking the Straits of Dover was erected. He died in 2000. Others have joined the Royal Air Force since, such as Wing Commander John Worrell.

A pacifist Oxford graduate who speaks Hebrew and Arabic, Emma Sky worked for the British Council in Jerusalem, Kabul and Gaza. After the fall of Saddam Hussein she volunteered for the Foreign and Commonwealth Office's administration team in Iraq, having been strongly opposed to the war. Through meeting General Odierno, eventually Commander of US forces in Iraq, she became his political adviser. As a result she claimed: 'I know that I have prevented loss of life on numerous occasions'. An expert on development and reconciliation, she so influenced US military policy that the *Times* described her as '...potentially the most influential Briton in the country...'. She was appointed MBE in 2003 and OBE in 2008.

As a young member of the Indian Police, Sir Philip Vickery CIE, OBE witnessed the Delhi Durbar of 1911 attended by the King-Emperor George V. He served in both world wars, after which he worked in the War Office and later in the Commonwealth Relations Office, not retiring until 1965. K.R.T. Goodale spent much of his time in various police forces abroad. He finally became Senior Superintendent of Police in the Royal Hong Kong Police Force. Also in the Royal Hong Kong Police was Henry Heath CMG, QPM, CPM, who became Commissioner in 1962.

Some ODs have joined the Metropolitan Police Force, of whom possibly the most senior to date has been Chief Inspector Neville Abraham, who served for 30 years in the latter half of the last century. James Butler is in the police on the Isle of Man. Possibly Emma Burrows is the first Dean Close girl to enter the police service; she joined West Mercia Police Force.

S. Montague Cleeve

Mike Barton is one of a few ODs who have entered Gloucestershire Police Force, eventually becoming a Chief Inspector. At one stage, as Head of Training, he found himself taking over what had been the old Wilton House in Lansdown Road, which for some years had been a part of Dean Close Junior School and in which he had had lessons as a boy! Another is Richard Cooper who was promoted Detective Chief Inspector in 2009 after fewer than 12 years in the Force.

In the arts, S. Montague Cleeve invented a new Viola d'Amore with 18 strings, which was considered a significant improvement on the traditional instrument. Its world premiére was at the Wigmore Hall in April 1962, where it was hailed by the press. On 10th November, 1964, he played it before the Queen Mother in the drawing room of St James's Palace in aid of charity.

Neil Jenkins

Organist Keri Dexter became Organist of St George's Chapel, Windsor in 1999 while Matthew Martin is organist of Westminster Cathedral.

On the classical singing front, Robert Johnston, tenor, has been a full-time member of the BBC Singers as well as doing solo work. Singer Emma Brain-Gabbott has appeared in a televised Promenade Concert as a soloist. Julie (Cooper) Vine has done much solo work and is also a member of The Sixteen and The King's Consort. In 2007, Neil Jenkins, the internationally known tenor, marked the 40th anniversary of his professional debut with a concert given by his choir, Sussex Chorus. Christopher Watson has also made his mark as a tenor soloist.

Alastair Milne was the founder of the Clarinet and Sax Society of England, himself playing in a clarinet choir when he wasn't about his day job of being a solicitor. Jessica Hayes is seen as a young but potentially distinguished cellist.

Brian Jones

Brian Jones, who attended the Junior School, became an international celebrity as a member of the 'Rolling Stones' pop group before his early tragic death in 1969. A cup for music is awarded annually in his memory in the Preparatory School.

In acting, Ernest Cossart (known as Emil von Holst at School), brother of Gustav Holst, had a remarkable career in Hollywood between 1916 and 1949, appearing in over 40 films, mostly in the 1930s and 1940s. Neil Williams, at present researching his life, has found that Ernest Cossart acted with most if not all the great stars of the era, such as Marlene Dietrich, Gary Cooper, Gladys Cooper and Humphrey Bogart to name but a few. Since then, a number of Old Decanians have tried the acting profession such as David Watson (professionally known as David Acton), Ellis Dale, who was said to be '…the finest schoolboy actor that…the vastly experienced C.A.P. Tuckwell (had) encountered…', who went to South Africa and was apparently heard of no more, and R.C. Winter (otherwise Richard Warwick), who appeared in several films directed by Franco Zeffirelli in minor roles but was probably best known for his staring role in Lindsay Anderson's *If.* He appeared in two films with Derek Jarman, *The Tempest* and *Sebastion,* was the title role in *The Breaking of Bumbo* and was in *White Hunter Black Heart* with Clint Eastwood. On the stage he was at different times a member of the National Theatre, Young Vic and Cambridge Theatre companies and was Antonio opposite Alec Guinness' Shylock at the Chichester. In 1986 he appeared at the Everyman, Cheltenham, as Higgins in *My Fair Lady.* He had several television credits and appeared as Tewkesbury author John Moore in BBC2's *The Brensham People*. More recently, there has been Hugh Quarshie, whose experience has ranged from Shakespeare to regularly appearing in the TV series *Holby City* and also as Captain Panaka, Head of the Palace Guard in the Star Wars film *The First Episode*. Frances Allberry has appeared in London's West End, and, it is said, television's *Brookside*. Currently there are a number of Old Decanians both in the United States and this country who are taking up acting as a profession.

Hugh Quarshie

Among the poets, mention has already been made of Professor Francis Berry and also Professor G.H. Luce but perhaps better known than them was James Elroy Flecker, son of the first Headmaster, whose work was cut short by his early death in 1915. However, he had already produced *A Bridge of Fire* (1907), *Thirty Six Poems* (1910) that was expanded to *Forty Two Poems* in 1911. Possibly his best known book of poems was *The Golden Road to Samarkand* (1913). *The Old Ships* was published posthumously in 1915. His *Collected Poems*, edited by J.C. Squire, was published in 1916. He also wrote a novel, *The King of Alsander* (1914) and two plays, *Hassan* and *Don Juan.* Mike Henry, who went to the Junior School in the early 1950s, has published four collections of poems, the last of which *After the Dancing Dogs* came out in 2008.

Playwrights have been few and far between, although A.L. Burke's play *Thank You, Phillips,* billed as a comedy, was produced on a London stage early in the 1920s, while Tom Kidd had his play *Samarkand* performed on BBC radio in January 1981. It portrayed the life of James Elroy Flecker and several scenes were set in Dean Close School.

It is thought that Jane Davis was the first female OD to be a published author, her *The Runes of War* being published by Harper Collins in December 1995. Amanda (McCardie) Parker was not far behind with *The Frog Ballet,* published in 1998. Eve Isherwood writes crime thrillers; her first book, *Absent Light* came out in 2007 but her publishers have decided that in future books, of which there are to be at least three, she will write under her married name of E.V. Seymour. Louisa Somerville, on the other hand, is a children's author. There are at least three male ODs who are also current authors: Richard Lyne-Pirkis published the historical novel *The Lion and the Rose* in 2007 under his *nom de plume* of Richard de Methley, while late in 2008 Naoise Rowley-Brooke, writing as Nick Brooke, published his first novel *New Head on the Block.* John Lewis's sixth book has recently been published; a previous book, *Foreman of the Bench,* includes a chapter about his years at Dean Close.

Lexicography is a minority occupation, but the current Chief Editor of the Oxford English Dictionary is OD John Simpson.

In music, mention has already been made of composer Professor Christopher Brown. Another OD who saw his setting of the Holy Communion Service (Rite A) published by Stainer and Bell was Christopher Boodle; in April 1992, his Oratorio *The Crown of Thorns* was performed in Gloucester Cathedral. John Metcalf had his opera *The Journey* performed by the Welsh National Opera at the 1981 Cheltenham Festival; he has composed for the BBC and has held Arts Fellowships in the USA and Wales.

Alistair Bland spent the first part of his career in contemporary dance before turning to social work.

The internationally acclaimed and respected artist Francis Bacon, of whom *The Times* said at his death in 1992 '…no other post-war painter transformed British art with as much energy, flair and obsessive conviction…' was described by Lord Gowrie, a former arts minister and Chairman of Sotheby's, as '…the greatest British painter since Turner…'. On the other hand, Margaret Thatcher saw him as '…that dreadful man who paints those horrible pictures…'. His work was shown in such places as New York, Tokyo, Liverpool, Paris, Moscow and Washington. It is suggested that he will be most remembered artistically for a large number of single images, at least 20 of his large

Francis Bacon

triptychs and many of his portraits. Andrew Graham-Dixon described much of his work thus: '...figures – usually male – (are) depicted as lurid agglomerations of bodily matter, raw flesh that seems on the point of putrefication. Their beauty is the beauty of rottenness...', and suggested that Francis Bacon's most famous paintings are the series of screaming heads he painted from the late 1940s onwards. His work tended to focus on the themes of sex and death, often violently expressed. Even before his death, his work commanded high prices: a 1973 triptych sold in 1989 at Sotheby's in New York for £3.75 million. Francis Bacon was said to have refused a knighthood.

Nadia Khairy was the only known OD to have made a living as a portrait artist, before her untimely death in 2007 at the age of 38.

Richard Bedford was recognized as a sculptor when he wasn't about his 'normal' job as Keeper of the Department of Sculpture and later Curator of Pictures, both at the Victoria and Albert Museum, London. He was nearly 30 when his talent as a sculptor was recognized and subsequently he exhibited a great deal. He died in October 1967.

Concerned with Wildlife Art is Lynn Burns who puts together such items for auction at Christie's.

Bishop Denis Wakeling

In the Church, fairly typical of quite a large number of early Old Decanians was the Revd R.P. Dodd, a Classical Scholar of St John's, Cambridge, who won the MC while Chaplain to the Forces in the First World War, subsequently becoming a missionary in Cawnpore; he later held a number of positions in England including that of honorary canon of Portsmouth Cathedral. The Very Revd J.E.B. Ashton was Dean of Killala, Ireland (1946-68) and was described as '...a rock of the Church of Ireland...'. The Revd Dr Jonathan Holmes, scientist and priest, was appointed Dean of Chapel at Queen's College, Cambridge in 1994.

Bishop B.M. Dale was consecrated Bishop of Jamaica in 1950, and organized the relief appeal following the Jamaican hurricane in 1951. He represented Jamaica at the Coronation in 1953. The Rt Revd W. Neville Welch was Bishop of Bradwell from 1968-73. The Rt Revd Denis Wakeling, MC, was a superb sportsman, a marine who won the MC in Corfu during the Second World War, coming out a Major, and a much-loved and hard-working Bishop of Southwell in the 1970s, as well as a School Governor. His brother, too, was in the Church.

Bishop Sherard Allison

Perhaps the family that made the greatest contribution to the Church that were all educated at Dean Close School were the four Allison brothers. The eldest, and most senior in the Church, was Sherard Allison who became Bishop of Winchester 1962-71. The second brother was Oliver Allison, Bishop in the Sudan 1953-74; the third was the Revd Canon Roger Allison, Rector of Christ Church, Jerusalem 1968-75 while the fourth was the Revd William Allison who stayed in parochial ministry in England.

The best known of all Dean Close bishops in the 21st century has been Bishop Jim Thompson, who died young, aged 67, in 2003,

Bishop Jim Thompson

latterly Diocesan Bishop of Bath and Wells, earlier Bishop of Stepney and before that Rector of Thamesmead. Throughout his ministry he was a champion of the socially deprived. Bishop Thompson was also an author and frequent BBC broadcaster. Perhaps the most brilliant scholar that the School has produced was Bishop Stephen Neill, ecumenist, missionary in India, church historian, Bishop of Tinnevelly 1939-44, and later in part responsible for some of the negotiations that resulted in the Church of South India in 1947; assistant bishop to the Archbishop of Canterbury, he wrote over 70 books, and at different times held professorships in Hamburg and Nairobi; elected FBA in 1969, he took his Cambridge DD aged 79 and held eight honorary degrees. Royalties from his books still swell the funds of Dean Close School Library, which benefitted under the terms of his will.

New expressions of church have involved Old Decanians, such as the Revd Paul Morris, Senior Minister of Tommy's Church for the Unchurched, Nottingham for some time, before becoming Director of the Australian Branch of 'Christian Witness to Israel', while others have continued to take on traditional responsibilities, such as the Revd Christopher Rowley, who became Rural Dean of Taunton in 2001. The Revd Tim Green worked at the Open Theological Seminary in Lahore but is believed to be currently leading the international congregation at St Thomas's, Church, Islamabad.

Bishop Stephen Neill

The Revd Marcus Morris OBE carved out a unique ministry in newspaper publishing. His Church career began conventionally with two curacies and incumbencies in Essex and Birkdale. Alarmed by what he saw as violent and indecent American comics flooding into Britain, he launched the *Eagle* for boys in 1950, which reached a circulation of 750,000 weekly, and was named after the design of a church lectern. It launched famous characters such as Dan Dare, Luck of the Legion and Harris Tweed and was known for its cutaway drawings. *Eagle* was soon followed by *Girl, Robin* and *Swift*, which together catered for children from the nursery through to adolescence, produced to far higher moral, intellectual and artistic standards than had been seen before, approved by both teachers and parents. Marcus moved on but without his inspiration, the *Eagle* gradually declined, merging with *The Lion* in 1967. He moved to the National Magazine Company where he later became managing director and editor-in-chief for nearly 20 years and influenced such magazines as *Harpers and Queen, The Connoisseur* and *Cosmopolitan*. He retired in 1983 and died six years later.

The Revd Marcus Morris

Not all those ordained have been into the Church of England, though that is true of the vast majority. Martin M'Caw was ordained into the Baptist Church in the 1960s, and has also done much in youth work, training and adoption work. Robert Stade is a priest in the Russian Orthodox Church Outside Russia, living in St Louis, Missouri.

Contributions to the work of the Church have not been confined to the ordained ministry. Iain Clayre, with his family, went to Borneo with the Borneo Evangelical Mission, based in Sarawak; he later obtained a Doctorate in Oriental Languages from Edinburgh University. A.L. Kensit was Secretary of the Protestant Truth Society and Editor of the Churchman's Magazine. A.G. Watts spent many of his latter years, after an earlier career in teaching, working for the Overseas Mission Fellowship in Toronto and then Nova Scotia. Andrew Clarke is a Lecturer in New Testament Studies at Aberdeen University, David Rogers worked for Mission Aviaton Fellowship in Central Africa, while Mary Grant has helped with the translation of the Bible into Bwamu. Mike Robinson did a great deal of missionary work in Zambia in the late 1990s; Heather (Clarke) Smethurst is a Clinical Research Nurse but is also youth ministries area co-ordinator for her church with 55 12-18 year-olds in her care, mostly boys. Sarah (Bastin) McCann is (part-time) worship leader at St Paul's, Hammersmith. Lay involvement in the work of the Church by Old Decanians was recognized in part in 2000 by the award of an OBE to Cliff Hodgetts for his contribution. Moreover, large numbers of ODs have filled voluntary roles within the Church, many as churchwardens, PCC members, running groups or active in pastoral or musical ministries.

Working with the disadvantaged or in charities has been something that many ODs have done, quite a few as an expression of their own Christian faith. Isaac Fisher has worked with the Weaver Clinic in Boston, USA, who work with children and adults with learning and attentional difficulties, Lucy (Tootell) Gooderham has been engaged in similar work with 11-16 year olds near Leicester, while David J. Howard was helping to run a centre for disadvantaged people in Bristol when he was sadly run over and killed at the age of 42. Richard Thomas has been Administrative Manager for the Treetops Hospice near Derby. For 20 years Gill (Munden) Cody was involved in helping 'the abused' through Christian counselling and being involved in projects in Africa and the Far East, such as building an orphanage. A rather adventurous way of supporting a charity was undertaken by Tom Fearnehough who led an expedition called Japan's 100-Mountain Trek, involving walking 4,000 miles and climbing 100 mountains in order to raise £20,000 for a charity called Adopt-A-Minefield (UK).

W.A.M. Edwards

In business, several ODs have achieved senior appointments, notably W.A.M. Edwards, who was General Manager of ICI from 1961-66 as well as being Chairman of the DCS Governors' Executive Committee 1966-73. He was a Governor for 51 years (1948-99) and was probably the School's greatest benefactor, certainly in the second half of the twentieth century.

Cecil Buckett, a fellow OD and Governor of many years' standing, has written of him '...(In) the difficult post-war years...his disciplined business approach was a major factor in ensuring the School survived...'. Through W.A.M. Edwards' very considerable generosity and foresight the Edwards' Building that today houses the Dining Hall and a classroom block became possible. He also gave substantially – hundreds of thousands of pounds – to fund scholarships. Kevan Swain has been European Sales and Development Director for the Clerical Medical Investment Group; Tim Tindle, now living in Norway, was a director of the multi-national agricultural machinery Kverneland Group; Tim Sanders was Executive Director of SBC Warburg and Ben Millington-Buck became President of Asia Equity, specializing in South East Asia stockmarkets, based in New York. Nick Mustoe was appointed in 1996 to '...to head up UK equities at Prudential Portfolio Managers, one of the world's biggest investment managers with more than £88bn under management...'. A similar world was inhabited by Simon Piney who went into investment banking, ending up as Head of Equity Capital Markets at BNP Paribas. F.E. Zollinger was a merchant banker who ended up on the Board of Lazards; he had had a very dangerous Second World War that had included at one stage being left for dead having been hit by an exploding grenade. Graham Jones was a partner in KPMG Management Consulting and spent much time in Nairobi, Algiers and latterly Paris. Tim Linford has been Chairman of Wessex Energy and Environmental Management Group and runs TJL Associates, which offers clients environmental and energy management skills.

Business at a more localised level has been the career of many ODs, including Martin Fowke, who in 1994 sent wine from his *Three Choirs Vineyard* near Newent express to Paris, in a neat reversal of wine being sent from the French vineyards to London. Another slightly unusual venture has been Adam Hodge's *Oxford Botanica*, supplying and caring for tropical plants. One local firm that has been the career of several ODs has been *Premiere Products* of Cheltenham. In 2004, the Chairman and Managing Director was Paul Hilltout, the Purchasing and Marketing Director was Richard Marquand, and the Assistant Managing Director was Andrew Marquand. Another has been *The Famous*, clothing retailers on Cheltenham High Street, whose Managing Director has been Ross N. Cole for many years. The firm also runs another shop in Exeter and 14 school shops.

Combining local business with contribution to the local community was Francis J.O. Martin, a son, father and grandfather of Decanians, who began in the family corn milling business at Tewkesbury, later founding and building up Tewkesbury Marine Services. He served for 25 years on Tewkesbury Town Council, being both Borough Mayor and Town Mayor, a JP for 26 years and Chairman of the Bench for five.

In industry, A.S. Dick was awarded the Royal Society of Arts' Benjamin Franklin Medal for 1961 for his contribution to industrial progress in the motor car industry.

In accountancy, H.F. Shapland was said to be the oldest practising Chartered Accountant in the country at his death, aged 90, having been in the profession 72 years, thus possibly also being the longest serving. In the Second World War he was in the Eighth Army at Alamein and Wadi Akarit and worked on the plans for the invasion of Normandy in 1944. A Major at 28, he was present at the German surrender on Luneberg Heath in 1945. He was awarded the Croix de Guerre with Palm, the Chevalier de l'Ordre de Leopold II with Palm and an MBE. He resumed his Accountancy career in Minehead and was a 'hobby' farmer but also founded the Minehead Barbarians Rugby Club, supported the Rotarians, the Nuffield Hospital, the Exmoor Show, being an auditor for many of them including the Old Decanian Society for some years, as well as being a JP.

In Architecture, E.U. Channon, FRIBA, was the RIBA Henry Jarvis Student in 1921 and RIBA Archibald Dawnay Scholar in 1922. His career took him to Singapore and he subsequently worked for Sir Edwin Lutyens on the New Delhi project. Later, he became Head of the School of Architecture at Plymouth, a position he held for over 20 years.

Aeronautical engineering was L.W. Nethercott's career, and he eventually rose to become Principal Inspector of Aircraft, having overseen the production of the Lancaster and Victor Bombers. In an allied, though not identical field, was the work of Alasdair Eales-White, a specialist in satellite and space communications who was awarded an OBE for his efforts.

In civil engineering, E.G. Hoare, brother of Stanley, worked on the Sydney Harbour Bridge in Australia, the high-level bridge at Newcastle-on-Tyne and was resident consultant engineer during the building of the Port Talbot Steel Works and the Spencer Steel Works, both in Wales. He also worked on projects in India. Similarly, Edward Foster was another civil engineer, who worked in Zambia and South Africa where he subsequently became a Director of LTA Construction. J.G. Wiltshire, a partner in Kennedy and Donkin, went to Uganda, Malawi, Libya and other parts of Africa building hydro-electric power stations; in 1977 he was elected to the prestigious Smeatonian Society of Civil Engineers, and was a Freeman of the City of London. Basil Montgomery, though badly wounded in the Second World War, was a successful chartered civil engineer who worked on the Snowy Mountain Hydro-Electric Scheme in Australia before being based in England. From the 1950s onwards he was particularly involved in the design of docks and harbours in the UK and abroad. He was also a Governor of the Royal National Lifeboat Institution.

Kenneth Pringle was a chartered land surveyor who undertook projects in the Sudan, Kenya, Tanzania, Libya, Nigeria and Ghana. Later, he supervised further projects in the Bahamas, Singapore, Burma and Bahrain. In 1970 he joined the Government's Joint Survey Service and was officer in charge in the West Indies. He became deputy Regional Controller in Scotland for seven years before being seconded to the Government of Malaysia as well as later working in Hong Kong and in the UK. He finally retired in 1997.

There have been several ODs in farming, especially just before and for some time after the Second World War. R.E.G. 'Bob' Finch not only farmed but bred and trained racing horses from his farm at Wiston, Suffolk. Robert Mawle, farming in Devon, is also something of a mathematician, having taken an external degree in it from Exeter University; Kate (Troughton) O'Connor farms dairy and beef on the West Coast of New Zealand's South Island; while Stuart Fuller-Shapcott not only farms in Scotland but also takes part in mountain rescue work. Mike Blanchard was a farmer in Southmoor, near Oxford and was an active member of the National Farmers' Union, holding a number of posts at national as well as local level.

H.J. Morris was a seismologist with the Royal Dutch Oil Company and travelled widely, notably in Nigeria, Borneo and the Dutch East Indies, while Martin Lednor was asked to assess the environmental impact of the trans-Russian oil pipeline in the 1990s.

Enthusing others, especially the young, in the great outdoors became the work of Col Jock Harrison OBE, who after some time with the 8th Punjab Regiment, took part in the first ever attempt on K1, losing most of his fingers and toes through frostbite. Later, he was Military Secretary and Comptroller of the Household at Government House, New Zealand, before becoming Executive Director of the New Zealand Outward Bound Trust in 1961.

George Adamson

George Adamson was best known for his work with lions, celebrated by the books *Born Free* and *Living Free* written by his wife Joy, the first subsequently being turned into a film starring Bill Travers and Virginia McKenna. The Adamsons' work inspired a whole new approach to animal conservation. There is a tree to his memory near the Bacon Theatre.

Others who have contributed to wildlife and environmental conservation include Dr H.F. Lamprey OBE who in the 1960s was Principal of the African Wildlife Management Training School in present-day Tanzania, training future African Game Wardens; later he became Director of the Serengeti Research Institute 1966-73. Then he worked for UNESCO for 11 years, after which he was the World Wildlife Fund representative for East and Central Africa.

Richard St Barbe Baker

Richard St Barbe Baker OBE was the founder of the Men of the Trees movement, the name being derived from his Swahili nickname, in 1924. He was one of the first hundred students at the new University of Saskatchewan, Canada, in 1913, where the archives of the movement are now kept. Later he studied at Cambridge University. His concern to plant trees was reinforced in his first professional job as an assistant forestry officer in Kenya in 1920. As such, he was two generations ahead of many who later realized the importance of trees to the well being of the planet. In his lifetime he was responsible for the planting of over 27,000 million trees worldwide, planted in large part as the result of his constant travelling and his meeting with government leaders. He wrote over 30 books, one of which, *Green Glory*, has been used as a standard text book in Russia for students of forestry.

In the media, R.L. Johns was in Israel as a Special Correspondent for *The Financial Times* during the 1967 Middle East War and narrowly escaped arrest by Israeli forces. He also worked in India and in Aden and was *The Financial Times* Middle East Editor 1973-82. He also completed a book started by his friend, David Holden, *The House of Sand* which received wide critical acclaim in 1980. Simon Harris won a Royal Television Society Award for Journalist of the Year in January 2003. Spencer Evans was to be heard '…every day…' on BBC Radio Gloucestershire in the late 1990s and Jason Gillot, who lives in Sweden, works in the media including freelancing for the BBC, while Simon Leung has worked for CAT FM Radio Station that serves both Cheltenham and Tewkesbury. Richard Synge is a writer, journalist and editor mainly for publications about Africa, and has links with Wolfson College and the African Studies Centre in Oxford while Stephen Cape has been the BBC Crime correspondent from the 1990s into the new millennium. Alison Stenlake is a journalist for BBC News Online and Lisa Creffield has been a foreign correspondent for *The Times* and other international news organizations working out of Sydney, Australia.

Charles Tanner has been a news cameraman in Strasbourg for a number of years. In a somewhat specialized area of the media, Charlie Parkin has been the 'man behind the microphone' at nine major racecourses.

Tim Davis runs a video/production company in Kenya and is heavily involved in that country's film industry, including wildlife productions. Jenny Dyer has spent 15 years as an art director in films and has also launched her own fashion and jewellery label.

In the world of retail, Chris Walker has been General Manager of the Marks and Spencer franchise in Gibraltar; at the same time he has been a top triathlete in Spain. In the hotel and allied industries, Alain Ridley became General Manager of the five star Princeton Hotel, Dubai in the 1990s.

Among the more unusual contributions was that of Dr O.J. Silberrad, sometime Superintendant of Research at the Royal Arsenal, Woolwich, between 1900 and 1906. He discovered how to detonate lyddite and TNT, and thus produced the high explosive shell that was introduced into the services in 1903. He discovered the cause of and a remedy for a form of erosion in ships' propellers, and as a result the entire Royal Navy and some of the world's great liners were fitted with propellers made of his bronze.

Another unconventional career was that of Dr H. Verrier Elwin, a former Vice Principal and Librarian at Wycliffe College, Oxford, who was a missionary to India. He became a disciple and close friend of Mahatma Ghandi, seeing in the British Raj the worst aspects of imperialism. He was one of two authors living in India who were awarded the Padma Bhushan for distinguished service of a high order, in his case in the field of anthropology, in 1960, having become a citizen of that country. He gave himself to working among the untouchables. He was the author of *The Muria and their Ghotul, The Religion of an Indian Tribe* and several other works. He eventually became a trusted advisor to the Indian Government.

A younger adventurer has been Adam Silver who won a Thomas Watson Fellowship in 1984 to study the sacred architecture of India and Nepal which he did for two years. He subsequently visited China, whose landscape painting he had studied and later settled in New York. Danny Edmunds has developed a career since 2003 as a photographer, diver, travel writer and boatdriver in some of the most remote parts of the world; he has driven Zodiac boats in the Indian Ocean, the Antarctic and the Arctic, worked on conservation projects in the Ecuadorian Andes and updated the Bradt Guide to Mozambique; he was

**Degree Choices made by Old Decanians**

| SUBJECT AREA | 1996/7 | | 2001/2 | | 2006/7 | |
|---|---|---|---|---|---|---|
| | **M** | **F** | **M** | **F** | **M** | **F** |
| Archaeology | 1 | 0 | 0 | 0 | 1 | 0 |
| Arts | 5 | 7 | 4 | 10 | 3 | 10 |
| Business St/Accountancy | 4 | 3 | 8 | 3 | 7 | 1 |
| Computer Studies/IT | 0 | 0 | 1 | 0 | 1 | 0 |
| Drama | 0 | 0 | 1 | 3 | 1 | 1 |
| Economics/Soc. Sciences | 4 | 8 | 4 | 4 | 8 | 9 |
| Engineering | 8 | 2 | 9 | 0 | 7 | 1 |
| Fine Art/ History of Art/Design | 0 | 6 | 2 | 6 | 1 | 10 |
| Hotel/Catering/Leisure | 2 | 1 | 1 | 0 | 1 | 1 |
| Law | 0 | 3 | 3 | 1 | 5 | 3 |
| Maths | 1 | 0 | 1 | 0 | 1 | 1 |
| Media Studies | 0 | 0 | 0 | 1 | 0 | 0 |
| Medicine/Nursing/Physiotherapy | 0 | 3 | 0 | 4 | 0 | 1 |
| Modern Languages | 1 | 3 | 0 | 1 | 2 | 4 |
| Music | 0 | 2 | 0 | 1 | 1 | 1 |
| Science | 5 | 4 | 7 | 1 | 1 | 5 |
| Sport Sc. | 1 | 0 | 1 | 1 | 4 | 1 |
| Theology | 1 | 2 | 1 | 0 | 0 | 1 |
| | 33 | 44 | 43 | 35 | 46 | 50 |

appointed Boating Officer at Rothera, the British Antarctic Survey base on the Antarctic peninsular in 2007. Dominic Faulkner, a teacher at Cheltenham College, led the British Expedition from the Dead Sea to the summit of Everest in 2006, the intervening distance being covered by bicycle; seven of his starting team of 12 reached the summit, rescuing a climber abandoned by another group *en route*. Rob Kinder took part in the Mongol Rally in July 2007 driving, with his co-driver, in a 1965 Morris Minor from Hyde Park to Istanbul, across Turkey, Georgia and Azerbaijan, across the Caspian Sea, Turkmenistan, Uzbekistan, Kazakhstan and into Mongolia, across the Gobi desert and finally to Ulaanbaatar, capital of Mongolia; it was all done for charity, with absolutely no back-up. The OD Society paid for the purchase of the car – £100.

Tamsin Barton won the 1993 Routledge Ancient History Prize with her book *Ancient Astrology* and subsequently became a research associate at the Indian Institute in Bangalore where she has worked as a Special Development Advisor for Water and Sanitation projects.

A 'different' career was that of R.M. Henderson who, although a businessman as a wine importer and Director of Dolamore Ltd, was also a composer and choral singer. A like-minded Old Decanian, but who has gone one further is Dr Adele-Louise Carter who is a Business Director for EDS, has a doctorate in Business Administration and Chartered Engineering Status, retired from the Intelligence Corps as a Captain, for which she was awarded the Territorial Decoration, and also spends time diving and travelling in search of wildlife.

J.N. Panes CBE sometime Principal of King's College, Lagos, Nigeria, became Government Secretary and Treasurer of the Isle of Man towards the end of the Second World War.

It is sometimes interesting to see what Old Decanians study at University and how it is changing. Indications are that while both Arts and Engineering options are still holding up quite well, Law, Fine Art/ History of Art and sports degrees are growing in their attraction to Old Decanians.

The late Ron Perry, thought to be the first OD centenarian, pictured shortly before celebrating that achievement in 2002 in Canada

Given Old Decanians' breadth of experience in many walks of life, it is to be hoped that many of them will feel able to respond to the recent request of the School to come and share their experiences and perspectives with present-day Decanians so that well-informed choices of career may be made by those just starting out.

Many Old Decanians feel a strong bond with the School and with the Old Decanian Society: long may this continue and flourish.

# Chapter 19

## Towards the Future

When the Revd Tim Hastie-Smith arrived in 1998, he was besieged with questions, not least what he saw as the School's strengths. He identified three. The first was the 'superb' way in which co-education worked, already honed for 30 years. The second was the rather small size of the School that '...(did) incredibly well in all sorts of areas...'. The sport was 'outstanding', academically the School did '...very well...' and the School was not particularly selective but all were helped by wonderful facilities. The third and key strength was the School's atmosphere, underpinned by its Christian ethos. He felt that the School had '...a strong spiritual sense...' that helped Decanians to come to terms with the world. However, he felt that change was inevitable, although it was important to hang on to '...enduring truths...' and quoted Edmund Burke's dictum that '...a state without the means of reform is without the means of its own preservation...'.

It is possible to see three distinct phases in the School's history thus far. The first was from 1886 to the arrival of Hugh Elder in 1938 and the Second World War in 1939, its 'Late Victorian' phase. Notwithstanding Percy Bolton's real efforts to modernise the School when he took over as Headmaster in 1924, including the introduction of houses, uniform changes, improvement in diet and changing facilities, building of the Tuckwell Theatre, encouragement of drama and the way senior boys especially looked at responsibilities, he was often severely restricted. Financial considerations, a slowly dwindling number of pupils and the perceived tradition of the School, jealously guarded by the Governors, slowed progress. Percy Bolton's Second Master, Edward Ellam, and senior staff were Flecker's appointees and most were with Percy Bolton throughout his headship. Thus changes that he brought about, important as they were, were not as radical as they probably would have been under different circumstances, especially if there had been no Wall Street crash or consequent slump this side of the Atlantic.

The second stage that emerged, beginning in 1938, might be called the 'Middle Twentieth Century' phase. During seven introductory years, a new, young Headmaster, Hugh Elder, began a new sport – rugby. The advent of the Second World War, and social, cultural, technological and educational changes, occurred, war being, as Professor A.J. Toynbee noted, the agent of greatest and quickest social change, including attitudes. The School was evacuated, and returned, surviving by the skin of its teeth. Domestic maids – in fact, virtually all School servants – disappeared. Within those same seven years two men who between them had held the School in an almost vice-like grip for its first 50 years, William Flecker and Edward Ellam, both died, as did Heller Nicholls. The same seven-year period saw the Junior School established as a separate entity, its uniform updated, although its Headmaster did not become a member of IAPS until 1949. Day boys were admitted – and welcomed – to both Schools. There was far less concern, if any, given to parental occupation than there had been earlier.

However, at that stage there was one thing the School, the staff particularly, had come to feel quite deeply; the importance of playing well in and as a team. Individualism was not really encouraged. There was a Christian ethos dimension to this, that taught the virtues of humility and of service to one's neighbour, rather than seeking one's own advance at the expense of others. Thus team sports were important, teaching Decanians to give their best efforts to the good of the whole rather than act as a *prima donna*. It explains why, when Hugh Cocksedge arrived at the end of the 1950s, anxious to start the Duke of Edinburgh Award Scheme which emphasized self-reliance, long-established teachers felt it was not good for the boys because it took the focus away from supporting others. Such was the initial feeling of some staff that mention of it was apparently vetoed in R.F. McNeile's history of the School. By contrast, the Headmaster was wholly for it and encouraged the Scheme.

The third phase began 30 years later in 1968 with the arrival of girls and again the immediate changes took roughly seven years to work through. Hot foot behind co-education was the beginning of the use and development of audio-visual and other technology: so this third phase could be seen as 'Co-education and Technology'. The changes were far-reaching. The arrival of girls – completely co-educational throughout the two Schools from 1973 – meant fundamental adjustments not only in how the School should educate but of what its education should consist. Areas of School life as diverse as phasing out corporal punishment, extending the curriculum, expanding the number of houses to eight, improving the financial health of the School and what activities were seen as being worthwhile were all, to a greater or lesser extent, affected by the advent of co-education. The technological dimension was heralded by the use of audio-visual equipment, especially for modern languages in the early 1970s and the arrival of the first computer, and the beginning of Computer Studies as a subject, in 1973. Decisions had to be taken against a background of long established cultural norms and expectations, and aspects of the Christian faith for which the School stood being challenged in part by the 'Swingin' Sixties', its aftermath and hedonistic ideas. Also the freedom of the individual and the desire of youth to experiment had to be remembered and put into the equation.

Tim and Joanne Hastie-Smith

As time has passed, so the way the individual Decanian has been perceived has also undergone change. This was probably hinted at firstly by the Duke of Edinburgh Scheme and secondly by the coming of co-education. Gradually there has come to be a shift of view to one that, while acknowledging the very great importance of teamwork that has enabled outward bound teams, choirs and hockey teams among others to achieve beyond expectation, nevertheless also takes a more individualistic line, advocated particularly strongly by Christopher Bacon and the Revd Tim Hastie-

Smith between 1979 and 2008, both of whom in their different ways were concerned to celebrate each individual's uniqueness in the eyes of God and wanting to give each individual Decanian as many opportunities for developing that uniqueness as was possible, so that their potential could be realized.

One of the changes that the Tim Hastie-Smith brought in was to end compulsory worship in both schools every Sunday. It was becoming more and more difficult to sustain in the light of parental wishes of day children and some boarders and the increasing number of key meetings, activities, sports and competitions held by outside bodies on Sundays. However, it was also critically important to maintain School worship other than assemblies. Thus Sunday worship was still required four or five times a year for both schools. Today, the Senior School worships on Friday afternoons while the Preparatory School worships on Saturday mornings.

The present generation of Trustees and the headship of Tim Hastie-Smith instituted other changes, such as a re-modelling of the governing body. Greater responsibility was devolved to those teachers in middle-management positions. New positions were established such as Senior Tutor (Chris Haslam), concerned about the working of the tutorial system throughout the School, and Senior Master (Rod Pellereau) concerned about staff and Common Room issues. Subjects on offer at A Level have been expanded, such as Physical Education, Psychology and Theatre Studies, while Spanish has grown considerably in popularity. Structurally, probably the most far reaching achievements have been the opening of

**The Governing Body**

The original constitution was finally enrolled in the High Court of Justice (Chancery Division) on 4th March, 1886. It was an unincorporated charity and so the Governors had to be the legal entity. That meant that in certain circumstances the entire governing body might have to sign legal documents. Moreover, if the School ran into debt, each Governor was '...jointly and severally...' personally liable. This may explain why Governors were always very wary about the level of School debt. Changes were effected in 2002 that eliminated those two drawbacks, brought the legal language into the 21st century and reorganized the structure, which is now as follows:

Dean Close School is an incorporated (charitable) company limited by guarantee. It has no shareholders but instead a self-electing body of Members, who include all who were formerly Governors, Life Governors and Vice-Presidents. They attend the Annual General Meeting, receive accounts and elect the Board of Directors. The Chairman of the Members is the President whose role is largely honorific. It is the Chairman of the Board who has executive authority.

The Board of Directors replaced the old Executive Committee. Those who are on it must be Members of the company. They receive no remuneration for their work. They are called Trustees and there may be up to 15 of them. The 'Treasurer' is a nominated Member of the Board who oversees the financial affairs of the School through the work of the Bursar. The Finance and General Purposes Committee is the main sub-committee of the Board, and anyone sitting on it must be a Trustee. There are some other sub-committees. The Bursar is now Clerk to the Trustees.

Thus the term 'Governor' is no longer strictly applicable. However, the term having been used correctly for nearly 120 years, it is still popularly if inaccurately applied to those who are Members or to the governing body as a whole.

One person who is invited to be *ex officio* is the Visitor who has always been the Bishop of Gloucester, currently the Rt Revd Michael Perham. His duties as such are not defined but in his capacity as Bishop of the Diocese he licenses and commissions the School's Chaplain and has a spiritual and pastoral interest in the whole Dean Close community.

## Sports Centre

The £3 million Sports Centre, sited between the Tuckwell Theatre and the Shelburne Road tennis courts, using space formerly used by three of the latter, was in use from the beginning of Michaelmas 2006. The formal Gala Opening was by Sir Geoff Hurst, of World Cup 1966 fame, on Thursday 26th April, 2007. The Sports Centre was deliberately sited to make it easily accessible to pupils of all three schools on the campus.

The Sports Centre includes a fitness studio, an aerobics studio, a seminar room, a viewing gallery and six changing rooms as well as offices. The sports hall is marked up for a full size hockey pitch, an indoor football pitch, five indoor cricket nets, two basketball courts, five badminton courts and two netball courts as well as being used as a gym.

The School Shop is also housed in the Sports Centre.

| Housemasters of Brook Court | |
|---|---|
| J.P. Watson | 1999-2004 |
| J. Slade | 2004-present |

the purpose built Pre-Preparatory School in 2003 and the opening of the Sports Centre for all three Schools in 2006, although the Millennium Building in the Preparatory School (2000), the new Brook Court (also 2000, opened by Prince Edward, Earl of Wessex, accompanied by the Countess), new Shelburne Hall (2003, opened by Estelle Morris MP), Turner Hall (also 2003, opened by the Revd Christopher Turner) and the major restoration and refurbishment of Tower House (2005, reopened by Bear Grylls, the explorer) must not be forgotten. A bonus to the building of the Sports Centre was the now required building of a road crossing on Shelburne Road, it having previously been refused by the local authorities for over 20 years. Maybe the most dramatic achievement was the transference of Tewkesbury Abbey Schola Cantorum from the Abbey School, Tewkesbury, to Dean Close Preparatory School, turning the latter into a choir school. It is a good example, it could be said, of Tim Hastie-Smith's oft quoted dictum, '*Carpe Diem*' – 'Seize the Day'.

Since 2002, in recognition of the needs of children and the sometimes complex lives of parents, there has been the development of 'Dayboarding' both at DCS and DCPS. It allows participants to belong to a boarding house although returning home most nights, and to stay for up to two nights a week in the Senior School and up to three nights a week in the Preparatory School, both regularly or occasionally. How flexible this arrangement is depends on an individual's circumstances and the availability of space in boarding houses.

Yet one or two tangible things have not changed. The School is still administered from, and classes taught in, the same building from which W.H. Flecker began; games are still played on Chapel Close, the first sports field; the clock (see page 19) that John Deacon, President of the School, gave that first Public or Prize Day in 1888 is still in the hallway by Reception and the number of boarding boys in

Upper Quad

1890 is almost as many of comparable ages as there are today – 170 to today's 195 – although the number of day boys today is far greater.

There have been memorable occasions, such as the Millennium Service in Gloucester Cathedral, attended by all three Schools on Friday, 28th January, 2000 or the BBC Any Questions that came to the School in the same year.

In October 1999, a group of former parents banded together to form Dean Close School Past Parents' Association. The original idea of bringing together those interested in the School but who were either no longer, or had never been, closely associated had been tried out earlier by Peter Lynam, OD and Governor, who was chairman of the Friends of Dean Close School which was set up in 1991. It was essentially a fund-raising organization that found that much of what they proposed was effectively already being done, and that general support was negligible, so they disbanded in 1994. This new organization was confined to former parents but was not aimed at fund-raising. Rather, it was providing ways to allow former parents to continue to take an interest in the School and join in some of its activities. It had its own Newsletter, *Close Call,* and under the leadership of James Moger, Doug Garner and Tim and Dorothy Odell the initial interest was considerable. Eventually it was closed in 2004 due to lack of support, its surplus funds given to the sports hall appeal.

There has been an increase in the number of interesting people willing to coming to talk to Decanians, trying to bring something of the 'real world' to them, from David Shepherd, wildlife artist, to Sir Bernard Ingham, Press Secretary to Margaret Thatcher; from Dame Elizabeth Butler-Sloss, first woman President of the High Court, to Jilly Cooper, novelist; from Jonathan Aitken, former disgraced politician, to Sir Ghilean Prance, a distinguished scientist. The point made to every Decanian is this: that each person is special and that each person leaving the School has the potential to achieve anything they wish – but in doing so they must realize and accept that everyone else is special, too. How they spend their time is key to their futures. All this has meant that careers advice, originally organized by Denys Carnill but now by David Fullerton, must be carefully tailored to the individual, reflecting the School ethos. In 2001, when A/S levels were being ushered in by the government, a part of an anonymous letter appeared in John Clare's column of the *Daily Telegraph*. It said: '…Could I reinforce the point…about the best things in education being those that can't be measured? Ten years after my daughter took A Levels at Dean Close, Cheltenham, every aspect of her life – career, hobbies, friends – stem from those parts of school that were outside the curriculum: acting, sport, music, even the cadet force. How tragic that time for them should be further reduced by yet more exams…'.

Decanians must learn from their experiences. One of the most poignant was for some members of the Lower Sixth in 2002 who visited the cemeteries associated with the First World War Battle of the Somme, and found the graves of brothers A.B. and E.B. Hatt, both of whom were young Old Decanians killed in the Battle. The party found that experience intensely moving. Readings were delivered and poppy wreaths were left at both headstones, together with a message that ran: '…We are the young whom you never lived to see. We have come from your old School, Dean Close. Our lives will not be the same because we have been here…'.

In that same spirit of honouring Old Decanians who fell in war, the Second Master, Richard Taylor, presented St George's Chapel, Ypres, with a plaque in remembrance of '…all Old Boys of Dean Close School who gave their lives in two world wars and other conflicts…' in 2007. It was dedicated and is now on the north wall of the chapel among a number of similar plaques from other schools. A copy of the plaque is in the Cloister by the entrance to the School Chapel.

**St George's Memorial Chapel, Ypres**

The chapel was dedicated in 1929 and stands in the centre of Ypres. It is the chapel in which the British community resident in the area worships and the memorial church for all who fought and died in Flanders' fields in both World Wars. Such was the slaughter around the town of Ypres in three great battles during the First World War that there are 160 Commonwealth war cemeteries in the area, and on the Menin Gate Memorial, through which a visitor passes as Ypres is entered, and at which the Last Post is sounded every day, 150,000 names are inscribed of British and Commonwealth war dead who have no known grave.

St George's is a living memorial. Nearly every item in the chapel has been given in memory of an individual or of a regiment, of a battalion of Chinese labourers or of the old boys of British schools.

Commemorative plaque at Ypres

The idea of present-day members of a school drawing on the lives and experiences of former generations is not new. Indeed, current Decanians are grateful for the time and trouble some Old Decanians give in advising leavers about future careers.

One other innovation came about as a result of the Revd Leonard Browne becoming Headmaster of the Preparatory School in 2003. Although the Revd Steve Gray was able to come temporarily for a valuable year before moving on, it was not until September 2005 that the new Chaplain finally took over. Dean Close School is believed to be the first co-educational boarding and day school to appoint a female Chaplain. The Revd Libby Talbot had experience of parish ministry

The Chaplaincy team in 2008: Alastair Groom, Laura Burton, the Revd Libby Talbot, Claire Tufnell and James Mears

in Southampton before coming to Dean Close School. With her arrival, the Chaplaincy emphasis on the pastoral was reinforced, the Chaplaincy team now including a lay Chaplain in the Preparatory School as well as two lay assistants in the Senior. Christian Union (CU), its house-parties and its series of Lent Addresses, were affirmed and encouraged as well as all the other areas of Chaplaincy involvement. Libby Talbot, her husband John and family moved into Bayley House, home of previous Preparatory School Headmasters, while Leonard Browne and his family remained in the former Chaplain's house.

In 2008 it was just over 80 years since houses first opened. Of the 138 participants in a short questionnaire, the results suggested that overall, regardless of sex, 94% felt loyalty to the School, virtually 98% as much or greater loyalty to their house. The house spirit of 1924 appears to be alive and well today.

Just as it always has been, academic rigour, while not being the only key mark of the health of the School has, nevertheless, been an important one from W.H. Flecker through to the present day. The last few years have seen improvements in performance that was already impressive, the best years thus far for results being 2004 for GCSEs and 2007 for A levels, up until 2008.

Inspections have become ever more common and searching but the three schools that make up the Dean Close campus have survived them with equanimity, and not a few plaudits. Although there was a boarding inspection in 2008, the last major inspection was in October 2005, when the Preparatory and Pre-preparatory Schools were described as providing '...a good all-round education for their day pupils and boarders. Pupils achieve good standards. The curriculum is wide-ranging and the provision and facilities for physical education and games are a major strength. The very good quality of pastoral care and the behaviour and attitudes of the children reflect the strong Christian ethos of the Schools. Pupils are very well prepared for the next stage of their education and the Schools are well led and managed...'.

The Senior School had its inspection at the same time and received the comment that '...Dean Close School is a happy and successful co-educational boarding and day school...It has a clear sense of purpose, based on strong Christian principles. Good teaching and excellent facilities contribute to the achievement of good standards in relation to pupils' abilities, to the very positive attitudes that pupils display in the classroom and in their extensive participation in School life. The quality and wide range of extra-curricular activities is excellent...'.

If that was what outsiders saw, looking in, it is also of interest to see what insiders felt. Joshua Powell, who rose through the Preparatory School to become DCS Head of School 2007-08, a talented musician, actor and sportsman, felt that the strengths

Still life by Alexander Edwards

**Baroness Cox of Queensbury, President 2001-present**

Caroline Cox trained as a nurse at the London Hospital, becoming a staff nurse at Edgeware General Hospital. Later, she achieved a B.Sc. (First Class) in Sociology and an M.Sc. (Econ), both from London University. A period as Research Associate at the University of Newcastle-Upon-Tyne was followed by a succession of appointments, emerging as Head of the Department of Sociology, Polytechnic of North London (1974-77) where she was targeted by Marxist lecturers and intellectuals because of her views and faith. Her book on this lengthy confrontation, *Rape of Reason: the Corruption of the Polytechnic of North London*, came out in 1975. When she was Director of the Nursing Education Research Council (1977-84), Margaret Thatcher sent her to the Lords (1982). Baroness Cox was Director of the Centre for Policy Studies (1983-88). She has been Chancellor of the University of Bournemouth (1992-2001) and became International President, Christian Solidarity Worldwide. She is President or Patron of organizations in Britain, Poland and Russia and has sought to alleviate suffering in Eastern Europe and the Sudan. She holds honorary doctorates from six British Universities, and at least three foreign ones. She holds the Commander's Cross, Order of Merit, from Poland. Books by her or in collaboration with others are on topics as diverse as Sociology; educational choice; ethnic cleansing; modern slavery; mental health and the maltreatment of Soviet orphans. Four of her grandchildren have been to the School.

of the School were that it was a School of excellence in Music, Drama, Sport, and academically – an 'all rounded' school, as he put it. It had a great sense of community and was '...a happy place to be...' with little bullying. He thought that everyone was aware of the Christian values that the School was run on. But the School had weaknesses, too, because it was such a safe environment, where a member of staff was always available to come to one's aid. It was a small school achieving a huge amount that consequently put pressures on a lot of people and expectations were high. It needed a certain strength to say 'no' to something sometimes.

Yet for those wishing to 'do their own thing', what may have been perceived once as being a rather restrictive institution is now viewed somewhat differently. Steph Simms, an A Level Decanian, answered in 2003 when asked what she enjoyed about studying Art at the School: '...the freedom to do what you want and the fact that you can express yourself so freely. Also, the chance to experiment with such a wide range of materials that you may never have the opportunity to use again. The Art School is fantastic: I was immediately impressed by the building, the exhilarating atmosphere and most importantly, the friendly, helpful staff...'.

Georgina Hildick-Smith OD, who left in 2003, only to return first as a member of the Speech and Drama Department in the Preparatory School and then the Senior School English Department in 2008, felt that the School had given her a love for her subject; interested her in fresh subjects and challenged her in an '...incredibly secure, stable, supportive environment...' where Christianity '...permeated the School...'. Intellectually, she felt that she left with increased assurance and self-confidence. When she arrived in 1998, the girls and boys were on a '...level playing field...' unlike earlier years when the girls

**Chairmen of the Board**
(known as the Executive Committee until 2000), **1922 to 2009**

1922-1929
The Revd Canon H.A. Wilson
Rector and Rural Dean of Cheltenham who resigned when appointed Bishop of Chelmsford

1929
Major T.E. Rickerby, TD
Officer in the Volunteers; Executive Governor of St Paul's and St Mary's Training Colleges

1930
Dr S.T. Pruen (Vice Chairman)

1931-1936
The Revd L.G.M. Sheldon
Rector and Rural Dean of Cheltenham

1936-1939
The Revd R.H.M. Bouth, JP
Rector of Elkstone; Magistrate

1939-49
Ian D. Yeaman, OD
Partner at Rickerby's, School Solicitors

1949-1959
Major H.H. Hardy, CBE
Headmaster of Cheltenham College, then Headmaster of Shrewsbury School, then Director of Studies, RMA Sandhurst

1959-1966
Sir Ian Yeaman, OD
President of the Law Society; Partner at Rickerby's, School Solicitors

1966-1973
W.A.M. Edwards, OD
General Manager, ICI

1973-1984
Sir Leonard (Joe) Hooper, KCMG, CBE
Cabinet Secretary, Director GCHQ

1984-1993
Steuart BonBernard
Colonial administrator; later Partner at Rickerbys, School Solicitors

1993-2001
Colin Cocks, OBE
Lawyer; Senior Director, Dowty's Engineering

2001-present
Mrs Patricia Napier
Parent DCJS/DCS; founding Chairman, the Baynards Zambia Trust

had possibly got away with rather more than the boys. Staff had a sense of camaraderie; were interested and interesting in their subjects and in each Decanian, and in the Sixth Form often became friends. However, the Protestant work ethic was still very much alive.

In previous chapters, musical, dramatic, sporting and other highlights and achievements have been traced. Some events are outside the normal, however, such as Baroness Cox agreeing to become President of the Council of Dean Close School in 2001; Dean Close School's first ever racing car, a Lotus Seven style kit car, which took a year to construct and was tested out at Silverstone by James Davies in the same year; the Dean Close Jubilee Festival that marked the Golden Jubilee of Her Majesty the Queen; the arrival of award winning artist Kim Williams

Patricia Napier

Margaret Bowen

| **Presidents of Dean Close School** | |
|---|---|
| 1884-1885* | The 7th Earl of Shaftesbury |
| 1885-1908* | John Deacon Esq. |
| 1908-1909 | Lord Wimborne |
| 1909-1919 | Sir John Kennaway |
| 1919-1947* | Sir Thomas Inskip, KC, CBE, MP (Later 1st Viscount Caldecote) |
| 1948-1960* | Lord Oaksey, PC, DSO, TD, DL (Later Lord Trevethin and Oaksey) |
| 1960-1990 | The 2nd Viscount Caldecote, DSC |
| 1990-2001 | The 4th Marquess of Reading |
| 2001-present* | The Baroness Cox of Queensbury |

* There are boxes on these Presidents elsewhere in the book.

as Artist in Residence and the retirement of Keith Davis after 36 years as the School's Head of Art, to be succeeded by Caroline Herd, now Mrs Evans; the sad news of the death of Colin Cocks, OBE, who had been Chairman of the Executive of the Governors, all of which occurred in 2002.

Then there was the graduation of the Marsh brothers, Andrew, Nicholas and David, in the same subject (engineering) on the same day in 2003 from Magdalen College Oxford; the 60$^{th}$ birthday of Margaret Bowen, a supervisor on the catering staff who came for just one week in 1972 and then stayed for over 32 years; the retirements of Dennis Artus, the School plumber, having completed 50 years' service in 2004; and that of Alan Cresswell of Tewkesbury after 33 years as the School barber, while the School became a principal sponsor of the Cheltenham Festival of Literature. There was also the death of former Headmaster Christopher Bacon after many years battling against leukaemia in April 2005. There was a mock election, and then Picasso arrived at the BonBernard Gallery, Dean Close School in 2006 in the shape of a National Touring Exhibition of 31 prints of his work arranged by the Hayward Gallery, called *Picasso: Histoire Naturelle* which several other preparatory schools came to see – and also take a quick look at an ever-expanding Art Department. In the same year the Senior Mistress, Emma Taylor, was appointed head of an HMC School, Christ's College, Brecon (from the following academic year), the first Dean Close School member of staff ever to go straight to heading an HMC School. She was succeeded as Senior Mistress by Jacquie Davis, who from 1986-89 had been a junior member of the Geography Department staff, and specialist in mountain craft, as Miss Crane.

Emma Taylor

In 2006 Edward Coram won a scholarship to the highly prestigious American Academy of Dramatic Art in Hollywood, and there has been a trickle of others, led by Tom Sword, following in his wake.

DCS International Summer School

In 2007 Dean Close School accepted a challenge to a Gun and Limber Race at Cheltenham College – and beat them. There are now matches every year at each others' schools. The same year, 2007, the Headmaster, the Revd Tim Hastie-Smith, was elected to the prestigious position of Chairman of the Headmasters' and Headmistresses' Conference (HMC) for the academic year 2008-09, the first to be elected from Cheltenham in the Conference's one hundred year history.

Viv Burroughs' examination candidates usually did well, but in 2007 James Melville gained the highest mark in the UK in the OCR Home Economics GCSE. This remarkable achievement necessitated receiving prizes from the Chief Executive of Sainsbury's at an award ceremony in London.

2007 was also when the Dean Close International Summer School opened that operates from the Senior School during the summer holidays for five weeks. Directed by Nick Albrecht, it involves a staff of about 26 of whom roughly half are teachers, the rest running activities and providing administrative and managerial back-up. It caters for children from 9 to 15 years old from a wide range of countries and backgrounds. It had a challenging beginning because of the torrential rain, flooding and consequent interruption to some mains services that affected the School, along with parts of Cheltenham and areas of Gloucestershire that first July and August, so much so that the International School had to

**GCSE Results 2007**

**A LEVEL**

| Subject | No. | Subject | No. | Subject | No. | Subject | No. |
|---|---|---|---|---|---|---|---|
| English | 18 | French | 14 | German | 1 | Spanish | 8 |
| Latin | 7 | Classical Greek | 3 | History | 25 | Geography | 11 |
| Religious Studies | 8 | Economics | 12 | Business Studies | 21 | Gov't & Politics | 5 |
| History of Art | 11 | Art & Design | 16 | Music | 5 | Mathematics | 39 |
| Further Maths | 22 | Physics | 19 | Chemistry | 16 | Biology | 11 |
| Phys. Education | 11 | Psychology | 28 | Drama & Theatre | 2 | Dutch | 2 |
| Chinese | 5 | Japanese | 1 | | | | |

**GCSE**

| Subject | No. | Subject | No. | Subject | No. | Subject | No. |
|---|---|---|---|---|---|---|---|
| English | 78 | English Lit. | 83 | French | 67 | German | 6 |
| Spanish | 18 | Latin | 14 | Greek | 7 | Class Civ. | 14 |
| History | 62 | Geography | 37 | Mathematics | 65 | Maths (AO) | 17 |
| Physics | 71 | Chemistry | 56 | Biology | 61 | Art & Design | 28 |
| Design Tech. | 26 | Home Economics | 24 | Music | 17 | | |

*A Level: Grades A to D; 103 candidates at 3.3 passes each. Two candidates achieved five straight A grades – Emma Brown and Yee Lam Kwan – thirteen achieved four straight A grades and another seven three straight A grades.*

*GCSE Grades A to C, i.e. a 'Good' Pass. 85 candidates at 7.6 good passes each. Two candidates achieved nine distinctions (A*) each, Peter Richardson and Emily Watkins, while Annabel Coaker, David Pritchett and Michael Strachan achieved eight distinctions each.*

*Please note: the AS results have not been used as there was nothing comparable in 1955. Please see chapter 6 for GCE comparison.*

*(Source: Results 2007)*

close prematurely. However, it has come through that ordeal and seems set fair for many years to come. Children come for two to five weeks and there are usually just over 180 students on the campus, over 400 being involved at one point or another in any one year. Already, it is not unknown for children from the International School to come back the following year or to subsequently transfer to either the Preparatory or Senior Schools.

2008 was the year in which Ben Marsden was the third known OD to be picked for the British Olympics Team, being selected for the hockey squad for Bejing and following D.A. Pringle, a pentathlon athlete in the 1936 Games, and R.I. Ireland who was picked to play hockey in the 1964 Tokyo games. It was also the year in which Jon Brock, Head of Biology and a key member of the Duke of Edinburgh Award Scheme, retired after 27 years.

If 2007 was the most successful year to date academically, 2008 was not far behind. At A level, the AB percentage was 75.7%, the second best result in the School's history. Of the 369 papers taken, just one was failed. 32 Decanians gained at least four A grade passes. One candidate achieved six A grades.

Tim Hastie-Smith was due to leave Dean Close at the end of Trinity 2009 to become principal of Kettering Academy; however, during Michaelmas 2008, a teacher whom he had employed to '...give him a second chance...' was struck off the General Teaching Council's register for at least four years for '...unacceptable professional conduct...' while at a previous school. On learning of this, the United Learning Trust, Kettering Academy's Christian backer, made it evident that they were deeply upset. Tim Hastie-Smith felt compelled to resign the Kettering appointment. Subsequently, he resigned from both Dean Close School and the Chairmanship of HMC. In a press statement he said: '...In the light of recent events, and given that I was planning to leave the School next summer I have, after careful thought, decided that it would be better to bring forward my leaving date…'. He and Joanne received many expressions of support and good wishes for the future. He has subsequently become a Team Vicar near Fairford, Gloucestershire.

As yet, it is far too early to assess Tim Hastie-Smith's headship. In the immediate aftermath of his resignation, the Trustees asked Jonathan Lancashire, the Bursar, to be Acting Headmaster. The selection process for a new Head had already begun via a firm of recruitment consultants as Tim Hastie-Smith was due to have left the following summer anyway. At the beginning of December, it was announced that Jonathan Lancashire himself was to be Headmaster. He took office formally on 1st January 2009. In his first letter to parents as Headmaster, he wrote: '…Having worked in a number of schools I know that Dean Close is unique; immediately on arriving in 2000 I was impressed by its qualities of Christian Faith; care and respect; confidence and freedom; and high achievement.

'All these are things to be preserved and enhanced, and my vision is to continue to educate the whole person, spiritual, intellectual, physical, creative and moral…'.

**Headmasters**

| | |
|---|---|
| 1886-1924 | The Revd Dr W.H. Flecker, DCL |
| 1924-1938 | P. Bolton, MA |
| 1938-1946 | H. Elder, MA |
| 1946-1953 | A.N. Gilkes, MA |
| 1954-1968 | The Revd D.L. Graham, MA |
| 1968-1979 | C.G. Turner, MA |
| 1979-1998 | C.J. Bacon, MA, Dip Ed |
| 1998-2008 | The Revd T.M. Hastie-Smith, MA, Cert.Theol |
| 2008-present | J.M. Lancashire, MA, FCA |

**Jonathan Lancashire, Bursar 2000-08, Headmaster 2008-present**

Yorkshire-born, he was educated at Malvern College, Worcs, gaining seven grade A passes at A level. A Mathematics graduate of St John's, Cambridge, he taught for seven years and was a head of department and an assistant housemaster at Radley College before switching to accountancy and the bursarial side of independent schools. He was bursar at Rishworth School, Yorkshire before becoming Bursar at Dean Close School in 2000. He served on the committee of the Bursary Schools Association and the Independent Schools' Council Education Forum and served as a governor of a preparatory school.

While brought up a Roman Catholic, he has worshipped in the Church of England for many years. As he put it himself, he '…has embraced (and been embraced by) the Evangelical stance of the School in which he firmly believes…'.

Outside the School, he has kept sheep and pigs on his smallholding, and qualified as a mountain leader and also as a RYA Day-skipper. An enthusiast for choral music, he became a Trustee of Tewkesbury Abbey Choral Scholarship Fund.

Jonathan Lancashire's wife, Sally, has been head of History and Politics at Cheltenham Ladies' College since 2000. Their children were in their late teens at the time of his appointment, Hannah being between school and university and William in the Sixth Form at Dean Close School.

In those words is not just an affirmation of the direction in which the School has been heading, but an echo, albeit couched in different language, of the Christian commitment, vision and ethos of the founding fathers of the School. Perhaps it is that unswerving adherence to that ethos down the years that caused the HMC Inspectors to write of the School in 1999: '...Dean Close is arguably one of the most successful small co-educational boarding schools in the country and members of the community are justly proud of the achievements...'.

Tony Marchand

The end of the academic year 2008-09 also ended on something of a bittersweet note, as Richard Taylor, now Deputy Headmaster, and Tony Marchand, Deputy Head (Academic), retired, the first having been at the School since 1983 and the latter since 1989, a total of 46 years' service. Richard Taylor, a former Head of History, had been Housemaster of both Court and Tower, while Tony Marchand had been the key driving force behind the improvement in academic performance over 20 years.

The tree that stands outside Chapel, known to generations of Decanians as Ellam's Oak, which photographs show was a mere sapling when the School opened but is now a mature oak, symbolises the School's growth and development over the 120 years and more of its existence.

May the School's success and achievements – however defined – continue with the same Christian spirit and ethos to produce articulate, well-rounded, self-confident, caring citizens of the future, equipped to fulfil their individual potential in the service of others.

**Senior Prefects/Heads of School**

| | | | | | |
|---|---|---|---|---|---|
| 1893 | T.F. Palmer | 1913 | *N.F. Herapath | 1930 | D.M. Hall |
| 1894 | R.F. McNeile | 1914 | H.L.O. Flecker | 1931 | H.G. Mullens |
| 1895 | *H.S. Snell | 1915 | R.E. Wilson | 1931 | P.J.H. Hornsby |
| 1896 | R.G. Brooke | 1915 | G. H. Hoare | 1932 | A.G. Watts |
| 1897 | R.G. Brooke | 1916 | D.E. Green | 1933 | H.J. Morris |
| 1898 | R.G. Brooke | 1917 | H.C. Neill | 1933 | J.D. Porter |
| 1899 | E.F. Unwin | 1918 | H.C. Barrett | 1934 | R.A.E. Cheales |
| 1900 | H.B. Cox | 1918 | S.C. Neill | 1935 | H.E.O. Hughes |
| 1901 | H.F.P. Knight | 1919 | L.R. Miller | 1936 | M.M. Johnson |
| 1902 | G.N. Rawlence | 1920 | I.W. Kerr | 1937 | J.B.C. Robinson |
| 1903 | *O.E. Windle | 1921 | E.S. Hoare | 1937 | R. Drown |
| 1904 | *O.E. Windle | 1922 | S.H.H. Johnson | 1938 | J.P.P. Crawford |
| 1905 | H.O. Cooper | 1923 | J.S. Smith | 1939 | D.M. Mills |
| 1906 | *H.C.H. Lane | 1924 | L.M.J. Kramer | 1939 | G.A. Tyers |
| 1906 | W.H. Anderson | 1925 | W.D. Kerr | 1940 | W. St. C. Tisdall |
| 1907 | G.H. Luce | 1926 | E. Fowler | 1940 | J.R. Reid |
| 1908 | *S.O. Monies | 1927 | E.R. Nash | 1941 | R.K. Thomas |
| 1909 | *R.W. Salter | 1928 | S.G. Bayliss | 1941 | R. Blyth |
| 1910 | *D.H. Bodley | 1928 | D. Powell | 1941 | G.L. Harrison |
| 1911 | F.G. Sellwood | 1929 | E.M. Cobb | 1942 | J.R. Blyth |
| 1912 | F.O. Hoare | 1929 | J. Bradley | 1943 | A.H. Knowles-Bolton |

1943 L.R. Griffiths
1944 G.N. Henderson
1944 F.B. James
1945 W.R. Edwards
1945 J.E. Pearson
1946 M. Mander
1946 H.S. Stringer
1947 P.D. House
1948 J.M.A. Parker
1949 C.G. Mallard
1949 C.H.R. Bell
1950 P.J. Habershon
1951 J. Stanley-Smith
1951 I.S. Blair
1951 I.F.C.S. Clayre
1952 M.R. Maloney
1952 C.L. Hodgetts
1952 D.W. Jones
1953 M.H.V. Bowles
1954 G. Jones
1955 G.A. Hutchings
1956 R.L. Johns
1957 P.D. Gaine
1958 J.N. Fuller-Shapcott
1958 L.H. Page
1959 A.R. Bailey
1960 M.C.L. Scott
1960 R.C. Padfield
1961 M.A. Campbell-White
1962 R.D. Lane
1962 R.G. Pearse
1963 T.L. Burton
1964 P.N. Johnston
1964 M.W. Bawden
1965 R.C.B. Clark
1966 G.H.C. Frankham
1966 R.D. Stewart
1967 C.V.G. Harries
1968 J.W. Cutts
1969 P.D. Badger
1970 A.D. Meek
1970 E.D. Kerr
1971 I.C. Gayward
1971 H.A.A.K. Quarshie
1972 S.J. Oxlade
1972 S. Bates
1973 W.R. Lucas
1974 *W.R. Lucas
1975 E.G.R. Speed
1976 M.J. Stocker
1977 R.C. Tupper
1977 A.J. Puttnam
1978 T.M.W. Green
1979 T.G. Graveney
1980 J.K. Wong
1980 Karen Sochart
1981 Karen Sochart
1982 R.J. Mitchell
1982 C.S. Thiagarajah
1983 K.P.H. Leech
1984 S.T. Kirby
1985 M.A. Hughes
1986 S.K.S. Chua
1987 Naomi Pickard
1988 Matthew Pickard
1989 Joanne Awre
1990 Sarah Pickard
1991 Melanie E. Bird
1992 Philip Marr
1993 Andrew Marsh
1994 Laura Jervis
1995 Nicholas Marsh
1996 Clare Marchand
1997 Kerrin Masterman
1998 Paul Marchand
1999 Emma Hines
2000 Jeremy Bidgood
2001 Isobel Shayle
2002 Rebecca Irvine
2003 Robbie McColl
2004 Francesca Hildick-Smith
2005 Jonty Strachan
2006 Alice Clayton
2007 Joshua Powell
2008 James Melville & Emily Watkin

*Those marked * are unconfirmed and/or have little or inconclusive proof that they were Senior Prefect.*
*From 1906-1980 there were many occasions when there were two, or occasionally three, Senior Prefects in the course of an academic year.*

# Appendix

## The layout of the School buildings

Lansdown Road aerial view

**1** Turner Hall. Boarding for Senior School girls as Shelburne Hall 1975-2003; Turner Hall for VI Form girls 2003-present.

**2** Dean Close House. Caynham House bought, renamed Dean Close House 1957.

**3** Fortfield. Boys' boarding House 1925-2001; DCPS girls' House 2001-present.

**4** Langhorne. Classrooms opened 1966; Hall opened 1967.

**5** Hardy. Purchased 1954; HM study, admin, also used briefly for Library & Boarding boys overflow 1955-1990; Music School from 1978; Girls' boarding House 1980-96, 1999-2001; Registry/ Marketing/Meeting from 2004; Choir School 2006-present.

**6** Wilton. Boarding for Juniors as The Hostel 1890s-1924; part of Walton Court House 1924-1939; Hostel requisitioned by Govt (including use as a US services Club) 1939-1945; Rickerby 1945-1990; Wilton 1990-present.

**7** Dining Hall. Opened 1971-2.

**8** Caldecote. Walton Court House, DCS 1890s-1939; requisitioned by Govt 1939-1942; renamed Caldecote & becomes JS boys' boarding House 1942-present.

**9** Shelburne. Boarding for Senior School girls from 2002; official opening 2003

**10** DCPPS. Site of Walton Court Stables / DCS Tuckshop 1880s-2002; DCPPS 2003-present.

**11** CPA. Opened 1978.

**12** Bayley House. Built 1983.

**13** Ferguson. Centenary 1987-97; Ferguson 1997-present.

**14** Rickerby. Site of School Porter's house until 1989; Rickerby opened 1990.

**15** Millennium. Opened 2000.

Shelburne Road aerial view

**1** Hm's Old House. Headmaster's House 1886-1957. School reception, 1886-present. School offices and Staff Common Room from 1957.

**2** Original school. First school teaching area 1886-present. First & second floor boys' boarding 1886-1924. First Floor Tower, second Floor Gate 1924-64. Gate only thereafter.

**3** Extension. Ground floor teaching 1888-present. Boys' boarding 1888-1924. First Floor Tower, second floor Gate 1924-1964. Gate thereafter. Also Dale 1973 onwards.

**4** Flecker Library. Old schoolroom / hall 1887-1996; Flecker Library 1997-present.

**5** Beaufort. Site of Fives Courts 1896-1908; Site of First (temporary) Chapel 1909-1923; Site of Old Chapel used as Brook Common Rooms 1923- c1959; Beaufort Block opened 1960, incorporating Field House.

**6** BonBernard Gallery & Art Dept. Site of CCF rooms 1956-1992; Opened 1993.

**7** CCF. Opened 1992.

**8** Pool / Gym. Opened 1964.

**9** WAM Edwards bldg. Site of Swimming Pool 1889-1964; Site of classrooms, workshops, stores etc 1889-c.1985; WAM Edwards building opened 1987.

**10** Bacon Theatre. Opened 1991.

**11** Prince Michael Hall & Music School. Opened 1997,

**12** Brook Court. Opened 2000.

**13** Estates & Maintenance. Built 1986.

**14** Astro: Carnill. Redgra opened 1961-1993, Astro laid 1993.

**15** Astro: Ellam. Opened 1988.

**16** Hoare Memorial Rose Garden. Site of Art & Design Dept 1973-1993; Garden opened 1993.

**17** Sports Centre. Used from 2006; Formally Opened 2007.

**18** Fawley. Ombersley bought 1961; Yearlings 1961-1973; Court 1973-1984; Fawley 1984-

# Select Bibliography And Sources


**Books**

Devereux, J and Sacker G., *Leaving All That Was Dear*, Promenade Publications, 1996

Gilbert, Rod (ed) *Rain on a Tin Roof, 100 Years of Hebron Experiences*, Hebron School Council, 1999

Harris, Khim, *Evangelicals and Education*, Paternoster Press, 2004

Hart, Gwen, *A History of Cheltenham,* Alan Sutton, second ed., 1981

Houghton, Elsie, *Christian Hymn Writers* Evangelical Press, Wales, 1982

Jackson, Dr E.M., *God's Apprentice, An Autobiography of Bishop Stephen Neill,* Hodder & Stoughton, 1991

Lace, A F., *A History of Monkton Combe School*, Monkton Combe, 1968

Girling, M.A., and Hooper, Sir Leonard, (Eds) *The First 100 Years*, Dean Close School, 1986

McNeile, RF., *A History of Dean Close School*, Dean Close School, 1966

Munden, Alan, *A Cheltenham Gamaliel*, Dean Close School, 1997

Padfield, Richard (ed) *The History of the Tuckwell Theatre 1926-1998* Dean Close School, 1998

Sacker, G., *Held in Honour – Cheltenham and the Second World War,* Promenade Publications, 2000

Sampson, A., & Blake, S., *A Cheltenham Companion,* Portico Press, 1993

Walker, Heather, *Roses and Rain: A Biography of James Elroy Flecker,* Melrose, 2006

Warr, Hedley, *Memoirs,* N. Warr 1978

Williams, Charles, *Flecker of Dean Close*, Canterbury Press, 1946

**Newspapers and Periodicals**

*Cheltenham Examiner, The* 1989

*Choir and Organ Magazine*, 2002

*Courtier, The* (Court House) various editions from 1927

*Church Times, The* (December 2007)

*Decanian, The* 1892-2008

*Decus* (Decanian sixth form magazine) 1979-80

*Gloucestershire Echo, The* various editions 1953-2008

*Impact* (Decanian Newsletter) 1963

*Lantern, The*, (Junior School) 1957

*Martian, The* (Gate House) various editions from 1927

*(Old) Decanian News, The* 1977-2008

*South Eastern College Magazine*, April 1901

*Times, The* various editions, 1895-2008

*Young Decanian, The* 1974-2008

*Youngest Decanian, The* 2007-2008

**Booklets/ Monographs**

Osmond, H.W., *The History of Dean Close School Chapel*, Dean Close School, 1993

Elder, H., *Dean Close School During Six Years of War 1939-1945* Batsford, 1946

Flecker, the Revd Dr. W.H., *et al*, *Edward Ellam, Dean Close School 1891-1941* (anon, prob. Dean Close School, *c*.1942)

Kramer, Dr L.M.J., *Another Look at Dr. W.H. Flecker* (Private) *c*.1974

McNeile, R.F., *Three Decanian Worthies,* The Wykeham Press, (Winchester), 1951

Whitney, C.E., *Dean Close School: 100 Years of Hockey*, Dean Close School, 2006

**Reference Books**
The Cheltenham Annuaire, 1882
Concise Oxford English Dictionary, 7th ed., 1982 & 1987
Crockford's Clerical Directories, 1929; 1959; 1971; 1977
Dictionary of Hymnology, John Murray, 1907 ed
Dictionary of National Biography, 2005
Good Schools Guide, The, 2007
Oxford Dictionary of National Biography, 2004
Who's Who 1989 and 2007 eds.

**Autobiographies by ODs (unpublished)**
Barker, B.J. *November Evenings*
Kramer, L.M.J. *Sir*
Preston, Peter F.B., *We Also Served*
Whittaker, Victor, *Flashbacks: An Autobiography*

**School Sources and Ephemera**
Brief History of Dean Close School 1886-2008
Dean Close Junior School Calendars 1949-1999
Dean Close Junior School Prospectuses, various from 1935
Dean Close (Memorial) School Executive Committee Minutes 1886-1936
Dean Close (Memorial) School Prospectuses, various from 1899
Dean Close Memorial School Register 1886-1927
Dean Close (Memorial) School, Report and Accounts 1886-1998
Dean Close Preparatory School Calendars 1999-2008
Dean Close School Calendars 1948-2008
Dean Close School House and Finance Committee 1941-1945
Dean Close School General Purposes Committee 1950-1953
Dean Close School Register 1927-1980
Hardingham, C.H., Le Poer Trench, C.E., Palmer, T.F., Report of the Executive Committee, 1896
Headmaster (DCS) letters to Parents, various from 1956 -2008
Headmaster (DC(J)PS) letters to Parents, various from 1957-2008
Old Decanian Registers 1884-1948, 1948-1990
Order of Services, St. Mark's Church, Cheltenham, 11.00 a.m., 11th November 1884
Order of Service for Laying the Corner Stone, 11th November 1884
Parker, A.S.R., 'Notes on His Time in Tower House,' *Tower House History,* unpublished, *c.*1986
Programmes of various Concerts and Theatrical Productions 1937-2008
Watkins, Lucinda, *Ideals of Masculinity: A Study of two Public Schools, Cheltenham College and Dean Close Memorial School, 1886-1914* BA Undergraduate Dissertation, Unpublished, University of York 2007

In addition, memories, extended letters and conversations with a large number of ODs, former and present members of staff and governors, a number of whom appear in the Acknowledgements.

# Cheltenham and School Index

PRINT: ordinary for general entry; *italics for photo captions*; **bold for box inclusion**

## Cheltenham


*A Cheltenham Gamaliel* 148
& County Harriers, 154
& District (Athletics) Championships 169
Air raids on 74
Airthrie School **115,** 135,313
Alma Road (and Land) 76, 94, **89**
Archdeacon of 40
Arle Court 153
Arle House 258
A.R.P. Wardens **75**
Art Gallery 85
Art Group Exhibition 78
Assn for Transport for Disabled, 259
Banbury & Cheltenham Railway **7**
Barn Farm 72
Barnfield 136,169
Battledown School 264
Benhall 257
Benhall Farm Fields *61,* 97
Berkhampstead School **115**
Bettridge School 258, 264, 280, *280*
British Empire Shakespeare Soc. 219
Cavendish House 259
Charlton Kings **7**
Choral Society 234
Christ Church **10,**235, 273, 284
Cleeve Hill 108, **206,** 208, 270
Coat of Arms **18**
College **10,**15,16,38,46,52,54, **55,** 62, **66,** 67, 98, 112, **118,** 126, 135, 163, 232, 343,
  Matches against 155, 163, 167-8, 186-7, 192-3, 197, 217
College Junior School 100, **115,** 279, 291
Competitive Festival 238, 286, 288
Daffodil, The 244
Delancey Hospital, donations to 259
Dowty Ltd **72**
Everyman Theatre *138,* 139, 143, 222, 286
  Youth Drama Festival 223
Family Space Project 267
Famous, The 339
Festival of Contemporary Art 90
Festival of Literature 355
Festival of Music 239
Fire Brigade 94, **140**
Flecker's Drive 153
GCHQ **72**
Glencairn Park Road 136
Gloucester Road 153
*Gloucestershire Echo* 236, 237
Glyngarth School **52,** 66-7, 100, **104,** ***105-6,*** 110, **111**
  Location 66,100
Grammar School **10, 66**
Matches against *165,* 168, 170
Hatherley Brook 6, 321
Hatherley Road 7, 94, 136, 153
Health Visitors 257
Holy Trinity Church **10**
Home Guard *73,* **73, 76, 111,** *200,* 201
Hospital 259
Jazz Festival 243- 5
Ladies' College **10,** 18, **66,** 67, **105, 115, 118,** 126, 168, 232, 236, 358,
  Choir of 235, 237
  Matches v 186-7, 293
Lance's Shop, High St 33
Lansdown Castle Post Office 21
Lansdown Rd **3,** 25, 136
Leckhampton **7**
Leckhampton Hill 90
Manor, lordship of 2
Mayors of 1, **2,** 189
Mayor's Fund for CLIC 189
New Court School **115,** 116, 269, 277
Operatic Society **221**
Pate's Grammar School 98
Pate's Grammar School for Girls 66
  Matches against 173, 182
Pittville Park 242
Pittville Pump Room 239, 244, 311
Plant, Thos., The Colonade, 100
Premiere Products 339
Prestbury 240
Prince of Wales Stadium, Pittville 169
Records at 169-70
Promenade *1,* 257
Queens Hotel **2**
Queen's Road *3*
Racecourse 259
Races at **88**
Railway Station 38
Rugby Club and All Blacks **184**
Ryland's Land *61,* **89,** 97
St Luke's Church **10**
St James' Chapel **10**
St John's Chapel **10**
St Mark's Church **2,** 13, 22, *23,* 32, **111, 120,** 237, 253
St Mary's Church **10**
St Mary's College **10**
  Choir of 235
St Mary's Convent **89,** 94
St Matthew's Church 237
St Paul's Church **10,** 238
St Paul's College **10,** 238
  Matches against 167, 188, 193
Salem Baptist Church 134
Samaritans 261
School of Art 60
Schools' Squadron, ATC 201
Scientific Society **55**
Shelburne Road 3,7, 24, 25, 30, 139, 153, 155
Smiths Industries **72**
Sports Achievement Award 198
Sue Ryder Home, Leckhampton 259
Sunrise Rotary Club of **265**
Tigers (Rugby) 296
Tivoli **285**
Town Band 13
Town Football Club 15
Town Hall, Pillar Room 187, 239, 240, 244
Town Hockey Team 161
Town Wednesday hockey XI 285
Transport for the Disabled 259
U.S. Army in 201
Warden Hill area 257


## Dean Close (Memorial) School


A levels **90,**125,**357,**138,352
Absalom 25-6
Academic Standards 16, **25,** 27, 31, 42-4, 51, 61, 81, 84-5, 87, 90, **90,** 97, 117,125, 129-31, 134, 138, 149, 352-3, **357,** 357
Acton (History) Club **97**
Air raids on **74, 79**
Air Training Corps (ATC) – see CCF
Allotments at 15
Alma Road Land **89**
Amnesty International at 261
Angling Club (Coarse) 126
Archaeology 126
Archibald the goat 25-6
Archives 141, 327
Archivist 140, 307
Arithmetic 31
Art 60, 81, 125,127, 353
Art and Pottery Society 96, **97**
Art History 136
Art Room/Dept 42, 44, 60, 85, 106, 123, 136, 139, 355
Art School 93, 123, **132,** *146,* 148, 353
Art Teaching staff *146,* 147
Art Technician 147
Artist-in-residence 147, 354-5
Assisted Places Scheme 134
Association Football – see under Sport
Astro-hockey pitches **132,** 136, 140, 175
Astronomical Society 97
Asylum Seekers, helping 267

Bacon Theatre **132,** 136, 211, 226, 229, 230, 241, 243-4, 277, 282, 284, 286
  Original opening **132,** 142, ***143,*** *144,* 225, 240
  Naming 149
  Steinway Grand Piano in 240
  Tree near 341
Badge/coat of arms ***18***
Balls/Dances 97-8, 135
Barnfield 153
Bayley House **132**
Beaufort Building 40, **89,** 93, **94, 139,** 148,153,167
'Bevan boy(s)' **75**
Bible, the
  Deuteronomy, Book of, **2**
  Hebrews, Epistle to the **82**
  Peter, First Epistle of **2**
  Proverbs, Book of 46
  Psalms, Book of, Number 119, 17-18
Big Field **24,** 24-5, 29, 32, *74,*135, 151, 153, 160, 164, 258
  Bomb in 152
Big Schoolroom 14-15, 18, *23,* 27, 30, 34, *37,* 37, 55, 67, **72, 80,** 106, **120,** 148, 219-20, 237, 238
Biology 81, **90,** 125, **129**
Blackberrying 7
Blackout, concerning 71,76
Boarding accommodation 123
Boer War 34, **35,** 36, 99
  Casualties **35**
  Change of School mood 34, 36
Boilers in 71
BonBernard Gallery 93, *146,* 147, 355
Boxer Rising, Decanian in **35**

Boxing – see under Sport
Branch Railway Line 6-7, **7**, 102
Signal box on 147
Bridge Club 136
Brook House (1924-1999) **25,** 56, *57, 61,* 66, **89, 94, 125, 132,** 135-7, 154, 158, **159,** 242, 260
Changing Rooms for 58
Drama involvement **250-1**
During evacuation 68
Housemaster List **57**
House Magazine **56**
Music and 235
Structural changes **132**
Relocation **89**
Wartime and 71
World Record Walk **260-1**
Brook Court House (1999-present)
Drama involvement 229, **251-2**
Housemaster List **349**
Opening of 349
Brown's (later music, medical) cottage 9, **61, 70,** 92-3
Bugle Band – see under CCF
Building of School 3-6
Buildings, state of repair 13,4 2, 51, 54, 57, 74, 87, 133-4
Bulgarides Family 240
Bullying 353
Bursars, list of **17**
Bursary 119, 123, 145
Business experience 123
Bus service 280

Cadet Corps – see under CCF
Canoe Club 127
Carlisle Cathedral 239
*Carmen* – see under School Song
Carnill's Hockey Pitch 162, 168, 175
Carpenter(s) 15, *15,* 34, **50**
Carpentry at 15
Carpentry workshop *15,* 104
Catering services 142
CCF (and OTC, JTC) 36, **39,** 39, 42, 68, 70, 73, **121,** 127, **129,** 130, 151, **159,** 186-7, 199-218, *200, 201, 211, 215, 217,*
Arduous training 204-6, 218
Army section 205, 207-9, 212, 217
Bugle Band 204, *214*
Buildings for **132**
Drum Corps *63,* 200-1, 206
Field Gun Competition *216,* **217,** 217
House Drill Comp. 254
HQ **89,** 146-7, 202, 204, *204*
House Platoons begun 206
Lord Lieutenant's Cadets 208, **209,** *210*
Motor Transport Section 209, 213
Orderly Room 199
OTC contract **39**
RAF Section 200-7, 209-10, 212, 213-5, 217
RN Section 202, 207- 9, 211-2, 214
RSMs/SSI 200, 208, **111,** 217-8
Shooting Ranges 43, *61,* 186, 199
Signals section 213, 218
CDT Centre **132,**139
Centenary Year 138-9, 209, 259
Changing Rooms 42, 58, *61,* **132**
Chapel 23, 38, 40, ***50, 51,*** 54, *61,* **68, 77,** 90, 93, *96,* 130, **132,** 146, 232, 328
Attendance at 58, 112, 124
Books of Remembrance 87
Confirmation classes 13, *22,* 22, 136, 253,
Confirmation Services 69, 258, *258,* 306-7
Crusader Meetings **53**
Foundation Stone laid 52
Friends of 86, 91
Furnishing of 126
Oak choir stalls 91
Oak Pews 134
Organs in **51,** 85-6, 119, ***120,*** *233,* 237, 241
Loft 86
Recitals 240
Specification 241
Pulpit **51**
Roll of Honour in 52, 211
Services in 76, 90, 103, 137, 235
Vestry & classrooms **51, 89,** 91
War Memorials in 86
West end balcony/gallery **51,** 86, **89,** 95
Chapel Choir **97,** 121, 124, 140, 236
Chapel Cloister **132,** 134, 350
Chapel Close 12-14, 29, *30,* 70, 149, 151, 173, 238
Chapel (temporary) 40, ***41,*** 253
Chaplain(s) **22,** 44, **53, 83,** *84,* 87, 119, 124, 136, 283, 299, 319, 351-2, *351*
Chaplain's House 133, 283, 352
Chaplain's Room **51**
Chaplaincy Team 264, *351*
Chemistry 44, **90,** 45
Chemistry (Junior) Group **97**
Chemistry Labs 24, 142-3
Chess (Club) at 85, **97,** 126
Children Act (1989) 141
Christian Aid at 267
Christian ethos of 64, 346, 359
Christian Union **97,** 119, 128, 141, 352
Christmas Ball 135, 238
Church attendance 96
Christmas tree 34
Cine club **97**
Citizenship 264
Clark Labs Building 39-40, *40,* 61, 71, **132**
Classrooms (general) 125
Claudia's Closet ***265,*** 265
Classics 136, 139
Climbing 127
Climbing Wall, The Talbot Griffith *141,* 141-2, **210,** 211
Coat of Arms/Badge 17, **18,** 28
Co-education 117-9, 124, 131-2, 150, 346
Arguments for **118**
Decision to go totally co-ed 123
Colours, awarding of 152
Colours of **24**
Commemoration as Remembrance 201, 235
Commemoration, explanation of 79
Commemoration Service(s) 98, 148
Commemoration Weekend 98,127, 130, 134, 141, 146, 192, 222-5, 238, 243-6, 264, 308
Common Room (place) **132**
Common Room (staff**),** 4, 91, 123, 220, 347
Common Room teams 172, 177, 195
Community Action Booklet 264
Community Work
Action day 264
Action Group 257, 264, 266-7
At School 63-4, 254-5
In the Depression 255
In the locality 257-62, 264-5, 267
Wartime 70-3, *71,72,* **72,** 76, 255
Computers at 125, 134, 140
Computers (laptop) 149
Computer Room **132**
Computer Studies 139, 346
Confirmation classes + services – see chapel
Cookery activity 136
Cora Lynn 'House' 19-21, 27
Corinium (Archaeology & Classics) Society **97**
Cornerstone, laying of the 1, **2**
Corporal punishment 15, 124
Cottage, (Brown's, later music, medical centre) 9, **61, 70,** 92-3
Court House (1957-1999) *(previously Walton Court)* 92
Housemaster list **55**
Move to Lansdown Rd 137
Crater Ground/Pitch 74, 152
Cricket – see Sport
Cubicles 20, **21,** 30
Curriculum (see also academic standards) 85, 97, 125, 135, 138, 139-40

'Dabbers' 33, 98, 100
Dale House 125, 134-5, 242
Drama involvement 229
List of Housemasters **125**
Dartmoor, expeditions to 204-5, 207-8
Dartmoor Letterbox **208**
Dayboarding 349
Day boys (also see under Dale and Field Houses) 17-8, 125, 149, 346
Day girls (also see under Mead House) 118, **119**
Dean Close House 89, 91, 125-6, **132**
Debating Society 16, 37, **97**
*Decanian* 14, 15, 17, 21, **24,** 27, 32-3, **35,** 36, 38, 42, **44,** 64, 66, 70, 76, **78, 82,** 85, 93, 118-9, 123-4, **125,** 126-7, 130, 135, 147, 150-1, 154, 158, 162-3, 185, 193, 204, 207, **220,** 223-4, *227,* **233,** 235-6, 253-4, 256-7, **271,** 271, 323, 332
Naming of 325
Weekly 95-6
Decanians, influences on 122
Decision to build at Cheltenham 3
*Decus 131, 133*
Deputy Head (Academic) 147
Design Technology Dept 95, **132**
Detention(s) – see under 'punishments'
Diet 21, 44, 58-9, 139
Dining Hall Block (old) 18, 33, *61,* 71, **80,** 124, **132,** 140
Dining Hall since 1987 – see under Edwards Building
Director of Studies 134, 147
Discipline problems 26-7, 122
Domestic Science (Home Ec) 58, 356
Domestic staff *20,* 22, 26, 67
Dormitories 54
Douglas Graham Memorial Lecture 142
Drama 59, 121, 219-31, *226-31,*353
Close Up Theatre 227, 229-30
Drama studio *228,* 229-30
Everyman Youth Festival 223
Junior Drama Group 223-4, 226, 229-30
List of productions **247-52**
Speech and Drama 227
Ten Play Challenge 229
Theatre Group **97**
Theatre Studies 226, 347
Theatre trips 47, 59
Dress – see uniform
Drill at 15, 31
Dri-ski activity 136
Driveway to Estates Dept. 136
Drugs at 128, 131
Drums – see under CCF
Duke of Edinburgh Award Scheme (DoE) 127, 145, *203-4,* 205-6, 208, 210, 212-3, 218, 257, 267, 346
Dyslexia at 130, 141

Edwards Building / Dining Hall 26, 74, **77**, 93, 136, 158, 339
opening of *139*
EFL (now EAL) 136
Electric light arrives 37
Ellam's Oak *21*, 359
Emily Kent Charitable Trust **264**, 265, 280
Engineering 31
English 31, 61, **90**, 120, 122, 131, 136, 139
Entrance to *11*
Estates Dept. 136
Euripedean (Greek & Modern Studies) Society **97**
Evacuation of 67-9
Evangelical nature of School 28

'fagging', lack of 27, 42, 254
Fairtrade group 265
Falconry club 96
Family Law Reform Act (1969) 124
Fawley House/Lodge 21, 86, **89**, 91, 97, 110, 123, 126, 129, 136, 137, *137*, 145, 149, 210
Badge / Crest 149
Drama involvement 229
Fire in **140**
Housemaster/mistress list **137**
Location **89**, 137
Fees at 16, 42, 63, 134
Field Club 37, **83**, 106
Field Day 259, 261-2, 267
Field House 91, **94**, 126, 135, 147, 149, 210
Drama involving 223, 229
Housemaster list **91**
Sporting success 193
Fifty mile walk **206**
Fights at 27
Fires at 94, **140**, 149
Fire watching at **72**, 73
First girl at 117-8, **119**
First girl through both Schools 135
First Sports Day 13
First World War 43-7, **45-6**, 48, 51-2, 62, **220**
Armistice Day 1, 79
Books of Remembrance 52, 211
Rationing 44
Sixth Form at cemeteries 350
Fives – see under Sport
Fives Courts *21*, 22, 153
Flecker Elms 80
Flecker Hall – see Big Schoolroom
Flecker Library *14*, **132**, **143**, 148
Flecker's Piece 70, 76, **97**, 153, 163-4
Flower borders at **25**
Food protests 76, 95-6
French 31, 61, **90**
Friends of 350

Garden, Stanley Hoare Rose **159**
Gardening 15
Gardener **46**, 148
Gate House 4, **54**, 55, 57, *78*, **83**, 91, **94**, **121**, **132**, 149, *221*
Changing rooms for 58
Drama involving 220, 223
During evacuation 68
House magazine **68**
Housemaster list 57
In wartime 71
GCSEs 138, 352, **357**
'General Election' in 263, 355
Geography & classrooms for 57, 61, **90**, 120, 122, 127, 149
German 31, **89**, **90**
Girl numbers 117, 119, 126, 129, 136, 149

Girling Room 57, 71, 119, 141
Gleaners Union 253
Governors / Trustees: 38, 64-6, 69, 128, 130, 134-7, 142, 149-50, 219, **270**, 273, 282, 306-8, 313-4, 321, 327, 338, 345, 347
Chairmen 87, 128-9
list of **354**
Constitution concerning **347**
Executive Committee of 17, 32, **35**, 36, 38-9, 40, 42-3, 46, 60, 63, 69, *145*, **270**
First women governors 121
Life Governors **25**, 69
Presidents, list of **355**
Gramophone Society **97**
'Grease Pit' 86
Greek 31, 61, **90**
Green Bicycle murder **47**, 47
Groundsmen 126
head 124
Gym 15, 24, 26, 34, **89**, *95*, 104, 129, 135, 153, 277, 285
Gymnastics – see under Sport

Hatherley Brook 6, 136, 156
Hatherley Road 7, 94
Head of School *32*, **35**, 134, 147, 152, 156, **159**, 352-3
List of **359-60**
Headmasters – see under names index
List of **358**
Headmaster's House (see also Dean Close House) 4, 6, 30
Headmaster's Garden 80, 220
Headmaster's Study 4, 57, 91
Health 31-2, 42, 92, 134
History (subject) 85, **90**
History of, seen as three stages 345-6
Hoare Memorial Rose Garden **159**
Hoare's Ground 139, 147
Hobbies Club **97**
Hockey – see under Sport
Home Economics (see Domestic Science)
Home Economics Room 138
Home Guard, School platoon in *73*, 73, 76, **76**, 255
Hooper Sundial & Quad 95, ***130***, 140, 349
Hostel 36, 48-9, 55, 79
House magazines **56**
House names 91-2, 152
House system begun 254
Houses – see under individual House entry
Humanities 136
'Humpty Dumpty' 7, 70

*Impact* *96*
Incorporation (School) 5
Influenza in 92, 134
Inspection(s) of 42-3, 83-4, 123, 141, 352
International Club 261, *261*
IQ testing 92
IT Department 21, 33

Joint Training Corps (JTC) – see CCF
Junior Drama Group – see under Drama

kitchen gardens *61*
kitchen pickets *71*, 71

Laboratories 24, **89**, 104, 106, 125, **132**, **139**, 142-3
Lamplighters 256
Lantern lectures 16
Last Post 98
Latin 31, 61, **90**, 122
Lecture, Douglas Graham Memorial 142

Lent Addresses 352
Librarian **125**
Library 128, **132**, 337
Literary Society **97**
Lower Quad 58, *96*
Loyalty survey 352

Madrigal Club – see Music
Malnutrition 44
Marketing Manager 138
Mathematics 31, 42, 44, 61, **90**
Mathematics Dept 24, 134
Mathematical Society **97**
Mead House 95, 120-1, 123, 126, 129, **139**, 148-9, 173, 212
Building 95
Drama involving 223-4, 229
List of Housemistresses **122**
Naming of 121
Swimming 188
Memorial Book(s) 87
metalwork 125
Meteorological Society **97**
Midsummer Fair at *127*, 238, 258-9, *260*, 261
Millennium appointments 263
Millennium Service 350
Millennium Walk 263
Mission to Lepers Group **97**
Missionary Sunday 253
Model Railway Club **97**
Modern Dance activity 136
Modern Languages 120, 136, **139**, 139
Modern Languages Society **97**
Monthly holidays 24
Motor Club **97**
Mottoes of 17-18, **18**
'Mufti' introduced 124, 129
Music 27, 31, 85, **90**, 123, 126, 232-46, 353
BBC broadcasts **232**, 233, **234**, 239, 241, 305, 311, 319, 334-5, 342
Chamber/Small Choir 239, 244
Chamber Orchestra 239-40, 241
Chapel/School Choir 81, **97**, 232, 233-4, **234**, 235-6, 239, 241, 243, 245
Choral Society **97**, 234-7, 239, 241-2, 245-6, 311
Concerts 34, 232-5, 237-8, 240-6
Directors of 27, **49**, **68**, ***232***, *233*, *235*, *237*, *242*, *245*, 311-2
Instrumental 31, 235, 237-8
Jazz 60, 135-6, 237, 242, 245-6
Jazz Band 232, 241-2
Jazz Combo 243, *243*, 244
Junior Choir **234**
Madrigal Club 235-6
Music Club **234**
National Youth Orchestra 241
Nightingale/McConnell Library 240, **240**
Orchestra 81, 122, **234**, 235-6, *244*, 244, 246
Practice rooms **89**, 123
Prep Schools Choral Course 239-40, 243
Recital Room **132**, 138
recordings 236, 239, 240-1
Rock 'n' roll 238
RocSoc 244-5
Sinfonia 244
Singing 31, 232
Staff 60, 125
Strings Day 244
Sunday concerts 233
Tovey Society **97**
Music School **132**, 138, 148, *148*, 149, 236, **242**
Opening of 241
Prince Michael Hall 149, 244-6

New Theatre – see Bacon Theatre
Numbers of girls in first co-ed years 117, 119, 126, 129, 136, 149
Numbers of pupils 7-8, 15-16, 18, 37, 47, 60, 62-4, 80-1, 87, 97, 125, 129, 131, 137, 141, 149

Object of the School 5
Officers' Training Corps – see CCF entry
Old (temporary) Chapel 40, **41**, *61*
Old Decanians 135, 141, 149, 160, 167-8, 203, 222, 323-44
advice by 351
and First World War 44-8, **45-6**
and Second World War **75-6**
and Oxbridge hockey matches 163, **177**
and 'Tanning' 124
Books of Remembrance 87
career choices 328, **328**
degree choices 343
gallantry & other wartime awards **75-6**
Roll of Honour 211
Old Decanian Register 313
Old Decanian Society 161, 38, 339, 343
branches **24**, 327
Colours of 326
Committee of 313, 324-5, 327
First Dinner 323-4
Funding of choral scholarship 312
Naming of Society 325
Officers of 147, **159, 323, 324, 325**
(Old) Decanian News **159**
Other dinners 34, 199, *326*
Presidents of 108, **159, 324**
Prize 327
Sports fixtures with School 155-6, 171, 182-3, 191-2, 326
Suggested objects of 324
Support of School building projects 327-8
Travel bursaries 327
Old Library – see Seminar Room
Old Swimming Pool *19, 26, 61*
Olympics
1936 Berlin: 129, 198, 357
1952 Helsinki: 161
1956 Melbourne: 161
1960 Rome: 161
1964 Tokyo: 198, 357
2008 Beijing: 176, 198, 357
Open Air Theatre – see Tuckwell Theatre
Opening of School 6, 8-9
Open Days 137, 308

Paper recycling 261
Past Parents Association 350
*Close Call 350*
*Pateronage* 96, **97**
Pavilions **24**, 24, **132**, 149, *157*
Photographic Club **97**
P.T./P.E. 125, *151*, 152-3
Physical Education A level 347
Physics 87, **90**
Picture framing 136
Pigs at 85, 126, *126*
Pioneers 63-4, 71, 205, 254
pottery 85, 146
Prayers at 22
Prefects 131
Attitudes to 'Tanning' 124
Badge 33
Canes 124, 129, 131
dress 131
President(s) of School: 17, **19**, 36, 52, 69, 84, **84**, 95, 263, 276, ***353***
List of Presidents **355**
Principles of 83
Prize Giving – see under Speech Day
Productions 219-31, **247-51**
Prospectus 29-32, 99
Protestant Work Ethic 354
Psychology 347
Public Day – see under 'Speech Day'
Punishments:
bread and water 16
detention(s) *16*, 16
lines 16
'tanning' 15, 124
Racing car (kit) 354
Railings surrounding School 278
Railway Land **89**, 97, **132**, 136
Railway **7**, *61*
Rationing
First World War 44
Second World War 76-7, 87
*Reaching Out* 267
Recital Room **132**, 138
*Recorder, The* 96
Recruitment 9, 13, 16-18, 37, 47, 60, 62-4, 80-1, 87, 97, 136, 137-8
Recycling paper 261
Register of *7*, 16
Registrar 138
Religious instruction 22,31
Religious Knowledge 31
Remembrance Day 201,202
Remembrance Sunday Parade alterations to 202
Requisition Order on 66,67
Roll of Honour 52, 211
Room 5 group 59
Rutherford (Science) Society **97**
Ryland's Land **89**, 91, 97

Sanatorium 19, **25**, 70, 92, **92**, **111**,126,136,148
Sanitation 31
'Scholars' 133
School Barber 138, 355
School Clock ***19***
School Dances 97-8, 135
School Golden Jubilee 255
School Hymn 33, **41**,79
School Mission, the 254-5
School numbers – see 'numbers of pupils'
School phases of development 345-6
School photo ***14***
School Porter 124,133
Schoolroom – see under Big Schoolroom
School shooting ranges 39, 43, 199
School shop – see Tuck shop
School slang 21, 23
School song **49**, 49, 232, **232**, **234**
School strengths 345
School work camps 255
Schools' Challenge Quiz 140
Science 24, 31, 42, 85, **90**
Science Society 85, 126
Scouts 207-8
Scripture **90**, 149
Second Master(s) **25**, 122, 135, 141, 147, 154, **159**
Second World War, 64, 67-9, **72**, **73**, 74, *74*, **75 -76**, 154, 212, 222, 255, 345
Arrival of U.S. forces 79
Battle of Britain at DCS **72**, **73**,73-4, 76-8, **78**
beginning of 67
Blackout regulations 71
Bomb damage 74, *74*
Book of Remembrance 52, 211
Evacuation to Monkton Combe School **54**, 66, 67-9, 160
Fire Watching, **72**
Home Guard **73**, **76**, **111**, *200*, 201
Rationing 76-77
Red Cross trains 78
U.S. officers' club 79
Victory in Europe 79
Volunteering for 77-78
Seminar Room (Old Library) 34, **35**, *57*, 119
Senior Prefect(s) – see under Head(s) of School
Servants *20*, 22, 26
Senior Master 347
Senior Mistress 140, 147, 355
Senior Tutor 347
Shelburne Hall/House **89**, *125*, 129, 135-6, **140**, 213
Claudia's Closet 265, ***265***
Drama involving 224
List of Houseparents **126**
Shelburne House (post 2002) 139,349
Shooting (Club) – see under Sport
Sisters (medical) **92**, 92-3,123
Sixth Form Common Room (Centre) 58
Sixth Form Film Society 126
Smith's Land **89**
Soccer – see Association Football
Social attitudes, changes in 124
Social Service activity 127, 257-9, *259*
Over sixties' Yearbook 259
Society of Contemporary Art 93
Spanish 347
Speech and Drama – see under Drama
Speech Day(s) 15, 17, **19**, 42,59, 60,80,86, **220**, 253, 324, 349
Bell Prize 36
Charles & Elizabeth Prize 37
Exhibitions 15, 85
Sport
Athletics 32,42, *62*, 62, 151, *153*, 153-4, *165*, 169-70
sports day(s) 12,13, 154
badminton 153, 167, 193
basketball 153, 167, 193
biathlon – see modern pentathlon
boxing 37, 167
chess 193
clay pigeon shooting 194
cricket *8*, 12,14,37, 42, 62, 147, 151, 154-7, *155-7*, **159**, *170*, 170-3, *171-2*
girls' cricket 173
tours 170,172
cross-country 62, *153*, *153-4*, *173*
Hatherley Run 153-4
Equestrian 173-4, *174*
Polo 173-4
Fencing 194, *194*
Fives 37, 42, 62, 151, 167
football (soccer) 15, 26, 37, 42, **53**, 62, 65, 80, 151, 158, **159**, 197
golf 147, 149, 167, 194-5, *195*
gymnastics 37-8, 42,62, 151, 153, 158, **159**, 197
hockey
boys 37,39, 42, 62, 130, 147, 149, 151, 153, 159-63, **159**, 175-7, *176*, *178*
centenary of **181**
change of heads 162
girls 122, 177-181, *178*, *179*
Astro pitches **132**, 136, 140, 175
redgra pitch 162, 175
tours (boys) 160-1, 175
tours (girls)122, 177-81, *178*,*179*
lacrosse 136, 196

martial arts 196
modern pentathlon 196
netball 122, 182
tour 182
orienteering *196*
rounders 196-7
rugby *9*, 15, 65, 80-1, 145, 153, 163-6, *164*, *165*, 182-4, *183*, **184**, *185*
girls' rugby 184
sevens 183-4
tours 166, 182, 184
sailing club 122, *127*, 167-8, 185-6
shooting 37, 39, 42, 62, **97**, 151, 168, 186-7, 206, 211-2, 217
ski-ing 197
soccer – see football
sport for girls 122
sporting giants 197, *197*
squash 149, 187-8, *187*
swimming 37, 62, 122, 151, 153, **159**, 166-7, 188-90
diving 166
life saving 166, 168
sports 37, 166
water polo 151, 153, 166, 190, 192
tennis 37, 122, **139**, 168, 190-2, *192*
trampolining 197-8
triathlon – see modern pentathlon
weight training 153
Sports Centre/Hall 176, ***348***
Sports 'Clubs' 42, 151
Sports Day 151, 154

Talbot Griffith Climbing Wall *141*, 141-2, **210**
'Tanning' – see under Punishments
Teachers pay for bursaries 62
Teachers' community help **267-8**
Teachers' pensions 43
Teachers' salaries, cut in 62, 66, 69, 128, 134
Teaching staff *13*, 63, **82**, 83, 129, 130, 13
Discipline of 37
Teetotal in 16, 36, 37, 253
Ten Tors Challenge 204, *205*, 205-6, 208-9, 211, 257
T.H. Clark Laboratories *40*, 40
Theatre Group – see Drama
Tovey Society – see under Music
Tower House 33, *33*, 42, 55, 57-8, **83**, **94**, 122, **132**, 135, 147, **219**, 359
Boilers in 128
Building of *32*
Changing Rooms 58
Drama involving 220, 224, 229
During evacuation 68
Housemaster list **57**
House Magazine **56**
In wartime 71
Music and 232
Treatment Room 92-3
Trustees – see under Governors/Trustees
Tuck Shop – see under School Shop
Tuckwell Open Air Theatre 64, 80, **83**, 130, **133**, **139**, 220, ***221***, 224-5, 230, 278, 284-6, 345, **348**
Opening of **222**
Site of *61*
Turner Hall 349

Uniform (boys) 23,98, 121
Uniform (girls) 121
Upper (Hooper) Quad ***130***, **132**
U.S. Army officers' club in 79

Vegetables grown at 76
Video of 138
Visitor, The School 273, 306-7, *307*

Walton Court House (1919-1957) (Thereafter see 'Court House') 49, 52, **53**, 55, *56*, 58, 65, 70, **83**, 92
Drama involving 223-4
During evacuation 68
Housemaster list **55**
Purchase of 49
House Magazine **56**
In wartime 71
Stables of become Tuckshop 59
War, verse from 34, 36
Washing facilities – see changing rooms
Winemaking Society 126
World Record Walk 209, **260**
Worship 100, 124, 347
Carol Services 137, 235
End of compulsory Sundays 347
Remembrance Services 79, 211, *211*
Special Services 27, **68**, 258

Yearlings House **89**, 91, 125, 137, **139**
Young Farmers' Club **83**, 85, **97**, *126*


## Dean Close Junior / Preparatory School


**65**, **69**, 72, 80-1, 84, **89**, 99-116, **109**, **115**, 137, 139, 147, 258, 269-302, 306-312, 345
as Choir School 349
Activities
Beddgelert Week 299
Canal boat holidays 300
Carpentry 103
Cruises *300*, 300
Cultural/Language French trips 300, *301*
Cycling proficiency 299
Dancing 274, 284
Drama 102, 106, 139, 285-6, *287*, *288*
Productions list **284-5**
Junior productions list **286**
Other activities 274, 302
Railways/Train Club *302*
Skiing 299-300
Admissions 283
Adventure Playground 275
Alton Towers visit 278
Argonauts 112, **113**, 270, 274, 296-9
Pathfinders 299
Ramblers 299
Art 270, 274, 282-3, 315
Art Room/Suite 113, 272, 279
Artslink 282

Bacon Theatre, use of 142
Bayley House **132**, 133, 272-3, **273**, 283
Becomes an IAPS prep. school 107-8
Begun 65
Bomb shelter in 106
Bullying 100
Bus service 280

Caldecote House 25, 49, *56*, 106-7, **108**, 109-10, **111**, 112, 269, 272-3, 275, 281, 318
Caldecote Stables 85
Housemaster in World War II 76
Housemaster list **106**
Support for T.A.S.C. Choristers 311
Centenary Building – see Ferguson Block
Centenary Service 273
Centenary Year 273-4
Change of name 279
Chapel 100, 103, 112, **273**, 347
Carol Services 235
Chapel Choir 236, 239, 245, 284, 286, *287*, 311
Choirgirl of the Year 286
Recordings 286
Tours 286
Chaplain(s) **113**, 114, 279, 283, 301, 351
lay 282, 352
Charity fund raising 257, 258-61, 263-5, 267-8
Christian Union 278, 301-2
Classics 101, 275
Co-education 269-302, 346
Common Room (staff) 112, 114, 241, 269, 309
Covered Play Area CPA) 271-2, **272**, 275, 318
Curriculum 31

Day boarding 349
day boys 80, 112, 346
'House' 112, **285**
Housemaster list **113**
Deacon House
Foundation **19**, 281
Housemasters/mistresses list **282**
Location 281, 283
Deputy head(s) 279, 282-3
Design & Technology Suite 279, 283
Dining Hall 283
Director(s) of Studies 276-7, 282
'Divisions' 107
dress code – see uniform

English 99, 101
Evacuation 67-70, 105-6

Ferguson Building 102, **132**, 275
Naming of 279
Site of 272
First girl at 269
First ideas about a JS 36
First OD girl working at 272
Fortfield House 58, 62, 65, 67, 69, 100-5, *101*, *104*, 107, 109, 110, **111**, 112, 115, 272, **273**, 275, 281-2
Cricket and *101*
Girls in, boys out 281-2
Hockey and *102*
Housemasters list **101**
Houseparents of **282**
stable block (later classrooms) 65, 74, *74*, 102, 106, 112-3
Tennis Courts at 102
French 99, 101, 112, 114

Geography 99, **273**, 284
Greek 99

Hardy House **89**, 272-3, 275, 278-9, 283, 285, 309
Housemistresses list **272**
Purchase of 'Lisnamoe' 112
Headmasters
Housing for 270
List of **270**
Role 270, 272, 351
Trips abroad 277, 280
Heads of School list **302**
*Hermes* **276**, 277, 282
Houses – see individual entries

Inspection(s) of 111-2, 141, 277, 282-3, 352
I.T. 283

Laboratories **89**, 275
Langhorne Hall **89**, 113, 272, 284-5, 315
Langhorne Hall Classrooms **89**, 113, 272
*Lantern, The* **271**
Latin drama 278, 286
Learning Support Dept. 277-8
Iris Long Suite 279
Leavers' Course **113**, 300-1
Library, Harper **285**, 275, 279, 283
Library(s), old 112
Lisnamoe – see under Hardy House
Lower School 110, 113

Marketing of 282
Masters of Juniors **101**
Mathematics 99, 101, 276, 279, 282
Challenge(s) 255
Medical Treatment Room 283
Millennium Building 91, 279, 283, 317
Opening of 280,349
Millennium Pilgrimage 280
Millennium Service 242, 280
'Morning Blub' 100
Music 274, 315
Music School 272

National Curriculum 276-7, 279
*Newspaper* **276**
Numbers in School 65, 68-9, 80, 87, 97, 101, 103-4, 106-7, 111-2, 131

Oaksey House **273**, 275, 279, 281
Housemaster list **282**
Location 272, 276
Organization of School (1949) **109**

Plays/revues – see Drama
Porter's lodge in 275, *276*
Pottery, plaque in 272
Pre-Prep (1949 model) – see lower school
Productions list **284-5**
Productions references 219-30
Prospectus(es) 99, 101
punishments 108

Railings surrounding School 278
Religious Instruction – see Scripture
Requisition Order on 105
Rickerby House (before 1990) 107-8, 110, **111**, 272, 274, 277, 285
Dining 110
Girls in 269
Girls out 271
Housemaster list **110**
Sickbay at 110
Rickerby Building (post 1990) 91, **132**, 276, 283

Science 99, 101, 270, **273**, 274
School name change 279
Scouts at 112, **113**
Scripture/Religious Instruction 99, 101, **273**
Second Master 276, 282
Senior Master **271**, 302
Senior Mistress 276-8, 282
Speech & Drama 353
Sport
Athletics *289*, 289
Cricket 100-1, *101*, 103-4, 274-5, 289-91, *290*
Records in 290
Six-a-side 290
Tredgett trophy 289-90
Tours 290
Cross-country *291*, 291
Equestrian 297
Fencing 297
Football (Soccer) 100-3
Golf 297
Stowe Putter 297
Gymnastics 274
Hockey (boys) 101, *102*, 103, 292-3
astroturf 292
GB player 292
Padfield Trophy 292
Hockey (girls) 293-4, *293*
Judo & Jujitsu 274, 298
Netball 294
Rounders 294-5, *294*
England squad player 295
Rugby 104, 275, 295-6, *295*, *296*
7-a-side 295
Shooting 274, 298
Ski-ing *298*, 298
Squash 298
Swimming 100, 296, 315
Tennis 297
Trampolining 274, 298
Sports Centre/Hall 283
Staff – see Common Room (staff)

Teams in sport 288
Tewkesbury Abbey Schola Cantorum **150**, 245, 309, *310*, 349
Abbey School 244, 283, 303-311, *306*
Abbey School Choir 283, 303-311
First broadcast 305
First CD 305
First service 304
Last service 309
Moving to DCPS 308
Schola Cantorum begins 309-311
Broadcasts 311
Choral Scholarship Fund 312, **358**
First CD 311
First services 311
Lay Clerks of 311
tours 311
Trustees **358**
Tewkesbury Abbey 138, 236, 284, 303-312
Vicars of 303, *307*

Uniform 100, 107

Video of Junior/Prep School 277

WH Smith Young Writers' Awards 274, *274*
Wilton House
Acquisition of 'Old' Wilton **89**, 112, *114*
Girls move in 271
Housemaster list of 'Old' Wilton **114**
Houseparent list of 'New' Wilton **282**
Location of 'Old' Wilton 272
'New' Wilton House 99, 100, **125**, 276, **279**, 281, 283
'Old' Wilton House 275, 333
Wilton Crocodile 276
Yeaman House 114, 269, 275, 277, 282
locations 114, 272, 274
Housemaster/mistress list **114**
Year numbering changes 277
*Young Decanian, The* ***271***, 271-3, 279, 290


## Dean Close Pre-Preparatory School 'The Squirrels'


135, **273**, 277-9, 313-22
Building of 85, *319*
Computers in *320*, 322
Early Years Partnership 321
First business meeting concerning 314
First concert 316
First Nativity play 316
First Parents' Meeting 315
First Sports Day 316
Forest School 321-22, *322*
Headmistress appointed ***317***, 321
Inspections of 317, 321, 352
Kindergarten begun 317
Langhorne Hall Classrooms and 314, *315*
Launch of 315
Learning support in 319
Millennium Pilgrimage 318
Millennium Service 318
Previous 'Pre-prep' children 313
Productions in **318**
Quality Assurance Award 321
Senior management team in 321
*Youngest Decanian* ***271***


## Dean Close International Summer School


356-7, *356*
Director of 356

# Names Index

PRINT: ordinary for general entry; *italics for photo captions*; **bold for box inclusion**


Abbas, Sam 193
Abbatt, Mrs Barbara 107
Abbott, Olivia 180
Abraham, Ch.Insp. Neville *155*, 333
Acheampong, Julian 197-8
Acton, David 334
Adams, C.S. 235
Adamson, George *341*, 341
Agg-Gardner, Sir James **2**, 52
Aiano, Sister Philippa **92**
Aiano, Stephen G.G. **55**, 224, **247**, **250-1**, 261
Ainslie, Scott **261**
Aitken, Jonathan 350
Akenhead, Dan 170, *316*, 316
Akenhead, Richard (Ricky) F. **57**, 170, *182*, 182, 184, 223, **249-50**
Akerman, Nick R. 183, **325**
Albrecht, Nick 356
Alcock, Sister **92**
Alder, John 170
Aldis, G.H. 160
Alexander, Richard **181**
Alexandra, HRH Princess *138*, 138, *273*, 273,
Alger, Beth 188-9, 194
Alger, Cathy 188-9
Allan twins 190
Allberry, Frances 191, 225, 297, 334
Allberry, Penny 190, 192
Allbut, Mrs Caroline 283
Allcock, Matron 106
Allen, Alexander **316**
Allen, Christian 193
Allen, Ciara 225, 229-30, 242
Allen, David 156
Allen, Geoff 148
Allen, Jacky 197
Allen, Jon 225, 251, **267**
Allington, Lloyd **91**, 142, 223-7, *228*, 229-30, **247**, **250-2**
Allison, Bishop Oliver336
Allison, the Revd Canon 336
Allison, Bishop Sherard F. **324**, 336
Allison, the Revd William 336
Allwood, Ralph 243
Amherst, Miles 303-5, **304-5**, 309, 311-2,
Amherst, William **304**
Anderson, Nick 197
Anderson, W.H. **359**
Anderson, W.R. **234**
Anderson, Lindsay 334
Andre, Benoit **309**
Andrew, Benjamin *176*, 177
Anne, HRH Princess **115**, 124, **260**, 311
Anstey, W. 220
Appleby, Major Harry 186, 208
Araujo, Fernando de 261
Aris, Dr Keith **137**, 137, **140**, 142, 145, 149, 258-9
Aris, Mrs Vanessa **137**, 137, **140**, 145, 149, **263**, *267*, 267
Armstrong, Dr (later Sir) Thomas 233
Artus, Dennis 355
Ash, Angela 146
Ashton, The Very Revd J.E.B. 336
Askwith, Myron 190
Astley-Weston, B. *38*
Atkins, Mrs Anne 145
Atkinson, Pip 182, 184
Auchinleck, Field Marshal Sir Claude 206
Auchinleck, Mark 206
Auckland, David *287*
August, Angela 188
Autarkanov, Arbi **302**
Averiss, Declan 184
Awrege, Sven **261**, 289
Awre, Joanne **360**
Axford, Lee 243
Ayers, C.H. 25, **31**
Ayrton, Randle **222**, 222

Bach, J.S. 235-6, 238, 311
Backhouse, T.W. *155*, 156
Bacon, Christopher J. **17**, 124, **130**, 131, *133*, **133**, 133-5, 138-9, *138*, *141*, 145, 147, 149-50, 189, 196, 212, 225, 241, 278-9, 346, 355, **358**
Bacon, Francis 60, *335*, 335-6
Bacon, Mrs Jill 131, *133*, **133**, 149, 225, 241
Bacon, Philippa **133**
Bacon, Stephanie **133**, 177
Bacon, Tamsin **133**, 182, **209**, 210
Bacon, Tom *178*, 213
Badger, Peter D. 163, 167, 290, **360**
Badham, Mrs Marion 321
Baggaley, K. **249**,
Bagshaw, C.F. **251**
Bailey, Miss **50**
Bailey, Dr A.R. **325**, **360**
Bailey, Clive 286
Bailey, Edgar 286
Bailey, Hannah **302**
Bailey, Mrs Lisa 309
Bailey, Pandora 173
Bailey, Sam 184
Baillie, A.N. 193
Baillie, Mrs Pam **115**, 117, **119**, 119, 123, 222, **325**
Baillie, Neil **119**
Baines, A.C. 'Tony' 237
Baird, Dickon **279**
Baird, Edmund **279**
Baird, George **279**
Baird, Mrs Liz 278, **279**, 279-81, **282**, 317
Baird, Stephen W. **270**, **279**, 278-80, **281**, 282, **285**, 286, 317, 319
Bairstow, Sir Edward 309
Baker, E.N. 32
Baker, Miss Frances (Fan) 111, **111**
Baker, Jane **147**
Baker, Dame Janet 138, 239
Baker, Malcolm 168
Baker, Richard *176*
Baker, Dr Richard St.Barbe *341*, 341
Baldwin, R. *161*
Ball, Nicholas **202**
Ball, Nick 172-3, 183-4
Ball, Richard **202**, 211
Ball, Sarah **202**
Ballance, H.C. **325**, 325
Bamber, Mr 15
Banks, Mrs Elaine 136
Banks, Garth *178*, 190, **202**
Banks, James 190
Baring, Edward **233**
Baring, Pauline **233**
Barker, Barry **49**
Barker, Derek 85, 91, 120, 125, **125**, **139**, 139, 168
Barker, J.K. 325
Barker, Mrs Joyce 120-1, **122**, 123, **139**
Barnado, Dr 253
Barnard, L.W. **50**
Barnes, Peter 183
Barnes, S.G. 206
Barraclough, Miss **115**
Barraclough, Rachael **181**
Barrett, H.C. **359**
Barrett, Sam *178*, **202**
Barrington-Earp, Mrs Susan **119**
Barritt, Victoria 225,
Barron, David *195*
Bart, Lionel 224
Bartlett, Major C.B. **45**
Barton, Ben 170, 195
Barton, Giles 197, 290, 298, *298*
Barton, J.E. 81
Barton, Ch.Insp. Mike 333
Barton, Tamsin 343
Barwell, Emily 187
Bassett-Smith, Ian **325**
Bastin, Melissa 241
Bastin, Sarah – see McCann
Bates, S. **360**
Bath, David **309**
Batten, Joanna 187
Batten, Nick *178*
Batten, Will 193
Battle, Jim 193
Batty, Kate 192
Bawden, M.W. 157, 163, 172, 328, **360**
Bayley, Claire – see under Harding
Bayley, John 133, 273
Baylis, Mrs Jane 322
Baylis, R. *155*
Bayliss, S.G. **359**
Beardsley, Miles 176
Beaufort, the Duke of 202
Becker, Randy 243
Becket, Samuel **88**, 222
Bedford, Richard 336
Beeching, Dr (later Lord) 97
Beethoven, Ludwig van 236-7
Bell, A.S. 36
Bell, C.H.R. 106, **360**
Bell, Linsey 192
Bell, R. 32
Bell, R.T. 76, **77**
Bell, the Revd Canon **3**
Bellwood, Laura 169, 170, *178*, 182, 184
Benians, RSM L.M. 168, **206**
Benn, Rt. Hon Anthony (Tony), M.P. 145
Bennett, Alan 223, 229
Bennett, Catherine **317**
Bennett, James **317**
Bennett, the Revd N. 31
Bennett, Dr R. Sterndale 235
Bennett, Richard Rodney 239
Bennett, Mrs Sue 316, **317**, 321
Benson, R.A. 'Bob' **113**, **282**, 301
Benton-Evans, W.J. 156, 162-3
Berkeley, Sir Lennox 239
Berry, Prof. Francis **220**, 329, 334
Berry, the Very Revd Nick **281**
Betjeman, Sir John 90
Bhandari, Neel 290
Bhushan, Padma 342
Bidgood, Jeremy **360**
Biennemann, The Revd F.W. 29, **31**, 36, 99

Billington, Susan – see under Barrington-Earp
Birch, Phillip 225
Bird, Anthony R. 213, **218**, 224, *286*, 290, **302**
Bird, Melanie E. **360**
Bishop, Robert **233**, 244, *245*, 245, 311
Black, Mary 178, 186
Blackwell, Angela 169
Blackwell, S. **251**
Blair, Andrew 238
Blair, I.S. **360**
Blair, Rt Hon Tony, M.P. 150
Blake, C.E.N. 156
Blake, N.M. **55**
Blampied, Amelia 192
Blampied, Eleanor192
Blampied, Katrina192
Blanchard, Mike 340
Bland, Alistair 335
Bliss, Lucas **316**
Bliss, Timothy V.P. 97
Blomfield, Richard **147**
Blyth, Dr A.G. **324**
Blyth, J.R. **359**
Blyth, R. **359**
Boardman, A.J. (Tony) **284**, 285
Bodley, A.L. 15
Bodley, Douglas 154
Bodley, the Revd D.H. 62, **359**
Bodvan-Griffiths, Lt-Col P.F. 331
Bogart, Humphrey 334
Bolton, Arthur **4**
Bolton, Edward 296
Bolton, Elaine **55**
Bolton, James **55**
Bolton, Mrs Madeleine **55**, **60**
Bolton, Percy **54-5**, 54-6, 58-60, **60**, 62-4, 87, 100, 152, 219, 253-4, **324**, 345, **358**
Bolton, Phoebe *293*, 294
Bolton, Richard 187
BonBernard, Steuart *145*, 145, **354**
Bond, Stuart *178*
Bone, Mr 126
Boodle, Christopher 237, 335
Booth, M.S. **114**
Bouquet, Mrs 190
Bourne, Rosemary 227
Bouth, the Revd R.H.M. **354**
Bowden, Martin 136-7, *136*, **137**
Bowden, Sister Jenny (née LeSeelleur) **92**, 137, 225, 230
Bowditch, Jasper 172
Bowen, D. 169
Bowen, Martyn 170
Bowen, Mrs Margaret *355*, 355
Bowes, Susan – see under Burke
Bowles, Michael H.V. 168, **360**
Bowman, James 307
Boyce, William 236, **240**
Boyd, Edward *178*, 291, 297
Boyd, Emma **147**
Boyd, Philippa 286
Boyd, Stephanie 174, 296
Boyle, R.C. **91**, 217
Bradby, Barbara **115**
Bradley, J **359**
Bradnack, B.O. 52, 56, **57**, 63-4, 153, 166, **220**, 220, 234, 254-5, 330
Bradstock, William 163
Brahms, Johann 237
Brain-Gabbott, Mrs A. **282, 125**
Brain-Gabbott, Emma 241, 333
Braithwaite, Nancy 140, 224
Brazell, Elizabeth **284**, 284-5
Brecht, Bertold 227
Brecht, Timothy **302**
Breese, D. **250**, **352**
Brennan, Roy 71
Brenninkmeijer, Vicky *215*
Bretherton, Melissa 286
Bretherton, Oliver 172
Brett, Stephen 209
Brewster, Mrs Debbie 277
Brewster, Paul 276-7, **276**, 314
Brian, F.R.H. 52, **55**, 56, 64, **68**, 80-1, **83**, 94, **221**
Brice, Richard 190, 194
Brick, Sarah *274*
Bright, G.E. **109**
Brignull, Liam *176*, 291-3, *292*, **302**
Bristow, Christopher 266
Bristow, David 266
Britten, Benjamin 236-7, 239
Brock, Jon 186, 213, 357
Bromford, R.F. 58
Brooke, Philip C.W. 241, 278, 315
Brooke, R.G. *32*, 33-4, **35**, 36, 99, 326, **359**
Brough, Paul **305**
Brown 153
Brown sisters 16, 22, 54, **54**
Brown, Alastair **276**, 283-4
Brown, David **130**
Brown, Emma 280, **357**
Brown, Jenny 173-4, *215*
Brown, Mrs L – see Laura Sorrell
Brown, Mrs Ruth 284
Brown, Phib 174
Brown, Prof Christopher 236, 239, 241, 329, 335
Brown, Rosanna 297
Brown, Sgt./Major R.E. 15
Brown, Sue **263**
Brown, Tim 189, 298
Browne, Katherine **283**
Browne, Mrs Alison **283**
Browne, Peter 184, **283**
Browne, Rebecca **283, 302**
Browne, the Revd Leonard J. **22**, **270**, 282-3, **283**, 288, 307, 311, 351-2
Browning, H. 78
Bruch, Max 242
Bruckland, Andrew **263**
Bruckland, Anna **302**
Bruckland, Mrs Diane **263**
Bruckland, Sarah **263**
Bruen, Lucy *274*
Bryan, P.J. (Pat) **114**, **271**, *275*, 275-6, 300
Buccleuch, Earl & Countess of **260**
Buchanan, Margaret – see under Ferguson
Buckett, C.J. **323, 325**, 327, 339
Buckett, Simon 291
Bufton, Air Vice Marshall S.O. 203, 332
Bulgarides Family 240
Bullingham, William 189
Bullock, Oliver **309**
Bunce, Becky 294
Bunce, James **302**
Bunce, John 282, **282**
Bunce, Mrs Liz 282, **282**
Burch, Ian **147**
Burgess, Susan **284**, 301
Burgon, Edward *229*
Burke, A.L. 335
Burke, Dr N.H.M. **324**, 330
Burke, Edmund 150, 345
Burke, Mrs Susan **119**
Burkitt, Dr Denis *329*, 329-30
Burnett-Hodd, F.A. 330
Burns, Jessica **302**
Burns, Lynn 177-8, 294
Burns, Nicholas 297
Burroughs, Lynn 183, 336
Burroughs, Mrs Viv A. **122**, **137**, 149, 356
Burrows, Emma 333
Burrows, Jim R.J. 208, *209*, 210-13, 215
Burton, Laura 182, 193, *351*
Burton, T.L. **360**
Butland, Isobel 180
Butler, James 290, 333
Butler, John 136
Butler, Karen 141
Butler, Matthew 169
Butler-Sloss, Dame Elizabeth 350
Byard, H. 234

Cahill, Mrs Jo **106**, 281-2, **282**, 301
Cahill, Steve A. **106**, **282**, 281-2, 286, 301
Cairns, Peter M. 119, 131, 142, 183, 223-6, 230, 237-41, **247-51**
Caldecote, 1st Viscount 52, 54, 69, **77**, 94, 106, **355**
Caldecote, 2nd Viscount 148, **355**
Calderbank, Paul 169
Calvert, Martina 191, 297
Cameron, Alexandra *191*
Campbell, Mrs E.R. 110
Campbell-White, Martin A. 236, **360**
Cannon, T.F. **60**, **325**
Cantelo, April 240
Canterbury, Archbishops of – see under individual names
Carey, George
Fisher, Geoffrey
Temple, William
Carden, Alex *230*
Cardoza, Lida **130**
Carey, Archbishop George 148
Carlisle, Alex *172*, 195, 290
Carmell, Chris 135, 194, 238, *238*
Carne, Lt.-Col. J.P., V.C. 203
Carnill, Denys 85, *91*, **91**, 123, 127, **147**, 156, **159**, *161*, 161-3, 166, 175, 257-9, 350
Carnill, Mrs Pam 277
Carpenter, Adrian D. **101**, **114**, 272
Carpenter, D.N.A. 162
Carpenter, F.W. 160
Carter, Dr Adele-Louise 343
Carter, H. **249**
Carter, Mr and Mrs **68**, **70**, 70
Carter, Neil 153
Cartwright, Jonathan *176*
Cary, Falkland 104
Cates, C.S. **60**
Catherwood, Lady 146
Catherwood, Sir Fred 146
Challenor, Emily 295
Challis, Miss M 121
Chan, Connie 298
Chandler, Christopher 188
Channon, E.U. 340
Chaplin, Mrs Rebecca **271**, 282, 309
Chapman, Major Ben 122-3, 126, **129**, 129, 153, 188, 195
Chapman, Mrs Evelyn 123, 126, **129**, 129
Chapman, Piers 329
Chapple, S.A.H. 157
Charania, Nadia *191*
Charania, Sheila 230
Charles, HRH Prince 135, **260**
Chatteris, Mr 33
Cheales, R.A.E. **359**
Chekhov, Anton 223

Cheltenham College – see under individual names
Headmasters of
Hardy, Major H.
Richardson, John
Waterfield, The Revd Canon
Cheltenham Ladies' College – see under individual names
Principal of:
Popham, Miss Mary
Housemistress:
Udell, Miss Kay
Cheltenham Mayors – see under individual names
Bullingham, William
Parsonage, George
Winterbotham, Clara
Cheltenham Rectors – see under individual names
Bell, the Revd Canon
Close, the Revd Francis
Roxby, the Revd Mr
Chesshire, Peter **82**
Chester, Kim 173, 225
Chick, Nicola 209, **209**, *210*, 210
Chitty, Col A.A. 201
Chiu, Jeff 289
Chorley, Mrs Joanna 305
Chorley, Simon 305-6
Chua, S.K.S. **360**
Chubb, Richard 290
Chukwueke, Enyinna 289
Chukwueke, Onyinye *289*
Churchill, Abigail **302**
Clare, John 350
Clark, Dr C.S. 253
Clark, R.C.B. **360**
Clark, the Revd T.H. **2**, 38-9, **41**
Clarke, (H.) G.T. 67, **101**, 101, **103**, *104*, 105,
Clarke, Andrew 338
Clarke, Heather – see under Smethurst
Clarke, Mrs (H.) G.T. 67, **103**, 103-5
Clarke, W. Graham 102
Claughton, Mr **46**
Clayre, Iain F.C.S. 164, 338, **360**
Clayton, Alice 243, **360**
Cleary, Andrew 227, 242, *242*, 244
Cleeve, S. Montague *333*, 333
Close, Admiral Francis Arden **2**, **41**
Close, Dean Francis 1, 3, **10**, ***10***, 148
Close, Mrs Anne (née Arden) **10**
Close, Mrs Mary **2**, 3, **10**, 34
Close, Mrs Mary (Hodgson) **10**
Close, The Revd Henry **10**
Coaker, Annabel 357
Coaker, Charlie *296*
Cobb, E.M. **359**
Cobb, J.F. 98, 206
Cocks, Colin *145*, 145, **354**, 355
Cocks, Gwyneth *145*
Cocks, Eleanor 106, **209**
Cocksedge, Hugh F. (later the Revd) **57**, 145, 203, 207, 257, 346
Codd, Farmer 208
Cody, Mrs Gill 338
Cogbill, Miss 22, 31, 67, 70, 92
Colbert-Smith, Mrs Tracey 138
Cole, Claire 209-10
Cole, Col Eric *95*
Cole, Ross 339
Cole, R. **251**
Cole, Saskia 264
Coleman, Mrs Maggie 300
Coleman, Paul **276**, 279, 283, 300, 302
Colley, Harriet 243
Collier, Mark *320*
Collins, Christopher 185
Collins, Mrs E. **116**
Collins, John 173, **202**
Collinson, Ian 196, 214
Colwill, Esther **262**
Connolly, Sarah 307
Constable, Gwen 274
Constantinou, Matthew **316**
Cook, Alastair **316**
Cook, Brig Jonathan 332
Cook, J.R.B. 206, 332
Cooke, Richard 289
Coombs, Rosemary 243
Cooper, Gary 334
Coope, Gladys 334
Cooper, Det.Ch. Insp. Richard 333
Cooper, H.O. 39, **359**
Cooper, Jilly 350
Cooper, Julie – see under Vine
Cooper, Michael J.R. 168, 186, 207-8
Cooper, Thomas M.A. **4**, **17**, 24, 27-9, 34, 52, *64*, 64, 324, **324**
Cooper, Vicki **202**
Coram, Edward 355
Cormack, Don 279
Cormack, Mrs Margaret 136
Cornwell, A.L. 257
Corry, Rachael 192
Corelli 232
Cossart, Ernest 334
Costin, Lucinda 127
Court-Hampton, Peter 328
Coward, Sir Noel 224
Cox, J.A.D. 154
Cox, Baroness (Caroline) 263, **353**, 354, **355**
Cox, H.B. **359**
Crabb, Mrs Sally 278
Crabbe, R.P. 154
Craig, Rebecca **202**
Crane, Jacquie – see under Mrs J.A. Davis
Crawford, J.P. 155, **359**
Crawley, Mrs V. **323**
Crawshaw, Derek A.J. **101**, 275
Crawshaw, Mrs Bridget **101**, 275, 277, 293
Creery-Hill, the Revd Anthony **113**, **114**, 299
Creffield, Lisa 342
Cresswell, Alan 138, 355
Crippen, Douglas *178*, 290, 292
Crisp, Jo 192
Crofts, Hilary 314-5
Crowley, Patrick 169
Cruger, Johann **41**
Crumplin, J.H.D. **60**
Cullen, O. **250**
Cunningham, Prof G C. 329
Curley, Carlo 240
Curry, Gavin *178*, 290
Curry, Scott 183
Cutts, J.W. 124, 168, **360**

Daintrey, Adrian 60
Dainty, Sister Gerry **92**
Dale, Bishop Basil M. 86-7, *87*, 336
Dale, Ellis 334
Daniels, Major G.P. *100*, **101**, 100-1, 200
Dann, A.C. **90**
Darch-Hopkins, Sian **316**
Darke, Peter 331
Darke, Rachel 197
Darvall, Air Vice-Marshall L. 203
Dash, M.G. 156
Davies, A.B.W. 96
Davies, Anthony 189, 296
Davies, Capt W.A. 202
Davies, Dr Anthony 330
Davies, Dr Cyril 330
Davies, I. Dai 224, **261**
Davies, James 175, *178*, **202**, 354
Davies, Jane 227
Davies, Malcolm 134
Davies, M.F. **114**, 282, 288
Davies, Moira 197
Davies, Mrs Sarah A. **282**, 300
Davies, Philip 166
Davies, Robin 213
Davies, Robin L. 282-3, 307
Davies, Rufus *321*
Davies, Sister Ceri **92**
Davies, Sophie 192
Davies, Vivian 188
Davies-Thomas, Huw 290
Davis, Jane 335
Davis, Keith 127, *146*, 146, **147**, 355
Davis, Mrs J.A. **202**, 355
Davis, Prof J.N. P. 329
Davis, R.T. 187
Davis, the Revd G.B. 253
Davis, Tim 342
Dawkins, the Revd C.H. **109**
Dawson, Matt 295
Deacon, A.F. **35**
Deacon, John 17, **18**, 36, 281, 349, 355
Dean Close Memorial School
Governors/ Trustees – see under individual names:
Bayley, John
Bird, Anthony R.
BonBernard, Steuart
Bruckland, Andrew
Buckett, Cecil
Challis, Miss M.
Clark, the Revd T.H.
Cocks, Colin
Cocks, Mrs Gwyneth
Edwards, W.A.M.
Ellam, Edward
Evans, Prof R.J.W.
Griffith, Miss Caroline
Griffith, Talbot
Hall, Mrs Val
Hardy, Mrs Sue
Holmes, the Revd Dr Jonathan
Hooper, Sir Leonard
Lachlan, John
Lynam, C. Peter
Napier, Mrs Patricia
Watson, the Revd Canon Tim
Went, Bishop John
Yeaman, Sir Ian
Headmasters – see Headmasters' list **358**
Housemasters/mistresses and other staff – see under individual names or under Housemaster/mistress lists for each House
Houses – see School index
Old Decanians – see under names
Old Decanian Society – see School index
Second Masters **25**, 122, 135, 141, 147, 154, **159**
Senior Mistresses 140, 147, 355
Dean Close International School – see under individual names
Dean Close Junior/ Preparatory School – see under individual names
Masters-in-Charge – see list **101**
Headmasters – see list **270**

Dean Close Pre-Preparatory School 'The Squirrels' – see under individual names
Headmistress – see **317**
Deans-Sidgreaves, James **309**
Delhanty, Denys **147**
Delius, Frederick **232**, **234**
Dennis, Simon 307
Derry, Simon **202**
Dexter, Keri 333
Dick, A.S. **324**, 339
Dickinson, J.R. 154
Dietrich, Marlene 334
Dimbleby, Jonathan 145
Dimoline, Major Gen W.A. **324**, 332
Dobbs, Matt 278
Dobbs, Mrs Colette 281, **282**, 300
Dodd, E. **324**
Dodd, the Revd R.P. **324**, 336
D'Oliveira, Basil 289
Donaldson, Rhona 170
Dorrell, Tracey 189
Dowdney, R.E. **250**
Dowler, James 302
Dowler, Matthew *195*, *203*
Dowler, Thomas *195*
Downes, Frankie *191*, 293
Downes, Sarah *178*, 179
Dowty, Ben 170, 291
Dowty, Harry 297
Dowty, Selina 192, 297
Doyle, Sir Arthur C. 60, 219
Dravers, P. *155*
Dring, Matthew **181**, 298
Drinkwater, John 79, 220
Drown, the Revd R. 'Dick' 266, **359**
Ducat, Mrs 19
Ducat, Sarah – see under Flecker
Duff, Ollie 173-4
Duffield, M. 169
Duffin, Sarah ***265***
Dunbar, Ian 170
Dunlop, Mrs J.M. **114**, 282, 300
Dunn, James **147**
Dunnett, Roderic 311
Durstan, David **147**
Duruty, Donald **78**
Dwerryhouse, W.F. 167
Dyer, Charlotte 196
Dyer, Ciaran 212
Dyer, Jenny 342

Eadon, Andrew 312
Eagleton, Thomas **262**
Eales-White, Alasdair 340
Eales-White, Prof Ian 329
Eames, K.E. 167
Easterfield, Edward 16, 29, 36, 99
Eastwood, Clint 334
Eaton, M.W. 206
Ede, Michael **263**, 279, 282, 302
Edge, Miss P. **116**
Edginton, Cathy 191
Edginton, Tom **181**, 193, **261**
Edkins, Bridget 182, 192
Edmondson, Sister Shona **92**
Edmunds, Danny 342-3
Edward VII, HM King 37
Edwards, Alex 174, *352*
Edwards, Samantha 186
Edwards, W.A.M. 98, 115, 139, *139*, 145, *153*, 153-4, **159**, 270, **324**, *338*, 338-9, **354**
Edwards, W.R. **360**
Elder, Hugh **49**, **53**, **54**, **65**, 65-7, 69, **70**, 71, 79-81, 93, 103, 105-7, 110, **129**, 150, 152, 158-9, 163, 234, 313, **324**, 345, **358**
Elder, Hugh J.M. **65**
Elder, Mrs Mary (née Stagg) **65**, **70**
Elder, Patricia (later Mrs Hurst) **68**
Elgar, Sir Edward 232
Elgood, Mrs 187
Elias, Mr **46**
Eliot, T.S. **220**
Elizabeth II, HM Queen, Coronation of 86
Golden Jubilee of 354
Elizabeth, HM Queen Mother 64
Elizabeth, HRH Princess 203
Ellam, Edward 14, **17**, 25, **25**, 28-9, 40, 46, **49**, 52, 55-6, **56**, **57**, 66, **68**, 69, 80, 153-4, 160, 162, 168, **221**, 232, **234**
Ellames, P. 168
Ellard, Stephen **302**
Ellis, G.C.J. 154, 168
Ellis, R.A. 203
Ellis, S.P.J. 168
El-Marazki, Hisham 290
Elwin, Dr H.Verrier 342
Emm, Mrs Mary 278
Emmerson, Marcus **309**
Emms, Richard 313
English, Gerald 236
Ensor, Simon 290, 292
Entwistle, R. **249**
Epps, J.R. 99
Etherington, Carleton 309, 312
Etherington, Mrs Katie 309
Evans, Dominic D. **217**, 217
Evans, David R. 147
Evans, Ffion 296
Evans, Jack 291
Evans, Lloyd 291
Evans, Miss 106
Evans, Mrs Caroline 355
Evans, Prof R.J.W. **4**, 24, 44, 142, **329**, *329*, 329
Evans, S.M. 119
Evans, Spencer 342
Evans, the Very Revd Seriol 90
Ewing, Sir Alexander 330
Eyres, David 173

Fair, James **181**
Fairclough, Lisa 182
Fanshawe, David 239
Farmer, A. *155*
Farquhason, Bill 124
Fateh, Alex 171, *178*, 190, 292, 297
Fateh, Isabella (Issey) *180*, **181**, *191*, 286
Fateh, Tamara *176*, *178*, 179-80, **181**, 291, 293-4
Faulkes, Prof Anthony 329
Faulkner, Dominic **202**, 209
Faulkner, Tegan *178*, **302**
Faull, Jonathan 242, *243*, 246
Faure, Gabriel 236-7
Fearnehough, Tom 338
Fenton, Georgina 184
Ferguson, David 198
Ferguson, Ian F.M. **270**, **271**, 272, **273**, *274*, 275-9, **282**, 282, 290, 313-4, 317
Ferguson, Mrs Margaret E. 272, **272**, **273**, 273, 277-9, 297, 301, 314, 317
Ferriman, D.G. **60**
Feydeau, Georges 223
Fick, James 290
Field, Christopher 169, 189, *287*, 289, 291, **302**
Fieldhouse, Prof D.K. **324**
Finch, David 194
Finch, R.E.G. 'Bob' 70, 340
Findlay, G.W.M. 330
Findlay, S.H. **76**
Fisher, Archbishop Geoffrey **53**
Fisher, Isaac 338
Fitton, David J.M. 163, 166
Fitton, J.M. **325**, 330
Fitzgerald, Alexander 190
Flanagan, Oliver 170
Flecker, (Herman) James Elroy **4**, ***5***, 43, *44*, 334-5
Flecker, Claire **4**
Flecker, H.L. Oswald **4**, 44, 46, 200, 359
Flecker, Issacher **4**
Flecker, Joyce **4**, 33-4, 44, 232
Flecker, Mrs Sarah (née Ducat) **4**, 8, ***5***, 27, 32, 38, 42-4, 47, **50**, 51, 84, 99, 232
Flecker, the Revd Dr. William H. 4, **4**, ***5***, *6*, 12-13, *13*, 15-18, **17**, **18**, 21, **22**, 22, 27-31, **31**, 32, 34, **35**, 36-9, **41**, 42-4, 46-7, **47**, 49, 51, 52, 54, **54**, 59, 80, 87, 99, 107, 119, 129, 145, 149, 150, **184**, 199, 219, 232, 253, 255, 309, 323-4, **324**, *326*, 345, 349, 352, **352**
Fletcher, Claire 177, 293-4
Fletcher, Mr 42
Flint, Ben 153, 156
Flower, R.K. 164
Foale, Ashley 186, 211, *287*
Forbes, A.C. (Tony) **126**, 135, 175
Forbes, Annabel 297
Forbes, Charlie 191, 297
Forbes, Justin *178*
Forbes, Lindy 135, **247**, **249**, **250**
Ford, Jack *176*
Fordham, Sister Mina **92**
Forrester, Edward **202**
Foss-Pedersen, Frederick 190
Foster, Anne 237
Foster, D.J. **202**
Foster, Edward 340
Foster, Philip **110**, **113**
Fothergill, Martin 238
Fowke, Martin 339
Fowler, E. 330, **359**
Fowler, G. **60**
Fowler, Sister Sally **92**
Fowler, W/Cdr Stuart G. **17**, 145
Foxall, Dennis **82**
Frankham, G.H.C. **360**
Fraser, R.H. **325**
Fredjohn, Wendy 188
Freemantle, the Very Revd **2**
French, Robert *185*
Friend, Dr 58
Frost, C.S. **35**
Fry, Christopher 224
Fuller-Shapcott, David C.J. 186
Fuller-Shapcott, J.N. 186, **323**, **325**, **360**
Fuller-Shapcott, Stuart I.J. 186, **260**, 340
Fullerton, David 350
Fulton, Joanna 192
Furnish, Alfred **82**, 235
Furno, Melissa 291

Gaine, P.D. **325**, **360**
Gale, Julian 242-3
Gall, Diana 185
Gall, John 185
Gallagher, Sister Sarah **92**
Gamman, Andrew **309**
Gandhi, Mahatma 342
Gane, Stuart 126, 139
Garbett, M.E. 193
Gardiner, A.C. **323**, **325**
Gardiner, Balfour 309

Gardner, Miss Alice 232
Gardner, Neil W. **305**, 305, 309
Gare, Mrs *52*
Garner, Doug 350
Garner, Peter J.J. 193
Garner, Richard **251**
Garrett, Emma **202**
Garrett, Will **202**
Garson, Rachel 185
Garstang, Rachel 186
Gaunt, Lt Col R.J.H. **324**
Gaussen, Major B. **17**
Gay, Oliver **309**, 311
Gay, Sister Catherine **92**
Gaye, Derek **82**, **109**, 235, *235*
Gaylard, Les *172*
Gayward, I.C. **360**
George V, HM King 254, 333
George VI, HM King 64, 254
George, Elizabeth **302**
Georgeson, Dudley 190, 192
George-Wallich, R. **17**
Gershwin, George 242
Gibbings, Grp Capt P.H. **324**
Gibbins, Rowena 186-7
Gibbons, Benjamin 184
Gibbons, Orlando 239
Gibbs, Col Sir Martin 142, *210*, 224
Gibbs, Jennifer – see under Mrs Pritchard
Gibson, Christopher **261**
Gibson, Guy W/Cdr 277
Gibson, the Revd D.I. **22**, **55**, 119, 124, 126, 137, 207, 224
Gibsin, Bishop E. 40, **41**
Gifford, Norman 289
Gilbert, Sam 193, 211, 225, **251**
Giles, Mrs Di 296
Gilkes, Antony (Tony) N. 81, **82**, 83-5, 87, 89, 93, 96, 107, **108**, 122, 129, 135, 153, *201*, 256, **324**, **358**
Gilkes, David **82**
Gilkes, Mrs Ruby (née Shaw) **82**
Gilkes, Patrick **82**
Gilkes, Robin **82**
Gilkes, Roger **82**
Gilliam, P.M. 170
Gillman, Jeremy *176*, ***184***
Gillot, Jason 342
Gilroy, Duncan 290
Gilson, Mr 51
Girling, M.A. **57**, 81, **82**, 87, *121*, 122, 124, 131, 135, 141, 149, 156-7, *161*, *172*, **325**, 327
Glanville, Prof Stephen **117**
Glover, Anna 170
Godwin, Claire *178*, 179, 286
Godwin, Helen 187
Golder, Major A.W. 52, *73*, **76**, 105-6, **109**, 110, **111**, 152, 158, 200, *201*, 201-2
Golder, Mrs Edith M. **111**
Gonner, E. *38*
Gooch, Lindsay 309
Goodale, K.R.T. 333
Gooderham, Mrs Lucy 338
Goodhew, Duncan 189
Goodwright, Mrs Vicky **272**, 279
Goodwright, Tim 227, **251**, **272**, 279, **285**
Gorton, M.G. 204
Goudie, James 258
Goudie, Prof Andrew 328
Gough, James **181**, 243
Gower, Tom 190, 290
Gowrie, Lord 335
Grace, Richard 185
Graham, James **88**
Graham, John **88**
Graham, Miss 70
Graham, Mrs Ann **88**, 154
Graham, the Revd Douglas L. 37, 79, 87, **88**, 89-98, 107, 116-7, 125, 135, 142, *161*, 162, 167, 222, 235, 256, **358**
Graham, Timothy **88**
Graham-Dixon, Andrew 336
Grant, Mary 338
Graveney, Tim G. **360**
Gray, E.R.B. **55**, **68**, 70, **76**
Gray, the Revd Steven J.N. **22**, 351
Greaves, R.H. **35**
Green, D.E. 151, **359**
Green, Mr 324
Green, R.N. 27, 232
Green, Rosie **276**
Green, Sister Vera **92**
Green, the Revd Tim 337
Green,T.M.W. **360**
Greening, M.R. **202**, 203
Gregory, Christopher 197, *197*
Gregory, Mrs W. **272**
Grieg, Edvard **233**, 236
Griffin, Bob 190
Griffin, Ian **305**
Griffith, Miss Caroline *141*, 142, **210**
Griffith, Mrs Mary **210**
Griffith, Talbot 141-2, **210**
Griffiths, L.R. **360**
Griffiths, the Revd Canon G.P. **2**, 13, 22, 25, 38, 40
Griffiths, Zoe 186
Grigg, D.B. 156
Groom, Alistair *351*
Groslin, J. **249**
Grylls, Bear 349
Guest, Mrs S. **282**
Guinness, Sir Alec 334
Gupta, Ashok 242, *243*, *245*, 245, 308
Guthrie, General Lord 217, *217*
Guy, Sister Wendy **92**
Gwilliam, Rhys 175, *176*, **181**, 184

Habershon, P.J. **360**
Hadfield, Ben **202**
Hague, Sarah 297
Hall, D.M. **359**
Hall, Jamie 213
Hall, Jeremy 289
Hall, Marie 60, **232**, **233**
Hall, Miss Val 121
Hallett, the Revd R.W. **22**, 90, 257
Halse, Lionel **46**, **51**
Hamill, Sean 226, 229, **252**
Hamlett, D.J.R. 168
Hammond, Jon 190
Hammond, Wally **159**
Handel, George F. 234, 236-7, 239, **240**
Handl, Jacob 239
Handy, I.G. **202**
Hanks, Joanna 196, 298
Hanks, Laura 298
Hanney, Sgt/Major 68
Hansford, Steve 170
Hanson, J. *155*
Haracz, Joanna **147**, 147
Harding, Claire 331
Harding, P.J. 163
Hardy, Major H.H. 112, **354**
Hardy, Mrs Sue 121
Hardy, Nicholas 135, *135*
Hardy, Thomas 36
Harmer, Tim 183
Harper, Bridget 259
Harper, D.H. 188
Harper, Duncan 328
Harper, G.H. 109, **109**, **110**, **113**, 269, 271, 275, **284**, 284-5, **285**
Harper, Mike 297
Harper, Miles **285**
Harper, Mrs P.E. (Liz) **116**, **285**
Harper, Shan 269, **285**
Harries, C.V.G. 123, **360**
Harries, G. Vaughan **57**, **82**, **125**
Harries, Angela – see under Brain-Gabbott
Harries, Mrs 236
Harris, Col 212
Harris, Col Jock 340
Harris, Eric 266, 302
Harris, Jon **106**, 282, 288
Harris, Mrs **115**
Harris, Mrs Fiona **106**, 282
Harris, Simon 342
Harris, Tom *176*
Harris, Vicky 289
Harrison, Alexander 280
Harrison, G.L. **359**
Harrison, Prof C.V. 329
Harrison, Richard 190
Harrison, Sian 297
Harriss, Louise 212
Harry, M.J.H. 257
Hart, Claude 33
Hart, George 69
Hart, S.S.I. Mike 187, 208, 210, 215, 217
Harvey, J.H. 7, 9, *13*, **31**, 324
Harvey, R.M. 153
Harwood, Cecil S. 'Mac' **101**, **106**, 109, **109**, *112*, 112, 114-5
Harwood, John 147
Harwood, Mrs Jean 115
Harwood-Smith, Michael 213
Haslam, Chris 229, **247**, **251-2**, 347
Hastie-Smith, the Revd Timothy M. **22**, **150**, 150, **184**, 225-6, **251-2**, **263**, 264, *266*, 266, 279, 305-7, 321, *346*, 345-7, 349, 356-8, **358**
Hastie-Smith, Alice **150**
Hastie-Smith, Edward **150**
Hastie-Smith, Emily **150**
Hastie-Smith, Mrs Joanne **150**, *346*, 358
Hatt, A.B. 350
Hatt, E.B. 350
Havers, Nigel 229
Hawes, Simon 185
Hawkesworth, M. 168
Hawkins, J.S.R. 205
Hawkins, Michael 185, 207
Hawley, Miss 44
Hay, Einar S. **57**, 85, 94, 203
Hay, Stuart 145
Haydn, Joseph 235-8, **240**
Hayes, Jessica 243, 334
Hayes, Sarah 286
Hayward, the Revd Edward 66, **68**
Head, Jasmin *289*
Heath, Henry 333
Heath, Malcolm 170
Heaton-Jones, Gordon 207, **261**
Henderson, G.N. **360**
Henderson, Mr & Mrs **221**
Henderson, R.M. 343
Henle, Sister Claire **92**
Henley, Susie 241
Henry, Mike 335
Hensley, Miss **111**

Henslow, Miss E.R. 'Hetty' – see under Mrs E.R. Campbell
Hensman, Col Jake R., R.M. 91, 248, **331**
Hepple, J.F. (later the Revd) **31**
Herapath, N.F. *38*, **359**
Herber-Davies, Elizabeth **302**
Herbert, Matthew 197-8, **261**, 289
Herbert, Mrs Jane **260**, **272**, 278
Herbertson, Kirsty 186, 194
Herd, Caroline – see under Evans
Herring, W.M. (Mike) 279, **282**
Heskell, John 102
Hewitt, Helen **233**, 241
Hewitt, Linda 188
Hewitt-Jones, Tony 241
Hewlett, Rebecca 169, 184
Hibberd, Jonathan 272
Hildick-Smith, Francesca **360**
Hildick-Smith, Georgina 196, 353
Hildick-Smith, Richard 170, 173, *190*, 190, 196, **209**
Hill, Chris *274*
Hill, Christopher 196
Hill, Joe *227*, 227
Hill, John 190
Hill, Mrs Sally **323**
Hill, P.S. **35**
Hill, R. **60**
Hill, R.G.154
Hill, Ryan 215
Hill, sisters **105**
Hill, Tessa 196, *196*
Hillier, A.G. **35**
Hillier, H.W. **35**
Hilltout, Paul 339
Hilton, R. **250**
Hindemith, Paul 237
Hines, Emma **360**
Hinton, Graham **140**
Hitchcock, Mr **46**
Hoare, E.G. 340
Hoare, E.S. 56, **57**, 62, **68**, **77**, 80-1, 94, 119, **121**, 122, 155, *156*, 159, **159**, *159*, 160-2, 201, **323**, **324**, **325**, 325, **359**
Hoare, F.O. *38*, **359**
Hoare, G.H. **359**
Hoare, Mrs Joan ***159***
Hoare, the Revd Canon 9
Hobbs, Paul 147
Hocking, Captain Muriel, RN 212
Hodges, Adam 339
Hodges, Horace 220, **247-8**
Hodges, Paul 225, **251**
Hodgetts, C.L. **360**
Hodgetts, Cliff 338
Hodgetts, Mr 162
Hodgkins, Catherine **302**
Hodgkins, Matthew *321*
Hoggett, Chris **147**
Holborow, R.W. 173
Holden, David 342
Holden, Dr Oscar M. **75**
Hole, R.D. 67
Holliday, S.W. **55**, **250**
Hollington, Ken 85, 110, **110**, **113**, **114**, 113, 270
Holloway, Charlotte 238
Hollows, Edward *178*
Holman, Col John 330
Holmes, Robert 189
Holmes, the Revd Dr Jonathan 112, 336
Holyfield, Mrs Jane 317
Honneyman, Daniel 169
Hooper, J.D. **101**, **282**
Hooper, Sir Leonard 'Joe' 118, 128, **130**, 130, 145, 327, **354**
Hopkin, John 212
Hopkin, Katy *178*, 186, 194, 298
Hopkins, A.J. 325
Hopkins, R.D. **17**, **145**
Hornby, Francesca 296
Hornby, Olivia 242-3, 286
Horncastle, A.W. **206**
Horne, I.M.E. 163
Hornsby, P.J.H. **359**
Horsefield, the Revd D.F. **22**, 52, **53**, 55, **55**, 58, 100, 136, 254-5, **324**
Horsfall, J.S.C. 'Jimmy' 237
Horsley, Francis 52, **53**, 62, 66-7, 80-1, 84, **101**, 101, 105, 107-8, 110, **111**
Horsley, John **53**, 106
Horsley, Margaret **53**
Horsley, Mrs Mary **53**, 107
Horsley, Robert **53**
Horton, G. 162
Hotchkiss, Christopher 183
House, P.D. **360**
Houseman, A.E. **88**
Hover, Roland 193
Howard, David J. 338
Howard, Rt Hon Michael, M.P. 145
Howarth, George 237-9
Howarth, Major D.J.G. **324**, **325**
Howell, Lucy *203*, 246
Howell, Megan **202**, **302**
Howell, Wesley 188, 193, 298
Howells, Herbert 309
Howells, M.S. 256
Howse, Frank 280
Huckvale, Guy **202**
Huckvale, Mrs Carol 277, 282
Huddleston, Fr Trevor, (later Archbishop) 257
Hudson, Sister Nancy **92**
Hughes, H.E.O. **359**
Hughes, Mark A. 208, **209**, **360**
Hughes, Simon 296
Hughes, Sue 185
Hume, Alex 171, *178*
Hunt, James *320*
Hunt, Rodney **261**
Hunt, Sir John 207
Hunter, Jack *178*
Hunton, Hugo 189
Hurst, A.W. **68**
Hurst, Mrs Patricia – see under Elder
Hurst, Sir Geoff 283, **348**
Hutchings, G.A. **360**
Hutchinson, I.D. 166
Huxtable, M. Claire 288
Hyde, Ben 183, *183*

Iles, Sgt **47**
Imlay, Major D.A. **17**
Ingham, Sir Bernard 350
Ings, Sarah *245*, 246
Inkin, Lt-Col Sir Geoffrey 332
Inskip, T.W.H. – see under Caldecote, 1st Lord
Ip, Patrick 188
Iredale, A. Linton **50**
Iredale, A.C. **324**
Ireland, R.I. **113**, 156, 162, **198**, 357
Irvine, Rebecca **360**
Isherwood, Eve – see under Seymour

Jacks, Sister Bridget **92**
Jackson, Samantha **202**
Jackson, Stephen 311
Jacob, Richard 188-90, *190*
Jacobsen, Mark 191-2
James, B.G. **206**, 206
James, F.B. **360**
James, Michael 274, 290
Jameson, Mrs Faith 277, 301
Jarman, Derek 334
Jarrett, Miss A. **109**
Jarrett-Kerr, Jake 123
Jarrett-Kerr, Lt.-Col C.E. 186
Jarvis, Toby **261**
Jary, Michael 187
Jeffries, Mr 153
Jeffries, T. 70
Jellings, H. **75**
Jenkins, D.M. 168
Jenkins, Gareth *178*
Jenkins, Joe *178*, 290
Jenkins, Neil 236-7, 239, 245, 333, *333*
Jenkins, T.W. 35, **35**
Jennings, Joanne **140**
Jensen, C.E. 154
Jervis, Laura **360**
Jessop, Andrew **262**
Johana, Pastor **262**
Johns, R.L. 154, 342, **360**
Johnson, Capt. R.H., R.N. **324**
Johnson, Lucy *178*, 298
Johnson, M.M. **359**
Johnson, Nicola 238
Johnson, R. *38*
Johnson, S.H.H. **359**
Johnson, Tom *178*, 183
Johnston, P.N. **360**
Johnston, Robert 241, 333
Joiner, Sara 177
Jones, A.J. 'Tony' 197-8, 211
Jones, Aled 311
Jones, Brian *334*, 334
Jones, Chris 123, 173, 223
Jones, Christina 175, *178*, 182, 187
Jones, D.W. **360**
Jones, David 198, 298, 302
Jones, E.S. 323
Jones, Edward 243, *246*, 246
Jones, G.M. 93
Jones, Gareth 198, 298
Jones, Gareth (Tewkesbury) **305**
Jones, Graham 339
Jones, H.I. **323**, **325**, 326
Jones, K.H., Surgeon, R.N. **35**
Jones, M.K. 157
Jones, Martin **181**
Jones, Willie 157, 170
Jose, S.W. 27, **323**
Joubert, John 237
Joyce, Margaret 169, 173
Judge, Alastair 173, *178*, *291*, 291
Judge, Andrew J. **101**, 224, **271**, 275, **276**, 281, **282**, **284-5**, 286, 288, 290, 300
Judge, Mrs Margaret F. **101**, 275, 281
Judge, Thomas 171-2, *178*, 290, 292, **302**
Judge, Victoria 184, **302**
Judson, William 28, 52, 61

Kaveh, Farman 193
Kay, the Revd A.I. 253
Kearns, J.W. 36
Keay, John *178*
Keiller, Robert 193
Kelly, Sir Gerald 90
Kemp, Alexander 169
Kemp, Lisa 193

Kennaway, Sir John 42, **35**
Kennedy, Cedric **76**, 78, 81, 85, *93*, 93, **109**
Kennedy, Peter 184
Kenny, Sarah 189
Kensit, A.L. 338
Kent, Bernard **264**
Kent, Emily **264**
Kent, Mrs Julie **122**, **126**, 149, 264, **264**
Kenyon, C.M. **57**, **91**, 97, **147**, 149, 157, 170, *172*, 187
Kenyon, Mrs Sarah 149
Kerr, E.D. **360**
Kerr, I.W. **359**
Kerr, W.D. **359**
Kettle, Lana **202**
Key, Pat **261**
Khairy, Nadia 336
Kidd, Tom 335
Kiddell, C.B. **82**, 167, 202
Kinder, Robert *178*, **202**, 343
Kinder, Will 175
Kindersley, David **130**
King, Aaron **309**
King, Bruce 185
King, Nathan **309**
King, Peter 163
King, Prof Peter 329
Kingston, E. **251**
Kingston, Joanna 178
Kirby, A.W 104
Kirby, R.I. **57**, **125**, 217
Kirby, Simon T. 259, **360**
Kitchener, Lord **35**
Klemz, Mrs Sylvia **323**
Knight, P.H. 156
Knight, G. Wilson 60, 102, 220, **220**, **247**
Knight, H.F.P. **359**
Knight, Richard O. 225, 239-42, **240**
Knowles-Bolton, A.H. **359**
Koufou, Savvas *287*
Kramer, Dr L.M.J. **4**, 55, **60**, **324**, **325**, **359**
Kreisler, Fritz **233**
Krick, Emma 288
Kvesic, Sister Jane **92**
Kwan, Yee Lam **357**
Kynaston, Neil 190, *191*

Lachlan, John 134
Lai, Eric *194*, 194, 297
Laing, Brig G. 204
Lamb, F.R. **60**
Lamb, T.N. 160
Lamprey, Dr H.F. 341
Lamprey, W.S. 106
Lancashire, Hannah **358**
Lancashire, Jonathan M. **17**, 307, **358**, *358*, 358
Lancashire, Mrs Sally **358**
Lancashire, William **358**
Lane, Dan 170
Lane, George 297
Lane, H.C.H. **359**
Lane, Joe *178*, 290
Lane, Rupert D. 157, 183, 328, **360**
Langford, David E. 168, 205
Langhorne, Eadward 84, **106**, 107, ***108***, 108-112, **109**, **270**, 270, 277
Langhorne, Mrs Rosemary ***108***, 110, 270
Langhorne, Sister Penelope **92**
Lansdown, Simon 163
Large, A.W. 37
Laszlo, D. **251**
Latham, J.M. 166
Lavis, T.H. **325**
Lawrence, Beatrice *230*
Lawrence, Geoffrey – see under Lord Oaksey
Lawrence, J.H. **324**, **325**
Lawrence, Lyn **252**
Lawrence, T.J. 170
Lawson, Flt/Sgt Roy, RAFVR 200
Le Bargy, Charles 297
Lea, Katie 196, 213
Leach, W.H. **60**
Leakey, Samuel **209**
Leavey, K. 60
Lednor, Martin 340
Lee, Charles 298-9
Lee, John **202, 251**
Lee, Lucinda *229*, **252,** ***265***
Lee, Mrs Christine 293-4
Lee, U.S. General John 79, 201
Leech, K.P.H. **360**
Leech, P.J. 156
Leeke, Mrs Amy *321*, 321
Lefeaux, Cdr J.M., R.N. 331
Leger, Hannah 182
Legg, Anna ***265***
Legg, Jamie **181**
Lehane, Margaret *316*, 316
Lehment, Henrik *178*
Lemon, R.L. 206
Leonard, Sir John **324**, 331
Leopold, Philip 185
Lepine, David 235-6
Letchworth, A.T. 154
Letchworth, Charles 332
Leung, Simon 342
Levett, Miss **68**, 70
Levick, Surgeon Cdr M. **202**
Lewin, A.H. 9, 323
Lewis, A.D. **324**, **325**
Lewis, Emma 173, *191*
Lewis, farmer 72
Lewis, Hywel 175, 297
Lewis, John 335
Lewis, Mrs Liz **106**, 275
Lewis, Trevor **106**, 275, 300
Lidderdale, F.J. 37, *38*, 158, **324**
Lidderdale, W.G. 37, *38*, 158
Light, Ronald 47, **47**
Lin, Yi-Lun 246
Lineham, Elliot 173
Lineham, Wesley 174
Linford, T.J. **206**, 206
Lingley, Matron **68**
Lister, George 331
Litt, Jessica **252**
Little, Ian 224, 239, 284
Liverton, Sister Gillian **92**
Llewelyn, Ivor 26
Llewelyn, Sir Leonard 26
Lloyd, S.S.I. Brian 218
Lloyd-Wood, Christopher 223, **248**
Lomas, Christopher 213
Long, George **284**, 285
Long, Mrs Iris **115**, **116**, *277*, 277, 300
Long, Richard **209**
Long, Tony 207
Losh, Jack *243*
Lott, Dame Felicity 238
Lovell, Julian T. **114, 271,** 277-8, 289
Lowe, Robert 290
Lucas, W.R. **360**
Luce, Prof G.H. 329, 334, **359**
Luce, Sir Richard 239
Luce, the Revd C.E. **50**, 55, 100
Luce, the Revd J.A. **22**, **31**, 44, **50**, 55
Lunt, Stephen 190
Luther, Martin **41**
Lutley, J.H. 162
Lutyens, Sir Edwin 340
Lynall, Richard 183
Lynam, C.P. **323**, **324**, **325**, 327, 350
Lyne-Pirkis, A. **251**
Lyne-Pirkis, Richard 335

M'Caw, Martin 338
Mac, Jenna 192
Macfarlane, Laura *178*, 293, **302**
Macgill, Mrs G.S. **122**
Machin, Antonia 188
MacIndoe, Sir Archibald 332
MacKenzie, Laura 248
Mackie, F.P. 26
Mackie, Neil 238
Mackinnon, Rachel 243
Macpherson sisters, the 47, 219
Macpherson, D.S. **125**, 135, **249**
Major, Richard 166
Mallard, C.G. **360**
Maloney, M.R. **360**
Malric-Smith, Michael 185
Mander, M. **360**
Mangue, Miriam 197
Mantell, Simon **181**
Marchand, A.R. 'Tony' 147, *359*, 359
Marchand, Clare 212, **360**
Marchand, Paul 172, 175, *178*, 183-4, 194, **360**
Marlow, Simon *195*
Marquand, Andrew 339
Marquand, Richard 339
Marr, Philip **360**
Marsden, Ben 175-6, *176*, *178*, **181**, **198**, 357
Marsh, Andrew 261, 355, **360**
Marsh, David B.W. **57**, 184, 355
Marsh, Nicholas 184, 290, 355, **360**
Marshall, Edward 246
Marshall, Mrs Janet 225, 230, 284
Marston, Joanne 197
Martin, Andrew *178*
Martin, C. 223, **249**
Martin, Col B.K. 332
Martin, Francis J.O. 339
Martin, Matthew 241, 333
Martin, Michael W.G. 185
Martin, Philippa *243*, 243, 316
Martin, R.C. **247**, **249, 250**
Martin, S.V. 157
Martin, Sarah 297
Martin, the Revd Richard 259
Martin, William *227*, **316**
Masefield, John **222**, 222
Maslin, Ted 124
Mason, Bill 124, *124*, 153
Mason, Pippa 195
Masterman, C. **251**
Masterman, Laura 170
Mathias, P/O Anthony, RAF 200
Mawle, Robert 340
Maxwell, Andrew *195*, *203*
Mbangwa, 'Pom' *172*, 172
McAdam, Catherine (Katy) 177, 186, 274, **302**
McAdam, Iain 209
McAleer, William *176*
McBane, Naomi 198
McCann, Mrs Sarah 338
McCardie, Amanda – see under Parker
McCloy, Sam **261**
McColl, Blaire 179
McColl, Robbie **360**

McConnell, Mrs **240**
McCulloch, Morag *274*
McDowall, Carol 230, 284
McElhinney-Kent, Charlotte **316**
McEwen, L.W. 166
McGhie, P. **248**
McGregor-Johnson, Richard 331
McGuffie, Robert 174
McKellar, Beverley 182
McKenna, Virginia 341
McKinnon, Stuart 331
McLellan, Dr E.A. 234-5
McLellan, Mrs Joyce (née Sadler) 235
McNeile, R.F. 7, 26-7, *27*, 54, 153, 167, **219**, 323, **324**, 346, **359**
Mears, James 183, *351*
Meek, A.D. **360**
Melrose, the Revd K.M.C. **76**, 106, **106**
Melville, Helen **181**, 182
Melville, James *176*, **302,** 355, **360**
Melville, Nigel 184, 295
Mendelssohn, Felix 240
Mercer-Wilson, Midshipman Stephen R. *75*
Mercer-Wilson, Peter 163
Metcalf, G.M. **324**, **325**
Metcalf, John 239, 335
Michael of Kent, HRH Prince 149, 241, **242**, **260**, 279
Michell, J. **251**
Middleton, Chloe 173
Miliffe, Sue 315
Millard, Rebecca – see under Smith, Dr Rebecca
Miller, Arthur 224, 226
Miller, Benjamin *176*
Miller, Kate 229, **252**
Miller, L.R. **359**
Millington-Buck, Ben 339
Mills, D.M. **359**
Mills, Peter 224, **250**, 277, **284**, 284, 295, *295*
Millward, T.J. 204
Milne, A. **325**, 334
Milne, A.W. 182
Milne, Sheila 191
Milton, Alan 160, 329
Milton, Jonathan **305**, *312*, 312
Minchin, Mrs Lesley 317
Mintram, Bryony **181**
Mitchell, R.J. **360**
Mitzner, Drew 193
Moger, Charlotte 173
Moger, James 350
Moiseiwitsch, Benno 234
Monaco, David 222
Money, George J. 328
Money, the Revd Canon W.T. 253-4, **255**
Monie, K.M. 66, 105, **105**
Monies, S.O. **359**
Montagu, Brig J.H. **17**, 187
Monteverdi 238
Montgomery, Basil 340
Montgomery, composer 236
Montgomery, Marion 239
Montgomery, Paul S. **91**, 211
Moor, Joe **202**
Moor, N.P. **57**
Moore, Dr Barbara **260**
Moore, G. **35**
Moore, Gerald **233**
Moore, Janet – see under Skidmore
Moore, John S. **55**, **68**, **76**, 80-1, 128, **129**, 154, 163-5, 207
Moore, Mr 104
Moore, Mrs Binnie **129**
Moore, Rob **181**
Moore, T.L. 157
Moos, Beth 294
Moran, M.D. 156
Moreland, Robert 331
Morgan, Christopher 296
Morgan, F.W. 149
Morgan, Kit 136
Morgan, T.R. *218*, **218, 325**
Morgan, the Ven Chandos C.H.M. **22**, 136
Morgan, W.E. 328
Morgans, David 183
Morris, H.J. 340, **359**
Morris, Jennifer 134
Morris, Miss 44
Morris, the Revd Marcus *337*, 337
Morris, the Revd Paul 337
Morrison sisters 18
Morse 153
Moses, N.C. 153
Mosley, Mrs N. **17**
Motum, Col Mike 332
Mould, W. Crafnant **17**
Moule, John 147, 193, **251**
Moule, the Revd G.W.H. **22**
Mountfort, the Revd C.C. **31**, *39*, 39, 46, 199
Mowat, M.G. 123
Mozart, Wolfgang A. 236-40, **240**
Mudway, Selby 156
Mudway, Tom 156
Mullan, Peter 291
Mullen, Chris 186
Mullens, H.G. **359**
Mullins, I. 222, 230, **248**
Munden, Gill – see under Cody
Munden, the Revd Dr Alan 148
Murray, C.S. 325
Murray, Tim 222-3, **247, 248**
Mustoe, Nick 339

Napier, Mrs Patricia 308, *354*, **354**
Nash, E.R. **359**
Nash, John 175
Nash, John 208
Nasralla, Patrick 213
Naylor, Amy – see under Leeke
Neal, Chris 190, 192
Needs, Aaron 191
Negus, Alastair 194
Neil, Charles C.S. 154
Neill, Bishop Stephen C. 44, 48, 52, 337, **359**
Neill, H.C. 56, **57**, 84, **220**, 220, **324**, **325**, 328, **359**
Neill, Henry 243, *245*, 246
Nelson, Mr 163
Nelson, Sister Fiona **92**
Nethercott, L.W. 340
Newall, Matthew **202**
Newell, Heather 173
Newiss, Robbie 184
Newman, B.R. 160
Newman, Christopher 190
Newnham, H.E. **324**, 327
Newport-Black, Nigel 297
Newsom, Sir John **118**
Newte, W.M. 110, 112, **113**
Newton, Howard 282
Newton, Robert 186
Niblett, Jeremy **263**
Nicholas, Benjamin 244-6, 305-9, *306*, 311-2
Nicholls, Ann 191
Nicholls, Major David, RM 209
Nicholls, W. Heller 27-9, **49**, 52, 80, 219, 232-3, **232**, **233**, **234**, **324**, 345
Nield, Guy **202**
Nipperess, K. **251**
Norman, Diana V. **272**, 278
Northcott, William **309**
Nutbeam, Mrs Sally **119**

O'Connor, Mrs Kate 340
O'Neill, Duncan 193
O'Neill, S.N. 167
Oakley, P.A. **55**
Oaksey, Lady **84**
Oaksey, The Rt Hon Lord **84**, 84, 94, **355**
Ochola, the Revd George **262**
Oddy, J.M. 156
Odell, Andrew 290
Odell, Mrs Dorothy 135, 242, 262, 282, 350
Odell, Steven **209**, *210*, 210
Odell, Tim G. **57**, **125,** 135, 238, 242, 350
Odell, William 225
Odierno, General 332
Oke, Mrs Jane 316
Oliver, Christian 198
Oliver, H.A.D. 331
Oliver, Howard 183
Omenai, Henry 154
Ong Chris 189
Ooi, Thomas **301**
Oram, Martin 236
Organ, Joyce 76
Organ, Simon 172
Orlebar, Miss **263**
Orr, Rebecca 291, **302**
Osborne, R.R. 140
Osmond, Humphrey **45**, **50**, *55*, **55**, **75**, 140, 224
Outhwaite, O.P. **101**
Owen, Trevor 239
Oxlade, Col Stephen J. 207, 332, **360**

Padfield, David 175
Padfield, Mrs Sue E. 125, *125*, **126**, 126, 135, 141, 147, 170, 178, 193, 207-8
Padfield, Richard C. **45**, **57**, **75**, **91**, *121*, 126, 135, 141, 147, 157, 162, 169, 175, **177**, 207-8, 224, 292, **323**
Padley, Mrs Mary 279, **281**, 282, 315
Page, L.H. **360**
Page, Neville 153, 194
Page, the Revd R.D. **22**, 90, 168
Page, W. *15*, 15, 34, **50**
Page, W/Cdr Geoffrey 332
Paget-Wilkes, Marcus 183, 203
Paine, Douglas 225
Palfreyman, Sister **92**
Pallett, Katherine 197
Palmer, Adrian 266
Palmer, T.F. **359**
Paltridge, Gil **284**
Panes, J.N. 343
Pantanay, Rebecca 193
Panting, the Revd J. **22**
Parfitt, Christine – see Lee, Mrs Christine
Pargiter, Mr 324
Paris, Sir E.T. **75**
Park, Trevor 173
Parker, Amanda 335
Parker, Arnold S.R. **57**, **82**, **121**, 202, **219**, 236, 325
Parker, J.M.A. 164-5, **218**, **360**
Parker, Alistair *176*
Parker, Claire 317
Parker, Sir Alan 226
Parker, Stephanie 182
Parkin, Charlie 342

Parlour, Selma **147**
Parsonage, George 1, **2**
Parsons, Geoffrey 239
Paul, Claudia **265**
Paul, Elaine **250**
Paul, Marcus K. **125**, 208
Payne, S.W. (later the Revd) **31**
Pearce, William 175, **181**
Pearse, Miss 70
Pearse, R.G. **360**
Pearson, Adam 298
Pearson, J.E. **360**
Pegg, Thomas 186
Pegrum, Mick 187, 209, 280
Pellereau, D.J.R. (Rod) **57**, 175, 347
Pellereau, Kate **316**
Penny, Michael *176*, *215*
Pentycross, Rhod 145, 166, 207
Peploe, Ben 174
Peploe, Jack 186
Peplow, Miss Eleanor **115**
Perham, Bishop Michael *306*, 306, 319, **347**
Perinpanayagam, Yshani *245*
Perry, Helen 192
Perry, R.H. 328, *343*
Peskett, Jonathan 188
Peterson, Michael D. *303*, 303
Petrencik, D. 193
Petrie, James 173
Phair, Mr 160, **247**
Philip, HRH Prince 48, 204, 213, **260**
Phillips, F.J. **323**, **325**
Phillips, John L. 275, 280-1, **282**, 292
Phillips, Michael **316**
Phillips, Mrs Rosie 275, 281, **282**, *315*, 316
Phillips, the Revd E.L.**22**
Philp, F.R.E. 9
Phinn, Prof Gervase 280
Pickard, Col E.C. 204, 331
Pickard, Matthew 291, **360**
Pickard, Naomi **360**
Pickard, Sarah **360**
Pieters, Ross 183
Pigg, Mr 34
Pihlens, David 225
Pihlens, Mark 175, *274*
Pike, Suzanne 178, 275
Pinches, Anthony 169
Piney, Jason 289
Piney, Simon 339
Pinnegar, Thomas *176*
Piper, Martin **106**, **284**, 285, 300
Piper, Mrs Jenny **106**
Pitt-Jones, Peter 168
Plumridge, Mr 86, 126
Poe, Major A. **17**
Polglase, Joe *237*, 237
Pope, Mrs Jean 278
Popham, Miss M. **66**
Porter, Abigail 180
Porter, Helen 244-5, *245*, 311
Porter, J.D. **359**
Pouncey, the Revd Canon Cosmo 303
Powell, Benjamin 242, *243*, *245*, 246
Powell, D. **324**, **359**
Powell, Joshua *195*, 243, *243*, 246, 352 3, **360**
Power, Jim 124
Poyner, Philip 185
Pragnell, Sheilagh 227
Prance, Sir Ghilean 350
Pratt, Elizabeth 197
Pratt, Henry 213
Prentis, Charles **302**
Preston, John 186, 215, *226*
Preston, Peter 70
Price, Ben 170
Price, Christopher 175, **181**, **202**
Price, J. **323**, **325**
Price, Natasha 179-80, *180,* **181**, *191*, **202**, **302**
Price, the Revd W.J. Allan **22**
Primrose, Mrs Alison *278*, 278-80
Pringle, Douglas A. 100, 154, **198**, 357
Pringle, Kenneth 340
Pringle, Major R.C. 332
Prior, D.I. 204
Pritchard, J. 13, *13*, **31**
Pritchard, Mrs J. **119**, 122, **323**, **325**
Pritchett, David **357**
Proctor, Gordon 190
Pruen, Dr S.T. **354**
Pruen, Miss 67
Purcaro, Joseph 184
Purchase, Miss 258
Pushman, Rosie 192, 197
Puttnam, A.J. **360**

Qualtrough, Katherine 187
Quarshie, Hugh A.A.K. 223, *334*, 334, **360**

Raghuram, Nina *318*
Raine, B.S. 328
Ramm, Selina 300
Rank, Rachel 173, 192
Rankin, Eleanor 189
Rawlence, G.N. **359**
Ray, Julian 187, 298
Rayner, W/Cdr 204
Reading, The 4th Marquis of *145*, **355**
Readings, D.G. 123
Redgrave, Sir Steve 197
Reed, B. *38*
Reed, R.D. 162
Reeve, Christopher 328
Reeve, Mrs J. (née Golder) **109**, 110, **111**
Reeve, Simon 207
Registe, Nigel **261**
Reicher, Michael **302**
Reid, Alastair 147, 175, **263**, 263, 302
Reid, Alistair 243
Reid, Alix *178*, 196
Reid, Helen 243
Reid, J.R. **359**
Reid, Mrs Rosalyn **263**, 286, 302
Reid, Naomi *178*, 293-4
Reuss, Professor Albert 78
Reynolds, M.S. **206**, 206, 236
Reynolds, Mrs Annette 317
Rhodes, S.D. 155
Ribeiro, Sir Bernard *330*, 330
Richards, Isabella *229,* **252**
Richards, the Revd C.L. 253
Richards, W.H. **35**
Richardson, Anna 194
Richardson, Cdr H.N.A., R.N. 331
Richardson, John R. 91, 135
Richardson, L. **251**
Richardson, Peter **357**
Rickerby, Major T.E. **354**
Ridley, Alain 342
Rigby, Miss Phyllis **115**
Righton, Anna 188, 195
Righton, E.G. 155
Rimell, Rebecca 225, **251**
Rinkart, Martin **41**
Ripon, Dean of (Freemantle, the Very Revd) **2**
Robathan, the Revd Canon .H. 119
Roberts, Lord **35**, 42, **43**
Robertson, Elizabeth 188
Robertson, V. – see under Crawley
Robins, Michael 168
Robinson, Bishop John A.C. 197
Robinson, Camilla 178
Robinson, Don **210**
Robinson, J.B.C. **359**
Robinson, J.H. 156
Robinson, Ken **261**
Robinson, Lucy 197
Robinson, M.T. 156
Robinson, Marjorie – see under Lady Oaksey
Robinson, Mike 338
Robinson, Mrs Jean *280*, 280
Robinson, Mrs Maureen **260**
Robinson, Paul **261**
Robinson, Ruth 197
Robinson, Sally – see under Nutbeam
Robinson, Steve **261**
Robson, Dr Walker **234**
Roebuck, S. **251**
Rogers, David 338
Rooke, Clive V.J. **114**, 277, 299
Rooney, Julie 277
Rose, Dr Bernard 235
Rose, Lewis 331
Rose, R.J. 157
Rose-Innes, Alexander *287*
Roth, James 187
Routledge, Guy 213, **251**
Routledge, Miss Patricia 229
Routledge, P.B. 166
Rowe, C.E. **17**
Rowlands, Jane 177, 188
Rowlands, Michael D. **113**, **114**, 302
Rowles, Alison 118
Rowles, Pam – see under Baillie
Rowles, Susannah 186
Rowley, the Revd Christopher 337
Rowley-Brooke, Naoise (Nick) 335
Rowley-Brooke, Roisin 215
Roxburgh, J.N. 27
Roxby, Mr 33
Rundall, Francis 312
Rusher, Robin 123
Ruskell, Louise 297
Russell, Prof Richard D. 329
Rutter, John 307, 309
Ryall, Richard P. **57**, 142, 225

Sackett, Andrew **305**
Safe, Jo 170
Sainsbury, E.J. 162
Salter, R.W. **359**
Sanders, Colin A.W. **270**, 270-1, 284
Sanders, Ian **270**
Sanders, Miss **115**
Sanders, Mrs Carol **270**, 293
Sanders, Ruth **270**
Sanders, Tim 339
Sanderson, sisters **105**
Santall, Reg 156
Sauer, Colin 240
Saunders, Rebecca *191*
Saunders, A. **251**
Savage, James 193, *203*
Savage, W.C.R. **35**
Sawyer, A.F. 169
Scamell, A.W. 99
Scarrott, Charlotte **316**
Scarrott, Elizabeth **316**
Schneider, Christopher 313, 328

Schneider, Miss Alice *89*, 120
Scott, Edward 225, **251**
Scott, Jane 223
Scott, John **10**
Scott, M.C.L. **360**
Scowcroft, D.J.M. **75**
Scrase, Andrew 170, *176*, 289
Scrase, Thomas *176*, 177
Searle, Beccy 242-3, 286
Seates, Harry **46**
Seavers, Jeremy 164
Sedgewick, Sister **92**
Sellwood, F.G. **359**
Senior, the Revd K.N. **22**
Senior, the Revd T.H. **31**, **323**, **325**
Serpell, S. **249**
Seymour, Mrs Eve 335
Seymour-Smith, Q.D. 204
Shaffer, Peter 227
Shaftesbury, 7th Earl of 1, 355
Shakespeare, William 223
Shapland, H.C.B. 157
Shapland, H.F. **304**, 339
Sharp, J.R.C. 158, 163
Sharpe, Jonathan 298
Sharples, Sister Deborah **92**
Shaw, Bishop E.D. **82**
Shaw, G.B. 223-4
Shaw, G.H. **60**
Shaw, S.W.E. 182
Shayle, Isobel *178*, 286, **360**
Sheldon, the Revd L.G.M. **354**
Shepherd, David 350
Shepherd, Sister Anita **92**
Sheppard, Philip 244
Sherratt, Colin 119, 239-41, *240*
Sherwood, E.C. **4**
Shouksmith, Rachel 317
Sidey, Phil 227, 230
Silberrad, Dr O.J. 342
Silver, Adam 342
Simeon, the Revd Charles 3, 9, **10**
Simmons, Claire 212
Simms, A.J. 104
Simms, Stephanie 353
Simons, Heather *227*, 229
Simpson, John 335
Simpson, Roy 190
Sinclair-Hill, N. 60
Skidmore, Mrs Janet **119**
Skinner, H.H. 331
Skinner, Mrs Jacky 278
Sky, Emma 332-3
Slabbert, Simon *176*
Slade, J. **252**, **349**
Slawson, Richard 142, **143**
Smallbone, Graham 236-7
Smallwood, F.G. **324**
Smethurst, Heather 338
Smith, A.N. 6, 23, **24**, **323**, **325**, 326
Smith, Alastair 184
Smith, C.G. 87
Smith, Cameron 188
Smith, Dr Rebecca 135
Smith, Instructor C. 158, 167
Smith, J.S. 158, **359**
Smith, Lisa 274
Smith, Lisa-Marie 178
Smith, Martyn 291
Smith, Miss Julie **272**, 275
Smith, Mr **46**
Smith, Mrs Lucy 328
Smith, P.E. **57**, 94
Smith, Rebecca *179*, **302**
Smith, Sally **263**
Snell, H.S. 158, **359**
Snow, Trevor N. **91**, 157, 163, 175
Sobers, Sir Gary 172
Sochart, Karen **360**
Somerville, Louisa 335
Sorensen family 240
Sorrell, Laura 283, 307
Spanner, David 194
Spear, the Revd Canon E.N. *161*
Speed, E.G.R. **360**
Spence, Catherine 187
Spencer, Lady Diana *135*, 135
Spicer, R.D.M. 93
Spreadbury, Lt Col W.E. **17**
Spurling, G. 168
Squire, J.C. 335
Stade, Fr Robert 338
Staelens, Henry 190
Stainer, John 232
Stammers, Prof A. Dighton 330
Stanford, C.V. 235-6
Stanley-Smith, J. 164, **360**
Stanley-Smith, M. **248**
Stanway, Nicola – see under Troughton
Stebbings, Claudia **302**
Stebbings, Imogen ***265***
Stenlake, Alison 342
Stephens, E.G. 154, 169
Steplewska, Hanna 197
Stern, Sonia **119**
Stevens, Simon *178*
Stewart, Martin 230
Stewart, R.D. **360**
Stocker, M.J. **360**
Stokes, Mrs Vicky *320*
Stokes, N.P. **57**, **125**
Stone, Eleanor *203*, **302**
Stoppard, Sir Tom 223-4
Stott, Sir Philip **221**
Stovold, Kyle **316**
Strachan, Jonty 172, 215, **360**
Strachan, Michael *176*, **357**
Stradling, Annette **137**, 137
Stradling, Nadia 197
Straker, Sister Mary **92**
Strand, Mr **46**
Stratton, G. **35**
Stringer, H.S. **360**
Stringer, Prudence **119**
Strong, Matthew 184
Struthers, M. *155*
Stuart, Grace *320*
Sturdy, Alice 212
Sullivan, Fay ***265***
Sutcliffe, Miss V. – see Troughton, Mrs V.
Sutherland, John 288
Sutton, Paul 243
Swain, Kevan 339
Swan, Mrs Hilary 178-80, **181**, 182, *191*
Swarbrick, Andy R. *195*, 195, 217
Swiss, Kenneth G. 330
Swiss, Sir Rodney 330
Sword, Nick 190, 215, 296, **316**
Sword, Tom **181**, **316**, 355
Symonds, M.S. **57**, **250**
Synge, Richard 342

Taffinder, M.A. 204
Tait, T.W. **60**
Talbot, J.W. 200
Talbot, John 283, 252
Talbot, Mr **46**
Talbot, the Revd E.L. (Libby) **22**, 283, 319, *351*, 351-2
Tanner, Charles 342
Tanner, the Revd E. Victor **22**, **45**, **51**, **57**, **78**, 80-1, **83**, **121**, 129
Tarsnane, K.P. 167
Tasker-Grindley, Christopher **181**, *187*, 190, 292, 297-8
Tasker-Grindley, Sam 187, *187*, 190, 292, 297-8
Taylor, Brig R.D.B. **17**
Taylor, Det Supt Herbert **47**
Taylor, E.H. **82**
Taylor, Ed 175, *178*, *215*
Taylor, Matt **181**
Taylor, Mrs Anne 137, *215*
Taylor, Mrs Emma L.C. 227, *355*, 355
Taylor, R.F. **55**, **57**, *121*, 137, *215*, 225, **251**, 261, 350, 359
Taylor, Stuart 183
Taylor, the Revd Harold 48
Temple, Nigel **147**
Temple, the Revd William (later Archbishop) 44
Terent'ev, Sergei 197
Terfel, Bryn 307
Thatcher, Rt Hon Mrs Margaret, M.P. 149, 335, 350
Thiagarajah, C.S. **360**
Thickett-Menghini, Nathan 170
Thomas, C.W. **60**
Thomas, Dr Stephanie 141
Thomas, Elizabeth 210
Thomas, Helen 184
Thomas, Matthew 169
Thomas, R. *155*
Thomas, R.C. **60**
Thomas, R.K. **359**
Thomas, R.M. 67, **68**, **73**, **76**, 80
Thomas, Richard 338
Thomas, Sister Gill **92**
Thomas, Will 170
Thompson, Anna *274*
Thompson, Anthony *171*, 171
Thompson, Bishop Jim 107, 148, 336, *337*, 337
Thompson, Dave 227, 230
Thompson, Herbert **221**
Thompson, Miss Barbara – see Mrs Abbatt
Thompson, Mrs Madge 107
Thompson, R.S. 154, *155*
Thornburgh, P.T. 17
Thornton, Barney **272**
Thornton, Magnus **272**
Thornton, Mrs Lyndall **272**, 293
Thornton, Samuel **272**
Thornton, Tim M. **270**, 271, **272**, 272, 278
Thynne, Phillippa 272
Tidmarsh, the Revd Philip R.W. **22**, *84*, 85, 90, 203
Tilley, Kate 198
Timson, Charlotte **262**
Tindall, James **181**
Tindle, Tim 339
Tisdall, W. St C. 156, **359**
Titterington, John C. **101**, **113**, 299
Tognazzi, S. **251**
Toms, S. **249**
Tonge, Chris **208**, 208
Tootell, Lucy – see under Gooderham
Tottenham, C.G. **324**
Tottenham, Rear Adml E.L. **324**, 331
Tottman, Mark D. **57**, 184
Tovey, Adml Lord *201*, 202
Townsend, Chris **91**, 170-1, *172*, 172
Townsend, James **202**, **209**, 227, **252**, 267
Toynbee, Prof. A.J. 345

Trapp, Allan **261**
Travers, Bill 341
Tredgett, Gary 175, *176*, 176-8, 180, **181**, 292
Tredgett, Hannah 180
Trevett, Capt 206
Trickery, Jo 207
Trist, David 170, 291
Troughton, Elisabeth 177
Troughton, Kate – see under O'Connor
Troughton, Mrs Nicola **119**, 122
Troughton, Mrs Viv. 278, 301, 314-6
Tschaikovsky, Peter 234
Tucker-Brown, Amy 173
Tuckwell, C.A.P. 52, 56, **57**, 59, **60**, 62, 64, **68**, *79*, 80-1, 119, 140, **143**, 159, **159**, 160, *161*, 162, **219**, 219-20, **220**, 334, **221**, **222**, 222, 226-7, 230, **247**, **248**
Tufnell, Claire *351*
Tugwell, D.B. 100, *155*
Tugwell, L.G. 13, *13*, 20-1, 27, **31**, 324
Tugwell, Mrs Alicia 20
Tully, Ben 170
Tunnell, Dominic 330
Tupper, R.C. **360**
Turnau, Will 224
Turnbull, Prof James 329
Turner Rosalie **117**
Turner, Catherine **117**
Turner, Christopher G. 107, 116-7, ***117***, **118**, 121-5, 127-31, 133, 135, 141, 238, 349, **358**
Turner, Glenn 289
Turner, Mark D. **114**, **276**, 277
Turner, Matthew **117**
Turner, Mrs Lucia *117*, 120, 131, 168, 259
Turner, P. *155*
Tyce, Jonathon **302**
Tyers, E.T.R. **35**
Tyers, G.A. **359**
Tyler, Wendy 282-3

Udell, Miss Kay 168
Unwin, E.F. **359**
Unwin, Maj Richard ***45***
Unwin, Richard 208
Upton, Justin *287*, 298

van Gils, Julian 173
Vaughan, Mervyn 93, 126
Vaughan, Sister Mary **92**, 93, 126, 148
Vaus, Mrs Sue 93, **122**, 123, 126, 140, 148
Venn, Mrs Marion *189*, 189, 192, 296
Vickers, E.S. **323**, **325**, 325
Vickery, Sir Philip 333
Victoria, HM Queen 37
Villar, J.G. **35**
Vincent, Paul 171, 290
Vine, Julie 225, 241, 333
Vines, Rebecca *226*, 226-7, 229, **247**, **252**
Virgin, Colette – see under Dobbs
von Holst, Ernest – see under Cossart
von Holst, Gustav 334

Wadsworth, Giles S. **282**, 282
Wadsworth, Rachel **282**, 282
Wait, E. **35**
Wakefield, Bishop of 237
Wakeling, Bishop J. Denis **222**, **324**, *336*, 336
Wales, HRH Prince of – see under Charles, HRH Prince
Walker, Chris **261**, 342
Walker, George 171, **202**
Walkley, Diana 241
Wall, Katherine 189
Walters, Sue 188
Walters, the Revd Preb E.E.F. 328
Walters, the Revd R. **22**
Walters, V.J. **248**
Walton, Mrs K. **17**
Walton, Sir William 234
Walwin, P/O 'Red', RAF 200
Warr, A. Hedley 52, **54**, 56, **56**, **57**, **58**, 65-7, **68**, 69, **78**, 80, **220**, 220,233, **247**, **248**, 254-5
Warr, E.H. **17**, 66, 80
Warren J.L.E. *38*
Warren, Sue 294
Warren, the Revd J.E.L. **45**
Warren, Tom 291
Warwick, Richard 334
Waterfield, the Revd Canon 46
Watkin, Emily **360**
Watson, Christopher 333
Watson, David – see under Acton
Watson, Giles 224
Watson, H. David 223, 237-8, **247**, **249**, 284
Watson, Hector **309**
Watson, Jess 174
Watson, John P. **55**, **125**, 141, 175, **349**
Watson, Kathryn **202**, 210
Watson, Mrs Paula **122**, 173, 182, 197
Watson, the Revd Canon Tim 266
Watt, G. 168
Watts, A.G. 338, **359**
Watts, J.R.C. 162
Weaver 153
Webb, Dr Gerald B. **323**, 323, 325, 330
Webb, India 243
Webber, P.R.H. **206**, 206
Webb-Peploe, the Revd Preb 28
Webster, Sister Sue **92**
Wedgebury, Kay **147**
Weighill, P.J. 188
Weighill, S.R.A. 193
Weitz, Liz 213
Welch, Bishop W. Neville 336
Welles, F.C. 156, 162, 165
Wells, Anabelle *321*
Wells, Denys 168
Wendon, Rosemary 246
Wenham, Mary 274
Went, Bishop John *258*, 280, 319
Wertenbaker, Timberlake 226
Wessex, Earl & Countess 349
West, Benjamin **302**
West, Naomi *274*
West, Tom 184
Westcott, Bishop B.F. **25**
Westcott, Dr Freddie G.K. 60, **68**, 80, **247**, *233*, 233-5, **234**
Westley, E. 99
Westmacott, Sister Frances **92**, 123
Weston, R.M. **50**
Weston, Sir Arthur 331
Westwood, Zoe 194, 212
Whalley, Caroline 182
Whetter, Benjamin *287*
White, C. **252**
White, J.M. 284
White, M.A. 96
White, Molly *294*
White, Seaton 60
Whitehead, Jessica **251**
Whitehead, John 173-4
Whitehead, Paul *174*, 174
Whiting, G.E.B. 186, 195
Whitney, A. Louise **262**
Whitney, Charles E. (later the Revd) 276, **276**, 279, 282, 309, 314
Whittaker, Dr V.P. 331
Wickham, H.F. **325**
Wigley, M.J.O'H. 157
Wilberforce, William **19**
Wilcox, the Revd A.J. **324**
Wilkin, Anna 297
Wilkins, David 169, **209**, 213, **218**, 225, 332
Wilks, Robert **309**
Willett, E.W. **323**, **324**, **325**, 326
Williams, Adam 176, *195*, *203*
Williams, Beth **302**
Williams, David 194
Williams, Garth T. **57**, 195
Williams, J.H. **35**
Williams, John, of St David's **130**
Williams, Kim 354
Williams, Linda 188
Williams, Neil 334
Williams, P.M.W. **109**
Williams, Ralph Vaughan **233**, 239
Williams, Ron 187
Williams, Rt Hon Baroness Shirley 145
Williams, the Revd Canon Paul R. *307*, 307, 309, 311-2
Williams, Ursula Vaughan **233**
Williams-Jones, B.W. **57**
Williams-Jones, Cerys *321*
Willington, M. *38*
Willington, V. *38*
Willis, Christopher **181**
Wills, Mrs **115**
Wilshire, Graham **271**
Wilson, A. 156
Wilson, A.B. 158
Wilson, Brian K. **57**, 97, 120, *121*, 134-5, 147, 165-7, 182
Wilson, David 297
Wilson, F.J. 188
Wilson, James 189
Wilson, Jenni **305**
Wilson, Miss Liz **115**
Wilson, P.M. **106**, 106
Wilson, Lt Col F.T.D. **35**
Wilson, Mrs Valerie 120-1, **122**
Wilson, R.E. **359**
Wilson, Rt Hon J. Harold **125**
Wilson, the Revd Canon H.A. (later Bishop) **354**
Wilton, Capt Harold **46**
Wiltshire, J.G. 340
Wimborne, Lady 36
Wimborne, Lord 36, 42, **355**
Winch, Victoria 289
Windle, O.E. **359**
Winkworth, Catherine **41**
Winpenny, David **271**
Winrow, Gary 230
Winrow, Sue 230
Winston, Prof Lord (Robert) *319*, 319
Winstone, Matthew 198
Winter, J.C.B. 157, *326*
Winter, R.C. – see under Warwick
Winterbotham, family 3, **4**, 24
Witts, Prof Noel 329
Witts, Ray 124, 133
Wodehouse, P.G. **78**
Wong, J.K. **360**
Wood, Christopher – see under Lloyd-Wood
Wood, A.D. **106**
Wood, Dr Thomas **234**
Wood, H.J. **60**
Wood, H.M. 34, **35**
Wood, Tom **302**

Woodard, the Revd Canon Nathaniel 3
Woodcock, Sister Naomi **92**
Woodcock, Will 291
Worrell, W/Cdr John 332
Wreford B. *38*
Wreford S. *38*
Wren, Sir Christopher 54
Wright, Annie Bella **47**
Wright, Cpl 204
Wright, M.P.L. 106, 164, **324**

Xiaowen, He 266

Yates, Bishop John 273
Yates, Neil 245
Yeaman, Sir Ian 87, **94**, 129, ***270***, **324**, 331, **354**
Yearwood, A.J. 170
Youde, Victoria 169, *274*, 289
Young, D.B. 157
Young, Helena 319
Young, Kathryn **262**
Young, Mrs Sue 279
Young, Paul **261**
Young, the Revd Daniel G.H. **22**, 136, 279, 301

Zhou, Carter 266
Zeffirelli, Franco 334
Zollinger, F.E. 339